教授"二次立法"
《申命记》与里昂地区的查理曼改革

Teaching the *Secunda Lex*
Deuteronomy and Church Reform at Lyon
in the Age of Charlemagne

刘　寅◎著

ZHEJIANG UNIVERSITY PRESS
浙江大学出版社

Preface

The English translations of the Vulgate, unless specified, are taken from the Douay-Rheims Bible. The English translations of the Septuagint, unless specified, are taken from Lancelot Charles Lee Brenton's edition.

On the basis of the marginal annotations in Paris, Bibliothèque nationale de France (BAF), NAL 1740, the subject of this book, is shortened as "the Lyon Annotations" for convenience. The author will call its composer "the Lyon Annotator." Throughout this book, the author will use Paul-Irénée Fransen's edition ("Un commentaire marginal lyonnais du Deutéronome du milieu du IXe siècle," *Revue Bénédictine* 117 (2007): pp. 31-63, 339-382) as basis, but consult Paris, BnF, NAL 1740 directly when necessary and make citation by folio number in the format "BnF, NAL 1740, fol. x, on Deut. y."

Abbreviations

BAV	Città del Vaticano, Biblioteca Apostolica
Bischoff, *Katalog*	Bernhard Bischoff, *Katalog der festländischen Handschriften des neunten Jahrhunderts (mit Ausnahme der wisigotischen)*
BnF	Bibliothèque nationale de France
BM	Bibliothèque municipale
CCCM	*Corpus Christianorum, Continuatio Mediaevalis*
CCSL	*Corpus Christianorum, Series Latina*
CLA	*Codices Latini Antiquiores: A Paleographical Guide to Latin Manuscripts Prior to the Ninth Century*
CSEL	*Corpus Scriptorum Ecclesiasticorum Latinorum*
GCS	*Die Griechischen Christlichen Schriftsteller*
MGH	*Monumenta Germaniae Historica*
PL	*Patrologia Latina*
PG	*Patrologia Graeca*
SC	*Sources Chrétiennes*

CONTENTS

PART I
TEXT AND CONTEXT

CHAPTER 1

INTRODUCTION: HISTORIOGRAPHICAL BACKGROUND

Manuscript NAL 1740 of the Bibliothèque nationale de France, a Bible codex from early medieval Lyon, contains an anonymous commentary on the book of Deuteronomy in the form of over 400 marginal or intercolumnar annotations written in Carolingian minuscule. Deuteronomy, "the second law" (*deuteros-nomos*), is the fifth book of the Old Testament, mainly consisting of three admonitory speeches of Moses to the people of Israel on the plains of Moab right before they entered Canaan, the Promised Land. This commentary — which is designated in this book "the Lyon Annotations" — has been little studied so far. Many questions are yet to be answered: Who composed this commentary, where, when, and why? In which circumstance was it copied in an old codex? Who read and utilized it? What was the exegetical tradition behind it? What was its exegetical scheme? What kind of theological and social messages was it designed to deliver?

This book aims to answer these questions as thoroughly and exhaustively as extant evidence and reasonable imagination of a historian allow. In a nutshell, the author will demonstrate the Lyon Annotations took shape during the first two decades of the ninth century, composed by a master active in the cathedral school of Lyon, then copied down by the episcopal scriptorium to create a commented Bible codex. While both its general scheme and part of its concrete expositions are rooted in the Latin exegetical tradition of Deuteronomy that is accumulated and evolved from Origen to the second half of the eighth century, it shows a high level of originality not commonly associated with the biblical exegesis of the Carolingian era, and creatively presents a Christian community self-identified as the "spiritual Israel," and the Jews as the "carnal Israel" (*prior populus*) as its theological antithesis.

Nevertheless, the horizon of this book is not only this single biblical commentary, but also the historical world that shaped it. This world, on a micro level, is Lyon under the reign of Archbishop Leidrad (r. 798–816); in a broader view, it is the epoch of Charlemagne, the initial stage of the so-called "Carolingian Renaissance" characterized by a realm-wide movement of cultural and social *renouatio*. Leidrad was a Bavarian and served the Frankish king in his court as a clerical courtier from sometime in the 780s. In 798, Charlemagne appointed him as archbishop of Lyon and ordered him to "emend the negligence" of the church there. During his episcopate, Leidrad carried out a remarkable reform program, including the restoration of church buildings, the reorganization of clerical and monastic institutions, the establishment of schools, and the promotion of book production. The Lyon Annotations was the product, legacy, and in a certain sense, mirror of Leidrad's reform. The intellectual resources, ambition, want, and anxiety of this historical world made the Lyon Annotations what it was.

The present introduction serves to clarify the general historiographical background of this book. Two topics will be examined in turn: the Carolingian Renaissance and Carolingian biblical exegesis. The research histories of specific issues will be reviewed throughout the main body of the book.

1.1   Carolingian Renaissance and Reform

The Lyon Annotations is a typical production of the cultural revival movement from the late eighth to the ninth century, customarily known as the "Carolingian Renaissance."[1] Since its first use by the French historian of literature Jean-Jacques Ampère in 1840, the term in the first place refers to the "rebirth" of learning, namely the boom of books, manuscripts, schools, teachers, and authors after the sixth- and seventh-century "Dark Age."[2]

At least for the first half of the Carolingian Renaissance, Carolingian rulers were the

---

1   For a convenient definition, see John Contreni, "The Carolingian Renaissance," *Renaissances before the Renaissance: Cultural Revivals of Late Antiquity and the Middle Ages*, ed. Warren Treadgold (Stanford: Stanford University Press, 1984), pp. 59-74, at 59: "The Carolingian renaissance formed part of a program of religious renewal that Carolingian political and clerical leaders sponsored and encouraged in the hope that it would lead to the moral betterment of the Christian people. As a conscious effort to improve man through knowledge of the Scriptures, the renaissance emphasized study, books, script, and schools. Although conceived and initially executed by an elite group of scholars, the first generation of which was largely foreign-born, the renaissance was aimed at society as a whole. It had a spectacular effect on education and culture in Francia, a debatable effect on artistic endeavors, and an unmeasurable effect in what mattered most to the Carolingians, the moral regeneration of society." For a defense of the use of the concept "Carolingian Renaissance" (against the Latin word *renouatio*), see Michel Sot, "*Renovatio*, renaissance et réforme à l'époque carolingienne: recherche sur les mots," *Au Moyen Âge, entre tradition antique et innovation: Actes du 131e Congrès des Sociétés Historiques et Scientifiques*, eds. Michel Balard, Michel Sot (Grénoble: Editions du Comité des Travaux Historiques et Scientifiques, 2009), pp. 117-140; also cf. G. W. Trompf, "The Concept of the Carolingian Renaissance," *Journal of the History of Ideas* 34 (1973): pp. 3-26.

2   "Par là, je suis amené à considérer le règne de Charlemagne sous son véritable point de vue, c'est-à-dire comme une *renaissance*." Jean-Jacques Ampère, *Histoire litteraire de la France avant le douzième siècle* (Paris: L. Hachette, 1839–1840), vol. 3, p. 32.

primary sponsors. Charlemagne's well-known circular letter *De litteris colendis*, delivered at the end of the eighth century, can be seen as the clearest manifesto of the Carolingian royal will to cultivate literary learning as well as the motive behind it:

> For let it be known to your piety pleasing to God, that we, together with our faithful, consider it useful that it be incumbent on the cathedrals and monasteries given into our rule by the favor of Christ to strive to teach, along with the order of the regular life and the way of life appropriate to holy religion, the study of letters (*litterarum meditationibus*) to those who are able to learn, each according to his own capacity. Just as the rule of living ordains and embellishes upright behavior, so also let the activity of teaching and learning order and embellish the flow of our speech, so that those who seek to please God by right living may not neglect to please Him by right speaking.[1]

What Charlemagne wanted was a more qualified clerical team consisting of "soldiers of the church internally pious, externally learned, chaste in good living, and scholarly in good speaking" (*ecclesiae milites, et interius deuotos et exterius doctos castosque bene uiuendo et scolasticos bene loquendo*) who could assist in governing and bettering his Christendom.[2] The cultivation of learning served a realm-wide social reform whose ultimate goal was to "correct" — an image (*correctio*) that Percy Ernst Schramm picked up as the *Zeitgeist* of the age of Charlemagne[3] — the past negligence, and to find out and promote the "standard of righteousness" (*norma rectitudinis*) — a notion important to the Carolingians, as Josef Fleckenstein insightfully grasped[4] — to worship, to teach, to believe, and to live. As Walter Ullmann cogently put it in his Birkbeck lectures published in 1969, "[t]he effect which this Carolingian Renaissance in the social sense was to produce in the public field was a 'baptism' on the largest conceivable scale."[5] The reform brought forth the "rebirth." It has been a trend for recent scholars to synonymize

---

1 "Notum igitur sit Deo placitae deuotioni uestrae, quia nos una cum fidelibus nostris considerauimus utile esse, ut episcopia et monasteria nobis Christo propitio ad gubernandum commissa praeter regularis uitae ordinem atque sanctae relegionis conuersationem etiam in litterarum meditationibus eis qui donante Domino discere possunt secundum uniuscuiusque capacitatem docendi studium debeant impendere, qualiter, sicut regularis normae honestatem morum, ita quoque docendi et discendi instantia ordinet et ornet seriem uerborum, ut, qui Deo placere appetunt recte uiuendo, ei etiam placere non neglegant recte loquendo." Luitpold Wallach, "Charlemagne's *De litteris colendis* and Alcuin: A Diplomatic-Historical Study," *Speculum* 26 (1951): pp. 288-305. The translation is based on Stephen Jaeger, *The Envy of Angels: Cathedral Schools and Social Ideals in Medieval Europe, 950–1200* (Philadelphia: University of Pennsylvania Press, 1994), p. 25, with certain modification.
2 Luitpold Wallach, "Charlemagne's *De litteris colendis*," p. 290.
3 Percy Ernst Schramm, "Karl Der Große: Denkart und Grundauffassungen. Die von Ihm Bewirkte *Correctio* ('Renaissance')," *Historische Zeitschrift* 198 (1964): pp. 306-345.
4 Josef Fleckenstein, *Die Bildungsreform Karls des Grossen als Verwirklichung der* Norma Rectitudinis (Bigge-Ruhr: Josefs-Druckerei, 1953), pp. 7-23.
5 Walter Ullmann, *The Carolingian Renaissance and the Idea of Kingship* (London: Methuen, 1969).

Carolingian Renaissance and Carolingian reform.[1]

While Ullmann's interest was mainly in abstract political and ecclesiological concepts, his student Rosamond McKitterick was among the pioneers in exploring how the Carolingian *renouatio* was practiced. At the center of the reform program was religious education of clerics and of common Christians through clerics.[2] Various written documents were produced, spread, and applied in order to facilitate the reform, which in turn stimulated the shaping of a Carolingian culture of "written words."[3] This picture of the pastoral mechanism of the Carolingian Renaissance has been enriched in later studies, for example, Susan Keefe's on Carolingian baptismal treatises (the implicit political ideology of which is further explored by Owen Michael Phelan[4]), explanations of the faith, and their manuscripts,[5] Carine van Rhijn's on episcopal statutes and handbooks for the use of local priests,[6] Yitzhak Hen's on canon law,[7] Rob Meens' on penitentials and their manuscripts transmission,[8] and Thomas Amos', Maximilian Diesenberger's, and James McCune's on sermons and sermon collections.[9]

One thing that the studies enumerated above tend to agree on is that, in the practice of

---

1 E.g., Giles Brown, "Introduction: The Carolingian Renaissance," *Carolingian Culture: Emulation and Innovation*, ed. Rosamond McKitterick (Cambridge: Cambridge University Press, 1994), pp. 1-51. For a helpful synthesis from a more political perspective, see Philippe Depreux, "Ambitions et limites des réformes culturelles à l'époque carolingienne," *Revue historique* 623 (2002): pp. 721-753.

2 Rosamond McKitterick, *The Frankish Church and the Carolingian Reforms, 789–895* (London: Royal Historical Society, 1977). For a useful recent survey, see Carine van Rhijn, "Charlemagne's *Correctio*: A Local Perspective," *Charlemagne: les temps, les espaces, les hommes. Construction et déconstruction d'un règne*, eds. Rolf Grosse, Michel Sot (Turnhout: Brepols, 2018), pp. 43-60.

3 Rosamond McKitterick, *The Carolingians and the Written Word* (Cambridge: Cambridge University Press, 1989).

4 Owen Michael Phelan, *The Formation of Christian Europe: The Carolingians, Baptism, and the Imperium Christianum* (Oxford: Oxford University Press, 2014).

5 Susan Keefe, *Water and the Word: Baptism and the Education of the Clergy in the Carolingian Empire* (Notre Dame: University of Notre Dame Press 2002); Susan Keefe, *A Catalogue of Works Pertaining to the Explanation of the Creed in Carolingian Manuscripts* (Turnhout: Brepols, 2012).

6 Carine van Rhijn, *Shepherds of the Lord: Priests and Episcopal Statutes in the Carolingian Period* (Turnhout: Brepols, 2014); Carine van Rhijn, "Manuscripts for Local Priests and the Carolingian Reforms," *Men in the Middle: Local Priests in Early Medieval Europe,* eds. Steffen Patzold, Carine van Rhijn (Berlin: De Gruyter, 2016), pp. 177-198.

7 Yitzhak Hen, "Knowledge of Canon Law Among Rural Priests: The Evidence of Two Carolingian Manuscripts from Around 800," *The Journal of Theological Studies* 50 (1999): pp. 117-134; Yitzhak Hen, "Educating the Clergy: Canon Law and Liturgy in a Carolingian Handbook from the Time of Charles the Bald," De Sion exibit lex et verbum domini de Hierusalem: *Essays on Medieval Law, Liturgy and Literature in Honour of Amnon Linder*, ed. Yitzhak Hen (Turnhout: Brepols, 2010), pp. 43-58.

8 Rob Meens, *Penance in Medieval Europe, 600–1200* (Cambridge: Cambridge University Press, 2012), pp. 101-140.

9 Thomas Amos, *The Origin and Nature of the Carolingian Sermon* (Ph.D. dissertation: Michigan State University, 1983); Maximilian Diesenberger, *Predigt und Politik im frühmittelalterlichen Bayern: Arn von Salzburg, Karl der Große und die Salzburger Sermones-Sammlung* (Berlin, De Gruyter: 2016); James McCune, "The Sermon Collection in the Carolingian Clerical Handbook, Paris, Bibliothèque nationale de France lat. 1012," *Mediaeval Studies* 75 (2013): pp. 35-92.

reform, more often than not, the person in charge was the bishop and the unit of reform was the diocese, within which policies were made, pastors instructed, and documents circulated.[1] As Keefe sharply put it: "The Carolingian Reform had encouragement from the royal palace, but in its actual implementation, it may only be possible to speak accurately of the 'Sens' Reform under Magnus, or the 'Lyonese Reform under Leidrad.'"[2]

This insight crucially pertains to the present book, because the Lyon Annotations was a product of the "Lyonese Reform under Leidrad." While pastoral care was certainly not absent from Leidrad's mind, the extant evidence suggested that his reform rather focused on the formation of a highly learned, doctrinally catholic, and well-disciplined religious elite, whose backbone was the urban canons, especially the cathedral canons. They constituted the primary audience of the Lyon Annotations, among whom we can identify Claudius of Turin and Agobard of Lyon. The strong concern of the commentary over the doctrine, order, and ethos of a Christian community under the leadership of a bishop and *doctores* (i.e., clerical elites known for their learning) reflects a certain self-imagination of Leidrad's reform. What the Lyon Annotations instructed is not only how to understand a particular biblical book, but also what an ideal *ecclesia* should be. The Lyon Annotations was a commentary both *of* reform and *for* reform.

How the Lyon Annotations was composed and taught naturally brings us to a crucial dimension of the Carolingian Renaissance: knowledge production and knowledge transmission. While scholars have held different opinions on whether there was continuity or breakthrough in intellectual life before and after the mid-eighth century,[3] the Carolingian era as a peak in the history of western learning is hard to deny. The number of all the extant Latin manuscripts prior to 800 is identified in Elias A. Lowe's

---

1   A study that particularly focuses on Carolingian bishops in the practice of reform is Franceen S. Hoyt, *The Carolingian Episcopate: Concepts of Pastoral Care as Set Forth in the Capitularies of Charlemagne and His Bishops (789–822)* (Ph.D. dissertation: Yale University, 1975).

2   Susan Keefe, *Water and the Word*, vol. 1, pp. 146-147.

3   For example, Erna Patzelt emphasized the continuity between the Carolingian Renaissance and the previous era, in her Habilitation: *Die karolingische Renaissance: Beiträge zur Geschichte der Kultur des frühen Mittelalters* (Wien: Österreichischer Schulbücherverlag, 1924). Patzelt was a student of Alfons Dopsch, whose view of the continuous social and economic development of the early medieval west very likely influenced her. Cf. Erna Patzelt, "Die Kontinuitätsfrage," *Wirtschaft und Kultur: Festschrift zum 70. Geburtstag von Alfons Dopsch* (Frankfurt: Verlag Sauer & Auvermann, 1966), pp. 18-33. Pierre Riché held a similar evolutionary view of the early Middle Ages, in Pierre Riché, *Education and Culture in the Barbarian West: Sixth through Eighth Centuries*, trans. John Contreni (Columbia: University of South Carolina Press, 1975). M. L. W. Laistner saw the Carolingian intellectual achievement, especially in the sense of the preservation of classical and post-classical Latin literature, as a breakthrough, in Laistner M.L.W., *Thought and Letters in Western Europe: A. D. 500 to 900* (Ithaca: Cornell University Press, 1957).

Codices Latini Antiquiores and supplemented by others in 1884.[1] According to the catalogue of Bernhard Bischoff, there are at least 7656 extant manuscripts produced in the Latin west (Spain excluded) in the ninth century.[2] A similarly striking contrast can be found in the number of authors of Gaul. The *Clauis Patrum Latinorum* of 1995 lists fewer than ten *scriptores Gallicae* known from the one century between Isidore of Seville (d. 636) and Bede the Venerable (d. 735);[3] in the already published sections of the project *Clauis scriptorum Latinorum Medii Aeui (Auctores Galliae)*, there are already more than 150 Gallic authors identified between 735 and 987, and this does not even cover all the authors whose names begin with A to H![4]

The institutional guarantee of this prosperous production of both knowledge and men of knowledge is school, scriptorium, and library. Thanks to, among others, Pierre Riché and John Contreni, we now have a general picture of how the Carolingian educational system functioned.[5] The capitulary *Admonitio generalis* of 789, Charlemagne's manifesto of reform, specifies school teaching and manuscript copying in the following words:

> Let schools be established in every monastery and bishopric for boys to read psalms, notes, chant, computus, grammar, and well corrected catholic books, for often when someone desires to beseech God effectively, they ask poorly because of uncorrected books. And do not let your boys, either in reading [dictating] or copying, corrupt the [catholic] books. If the task is to copy a gospel book, Psalter, or missal, let men of mature age do the copying with all diligence.[6]

Contreni recently points out that "psalms, notes, chant, computus, grammar, and

---

1 Elias Lowe, *Codices Latini Antiquiores: A Palaeographical Guide to Latin Manuscripts Prior to the Ninth Century* (Oxford: Clarendon Press, 1934–1971); Bernhard Bischoff, Virginia Brown, "Addenda to *Codices Latini Antiquiores*," *Mediaeval Studies* 47 (1985): pp. 317-366; Bernhard Bischoff, Virginia Brown, James J. John, "Addenda to *Codices Latini Antiquiores* (II)," *Mediaeval Studies* 54 (1992): pp. 286-307.

2 Bernhard Bischoff, *Katalog der festländischen Handschriften des neunten Jahrhunderts (mit Ausnahme der wisigotischen)*, in 4 vols. (Wiesbaden: Harrassowitz, 1998-2017). Cf. David Ganz' "Carolingian Manuscripts: The Verdict of the Master," *Francia* 42 (2015): pp. 252-274.

3 Eligius Dekkers, Emil Gaar, *Clavis patrum Latinorum* (Turnhout: Brepols, 1995).

4 Marie-Hélène Jullien, *Clavis scriptorum Latinorum medii aevi: Auctores Galliae 735–987* (Turnhout: Brepols, 1994-2015).

5 Pierre Riché, *Les écoles et l'enseignement dans l'Occident chrétien de la fin du Ve siècle au milieu du XIe siècle*. 3rd ed. (Paris: Picard, 1999); John Contreni, *Carolingian Learning, Masters and Manuscripts* (Aldershot: Variorum, 1992); John Contreni *Learning and Culture in Carolingian Europe: Letters, Numbers, Exegesis, and Manuscripts* (Farnham: Variorum, 2011).

6 "Et ut scolae legentium puerorum fiant. Psalmos, notas, cantus, compotum, grammaticam per singula monasteria uel episcopia et libros catholicas bene emendate, quia sepe, dum bene aliqui Deum rogare cupiunt, sed per inemendatos libros male rogant. Et pueros uestros non sinite eos uel legendo uel scribendo corrumpere. Et si opus est euangelium, psalterium et missale scribere, perfectae aetatis homines scribant cum omni diligentia." *Admonitio generalis*, LXX, MGH Fontes iuris Germanici antiqui in usum scholarum separatim editi XVI, eds. Hubert Mordek, Klaus Zechiel-Eckes, Michael Glatthaar (Hannover: Hahnsche, 2012), p. 224.

well corrected catholic books" could refer to a "reading program... in progressive steps... intended for boys taking their first steps toward becoming religious men."[1] A higher level of education in liberal arts, patristic theology, and ultimately the "spiritual understanding" of the Bible was also taught by masters in cathedral and monastic schools (according to one estimation, around 70 active in Carolingian Europe[2]) to train scholars, as Contreni has demonstrated in closest detail in several of his great syntheses.[3] They were usually accompanied by scriptoria and libraries in which books, the essential resource of education and learning, were copied and preserved.[4] Some of these Carolingian centers of learning have been comprehensively studied, such as David Ganz' Corbie and Contreni's Laon.[5]

If we limit ourselves to the era of Charlemagne (d. 814),[6] Leidrad's Lyon is one of a few ideal cases in which we can find sufficient evidence of both active schools and an active scriptorium. Leidrad established both schools of chanters and "schools of readers who not only carry out the readings of services, but also grasp the fruits of spiritual understanding in the study of divine books." The latter trained students to understand different biblical books "according to spiritual sense."[7] The Lyon Annotations was primarily composed, either in oral or in written form, by a master from these schools in order to supplement the exegetical curriculum for the Pentateuch. It was soon copied in "small and neat Lyon minuscule of late Leidrad-script" (according to Bernhard Bischoff) in MS Paris, BnF, NAL 1740 as marginalia. This old codex of the Vulgate Bible subsequently functioned as an édition commentée. As Margaret Gibson, Louis Holtz, and

---

1 John Contreni, "Learning for God: Education in the Carolingian Age," *The Journal of Medieval Latin* 24 (2014): pp. 89-129.

2 Pierre Riché, *Les écoles et l'enseignement*, pp. 97-110; John Contreni, "The Carolingian Renaissance: Education and Literary Culture," *The New Cambridge Medieval History*, vol. 2, ed. Rosamond McKitterick (Cambridge: Cambridge University Press, 1995), pp. 709-757.

3 For one of the best surveys of the Carolingian classroom experience, see John Contreni, "The Pursuit of Knowledge in Carolingian Europe," *The Gentle Voices of Teachers: Aspects of Learning in the Carolingian Age*, ed. Richard Sullivan (Columbus: Ohio State University Press, 1995), pp. 106-141.

4 Cf. Bernhard Bischoff, *Manuscripts and Libraries in the Age of Charlemagne*, trans. ed. Michael Gorman (Cambridge: Cambridge University Press, 1994); Rosamond McKitterick, "Manuscripts and Scriptoria in the Reign of Charles the Bald, 840–877," *Giovanni Scoto nel suo tempo. L'organizzazione del sapere in eta Carolingia*, eds. Claudio Leonardi, Enrico Menestò (Spoleto: Centro italiano di studi sull'alto medioevo, 1989), pp. 200-233.

5 David Ganz, *Corbie in the Carolingian Renaissance*, Beihefte der Francia 20 (Sigmaringen: Thorbecke Verlag, 1990); John Contreni, *The Cathedral School of Laon from 850 to 930: Its Manuscripts and Masters* (München: Arbeo-Gesellschaft, 1978).

6 Pierre Riché, *Les écoles et l'enseignement*, pp. 102-103.

7 "Preter hec, habeo scholas lectorum, non solum qui officiorum lectionibus exercentur, sed eciam qui in diuinorum librorum meditacione spiritalis intelligencie fructus consequantur. Ex quibus nonnulli de libro Euangeliorum sensum spiritalem iam ex parte adipisci possunt. Alii adiuncto libro etiam Apostolorum, plerique uero librum Prophetarum secundum spiritalem intelligentiam ex parte adepti sunt. Similiter libros Salomonis uel libros Psalmorum atque eciam Iob." Leidrad, *Report to Charlemagne*, in Alfred Coville, *Recherches sur l'Histoire de Lyon du Ve siècle au IXe siècle (450–800)* (Paris: Picard, 1928), pp. 284-285.

Michele Camillo Ferrari have shown, this codicological format, pioneering at that time, facilitated readers' ability to simultaneously grasp the biblical text and its exposition.[1] Therefore, on one hand, as carefully designed and elegantly copied marginalia, the Lyon Annotations enrich the picture of the active book production in Lyon in the earlier stage of the Carolingian Renaissance explored by Sigmund Tafel and Holtz;[2] on the other hand, as an elaborately composed biblical commentary, they witness the great intellectual creativity of Leidrad's Lyon — an issue still wanting substantial study — along with other products such as the canon law collection *Dacheriana* and the first Lyon martyrology.

The concrete expositions in the Lyon Annotations reflect an exegete who had both the extensive knowledge of patristic tradition and the confidence and skills to integrate them in an exegetical scheme of his own. As Paul Lehmann and many scholars after him have pointed out, the Carolingians *renouatio* was based on the recovery and absorption of tradition.[3] Richard Sullivan in the editorial introduction of an influential volume of 1995 expressed this idea cogently: "The Carolingian cultural renewal was a phenomenon shaped and driven by a conscious public policy aimed at serving the public weal by utilizing education to recover and transmit behavioral norms defined in the distant past. Its achievements can best be assessed in terms of the capacity of its agents to capture, adapt, and apply that tradition in ways that modified the behavioral patterns of a troubled, 'backward' society seeking to renew itself."[4] Thomas F. X. Noble in his study of *Opus Caroli* crystallized three words to grasp the spirit of Charlemagne's reform: the pursuit

---

1   Margaret Gibson, "Carolingian Glossed Psalters," *The Early Medieval Bible: Its Production, Decoration and Use*, ed. Richard Gameson (Cambridge: Cambridge University Press, 1994), pp. 78-100; Louis Holtz, "Les manuscrits latins à gloses et à commentaires de l'Antiquité à l'époque carolingienne," *Il Libro e il Testo: Atti del Convegno Internazionale: Urbino, 20–23 Settembre 1982*, eds. Cesare Questa, Renato Raffaelli (Urbino: Università degli Studi di Urbino, 1984), pp. 139-167; Michele Camillo Ferrari, "Before the 'Glossa ordinaria': The Ezekiel Fragment in Irish Minuscule Zürich, Staatsarchiv W3.19.XII, and Other Experiments towards a 'Bible commentée' in the Early Middle Ages," *Biblical Studies in the Early Middle Ages*, eds. Claudio Leonardi, Giovanni Orlandi (Firenze: Edizioni del Galluzzo, 2005), pp. 283-307.

2   Sigmund Tafel, "The Lyons Scriptorium," *Palaeographia Latina* 2 (1923): pp. 66-73; Sigmund Tafel, "The Lyons Scriptorinm," *Palaeographia Latina* 4 (1925): pp. 40-70; Louis Holtz, "Leidrat, évêque de Lyon (798–814): ses livres, son écriture," *Amicorum societas: mélanges offerts à François Dolbeau pour son 65e anniversaire*, eds. Jacques Elfassi, Cécile Lanéry, Anne-Marie Turcan-Verkerk, François Dolbeau (Firenze: SISMEL edizioni del Galluzzo, 2013), pp. 315-333; Louis Holtz, "La bibliothèque de Florus de Lyon," *Le sense du temps: actes du VIIe Congres du Comite International de Latin Medieval (Lyon, 10–13.09.2014)*, eds. Pascale Bourgain, Jean-Yves Tilliette (Genève: Librairie Droz, 2017), pp. 897-914.

3   Paul Lehmann, "Das Problem der Karolingischen Renaissance," *I Problemi Della Civiltà Carolingia* (Spoleto: Centro italiano di studi sull'alto medioevo, 1954), pp. 309-358.

4   Richard Sullivan, "The Context of Cultural Activity in the Carolingian Age," *The Gentle Voices of Teachers: Aspects of Learning in the Carolingian Age*, ed. Richard Sullivan (Columbus: Ohio State University Press, 1995), pp. 51-105.

of a new *order* securely anchored in old *tradition* for the sake of correct *worship* of God.[1] Even if we limit ourselves to the sphere of scholastic learning — that is, leaving the more general "use of the past" or "resources of the past" aside[2] — the tradition accepted, transmitted, and absorbed by Carolingians is multidimensional. It was fundamentally biblical (as we will survey in detail below), to no little degree classical,[3] arguably Irish,[4] but overwhelmingly patristic.

Carolingians diligently copied and zealously preserved the works of Church Fathers.[5] One could even say that the earliest "patrology" of the Latin west, namely a conscious practice of systematizing patristic knowledge, took shape in the ninth century.[6] Moreover, when Dominique Alibert called the Church Fathers "un héritage vivant et assumé" for Carolingians, he meant a fully digested and internalized tradition.[7] Willemien Otten demonstrated how Carolingian authors not only transmitted the opinions of the Church Fathers but also altered and developed them in their own theological, moral, and philosophical writings.[8] Owen Michael Phelan showed us how Alcuin's adaptation of an Augustinian work reflected "Carolingian innovative deference to the Fathers of the Church: a conscious and clever capacity to recast the language and ideas of the Fathers of the Church into new moulds more directly applicable to the world of the late eighth

1   Thomas F. X. *Noble, Images, Iconoclasm, and the Carolingians* (Philadelphia: University of Pennsylvania Press, 2009). Also cf. idem, "Tradition and Learning in Search of Ideology: The *Libri Carolini*," *The Gentle Voices of Teachers: Aspects of Learning in the Carolingian Age*, ed. Richard Sullivan (Columbus: Ohio State University Press, 1995), pp. 228-260.

2   Yitzhak Hen, Matthew Innes, eds., *The Uses of the Past in the Early Middle Ages* (Cambridge: Cambridge University Press, 2000); Rosamond McKitterick, *History and Memory in the Carolingian World* (Cambridge: Cambridge University Press, 2004); Clemens Gantner, Rosamond McKitterick, Sven Meeder, eds., *The Resources of the Past in Early Medieval Europe* (Cambridge: Cambridge University Press, 2015).

3   Among many others, see Mariken Teeuwen, "Carolingian Scholarship on Classical Authors: Practices of Reading and Writing," *Manuscripts of the Latin Classics 800–1200*, ed. Erik Kwakkel (Leiden: Leiden University Press, 2015), pp. 23-52; Sinéad O'Sullivan, "Glossing Vergil and Pagan Learning in the Carolingian Age," *Speculum* 93 (2018): pp. 132-165.

4   Cf. Sven Meeder, "The Irish Foundations and the Carolingian World," *L'Irlanda e gli Irlandesi nell'alto Medioevo* (Spoleto: Centro italiano di studi sull'alto medioevo, 2010), pp. 467-494.

5   See Bernice Kaczynski, "The Authority of the Fathers: Patristic Texts in Early Medieval Libraries and Scriptoria," *Journal of Medieval Latin* 16 (2006): pp. 1-27.

6   Especially in the case of Notker the Stammerer, cf. Bernice Kaczynski, "Reading the Church Fathers: Notker the Stammerer's 'Notatio de illustribus viris,'" *Journal of Medieval Latin* 17 (2007): pp. 401-412.

7   Dominique Alibert, "La transmission des textes patristiques à l'époque carolingienne," *Revue des Sciences philosophiques et théologiques* 91 (2007): pp. 7-21.

8   Willemien Otten, "The Texture of Tradition: The Role of the Church Fathers in Carolingian Theology," *The Reception of the Church Fathers in the West: From the Carolingians to the Maurists*, ed. Irena Backus (Leiden: Brill, 1997), pp. 3-50.

century," and this argument was applicable to the ninth century as well.[1] In fact, where Carolingian authors encountered Church Fathers most intimately was exactly in the literary genre of the Lyon Annotations: biblical exegesis.

1.2   Carolingian Biblical Studies and Biblical Culture

Dearest sons, let your adolescence run through these paths [i.e., the seven steps of literal arts] every day, until the more perfect age and the soul stronger in understanding reaches the summits of sacred scriptures, to the point that you then become the well-armed defenders of the true faith and the invincible protectors of the truth in all the ways.[2]

Brethren, understand what you read, do not invent new and unknown names, but hold what are found in the Holy Scripture. For what are found there about Christ the God have distinguished meanings beneficial to our salvation. Do not be swayed by human inventions, but reinforce yourselves in the solidarity of sacred scriptures. Read them and teach them, because there is eternal life in them. Again and again, you shall inculcate and repeat affirming harmonious testimonies from Holy Fathers.[3]

The first passage above from Alcuin's *De Grammatica* represents the basic Carolingian attitude toward biblical learning: it is the highest knowledge, to which secular learning must lead; essential to cultivate a qualified advocate of the faith, it is the natural pursuit for any mature scholar. The second passage above from the synod of Frankfurt of 794 reflects the official Carolingian affirmation of the crucial pertinence of biblical knowledge to salvation and of patristic testimony as the only reliable guide to approaching divine knowledge. Maybe none of these was absolutely new as *idea*, but it was the Carolingians who put them in *practice* through a realm-wide educational project.

---

1   Owen Michael Phelan, "Catechising the Wild: The Continuity and Innovation of Missionary Catechesis under the Carolingians," *The Journal of Ecclesiastical History* 61 (2010): pp. 455-474; Owen Michael Phelan "New Insights, Old Texts: Clerical Formation and the Carolingian Renewal in Hrabanus Maurus," *Traditio* 71 (2017): pp. 63-89.

2   "Per has uero, filii charissimi, semitas uestra quotidie currat adolescentia, donec perfectior aetas et animus sensu robustior ad culmina sanctarum Scripturarum perueniat. Quatenus hinc inde armati uerae fidei defensores et ueritatis assertores omnimodis inuincibiles efficiamini." Alcuin, *De Grammatica*, PL 101, col. 853.

3   "Intellegite, fratres, quae legitis et nolite noua et incognita nomina fingere, sed quae in sancta scriptura inueniuntur tenete. Illa enim, quae ibi inueniuntur de Christo Deo, honestas habent significationes et nostrae saluti conuenientes. Et nolite per humanas inuentiones fluctuare, sed in soliditate sanctarum scripturarum uosmetipsos roborate. Illas legite, illas docete, quia in illis est uita aeterna. Inculcastis iterum iterumque replicastis uos consona sanctis patribus ponere testimonia." *Concilia aevi Karolini [742–842]. Teil 1 [742–817]*, no. 19, MGH Leges, ed. Albert Werminghoff (Hannover and Leipzig: Hahnsche, 1906), p. 156.

Besides large production of Bible copies (pandects or not) and the achievement of Maudramnus, Alcuin, and Theodulf in textual correction of the Vulgate,[1] its outcome was a quantitative boom of exegetical treatises. More than 100 commentaries, *collectanea*, or glosses — not even including homilies of an exegetical nature — can be safely identified as the works of authors active in the realm under the control of the Carolingian dynasty between 775 and 875;[2] between 750 and 1000, there were more than 50 known Latin exegetes.[3] In contrast, according to *Clauis Patrum Latinorum*, there were only 35 extant biblical commentaries from the Latin west between 500 and 750 (fourteen of which are Bede's);[4] there were only three extant biblical commentaries from Merovingian *Francia*.[5] It is no exaggeration for Sumi Shimahara to propose a "renaissance carolingienne de l'exégèse."[6]

Meanwhile, it is more difficult to evaluate justly the achievement of Carolingian biblical exegesis in a qualitative sense, especially if one takes original theological speculation or modern higher criticism as caliber. In most cases, Carolingian exegetes worked as collectors or abbreviators of patristic exegesis and preferred the seemingly uncritical and arbitrary allegorical interpretation. Beryl Smalley in her magisterial *The Study of the Bible in the Middle Ages* (revised edition published in 1952) bluntly stated that "to study the commentaries of Alcuin, Claudius of Turin, Raban Maur and Walafrid Strabo his pupil, to mention outstanding names, is simply to study their sources... the *pauperculus*

---

1   Cf. Bonifatius Fischer, "Bibeltext und Bibelreform unter Karl Dem Grossen," *Karl der Grosse: Lebenswerk und Nachleben*, vol. 2, ed. Bernhard Bischoff (Düsseldorf: L. Schwann, 1965), pp. 156-216; François Louis Ganshof, "Charlemagne et la revision du texte latin," *Bulletin de l'Institut historique belge de Rome* 44 (1974): pp. 271-281; David Ganz, "Mass Production of Early Medieval Manuscripts: The Carolingian Bibles from Tours," *The Early Medieval Bible: Its Production, Decoration and Use*, ed. Richard Gameson (Cambridge: Cambridge University Press, 1994), pp. 53-62; idem, "Carolingian Bibles," *The New Cambridge History of the Bible from 600 to 1450*, eds. Richard Marsden, Ann Matter (Cambridge: Cambridge University Press, 2012), pp. 325-337.
2   Rossana Guglielmetti, "Un'esegesi incontentabile," *Il secolo di Carlo Magno: istituzioni, letterature e cultura del tempo carolingio*, eds. Ileana Pagani, Francesco Santi (Firenze: SISMEL edizioni del Galluzzo, 2016), pp. 177-200. A list of these exegetical treatises in Guglielmetti's footnote is very helpful. However, this list is certainly not an exhaustive one, because at least the Lyon Annotations is absent!
3   The count is based on the list in progress "The Transmission of Carolingian Bible Commentaries in Manuscripts and Printed Editions" by Burton Van Name Edwards, available in https://risd.digication. com/bvnedwards/Bibliography, last accessed September 14, 2021.
4   John Contreni, "Carolingian Biblical Culture," *Iohannes Scottus Eriugena: The Bible and Hermeneutics*, eds. Gerd van Riel, Carlos Steel, and James McEvoy (Leuven: Leuven University Press, 1996), pp. 1-23. However, as Contreni cautioned, most of the early Irish biblical commentaries are not included in *Clauis Patrum Latinorum*.
5   Cf. Yitzhak Hen, "A Merovingian Commentary on the Four Gospels," *Revue des Études Augustiniennes* 49 (2003): pp. 167-187.
6   Sumi Shimahara, "*Renovatio* et réforme dans l'exégèse carolingienne," *Au Moyen Âge, entre tradition antique et innovation: Actes du 131e Congrès des Sociétés Historiques et Scientifiques*, eds. Michel Balard, Michel Sot (Grénoble: Editions du Comité des Travaux Historiques et Scientifiques, 2009), pp. 57-74.

lector, for whom, they tell us in their prologues, their work was intended, was getting his Fathers at third or fourth hand."[1]

The most remarkable development in the academic field of Carolingian exegesis in the past decades is a common shift of focus from the commentators' patristic sources to their *use* of these sources. Behind this new approach are two major scholarly advances. First, experts on early medieval education, especially Riché and Contreni, have persuasively demonstrated that the seemingly unproductive exegetical practices typical of the Carolingian era, such as epitomizing and compiling, were deliberately chosen out of pedagogical consideration, namely for the sake of teaching secured and easy-to-digest biblical knowledge to students, to political *potestates*, and in fact, to a Christian society in general. Carolingian exegetes carried out their duty most effectively.[2]

Second, scholars have found ways to appreciate the innovation in Carolingian exegetical techniques of "repackaging" the patristic tradition within the scheme of their own "editorial intention."[3] When Silvia Cantelli defined Carolingian exegesis as "exegesis of [patristic] exegesis," and described the Carolingian exegetical practice as "inexhaustible work of reading, cutting, and weaving," she was appreciating a complex intellectual achievement.[4] In an insightful paper, Rossana Guglielmetti showed us how Carolingians exegetes of different generations shared the habit of reorganizing and adjusting the

---

1 Beryl Smalley, *The Study of the Bible in the Middle Ages*, (Oxford: Basil Blackwell, 1952), pp. 37-38. Smalley reserved mere seven pages (pp. 37-43) for the Carolingian era, while the whole book is of 406 pages, and the twelfth-century Victorines, Smalley's heroes who "rediscovered" the literal or historical meaning of the Bible, occupies more than 100 pages.

2 Pierre Riché, "Divina pagina, ratio et auctoritas dans la theologie carolingienne," *Nascita dell'Europa ed Europa carolingia, un'equazione da verificare* (Spoleto: Centro italiano di studi sull'alto medioevo, 1980–1981), vol. 2, pp. 719-758; Pierre Riché, "Instruments de travail et méthodes de l'exégète à l'époque carolingienne," *Le Moyen Âge et la Bible*, eds. Pierre Riché, Guy Lobrichon (Paris: Beauchesne, 1984), pp. 147-161; John Contreni, "Carolingian Biblical Studies," *Carolingian Essays: Andrew W. Mellon Lectures in Early Christian Studies*, ed. Uta-Renate Blumenthal (Washington, D.C.: Catholic University of America Press, 1983), pp. 71-97; John Contreni, "Carolingian Biblical Culture." Also cf. Ann Matter, "Exegesis and Christian Education: The Carolingian Model," *Schools of Thought in the Christian Tradition*, ed. Patrick Henry (Philadelphia: Fortress Press, 1984), pp. 90-105.

3 For a general survey, see Thomas O'Loughlin, "Tradition and Exegesis in the Eighth Century: The Use of Patristic Sources in Early Medieval Scriptural Commentaries," *The Scriptures and Early Medieval Ireland: Proceedings of the 1993 Conference of the Society for Hiberno-Latin Studies on Early Irish Exegesis and Homilectics*, ed. Thomas O'Loughlin (Turnhout: Brepols, 1999), pp. 217-239; John Contreni, "The Patristic Legacy to c. 1000," *The New Cambridge History of the Bible from 600 to 1450*, eds. Richard Marsden, Ann Matter (Cambridge: Cambridge University Press, 2012), pp. 505-535; Sumi Shimahara, "Citations explicites ou recours implicites? Les usages de l'autorite des Pères dans l'exegese carolingienne," *Les réceptions des Pères de l'Église au Moyen Âge: le devenir de la tradition ecclésiale*, eds. Rainer Berndt, Michel Fédou (Münster: Aschendorff Verlag, 2013), vol. 1, pp. 369-388.

4 Silvia Cantelli, *Angelomo e la scuola esegetica di Luxeuil* (Spoleto: Centro Italiano di Studi sull'alto Medioevo, 1990), vol. 1, pp. 15-87 on Carolingian exegesis in general; quotations are from pp. 61-63. Also cf. Silvia Cantelli "L'esegesi della rinascita carolingia," *La Bibbia nel medioevo*, eds. Giuseppe Cremascoli, Claudio Leonardi (Bologna: Dehoniane, 1996), pp. 167-198.

established biblical expositions of the Fathers and their own contemporaries to fit concrete teaching circumstances. This phenomenon of "never-satisfied exegesis" (*esegesi incontentabile*) explains the boom of exegetical treatises and reflects great intellectual confidence.[1]

New perspectives have aroused new interest in Carolingian biblical commentaries, which in turn has brought about a series of critical editions (most of them were published in CCCM) and many delicate studies of the exegetical practice of certain Carolingian authors, including but not limited to Wigbod,[2] Alcuin,[3] Claudius of Turin,[4] Hrabanus Maurus,[5] Angelomus of Luxeuil,[6] Florus of Lyon,[7] and Haimo of Auxerre;[8] and of the Carolingian treatment of certain biblical books, including but not limited to Genesis,[9]

1 Rossana Guglielmetti, "Un'esegesi incontentabile," *Il secolo di Carlo Magno: istituzioni, letterature e cultura del tempo carolingio*, eds. Ileana Pagani, Francesco Santi (Firenze: SISMEL edizioni del Galluzzo, 2016), pp. 177-200.

2 Michael Gorman, "The Encylopedic Commentary on Genesis Prepared for Charlemagne by Wigbod," *Recherches Augustiniennes et Patristiques* 17 (1982): pp. 173-201; idem, "Wigbod and the *Lectiones* on the Hexateuch Attributed to Bede in Paris Lat. 2342," *Revue Bénédictine* 105 (1995): pp. 305-347; idem, "Wigbod and Biblical Studies under Charlemagne," *Revue Bénédictine* 107 (1997): pp. 40-76; idem, "Charlemagne's Commentator: The *Quaestiunculae super Euangelium*," *Revue Bénédictine* 117 (2004): pp. 5-74; idem, "The Epitome of Wigbod's Commentaries on Genesis and the Gospels," *Revue Bénédictine* 118 (2008): pp. 5-45.

3 Michael Fox, "Alcuin the Exegete: The Evidence of the *Quaestiones in Genesim*," *The Study of the Bible in the Carolingian Era*, eds. Celia Chazelle, Burton Van Name Edwards (Turnhout: Brepols, 2003), pp. 39-60; Michael Fox, "Alcuin's *Expositio in epistolam ad Hebraeos*," *The Journal of Medieval Latin* 18 (2008): pp. 326-345; Michael Gorman, "Rewriting Augustine: Alcuin's Commentary on the Gospel of John," *Revue Bénédictine* 119 (2009): pp. 36-85.

4 Michael Gorman, "The Commentary on Genesis of Claudius of Turin and Biblical Studies under Louis the Pious," *Speculum* 72 (1997): pp. 279-329; Pascal Boulhol, *Claude de Turin: un évêque iconoclaste dans l'Occident carolingien: Étude suivie de l'édition du Commentaire sur Josué* (Paris: Institut d'études augustiniennes, 2002).

5 Silvia Cantelli, *Hrabani Mauri opera exegetica: repertorium fontium* (Turnhout: Brepols, 2006); relevant papers in *Raban Maur et son temps*, eds. Philippe Depreux, Stéphane Lebecq, Michel Perrin, Olivier Szerwiniack (Turnhout: Brepols, 2010); Caroline Chevalier-Royet, "Entre tradition et innovation: Raban Maur, un érudit carolingien face à ses sources," *Érudition et culture savante de l'Antiquité a l'époque moderne*, eds. François Brizay, Véronique Sarrazin (Rennes: Presses universitaires de Rennes, 2015), pp. 53-70.

6 Silvia Cantelli, *Angelomo e la scuola esegetica di Luxeuil*; Michael Gorman, "The Commentary on Genesis of Angelomus of Luxeuil and Biblical studies under Lothar," *Studi medievali* 40 (1999): pp. 559-632.

7 Pierre Chambert-Protat, Franz Dolveck, Camille Gerzaguet, eds., *Les douze compilations pauliniennes de Florus de Lyon: Un carrefour des tradition patristiques au IXe siècle* (Rome: École française de Rome, 2017).

8 Sumi Shimahara, *Haymon d'Auxerre, exegete carolingien* (Turnhout: Brepols, 2013); eadem, ed., *Études d'exégèse carolingienne: Autour d'Haymon d'Auxerre* (Turnhout: Brepols, 2007); Michael Gorman, "The Commentary on the Gospel of John by Haimo of Auxerre," *Revue Bénédictine* 105 (1995): pp. 61-111.

9 Cf. the papers of Michael Gorman as listed in the preceding footnotes. Most of them are available in two collections of his: *Biblical Commentaries from the Early Middle Ages* (Firenze: SISMEL edizioni del Galluzzo, 2002); *The Study of the Bible in the Early Middle Ages* (Firenze: SISMEL edizioni del Galluzzo, 2007).

four books of Kings,[1] and Pauline epistles.[2]

Pertinent to the present book, scholarship in the past three decades has also greatly enriched our understanding of the Carolingian exegesis of Deuteronomy. Beda Paulus published the *editio princeps* of Paschasius Radbertus' *De benedictionibus patriarcharum Iacob et Moysi*, a comparative exposition of the Blessings of Jacob (Genesis 49) and the Blessings of Moses (Deuteronomy 33) dedicated to the monks of St-Riquier.[3] Dom Paul-Irénée Fransen, besides editing the marginal annotations in Paris, BnF, NAL 1740, the subject of the present book (for the detailed historiographical review, see Chapter 2.2), supplemented the ending of Hrabanus Maurus' commentary on Deuteronomy that was previously unedited. This commentary is the fifth section of the expository series on the whole Pentateuch composed by Hrabanus between 822 and 829 for Freculf, the newly-elected bishop of Lisieux.[4] Burton Van Name Edwards introduced two more ninth-century commentaries on Deuteronomy, so far still unedited, respectively attributed by him to Walahfrid Strabo and Haimo.[5]

---

1 Caroline Chevalier-Royet, *Les Livres de Rois dans l'empire carolingien: Exégèse et actualité* (Paris: Classiques Garnier, 2021).

2 Johannes Heil, *Kompilation oder Konstruktion? Die Juden in den Pauluskommentaren des 9. Jahrhunderts* (Hannover: Hahnsche, 1998); Pierre Boucaud, "Corpus Paulinum: L'exégèse grecque et latine des Épîtres au premier millénaire," *Revue de l'histoire des religions* 230 (2013): pp. 299-332.

3 Paschasius Radbertus, *De benedictionibus patriarcharum Iacob et Moysi*, CCCM 96, ed. Beda Paulus (Turnhout: Brepols, 1993). Pierre Blanchard discovered this text in a lone manuscript. Cf. Pierre Blanchard, "Un traité de Benedictionibus Patriarcharum de Paschase Radbert?" *Revue Bénédictine* 28 (1911): pp. 425-432. For a rich exegetical tradition on the blessings of Jacob before Radbertus, including that of Gregory of Elvira, Ambrose, Jerome, Rufinus, Augustine, Paulinus of Nola, Gregory the Great, Isidore, Bede, and Alcuin, see Henri Moretus, "Les Bénédictions des Patriarches dans la littérature du IVe au VIIIe Siècle," *Bulletin de Littérature Ecclésiastique*, ser. 4th, 1 (1909): pp. 398-411; ser. 4th, 2 (1910), pp. 28-40, 83-100. Radbertus' contemporary Adrevald of Fleury also composed a commentary on *Benedictiones de filiis Iacob*, in PL 20, cols. 715-732, cf. André Wilmart, "Le commentaire des Bénédictions de Jacob attribué a Paulin de Milan," *Revue Bénédictine* 10 (1920): pp. 57-63. Radbertus's goal was to compose an exposition of the blessings of Moses in Deuteronomy 33, a passage "obscure matters of which [have] not been expounded thoroughly by any Latin writers." He adopted a remarkable comparative method to use an already well interpreted biblical passage (Genesis 49) to illuminate a much less interpreted one (Deuteronomy 33). Unfortunately, this creative exegetical treatise has drawn little attention of scholars of Carolingian history.

4 Paul-Irénée Fransen, "La fin inédite du commentaire de Raban Maur sur le Deutéronome," *Revue Bénédictine* 108 (1998): pp. 80-103. The edition of Hrabanus's *Enarratio super Deuteronomium* in PL 108, cols. 837-998 breaks in the middle of Deut. 33. For a critical survey, see Rossana Guglielmetti, "Hrabanus Maurus," *La trasmissione dei testi latini del Medioevo*, eds. Paolo Chiesa, Lucia Castaldi (Florence: SISMEL, Edizioni del Galluzzo, 2004–2013), vol. 3, pp. 275-332.

5 Burton Van Name Edwards, "Deuteronomy in the Ninth Century: The Unpublished Commentaries of Walahfrid Strabo and Haimo of Auxerre," *The Study of the Bible in the Carolingian Era*, eds. Celia Chazelle, Burton Van Name Edwards (Turnhout: Brepols, 2003), pp. 97-113. Both of them use Hrabanus' commentary as a major source. Edwards is preparing the editions of both commentaries for CCCM. The doubt on Haimo's authorship, see Christopher A. Jones's review in *The Medieval Review*, 04.11.14. But this authorship is accepted by Sumi Shimahara in her monograph *Haymon d'Auxerre, exegete Carolingien*.

Thus, besides homilies of an exegetical nature,[1] we have five commentaries on Deuteronomy extant from the ninth century: the Lyon Annotations (composed before the middle of the second decade), Hrabanus' (the end of third decade), Walahfrid's (the 830s or 840s), Haimo's (mid-ninth century), and Radbertus' (only on Deut. 33, composed at his old age, namely in the 860s). To investigate all these commentaries systematically is not among the goals of the present book. It is sufficient to say that each of them shows a distinctive way to integrate earlier exegesis without sacrificing innovation. Among them, the Lyon Annotations is the earliest, and, if we dare to say so, the most creative.

In the preface to his commentary on Deuteronomy, Hrabanus laments to Freculf that "I did not find anybody's interpretation particularly on this book."[2] What Hrabanus actually meant was that there was no major running commentary on Deuteronomy from Church Fathers, like Augustine's on the Gospel of John and Bede's work on the Song of Songs, convenient for him to epitomize and supplement. But it is far from true that there was no Latin exegetical tradition for Deuteronomy before the Carolingian era. Despite the loss of his homilies, Origen's exegesis of Deuteronomy, especially his typological motif that Deuteronomy foreshadows the Gospel, was inherited by western authors via the translation of other works of his. Jerome developed the "Deuteronomy-Gospel" motif and made it a standard hermeneutical principle, and his Hebrew etymologies turned out to be an important exegetical source as well. Ambrose expounded Deuteronomic precepts in a moralistic way. Augustine's philology-oriented exegesis of the same book can be found in his *Quaestiones in Heptateuchum*; his allegorical expositions were scattered in *Contra Faustum*, and were collected by John the Deacon in his *Expositio in Heptateuchum*. There are two entries for Deuteronomy in Eucherius of Lyon's *Intructiones*; his *Formulae* contains a handful of Deuteronomic symbols. Verecundus of Junca expounded Deut. 32 (socalled "the Song of Moses") closely in his *Commentarii super cantica ecclesiastica*. Paterius' *Liber testimoniorum* transmitted Gregory the Great's spiritual exposition of 22 Deuteronomic passages. The fifth section of Isidore of Seville's *Expositio in uetus testamentum* marks a watershed in Latin Deuteronomy exegetical history (which I call "the Isidorian moment"), and constitutes a dominant source for the exegetical practice of the same book until the end of the eighth century, as is shown in the three recensions

---

1   For example, in the three-book homiliary composed by Hrabanus Maurus for Emperor Lothair I shortly before 855, there are at least two original expository pieces of Deuteronomic verses: I.94 and I.95 (Cf. Raymond Étaix, "L'homéliaire composé par Raban Maur pour l'empereur Lothaire," *Recherches Augustiniennes* 19 (1984): pp. 211-240). The ending section of II.90 (Cf. PL 100, cols. 135-468) is original as well. For this homiliary, see Caroline Chevalier-Royet, "Des prédicateurs au service de la réforme de la société carolingienne: l'exemple des homélies de Raban Maur (vers 780-856)," *Gouverner les hommes, gouverner les âmes. XLVIe Congrès de la SHMESP* (Paris, Publications de la Sorbonne: 2016), pp. 49-58.
2   "Sed quia in hunc librum cuiuspiam explanationem proprie non inueni, necesse habui ut perfectis anteriorum librorum expositionibus, inde ad huius libri enodandas quaestiones assumerem facultatem." Hrabanus Maurus, *Enarratio super Deuteronomium*, PL 108, cols. 838-839.

of the Pseudo-Bedan Pentateuch commentary, the *Irish Bibelwerk*, and Wigbod's *Quaestiones in Octateuchum* and his *Lectiones* on the Hexateuch.

The author of the Lyon Annotations had a wide knowledge of this patristic tradition. He probably consulted Origen, Jerome, Ambrose, Eucherius (and maybe *De diuinis nominibus* of Pseudo-Eucherius), Paterius, Gregory (independent of Paterius), Isidore, and maybe one of the recensions of Pseudo-Bede. Meanwhile, there is rarely a single entry in the Lyon Annotations that is copied verbatim from a certain patristic source. Abridging, paraphrasing, pasting, adapting, and re-contextualizing are the author's major exegetical techniques. What's more, only a small portion of the Lyon Annotations can be traced back to known patristic sources. Both the flexible use of the Church Fathers and the large amount of original exegesis make the Lyon Annotations a rare sample for evaluating the vitality of exegetical practice in the earlier phase of the Carolingian Renaissance which is still largely underrated in current scholarship (for the detailed historiographical review, see Chapter 6.7).

Source criticism is not the only effective approach to Carolingian biblical exegesis. Scholars recently have developed great sensitivity to the public function of the Bible and of its interpretation. As the papers in the collection *The Study of the Bible in the Carolingian Era* of 2003 demonstrate, biblical exegesis was deeply immersed in every intellectual sphere: political discourse, theological controversy, "art talk," hagiography, legal compilation, etc.[1] The Holy Scripture played a fundamental role in various aspects of political life in the early medieval west, including the Carolingian era.[2] The biblical model as exemplum for the ideological building of Carolingian rulership has been a subject of multiple fine studies.[3] As Mayke de Jong's many revealing studies have shown, Carolingian secular elites, male and female, royal and non-royal, consciously patronized, read,

---

1 Celia Chazelle, Burton Van Name Edwards, eds., *The Study of the Bible in the Carolingian Era* (Turnhout: Brepols, 2003).

2 Walter Ullmann, "The Bible and Principles of Government in the Middle Ages," *La bibbia nell'alto medioevo* (Spoleto: Centro italiano di studi sull'alto medioevo, 1963), pp. 181-228; Pierre Riché, "La Bible et la vie politique dans le haut Moyen Âge," *Le Moyen Âge et la Bible*, eds. Pierre Riché, Guy Lobrichon (Paris: Beauchesne, 1984), pp. 385-400; Mayke de Jong, "Carolingian Political Discourse and the Biblical Past: Hraban, Dhuoda, Radbert," *The Resources of the Past in Early Medieval Europe*, eds. Clemens Gantner, Rosamond McKitterick, Sven Meeder (Cambridge: Cambridge University Press, 2015), pp. 87-102.

3 E.g., John M. Wallace-Hadrill, "The via regia of the Carolingian Age," *Trends in Medieval Political Thought*, ed. Beryl Smalley (Oxford: Blackwell, 1965), pp. 22-41; Hans Hubert Anton, *Fürstenspiegel und Herrscherethos in der Karlolingerzeit* (Bonn: L. Röhrscheid, 1968), pp. 419-436; Mary Garrison, "Letters to a King and Biblical Exempla: The Examples of Cathuulf and Clemens Peregrinus," *Early Medieval Europe* 7 (1998): pp. 305-328; Rachel Stone, "Beyond David and Solomon: Biblical models for Carolingian laymen," *Gott handhaben: Religiöses Wissen im Konflikt um Mythisierung und Rationalisierung*, eds. Steffen Patzold, Florian Bock (Berlin: De Gruyter, 2016), pp. 189-202. An old but still valuable study is Ernst Rieber, Die Bedeutung alttestamentlicher Vorstellungen für das Herrscherbild Karls des Grossen und seines Hofkreises (Ph.D. dissertation: Universität Tübingen, 1949).

and internalized biblical exegesis.[1] Sumi Shimahara recently proposed the possibility that Charlemagne was the first royal sponsor of biblical exegesis in the Latin west.[2] The principles of Carolingian reform were forged in biblical language and exegetical mentality.[3] The churchmen in the age of Charlemagne, namely the contemporaries of the author of the Lyon Annotations, were accustomed to experience and address present issues via the Bible.[4]

Certain biblical books are inclined to evoke exegesis with specific political or ecclesiological implications. As Eric Miller and Caroline Chevalier-Royet have shown, Carolingian exegetes used books of Kings for the ideological construction of Christian kingship.[5] Similarly, the books of Prophets are ideal conduits for churchmen to express social and

---

1 Mayke de Jong, "The Emperor Lothar and His *Bibliotheca Historiarum*," *Media Latinitas: A Collection of Essays to Mark the Occasion of the Retirement of L. J. Engels*, eds. R. I. A. Nip, H. van Dijk, E. M. C. van Houts, C. H. J. M. Kneepkens, G. A. A. Kortekaas (Turnhout: Brepols, 1996), pp. 229-235; Mayke de Jong, "The Empire as *Ecclesia*: Hrabanus Maurus and Biblical *Historia* for Rulers," *The Uses of the Past in the Early Middle Ages*, eds. Yitzhak Hen, Matthew Innes (Cambridge: Cambridge University Press, 2000), pp. 191-226; Mayke de Jong, "Exegesis for an Empress," *Medieval Transformations: Texts, Power, and Gifts in Context*, eds. Esther Cohen, Mayke de Jong (Leiden: Brill, 2001), pp. 69-100. Also cf. Janet Nelson, "Lay Readers of the Bible in the Carolingian Ninth Century," *Reading the Bible in the Middle Ages*, eds. Janet Nelson, Damien Kempf (London: Bloomsbury Academic, 2015), pp. 43-56.
2 Sumi Shimahara, "Charlemagne, premier souverain chrétien commanditaire d'exégèse biblique?" *Charlemagne: les temps, les espaces, les hommes. Construction et déconstruction d'un règne*, eds. Rolf Grosse, Michel Sot (Turnhout: Brepols, 2018), pp. 101-117. Also cf. eadem, "Gouverner avec la Bible: Les lettres de dédicace adressées aux souverains à l'époque carolingienne," *Épistolaire politique*, ed. Bruno Dumézil (Paris: Presses de l'Université Paris-Sorbonne, 2014), vol. 1, pp. 107-141.
3 Wilfried Hartmann, "Die Karolingische Reform und die Bibel," *Annuarium Historiae Conciliorum* 18 (1986): pp. 58-74.
4 E.g., Mary Garrison, "The Bible and Alcuin's Interpretation of Current Events," *Peritia* 16 (2002): pp. 68-84; Mary Alberi, "'The Sword Which You Hold in Your Hand': Alcuin's Exegesis of the Two Swords and the Lay *Miles Christi*," *The Study of the Bible in the Carolingian Era*, eds. Celia Chazelle, Burton Van Name Edwards (Turnhout: Brepols, 2003), pp. 117-131; Thomas F. X. Noble, "The Varying Roles of Biblical Testimonies in the Carolingian Image Controversies," *Medieval Transformations: Texts, Power, and Gifts in Context*, eds. Esther Cohen, Mayke de Jong (Leiden: Brill, 2001), pp. 101-119; Pierre Boucaud, "Tous libres devant Dieu: Société carolingienne, Église et esclavage d'après l'exégèse de Claude de Turin († ca. 827/828)," *Revue de l'histoire des religions* 228 (2011): pp. 349-387. For a slightly later period, cf. Mayke de Jong, "Becoming Jeremiah: Paschasius Radbertus on Wala, Himself and Others," *Ego Trouble: Authors and Their Identities in the Early Middle Ages*, eds. Richard Corradini, Matthew Gillis, Rosamund McKitterick, Irene van Reenswoude (Wien: Verlag der Österreichischen Akademie der Wissenschaften, 2010), pp. 185-196; Mayke de Jong, "Jeremiah, Job, Terence and Paschasius Radbertus: Political Rhetoric and Biblical Authority in the *Epitaphium Arsenii*," *Reading the Bible in the Middle Ages*, eds. Janet Nelson, Damien Kempf (London: Bloomsbury Academic, 2015), pp. 57-76.
5 Eric Miller, "The Political Significance of Christ's Kingship in the Biblical Exegesis," *Biblical Studies in the Early Middle Ages*, eds. Claudio Leonardi, Giovanni Orlandi (Firenze: Edizioni del Galluzzo, 2005), pp. 193-213; Caroline Chevalier-Royet, "Saül et David, premiers rois oints: L'interprétation de ces modèles royaux par deux exégétes carolingiens, Raban Maur et Angélome de Luxeuil," *The Multiple Meaning of Scripture: The Role of Exegesis in Early-Christian and Medieval Culture*, ed. Ineke Van't Spijker (Leiden: Brill, 2008), pp. 61-76.

political admonition, sometimes harsh, in the *persona* of biblical prophets.[1] Hannah Matis recently argued persuasively that the Carolingian commentaries on the Song of Songs functioned to elaborate a collective identity for the Carolingian *doctores*, ecclesiastical leaders.[2]

In Deuteronomy, the biblical book in the spotlight of the present book, Moses repeatedly called Israel God's chosen people, promised the land flowing with milk and honey to them, and admonished them to observe his precepts. The author of the Lyon Annotations inherited the typological motif from his patristic tradition that the Deuteronomic law signifies the Gospel, and developed it further by expounding the true recipient of Deuteronomy, the "spiritual Israel," as a Christian *ecclesia*. Within this innovative exegetical scheme, the Mosaic precepts in Deuteronomy are effectively transformed into teachings that cultivate the right way of life of a Christian church via both allegorical (*spiritaliter*) and literal (*secundum litteram*) interpretation. An imagined Christian community emerges from the teachings of Deuteronomy.

A constant theme of Carolingian exegesis concerns Jews. In an era usually considered a "golden age" for Jews characterized by tolerant royal policy and intimated Jewish-Christian connections (including communication of biblical learning),[3] ironically, as Johannes Heil put it, "the innumerable references to Jews in Carolingian biblical commentaries are in general unfriendly, even hostile, continuing the 'doctrine of

---

1 John Contreni, "'By Lions, Bishops are Meant; by Wolves, Priests': History, Exegesis, and the Carolingian Church in Haimo of Auxerre's Commentary on Ezechiel," *Francia* 29 (2002): pp. 29-56; Sumi Shimahara, "Daniel et les visions politiques à l'époque carolingienne," *Médiévales: Langues, Textes, Histoire* 55 (2008): pp. 19-32; eadem, "Prophétiser à l'époque carolingienne: l'exégète de la Bible, nouveau prophète et prédicateur par l'écrit," *Études d'exégèse médiévale offertes à Gilbert Dahan par ses élèves*, ed. Annie Noblesse-Rocher (Turnhout: Brepols, 2012), pp. 51-80; eadem, "Prophètes scripturaires et hagiographie à l'époque carolingienne," *Hagiographie et prophétie (VIe-XIIIe siècles)*, eds. Patrick Henriet, Klaus Herbers, Hans-Christian Lehner (Firenze: Edizioni del Galluzzo, 2017), pp. 71-110.

2 Hannah Matis, *The Song of Songs in the Early Middle Ages* (Leiden: Brill, 2019).

3 Cf. Bernard Bachrach, *Early Medieval Jewish Policy in Western Europe* (Minneapolis: University of Minnesota Press, 1977); David Malkiel, "Jewish-Christian Relations in Europe, 840–1096," *Journal of Medieval History* 29 (2003): pp. 55-83; Philippe Depreux, "Les juifs dans le droit carolingien," *Jews in Early Christian Law: Byzantium and the Latin West, 6th–11th Centuries*, eds. Capucine Nemo-Pekelman, Laurence Foschia, John V. Tolan, Nicholas de Lange (Turnhout: Brepols, 2014), pp. 131-152; Avrom Saltman, "Rabanus Maurus and the Pseudo-Hieronymian *Quaestiones Hebraicae in Libros Regum et Paralipomenon*," *The Harvard Theological Review* 66 (1973): pp. 43-75; Johannes Heil, "Theodulf, Haimo, and Jewish Traditions of Biblical Learning: Exploring Carolingian Culture's Lost Spanish Heritage," *Discovery and Distinction in the Early Middle Ages: Studies in Honor of John J. Contreni*, eds. Cullen Chandler, Steven Stofferahn (Kalamazoo: Medieval Institute Publications, Western Michigan University, 2013), pp. 88-115. A cautious revision of this traditional view, see Johannes Heil, "Goldenes Zeitalter? Juden und Judentum in der Karolingerzeit," *"Wie schön sind Deine Zelte, Jakob, deine Wohnungen, Israel?"*: *Beiträge zur Geschichte europäisch-jüdischer Kultur*, ed. Rainer Kampling (Frankfurt am Main: Peter Lang, 2009), pp. 99-114.

contempt' first articulated in the patristic era."[1] More than other literary genres did biblical exegesis contribute to the Carolingian *contra Iudaeos* discourse, as Heil, Bat-Sheva Albert, and other scholars have clearly shown.[2]

The anti-Jewish exposition in the Lyon Annotations is far more extensive and harsher than in any earlier Latin commentary on Deuteronomy, which very likely reflects the intellectual pressure that contemporary Christian ecclesiastics of Lyon felt from the neighboring Jewish community. From the 820s on, Agobard and Amulo adopted it as a source to develop a more radical anti-Jewish rhetoric. The Lyon Annotations in this sense witnesses a so far neglected stage of the evolution of the anti-Judaism in Carolingian Lyon.

1.3 Chapter Plan

The main body of this book is divided into three large sections. Part I "Text and Context" contains three chapters. Chapter 1 introduces the historiographical background of the main text. Chapter 2 introduces a thorough examination of the codicological and textual features of the Deuteronomy annotations in Paris, BnF, NAL 1740, as well as their research history. It also demonstrates in depth why these annotations were most likely the production of the biblical school and the enlivened scriptorium of the episcopal church of Lyon during the time of Leidrad. Chapter 3 depicts in detail the immediate historical context of the making of the Lyon Annotations: Leidrad's church reform of Lyon in the years 798–816. Not only Leidrad's personality and intellectual horizon but also the institutional outcomes of his reform (library, scriptorium, schools, and a team of clerical elite) brought about the birth of the Lyon Annotations, and the latter in turn served the reform with teaching biblical knowledge and inculcating the ideal of a *plebs ecclesiastica*.

Part II "Tradition and Innovation" reviews the Latin Christian exegetical history of Deuteronomy from the beginning to 800. Three chapters are arranged in chronological order. Chapter 4 mainly surveys three exegetes, Origen, Jerome, and Ambrose, who left a fundamental inheritance of Christian interpretation of Deuteronomy, especially the

---

1 The quotation is from idem, "Labourers in the Lord's Quarry: Carolingian Exegetes, Patristic Authority, and Theological Innovation, a Case Study in the Representation of Jews in Commentaries on Paul," *The Study of the Bible in the Carolingian Era*, eds. Celia Chazelle, Burton Van Name Edwards (Turnhout: Brepols, 2003), pp. 75-95.

2 Idem, *Kompilation oder Konstruktion*; Bat-Sheva Albert, "*Adversos Iudaeos* in the Carolingian Empire," *Contra Iudaeos: Ancient and Medieval Polemics between Christians and Jews*, eds. Ora Limor, Guy G. Stroumsa (Tübingen: Mohr, 1996), pp. 119-142; idem, "Anti-Jewish Exegesis in the Carolingian Period: the Commentaries on Lamentations of Hrabanus Maurus and Pascasius Radbertus," *Biblical Studies in the Early Middle Ages*, eds. Claudio Leonardi, Giovanni Orlandi (Firenze: Edizioni del Galluzzo, 2005), pp. 175-192; Jonathan Elukin, "Judaism: From Heresy to Pharisee in Early Medieval Christian Literature," *Traditio* 57 (2002): pp. 49-66.

"Deuteronomy-Gospel" typological motif. Chapter 5 examines five pre-Isidorian Latin commentaries, from Augustine to Gregory, and their diverse hermeneutical approaches to this biblical book. Chapter 6 focuses on Isidore's exegetical synthesis and his dominant influence in later expositions of Deuteronomy before 800. The detailed study of each of these exegetical enterprises is accompanied by a discussion of how it is used (or not used) in the Lyon Annotations. A conclusion will summarize the source criticism of the Lyon Annotations against the patristic tradition excavated in Part II, and its flexible expository techniques. The highly innovative and confident exegetical practice of the Lyon Annotations enriches the common understanding of biblical studies in the age of Charlemagne.

Part III "Old and New" turns to analyze the ecclesiastical imaginary in the Lyon Annotations, namely, how the Christian church, its history, and its opponents (pagans, heretics, and Jews) are presented via exegetical language. It has two chapters. Chapter 7 describes how the Lyon Annotations presents a Christian community, its self-identity as the "spiritual Israel," internal hierarchy, and specific moral concerns. Chapter 8 focuses on how the Lyon Annotations talks about Jews and their position in the history of salvation, and how it represents a comparatively mild anti-Jewish tradition in Carolingian Lyon prior to Agobard's radicalization.

CHAPTER 2
THE LYON ANNOTATIONS: A PRIMARY SURVEY

This chapter aims to provide in a thorough way a survey of the physical presentation and the research history of the Deuteronomy annotations of Paris, BnF, NAL 1740, and an investigation of their most likely compositional date, background, and authorship. It will pave the way for the deeper study of their historical context (Chapter 3), exegetical tradition (Chapters 4–6), and social imagination (Chapters 7–8).

The fundamental question to ask here is: to what extent can we connect the making of these annotations with Lyon, especially the Lyon during the episcopate of Leidrad; in other words, is it reasonable for us to give them the collective name "the Lyon Annotations"?

2.1 Paris, BnF, NAL 1740

Manuscript NAL 1740 of the Bibliothèque nationale de France is a two-column *de luxe* codex of 236 folios (330 × 260 mm). It contains the Vulgate of Deuteronomy, Joshua, Judges, and most of Ruth.[1] It is one of the oldest extant manuscripts of the Vulgate Bible.[2] The biblical text was written in well-formed uncial. The title and colophon for each biblical book are in highly decorative three-colored capital. Elias Lowe proposed that the script of the main text in Paris, BnF, NAL 1740 resembled that of two manuscripts, the *Missale Francorum* (BAV, Vat. Reg. Lat. 257) and the *Psalterium Duplum* (BAV, Vat Reg. Lat. 11), and accordingly located the origin of Paris, BnF, NAL

---

1 The text of Ruth breaks off at *neque enim posteritatem familiae meae delere debeo: tu meo ute(re)...* (4:6), presumably due to the missing of the last several folios. For the online facsimile of Paris, BnF, NAL 1740, see http://gallica.bnf.fr/ark:/12148/btv1b85856056, last accessed September 14, 2021.
2 As Manuscript F in the Benedictine edition of the Vulgate. Cf. *Biblia sacra iuxta latinam Vulgatam versionem ad codicum fidem*, III: Libros Numerorum et Deuteronomii (Rome: Typis Polyglottis Vaticanis, 1936), p. XI.

1740 to northern France in the early eighth century.[1]

The manuscript had reached Lyon by the ninth century. The replacement quire of fols. 193-197 was written in Carolingian minuscule. André Wilmart pointed out that the script of these five folios strongly recalled that of two other manuscripts: Lyon, BM, 402 (Origen's Homilies on Joshua, Judge, Kings, and Chronicles) and Lyon, BM, 599 (Gregory of Nazianzus's *Liber apologeticus* and several other works of his).[2] Both of them are thought to have been copied in Lyon at the end of the eighth century or the beginning of the ninth century.[3] The cathedral scriptorium produced them for the personal use of Archbishop Leidrad. In the former manuscript, Leidrad collated the text by his own hand. In the latter, he left an autographical *ex-dono* (*Leidrat, licet indignus, tamen episcopus/Istum librum tradidi ad altare sancti Stephani* in fol. 1r) when he donated it to the episcopal library.[4] The replacement folios of Paris, BnF, NAL 1740 thus was probably copied by the cathedral scriptorium as well ca. 800, probably under Leidrad's command. There are also a large number of minuscule collations visible in Paris, BnF, NAL 1740 by different hands.[5] It seems that the cathedral scriptorium took efforts to emend the manuscript by both supplementing its lost folios and correcting its textual errors upon its arrival at Lyon. It could echo Charlemagne's order to regularize the biblical text and the effort to revise the Vulgate by Alcuin of York and Theodulf of Orléans, both of whom were Leidrad's acquaintances.[6]

As early as the ninth century, Paris, BnF, NAL 1740 was available to the clergy of St-Stephen, the collegiate church of Lyon cathedral. In fol. 225v, among many ninth- and tenth-century *probationes pennae*, three of them refer to the church of St-Stephen: *ad*

---

1 "The characters bear the strongest resemblance to two well-known MSS. In the Regina collection of Vatican, namely, MS. 11, a Psalter, and MS. 257, The Missale Francorum." Elias A. Lowe, *Codices Lugdunenses Antiquissimi. Le scriptorium de Lyon, le plus ancienne école calligraphique de France* (Lyon: Aux dépens des "Amis de la Bibliothèque de Lyon," 1924). "Written doubtless in the same French scriptorium as produced the Missale Francorum and the Psalterium Duplum (CLA, I.101 and 103)." CLA, V.691.

2 "Il est vrai seulement que Lyon 402, Lyon 599 et Paris B. N. Acu. 1740, fol. 193-197 (provenant de Lyon), sont d'un type graphique voisin de celui d'Autun-Flavigny." André Wilmart, "Membra Disiecta," *Revue Bénédictine* 36 (1924): pp. 131-136. Cf. Bernhard Bischoff, *Katalog*, 5113a: "Erg. Der Unz.hs. in kräftiger rundlicher Lyoneser Min.; vergleiche die von Eb. Leidrad der Kathedrale St. Stephan übergebene Hs. LYON, BM, Ms. 599 (515)."

3 Lyon, BM, 402: "Vorkarol. Min. Lyon, s. VIIIex." Bischoff, *Katalog*, 2547b; Lyon, BM, 599: "Vielleicht Lyon, VIII./IX. Jh.." Bischoff, *Katalog*, 2568.

4 See Louis Holtz, "Leidrat, évêque de Lyon," pp. 319-320.

5 For example: "EN POPVLVS SAPIENS ET INTELLIGENS, ᵍᵉⁿˢ MAGNA." (Deut. 4:6, fol. 12v); "DOMINVM DEVM TVVM TIMEBIS, ET ILLI ˢᵒˡⁱ SERVIES, AC PER NOMEN ILLIVS IVRABIS." (Deut. 6:13, fol. 21r); "QVI SVNT POPVLVS TVVS ET HAᵉʳEDITAS TVA, QVOS EDVXISTI IN FORTITVDINE TVA MAGNA, ET IN BRACHIO TVO EXTENTO." (Deut. 9:29, fol. 29r); "TRIBVS VICIBVS PER ANNVM APPAREBIT OMNE MASCVLINVM ᵗᵘᵘᵐ IN CONSPECTV DOMINI DEI TVI IN LOCO QVEM ELEGERIT." (Deut. 16:16, fol. 46v).

6 Cf. François Louis Ganshof, "Charlemagne et la revision du texte latin." For Leidrad's personal relationship with Alcuin and Theodulf, see Chapter 2.

altare Sancti Stefani, Rudoltus sancti Stefani, and *iste liber est Daniele clerice sancti Stephani episcopatus bonum*. Other *probationes pennae* written in the same period of time show that people named Artoldus, Autgarius, Alimarus, and Girbertus, all possibly being canons of St-Stephen, had once consulted this manuscript, probably for personal study.[1] In fol. 231v, there is a minuscule intercolumnar note — *Orate pro illo qui istum librum suscripsit, tercio kalendas agustas, regnante Lottario rege* — apparently by a cleric who used the manuscript during the reign of King Lothair II (r. 863–869). Meanwhile, there are numerous punctuation marks added to the biblical text in the ink darker than the original handwriting, an indication that, besides personal silent reading, the manuscript could also have been read aloud, either for liturgical use or on gathering occasions such as chapter meeting or common refectory.

In modern times, prior to its migration to the Bibliothèque Nationale in 1894, Paris, BnF, NAL 1740 was preserved in the library of the Baron Dauphin de Verna (as No. 1234 of the sale catalogue) in Crémieu, Isère, a short distance (25 miles) from the city of Lyon. The manuscript thus stayed in the Lyonnais until the end of the nineteenth century.

2.2   The Marginal and Intercolumnar Annotations in Paris, BnF, NAL 1740

Paris, BnF, NAL 1740 preserves an anonymous commentary on Deuteronomy. The commentary consists of more than 400 annotations alongside the annotated Deuteronomic verses through fols. 1r-94r (including 27bis and 81bis), either in page margins or between columns. These annotations vary in style, from succinct etymological gloss to elaborate spiritual exposition. While some are blurry due to the long time and the wear on manuscript margin, they are generally legible. The annotations are connected to the main text by proximate placement and/or pairs of *signes de renvoi*, or tie marks.[2] Léopold Delisle was the first scholar who paid attention to these annotations. In his survey of 1895 for certain manuscripts from the Library of the Baron Dauphin de Verna, Delisle described these annotations as "en caractères minuscules très élégants, pouvant remonter au IXe siècle." He also took pain to transcribe a part of them.[3] After Delisle, no scholar had undertaken specific investigation into these annotations, until Paul-Irénée Fransen rediscovered them in a paper published in 1997. Fransen commented that "quoique disparates, ces notes ne manquent pas d'unite et dans la pensée et dans

---

1   "Artoldus bonus omo" in fol. 58r; "Autgarius istum librum legit" in fol. 162v; "Alimarus suscripsit" in fol. 163r; "tus ber gir (=Girbertus)" in fol. 167v.
2   62 types of tie mark shapes are detected in total.
3   Léopold Delisle, "Notes sur quelques manuscrits du Baron Dauphin de Verna," *Bibliothèque de l'École des Chartes* 56 (1895): pp. 651-655.

l'expression," and defined their central theme as "la discipline de l'Église."[1] As the major editor of the *opera* of Florus of Lyon, the most prolific Carolingian compiler of patristic exegesis who served as deacon (early 820s–860s) and scriptorium director at Lyon,[2] Fransen expected to connect the anonymous Deuteronomy annotations, together with the anti-heretical and anti-Jewish expositions in them, to Florus and his polemical writings, although he conceded that the script of the annotations does not match the deacon's handwriting.

In the same paper, Fransen also promised an edition of these annotations, the fulfillment of which appeared in the 2007 volume of *Revue Bénédictine*.[3] In his introduction to the edition, Fransen noted that the annotations varied in nature, including "etymological notes, references to history, theological reflections and explications of the biblical text," which altogether reflected "the personality of a thinker, an erudite, and a church man."[4] Fransen summarized his evaluation gracefully in the following words:

> The work is attractive. It is characterized by a profound theology about salvation, based on the life of a living community which reads and interprets the Bible. It presents personal notes which illustrate precisely and humorously the way of thinking of an insightful observer of the Christianity of his own times. It is an original testimony of an epoch that was concerned with its roots and its future.[5]

Fransen's edition also contains a two-layered editorial apparatus which shows the biblical references inside these annotations, the correcting traces left on the annotations, and his suggestions on difficult readings. The edition is professionally produced and generally reliable, but not without minor problems. The corrections are listed in the following *corrigenda* (Table 2.1).

---

1 Paul-Irénée Fransen, "La discipline de l'Église dans un commentaire anonyme au Deutéronome écrit à Lyon au IXe siècle," *Zeitschrift der Savigny-Stiftung für Rechtsgeschichte* 83 (1997): pp. 52-66.

2 *Collectio ex dictis XII Patrum I* (CCCM 193); *Collectio ex dictis XII Patrum II* (CCCM 193A); *Collectio ex dictis XII Patrum III* (CCCM 193B); *Expositio in epistolas beati Pauli ex operibus s. Augustini III* (CCCM 220B).

3 Paul-Irénée Fransen, "Un commentaire marginal lyonnais du Deutéronome du milieu du IXe siècle," *Revue Bénédictine* 117 (2007): pp. 31-63, 339-382.

4 Ibid., p. 31.

5 "L'oeuvre est attachante. Elle est marqueée par une profonde théologie du Salut, fondée sur la vie d'une communauté vivante qui lit la Bible et sait l'interpréter. Elle apporte des notes personnelles qui illustrent avec précision et non sans un certain humour la maniére de penser d'un observateur perspicace du christianisme de son temps. Elle est un témoignage original d'une époque attentive à ses racines et soucieuse de son avenir." Ibid., pp. 35-36.

Table 2.1 *Corrigenda* of Fransen's edition

	Fransen's edition	Correction
fol. 10r; on Deut. 3:11	Lectus eius ferreus **uiri sunt** impii atque peccatores... (p. 36)	Lectus eius ferreus **homines** impii atque peccatores...[1]
fol. 16v; on Deut. 4:43	Ramoth excelsa **mons**. (p. 38)	Ramoth excelsa **mors**.
fol. 18r; on Deut. 5:14	Cum dicitur tui, doctoribus ecclesie loquitur... (p. 40)	Cum dicitur tui, doctoribus ecclesie loquitur... doctores*: doctoribus *cor.*[2]
fol. 18r; on Deut. 5:14	... utriusque sexus **religiosus** appellat... **per] peregrinans populus** gentium... (p. 40)	... utriusque sexus **religiosas** appellat... **peregrinus populum** gentium...
fol. 19r; on Deut. 5:29	Ø	NOTA[3]
fol. 23v; on Deut. 7:14	Ø	Tam in doctoribus quam auditoribus.[4]
fol. 30r; on Deut. 10:15	... eorum **in** posteritate de uirginem adsumpsit. (p. 46)	... eorum posteritate de uirginem dsumpsit.
Fol. 34r; on Deut. 11:29	Plerique in montem Ga<rizim> Euangelium et nouu<m> populum **accipiun<tur>**.	Plerique in montem Ga<rizim> Euangelium et nouu<m> populum **accipiun<t>**.[5]
fol. 36v; on Deut. 12:15-18	... permixtus populus tamquam **aduersa** animalia quasi **ceci dantur** cum baptizantur et quasi <**carnem**> **comedamur**... (p. 50)	... permixtus populus tanquam **diuersa** animalia quasi **occidentur** cum baptizantur et quasi **comedantur**...
fol. 37v	*On Deut. 12:25:* Non de carnalibus filiis dicit sed potius spiritalibus de quibus in psalmo scriptum est... (p. 51)	*This annotation is on Deut. 12:28 ("Observa et audi omnia quae ego praecipio tibi, ut bene sit tibi et filiis tuis post te in sempiternum...")*
fol. 39v	*On Deut. 13:15:* Iuxta historiam in priori populo... (p. 52)	*The annotation is on Deut. 13:12 (-15) ("Si audieris in una urbium tuarum quas Dominus Deus tuus, dabit tibi ad habitandum...")*
fol. 41r	Per sus id est **porcorum** eosdem Iudeos... (p. 53)	Per sus id est **porcum** eosdem Iudeos...
fol. 47r; on Deut. 16:21	... illi enim lucum uel quamlibet arborem infructuosa iuxta altare domini plantare conantur qui in **sinceritate** fidei... (p. 58)	... illi enim lucum uel quamlibet arborem infructuosa iuxta altare domini plantare conantur qui in **sinceritatem** fidei...

---

1 The word(s) between "ferreus" and "impii" is ambiguous, but Fransen's reading ("uiri sunt") is doubtful. Maybe the most likely reading is "homines," not only for paleographical reasons, but also because "homines impii" as a phrase appears several times in other annotations.

2 In this annotation, a scribe corrected "doctores" to "doctoribus."

3 Fransen missed a "Nota" sign connected to Deut. 5:29 ("Quis det talem eos habere mentem, ut timeant me et custodiant uniuersa mandata mea in omni tempore, ut bene sit eis et filiis eorum in sempiternum?") by a pair of tie marks.

4 Fransen missed the annotation on Deut. 7:14 ("Non erit apud te sterilis utriusque sexus, tam in hominibus quam in gregibus tuis.")

5 It is more reasonable to read the last word as "accipiunt" than as "accipiuntur."

Continued

	Fransen's edition	Correction
fol. 56r; on Deut. 21:1	... hoc quippe demonstrat cum dicit: Ignoratur cedis reus; sicut est illud in psalmo: Que **ignorabant me**, interrogabant me.	... hoc quippe demonstrat cum dicit: Ignoratur cedis reus; sicut est illud in psalmo: Que **ignorabant**, interrogabant me.
fol. 58r; on Deut. 21:22-23	Homo iste significat Adam qui primus peccauit, quod morte **plectendus non** fuit. (p. 344)	Homo iste significat Adam qui primus peccauit, quod morte **plectendus** fuit. plectendum*; plectendus: cor.[1]
fol. 71r; on Deut. 28:4	... armenta **boum** ordinem clericorum... (p. 357)	... armenta **bouum** ordinem clericorum...
fol. 88r; on Deut. 32:27	... **reseruatus** enim ad penitentiam propter illos qui ex ipsa gente secus fine mundi Christo credituri sunt. (p. 370)	... **reseruatur** enim ad penitentiam propter illos qui ex ipsa gente secus fine mundi Christo credituri sunt.
fol. 91r; on Deut. 33:8-9	... per passionem probabit qui dixit patri uel matri, id est sinagoge et fratribus, hoc est iudeis qui in eum **crediderunt**... (p. 374)	... per passionem probabit qui dixit patri uel matri, id est sinagoge et fratribus, hoc est iudeis qui in eum **credere noluerunt**...

Throughout this book, Fransen's edition is used as basis, and Paris, BnF, NAL 1740 is consulted directly when necessary and make citation by folio number.

Fransen pointed out a fair number of spelling and grammatical irregularities. The copyist, if not the author, of these marginal and intercolumnar annotations shows a predilection to adopt *b* for *v* (e.g., *obes* instead of *oves* in the annotation for Deut. 28:16-19), *b* for *p* (e.g., *obtimus* instead of *optimus* in the annotation for Deut. 28:12), *p* for *b* (e.g., *prespiteros* instead of *presbiteros* in the annotation for Deut. 17:14), and *u* for *b* (e.g., *improuis* instead of *improbis* in the annotation for Deut. 28:16-19). Fransen also remarked that the declension after preposition often breaks from regular Latin grammar: ablative after *ad*, *iuxta*, *inter*, *per*, and *propter*, and accusative after *de*, *ex*, *in*, *pro*, and *sub*.[2] To Fransen's observation, we can also supplement the occasional non-standard use of *h*, e.g., *abere* instead of *habere*, and *ehbrei* instead of *hebrei*.[3] One may ask whether such systematic linguistic irregularity should be explained by the oral origin of these marginal and intercolumnar annotations, rather than, as Fransen believed, merely by the negligence of the copyist. Another group of evidence is the occasional dialogic tone occasionally expressed in the commentary, such as *subaudis*, *repperies*, *nota*, *nota aperta*

---

1 In this annotation, a scribe corrected "plectendum" to "plectendus."

2 Paul-Irénée Fransen, "Un commentaire marginal lyonnais," p. 34.

3 "Id est stultum quemlibet sapienti in predicatione ne socies. Aliter: Ita religionem cristianam fide et opere retine, ut cum subprestitionibus Iudeorum nullam societatem abere uelis, ne utroque pede claudus efficiaris." Paris, BnF, NAL 1740, fol. 59r, on Deut. 22:10; "Romanos dicit quorum linguam tempore illo ehbrei non sciuerunt." Paris, BnF, NAL 1740, fol. 75v, on Deut. 28:49.

sententia..., ut suspicor, and *ut reor*.[1] We are probably hearing here the record of a living voice of a Carolingian exegetical doctor.

Two of the best paleographers, Elias A. Lowe and Bernhard Bischoff, gave opinions on the script of these annotations. Lowe agreed with Delisle on dating them to the ninth century and called the annotations "neatly copied marginal glosses in small Lyonese minuscule saec. IX."[2] Bischoff offered a more specific judgment by depicting the handwriting of these annotations "small and neat Lyon minuscule of late Leidrad-script." He also noted that the person who wrote down these annotations also left his handwriting in two corrections on the biblical text in the same manuscript in fol. 77v and 130r.[3] It is an important observation in helping us to glimpse this anonymous copyist: If he had the knowledge as well as the authority to correct the biblical text in an old codex, the scribe of the marginal and intercolumnar annotations in Paris, BnF, NAL 1740 was very probably a schoolmaster in the episcopal church of Lyon.

Scholars so far have paid little attention to these annotations. As far as we know, they are only briefly mentioned or treated in the works of four scholars. Abigail Firey cited the annotation on Deut. 24:10 in a footnote that discusses coercive penance in the Carolingian era.[4] Also only in footnote, Burton Van Name Edwards in his paper on two Carolingian commentaries on Deuteronomy (attributed by him to Walahfrid Strabo and Haimo of Auxerre) mentioned the annotations and commented that they are "completely independent of the two commentaries I have analyzed here."[5] Both Anna Langenwalter and Warren Pezé emphasized the omnipresent references to Jews, the "carnal Israel," in the annotations, and suggested contextualizing them in the anti-Jewish trend at Lyon during the episcopate of Leidrad's successor Agobard.[6]

---

1   "Subaudis": BnF, NAL 1740, fol. 15r, on Deut. 4:34; fol. 19r, on Deut. 5:28; fol. 86r, on Deut. 32:6;
"Repperies": fol. 13r, on Deut. 4:9; fol. 44, on Deut. 15:12; fol. 64r, on Deut. 24:16; fol. 82, on Deut;
31:2.
"Nota... ": , fol. 26r, on Deut. 8:12-14; fol. 60r, on Deut. 22:24-25; fol. 80, on Deut. 30:5; fol. 84r, on
Deut. 31:19; fol. 90v, on Deut. 33:6;
"Nota aperta...": fol. 17r , on Deut. 5:2-3; fol. 49v, on Deut. 18:1; fol. 78r, on Deut. 29:2-4; fol. 80r, on
Deut. 30:1-3;
"Hoc habes in...": fol. 20r, on Deut. 6:5;
"Ut opinor": fol. 47r, on Deut. 16:22;
"Ut suspicor": fol. 56r, on Deut. 21:1;
"Ut reor": fol. 57r, on Deut. 21:18-21.
2   CLA, V.691.
3   "Zum Dt zahlreiche, z.T. lange Erklarungen am Rd. u. zwischen den Sp. in kleiner gleichm. Lyoneser
Min. der späteren Leidrad-Schr." "In gleicher Schrift Textkorr. (77v, 130r)." "Lyon, IX. Jh., ca. 1./2.
Viertel." Bischoff, *Katalog*, III, 5113b.
4   Abigail Firey, *A Contrite Heart: Prosecution and Redemption in the Carolingian Empire* (Leiden:
Brill, 2009), p. 219, n. 27.
5   Burton Van Name Edwards, "Deuteronomy in the Ninth Century," p. 107, n. 35.
6   Anna Langenwalter, *Agobard of Lyon: An Exploration of Carolingian Jewish-Christian Relations* (Ph.
D. dissertation: University of Toronto, 2009), pp. 117-119; Warren Pezé, "Amalaire et la communauté
juive de Lyon: À propos de l'antijudaïsme lyonnais à l'époque carolingienne," *Francia* 40 (2013): pp.
1-25.

2.3   The Annotations in Paris, BnF, NAL 1740 as Marginalia

The more than 400 annotations in Paris, BnF, NAL 1740 together constitute a commentary on Deuteronomy. When Fransen in his edition collected them from the margins of the manuscript, supplemented the expounded biblical lemmata, and presented them in order, we see a running commentary not really distinguishable in outlook from other early medieval biblical commentaries. This being said, however, the fact that this commentary on Deuteronomy presents itself as marginalia is crucial to our understanding of this text in its historical context. The study of annotating practice in early medieval manuscripts has recently become an academic hotspot.[1] As an ancient technique of scribal culture, marginalia (including all notes and markings that were entered in the margins of a manuscript) were present in close to 60 out of approximately 1400 manuscripts catalogued by Lowe in *Codices Latini Antiquiores*.[2] Marginalia experienced a huge expansion in the Carolingian era. In Mariken Teeuwen's estimation, more than 80% or even 90% of Latin manuscripts from the ninth century onwards contain marginalia. Besides, the layout of the post-800 manuscripts more and more frequently leaves room for intended or potential marginal or interlineal annotations.[3]

This contrast gives us a general context in which we may locate the annotating practice found in Paris, BnF, NAL 1740. More specifically, David Ganz in his fundamental study of Carolingian Corbie claimed that "[i]n the Merovingian kingdoms, only Lyons seems to have preserved a tradition of annotations." He mentions sporadic marginal entries in cursive, uncial, or half-uncial in four pre-800 Lyon manuscripts.[4] This local tradition of marginal scholarship was inherited and developed to a great extent in the mid-ninth century by Florus. The master of cathedral scriptorium extensively added annotations and different types of signs (technical signs, *Nota* signs, and source marks) to the margins of the manuscripts preserved and produced in Lyon at that time,

---

1   E.g., the project "Marginal Scholarship: The Practice of Learning in the Early Middle Ages (c. 800– c. 1000)", see the website https://www.marginalscholarship.nl/, last accessed September 14, 2021. It includes a database of more than 350 annotated manuscripts of eighth-tenth centuries. Also cf. Mariken Teeuwen and Irene van Renswoude, eds., *The Annotated Book in the Early Middle Ages: Practices of Reading and Writing* (Turnhout: Brepols, 2018).

2   The count is initially proposed by David Ganz and adopted by Mariken Teeuwen, "Writing in the Blank Space of Manuscripts: Evidence from the Ninth Century," *Ars Edendi Lecture Series*, Volume IV, eds. Barbara Crostini, Gunilla Iversen, Brian M. Jensen (Stockholm: Stockholm University Press), pp. 1-25.

3   Ibid., pp. 2-3.

4   David Ganz, *Corbie in the Carolingian Renaissance*, p. 71. The four examples that he gives are based on Elias A-Lowe, *Codices Lugdunenses Antiquissimi*: Paris, BnF, lat. 9550 (p. 31; a codex of Eucherius' *Formulae spirituales*); Lyon, BM, 426 + Paris, BnF, lat. 1629, fols. 7-14 (p. 34; Augustine's *Enarationes in Psalmos*); Lyon, BM, 483 (p. 36; Origen's commentary on Pauline epistles); Lyon, BM, 607 (p. 43; Augustine's *De ciuitate Dei*). We can add Lyon, BM, 443 + Paris, BnF, lat. 1591 (p. 38; Origen's homilies on Genesis, Exodus, and Leviticus).

not least in aid of his great project of editing patristic compilations. To his path-breaking
paper on Florus published in 1945, Dom Célestin Charlier appended a list of about 100
manuscripts "qui se trouvaient certainement à Lyon au ixe siècle," in about 40 of which
he detected "traces de la main de Florus."[1]

Charlier did not see Florus' handwriting in Paris, BnF, NAL 1740, but Bischoff sus-
pected that a "critical note" on the left margin of fol. 94bisv was left by Florus.[2] However, the expositional annotations on Deuteronomy are certainly not Florus' own, and,
if we trust Bischoff's judgment of their script ("Lyoneser Min. der späteren Leidrad-
Schr."), they must have been produced prior to Florus' intellectual career. What's more,
quite different from Florus' spontaneous and concise ad-hoc marginal notes written down
during reading, the Deuteronomy annotations in Paris, BnF, NAL 1740 are characterized
by their great quantity (more than 400 annotations on less than 50 folios, and many very
long), consistent handwriting, neat ruling, proper management of marginal space, and
well-structured layout. These features alone distinguish Paris, BnF, NAL 1740 from all
other annotated manuscripts conserved at Lyon in the ninth century.

It is thus tempting to define these Deuteronomy annotations as "copied annotations,"
that is copied directly from a set exemplar.[3] But such a hypothesis is somehow vitiated
by the fact that there are some *signes de renvoi* marked on the main text *without* paired
annotations.[4] This curious phenomenon makes it possible to treat labeling Deuteronomic
verses planned to be annotated (by tie marks) and copying annotations (*maybe* from a set
exemplar) as two separate, if not sequential steps. It is hard to tell whether those unpaired
tie marks are the evidence of incompleteness or rather of openness to updating.

Concerning the educational and academic function of marginal annotating, Gernot
Wieland in 1970s famously hypothesized that glossed medieval books were classbooks
used in the schoolroom and that the glosses may reflect spontaneous reactions in teaching
and learning. Michael Lapidge argued against the generalization of this hypothesis and
cautioned that, in many cases, marginal glosses were not spontaneously made but rather

---

1   Célestin Charlier, "Les manuscrits personnels de Florus de Lyon et son activité littéraire," *Mélanges
Emmanuel Podechard. Études de sciences religieuses offertes pour son éméritat au doyen honoraire
de la faculté de théologie de Lyon* (Lyon: Faculté de théologie catholique: 1945): pp. 71-84. Charlier's
list is not a definite one. Pierre Chambert-Protat has provided a revised list based on Charlier's in
his blog and promised to update it: see https://florus.hypotheses.org/liste-de-charlier, last accessed
September 14, 2021. Also cf. Holtz, "La bibliothèque de Florus de Lyon."
2   "94bisv am ob. Rd. eine kritische Notiz von Florus (?)." Bischoff, *Katalog*, 5113b.
3   For the discussion of "copied" vs. "ad hoc" annotations in early medieval marginal scholarship,
see Mariken Teeuwen, "Voices from the Edge: Annotating Books in the Carolingian Period," *The
Annotated Book in the Early Middle Ages: Practices of Reading and Writing*, eds. Mariken Teeuwen,
Irene van Renswoude (Turnhout: Brepols, 2018), pp. 13-36.
4   There are at least two clear cases: the tie mark ⟩ in fol. 15v on "... extentumque brachium, et
horribiles uisiones iuxta omnia quae fecit pro uobis Dominus Deus uester in Aegypto..." (Deut. 4:34);
ꝝ in folio 36r on "... et quidquid praecipuum est in muneribus, quae uouebitis Domino." (Deut.
12:11)

copied in more than one extant manuscript, and that many annotated books were more likely to be conserved in libraries for clerics or monks to borrow for private reading.[1] Recent scholars have proposed a more dynamic perspective to see the manuscript margin as a communicating, negotiating, and debating space for scholars to accumulate, to collect, and even to debate learning.[2]

While this academic debate so far has been largely limited to secular learning, namely the annotated manuscripts of arts and classical literature, it can be usefully applied to the present case. Thanks to the ninth- and tenth-century *probationes pennae* and short notes left on the last folios (cf. Chapter 2.1), we can safely say that Paris, BnF, NAL 1740 was used as a library book available to the clerics of Lyon Cathedral in the Carolingian era. More significantly, it is proper to say that the added marginal annotations "upgraded" this early-eighth-century Bible manuscript to a *de facto* "commented edition."

Édition commentée is a term popularized by Louis Holtz to refer to a manuscript whose layout was *designed* to have gloss and commentary between the lines and in the margins of the main text. The main text (in the central column) and the comments — both the long expositions in the two columns on each side of the main text and the interlineal short glosses — were usually copied by the same hand but distinguished from each other by font, and linked by tie mark rather than lemma. Holtz saw the édition commentée as a codicological invention that first appeared in Carolingian Europe in the manuscript production of classical, especially Virgilian, works, and was slowly adapted to Bible manuscripts, the ultimate form of which was the well-known *Glossa ordinaria*.[3] However, Holtz' hypothesis on the development of the application of the "commented edition" to sacred text seems too conservative. It is worth noting that, while the extant Virgil manuscripts of this kind originated from the scriptoria of west *Francia* (Tours and Fleury), east *Francia* appeared to have been a pioneer in adopting this new technique to Bible production. Using this layout to integrate biblical text and comments was already

---

1 Arthur Rigg, Gernot Wieland, "A Canterbury Classbook of the Mid-Eleventh Century (the 'Cambridge Songs' Manuscript)," *Anglo-Saxon England* 4 (1975): pp. 113-130; Michael Lapidge, "The Study of Latin Texts in Late Anglo-Saxon England: The Evidence of Latin Glosses," *Latin and the Vernacular Languages in Early Medieval Britain*, ed. Nicholas Brooks (Leicester: Leicester University Press, 1982), pp. 99-140. Wieland accepted Lapidge's criticism in general, and returned to his research with a more specific definition of classbook as a "glossed manuscript which was designed to be used in the classroom." Cf. his "The Glossed Manuscript: Classbook or Library book?" *Anglo-Saxon England* 14 (1985): pp. 153-173.

2 E.g., Mariken Teeuwen, "Marginal Scholarship: Rethinking the Function of Latin Glosses in Early Medieval Manuscripts," *Rethinking and Recontextualizing Glosses: New Perspectives in the Study of Late Anglo-Saxon Glossography*, eds. Patrizia Lendinara, Loredana Lazzari, Claudia Di Sciacca (Turnhout: Brepols, 2011), pp. 19-37; Sinéad O'Sullivan, "Text, Gloss, and Tradition in the Early Medieval West: Expanding into a World of Learning," *Teaching and Learning in Medieval Europe: Essays in Honour of Gernot R. Wieland*, eds. Greti Dinkova-Bruun, Tristan Major (Turnhout: Brepols, 2017), pp. 3-24.

3 Louis Holtz, "Les manuscrits latins à gloses," pp. 156-166.

common in Psalter copying at St-Gall ca. 800.[1] By the mid-ninth century, the same format had become standard in the making of the commented Pauline epistles in the scriptorium of the monastery of Wissembourg.[2]

If we follow Michele Ferrari in seeing the emergence of édition commentée as a more general trend at the end of the eighth and beginning of the ninth centuries to experiment with different methods so as to efficiently combine text and commentary into a single codex,[3] the making of the Deuteronomy annotations in Paris, BnF, NAL 1740 can easily fit in this story. It may not be irrelevant that one of the "failed" experiments in this trend, Budapest, Országos Széchényi Könyvtár, Clmae 1, in which the Pauline text and its late antique commentary were copied in a single column in an irregular and confusing way, was produced in St-Amand from the circle of Arn of Salzburg, Leidrad's ex-colleague at Freising and lifelong friend.[4] This new codicological technique would not have been strange to the archbishop of Lyon.

To sum up, Paris, BnF, NAL 1740 is not an édition commentée in the strict sense, since it was not originally designed as a commentary carrier. However, when the Deuteronomy annotations were added at the beginning of the ninth century, it was transformed to function as one.

2.4   Provenance and Date

Fransen chose to call the annotations in Paris, BnF, NAL 1740 "un commentaire marginal lyonnais du Deutéronome." But whether the annotations were not only copied but also *composed* in Lyon is a matter that needs verifying. There is no direct information on the identity of their author. What we can tell is that he was an able exegete of independent mind, apt at using a repertoire of exegetical formulae all through (*iuxta historiam, non iuxta litteram sed spiritaliter, iuxta anagogem, moraliter, tropologice, quid per... nisi... significat, de... dicit..., hoc est,* etc.) and at merging the patristic exegesis into his own original exegetical scheme (cf. Part II). In fact, we may even say that anonymity was part of his literary achievement. Impersonality and tradition, rather than personality and

---

1   Cf. Margaret Gibson, "Carolingian Glossed Psalters," pp. 79-80. The best example is the Frankfurt Psalter (Frankfurt, Stadt- und Universitätsbibliothek, Barth. 32).

2   Cinzia Grifoni, "Reading the Catholic Epistles: Glossing Practices in Early Medieval Wissembourg," *The Annotated Book in the Early Middle Ages: Practices of Reading and Writing*, eds. Mariken Teeuwen, Irene van Renswoude (Turnhout: Brepols, 2018), pp. 705-742. The earliest of this group of manuscripts is Wolfenbüttel, Herzog August Bibliothek, Weissenburg 59, composed by Otfrid.

3   Michele Ferrari, "Before the 'Glossa ordinaria.'" Ferrari's model is the Ezekiel fragments (Zürich, Staatsarchiv, W3.19.XII).

4   Ibid., pp. 302-303. For plates of this manuscript, see Hermann Josef Frede, *Ein neuer Paulustext und Kommentar* (Freiburg: Herder, 1973), vol. 1, pp. I-III.

innovation, characterize a successful early medieval exegetical or theological treatise.[1]

To explore the provenance and date of the Deuteronomy annotations in Paris, BnF, NAL 1740, we have to appeal to indirect evidence.

2.4.1 Evidence (1): Codex Lugdunensis

The first set of internal evidence is the link between certain biblical references in the annotations with a codex of the *uetus latina* Heptateuch, Lyon, BM, 403 + Lyon, BM, 1964, customarily called *Codex Lugdunensis*. The codex was in Lyon in the sixth century,[2] and, witnessed by Florus' notes, remained in use at the episcopal library throughout the Carolingian age.[3] The annotation in Paris, BnF, NAL 1740 on Deut. 14:21 "Thou shalt not boil a kid in the milk of his dam" (*Non coques haedum in lacte matris suae*) is:

> Elsewhere (*alibi*), it reads lamb (*agnum*), but both kid (*haedum*) and lamb on different occasions signify the one Lord who was crucified by Jews thirty years after the days when He was conceived.[4]

Fransen suggested that the *alibi* in this annotation refered to Exodus 12:5 and Numbers 15:12, both verses mentioning the lamb as a sacrifice to God.[5] This reading is vitiated by the fact that Deut. 14:21 is not about the rite of sacrifice like Exodus 12:5 and Numbers 15:12 at all, but about a food taboo for the Israelites. It is hard to see why the annotator would want to lead readers to either of the two biblical verses on an irrelevant topic. My alternative proposal is that this annotation refers to a Latin translation different from the Vulgate reading in Paris, BnF, NAL 1740. *Codex Lugdunensis* reads Deut. 14:21 as *Non coques agnum in lacte matris suae.*[6] This annotation makes perfect sense if both the author and the target audience were ecclesiastics of Lyon Cathedral familiar with the *uetus latina* as recorded in *Codex Lugdunensis*. Similarly, the annotation in Paris, BnF, NAL 1740 for "a jealous God" (*Deus aemulator*, Deut. 5:9) is "Hemulator

---

1 Cf. Thomas O'Loughlin, "Tradition and Exegesis in the Eighth Century," pp. 238-239; idem, "Individual Anonymity and Collective Identity: The Enigma of Early Medieval Latin Theologians," *Recherches de théologie et philosophie médiévales* 64 (1997): pp. 291-314.

2 Elias A. Lowe, *Codices Lugdunenses Antiquissimi*, pp. 32-33. For the authoritative study and the edition of *Codex Lugdunensis*, see Ulysse Robert, *Pentateuchi versio latina antiquissima e Codice Lugdunensis* (Paris: Librairie de Firmin-Didot, 1881) and idem, *Heptateuchi partis posterioris versio latina antiquissima e Codice Lugdunensi* (Paris: A. Rey et cie, 1900).

3 Célestin Charlier, "Les manuscrits personnels," p. 266.

4 "Alibi agnum dicit sed utrumque pro diuersitate causarum unum significat Dominum quae in his diebus quibus conceptus est, a Iudeis post annos triginita crucifixus est." Paris, BnF, NAL 1740, fol. 41v.

5 Paul-Irénée Fransen, "Un commentaire marginal lyonnais," p. 54.

6 Ulysse Robert, *Heptateuchi versio*, p. 9.

id est zelator,"[1] and the *uetus latina* for the same lemma in *Codex Lugdunensis* is "Deus zelans..."[2]

Even more revealing is the annotation for Deut. 18:3 "... they shall give to the priest the shoulder and the belly" (... *dabunt sacerdoti armum ac uentriculum*). The portions of the sacrifice are originally interpreted as the virtues that qualify a Christian priest. The four portions are said to correspond to four virtues: shoulder (*armum*) as "right activity and detachment from vulgar way of life," breast (*pectusculum*) as "understanding and highest contemplation," jawbone (*maxilla*) as "speech of preaching," and belly (*uentriculum*) as "abstinence of the belly and of what are beneath the belly."[3] While *pectusculum* as the sacrifice reserved to Aaron and his sons can be found in Exodus 29:27-28, as Fransen suggested in the apparatus of his edition, *maxilla* in the annotation does not appear in either the vulgate Exodus 29:27-28 or Deut. 18:3. In fact, the word never appears throughout the whole Vulgate. Once again, the *uetus latina* Deut. 18:3 in *Codex Lugdunensis* presents "*dabit sacerdoti armum et maxillam et interanea.*"[4]

Unless one takes all these connections as pure coincidence, they strongly suggest that the annotator had the biblical text recorded in *Codex Lugdunensis* in mind. It is thus very likely that he was an ecclesiastic of Carolingian Lyon.

2.4.2   Evidence (2): Enumeration of Capital Sins

As mentioned above, Bischoff's paleographical diagnosis for the annotations in Paris, BnF, NAL 1740 is "small and neat Lyon minuscule of late Leidrad-script." Leidrad was the archbishop of Lyon between 798 and 816. If we trust Bischoff's judgment, Leidrad's later reign, namely the early ninth century, could be seen as the *terminus ante quem* of the composition of these Deuteronomy annotations.

The connection with Leidrad also emerges from an intriguing trace inside the annotations. It is the annotation for Deut. 7:1 in which Moses ordered the Israelites to destroy the seven Canaanite nations on their way to the Promised Land:

These seven nations signify all the nations which the Apostles and other preachers accepted into their possession. But in the moral sense (*tropologice*), they refer to

---

1   Paris, BnF, NAL 1740, fol. 17v.
2   Ulysse Robert, *Heptateuchi versio*, p.14.
3   "Alibi armum atque pectusculum siue maxillas quod secum legem sacertibus a populo accipere preceptum erat, sub Nouo Testamento boni sacerdotes non carnaliter sed spiritaliter a semetipsis Deo offerre debent. In armo quippe figuratur recta operatio et uulgari conuersatione seiuncta; in pectusculo autem intellectus et superna contemplatio; in maxilla sermo predicationis. In uentriculo uero continentia uentris et ea quae sub uentre sunt. Quicumque autem has quattuor uirtutes principlaes habuerit, perfectum sacerdotium absque culpa retemptabit." Paris, BnF, NAL 1740, fol. 50r.
4   Ulysse Robert, *Pentateuchi versio*, p. 321.

the seven capital sins, that is gluttony, fornication, avarice, anger, melancholy, envy, *cendoxia* (that is vainglory), and, the last queen of all of them, pride.[1]

To interpret the Canaanite nations as capital sins was no Carolingian invention.[2] In one of his homilies on Joshua (translated into Latin by Rufinus of Aquileia ca. 400), Origen calls Canaanite peoples *omnes gentes istae uitiorum*.[3] John Cassian, following a Greek anchoritic tradition,[4] was among the first in the Latin west to elaborate the same motif by combining it with eight capital sins: gluttony (*gastrimargia*), fornication (*fornicatio*), avarice (*philargyria*), anger (*ira*), melancholy (*tristitia*), sloth (*acedia*), vainglory (*cenodoxia*), and pride (*superbia*).[5] According to Cassian, the Israel had already conquered Gluttony when they left "the intellectual Egypt." The rest seven

---

1 "Septem hec gentes, licet omnes gentes quas apostoli et ceteri predicatores, in possesionem acceperunt significent; tropologice uero septem principalia vitia insinuant id est ingluuies, forncationem, auaritiam, iram, tristiam, inuidiam, cendoxia, id est vana g<loria> atque nouissima har<um> omnium regina, superbia." Paris, BnF, NAL 1740, fol. 22r.

2 For a systematic theological study of Deuteronomy 7, see Arie Versluis, *The Command to Exterminate the Canaanites: Deuteronomy 7* (Leiden: Brill, 2017). Also cf. Douglas Earl, "The Christian Significance of Deuteronomy 7," *Journal of Theological Interpretation* 3 (2009): pp. 41-62.

3 "Sub Moyseo non est dictum hoc, quod sub Iesu dicitur quia: Cessauit terra a proeliis. Certum est quod et terra nostra haec, in qua agones habemus et certamina sustinemus, solius Iesu Domini uirtute cessare poterit a proeliis. Intra nos etenim sunt omnes gentes istae uitiorum, quae animam iugiter et indesinenter oppugnant. Intra nos sunt 'Chananaei, intra nos sunt 'Pherezaei,' hic sunt 'Iebusaei.'" Origen, *Homiliae in Iesu Nave secundum translationem Rufini*, I.7, GCS 30, ed. Wilhelm Baehrens (Leipzig: J. C. Hinrichs, 1921), pp. 294-295.

4 The crucial figure of this Greek tradition was Evagrius Ponticus (345–399). For the pre-Cassianic development of the notion of capital sin, cf. Morton W. Bloomfield, *The Seven Deadly Sins: An Introduction to the History of a Religious Concept, with Special Reference to Medieval English Literature* (East Lansing: Michigan State College Press, 1952).

5 "Ita enim dicitur: cum introduxerit te dominus deus tuus in terram, quam possessurus ingrederis, et deleuerit gentes multas coram te, Chettaeum et Gergesaeum et Amorraeum, Chananaeum, et Ferezaeum, et Euaeum, et Iebusaeum, septem gentes multo maioris numeri quam tu es, et robustiores te: tradiderit que eas dominus tibi, percuties eas usque ad internicionem... Quae cum sint multo maioris numeri quam uirtutes, deuictis tamen illis octo principalibus uitiis, ex quorum natura eas certum est emanare, omnes protinus conquiescunt ac perpetua pariter cum his internicione delentur. De gastrimargia... de fornicatione... de philargyria... de ira... de tristitia... de acedia... de cenodoxia... de superbia..." John Cassian, *Collationes*, CSEL 13, V.16, ed. Michael Petschenig (Vienna: Verlag der Österreichischen Akademie der Wissenschaften, 1886), pp. 140-143. Also cf. John Cassian, *De institutis coenobiorum*, CSEL 17, V.1, ed. Michael Petschenig (Vienna: Verlag der Österreichischen Akademie der Wissenschaften, 1888), p. 81: "Nam post quattuor libellos, qui super institutis monasteriorum digesti sunt, nunc arripere conluctationem aduersus octo principalia uitia uestris orationibus Domino confortante disponimus, id est primum gastrimargiae, quae interpretatur gulae concupiscentia, secundum fornicationis, tertium filargyriae, quod intellegitur auaritia, uel ut proprius exprimatur, amor pecuniae, quartum irae, quintum tristitiae, sextum acediae, quod est anxietas siue taedium cordis, septimum cenodoxiae, quod sonat uana seu inanis gloria, octauum superbiae." Each of the last eight books of Cassian's *Institutes* is themed with one capital sin.

sins are signified by the seven Canaanite nations.[1] The Spanish Eutropius of Valencia
followed Cassian's interpretation of Deut. 7:1 in his own epistolary treatise *De octo
uitiis*, but interpreted the Canaanite nations as the first seven sins (from gluttony to
vainglory), and singled out pride as "the queen and mother of all the sins."[2] Isidore of
Seville copied Cassian's exposition of Deut. 7 in his *Expositio in uetus testamentum* with
subtle modification (cf. Chapter 6.1), but kept Cassian's list of sins untouched.[3]

There was another list of capital sins popular in the early medieval west. Gregory
the Great was its primary advocate. In his *Moralia in Iob*, to interpret Job 39:25 ("the
encouraging of the captains, and the shouting of the army"), Gregory proposed the image
of the troop of sins led by pride, "the queen of sins" and "the root of all evils," who had
seven capital sins as her generals and offspring: vainglory (*inanis gloria*), envy (*inuidia*),
anger (*ira*), melancholy (*tristitia*), avarice (*auaritia*), gluttony (*uentris ingluuies*), and
lust (*luxuria*). Compared with Cassian's list, Gregory dropped sloth and added envy; he

---

1   "Octo esse principalia uitia quae inpugnant monachum, cunctorum absoluta sententia est. Quae
    figuraliter sub gentium uocabulo nominata, idcirco nunc omnia non ponuntur, eo quod egressis iam
    de Aegypto et liberatis ab una gente ualidissima, id est Aegyptiorum, Moyses uel per ipsum Dominus
    in Deuteronomio loquebatur. Quae figura in nobis quoque rectissime stare deprehenditur, qui de
    saeculi laqueis expediti gastrimargiae, id est uentris uel gulae uitio caruisse cognoscimur. et habemus
    iam contra has residuas septem gentes simili ratione conflictum, prima scilicet quae iam deuicta est
    minime conputata. Cuius etiam terra in possessionem Israeli non datur, sed ut deserat eam perpetuo et
    egrediatur ab ea Domini praeceptione sancitur." Cassian, *Collationes*, V.18, CSEL 13, pp. 143-144.
2   "Et ideo in catalogo quidem dinumerantur septem nationes, in expugnatione uero earum sine numeri
    adscriptione ponuntur. Ita enim dicitur: Et deleuerit gentes multas coram te. Numerosior est enim
    quam Israel carnalium passionum populus qui de hoc septenario fomite uitiorum ac radice procedit,
    atque de octauo qui notior est omnibus, regina, ut ita dicam, atque mater omnium uitiorum."
    Eutropius, *Epistola de octo vitiis ad Petrum Papam*, in *Anecdota Wisigotica I*, Manuel Díaz y Díaz
    (Salamanca: Universidad de Salamanca, 1958), p. 33.
3   "Numerosior est enim quam Israel carnalium passionum populus, qui de hoc septenario fomite ac
    radice procedit uitiorum. De gastrimargia namque nascuntur... De fornicatione... De philargyria...
    De ira... De tristitia... De accidia... De cenodoxia... De superbia contemptus, inuidia, inobedientia,
    blasphemia, murmuratio, detractio, aliaquequam plurima similia, quae cum sint multo majoris numeri
    quam uirtutes, deuictis tamen illis septem principalibus uitiis, ex quorum natura ista procedunt,
    omnes protinus conquiescunt, ac perpetua pariter cum his internicione delentur." Isidore, *Expositio in
    uetus testamentum*, V.16, PL 83, cols. 366-367.

also adjusted the order by placing the five spiritual sins ahead of the two carnal ones.[1] Modern scholars have recognized the theological significance of Gregory's revision of Cassian's sin list as a shift of focus from "a growing liberation of the individual from the material constraints to meditation" to "the absolute necessity for a monk to diminish that very individualism which lies behind all sin, for him to internalize a disposition of humility towards God."[2]

In comparing the annotation for Deut. 7:1 in Paris, BnF, NAL 1740 with these two traditional lists of capital sins, we find that its ordering is Cassianic (from gluttony to pride), but the replacement of sloth with envy is rather Gregorian. In fact, when Carolingian moralists commented on sin, they all faced these two authorities (Cassian and Gregory), and had to make their own choice about how to deal with such patristic discrepancy. The solutions that they offered varied. For our purpose here, the multiple Carolingian enumerations of capital sins provide an opportunity to position the Deuteronomy annotations in Paris, BnF, NAL 1740 into a more specific micro-intellectual tradition. The author will first describe briefly five cases of enumerating capital sins in the late eighth century and the early ninth century: Alcuin of York, Theodulf of Orléans, Halitgar of Cambrai, Hrabanus Maurus and the anonymous penitential *Quadripartitus* then will show how the rationale behind list of capital sins in this annotation can be found in a treatise composed by Leidrad.

---

1 "Ipsa namque uitiorum regina superbia cum deuictum plene cor ceperit, mox illud septem principalibus uitiis, quasi quibusdam suis ducibus deuastandum tradit. Quos uidelicet duces exercitus sequitur, quia ex eis procul dubio importunae uitiorum multitudines oriuntur. Quod melius ostendimus, si ipsos duces atque exercitum specialiter, ut possumus, enumerando proferamus. Radix quippe cuncti mali superbia est, de qua, scriptura attestante, dicitur: initium omnis peccati superbia. Primae autem eius soboles, septem nimirum principalia uitia, de hac uirulenta radice proferuntur, scilicet inanis gloria, inuidia, ira, tristitia, auaritia, uentris ingluuies, luxuria. Nam quia his septem superbiae uitiis nos captos doluit, idcirco redemptor noster ad spiritale liberationis proelium spiritu septiformis gratiae plenus uenit. Sed habent contra nos haec singula exercitum suum. Nam de inani gloria inoboedientia, iactantia, hypocrisis, contentiones, pertinaciae, discordiae, et nouitatum praesumptiones oriuntur. De inuidia, odium, susurratio, detractio, exsultatio in aduersis proximi, afflictio autem in prosperis nascitur. De ira, rixae tumor mentis, contumeliae, clamor, indignatio, blasphemiae proferuntur. De tristitia, malitia, rancor, pusillanimitas, desperatio, torpor circa praecepta, uagatio mentis erga illicita nascitur. De auaritia, proditio, fraus, fallacia, periuria, inquietudo, uiolentiae, et contra misericordiam obdurationes cordis oriuntur. De uentris ingluuie, inepta laetitia, scurrilitas, immunditia, multiloquium, hebetudo sensus circa intellegentiam propagantur. De luxuria, caecitas mentis, inconsideratio, inconstantia, praecipitatio, amor sui, odium dei, affectus praesentis saeculi, horror autem uel desperatio futuri generatur. Quia ergo septem principalia uitia tantam de se uitiorum multitudinem proferunt, cum ad cor ueniunt, quasi subsequentis exercitus cateruas trahunt. Ex quibus uidelicet septem, quinque spiritalia, duo que carnalia sunt." Gregory, *Moralia in Iob*, XXXI.45, CCSL 143B, ed. Marci Adriaen (Turnhout: Brepols, 1985), pp. 1610-1612.

2 Richard Newhauser, "The Treatise on Vices and Virtues in Latin and the Vernacular," *Typologie des Sources du Moyen Âge Occidental 68* (Turnhout: Brepols, 1993), p. 188. Also see Carole Straw, "Gregory, Cassian, and the Cardinal Vices," *In the Garden of Evil: The Vices and Culture in the Middle Ages*, ed. Richard Newhauser (Toronto: Pontifical Institute of Mediaeval Studies, 2005), pp. 35-58.

***

Alcuin in his *Liber de uirtutibus et uitiis*, a moral treatise written for Wido count of Brittany ca. 800, enumerated capital sins as "pride, gluttony, fornication, avarice, anger, sloth, melancholy, and vainglory." The master from York adopted Cassian's list, but conspicuously singled out pride, placed it first, and called it "the queen of all evils," a treatment showing Gregorian influence.[1] Thanks to this treatise's great popularity, other Carolingian authors adopted the same list as Alcuin's. For example, it appears in Jonas of Orléans' *De institutione laicali*, a moral manual written in 828 for Matfrid count of Orléans, with clear acknowledgement of its indebtedness to Alcuin.[2]

Alcuin's contemporary Theodulf Bishop of Orléans enumerated capital sins as "gluttony, fornication, sloth or melancholy, avarice, vainglory, envy, anger, and pride," in both of his episcopal statutes promulgated shortly after 800 to the clerics of his diocese, stipulating that whoever commits these sins should make confession and priests have the obligation to absolve.[3] Theodulf kept the Cassianic ordering, but added envy, and combined *tristitia* and *acedia*. Similar understanding of capital sins can also be found in

---

1 "CAPUT XXVII De octo uitiis principalibus, et primo de superbia." "CAPUT XXVIII De gula." "CAPUT XXIX De fornicatione." "CAPUT XXX De auaritia." "CAPUT XXXI De ira." "CAPUT XXXII De acedia." "CAPUT XXXIII De tristitia." "CAPUT XXXIV De cenodoxia, id est, uana gloria." Alcuin, *Liber de uirtutibus et uitiis*, PL 101, cols. 632-635.

2 "De octo vitiis principalibus... Hi sunt, ut uenerabilis magister Alcuinus scribit..." Jonas of Orléans, *De institutione laicali*, III.6, PL 106, cols. 244-247. Cf. Luitpold Wallach, "Alcuin on Virtues and Vices: A Manual for a Carolingian Soldier," *Harvard Theological Review* 48 (1955): pp. 175-195. The fact that Chapters 27–34 of Alcuin's treatise had an independent transmission shows that his version of capital sins won status as somewhat standard. Cf. Paul Szarmach, "The Latin Tradition of Alcuin's 'Liber de Virtutibus et Vitiis,'" *Mediaevalia* 12 (1986): pp. 13-41.

3 "Confessiones dandae sunt de omnibus peccatis, quae siue in opere siue in cogitatione perpetrantur. Octo sunt principalia uitia, sine quibus uix ullus inueniri potest. Est enim castrimargia, hoc est uentris ingluuies, secunda fornicatio, tertia accidia siue tristitia, quarta auaritia, quinta uana gloria, sexta inuidia, septima ira, octaua superbia. Quando ergo quis ad confessionem uenit, diligenter debet inquiri, quomodo aut qua occasione peccatum perpetrauerit, quod peregisse se confitetur. Et iuxta modum facti debet ei paenitentia iudicari. Debet ei persuaderi, ut de peruersis cogitationibus faciat confessionem. Debet ei etiam iniungi, ut de octo principalibus uitiis faciat suam confessionem. Et nominatim ei debet sacerdos unumquodque uitium dicere et suam de eo confessionem accipere." Theodulf, *Erstes Kapitular*, XXXI, *Capitula episcoporum Teil 1*, MGH Leges, ed. Peter Brommer (Hannover: Hahnsche, 1984), pp. 128-129. "Sacerdos cum a fidelibus confessionem accipit, inter cetera debet confitentem ammonere, ut de octo principalibus uitiis confessionem faciat et emendationem promittat et penitentiae medicinam animae suae suscipiat. Vitiorum autem principalium octo, sicut hic continentur, nomina per singula interroget, et ille confiteatur et de omnibus, sicut praemissum est, confessionem faciat; et tunc ei medela poenitentiae adhibeatur. Principalia uitia, sine quibus uix ullus inueniri potest, haec sunt: Primum castrimargia, hoc est uentris ingluuies, secundum fornicatio, tercium accidia siue tristitia, quartum auaritia, quintum uana gloria, sextum inuidia, septimum ira, octauum superbia." Theodulf, *Zweites Kapitular*, X.1, *Capitula episcoporum Teil 1*, MGH Leges, ed. Peter Brommer (Hannover: Hahnsche, 1984), p. 172.

his *Opus Caroli* composed on the command of Charlemagne ca. 790.[1]

The stipulation about the confession for *octo principalia uitia* can also be found in the *acta* of the council of Chalon held in 813, although the sins are not enumerated.[2] The list of capital sins in pastoral practice was by no means standardized in the early ninth century, though. In the 820s, at the request of Ebo of Rheims to compose a penitential for the use of priests in confession, Halitgar bishop of Cambrai compiled a six-book work. Its first book is about "the eight capital sins and their remedies." Different from Theodulf, Halitgar chose to copy verbatim Gregory's eight sins and made explicit acknowledgement to him.[3]

Hrabanus Maurus, the Carolingian intellectual guru of a generation junior to Alcuin and Theodulf, held a more eclectic attitude toward the issue of capital sins. In his commentary on Deuteronomy, Hrabanus quoted Isidore's exposition of Deut. 7:1

---

1   "In illis inueniuntur arma, quibus contra aduersa confligatur; quibus uitia reprimantur; quibus uirtutes erigantur; quibus gulae concupiscentia uigiliis et conpunctione cordis reprimatur; quibus fornicatio contritione cordis et corporis afflictione, orationum instantia, laboris exercitio metuque suppliciorum uel amore aeternae patriae refrenetur; quibus inuidia amore fraternae dilectionis et caelestis regni desiderio, quod non nisi concordes adipiscuntur, superetur; quibus ira modestissimae patientiae grauitate et acumine rationis et aequanimitatis munere frangatur; quibus auaritia aelemosynis et spe aeternae retributionis calcetur; quibus tristitia fraternis alloquiis, assiduis lectionibus uel orationibus pellatur; quibus arrogantia metu amittendarum uirtutum, cum qua illae haberi non possunt, et accessus uanae gloriae, qui est uirtutum inimicus, secluditur; in quibus superbia metu diabolicae ruinae et exemplo humilitatis Christi conteritur." Theodulf, *Opus Caroli regis contra synodum*, II.30, MGH Concilia II Supplementum I, ed. Ann Freeman (Hannover: Hahn, 1998), pp. 311-312.

2   "Instruendus est itaque peccatorum suorum confessor, ut de octo principalibus uitiis, sine quibus in hac uita difficile uiuitur, confessionem faciat, quia aut cogitatione aut, quod est grauius, opere eorum instinctu peccauit." Concilium Cabillonense, XXII, *Concilia aevi Karolini [742–842]. Teil 1 [742–817]*, no. 37, p. 279.

3   "Libellum de uitiis octo principalibus, eorumque remediis: quem in libris Gregorii, Augustini, nec non Prosperi excerpsimus, in capite praeponimus, post praefationem hanc, quam excerpsimus." PL 105, col. 658. For Halitgar's penitential (PL 105, cols. 652-710), see Raymund Kottje, *Die Bussbücher Halitgars von Cambrai und des Hrabanus Maurus: Ihre Überlieferung und ihre Quellen* (Berlin: de Gruyter, 1980); Rob Meens, *Penance in Medieval Europe*, pp. 130-139.

which contains the Cassianic list.[1] In the commentary on Exodus, however, he quoted the passage of Gregory's *Moralia*.[2] Hrabanus compiled both commentaries in the 820s at the earlier stage of his intellectual career when he was the abbot of Fulda. In the mid-840s, during the years of his retirement from the abbacy, Hrabanus composed for Reginbald chorbishop of Mainz a three-book *De ecclesiastica disciplina* as a guide to clergy training.[3] In Book 3 titled *De agone christiano* and themed with virtues and sins, Hrabanus rendered eight capital sins as "pride together with (*cum*) vainglory, anger, envy, avarice, gluttony, lust, melancholy, and sloth," and elaborates each of them in sequence.[4] The list is basically Gregorian, but includes sloth which appears in Cassian's list, and Hrabaus offered an independent treatment for it.[5]

The final case to treat here is an obscure penitential known as *Quadripartitus*, now

---

1   "Septem istae gentes septem sunt principalia uitia, quae per gratiam Dei unusquisque spiritalis miles exsuperans, exterminare penitus admonetur. Quod uero maioris numeri esse dicuntur, haec ratio est quia plura sunt uitia quam uirtutes. Et ideo quidem in catalogo dinumerantur septem nationes: in expugnatione uero earum, sine numeri ascriptione ponuntur. Ita enim dicitur: Et deleuerit gentes multas coram te. Numerosior est enim quam Israel carnalium passionum populus, qui de hoc septenario fomite uitiorum ac radice procedit. De gastrimargia namque nascuntur comessationes, ebrietates. De fornicatione, turpiloquia, scurrilitas, ludicra atque stultiloquia. De philargyria, mendacia, fraudatio, facta, periuria, turpis lucri appetitus, falsa testimonia, uiolentiae, immanitas ac rapacitas. De ira, homicidia, clamor et indignatio. De tristitia, rancor, pusillanimitas, amaritudo, desperatio. De acedia, otiositas, somnolentia, importunitas, inquietudo, praeuaricatio, instabilitas mentis et corporis, uerbositas et curiositas. De cenodoxia, contentiones, haereses, iactantia ac praesumptio nouitatum. De superbia, contemptus, inuidia, inobedientia, blasphemia, murmuratio, detractio, aliaque quam plurima similia. Quae cum sint multo maioris numeri quam uirtutes, deuictis tamen illis septem principalibus uitiis, ex quorum natura ista procedunt, omnes protinus conquiescunt, ac pariter perpetua cum his intentione delentur. Quod autem hae pestes etiam robustiores sunt, manifeste naturae ipsius impugnatione sentimus. Fortius enim militat in membris nostris carnalium passionum quam studia uirtutum: quae nisi summa contritione cordis et corporis non acquiruntur. Quod uero istarum perniciosarum gentium regiones salubriter possidere praecipimur, ita intelligitur. Habet enim unumquodcunque uitium in corde nostro stationem propriam. Sed si cum Israelis populo, id est uirtutibus contra se dimicantibus fuerint uitia superata, locum quem sibi in corde nostro concupiscentiae uel fornicationis spiritus retentabat, deinceps castitas obtinebit. Quem furor ceperat, patientia uindicabit. Quem tristitia mortem operans occupauerat, salutaris ex pleno gaudio laetitia possidebit. Quem acedia uastabat, incipit excolere fortitudo. Quem superbia uastabat, incipit excolere humilitas. Et ita singulis uitiis expulsis, eorum loca, id est animae, uident Deum." Hrabanus, *Enarratio super Deuteronomium*, PL 108, col. 867.

2   "Primae autem eius soboles, septem nimirum principalia uitia, de hac uirulenta radice proferuntur: scilicet inanis gloria, inuidia, ira, tristitia, auaritia, uentris ingluuies, luxuria. Nam quia his septem superbiae uitiis nos captos doluit, idcirco Redemptor noster ad spirituale liberationis praelium, spiritu septiformis gratiae plenus uenit." Hrabanus, *Commentaria in Exodum*, PL 108, col. 131.

3   PL 112, cols. 1191-1262. It is considered an authentic work by Hrabanus, but no manuscript survives, cf. Raymund Kottje, *Verzeichnis der Handschriften mit den Werken des Hrabanus Maurus* (Hannover: Hahnsche, 2012), p. 248

4   "Ut ergo contra tentamenta diaboli, et contra carnis desideria ordinate et fortiter pugnare et resistere possimus, primum nos oportet scire octo uitia esse principalia, per quae diabolus humanum genus corrumpere et decipere gestit, id est, superbiam cum uana gloria, iram, inuidiam, auaritiam, gulam, luxuriam, tristitiam, et acediam." Hrabanus, *De ecclesiastica disciplina*, III.6, PL 112, col. 1240.

5   Ibid., cols. 1240-1253: "De superbia." III.7; "De ira." III.8; "De inuidia." III.9; "De auaritia." III.10; "De gula." III.11; "De fornicatione." III.12; "De tristitia." III.13; "De acedia." III.14.

generally considered as an anonymous work composed in the second or third quarter of the ninth century in northern Gaul, probably Rheims or nearby.[1] *Quadripartitus* has four books, and, according to its general preface, consists of "blossoms" clipped from "the blooming fields of many Fathers." Its goal is to prepare confessors for the service of penance.[2] In Book 3, the author remarkably raised the question why Cassian and Gregory listed the capital sins in differently ways. Two discrepancies are pointed out. First, Cassian enumerated *philargiria* and *accedia*, but Gregory enumerated *inuidia* and *auaritia*. Second, pride is Cassian's last sin but Gregory's first. The solution offered by this anonymous author is that these are not real discrepancies: *philargiria* is the Greek word for *auaritia*; Cassian had envy as a derivative sin of pride, and Gregory similarly categorized sloth as a derivative sin of melancholy; pride appears last in the battle against

---

1 See Franz Kerff, *Der Quadripartitus: ein Handbuch der karolingischen Kirchenreform: Überlieferung, Quellen und Rezeption* (Sigmaringen: J. Thorbecke, 1982). Also cf. Rob Meens, *Penance in Medieval Europe*, pp. 134-135. No edition of the whole *Quadripartitus* is available yet. But for our purpose here, an imperfect edition of the general preface is available in *Veterum scriptorum et monumentorum historicorum, dogmaticorum, moralium amplissima collectio*, ed. Edmond Martène (Paris, 1724–1733), vol. 1, cols. 70-71; an edition of Book 3 based on a lost manuscript is available in PL 112, cols. 1337-1398, copied from Georg Colvener, *Hrabani Mauri opera omnia in sex tomos distincta, collecta primum industria Jac. Pamelii... nunc vero in lucem emissa cura Antonii de Henin... ac studio et opera Georgii Colvenerii* (Cologne, 1626–1627), vol. 6, pp. 130-154, mistakenly attributed to Hrabanus Maurus under the title *De uitiis et uirtutibus*. For the doubtful attribution of *Der Quadripartitus* to Halitgar, see Mary Bateson, "The Supposed Latin Penitential of Egbert and the Missing Work of Halitgar of Cambrai," *The English Historical Review* 34 (1894): pp. 320-326.

2 "Haec pauca beatitudo uestra gratifica, quaeso, excipiat deflorata, quae non ex uno unius doctoris prato diuinae auctoritatis studui decerpere, sed per multorum patrum florigera rura cordis & corporis ceruice summissa studiose, succinctim celeriterque ut jussio sanctitatis exstitit uestrae, cucurri & ex his hos odoriferos domino largiente, prout potui, flores excerpsi, hancque quadriformem huius uoluminis intexui coronulam, sicut in praefatiuncula subsequenti uestra sancta dinoscere poterit industria. Ex quibus uero auctoribus uel opusculis, ac institutis haec sunt excerpta, in margine uel titulis huius opusculi nomina eorum retinentur ascripta." *Quadripartitus*, "Preface," *Veterum scriptorum*, cols. 70–71.

sins, but it is the first sin in the sense of origin.[1] Besides harmonizing the two lists, the author showed respect to the authority of both of them, by adopting a clumsy strategy when it came to the discussion of individual sins. He examined the sins according to Gregory's list first, and then did so for the second round according to Cassian's, with unavoidable repetition.[2]

From the quick survey above, it is clear that Carolingian authors were generally conscious of the apparent difference between the two patristic lists of capital sins, and that they developed multiple solutions to this dilemma. The fact that each of these Carolingian authors showed rather independent initiative in deciding how to take a step when facing diverging patristic paths, makes the list of capital sins a sample of the "inharmonious harmony" of the Carolingian Renaissance.[3]

But for the present purpose here, it deserves special attention that the enumeration of sins in the annotation for Deut. 7:1 in Paris, BnF, NAL 1740 shows a pattern distinct from those that we have just examined above (Table 2.2).

---

1 "Hactenus haec pauca de octo principalibus uitiis Cassiani facundissimi doctoris sunt dicta, quaeritur autem cur Cassianus et Gregorius in Catalogo eorumdem principalium uitiorum inter se dissentiant, ita ut Cassianus in eorum numero philargyriam et acediam adnumeret: e contra Gregorius non haec duo uitia, philargyriam scilicet et acediam in eorum ponit numero, sed inuidiam et auaritiam inter eadem adnumerat uitia, quod Cassianus nullatenus facit; ait enim Cassianus quod aduersus octo principalia uitia, adiuuante Domino, colluctationem debemus arripere... Soluta est autem ueraciter ab eruditis doctoribus ita haec quaestio: Auaritia, inquiunt, quae in Graeco dicitur philargyria. Unde et Cassianus: Non solum eam Apostolus radicem esse omnium malorum, uerum etiam idolorum seruitutem pronuntiauit, dicens: Et auaritia, quod in Graeco dicitur philargyria, *quae est simulacrorum seruitus*. Claret autem quia hi duo doctores, Gregorius et Cassianus, quamuis unus diceret philargyriam, alter auaritiam, nullatenus inter se in hoc nomine discrepauerunt, quia unum est auaritia et philargyria. Inuidiam autem quam Cassianus inter caetera uitia non dinumerauit, dicunt sub titulo superbiae eam intellexisse, ideo quia diabolus per superbiam de coelo decidisset, inuidendo autem de sedibus paradisi, primos homines expulisset, ob hoc unum uolunt esse morbum; unde Prosper ait: In tantum unum est malum ut nec superbus sine inuidia, nec inuidus sine superbia possit inueniri: Acediam autem unde Gregorius in supra dicta principalium uitiorum dinumeratione nil dixit, aiunt eam sub tristitiae nomine intelligere uoluisse, unde et Cassianus: Acedia, quam nos, inquit, taedium siue anxietatem cordis possumus nuncupare affinis est tristitiae. His autem sententiis manifeste probatur quia Gregorius et Cassianus de octo principalibus uitiis uniformiter senserunt. Quaeritur et illud cur Gregorius in ipsa uitiorum adnumeratione primum uitium superbiam ponit, et Cassianus ultimum, ipse enim dicit: Licet morbus superbiae octauus et ultimus sit, in conflictu uitiorum atque in ordine ponatur extremus, origine tamen et tempore primus est; item alio loco, cum sit superbia posterior in ordine conflictuum, origine tamen anteriorem esse omnium peccatorum et criminum principium, et cunctarum interfectricem uirtutum." *Quadripartitus*, III.2, PL 112, cols. 1349-1350.

2 III.3-III.48 (PL 112, cols. 1351-1374) follows the Gregorian list; III,49-III.61 (cols. 1374-1382) follows the Cassianic list.

3 On this concept, cf. John Contreni, "Inharmonious Harmony: Education in the Carolingian World," *Annals of Scholarship: Metastudies of the Humanities and Social Sciences* 1 (1980): pp. 81-96.

Table 2.2 Enumeration of capital sins

Cassian	Gluttony, fornication, avarice, anger, melancholy, **sloth**, vain glory, pride
Eutropius of Valencia	
Isidore, *Expositio in uetus testamentum*	
Hrabanus, *Commentary on Deuteronomy*	
Quadripartitus, III,49-III.61	
Gregory	Pride: vain glory, **envy**, anger, melancholy, avarice, gluttony, lust
Halitgar	
Hrabanus, *Commentary on exodus*	
Quadripartitus, III.3-III.48	
Alcuin, *Liber de uirtutibus et uitiis*	Pride, gluttony, fornication, avarice, anger, **sloth**, melancholy, vain glory
Jonas, *De institutione laicali*	
Theodulf, Episcopal statutes	Gluttony, fornication, **sloth or melancholy**, avarice, vain glory, **envy**, anger, pride
Hrabanus, *De ecclesiastica disciplina*	Pride *cum* vain glory, anger, **envy**, avarice, gluttony, lust, **melancholy and sloth**
Annotation in Paris, BnF, NAL 1740, fol. 22r	Gluttony, fornication, avarice, anger, melancholy, **envy**, vain glory, pride

As our source criticism in Part II will show, Isidore's *Expositio in uetus testamentum* serves as a major source for the annotations in Paris, BnF, NAL 1740. The question thus is why the annotator deliberately substituted envy for sloth. Among all the known early medieval Latin texts, only in an epistolary treatise of Leidrad we find an explanation for this substitution.

In 811/812, Charlemagne sent an encyclical letter to ecclesiastical leaders of his empire, asking a series of questions on the rites of the baptismal liturgy. Leidrad, already the archbishop of Lyon for more than a decade at that time, wrote a treatise to expound the local baptismal *ordines* as a response to the emperor.[1] Charlemagne later asked Leidrad to elaborate his reply, especially concerning the renunciation of the devil in the baptismal rite. Leidrad took this opportunity to compose for the emperor a moral/political treatise on the nature of sins and virtues in human life, known as *De abrenuntiatione diaboli*.[2] This treatise is a patchwork of excerpts from Church Fathers including Augustine, Julianus Pomerius, Jerome, Cassian, and Gregory the Great. But Leidrad spoke his own words now and then, and one of his original passages was relevant to capital sins:

> But about other sins, they are either spiritual, such as heresy, schism, ostentation, envy, impetuosity, conceit, and hatred, or carnal (that is, they are perpetrated not only

---

1 Cf. Owen Michael Phelan, *Formation of Christian Europe*, pp. 147-206; Susan Keefe, *Water and the Word*. Leidrad's first response (*Baptismal Exposition*), formerly known as *Leidradi liber de sacramento baptismi ad Carolum Magnum imperatorum*, see ibid., vol. 2, no. 25, pp. 353-384.

2 PL 99, cols. 873-884. Cf. Yin Liu, "Baptismal Renunciation and the Moral Reform of Charlemagne's Christian Empire," *Traditio* 76 (2021): pp. 132-141.

by soul by also by body), such as excessive appetite, drunkenness, immoderate sexual desire, and adultery. Church doctors say that they proceed from seven capital sins, that is vainglory, envy, anger, melancholy, avarice, gluttony, and lust. These sins have pride as their mother and queen whom they followed like generals with their own armies. These seven sins are signified by the nations which the Lord wanted sons of the Israel to delete, namely the Hethite, the Gergezite, the Amorrhite, the Chanaanite, the Pherezite, the Hevite, and the Jebusite. God removed, devastated, and deleted various nations by the hands of other kings and other peoples. But he wanted these seven nations to be extinguished by sons of the Israel in order to indicate that these sins in the number of seven should be conquered and crushed by His chosen people.[1]

But other people, mostly Egyptian holy fathers, said that there are eight capital sins, and they placed those regarded as carnal here first, namely *gastrimargia*, which means gluttony, and fornication, which is named lust here under its general name. The third is *philargyria*, that is love of money, which we name avarice. The fourth is anger, the fifth melancholy, the sixth sloth, that is anxiety or weariness of heart, which our authors are accustomed to name inconstancy or wandering. The seventh is *cenodoxia*, which we call vainglory. The eighth is pride. They omitted envy, the greatest offspring and company of pride, but added sloth, which the doctors of the Church did not place among capital sins but rather regarded it born from melancholy or lust. For it seems that sloth is a sin particular to monks. Among all the faithful in general (*generaliter in cunctis fidelibus*), it seems to be much less bad than envy, because envy is found to be recorded in sacred letters with greater renunciation than mind wandering.[2]

---

1   "De caeteris uero uitiis, siue sint spiritalia, ut haereses, schismata, iactantia, inuidia, animositas, elatio, odium; siue sint corporalia, id est quae non solo animo sed corpore perpetrantur; ut est auiditas, ebrietas, intemperantia fornicatio, adulterium: ecclesiastici doctores dicunt, quod de septem principalibus uitiis procedant, id est de inani gloria, inuidia, ira, tristitia, auaritia, uentris ingluuie, atque luxuria. Quae uitia habent matrem et reginam superbiam, cui quasi duces cum suis exercitibus obsequuntur. Haec septem uitia significata per illas gentes, quas uoluit Dominus deleri per filios Israel, Ethaeos uidelicet et Gergessaeos, et Amorrhaeos, et Chananaeos, et Pheresaeos, et Euaeos, et Gebusaeos. Et reuera multas et uarias per alios atque alios reges et populos Dominus aut transtulit aut uastauit atque deleuit. Has autem gentes idcirco per filios Israel uoluit exstingui, ut significaret in septenario numero haec uitia ab electis suis uincenda atque calcanda..." PL 99, col. 880.
2   "Alii autem, maxime sancti Patres Aegyptii, octo dixerunt esse principalia uitia, et prima posuerunt ea quae hic carnalia dicta sunt, id est gastrimargiam, quod sonat uentris ingluuiem, et fornicationem, quod hic generali nomine luxuria nominatur. Tertium philargyriam, id est amorem pecuniae, quod nos auaritiam nominamus. Quartum iram, quintum tristitiam, sextum acediam, id est anxietatem seu taedium cordis, quod nostri inconstantiam uel uagatitatem nominare solent. Septimum cenodoxiam, quod nos inanem gloriam dicimus. Octauum superbiam. Praetermiserunt uero inuidiam, maximum superbiae prolem ac comitem; addiderunt autem acediam, quod doctores Ecclesiae inter principalia uitia non posuerunt, sed magis illud de tristitia, siue luxuria nasci dixerunt: quia et reuera quasi proprium uidetur esse monachorum. Nam generaliter in cunctis fidelibus multo minus malum uidetur esse, quam inuidia: quia et in diuinis litteris majori detestatione notatum inuenitur inuidia, quam uagatio mentis." Ibid., col. 881.

Leidrad was clearly aware of the existence of the two different sin lists, one of *ecclesiastici doctores* (Gregorian) and the other of *sancti patres Aegyptii* (Cassianic). What is remarkable is that he explicitly explained why it is more proper to take envy rather than sloth as a capital sin: the latter is a sin particularly noxious to monks, but the former much worse to "all the faithful in general."

In other words, by replacing sloth with envy, a list of capital sins particularly designed for a monastic community is converted to one suitable to the whole Christian society. The exactly identical treatment of capital sins in the annotation for Deut. 7:1 in Paris, BnF, NAL 1740 very likely reveals the same pastoral concern as Leidrad's. The reasonable explanation must be the shared intellectual atmosphere in Lyon at the beginning of the ninth century, or even Leidrad's direct influence on this anonymous annotator or vice versa.

2.4.3 *Biblical Education in Lyon during the Episcopate of Leidrad*

We now turn to examine the revival of biblical education in Lyon during Leidrad's episcopate. It arguably serves as a background for the making of the commentary on Deuteronomy recorded in Paris, BnF, NAL 1740.

The crucial testimony comes from a letter from Leidrad to Charlemagne. The archbishop reported to his "most glorious lord, the constant and holy emperor" the results of the church reform that he had achieved in Lyon since Charlemagne had sent him to "govern the church" to "emend the negligence" there. Leidrad enumerated in detail how he, in the diocese, had established clerical schools, promoted book productions, repaired and edified church buildings, introduced the Rule of Benedict and the rule for canons, and increased the number of clerics and monks.[1] Among them, Leidrad mentioned the *scholae lectorum* that he established:

> Besides these, I have schools of readers (*scholas lectorum*) who not only carry out the "readings of services" (*officiorum lectionibus*), but also grasp fruits of spiritual

---

1 "Domine mi, gloriosissime, constans et sacer Imperator... Olim me exiguissimum famulorum uestrorum ad regimen ecclesie Lugdunensis destinare uoluistis, cum ego huic officio impar existerem et indignus. Sed uos qui non attenditis hominum merita, sed uestram solitam clemenciam, egistis de me sicut ineffabili pietati placuit nullo existente merito meo, quo tempore ad praefatam ecclesiam regendam micteretis et nominare michi dignati estis quasdam negligencias que in supraedicta ecclesia perpetrate noscebantur; pro qua re me ammonere dignati estis ut ego solicitudinis curam gererem et ut perpetrate neglegencie emendarentur et perpetrande uitarentur. Erat enim tunc dicta ecclesia multis in rebus destituta interius exteriusque tam in officiis quam in edificiis uel ceteris ecclesiasticis ministeriis." The author follows Alfred Coville's critical edition of Leidrad's report in Alfred Coville, *Recherches sur l'Histoire de Lyon du Ve siècle au IXe siècle (450–800)* (Paris: Picard, 1928). The complicated manuscript transmission of this letter, see ibid., pp. 281-283.

understanding (*spiritalis intelligencie*) in the study (*meditacione*) of divine books. Some of them are able to partially interpret the spiritual sense of the Gospels, others are able to interpret the book of apostles (*libro apostolorum*), while most can at least partially interpret the books of prophets (*librum prophetarum*), the books of Solomon, the Psalms, and Job according to the spiritual sense.[1]

This short passage is perhaps the most valuable piece of evidence of biblical education in the Carolingian era. It deserves the closest scrutiny. The word *schola*, whose original meaning is a group of any sort, from the late eighth century on came to mean "a group of students or disciples around a master pursuing studies that were at once academic and spiritual."[2] In the same letter right before this passage, Leidrad mentioned the *scholae cantorum* that he established with the help of a cleric of Metz whom he requested sent to Lyon to "restore the *ordo psallendi*."[3] It is possible that Leidrad's *scholae lectorum* were also organized around one master or more.

As for the word *lector* here, it is less likely that it refers to the order of lector in the ecclesiastical hierarchy.[4] In Charlemagne's well-known capitulary *Admonitio generalis* (789), we find the command to establish *scolae legentium puerorum*, which could simply mean "schools to train boys to read."[5] Similarly, Leidrad's *scholae lectorum* could generally mean "the schools to train qualified readers of the Bible." Interestingly, one Deuteronomy annotation in Paris, BnF, NAL 1740 (on Deut. 30:5) addresses his reader by saying *Nota, lector...*[6]

But who were these *lectores*? The primary candidates were the cathedral canons. Leidrad introduced to Lyon the institution of canonical cleric created by Chrodegang

---

1   "Preter hec, habeo scholas lectorum, non solum qui officiorum lectionibus exercentur, sed eciam qui in diuinorum librorum meditacione spiritalis intelligencie fructus consequantur. Ex quibus nonnulli de libro Euangeliorum sensum spiritalem iam ex parte adipisci possunt. Alii adiuncto libro etiam Apostolorum, plerique uero librum Prophetarum secundum spiritalem intelligentiam ex parte adepti sunt. Similiter libros Salomonis uel libros Psalmorum atque eciam Iob." Leidrad, *Report to Charlemagne*, pp. 284-285.
2   John Contreni, "Pursuit of Knowledge," pp. 111-112.
3   "Et ideo officio pietatis uestre placuit, ut ad peticionem meam michi concederetis unum de Metensi ecclesia clericum, per quem, Deo iuuante et mercede uestra annuente, ita in Lugdunensi ecclesia instauratus est ordo psallendi, ut iuxta uires nostras secundum ritum sacri palatii omni ex parte agi uideatur quicquid ad diuinum persoluendum officium ordo exposcit." Leidrad, *Report to Charlemagne*, p. 284.
4   For *lector*, cf. Roger Reynolds, "Clerics in the Early Middle Ages: Hierarchies and Functions," *Clerics in the Early Middle Ages: Hierarchy and Image*, Roger Reynolds (Brookfield: Ashgate, 1999), pp. 1-31.
5   "Et ut scolae legentium puerorum fiant. Psalmos, notas, cantus, compotum, grammaticam per singula monasteria uel episcopia et libros catholicas bene emendate, quia sepe, dum bene aliqui Deum rogare cupiunt, sed per inemendatos libros male rogant. Et pueros uestros non sinite eos uel legendo uel scribendo corrumpere. Et si opus est euangelium, psalterium et missale scribere, perfectae aetatis homines scribant cum omni diligentia." *Admonitio generalis*, LXX, p. 224.
6   "Nota, lector, quanta multitudo credentium ex Iudeis circa fine mundi erit ut antiquorum patrum et primitiue ecclesiae numero superent." Paris, BnF, NAL 1740, fol. 81r.

of Metz. In the early ninth century, the number of canons of the collegiate church of St-Stephen was between 52 and 68 (cf. Chapter 3.2). They were the elite clerics closest to the archbishop, and would naturally be the primary beneficiaries of Leidrad's revival of biblical education. Florus, one of the most learned biblical scholars of his age, was a canon of St-Stephen, as the *Liber memorialis* of Reichenau (complied ca. 824) testifies.[1] Meanwhile, training canons to be qualified readers of the Bible was part of Charlemagne's realm-wide policy, as we can glimpse from a capitulary issued between 805 and 813: "Bishops should urge their canons to learn the Holy Scripture according to canonical discipline, as our Emperor the Lord orders in every meeting of his."[2]

By *officiorum lectiones*, Leidrad could certainly refer to the lesson reading at Mass according to the Roman rite. However, if Leidrad's canons were required to follow the *Regula canonicorum* of Chrodegang of Metz,[3] biblical recital would also be an essential part of the daily chapter meeting[4] and communal meal.[5] Moreover, the liturgical duty of *lectio* was not limited to the recital of the Holy Scripture, but also involved its interpretation. In an encyclical to "the pious *lectores* under my rule", Charlemagne exhorted

---

1 "Nomina Kanonicorum Domus Sancti Stephani Protomartyris... Florus *et amicis*." *Confraternitates Augienses*, MGH Antiquitates, Supplement: Libri confraternitatum Sancti Galli, Augiensis, Fabariensis, ed. Paul Pieper (Berlin: Weidmann, 1884), p. 257. For the facsimile, see Johanne Autenrieth, Dieter Geuenich, Karl Schmid, eds., *Das Verbrüderungsbuch der Abtei Reichenau*, MGH Libri memoriales et Necrologia, Nova series I (Hannover: Hahnsche, 1979), fol. 94A4. For the biography of Florus, see Klaus Zechiel-Eckes, *Florus von Lyon als Kirchenpolitiker und Publizist: Studien zur Persönlichkeit eines karolingischen "Intellektuellen" am Beispiel der Auseinandersetzung mit Amalarius (835–838) und des Prädestinationsstreits (851–855)* (Stuttgart: Thorbecke, 1999).

2 "Ut episcopi canonicos suos ad discendam divinam scripturam canonica disciplina constringant, sicut ipse domnus noster imperator in omni placito suo iubet..." *Caroli Magni capitulare ecclesiasticum*, 9, Hubert Mordek, *Bibliotheca Capitularium Regum Francorum Manuscripta: Überlieferung und Traditionszusammenhang der fränkischen Herrschererlasse* (München: Monumenta Germaniae Historica, 1995), no. 12, p. 985.

3 Charlemagne promoted *the Rule of Chrodegang* for clerics in *Francia*, and it is hard to imagine that the practice of *Regula canonicorum* was not part of the reform program of Leidrad who followed Charlemagne's policy more closely than others. See Julia Barrow, "Chrodegang, His Rule and its Successors," *Early Medieval Europe* 14 (2006): pp. 200-212.

4 "Necesse est ut omnis clerus canonicus ad Capitulum ueniant, ibidem uerba Dei audiant et istam instituciunculam nostram, quam propter illorum utilitatem ad eorum animas saluandas." *S. Chrodegangi Metensis Episcopi (742–766) Regula canonicorum, aus dem Leidener Codex Uossianus Latinus 94 mit Umschrift der Tironischen Noten*, VIII, ed. Wilhelm Schmitz (Hannover: Hahnsche, 1889), p. 7.

5 "Clerus uero in refectorio omnino silentium teneant interim quod exinde foris egrediuntur, qualiter illam lectionem diuinam possit audire et in corde meditare, quia sic est necesse, ut, quando cibum corporalem recepit, et tunc anima cibum spiritale reficiatur." Chrodegang, *Regula canonicorum*, XXI, p. 14.

them to use in night office the homiliary compiled by Paul the Deacon.[1] Also, according to Chrodegang's Rule, during the intervals in the nocturnal chanting, canons should read aloud, sing, and study the Psalms or *lectio*.[2]

Besides serving "readings of services," Leidrad presented the other educational goal of his biblical schools as training clerics to grasp the spiritual senses of the Bible. Louis Holtz proposed that the repetitive appearance of *spiritalis intelligentia* or *sensus spiritalis* in this passage of Leidrad's letter implied the influence of the exegetical manual *Formulae spiritalis intellegentiae* of Eucherius, the fifth-century bishop of Lyon.[3] But the "spiritual" (in contrast with merely "literal" or "carnal") understanding of the Bible was a pursuit common for early medieval biblical education. For example, Charlemagne in his well-known *De litteris colendis* urged the use of literary skill to "spiritually understand" (*spiritaliter intellegit*) the Bible.[4] Noticeably, *spiritalem... intellectum in sacra Scriptura* is the subject of one annotation in Paris, BnF, NAL 1740 (on Deut. 28:12).[5] *Spiritalem intellegentiam* also appears in another annotation (on Deut. 28:64).[6]

Leidrad mentioned several groups of biblical books specifically: *liber euangeliorum, liber apostolorum, liber prophetarum, libri Salomonis, libri psalmorum*, and *Iob*. It is very likely that the archbishop used the Isidorian division of biblical canons. Isidore in Book 4 of his *Etymologiae* divided the Old Testament books into three *ordines* and the New Testament books into two: Law (*Lex*), Prophets (*Propheta*) and Sacred Writings (*Hagiographa*); Gospel (*euangelicus*) and Apostolic (*apostolicus*). Thus, Leidrad's enu-

---

1 "Karolus, Dei fretus auxilio rex Francorum et Langobardorum ac patricius Romanorum, religiosis lectoribus nostrae ditioni subiectis... Idque opus Paulo diacono, familiari clientulo nostro, elimandum iniunximus, scilicet ut, studiose catholicorum patrum dicta percurrens, ueluti e latissimis eorum pratis certos quosque flosculos legeret, et in unum quaeque essent utilis quasi sertum aptaret. Qui nostrae celsitudini deuote parere desiderans, tractatus atque sermones diuersorum catholicorum patrum perlegens et optima quaeque decerpens, in duobus uoluminibus per totius anni circulum congruentes cuique festiuitati distincte et absque uitiis nobis obtulit lectiones. Quarum omnium textum nostra sagacitate perpendentes, nostra eadem uolumina auctoritate constabilimus uestraeque religioni in Christi ecclesiis tradimus ad legendum." *Karoli epistola generalis, Capitularia regum Francorum I*, MGH Leges, no. 30, ed. Alfred Boretius (Hannover: Hahnsche, 1883), pp. 80-81.

2 "Et qui psalterium uel lectionem aliquid indigent, meditationem inseruiantur; et meditent in ipso interualle quod possint capere; et qui non possunt, in ecclesia omnes aut cantant aut legant." Chrodegang, *Regula canonicorum*, V, pp. 6-7.

3 Leidrad probably arranged to bring a copy of the *Formulae* (Paris, BnF, Lat. 9550) to his episcopal library. Another copy (Paris, BnF, Lat. 12236) of the same work was available in Lyon at the beginning of the ninth century. Louis Holtz, "La tradition lyonnaise d'Eucher de Lyon et le manuscrit Paris, BNF, lat. 9550," *Revue d'Histoire des Textes* 3 (2008): pp. 135-200.

4 "Cum autem in sacris paginis scemata, tropi et caetera his similia inserta inveniantur, nulli dubium est, quod ea unusquisque legens tanto citius spiritaliter intellegit, quanto prius in litterarum magisterio plenius instructus fuerit." Charlemagne, *De litteris colendis*, p. 290.

5 "Thesaurus Dominus obtimus spiritalem significat intellectum in sacra Scriptura, quem ipse Dominus per semetipum apostolis reserabit dicente Euangelista: Tunc aperuit illis sensum ut intelligerent Scripturas." Paris, BnF, NAL 1740, fol. 71v.

6 "Manifestus sensus spiritalem intellegentiam non indiget. Vniuersa enim mala haec Iudeis post Domini resurrectionem accedisse quis dubitat." Paris, BnF, NAL 1740, fol. 77r.

meration here could be read in the following way: *Liber euangeliorum* refers to the four gospels; *liber apostolorum* refers to all the Epistles, the Acts of Apostles, and the Apocalypse of John; *liber prophetarum* refers to Joshua, Judges (including Ruth), four books of Kings, Isaiah, Jeremiah, Ezekiel, and the Twelve Prophets; *libri Salomonis* (Proverbs, Ecclesiastes, and the Song and Songs) together with Psalms and Job constitute the major part of *hagiographa*.[1]

The very first *ordo* in Isidore's catalogue, the Pentateuch, is conspicuously absent in Leidrad's statement. Leidrad composed his report of reform in an accurate and discreet way. For example, he gave the exact numbers of monks and nuns of individual monasteries of Lyon, and named the churches that he built or restored. The lacuna of the Pentateuch suggests that the exegetical curriculum for these five biblical books was not yet in place at the time when Leidrad composed this letter.

This brings us to the question about the compositional date of this letter. It is an issue that scholars have been struggling with for centuries but have not yet reached a satisfactory consensus. As early as the eighteenth century, Carolus Le Cointe claimed that there was no way to determine the date of the letter.[2] Ernst Dümmler in the nineteenth century dated the letter to ca. 813–814. Dümmler paid special attention to Leidrad's emphasis on his bad health, and thus assumed that the letter must have been written not long before Leidrad retired from his episcopal position into the monastery and died soon after.[3]

Dümmler's dating is questionable. It is true that Leidrad talked about his physical weakness and expectation to die soon, and expressed it as his motive to send this report to make sure that "the reform in Lyon would not cease after my death."[4] However, Leidrad had never been totally well in body at least since he took the episcopal position in Lyon. According to correspondence between Alcuin and Arn of Salzburg, both being the best

---

1 Isidore of Seville, *Etymologiarum siue Originum libri XX*, VI.I, ed. W. M. Lindsay (Oxford: Oxford University Press, 1911). The Isidorian division of biblical canons was well received in the Carolingian era. E.g., *Disputatio puerorum*, a Pseudo-Alcuinian pedagogical dialogue composed around 800, ed. Liam Ethan Felsen, *The Disputatio puerorum: A Ninth-Century Monastic Instructional Text Edited from Vienna, Österreichische Nationalbibliothek, 458* (Toronto: the Pontifical Institute of Mediaeval Studies: 2017), V-VI, pp. 57-70; Theodulf's preface for his biblical edition, see PL 105, col. 305; Hrabanus Maurus, *De clericorum institutione*, III.7, ed., trans. Detlev Zimpel (Turnhout: Brepols, 2006), vol. 2, pp. 482-483; idem, *De universo*, V.1, PL 111, col. 105.

2 Carolus Le Cointe, *Annales Ecclesiastici Francorum* (Paris: Typographia regia, 1665-1683), vol. 7, p. 87.

3 *Epistolae Karolini aevi (II)*, MGH Epistolae 4, ed. Ernst Dümmler (Berlin: Weidmann, 1895), p. 542.

4 "Dominus omnipotens michi testis est, non tali intencione ea uobis, patefacio que dicturus sum, ut propterea in rebus augeri merear; neque aliquid tale in cogitacione mea composui ut acquisitionis michi occasio sit, sed idcirco hec suggero quoniam quotidie exitum a rebus humanis suspicor propter infirmitatem meam et incessanter de morte suspectus sum. Et ideo hec suggero ut cum benignissimis auribus uestris presentata fuerint et clementer inspecta, in posterum diuina uestra mansuetudo prouideat, si qua bene et secundum uoluntatem uestram gessi, post meum discessum non defficiant aut pereant, sed pocius proficiant et permaneant." Leidrad, *Report to Charlemagne*, p. 284.

friends of his, Leidrad was weak for the whole year not long after his promotion to the archbishopric.[1] His state of health was not stable thereafter, witnessed by a letter of his to an anonymous nun written ca. 811.[2] Thus, there is no sufficient reason to take Leidrad's self-statement of bad health as a definite sign of his plan to retire. In fact, even after 814, Leidrad was healthy enough to visit Mâcon as the missus of the new ruler Louis the Pious.[3] Also, Leidrad did *not* die soon after his retirement to the monastery of St-Médard in 816 as Dümmler believed,[4] but lived there for at least five years.[5] Therefore, Leidrad's statement of bad health, even if it was not merely a rhetorical excuse for his report, cannot be used to verify that the letter was written at the end of his episcopal career.

Alfred Coville approached the dating issue from another angle. He noticed that the reform achievements that Leidrad listed in his report showed great similarity with certain entries in two capitularies of Charlemagne, *Capitulare missorum Niumagae datum* of 806 and *Capitula de causis diuersis* of 807. Coville surmised that Leidrad undertook the reform measures depicted in his letter according to Charlemagne's order of church reform issued ca. 806/807 as presented in the two capitularies. Since it would have taken some more years to realize them, the report probably was not written earlier than 809, but most likely between 809 and 812.[6] Coville's dating is well received in modern scholarship.[7] But it is flawed as well. Coville's assumption that Leidrad had not initiated his reform until 806/807 does not agree with the archbishop's clear self-statement at the very beginning of the report that Charlemagne sent him to Lyon (in 798) specially

---

1   "[E]t quid Laidrado demandare uelis. Vix uiuit, si facies nostras non uidebit pariter. Fuit enim toto anno infirmus ualde; et dissolutae animae suae consiliare nobiscum cupit. Multa bona-gloria Deo-habet in illis partibus facta. Dubitat uero, an melius sit laborare in praedicationis ministerio uel quietam ducere uitam. Sed certius ab illo ipso permittente Deo haec audituri erimus." Alcuin, Letter 165, *Epistolae Karolini aevi (II)*, pp. 267-268.

2   "Cognoscere dignetur prudentia almitatis tuę nos iuxta donum donantis Dei uiribus corporis aliquantisper ualere et secundum quod se incerta salus propter suspectos casus uitae huius habet, de salute nostra gratias Deo debere." *Epistolae Karolini aevi (II)*, pp. 545-546.

3   "Nos interea missum nostrum uenerabilem scilicet [uirum] Leidrardum archiepiscopum ad hanc rem inuestigandam et diligenter inquirendam misimus..." *Die Urkunden Ludwigs des Frommen*, MGH Diplomata [Urkunden], eds. Theo Kölzer, Jens Peter Clausen, Daniel Eichler (Wiesbaden: Harrassowitz Verlag, 2016), no. 80, pp. 196-197.

4   *Epistolae Karolini aevi (II)*, p. 542. Dümmler was influenced by Georg Waitz, who proposed the view that Leidrad died ca. 817, see Ceory Waitz, "Handschriften der Bibliothek zu Lyon," *Archiv der Gesellschaft für Ältere Deutsche Geschichtskunde zur Beförderung einer Gesamtausgabe der Quellenschriften deutscher Geschichten des Mittelalters* 7 (1839): pp. 211-214.

5   Witnessed by a letter written by Theutmirus abbot of Psalmody to Claudius of Turin in 821: "Nam et uenerabilis pater Leidrath, quondam episcopus Lucdunensis, cum hoc audisset, gauisus est et ipse rogauitque eum michi multum ad scribendum et miratus fuit, cur epistolam illi non misistis ex tanto tempore, et promisit, quod ipse suam epistolam uobis missurus sit. Valde enim desiderat uisionem uestram, si fieri potuisset, et si non uisione corporea, uel epistola." Claudius, Letter 8, *Epistolae Karolini aevi (II)*, p. 605.

6   Alfred Coville, *Recherches sur l'Histoire de Lyon*, pp. 295-296.

7   Accepted, for example, by Mayke de Jong in her "Charlemagne's Church," *Charlemagne: Empire and Society*, ed. Joanna Story (Manchester: Manchester University Press, 2005), pp. 103-135.

in order to emend the *negligentias* there, and that he undertook his task "upon arriving there."[1]

But there is indeed undeniable similarity, both in content and in language, between Leidrad's report and the reform instruction given in the two capitularies of 806/807 about "the emendation and restoration of church buildings and ornament," "the reading, chanting, and other related disciplines of ecclesiastical rules,"[2] "the ecclesiastical treasures of the church,"[3] and "walls" and "roofs" of the churches.[4] It is possible to see a connection between them, although not the connection suggested by Coville. A more reasonable proposal is that either Leidrad composed his report with these capitularies in mind, or, the other way around, the measures of church reform exhorted in the capitularies were modeled on Leidrad's report.

---

1 "Sed uos qui non attenditis hominum merita, sed uestram solitam clemenciam, egistis de me sicut ineffabili pietati placuit nullo existente merito meo, quo tempore ad praefatam ecclesiam regendam micteretis et nominare michi dignati estis quasdam negligencias que in supraedicta ecclesia perpetrate noscebantur; pro qua re me ammonere dignati estis ut ego solicitudinis curam gererem et ut perpetrate neglegencie emendarentur et perpetrande uitarentur. Erat enim tunc dicta ecclesia multis in rebus destituta interius exteriusque tam in officiis quam in edificiis uel ceteris ecclesiasticis ministeriis. Ego quoque, humillimus seruulus uester, postquam ibidem perueni, que cum Dei adiutorio et uestro peregi, dignemini audire." Leidrad, *Report to Charlemagne*, pp. 283-284.

2 "... et diligenter inquirant de conuersatione singulorum uel quomodo emendatum habeant quod iussimus de eorum lectione et canto caeterisque disciplinis aecclesiasticae regulae pertinentibus." *Capitulare missorum Niumagae datum* (806), *Capitularia regum Francorum I*, no. 46, p. 131. Cf. Leidrad, *Report to Charlemagne*, pp. 284-285. "Et ideo officio pietatis uestre placuit, ut ad peticionem meam michi concederetis unum de Metensi ecclesia clericum, per quem, Deo iuuante et mercede uestra annuente, ita in Lugdunensi ecclesia instauratus est ordo psallendi, ut iuxta uires nostras secundum ritum sacri palatii omni ex parte agi uideatur quicquid ad diuinum persoluendum officium ordo exposcit. Nam habeo scholas cantorum, ex quibus plerique ita sunt eruditi ut etiam alios erudire possint. Preter hec, habeo scholas lectorum..."

3 "Ut praedicti missi per singulas ciuitates et monasteria uirorum et puellarum praeuideant, quomodo aut qualiter in domibus aecclesiarum et ornamentis aecclesiae emendatae uel restauratae esse uidentur... Ut singuli episcopi, abbates, abbatissae diligenter considerent thesauros ecclesiasticos, ne propter perfidiam aut neglegentiam custodum aliquid de gemmis aut de uasis, reliquo quoque thesauro perditum sit..." *Capitulare missorum Niumagae datum* (806), *Capitularia regum Francorum I*, no. 46, p. 131. Cf. Leidrad, *Report to Charlemagne*, p. 285. "Similiter uestimenta sacerdotum et ministeria procuraui." According to Fresne du Cange, *ministerium sacrum* refers to "Ecclesiasticum, Sacrorum uasorum, donariorum, et ornamentorum, atque adeouestimentorum Ecclesiæ congeries et apparatus, quod ad Dei ministerium haec omnia consecrata sint." *Glossarium Mediae et Infimae Latinitatis*, ed. Léopold Favre (Niort: L. Favre, 1883–1887), vol. 5, col. 399.

4 "Primum de aecclesiis, quomodo structae aut destructae sint in tectis, in maceriis siue parietibus siue in pauimentis necnon in pictura etiam et in luminariis siue officiis." *Capitula de causis diuersis* (807), *Capitularia regum Francorum I*, no. 49, p. 136. Cf. Leidrad, *Report to Charlemagne*, pp. 285-286. "De restauracione eciam ecclesiarum, in quantum ualui, non cessaui, ita ut eiusdem ciuitatis maximam ecclesiam que est in honorem sancti Ioannis Baptiste, a nouo operuerim et macerias ex parte erexerim. Similiter ecclesie Sancti Stephani tegumentum de nouo reparaui... in honorem sancti Georgii quam de nouo operui et ex parte macerias eius a fundamentis erexi... Monasterium quoque Insule Barbare situm in medio Araris fluuii, in honorem sancti Martini dedicatum, ita restauraui ut tecta de nouo fierent et aliqua de maceriis a fundamentis erigerentur... Similiter aliud monasterium in honorem sancti Ragneberti aedificatum, ubi eiusdem sancti corpus requiescit, de nouo totum reparatum est, siue in parietibus, siue in tectis uel eciam in ecclesiis..."

Either of these two surmises leads us to date Leidrad's letter to Charlemagne ca. 806/807, namely the midpoint of his episcopal career (798–816), rather than the end according to the prevailing scholarly common wisdom.[1] Thus, the absence of the Pentateuch in Leidrad's report could suggest that the exegetical curriculum for the Pentateuch had not been available in Leidrad's schools until the second half of his episcopate.

To establish such a curriculum would have required much work. Leidrad once ordered the Lyon scriptorium to repair an old codex (Lyon BM, 443 + Paris, BnF, NAL 1591; CLA, IV.774a-c, Bischoff, *Katalog*, 2549a) which contained Origen's homilies on Genesis, Exodus, and Leviticus by remaking certain folios (Lyon BM, 443, fols. 7-11, 77 and 227-331).[2] It would have worked as a reference book for both master and student.

On a handful of occasions, the author of the Deuteronomy annotations in Paris, BnF, NAL 1740 named other biblical books and asked readers to consult them for reference. 13 of all 15 cases of such refer to the books of the Pentateuch: Genesis once, Exodus

---

1   To verify this dating, a piece of indirect evidence can be offered here. In his old age, Charlemagne tended to hold a more internalized view of church reform, the best witness of which is a capitulary known as *Capitula de causis cum episcopis et abbatibus tractandis* issued in 811 [*Capitularia regum Francorum I*, no. 72; François Louis Ganshof, "Note sur les 'Capitula de causis cum episcopis et abbatibus tractandis' de 811," *Studia Gratiana* 13 (1967): pp. 1-25. Cf. Heinrich Fichtenau, *The Carolingian Empire*, trans. Peter Munz (Oxford: Blackwell, 1957), pp. 181-185]. Charlemagne in this capitulary spoke in a preaching tone and Janet Neslon claimed that one can hear "Charlemagne's voice" in it. Cf. "The Voice of Charlemagne," *Belief and Culture in the Middle Ages: Studies Presented to Henry Mayr-Harting*, eds. Richard Gameson, Henrietta Leyser (Oxford: Oxford University Press, 2001), pp. 77-88. In one *capitulum*, Charlemagne rebuked a *magister*'s pursuit of "more men rather than good men," and the exclusive attention to chanting, reading, and the beauty of church building at the cost of the virtuous living of the clerics: "Quam paucitatem conferat ecclesie Christi quod is qui pastor uel magister cuiuscumque uenerabilis loci esse debet, magis studet in sua conuersatione habere multos quam bonos et non tantum probis quam multitudine hominum delectatur, plus studet ut suus clericus uel monachus bene cantet et legat quam iuste et beate uiuat, quamquam non solum minime in ecclesia contempnenda sit cantandi uel legendi disciplina, sed etiam omnimodis exercenda; sed si utrumque cuilibet uenerabili loco accedere potest, tolerabilius tamen ferendum nobis uidetur inperfectione cantandi quam uiuendi. Et quamuis bonum sit ut ecclesie pulchra sint edificia, praeferendus tamen est edificiis bonorum morum ornatus et culmen; quia in quantum nobis uidetur structio basilicarum ueteris legis quandam trahit consuetudinem, morum autem emendatio proprie ad nouum testamentum et Christianam pertinet disciplinam." Franois Louis Ganshof, "Note," p. 25. It is hard to imagine that, after such a turn of reform policy, Leidrad would write to his lord in the 810s a report that highlights the increase of clerics and religious persons, the establishment of schools of chanting and reading, and the improvement of church buildings, but says nothing concerning the clerical *conuersatio*.

2   Cf. Louis Holtz, "Leidrat, évêque de Lyon," pp. 316, 320.

six times, Leviticus twice, and Numbers five times.[1] It could be the indication that these Deuteronomy annotations originally served as part of the pedagogical program of teaching the Pentateuch.

The best witness to the exegesis of the Pentateuch in Leidrad's Lyon was Claudius of Turin. Born a Spaniard, Claudius went to Lyon at the end of the eighth century, probably in company with the Adoptionist Felix of Urgel who lived in Lyon under custody after being condemned as a heretic. Claudius turned out to be one of the first Carolingian professional exegetes and an author of many biblical commentaries.[2] His exegetical career started in Lyon. According to the preface to his commentary on Genesis accomplished not long after he left Lyon for the court of Louis the Pious, then king of Aquitaine, at Chasseneuil in 811, he recalled that he had begun to compose this commentary when he was in Lyon:

> The work [Commentary on Genesis] I began in Lyons when I was with the venerable father Leidrad, by the grace of God archbishop of the church there, when we advanced to some extent in our knowledge of the Bible, thanks to his effort and God's help.[3]

Scholars tend to read *apud uenerabilem patrem Leidrad* in this passage as evidence that Claudius learned biblical exegesis with Leidrad.[4] But Claudius here could simply mean that Leidrad was the head of the Lyon church and the organizer of the biblical

---

1 "... huic simile uidetur et illud quod in Genesi de Cam filio Noe scriptum est..." Paris, BnF, NAL 1740, fol. 66r, on Deut. 25:11-12; "Hoc in Exodo legitur quod Moyses per consilium Ietro cogniti sui fecerit." Fol. 2r, on Deut. 1:13; "Lege in Exodo et ibi repperies quae in hoc libro iterate sunt." Fol. 13r, on Deut. 4:9; "Hec sunt decem mandata legis que in libro Exodi continentur..." Fol. 17v, on Deut. 5:7; "Haec omnia in libro Exodi premissa et predicta sunt." Fol. 29v, on Deut. 10:1; "Hoc preceptum in libro Exodi similiter repperies..." Fol. 44r, on Deut. 15:12; "Hoc iudicium in libro Exodi et in Leuitico similiter premissum est..." Fol. 53v, on Deut. 19:21; "Hoc in libro Numeri de his exploratoribus scriptum est quod <preci>piente Domino ad explorandam terram repromissionis missi sunt." Fol. 3r, on Deut. 1:23; "Haec omnia in libro Numeri latius dicta sunt; in hoc uero rememoratio est preteritorum." Fol. 10v, on Deut. 3:18; "Tres ciuitates quas separauit Moyses ad refugium fugitiuorum, sicut superius in libro Numeri predictum est..." Fol. 16r, Deut. 4:41; "Filios Enahim de quibus in libro Numeri latius predictum est..." Fol. 27r, Deut. 9:2; "Haec uniuersa que de lebitis replicata sunt, in libro Numeri plenius predicta sunt." Fol. 30r, Deut. 10:8; "Hoc quippe significat in presenti libro annus remissionis septimus quod et [in libro Leuitico annus requietionis dicitur]." Fol. 42v, on Deut. 15:1. Cf. "Hoc et in Euangelio Dominus diabolo respondisse legitur." Fol. 25v, on Deut. 8:3; "Hoc enim et in Hieremia propheta et in Eze<c>hihel similiter repperies." Fol. 64r, on Deut. 24:16.

2 For a summary of Claudius' life and career, cf. Pascal Boulhol, *Claude de Turin*, pp. 15-32. The list of Claudius' exegetical works, see pp. 331-344.

3 "Quod ego in Lucduno ciuitate apud uenerabilem patrem Leidrad, gratiae Dei iamdictae aecclesiae archiepiscopo, incoaui, quo faciente et Deo donante aliquantulum in scripturarum scientiam profecimus." Claudius, Letter 1, *Epistolae Karolini aevi (II)*, p. 592.

4 E.g., Michael Gorman, "Commentary on Genesis of Claudius of Turin," pp. 279-280: "In the first decade of the ninth century he was studying with Leidrad."

schools. In fact, that the archbishop was ever a master of biblical exegesis himself is no more than a hypothesis verified by no solid evidence, although generally assumed.[1] A more reasonable reading of this passage of Claudius is that he was recalling his times in Lyon *not* as a student but as a master who was already qualified to start to compose a commentary of his own. In other words, before Claudius arrived at Louis' court in 811 to teach the Bible there (thanks to Leidrad's recommendation?), he had probably already been a *magister* in Leidrad's biblical schools in Lyon.

The Pentateuch is among Claudius' first exegetical targets.[2] He commented on Genesis (published ca. 811), Exodus (ca. 821, now lost), Leviticus (ca. 823), Numbers (before 825, now lost), but passed over Deuteronomy, "the book which I already expounded in part according to literal and spiritual senses in the previous books, that is Exodus, Leviticus, and Numbers."[3] In the preface to his commentary on 1 and 2 Corinthians (c. 820), Claudius made it clear that his commentaries on the Pentateuch as well as these two Pauline epistles grew out of the lectures that he delivered *uiua uoce*. He wrote them down at the request of Louis and at the urge of his disciples of the school.[4]

One may wonder whether the Deuteronomy annotations in Paris, BnF, NAL 1740 also originated from the same kind of classroom lecture. It could also be possible that it was the disciples in the classroom who had taken down the notes from a lecture, and that these notes were then edited into the archetype of these Deuteronomy annotations. After all, such a practice was not unknown in the Carolingian era.[5]

Claudius, in the preface to his commentary on Joshua, called Deuteronomy *secunda lex uel certe iteratio legis interpretetur, quod est figura euangelii.*[6] This is remarkably

---

1   E.g., Janneke Raaijmakers, "I, Claudius. Self-Styling in Early Medieval Debate," *Early Medieval Europe* 25 (2017): pp. 70-84, at 77: "… he was well-versed in biblical learning, having studied with the great exegetical expert Leidrad of Lyons."

2   In his correspondence with Michael Gorman, Iain Douglas suggested that "Claudius might have been told to concentrate on certain works at that point in his career," when he was in Lyon. See Michael Gorman, "Commentary on Genesis of Claudius of Turin," p. 280, n. 6.

3   "Et ob hoc omitto Deuteronomii librum, qui pene in superioribus libris, id est Exodo, Leuitico atque Numerorum magna ex parte iuxta litteram et spiritum a nobis iam expositus est..." Claudius, Letter 11, *Epistolae Karolini aevi (II)*, p. 609.

4   "Et uere fateor me primitus inuitus accessisse, et in hoc opus et in Pentatico quem postulas, imperantibus fratribus in scola constitutis, quibus uiua uoce scripturas tradebam, precipiente pio principe Hludowico imperatore. Compulsus etiam a memorato principe, ut non tantum uerba per obliuionem palantem traderem, sed etiam calamo diu permanentem scriberem, ut quod ore promebam calamo scriptitarem. De ammonitione fratrum et exhortationem unde rogasti quod scriberem, ut uotum quod uouerunt Domino reddant; et uotum ut dico non propositum quod scripsisti, quod solius Dei est." Claudius, Letter 4, *Epistolae Karolini aevi (II)*, p. 601.

5   A Carolingian case of a disciple copying down the exegetical lecture of the master can be found in a letter from Ercanbert of Fulda to his master Rudolf. Ercanbert dedicated to Rudolf the latter's oral commentary on the Gospel of John taken down by him from dictation. *Epistolae Karolini aevi (III)*, pp. 358-359. Cf. John Contreni, "Pursuit of Knowledge," p. 121.

6   "... annuente pietate diuina et bonitate indebita, accedere uolo, cuius tanta auctoritas est, ut secunda lex uel certe iteratio legis interpretetur, quod est figura euangelii. De quo solo libro testimonia Dominus temtatori suo diabolo protulit." Claudius, Letter 11, *Epistolae Karolini aevi (II)*, p. 609.

close to one annotation in Paris, BnF, NAL 1740: *Deuteronomium id est iteratio legis, figura est euangelii...* (fol. 49r, on Deut. 17:18), and the exactly identical wording cannot be found in any other early medieval writing. It could be a trace that Claudius had known the exegesis in these annotations in either a textual or an oral way.

Another witness to the contemporary reception of these Deuteronomy annotations is Agobard, the successor to Leidrad as archbishop of Lyon (r. 816–840). In Chapter 8, we will discuss in detail how he used the same exegesis of Moses' curses to the transgressors of the Law as recorded in Paris, BnF, NAL 1740 for his own polemical purpose.

***

This chapter provides a primary survey of the Deuteronomy annotations conserved in Paris, BnF, NAL 1740. Taking all the evidence together, the most reasonable deduction that we can draw about these annotations is that they were composed by a master — or originated from a master's lecture — in the biblical schools organized by Leidrad in the episcopal church of Lyon, copied soon after by a scribe of the Lyon cathedral scriptorium in the form of marginalia in order to make the manuscript a "commented biblical edition," and was preserved in the episcopal library accessible to clerics. We can now safely call them "the Lyon Annotations."

The analysis also suggests that the making of the Lyon Annotations is directly related to the broad context of the revival of biblical education promoted by Leidrad during his episcopate. In the next chapter, we will zoom out even farther, to see Leidrad's church reform in Lyon, and to contextualize the Lyon Annotations in this more general historical picture.

CHAPTER 3

HISTORICAL SETTING: LEIDRAD AND THE CAROLINGIAN REFORM IN LYON (798–816)

3.1   Leidrad: the Life of a Carolingian Reformer

Deuteronomy, namely the repetition of the Law (*iteratio legis*), is the figure of the Gospel, which all who preside in the church should study day and night, as the blessed Apostle Paul said to his disciple Timothy who was a bishop himself: 'Till I come, attend unto reading, to exhortation, and to doctrine (1 Timothy 4:13),' and slightly later, 'Take heed to thyself and to doctrine: be earnest in them. For in doing this thou shalt both save thyself and them that hear thee (1 Timothy 4:16).'[1]

This is the expositional entry for Deut. 17:18-19 in the Lyon Annotations. In this Deuteronomic verse, Moses admonished the king elected by the Israel to "copy out to himself the Deuteronomy of this law in a volume" and to "read it all the days of his life." In the historical world in which the Lyon Annotations was composed, the one who "preside[d] in the church" was Leidrad, and as we have seen in Chapter 2, the making of the Lyon Annotations was intrinsically related not only to the archbishop's own writings but also to the biblical schools organized by him. There has been yet no satisfactory modern biography of Leidrad.[2] The task of this subchapter is to present the life of this great figure of the age of Charlemagne as thoroughly as possible, by collecting and stitching together all the relevant information from extant sources.

---

1   "Deuteronomium id est iteratio legis, figura est Euangelii quam omnes qui presunt ecclesiae die ac nocte meditare debent, dicente beato Paulo apostolo ad Timotheum discipulum suum, qui et ipse erat episcopus: Dum uenio, adtende lectioni et exortatione doctrine; et post pauca: Adtende tibi doctrine, insta in illis: hoc enim faciens, et teipsum saluum facies et qui te audierint." Paris, BnF, NAL 1740, fol. 49r.

2   "Laidradus" "Leidradus" "Leidrardus" "Liobradus" or the Germanized "Leidrat" used by himself for *ex-dono*. His life, cf. Hubert Mordek, "Leidrad, Bischof von Lyon (797–814/816)," *Lexikon des Mittelalters* (Stuttgart: Metzler, 1977–1999), vol. 5, col. 1855; Philippe Depreux, *Prosopographie de l'Entourage de Louis le Pieux (781–840)* (Sigmaringen: Thorbecke, 1997). The sole modern but far from critical biography is a late-nineteenth-century dissertation: H. Favier, *Essai historique sur Leidrad Archevêque de Lyon (740?–816/817)* (Lyon: Typographie et lithographie J. Gallet, 1898).

We do not know the exact year of Leidrad's birth. The earliest evidence comes from the colophon of a charter issued at the episcopal residence of Arbeo bishop of Freising on February 20, 779. The charter recorded that a priest called Uuicpot donated his property to the church of St-Maria at Reichertshausen. The colophon reads: "I, Leidrad the deacon, wrote down under the command from the mouth of the bishop Arbeo."[1] Another charter issued in 782, at Freising as well, ends with "I, Leidrad, an unworthy sinner but a deacon (*licet indignus et peccator tamen diaconus*), drew up this charter of delivery under the command of Tassilo, the highest prince."[2] This colophon associated this deacon of Freising with the later archbishop of Lyon, because the formula *licet indignus... tamen* was also used in the archbishop's autographic *ex-dono* found in no fewer than five manuscripts donated by him to the collegiate church of Lyon: *Leidrat, licet indignus, tamen episcopus, istum librum tradidi ad altare sancti Stephani.*[3] Leidrad was thus a deacon in the church of Freising and worked as Bishop Arbeo's notary there in the 770s and 780s. If we take the usual canonical standard of the minimum age of 25 for deacon and 30 for priest,[4] he should have been born in ca. 750.

Leidrad was a local Bavarian. In Theodulf of Orléans' poem *Contra iudices*, whose theme is the mission of himself and Leidrad to southern Gaul as Charlemagne's *missi dominici*, Leidrad was described as "begotten by Bavaria (*Noricus*)."[5] His family background is little known, but may be glimpsed through a donation charter in 810. A person named Leidrat appears as one of the witnesses for the recipient of the donation, Adalwin bishop of Regensburg. If this namesake was a relative of the then archbishop of Lyon, it is likely that the latter was from a family that held high status in Bavarian ecclesiastical politics. It would explain how he grew up in the church of Freising and became a close assistant of Bishop Arbeo.

Arbeo was an able and learned bishop. During his episcopate, the church of Freising experienced huge development in ecclesiastical authority, wealth, and culture (school,

---

1 "Ego Leidraad diaconus iussus ex ore Heredis episcopi conscribsi." *Die Traditionen des Hochstifts Freising, 744–926*, ed. Theodor Bitterauf (Aalen: Scientia-Verlag, 1967), no. 95, p. 114.

2 "Scripsi autem hanc cartulam traditionis ego Leidrat licet indignus et peccator tamen diaconus iussus a principe summo Tassilone." *Traditionen des Hochstifts Freising*, no. 106, p. 123.

3 Cf. Sigmund Tafel, "Lyons Scriptorium," 4 (1925): pp. 51-52; Louis Holtz, "Leidrat, évêque de Lyon," pp. 318-320.

4 Cf. Julia Barrow, "Grades of Ordination and Clerical Careers, c.900-c.1200," *Anglo-Norman Studies: Proceedings of the Battle Conference* 30 (2007): pp. 41-61.

5 "Haeserat hac nobis Laidradus sorte sodalis,/Cederet ut magnus hoc relevante labor./Noricus hunc genuit, hunc tu, Lugdune, futurum/Pontificem speras relligionis ope." Theodulf, *Contra iudices*, *Poetae Latini aevi Carolini (I)*, MGH Poetae Latini medii aevi 1, ed. Ernst Dümmler (Berlin: Weidmann, 1881), no. 28, p. 496.

library, and scriptorium).[1] It is tempting to surmise that Leidrad later modeled Arbeo
to carry out the church and cultural reform of his own in Lyon. It is without doubt that
Leidrad received good education at Arbeo's Freising, including the training as a scribe.
Bischoff recognized his handwriting in two manuscripts produced in Freising in the later
eighth century: Munich, Bayerische Staatsbibliothek, Clm 6305 (Jerome's commentary
on the Gospel of Matthew and his letters; Bischoff, *Katalog*, 3040) and Munich, Bayerische Staatsbibliothek, Clm 6393 (various *vitae* composed by Rufinus, Jerome, and Atha-
nasius; Bischoff, *Katalog*, 3070).[2]

In the colophon of the charter of 782 mentioned above, Leidrad stated that he wrote
it under the command of *princeps summus Tassilo*. However, in the political tension
between Charlemagne and Tassilo in the 770s and 780s, it is very likely that Leidrad
followed his bishop Arbeo in standing with the Carolingian.[3] This explains how Leidrad
turned out to leave Bavaria for *Francia* to work for Charlemagne before or soon after
the fall of Tassilo in 788. It is likely that he once served the Carolingian king as an ecclesiastical courtier. In his epistolary report to Charlemagne which we have examined in
detail in Chapter 2.4.3, Leidrad claimed that he had reformed the order of Psalm singing
"according to the rite of the sacred palace," which he may have experienced personally.[4]
He also built an episcopal residence with a *solarium* for Charlemagne to reside in if the
latter ever visited Lyon, which implies his knowledge of the architectural design of Char-

---

1   Heinz Löwe, "Arbeo von Freising: Eine Studie zu Religiosität und Bildung im 8. Jahrhundert," *Von
    Cassiodor zu Dante: Ausgewählte Aufsätze zur Geschichtsschreibung und politischen Ideenwelt des
    Mittelalters* (Berlin: De Gruyter, 1973), pp. 75-110; Hubert Glaser, "Bischof Arbeo von Freising,"
    *Christenleben im Wandel der Zeit: Lebensbilder aus der Geschichte des Erzbistums München und
    Freising*, ed. Georg Schwaiger (Munich: E. Wewel, 1987), pp. 21-34. For Arbeo's involvement in
    politics, see Joachim Jahn, "Bischof Arbeo von Freising und die Politik seiner Zeit," *Ethnogenese
    und Überlieferung: Angewandte Methoden der Frühmittelalterforschung*, eds., Karl Brunner, Brigitte
    Merta (Vienne: Oldenbourg, 1994), pp. 157-162. For Arbeo's promotion of the library and the book
    production at Freising, see Bernhard Bischoff, *Die südostdeutschen Schreibschulen und Bibliotheken
    in der Karolingerzeit* (Wiesbaden: Harrassowitz, 1960-1980), pp. 60, 64, 83-85. For Arbeo as the
    author of the vitae of Emmeram and Corbinian, see Jonathan Couser, "A Usable Past: Early Bavarian
    Hagiography in Context," *Studies in Medieval and Renaissance History III* 4 (2007): pp. 1-56; Carl
    Hammer, "Arbeo of Freising's Life and Passion of St Emmeram: The Martyr and his Critics," *Revue
    d'histoire ecclésiastique* 161 (2006): pp. 5-36. For Edward Roberts' preliminary but promising
    project to study the church-building in Freising under Arbeo, see http://www.charlemagneseurope.
    ac.uk/blog/church-building-in-bavaria-under-bishop-arbeo-of-freising/, last accessed September 14,
    2021.
2   Bernhard Bischoff, *Die südostdeutschen Schreibschulen*, Teil I, pp. 83-85.
3   Friedrich Prinz, "Arbeo von Freising und die Agilulfinger," *Zeitschrift für Bayerische
    Landesgeschichte* 29 (1966): pp. 580-590.
4   "Et ideo officio pietatis uestre placuit, ut ad peticionem meam michi concederetis unum de Metensi
    ecclesia clericum, per quem, Deo iuuante et mercede uestra annuente, ita in Lugdunensi ecclesia
    instauratus est ordo psallendi, ut iuxta uires nostras secundum ritum sacri palatii omni ex parte
    agi uideatur quicquid ad diuinum persoluendum officium ordo exposcit." Leidrad, *Report to
    Charlemagne*, p. 284.

lemagne's royal residence.[1]

His working experience at Charlemagne's court could explain the intimate relationship that Leidrad developed with Alcuin who spent a long time as master in Charlemagne's court between 782 and 796. Alcuin's close friend Arn (nicknamed "Aquila") played a crucial role in this friendship. Leidrad appeared now and then as common friend in correspondence between these two dominant ecclesiastical figures of that time.[2] Like Leidrad, Arn also came from Freising Cathedral, so the two probably had known each other well there. Arn became the bishop of Salzburg in 785, and one of the most trusted confidants of Charlemagne not long after the fall of Tassilo.[3] One may wonder whether it was Arn who first introduced Leidrad to Alcuin who called Leidrad "my comrade and friend" (*consocius et amicus meus*). Leidrad was psychologically attached to these two older friends of his (Arn was older than he by around 10 years, and Alcuin by around 20) and very dependent on their suggestions.[4]

In 798, as mentioned above, Charlemagne sent Leidrad as a *missus dominicus* to Southern Gaul together with Theodulf. Their route was from Lyon to Vienne, Narbonne, Arles, Marseille, and so on. Theodulf commemorated this judicial mission in his poem *Contra iudices* themed with satire against bribery and admonition against the avarice of judges. He depicted his partner as "reputed for knowledge, vigorous in understanding, and abundant with virtue, to whom this life remains a passage to the heavenly one."[5] We

---

1 "Aliam quoque domum cum solario de nouo aedificaui et duplicaui et hanc propter uos paruui, ut si in illis partibus uester esset aduentus, in ea suscipi possetis." Leidrad, *Report to Charlemagne*, p. 285. On *solarium* and Charlemagne's palace, see Mayke de Jong, "Charlemagne's Balcony: The Solarium in Ninth-Century Narratives," *The Long Morning of Medieval Europe: New Directions in Early Medieval Studies*, eds. Jennifer R. Davis, Michael McCormick (Burlington: Ashgate, 2008), pp. 277-290.

2 Alcuin, Letter 10 (c. anno 790), *Epistolae Karolini aevi (II)*, p. 36; Letter 165 (799), ibid., pp. 267-268; Letter 194 (800), ibid., pp. 321-322; Letter 207 (800), ibid., pp. 343-345; Letter 208 (800), ibid., p. 346.

3 Donald Bullough, "Three 'Men of God' in Charlemagne's Service: Alcuin, Hildebald, Arno," *Charlemagne: Empire and Society*, ed. Joanna Story (Manchester: Manchester University Press, 2005), pp. 136-150; Meta Niederkorn-Bruck and Anton Scharer, eds., *Erzbischof Arn von Salzburg* (Wien: R. Oldenbourg Verlag), esp. the paper by Maximilian Diesenberger and Herwig Wolfram, "Arn und Alkuin 790 bis 804: Zwei Freunde und ihre Schriften," pp. 81-106.

4 "Saluta, obsecro, Laedredum, consocium et amicum meum. Sequenti anno certum eum faciam; si ille certus erit, quid uelit uel quid possit." Alcuin, Letter 10 (to Arn), *Epistolae Karolini aevi (II)*, p. 36. "Quod uero me interrogare uoluisti de certitudine uoluntatis uel loci, nihil tibi certum adhuc remandare habeo, nisi Deo miserante et uita comite adhuc uisurus eris faciem meam, licet nesciam propter occupationes meas uel uestras, ubi aut quando. Multoties secundum oportunitatem portantium litteras mihi dirigere satage, ut habeam curam tuae caritati rescribendi, uel etiam demandandi, quodcumque ueniat mihi." Alcuin, Letter 141 (to Leidrad), *Epistolae Karolini aevi (II)*, p. 223. "Sed festina rescribere mihi, quantum sciri posset tempus mansionis tuae apud Sanctum Amandum; et quid Laidrado demandare uelis. Vix uiuit, si facies nostras non uidebit pariter. Fuit enim toto anno infirmus ualde; et dissolutae animae suae consiliare nobiscum cupit. Multa bona - gloria Deo - habet in illis partibus facta. Dubitat uero, an melius sit laborare in praedicationis ministerio uel quietam ducere uitam. Sed certius ab illo ipso permittente Deo haec audituri erimus." Alcuin, Letter 165 (to Arn), ibid., p. 268.

5 "Arte cluit, sensuque uiget, uirtute redundat;/Cui uita ad superam transitus ista manet." Theodulf, *Contra iudices*, *Poetae Latini aevi Carolini (I)*, no. 28, p. 497.

find in the Lyon Annotations an orally styled exposition of Deut. 16:19 ("Thou shalt not accept person nor gifts"): "Let the avaricious judges hear this and cease accepting persons, driven by avarice."[1] Does it reflect Leidrad's moral teachings shaped in this journey with the bishop of Orléans?

Lyon was the point of departure of Leidrad's and Theodulf's official journey.[2] What *Contra iudices* also alludes to is that Leidrad had already been appointed as the bishop of Lyon when the journey started.[3] Around the same time, in a letter to Leidrad, Alcuin called him "bishop... elected."[4] The only quasi-contemporary account of this promotion was given by Ado of Vienne in his *Chronicon* composed ca. 870:

> At that time, Ursio ruled the church of Vienne, and Ado ruled the church of Lyon. After Ado, his younger relative (*nepos*) Ilduinus held the church of Lyon for a while, but not as bishop (*non episcopus*); he withdrew and took up the monastic life in the monastery of the island of Lérins. Post Ursio, a bishop too naïve (*nimiae simplicitatis episcopum*), the Bavarian Wifer whom they call by the paternal name *Vultreia*, took up the episcopate of Vienne. Hereafter, Leidrad, a man most earnest in secular authority and useful to the goodness of the state (*seculari dignitati intentissimus et honori reipublicae utilis*) ruled the church of Lyon...[5]

We know very little about either this Ado or his *nepos* Ilduinus, but Ado of Vienne seemed to insinuate that Ilduinus had attempted to "inherit" the episcopate of Lyon after the death of his relative, but did not manage to obtain the *nomen* of bishop, and finally retired to a monastery. His replacement was Leidrad. The power behind this was no doubt Charlemagne, as Leidrad recalled explicitly in his reform report to Charlemagne:

> At that time, you wanted to send me, the pettiest servant of yours to govern the church of Lyon (*ad regimen ecclesie*), although I did not deserve this office and was not qualified. But you do not care about people's good deeds, and treat me with your habitual mercy. As if with ineffable piety, you were happy to send me to rule the

---

1 "Audiant haec auari iudices et desinant contemplatione auaritie, personarum acceptores fieri." Paris, BnF, NAL 1740, fol. 47r.

2 "Iam, Lugdune, tuis celsis post terga relictis/Moenibus, adgredimur, causa quod optat, iter." Theodulf, *Contra iudices*, *Poetae Latini aevi Carolini (I)*, no. 28, p. 497.

3 "Noricus hunc genuit, hunc tu, Lugdune, futurum/Pontificem speras relligionis ope." Ibid., p. 497.

4 "Pontifici, Fratri, Amico Liobrado Electo Albinus Salutem..."Alcuin, Letter 141 (to Leidrad), *Epistolae Karolini aevi (II)*, p. 223.

5 "Viennensem tunc temporis ecclesiam Ursus, Ado Lugdunensem ecclesiam regebat. Post Adonem nepos eius Ilduinus paululum Lugdunensem ecclesiam, non episcopus, tenuit; et abscedens, Lirinis insulae monasterio monachalem conuersationem suscepit. Post Ursum, nimiae simplicitatis episcopum, Vulferi, quem Vultreiam patrio nomine appellarunt, Baioarius, Viennensem episcopatum suscepit. Porro Lugdunensem Leidradus, uir seculari dignitati intentissimus et honori reipublicae utilis, rexit ecclesiam..." Ado of Vienne, *Chronicon*, MGH Scriptores 2, ed. Georg Heinrich Pertz (Hannover: Hahnsche, 1829).

above mentioned church at that time (although I do not have the merit) and deigned to enumerate to me certain negligences (*negligencias*) that were known to have been perpetrated in the above mentioned church. You deigned to admonish me to take care of this problem, to emend the negligence perpetrated, and to prevent it from being perpetrated in the future. At that time, the mentioned church was destitute in many respects, both internal and external, in liturgical offices, church buildings, and other ecclesiastical utensils.[1]

The promotion of Leidrad to the bishopric needs to be understood as Charlemagne's intervention in the local ecclesiastical politics through one of his *fideles*.[2] Leidrad's connection with and accountability to the Carolingian ruler in the North was implied in Ado of Vienne's depiction of him: *seculari dignitati intentissimus et honori reipublicae utilis*. It is also tempting to ask whether Alcuin was involved in Leidrad's promotion. A letter sent by Alcuin to Charlemagne, usually dated to 798, consists of 12 pieces of advice, whose context is very ambiguous.[3] Items 7–10 are about election. Item 9 famously contains the first known appearance of the Latin phrase *uox populi, uox Dei*:

> The people are to be led in accordance with divine law, not followed. And when witnesses are needed, men of position are to be preferred. Nor are those to be listened to, who are accustomed to say "The voice of the people is the voice of God." For the clamor of the crowd is ever next to madness.[4]

If this clause reflected Alcuin's advice on the episcopal election, as Edward Peters

---

1 "Domine mi, gloriosissime, constans et sacer Imperator... Olim me exiguissimum famulorum uestrorum ad regimen ecclesie Lugdunensis destinare uoluistis, cum ego huic officio impar existerem et indignus. Sed uos qui non attenditis hominum merita, sed uestram solitam clemenciam, egistis de me sicut ineffabili pietati placuit nullo existente merito meo, quo tempore ad praefatam ecclesiam regendam micteretis et nominare michi dignati estis quasdam negligencias que in supraedicta ecclesia perpetrate noscebantur; pro qua re me ammonere dignati estis ut ego solicitudinis curam gererem et ut perpetrate neglegencie emendarentur et perpetrande uitarentur. Erat enim tunc dicta ecclesia multis in rebus destituta interius exteriusque tam in officiis quam in edificiis uel ceteris ecclesiasticis ministeriis." Leidrad, *Report to Charlemagne*, p. 283.

2 Among the enormous studies of the personal bond between rulers and aristocracy (both lay and ecclesiastical) in Carolingian politics, see esp. Stuart Airlie, "The Aristocracy in the Service of the State in the Carolingian Period," *Staat im frühen Mittelalter*, eds. Stuart Airlie, Walter Pohl, Helmut Reimitz (Wien:Verlag der Österreichischen Akademie der Wissenschaften, 2006), pp. 93-111.

3 Alcuin, Letter 132, *Epistolae Karolini aevi (II)*, pp. 198-199.

4 "Populus iuxta sanctiones diuinas ducendus est, non sequendus; et ad testimonium personae magis aliguntur honestae. Nec audiendi qui solent dicere: "Vox populi, vox Dei," cum tumultuositas vulgi semper insaniae proxima sit." Ibid., p. 199. The translation is based on Edward Peters' in his "Vox populi, vox Dei," *Law in Medieval Life and Thought*, eds. Edward King, Susan Ridyard (Sewanee: The University of the South, 1990), pp. 91-120.

suggested,[1] is it possible that Alcuin was encouraging Charlemagne to exercise his authority to impose Leidrad upon the church of Lyon at the expense of its local tradition (*uox populi*)? If so, Charlemagne obviously took Alcuin's advice and made this happen in the same year.

However obscure his promotion in 798 was, it is clear that Leidrad did not disappoint his master and his friend. Our next subchapter will focus on Leidrad's reform measures and their impact on this ancient city. Here, we first examine Leidrad's involvement in a big politico-religious event outside Lyon: the movement against Spanish Adoptionism.

The doctrine called Adoptionism holds that Christ is the adoptive son of God, and that his Incarnation should thus be described as *adoptiuus* rather than *assumptus*.[2] In the late eighth century, this Christological stance originated from a doctrinal controversy inside the Iberian territory under Umayyad rule. Its early major advocate was Elipandus archbishop of Toledo (717–808). Charlemagne's military expansion into the Spanish March and Septimania from the 770s made Adoptionism a Frankish problem, and Felix bishop of Urgel (in Catalonia), a follower of Elipandus' Christology, turned out to be the target of the "orthodox" Frankish clerics. Felix was condemned in the council of Narbonne of 788, forced to recant in the council of Regensburg of 792, and recanted again in Rome under the custody of Angilbert abbot of St-Riquier. However, once permitted to return to his diocese, Felix fled to Elipandus' Toledo. The well-known council of Frankfurt of 794 condemned "the impious and abominable heresy of Elipandus... Felix... and their disciples."[3] Alcuin played a leading role in this council. His severe theological battle against Adoptionism culminated in a seven-book *Contra Felicem Urgellitanum*.[4] Not long after its completion (799), Alcuin and Felix had a debate in Aachen in front of Charlemagne. Alcuin won, and Felix recanted his heretical thought publically.[5]

---

1   The strength of Peter's argument lies in the fact that this clause is quoted from a letter of Pope Celestine, and the original context of this papal letter is episcopal election. For other interpretations, see Brigitte Kasten, "Alkuins erbrechtliche Expertise für Karl den Großen?" *Annales de Bretagne et des Pays de l'Ouest* 111 (2004): pp. 301-315.

2   The best historical account in English is still Cullen Chandler, "Heresy and Empire: The Role of the Adoptionist Controversy in Charlemagne's Conquest of the Spanish March," *The International History Review* 24 (2002): pp. 505-527. Cf. Florence Close, Uniformiser la foi pour unifier l'Empire: Contribution à l'histoire de la pensée politico-théologique de Charlemagne (Bruxelles: Académie royale de Belgique, 2011). For the theological perspective, see John Cavadini, *The Last Christology of the West: Adoptionism in Spain and Gaul, 785–820* (Philadelphia: University of Pennsylvania Press, 1993).

3   "Ubi in primordio capitulorum exortum est de impia ac nefanda erese Elipandi a Toletane sedis episcopi et Felicis Orgellitanae eorumque sequacibus qui male sentientes in Dei filio adserebant adoptionem." *Synodus Franconofurtensis*, *Capitularia regum Francorum I*, no. 28, p. 73.

4   PL 99, cols. 343-468.

5   Cf. Rutger Kramer, "Adopt, Adapt and Improve: Dealing with the Adoptionist Controversy at the Court of Charlemagne," *Religious Franks: Religion and Power in the Frankish Kingdoms: Studies in Honour of Mayke de Jong*, eds. Rob Meens, Dorine van Espelo, Bram van den Hoven van Genderen, Janneke Raaijmakers, Irene van Renswoude, Carine van Rhijn (Manchester: Manchester University Press, 2016), pp. 32-50; Irene van Renswoude, "The Art of Disputation: Dialogue, Dialectic and Debate around 800," *Early Medieval Europe* 25 (2017): pp. 38-53.

It was Leidrad who brought Felix to Aachen for the debate.[1] The archbishop of Lyon may have already participated in the anti-Adoptionist propaganda in Septimania by then.[2] He seemed to have built a trustful relationship with the bishop of Urgel. Felix sent him a polemical treatise which recorded his dispute with a Moor.[3] According to Felix, the *uenerabilis domnus Laidradus episcopus* promised his safety from violence and license to speak freely in the debate of Aachen.[4] After Felix lost the debate, he stayed in Lyon under the custody of Leidrad according to Alcuin's arrangement.[5] At a certain time, Leidrad even accompanied him to visit Alcuin at Tours.[6]

After the council of Aachen, together with Nifridius archbishop of Narbonne and Benedict of Aniane, Leidrad came to *Gothia prouintia*, the Pyrenean area where the influence of Adoptionism was still present, and undertook "the work of the most pious preaching under the command of the glorious and most devout prince of all goodness, King Charles." Alcuin was zealous to equip them in timely fashion with a manual of his

---

1 "Iam Deo uolente medio mense Maio apud regem cogito esse, quia Laidradus, filius noster, adducere habet Felicem illum, cum quo nobis sermonis contentio est." Alcuin, Letter 194 (to Arn, March 19, 800), *Epistolae Karolini aevi (II)*, p. 36. "Quod uero me interrogare uoluisti de certitudine uoluntatis uel loci, nihil tibi certum adhuc remandare habeo, nisi Deo miserante et uita comite adhuc uisurus eris faciem meam, licet nesciam propter occupationes meas uel uestras, ubi aut quando. Multoties secundum oportunitatem portantium litteras mihi dirigere satage, ut habeam curam tuae caritati rescribendi, uel etiam demandandi, quodcumque ueniat mihi." Alcuin, Letter 141 (to Leidrad), ibid., p. 322.

2 Witnessed by two pieces of evidence from Alcuin. Letter 137 is Alcuin's religious exhortation to a Christian community in Septimania ca. 798, including his warning against the danger of Adoptionism. He claimed that he heard of them from Leidrad: "Religiosae in Christo conuersationis uestrae per Laidradum electum pontificem laudabilem audiens sollicitudinem, magno me esse gaudio delibutum fateor..." Ibid., p. 210. Alcuin stated in Letter 165 (to Arn, c. January 799) that Leidrad had achieved many good things *in illis partibus*. Dümmler read *illes partes* as *Hispaniae*, ibid., p. 268.

3 Documented by Alcuin: "Disputationem itaque Felicis cum Sarraceno nec uidi nec apud nos inuenta est; immo nec audiui nomen illius antea. Tamen, dum diligentius quaesiui, si quis ex nostris famam illius audiret, dictum est mihi, quod apud Laidradum episcopum Lugdunensem inueniri potuisset. Quapropter sub festinatione direxi missum nostrum ad praefatum episcopum, si forte ibi inuenire potuisset, ut quam citissime uestrae praesentiae dirigeretur." Letter 172 (to Charlemagne, April-May 799), ibid., p. 284.

4 "De caetero ad agnitionem uestram reducimus, quia, postquam ad praesentiam domini nostri ac piissimi gloriosique Caroli regis perductus sum et eius conspectui praesentatus, licentiam ab eo, secundum quod et uenerabilis domnus Laidradus episcopus nobis in Orgello pollicitus est, accepimus, qualiter in eius praesentiam in conspectu episcoporum, quos ad se ordinatio gloriosi principis nostri conuenire fecerat, sententias nostras, quas ex libris sanctorum habere nos de adoptione carnis in filio Dei seu nuncupatione in humanitate eius credebamus, praesentaremus; qualiter non in uiolentia, sed ratione ueritatis nostra adsertio rata iudicaretur, si ab illis per auctoritatem sanctorum patrum minime repudiarentur." Felix, *Confession in the Council of Aachen*, ibid., p. 329.

5 "Nos uero, cordis illius secreta nescientes, occultorum iudici causam dimisimus; dantes eum Laidrado episcopo, carissimo nostro filio, ut secum teneret eum et probaret: si uerum esset, quod se ait credidisse, et si per epistolas suas damnare uoluisset pristinum errorem, quem antea pertinaciter praedicauit." Alcuin, Letter 207 (to Arn, June 26, 800), ibid., p. 334.

6 "De ipso Felice, iam prius per litteras nostras uel magis aliorum relatione audisti, quid gestum fuit. Et modo fuit ad Sanctum Martinum apud praefatum filium nostrum. Et multum me amat; totumque odium, quod habuit in me, uersum est in caritatis dulcedinem." Alcuin, Letter 208, ibid., p. 346.

anti-adoptionist writings.[1] Leidrad carried out his job excellently. He was said to "make progress every day," and "to have converted as many as 2000 people among bishops, priests, and monks, both male and female" who renounced their "previous error" and embraced the orthodox faith.[2]

Exegesis pointing to the "orthodox" Christology appears now and then in the Lyon Annotations, including the use of "assumptus" for the Incarnation and the human nature of Christ.[3] One entry also mentions "the teachers who hold different understandings of the dispensation of the Incarnation of the Lord."[4] But since the concern over Christology was so common in the age of Charlemagne,[5] it is hard to determine whether there is indeed a specific anti-adoptionist implication in the Lyon Annotations.

The direct intellectual output from the involvement of Leidrad's Lyon in this anti-heretical movement, is a supplement of 36 *capitula* attached to the canonical collection known as *Collectio Dacheriana* (For *Dacheriana* in detail, see Chapter 3.2). The Supplement can be found in five of its extant manuscripts. According to Abigail Firey, it is "a late eighth or early ninth century southern Gallic contribution to the Adoptionist Controversy which was exercising Spanish and Gallic clerics in that period... reflect[ing] both the political and theological dimensions of the controversy," and "might have been compiled in Lyons during or soon after the punitive exile there of the Adoptionist bishop Felix of Urgel after his condemnation at the Council of Aix," by someone who "was aware of the Spanish perspectives on the problem and who responds to them rather more

---

1   "Ad cuius piissime praedicationis uenerabile opus, mandante glorioso principe et deuotissimo in omni bonitate Carolo rege, uos iterum ituros esse audiuimus. Quapropter paucorum arripui laborem dierum in solacium sanctissimi itineris uestri, quatenus haberetis in manibus cuiusdam aepistolae, meo nomni directae ab Elipanto Toletano episcopo, pias et pernecessarias responsiones, ne forte aliquorum ex eiusdem epistolae lectione mentes maculentur, quia easdem audiuimus litteras in aliorum prius peruenire manus, quam nobis, cui missae sunt, redditae essent." Alcuin, Letters 200, *Epistolae Karolini aevi*, p. 331. Also cf. Alcuin, Letters 201, ibid., pp. 333-336.

2   "Sciat tamen dilectio uestra, quod filius noster Laidradus episcopus, frater uester, magnum profectum in illis partibus Deo donante egit cotidieque agit. Ut mihi uere dixerunt ex illis partibus uiri relegiosi et ueraces, usque uiginti milia conuersi sunt inter episcopos sacerdotes monachos populum, uiros et feminas; plangentes pristinum errorem, gaudentesque cotidie Deo agentes gratias in agnitione ueritatis et in catholicae fidei firmitate." Alcuin, Letters 208, ibid., p. 346.

3   E.g., "De hereticis dicit qui Filium Dei non creatorem omnium cum Patrem se creaturam adfirmare conantur sicut Arriani et Eunamiani." Paris, BnF, NAL 1740, fol. 18r, on Deut. 5:11. "Dominum mort<i> tradiderunt. Vitul<am> de armento, eiusdem d<omini> carnem et patriarch<a>rum posteritatem, carnem assumptam a Filio Dei significat..." Paris, BnF, NAL 1740, fol. 56r, on Deut. 21:3.

4   "Viri iurgientes inter se, doctores significant ecclesiam de dispensationem dominice incarnationis diuersa sentientes, e quibus ille qui aduersus alterum preualet, de catholicum demonstrat qui per auctoritatem ueritatis, hereticum conuicit et refutat. Cuius heretici uxor dicitur plebs carnalis uel qulilibet fautor hereticorum, qui de incarnatione Domini male sentiendo blasphemat, cuius presumptio, uelut manus, ab ecclesia abscidatur." Paris, BnF, NAL 1740, fol. 66r, on Deut. 25:11-12.

5   Cf. Celia Chazelle, *The Crucified God in the Carolingian Era. Theology and the Art of Christ's Passion* (Cambridge: Cambridge University Press, 2001).

directly than did Alcuin."[1]

One of the 36 entries reveals a direct connection with the archbishop. The first part of the Supplement consists of eight papal decretals, all directed to Spain in the fifth or sixth century. They are drawn from the canon law collection *Collectio Hispana*. Among them, Entry 5 is Gregory's response to Leander of Seville on the question of triple immersion in Baptism.[2] Firey commented that this entry refers to "previous instances of heresy in Spain and responses to them."[3] Triple immersion was indeed a crucial matter in the Adoptionist controversy. Alcuin explicitly supported triple immersion and viewed it as signifying the Trinity. Favoring single immersion was thought to be an Adoptionist stance.[4] In Charlemagne's baptism inquiry of 811/812, at least five extant responses — of Jesse of Amiens, of Leidrad of Lyon, of Magnus of Sens, of Theodulf of Orléans, and of an anonymous author — mentioned triple immersion and interpreted it as a sign of the Trinity.[5] Revealingly, among all of them as well as Alcuin himself, Leidrad was the only one who quoted Gregory's letter to Leander to support his preference for triple immersion.[6] This clue indicates the possibility that Leidrad himself participated in the compilation of the *Dacheriana* Supplement.

There are four extant pieces of Leidrad's writing. We have already met three of them,

---

1   Abigail Firey, "Carolingian Ecclesiology and Heresy: A Southern Gallic Juridical Tract against Adoptionism," *Sacris erudiri* 39 (2000): pp. 253-316. Also cf. eadem, "A Carolingian Lyonnaise Supplement to the *Collectio Dacheriana*," *Proceedings of the Tenth International Congress of Medieval Canon Law: Syracuse, New York, 13–18 August 1996*, eds. Kenneth Pennington, Stanley Chodorow, Keith Kendall (Città del Vaticano: Biblioteca apostolica Vaticana, 2001), pp. 27-54.

2   Cf. Gregory, *Epistolae*, I.41, CCSL 140, ed. Dag Norberg (Turnhout: Brepols, 1982), p. 48.

3   Abigail Firey, "Carolingian Ecclesiology and Heresy," p. 268.

4   "Tertia quoque nobis de Hispania — quae olim tyrannorum nutrix fuit, nunc uero scismaticorum — contra uniuersalem sanctae ecclesiae consuetudinem, de baptismo quaestio delata est. Adfirmant enim quidam sub inuocatione sanctae Trinitatis unam esse mersionem agendam... Haec uero praecipui doctores et sanctissimi patres nobis reliquerunt in suis testimonia dictis. Nobis uero iuxta paruitatem ingenioli nostri uidetur, ut, sicut interior homo in fide sanctae Trinitatis ad imaginem sui conditoris reformandus est, ita exterior trina mersione abluendus est; ut, quod inuisibiliter spiritus operatur in anima, hoc uisibiliter sacerdos imitetur in aqua." Alcuin, Letter 137, *Epistolae Karolini aevi (II)*, pp. 212-214.

5   See Susan Keefe, *Water and the Word*, vol. 2, pp. 424, 370, 266, 302, and 326. Cf. Owen Michael Phelan, *Formation of Christian Europe*, pp. 147-206.

6   "Quidam enim senserunt trinam fieri mersionem propter trinitatis uenerationem; quidam autem propter triduanae sepulturae sacramentum. Sed beatus gregorius papa cuidam se interroganti de trina et simpla mersione sic respondit: 'De trina uero mersione baptismatis, nihil responderi uerius potest quam ipsi sensistis, quia in una fide nihil officit sanctae ecclesiae consuetudo diuersa. Nos autem quod tertio mergimus, triduanae sepulturae sacramenta signamus ut dum tertio ab aquis infans educitur, resurrectio triduani temporis exprimatur. Quod si quis forte etiam pro summae trinitatis uenerationae aestimet, neque ad hoc aliquid obsistit, baptizando semel in aquis mergere, quia dum in tribus subsistentiis una substantia est, reprehensibile esse nullatenus potest infantem in baptismate uel ter uel semel mergere, quando et in tribus mersionibus personarum trinitas, et in una potest diuinitatis singularitas designari.' Sed quamuis in morte christi secundum apostolum baptizemur, si praetermissa qualibet trinitatis persona baptismus detur in regenerationis sollemnitate, nihil agitur nisi tota trinitas inuocetur, quia nonnisi in uno nomine patris et filii et spiritus sancti baptismi sanctificatur officium." Susan Keefe, *Water and the Word*, vol. 2, p. 370.

and they were all composed for his master Charlemagne: the reform report (ca. 806/7); the response to Charlemagne's baptism inquiry of 811/2 (known as *Liber de sacramento baptismi*); the supplementary exposition of the renunciation of the devil in the ritual of baptism (known as *De abrenunciatione diaboli*). The fourth extant writing of Leidrad is a letter of consolation to a *soror* (either his consanguine sister or a nun) for the death of her son and brother.[1] It is structured on a poem of the sixth-century poet Venantius Fortunatus.[2] If *Liber de sacramento baptismi* reflects the archbishop's good theological learning, and *De abrenunciatione diaboli* reflects his familiarity with the works of Church Fathers (including Augustine, Julianus Pomerius, Jerome, Cassian, and Gregory the Great), this consolation letter demonstrates his interest in literature.

Leidrad's intellectual taste is also reflected in the five extant personal manuscripts of his witnessed by his autographic *ex-dono* (Table 3.1).[3]

Table 3.1 Leidrad's autographic *ex-dono*

Shelf mark	Content	Provenance
Lyon, BM, 466 + Paris, BnF, Lat. 152, fols. 21-25	Jerome, *Commentary on Isaiah*	Lyon[4]
Lyon, BM, 599	Gregory of Nazianzus' works	"Vielleicht Lyon"[5]
Lyon, BM, 608	Augustine, a series of shorter treatises on the theme of Grace	Lyon[6]
Lyon, BM, 610	Augustine, *Contra Faustum*	St-Amand[7]
Rome, Archivio della Casa Generalizia dei Padri Maristi, AII.1	*Codex pagesianus*	"Written presumably at Lyon... Corrections in his [Leidrad's] hand occur in this MS..."[8]

Two of the five deserve special attention. Lyon, BM, 610 was not produced in the scriptorium of the archbishop's own cathedral, but in that of the monastery of St-Amand whose abbot from 782 on was, Arn of Salzburg, Leidrad's close friend.[9] Rome, Archivio della Casa Generalizia dei Padri Maristi, the so-called *Codex pagesianus*, is an anthology of various pieces of treatises and excerpts.[10] The first set (fols. 2r-106r) constitutes the

---

1 *Epistolae Karolini aevi (II)*, pp. 544-546.
2 Venantius Fortunatus, *Carmina*, IX.2, MGH Auctores antiquissimi 4.1, ed. Friedrich Leo (Berlin: Weidmann, 1881), pp. 205-209.
3 Cf. Sigmund Tafel, "Lyons Scriptorium," 4 (1925): pp. 51-52; Louis Holtz, "Leidrat, évêque de Lyon," pp. 318-320.
4 According to Bernhard Bischoff, Katalog, 2558.
5 According to Bernhard Bischoff, Katalog, 2568.
6 According to Bernhard Bischoff, Katalog, 2575.
7 According to Bernhard Bischoff, Katalog, 2577.
8 According to CLA, IV.417.
9 For St-Amand's manuscript production during the reign of Arn, cf. Bernhard Bischoff, *Die südostdeutschen Schreibschulen und Bibliotheken in der Karolingerzeit* (Wiesbaden: Harrassowitz, 1960-1980), Teil 2, pp. 61-72.
10 Cf. Anthony Ward, "The Codex Pagesianus: Witness to Church Renewal," *American Benedictine Review* 44 (1993): pp. 308-333.

oldest surviving collection of Latin works on dialectic or logic, including Porphyry's *Isagoge* (translated by Boethius), Pseudo-Augustine's *Categoriae decem*, Apuleius' *Periermenias*, Boethius' first commentary on Aristotle's *De interpretatione*, and Alcuin's *De Dialectica*. It, according to Bischoff, "reflects the rediscovery of dialectic as a subject of instruction under Charlemagne and its introduction at the court by Alcuin."[1] What follows these dialectic treatises in the manuscript is a short treatise on human dignity known as *Dicta Albini* (fols. 106v-107r). While its authorship is still a matter of debate, this text can certainly be seen a product of the intellectual "circle of Alcuin."[2] The rest of the manuscript (fols. 107r-114v) consists of excerpts of creeds and expositions of Psalms.

These two manuscripts owned by Leidrad once again connect him with two of his best friends, Arn and Alcuin. This triangular friendship was not only of great geo-religious significance — given that Alcuin imposed his influence both on the enterprise of converting the Avars via Arn[3] and on the mission against Adoptionism in *Gothia* via Leidrad — but also an important part of a contemporary intellectual network.

Another personal manuscript of Leidrad's was Lyon, BM, 402, a codex of Origen's homilies on Joshua, Judges, and Kings in Rufinus' Latin translation (CLA, VI.770; Bischoff, *Katalog*, 2547b). Leidrad's autographic *ex-dono* could have been presented in the first folio of the codex but is now lost. However, the corrections made by Leidrad's own hands in fols. 17v, 18, 22v, etc. betray its ownership. This codex not only revealed the archbishop's exegetical interest in the Old Testament, but also his competence in manuscript collation, a habit that he could have developed in his youth as a professional scribe in Freising. If we follow Louis Holtz's suggestion, Leidrad's personal handwriting left influence on the scriptorium of Lyon, especially on the writing style of Florus.[4]

Leidrad was one of the witnesses of Charlemagne' testament in 811.[5] Not long after Charlemagne's death in 814, Leidrad began to arrange his own retirement, and chose the *chorepiscopus* Agobard as his successor. He apparently had Agobard consecrated

---

1 Bernhard Bischoff, "The Court Library of Charlemagne," *Manuscripts and Libraries in the Age of Charlemagne*, idem, trans., ed. by Michael Gorman (Cambridge: Cambridge University Press, 1994), pp. 56-75.

2 John Marenbon took it as an authentic work of Alcuin in John Marenbon, *From the Circle of Alcuin to the School of Auxerre: Logic, Theology and Philosophy in the Early Middle Ages* (Cambridge: Cambridge University Press, 1981), pp. 33-43; Donald Bullough regarded it "a late-Patristic one, which resurfaced at the Court and was subsequently exploited by Alcuin and his pupils," in his *Alcuin: Achievement and Reputation. Being Part of the Ford Lectures Delivered in Oxford in Hilary Term 1980* (Leiden: Brill, 2004), p. 6. The critical edition of *Dicta Albini*, see John Marenbon, *Circle of Alcuin*, pp. 158-161.

3 Cf. Owen Michael Phelan, "The Carolingian Renewal and Christian Formation in Ninth Century Bavaria," *Texts and Identities in the early Middle Ages*, ed. Richard Corradini (Vienna: Verlag der Österreichischen Akademie der Wissenschaften, 2006), pp. 389-399.

4 Louis Holtz, "Leidrat, évêque de Lyon," pp. 325-328.

5 Cf. Einhard, *The Life of Charles the Emperor*, c. 33, *Charlemagne and Louis the Pious: Lives by Einhard, Notker, Ermoldus, Thegan, and the Astronomer*, trans. Thomas F. X. Noble (University Park: Pennsylvania State University Press, 2009), p. 50.

as bishop by three bishops prior to his own formal resignation, which violated canon law and thus aroused certain censure. But the succession was finally sanctioned by both the new emperor Louis the Pious and the synod of Aachen of 816. Leidrad entered the monastery of St-Médard at Soissons.[1] He may have had this idea in mind for years. His health seems never to have been stable (cf. Chapter 2.4.3). As early as 799, according to a letter of Alcuin's, Leidrad was not sure whether he should remain "working in the office of preaching" or to retire to monastery to "lead a peaceful life," and he wanted advice from Alcuin and Arn.[2] Perhaps the death of his old lord Charlemagne in 814 made him finally make up his mind. He spent at least five years in St-Médard. According to a letter of 821 from Theutmirus abbot of Psalmody to Claudius, once a priest and master in Leidrad's church of Lyon and then the archbishop of Turin, Leidrad was happy to hear about Claudius' new biblical commentaries, and was eager to see him or his correspondence.[3] This was the last time that Leidrad showed up in the sources. Presumably, he died soon after on December 28, but it is not clear in which year.[4]

3.2   The Making of a Carolingian *Plebs Ecclesiastica*: Leidrad's Church Reform

In his report to Charlemagne, Leidrad repeatedly used the word *negligentia* to describe the condition of the church of Lyon before his reform. This word in the Carolingian ecclesiological context has the connotation of "sin of omission," that is failure to

---

1   "Qui initio imperii Ludouici imperatoris Suessionis monasterii locum petiit, et in loco eius Agobardus, eiusdem ecclesiae chorepiscopus, consentiente imperatore et uniuersa Gallorum episcoporum synodo, episcopus substitutus est; quod quidam defendere uolentes, dixerunt eumdem uenerabilem Agobardum a tribus episcopis in sede Lugdunensi iubente Leidrado fuisse ordinatum: sed canonica auctoritas est, in una ciuitate duos episcopos non esse, nec uiuente episcopo successorem sibi debere eligere, ac idcirco ulla quacumque causa regulae ecclesiae praeteriri in tanto ordine fixae non debent." Ado of Vienne, *Chronicon*, p. 320. Cf. *Annales Lugduneses*, MGH Scriptores 1, ed. Georg Pertz (Hannover: Hahnsche, 1826), p. 110: "816. Isto anno cathedra potitur mense octauo."

2   "Sed festina rescribere mihi, quantum sciri posset tempus mansionis tuae apud Sanctum Amandum; et quid Laidrado demandare uelis... Dubitat uero, an melius sit laborare in praedicationis ministerio uel quietam ducere uitam. Sed certius ab illo ipso permittente Deo haec audituri erimus." Alcuin, Letter 165 (to Arn), *Epistolae Karolini aevi (II)*, p. 268.

3   "Nam et uenerabilis pater Leidrath, quondam episcopus Lucdunensis, cum hoc audisset, gauisus est et ipse rogauitque eum michi multum ad scribendum et miratus fuit, cur epistolam illi non misistis ex tanto tempore, et promisit, quod ipse suam epistolam uobis missurus sit. Valde enim desiderat uisionem uestram, si fieri potuisset, et si non uisione corporea, uel epistola." Claudius, Letter 8, ibid., p. 605.

4   According to a *necrologium* of the Lyon church in a twelfth-century manuscript Lyon, BM, 1385. See Marie-Claude Guigue, ed., *Obituarium Lugdunensis Ecclesiae: Nécrologe des Personnages Illustres et des Bienfaiteurs de l'Église Métropolitaine de Lyon du IXe au XVe Siècle, Publié pour la Première Fois avec Notes et Documents Inédits* (Lyon: N. Scheuring, 1867), p. 169.

carry out the one's pastoral duty for the church committed to him.[1]

In the same report, Leidrad recalled that the church of Lyon had been "destitute in many respects."[2] It may not be exaggeration on Leidrad's part. Lyon was an ancient city located at the confluence of two rivers, Rhône and Saône. Its establishment can be traced back to the Roman era.[3] Geo-politically speaking, Lyon connects northern and southern Gaul.[4] It was also among the first Gallic cities where Christian belief and organization were introduced and established.[5] In the fifth and sixth centuries, the Burgundian barbarians settled in the Rhône-Saône area, and Lyon was one of their capitals during the reign of Gundobad.[6] By the 530s, this area, known as Burgundy, was conquered by the Merovingian Franks, but never fully integrated into the dynastic authorities centered in northern *Francia*.[7] In the late seventh century, power in many Burgundian cities gradually fell into the hands of local bishops. Eugen Ewig famously named them "Bistumsrepubliken." One of them was Lyon, described by Ewig as "eine Art Kirchenstaat" ca. 700.[8] In the first half of the eighth century, those largely autonomous "episcopal republics" faced pressure from both sides: the occasional raid of Saracens from the Spanish South and military intervention of the Carolingians from the Austrasian North. The impact of the latter was greater than that of the former.[9] The Continuator of Fredegar's *Chronicle* recorded twice Charles Martel's military intrusion and establishment of his secular fol-

---

1 Mayke de Jong, *The Penitential State: Authority and Atonement in the Age of Louis the Pious, 814–840* (Cambridge: Cambridge University Press, 2009).

2 "Pro qua re me ammonere dignati estis ut ego solicitudinis curam gererem et ut perpetrate neglegencie emendarentur et perpetrande uitarentur. Erat enim tunc dicta ecclesia multis in rebus destituta interius exteriusque tam in officiis quam in edificiis uel ceteris ecclesiasticis ministeriis." Leidrad, *Report to Charlemagne*, p. 283.

3 For general reference, see François Bayard, Pierre Cayez, *Histoire de Lyon, des origines à nos jours. Tome I, Antiquité et Moyen Âge* (Le Coteau: Horvath, 1990).

4 Christopher Wickham, *Framing the Early Middle Ages: Europe and the Mediterranean, 400–800* (Oxford: Oxford University Press, 2005).

5 For The origin of the Lyon Christian church, see Jacques Gadille, René Fédou, Henri Hours, Bernard de Vregille, *Le Diocèse de Lyon* (Paris: Beauchesne, 1983).

6 Cf. Herwig Wolfram, *The Roman Empire and Its Germanic Peoples*, trans. Thomas Dunlap (Berkeley: University of. California Press, 1997), pp. 248-259.

7 Cf. Ian Wood, *The Merovingian Kingdoms 450–751* (London: Longman, 1994), pp. 51-54.

8 Cf. Eugen Ewig, "Milo et eiusmodi similes," *Spätantikes und fränkisches Gallien: gesammelte Schriften (1952–1973)*, idem, eds. Hartmut Atsma, Matthias Becher (München: Artemis Verlag, 1976-2009), vol. 2, pp. 189-219. Also cf. Friedrich Prinz, "Aristocracy and Christianity in Merovingian Gaul," *Gesellschaft, Kultur, Literatur: Rezeption und Originalität im Wachsen einer europäischen Literatur und Geistigkeit. Beiträge Luitpold Wallach gewidmet*, ed. Karl Bosl (Stuttgart: Hiersemann, 1975), pp. 153-165.

9 Cf. Paul Fouracre, *The Age of Charles Martel* (Harlow: Longman, 2000), pp. 89-99.

lowers as the new local authority in Lyon, respectively in 734 and 736.[1] The expropriation of church property was certainly involved. Pippin the Short seemed to follow his father's southern policy. According to the vivid record for Year 752 of Ado of Vienne in his *Chronicon*:

> When the Franks expropriated the sacred utensils of the Church for their own use with furious and greatly insane mind, the same Wilicarius [bishop of Vienne] after seeing his own church of Vienne humiliated in an indecent way, left his episcopacy, entered the monastery of the holy martyr Agaune and led a venerable life there. The provinces of Vienne and Lyon were devastated and plundered, both churches remained without a bishop for a few years, and laymen obtained the sacred utensils of the churches sacrilegiously and barbarously.[2]

Between 712 and 798, we only hear of two bishops of Lyon, and little more than their names are known.[3] It was Leidrad's reform that restored Lyon as an "ecclesiastical city" (the words used by Leidrad himself).[4] However, Lyon after Leidrad was not an autonomous "episcopal republic" any more, but a "Carolingian" church with close connection with the dynasty and in the same rhythm of the realm-wide reform program.

The most visible achievement of Leidrad's reform was the rehabilitation of churches (*de restauratione... ecclesiarum*).[5] Scholars have counted between 14 and 23 churches

---

1   *The Fourth Book of the Chronicle of Fredegar: With its Continuations*, ed., trans. John M. Wallace-Hadrill (London: Nelson, 1960), XIV, p. 91. "Praecedente alioquin anno sequente egregius bellator Carlus princeps regionem Burgundie sagaciter penetrauit, fines regni illius leudibus suis probatissimis uiris industriis ad resistendas gentes rebelles et infideles statuit, pace patrata Lugdono Gallia suis fidelibus tradidit. Firmata foedera iudiciaria reuersus est uictor fiducialiter agens." XVIII, p. 93: "Idcirco sagacissimus uir Carlus dux commoto exercitu, partibus Burgundie dirigit Lugdunum Gallie urbem maiores natu atque praefectus eiusdem prouintie sua dicione rei publice subiugauit, usque Marsiliensem urbem uel Arelatum a suis iudicibus constituit, cum magnis thesauris et muneribus in Francorum regnum remeauit in sedem principatus sui."
2   "Idem Wilicarius, cum furioso et insano satis consilio Franci res sacras ecclesiarum ad usus suos retorquerent, uidens Viennensem ecclesiam suam indecenter humiliari, relicto episcopatu, in monasterium sanctorum martyrum Agaunensium ingressus, uitam uenerabilem duxit. Vastata et dissipata Viennensis et Lugdunensis prouincia, aliquot annis sine episcopis utraque ecclesia fuit, laicis sacrilege et barbare res sacras ecclesiarum obtinentibus." Ado of Vienne, *Chronicon*, p. 319.
3   Jacques Gadille, René Fédou, Henri Hours, Bernard de Vregille, *Diocèse de Lyon*, pp. 27-29; Heribert Müller, "Die Kirche von Lyon im Karolingerreich: Studien zur Bischofsliste des 8. und 9. Jahrhunderts," *Historisches Jahrbuch* (107) 1987, pp. 225-253.
4   "[E]t propterea debent praedicari Scripturae, debet sonare Euangelium, debent annuntiare et terrores comminationum et blandimenta consolationum, quia in plebe ecclesiastica exsistunt et duricordes quibus utilia sunt tonitrua et grando sermonum Dei quae primum percutiant et postea irrigent, existunt et mites quibus tantummodo lenis et placidus sermo uerbi diuini expedit." Leidrad, *Baptismal Exposition*, Susan Keefe, *Water and the Word*, vol. 2, p. 383.
5   For a modern account of Leidrad's reform, see Jacques Gadille, René Fédou, Henri Hours, Bernard de Vregille, *Diocèse de Lyon*, pp. 50-61; Michel Rubellin, "Lyon aux temps carolingiens," *Eglise et société chrétienne d'Agobard à Valdès*, (Lyon: Presses Universitaires Lyon, 2003), pp. 133-177.

in Lyon in the early Middle Ages.[1] Leidrad mentioned in his report that he had restored
or renovated ten churches in his diocese, including the "episcopal group" of St-John-
the-Baptist and St-Stephan (as well as a set of episcopal residences); three churches of
canons: St-Nizier, St-George and St-Paul; three monastic churches: St-Martin at Ile-
Barbe (for monks), St-Ragnebertus (for monks), and St-Peter (for nuns); St-Willibadus
(a parish church for local cult of the namesake saint); one hospice, St-Maria.[2] Seven of
these ten — apart from St-Ragnebertus, St-Willibadus, and St-Martin at Île-Barbe —
were located inside the city which then consisted of two spheres: the area at the foot
of Fourvière Hill and on the left bank of Saône, and the peninsula between Rhône and
Saône. The size of the whole area was no more than 40 hectares. Leidrad's renovation
of seven church buildings within such a small area within less than a decade no doubt
caused great change in the city's landscape and had a great impact on the living and
religious experience of its citizens.[3]

For some of these churches, Leidrad made (*maceriae*) walls roofs (*tegumenta*), and

---

1   Jacques Gadille, René Fédou, Henri Hours, Bernard de Vregille, *Diocèse de Lyon*, p. 32 counts
    fourteen churches; Brigitte Beaujard, Paul-Albert Février, Jean-Charles Picard, Charles Pietri, Jean-
    François Reynaud, *Topographie chrétienne des cités de la Gaule des origines au milieu du VIIIe
    siècle. 4, Province ecclésiastique de Lyon (Lugdunensis prima)* (Paris: De Boccard, 1986), pp. 22-35
    counts twenty-three church buildings (including one episcopal house and three churches of uncertain
    dates).

2   "De restauracione eciam ecclesiarum, in quantum ualui, non cessaui, ita ut eiusdem ciuitatis
    maximam ecclesiam que est in honorem sancti Ioannis Baptiste, a nouo operuerim et macerias ex
    parte erexerim. Similiter ecclesie Sancti Stephani tegumentum de nouo reparaui. Ecclesiam quoque
    Sancti Nicetii de nouo eciam reaedificaui. Similiter ecclesiam Sancte Marie. Preter monasteriorum
    reparaciones, domus quoque episcopales inter quas unam restauraui que iam pene destructa erat,
    quam operui. Aliam quoque domum cum solario de nouo aedificaui et duplicaui et hanc propter uos
    paraui, ut si in illis partibus uester esset aduentus, in ea suscipi possetis. Claustrum quoque clericorum
    construxi, in quo nunc omnes sub uno conclaui manere noscuntur. In eadem ciuitate, alias restauraui
    ecclesias: unam quidem in honorem sancte Eulalie ubi fuit monasterium puellarum, in honorem
    sancti Georgii quam de nouo operui et ex parte macerias eius a fundamentis erexi. Alia quoque
    domus in honorem sancti Pauli de nouo operta est. Monasterium quoque puellarum in honorem sancti
    Petri dedicatum, ego a fundamentis tam ecclesias quam domum restauraui, ubi nunc sanctimoniales
    numero XXXII secundum institutionem regularem uiuentes habitare uidentur. Monasterium quoque
    Insule Barbare situm in medio Araris fluuii, in honorem sancti Martini dedicatum, ita restauraui ut
    tecta de nouo fierent et aliqua de maceriis a fundamentis erigerentur, ubi nunc monachi secundum
    regularem disciplinam numero XC habitare uidentur. Similiter aliud monasterium in honorem sancti
    Ragneberti aedificatum, de nouo totum reparatum est, siue in parietibus, siue in tectis uel eciam
    in ecclesiis, ubi nunc monachi numero LVI secundum regularem custodiam habitant. In quibus
    monasteriis, unum puellarum et duo quoque monachorum, nemo antea erat qui regularem uitam
    immitari nosset aut uellet, propter quod plurimum laborem et studium impendi ut ad hanc regularis
    uite obseruanciam peruenire potuissent, quo nunc peruenisse, Deo auxiliante, uidentur. Aliam quoque
    ecclesiam in eadem parochia, que est in honorem sancti Vuldaldi, restauraui." Leidrad, *Report to
    Charlemagne*, pp. 285-287.

3   Cf. the "plan de Lyon" in Brigitte Beaujard, Paul-Albert Février, Jean-Charles Picard, Charles Pietri,
    Jean-François Reynaud, *Topographie chrétienne 4*, p. 17. According to René Fédon, "*Les temps
    obscurs (Ve–Xe siècles)*," *Histoire de Lyon et du Lyonnais*, ed. André Latreille (Toulouse: Université
    de la France, 1975), pp. 61-75, at 68: "Evêque bâtisseur, Leidrad transforma sa ville en un vaste
    chantier."

ceilings (*tecta*); for others, he had them rebuilt thoroughly (*a fundamentis... restauraui*) or repaired anew (*de nouo... reaedificaui*). Leidrad also mentioned in his report how he had acquired clerical vestments and ecclesiastical utensils.[1] It is natural to wonder about the financial support behind these material improvements. Tithes were certainly one of the major resources. The episcopal control of the tithe was tightened in the Carolingian era. It is difficult to know for sure which rule of distribution was in application in Leidrad's Lyon. However, according to contemporary custom, one third or one fourth of the tithe was supposed to be reserved for the use of *ornamentum ecclesiae*.[2]

An even larger income must have come from land revenue. We have a land inventory attached to three copies of Leidrad's report to Charlemagne. According to this inventory, there were 760 *colonicae* (the land unit used in southern Gaul, basically equal to *mansus* or 16 hectares) at Leidrad's disposal *besides* those landed properties whose revenues were reserved for chorbishops, canons, hospices, and monasteries.[3] One may wonder to what extent Charlemagne helped Leidrad protect the church properties in Lyon or restore those alienated during the time of his grandfather, father, and even his own, but there is no direct evidence.

Apart from material amelioration, institutional, intellectual, and spiritual improvement of the clerical class was at the center of Leidrad' reform. Judging from his reply to Charlemagne's baptism inquiry, Leidrad took it seriously to instruct the clergy and, through them, the lay population, about the rites of catechesis and baptism and the symbolic meanings of every step in them.[4] In Chapter 2.4.3, we have discussed in detail Leidrad's establishment of biblical schools and his revival of exegetical education. In

---

1   "Similiter uestimenta sacerdotum et ministeria procuraui." Leidrad, *Report to Charlemagne*, p. 285.

2   Cf. Giles Constable, *Monastic Tithes: From Their Origins to the Twelfth Century* (Cambridge: Cambridge University Press, 1964), pp. 31-56.

3   "Habet Leidradus episcopus ad suum opus inter totum colonicas uestitas DCCXXVII, absas XXXIII. Habet Amalbertus episcopus colonicas uestitas XXX, absas XVII. Habet Agobardus episcopus colonicas uestitas XLIIII, absas IIII. Sunt in domo sancti Stephani canonici clerici numero LII, habent in beneficio colonicas uestitas LXXXIII, absas L. Habent in Sancto Paulo canonicos XXIIII. Habent in beneficio colonicas uestitas XXII, absas XXI, et sunt pauperes numero XII, qui de suprascriptis rebus accipiunt terciam portionem. Ad hospitale quoque Sancti Romani, habent colonicas uestitas XXII, absas X . Et ad hospitale sancti Genesii habent colonicas uestitas VI, absas II. Et in monasterio uero [praedicto] sancti Petri puellarum, habet colonicas uestitas CLXXXVIII, absas XLVII. Et in monasterio Insule Barbare sont sunt colonice uestite CV, absas LIII. Et in monasterio sancti Ragneberti, habent colonicas uestitas XL." Alfred Coville, *Recherches sur l'Histoire de Lyon*, pp. 287-288. For the discussion of the nature of this inventory, see ibid., 288-293. For "colonica," see Adriaan Verhulst, *The Carolingian Economy* (Cambridge: Cambridge University Press, 2002), pp. 53-54. For "colonica absa," see Jean-Pierre Devroey, "'Mansi absi': indices de crise ou de croissance de l'économie rurale du haut Moyen Âge?" *Le Moyen Âge* 31 (1976): pp. 421-452.

4   "Praecipere nobis dignati estis, ut aut per nostra scripta aut per nos ipsos cognoscatis, qualiter nos et suffraganei nostri doceamus et instruamus sacerdotes Dei, et plebem nobis commissam de baptismi sacramento, et caeteris quae circa baptismum celebrantur. Deinde si in hoc quod praedicamus, nos ipsos custodiamus... maxime quia dicitis uos uelle cognoscere qualiter doceamus et instruamus plebem et sacerdotes." Leidrad, *Baptismal Exposition*, Susan Keefe, *Water and the Word*, vol. 2, pp. 353-355.

order to train "clerics qualified in liturgy" (*clerici officiales*), [1] Leidrad also established *scholae cantorum* by inviting a cleric of Metz via Charlemagne to "restore the order of psalm-singing" (*instauratus est ordo psallendi*) "according to the rite of the sacred palace."[2] Metz was well known for its introduction of the Roman liturgy (*Romana... cantilena*) during the episcopate of Chrodegang (r. 742–748).[3] Charlemagne promoted the *cantum Romanum* in his realm, and Leidrad's Lyon was one of a few cases, if not the single one, in which we know for certain the effect of this so-called "Romanization of liturgy."[4] However, we should not ignore Leidrad's wording "restore" (*instauratus*). According to an anonymous treatise of mid-eighth century known as *Ratio de cursus qui fuerunt eius auctores*, Lyon was thought to be one of the first Gallic dioceses to adopt *cursus Romanus* thanks to Photinus, the disciple of St. Peter as well as the first bishop of Lyon.[5] *Ritum sacri palatii*, *mos Romanus*, and the local memory of liturgical past converged. When Amalarius, the most accomplished Carolingian liturgist who had originated from Metz and once travelled to Rome to study liturgy, was appointed by Louis the Pious as archbishop of Lyon after 834 and carried out a liturgical reform there, he met furious resistance from the local clergy, whose leader, Florus, accused him of "raging with his stupidity and malice against our holy church, that is Lyon... as if she had not carried out the rites of divine chanting rightly, according to paternal custom or old

---

1 According to Fresne du Cange, *clerici officiales* refers to "Clerici ac sacerdotes qui ecclesiam deseruiunt." *Glossarium Mediae et Infimae Latinitatis*, vol. 6, col. 35. But the *officialis* in Leidrad's context should mean "related to liturgy," cf. Jesse D. Billett, *The Divine Office in Anglo-Saxon England, 597–c.1000* (Woodbridge and Rochester: Boydell Press, 2014), p. 55.

2 "Et ideo officio pietatis uestre placuit, ut ad peticionem meam michi concederetis unum de Metensi ecclesia clericum, per quem, Deo iuuante et mercede uestra annuente, ita in Lugdunensi ecclesia instauratus est ordo psallendi, ut iuxta uires nostras secundum ritum sacri palatii omni ex parte agi uideatur quicquid ad diuinum persoluendum officium ordo exposcit." Leidrad, *Report to Charlemagne*, p. 284.

3 According to Paul the Deacon, *Gesta episcoporum Mettensium*: "Ipsumque clerum abundanter lege diuina Romanaque imbutum cantilena, morem atque ordinem Romanae ecclesiae seruare praecepit, quod usque ad id tempus in Mettensi ecclesia factum minime fuit." MGH Scriptores 2, ed. Georg Heinrich Pertz (Hannover: Hahnsche, 1829), p. 268. Cf. Cyril Vogel, "Saint Chrodegang et les débuts de la romanisation du culte en pays Franc," *Saint Chrodegang: Communications présentées au colloque tenu à Metz à l'occasion du 12e centenaire de sa mort* (Metz: Lorrain, 1967), pp. 91-109; Martin Claussen, *The Reform of the Frankish Church: Chrodegang of Metz and the Regula canonicorum in the Eighth Century* (Cambridge: Cambridge University Press, 2004), pp. 263-276.

4 "Omni clero. Ut cantum Romanum pleniter discant, et ordinabiliter per nocturnale uel gradale officium peragatur secundum quod beatae memoriae genitor noster Pippinus rex decertauit ut fieret, quando Gallicanum tulit ob unanitatem apostolicae sedis et sanctae Dei ecclesiae pacificam concordiam." *Admonitio generalis*, LXXVIII, p. 230. Cf. Yitzhak Hen, "The Romanization of the Frankish Liturgy: Ideal, Reality, and the Rhetoric of Reform," *Rome across Time and Space, c. 500-1400: Cultural Transmission and the Exchange of Ideas*, eds. Claudia Bolgia, Rosamond McKitterick, John Osborne (Cambridge: Cambridge University Press, 2011), pp. 111-124.

5 "Beatus Trofimus episcopus Arelatensis et sanctus Photinus martyr et episcopus Lugdunensis discipulus sancti Petri apostoli sicut et refert Iosiphus et Eusebius Caesariensis episcopus cursum Romanum in Galleis tradiderunt." *Consuetudines saeculi octavi et noni*, ed. Kassius Hallinger, Corpus Consuetudinum Monasticarum 1 (Siegburg: F. Schmitt 1963), pp. 83-91.

liturgy."[1] The liturgy established by Leidrad had become a tradition in the next generation among the clergy of Lyon.[2]

It was probably also based on the model of Metz that Leidrad reformed the institution of canonical clergy in Lyon, as he claimed in the report: "I also built the cloister (*claustrum*) of clerics, in which all of them are known to live in a single enclosed space (*sub uno conclaui*) altogether."[3] This institution, characterized by the communal life of clergy under the bishop's leadership, was created by Chrodegang, who composed a *Regula canonicorum*. This canonical rule became the blueprint of the Carolingian reform of canonical clergy which culminated in Louis the Pious' council of Aachen of 816 and the official *Institutio canonicorum*.[4] Charlemagne's promotion of the same institution in his realm, although not as determined and thorough as that of his son, was clearly detectable in his capitularies.[5] There were probably no fewer than five churches of canons in Leidrad's Lyon: St-Stephen under the direct leadership of the archbishop himself, St-Irénée-and-St-Just and St-Paul respectively under a chorbishop, and St-Nizier and St-George respectively under an *abba*.[6] The inventory attached in Leidrad's report mentioned above and a confraternity book of Reichenau composed ca. 830[7] give us a

---

1 "Qvia Nvper Stvltvs Et Improbvs Ipsa Qve Stvltitia et improbitate sua omnibus notus calumniator erupit, qui sanctam ecclesiam nostram, id est Lugdunensem, non solum uerbis, sed etiam scriptis lacerare non cessat, quasi non recte nec more paterno siue usu antiquo diuine decantationis sollemnia peragentem, necesse fuit omnem sacrorum officiorum seriem, quae solito cantorum ministerio per totum anni circulum in ecclesiasticis conuentibus exhibetur, sicut in eadem ecclesia fauente dei gratia custoditur, diligentius et plenius in libello, quem usitato uocabulo antiphonarium nuncupant, colligere atque digerere, praemissa scilicet praefatione pii et orthodoxi patris, cuius probatissima fides atque doctrina in munere domini dei nostri omnibus examinata ac declarata caelebriter innotuit, ut omnes pacifici et prudentes ecclesiae filii, in quorum manus eiusdem libelli textus uenerit, uerissime et euidenter agnoscant praefatam Christi ecclesiam eodem Christo domino gubernante ac protegente nec a recto fidei tramite deuiasse et paternum morem, quam statuta ecclesiastica declarant, fideliter custodire ac per hoc ab antiquo ecclesiae dei usu nullatenus discrepare nec contempnere alicuius diuersum morem, si constat esse probabilem, sed, iuxta apostolum, ea, quae utiliora et potiora sunt, sequi." Florus of Lyon, *Liber de diuina psalmodia*, CCCM 260, eds. Klaus Zechiel-Eckes, Erwin Frauenknecht (Turnhout: Brepols, 2014).
2 For the continuous tradition of Leidrad's schools of chanting in Lyon, cf. Joseph Pourrat, *L'antique école de Leidrade: XIe centenaire de sa fondation* (Lyon: E. Vitte, 1899).
3 "Claustrum quoque clericorum construxi, in quo nunc omnes sub uno conclaui manere noscuntur." Leidrad, *Report to Charlemagne*, p. 285.
4 Cf. Julia Barrow, "Chrodegang," pp. 200-212.
5 E.g., *Admonitio generalis* (789), LXXI, p. 226: "Similiter qui ad clericatum accedunt, quod nos nominamus canonicam uitam, uolumes, ut illi canonice secundum suam regulam omnimodis uiuant, et episcopus illorum regat uitam , sicut abbas monachorum." The Synod of Tours (813), XXIII, *Concilia aevi Karolini [742–842]. Teil 1 [742–817]*, no. 38, p. 289: "Canonici clerici ciuitatum, qui in episcopiis conuersantur, considerauimus, ut in claustris habitantes simul omnes in uno dormitorio dormiant simulque in uno reficiantur refectorio, quo facilius possint ad horas canonicas celebrandas occurrere ac de uita et conuersatione sua admoneri et doceri. Victum et uestitum iuxta facultatem episcopi accipiant, ne paupertatis occasione compulsi per diuersa uagari ac turpibus se implicare negotiis cogantur dimissoque eclesiastico officio incipiant indisciplinate uiuere et propriis deseruire uoluptatibus."
6 Michel Rubellin, "Lyon aux temps carolingiens," p. 151.
7 *Confraternitates Augienses*, pp. 257, 259.

glimpse of the scale of the canonical clergy in Lyon (Table 3.2).

Table 3.2 Canonical clergy in Lyon

Church	Leader	Number of canons	Total
St-Stephan	Bishop	52–68	
St-Irénée-and-St-Just	Chorbishop	25	
St-Paul	Chorbishop	24–27	140–159
St-Nizier	*Abba*	20	
St-George	*Abba*	19	

These numbers certainly represented only part of the ecclesiastical faculty in the city in the early ninth century, but the amount was still considerable, especially in consideration the total urban population of Lyon at that time was rather low.[1]

Leidrad in his report mentioned three monasteries: St-Martin (at Île-Barbe in the middle of Saône, around 3 miles north of the city),[2] St-Ragnebertus (in Bugey area, around 40 miles east of the city along Saône),[3] and the convent St-Peter (inside the city, on the left bank of Saône).[4] Leidrad was proud not only of the amelioration of monastic buildings and the increase of monastic population (32 nuns in St-Peter, 90 monks in St-Martin, and 56 in St-Ragnebertus),[5] but also of his success in the imposition of *Regula Benedicti*: "In these monasteries, one of nuns and two of monks, no one knew or wanted to follow the regular life before. In view of this, I devoted great labor and zeal so that they observe the regular life. Thanks to God's help, they seem to follow it now."[6] Similar to the case of the canonical rule, Leidrad's monastic policy followed Charlemagne's

---

1 According to Bernard Gauthiez' estimation in "La topographie de Lyon au Moyen Âge," *Archéologie du Midi médiéval* 12 (1994): pp. 3-38, the lay population of Lyon in the age of Leidrad was between 800 and 1000.

2 Michel Rubellin, "Les monastères du diocèse de Lyon: Le poids de l'héritage carolingien," *Eglise et société chrétienne d'Agobard à Valdès* (Lyon: Presses Universitaires Lyon, 2003), pp. 243-294.

3 Jacques Dubois, "Moines et monastères du Bugey," *Le Bugey* 49 (1962): pp. 1-63, reprinted in idem, *Histoire monastique en France au XIIe siècle: les institutions monastiques et leur évolution* (London: Variorum, 1982), VII.

4 Jacques Gadille, René Fédou, Henri Hours, Bernard de Vregille, *Topographie chrétienne. 4*, pp. 33-34.

5 "Monasterium quoque puellarum in honorem sancti Petri dedicatum, ego a fundamentis tam ecclesias quam domum restauraui, ubi nunc sanctimoniales numero XXXII secundum institutionem regularem uiuentes habitare uidentur. Monasterium quoque Insule Barbare situm in medio Araris fluuii, in honorem sancti Martini dedicatum, ita restauraui ut tecta de nouo fierent et aliqua de maceriis a fundamentis erigerentur, ubi nunc monachi secundum regularem disciplinam numero XC habitare uidentur. Similiter aliud monasterium in honorem sancti Ragneberti aedificatum, de nouo totum reparatum est, siue in parietibus, siue in tectis uel eciam in ecclesiis, ubi nunc monachi numero LVI secundum regularem custodiam habitant." Leidrad, *Report to Charlemagne*, pp. 285-287.

6 "In quibus monasteriis, unum puellarum et duo quoque monachorum, nemo antea erat qui regularem uitam immitari nosset aut uellet, propter quod plurimum laborem et studium impendi ut ad hanc regularis uite obseruanciam peruenire potuissent, quo nunc peruenisse, Deo auxiliante, uidentur." Ibid., p. 287.

interest in promoting *Regula Benedicti* in his realm.[1] We had the opportunity to see in more detail how Leidrad carried out his monastic reform in the case of St-Martin at Ile-Barbe, the oldest monastery of the Lyonnais and one of the oldest in the whole of Gaul. According to Ardo Smaragdus, in response to Leidrad's wish to "rebuild the monastery of Ile-Barbe", Benedict of Aniane (ca. 747–821), the greatest Carolingian monastic reformer, sent 20 disciples of his there to display "the beginning of the good life."[2] Île-Barbe was also described as among the 12 monasteries in the Frankish kingdom which Benedict of Aniane "held under governance" (*habuit sub regimine*).[3] Leidrad was acquainted with Benedict. They carried out the anti-Adoptionist campaign in *Gothia* together at the beginning of the ninth century.[4] This personal connection contributed to the foundation of Benedictine monasticism in Lyon.

Concerning the intellectual life of the clergy, Leidrad reported to Charlemagne that

---

1   Charlemagne asked for a copy of *Regula Benedicti* from Monte Cassino in 787, cf. *Epistolae Karolini aevi (II)*, p. 510: "Qua de re quia ad beati patris nostri Benedicti doctrinam et luculenta exempla aliquos monachorum regionis illius uestrae clementiae informari placuit, iuxta preceptionem uestram en uobis regulam eiusdem beati patris, de ipso codice quem ille suis sanctis manibus exarauit transscriptam, direximus." The effort to promote *Regula Benedicti* can be found in his capitularies frequently, e.g., *Synodus Franconofurtensis* (794), *Capitularia regum Francorum I*, no. 28, XIII, XIV, XVI, XX, pp.75-76. The observation of the Rule was also the one of the major themes of the Council of Aachen of 802, cf. *Annales Laureshamenses*, XXXV: "Similiter in ipso synodo congregauit uniuersos abbates et monachos qui ibi aderant, et ipsi inter se conuentum faciebant, et legerunt regulam sancti patris Benedicti, et eum tradiderunt sapientes in conspectu abbatum et monachorum, et tunc iussio eius generaliter super omnes episcopos, abbates, presbyteros, diacones seu uniuerso clero facta est, ut unusquisque in loco suo iuxta constitutionem sanctorum patrum, siue in episcopatibus seu in monasteriis aut per uniuersas sanctas ecclaesias, ut canonici iuxta canones uiuerent, et quicquid in clero aut in populo de culpis aut de negligentiis apparuerit, iuxta canonum auctoritate emendassent, et quicquid in monasteriis seu in monachis contra regula sancti Benedicti factum fuisset, hoc ipsud iuxta ipsam regulam sancti Benedicti emendare fecissent." MGH Scriptores 1, ed. Georg Heinrich Pertz (Hannover: Hahnsche, 1826), p. 39. Cf. Josef Semmler, "Karl der Große und das Fränkische Mönchtum," *Karl der Grosse: Lebenswerk und Nachleben*, eds. Helmut Beumann, Wolfgang Braunfels (Düsseldorf: L. Schwann, 1965–1968), vol. 2, pp. 255-289.
2   "Interea audientes eius sanctitatis famam gregisque eius sanctam opinionem, postulare instanter exempli gratia monachos nonnulli episcopi coeperunt, de quibus Leidradus Lugdunensium pontifex uolens monasterium quod uocatur Insula-Barbara rehedificare, quaesiuit instanter qui ei initium bonae uitae ostenderent, et accepit siquidem electos ferme a grege 20 discipulos, quibus preposuit rectorem eosque Burgundiae partibus ad habitandum direxit. Quo, prestante Christo domino, nunc in sancta religione pollentes et florentes, pregrandis est turba aggregata monachorum." Ardo Smaragdus, *Vita Benedicti abbatis Anianensis et Indensis*, XXII, Scriptores 15.1, ed. Georg Waitz (Hannover: Hahnsche, 1887), p. 209. On Benedict of Aniane, cf. Clemens Radl, "The Second Benedict: A Review of Recent Scholarship," *Benedict of Aniane, the Emperor's Monk: Ardo's Life*, trans. Allen Cabaniss (Kalamazoo: Cistercian Publications: 2008), pp. 1-26.
3   "Hic habuit sub regimine suo monasteria 12, id est Anianum, Gellonem, Casam-nouam, Insulam-Barbaram, Menatem, Sanctum Sauinum, Sanctum Maximinum, Maciacum, Cormariacum, Cellam-nouam in Tolosano, Monasterium-Maurum in Elizaz, Indam ex iussu imperatoris ob illius ac discipulorum eius [usum] hedificatam et de fiscis regalibus ditatam." Smaragdus, *Vita Benedicti*, XLII, p. 219.
4   Cf. Alcuin, Letters 200, *Epistolae Karolini aevi (II)*, pp. 330-333; Letters 201, ibid., pp. 333-336.

"I took pains to have books copied in this church as best as I could."[1] The scriptorium of Lyon was among the most productive non-monastic scriptoria in Gaul in the age of Charlemagne. The following table shows more than 20 books, fragments, or folios produced (or possibly produced) in the cathedral scriptorium at the end of the eighth century or the early ninth century (Table 3.3).

Table 3.3 Book production in the scriptorium of Lyon cathedral ca. 800

Shelf mark	Content	Description
Lyon, BM, 336 + Paris, BnF, Baluze 270, fols. 74-75	*Collectio Hispana systematica*	"Lyon, IX. Jh., 1. Viertel"[3]
Lyon, BM, 375	*Lex Romana Visigothorum*	"Min. mehrerer Hde.; häufig die für die Leidrad-Zeit (bis 814) und Nach-Leidrad-Zeit in Lyon charakteristische *a*-Form"[4]
Lyon, BM, 402	Origen-Rufinus, *Homilies on Joshua, Judges and Kings*	"Written presumably at Lyon. Certainly collated there by Archbishop Leidrad (†816)."[5]
Lyon, BM, 443, fols. 7-11, 77, 227-331	Origen-Rufinus, *Homilies on Genesis, Exodus and Leviticus* (supplement folios to an older codex)	"Written in France in a centre with Spanish connections and presumably at Lyon itself, considering the close relations with Spain maintained by Leidrad (†816) and Agobard (796–840) who both became bishops of Lyon."[6]
Lyon, BM, 448, fols. 1-149 + Paris, BnF, Lat. 152, fols. 26-29	Jerome, *Commentary on Jeremiah*	"Kräftige, gleichm. Min. von mehr als einer Hd.; häufig *a* wie in LYON, BM, Ms. 375 (303)"[7]
Lyon, BM, 466 + Paris, BnF, Lat. 152, fols. 21-25	Jerome, *Commentary on Isaiah*	Ordered by Leidrad to copied for personal use with his *ex-dono*[8]
Lyon, BM, 475	Ambrose, *Expositio euangelii secundum Lucam*	"Min. mehrerer Hde. des auf die Leidrad-Min. folg. Stils; häufig *a* wie in LYON, BM, Ms. 375 (303)"[9]
Lyon, BM, 599	Gregory of Nazianzus, *Liber apologeticus*; *De natiuitate Domini*; *De Epiphania*; *De Pentechosten et de Spiritu Sancto*	Ordered by Leidrad to copied for personal use with *ex-dono*[10]

---

1 "In libris conscribendis in eadem ecclesia, in quantum potui, elaboraui." Leidrad, *Report to Charlemagne*, p. 285.
2 According to Bernhard Bischoff, *Katalog*, 2546.
3 According to Bernhard Bischoff, *Katalog*, 2547.
4 According to CLA, VI.770. Cf. Bernhard Bischoff, *Katalog*, 2547b.
5 According to CLA, VI.774c. Cf. Bernhard Bischoff, *Katalog*, 2549a.
6 According to Bischoff, *Katalog*, 2551.
7 Cf. Sigmund Tafel, "Lyons Scriptorium," 4 (1925): pp. 51-52; Louis Holtz, "Leidrat, évêque de Lyon (798–814)," pp. 318-320.
8 According to Bernhard Bischoff, Katalog, 2562.
9 Cf. Sigmund Tafel, "Lyons Scriptorium," 4 (1925): pp. 51-52; Louis Holtz, "Leidrat, évêque de Lyon," pp. 318-320.

Continued

Shelf mark	Content	Description
Lyon, BM, 608	Augustine, a series of shorter treatises on the theme of Grace	Ordered by Leidrad to copied for personal use with his *ex-dono*[1]
Lyon BM, 788, fols. 67-74 + Lyon, BM, 603	Augustine, *De pastoribus, De ouibus, De baptismo, De peccatorum meritis et de baptismo paruulorum, De unico baptismo and De spiritu et littera*	"Min. mehrerer Hde. im späten Leidrad-Stil."[2]
Lyon BM, 788, fols. 87-88 + Paris, BnF, Baluze 270, fols. 107-108, 132-158	Bede, *De templo Salomonis*	"Neben einer typischen Leidrad-Hd."[3]
Lyon BM, 788, fols. 100-101 + Paris, BnF, Baluze 270, fols. 177-178	*Epitome Hispana* (fragments)	"Lyon, IX. Jh., 1. Viertel"[4]
Paris, BnF, Lat. 2812	"Sacramentary of Arles"[5]	"Lyon, IX. Jh., 1./2. Viertel"[6]
Paris, BnF, Lat. 8093, fols. 1-38 + Leiden, Bibliotheek der Riksuniversiteit, Voss. Lat. 111	Poems and hymns of Coelius Sedulius, Ausonius, Engenius II of Toledo and etc.	"Lyon (?), IX. Jh., 1. Viertel (wohl vor 821)"[7]
Paris, BnF, Lat. 11709	*Collectio Hispana systematica*	With non-autographical *ex-dono* "Leydrat licet indignus tamen episcopus"[8]
Paris, BnF, Lat. 12446	*Collectio Dionysio-Hadriana* and etc.	"Etwa Lyon (?) oder Mitte Frankreiches (?), IX. Jh., 1./2. Viertel"[9]
Paris, BnF, NAL 1740, fols. 193-197	Bible books of Deuteronomy, Joshua, Judges and most of Ruth (supplement folios to an older codex)	"Erg. Der Unz.hs. in kräftiger rundlicher Lyoneser Min.; vergleiche die von Eb. Leidrad der Kathedrale St. Stephan übergebene Hs. LYON, BM, Ms. 599 (515)."[10]

1   Cf. Sigmund Tafel, "Lyons Scriptorium," 4 (1925): pp. 51-52; Louis Holtz, "Leidrat, évêque de Lyon," pp. 318-320.
2   According to Bernhard Bischoff, *Katalog*, 2572.
3   According to Bernhard Bischoff, *Katalog*, 2585.
4   According to Bernhard Bischoff, *Katalog*, 2587.
5   Cf. Michael McCormick, "A New Ninth-Century Witness to the Carolingian Mass Against the Pagans (Paris, B.N., Lat. 2812)," *Revue Bénédictine* 97 (1987): pp. 68-86.
6   According to Bernhard Bischoff, *Katalog*, 4234.
7   According to Bernhard Bischoff, *Katalog*, 4529.
8   Louis Holtz, "Leidrat, évêque de Lyon," pp. 320-321: "Roger E. Reynolds, sans doute le meilleur connaisseur de son contenu, a montré que des interpolations entrées dans le texte, sans doute avant sa diffusion en Gaule, étaient de nature à conforter certains aspects de la politique ecclésiale d'Agobard, mais à mon avis cela n'exclut pas que ce manuscrit, dont l'écriture est truffée de symptômes wisigothiques, ait été copié à Lyon du temps de Leidrat." But cf. Bischoff' doubt in *Katalog*, 4705.
9   According to Bernhard Bischoff, *Katalog*, 4835; cf. Lotte Kéry, *Canonical Collections of the Early Middle Ages (ca. 400–1140): A Bibliographical Guide to the Manuscripts and Literature* (Washington, D.C.: Catholic University of America Press, 1999).
10   According to Bernhard Bischoff, *Katalog*, 5113a.

Continued

Shelf mark	Content	Description
Autun, BM, 24, fols. 64-136, 138-142, 105 bis+Paris, BnF, NAL 1628, fols. 5-14	Gregory, *Moralia* (fragments)	"Burgund (Lyon?), VIII./IX. Jh."[1]
Ghent, Rijksuniversiteit, Centrale Bibliotheek, 238	Augustine, *Enarrationes in Psalmos cixx-cxxxiii*	"Lyon, IX. Jh., 1./2. Viertel"[2]
Rome, Archivio della Casa Generalizia dei Padri Maristi, AII.1	*Codex pagesianus*	"Written presumably at Lyon... Corrections in his [Leidrad's] hand occur in this MS..."[3] With Leidrad's autographic *ex-dono*
Rome, Biblioteca Vallicelliana, E.26	Bede, *De temporum ratione*; *Annales Lugdunenses* and etc.	"Le manuscrit date du 1er quart du IXe siècle, mais sa datation de l'époque de Leidrat reste incertaine."[4]
Florence, Biblioteca Medicea Laurenziana, Pl.XIV.21, fols. 1-159	Ambrose, *Expositio psalmi cxviii*	"Lyoneser Min., spätere Leidrad-Zeit."[5]
Chicago, University of Chicago Library, PQ 4617 C 75 P 4	Bible book of Judges (fragments)	"Lyon, IX. Jh., 1.(-2.) Drittel"[6]

In at least three of them (Lyon, BM, 443, fols. 7-11, 77, 227-331; Paris, BnF, Lat. 8093, fols. 1-38 + Leiden, Bibliotheek der Riksuniversiteit, Voss. Lat. 111; Paris, BnF, Lat. 11709), scholars have detected "the handwriting of Visigothic emigrants who had retained their native writing habits."[7] The connection between Lyon and Spain built up during Leidrad's participation in the anti-Adoptionist movement — which brought Felix of Urgel and maybe his followers, probably including Claudius, to Lyon — certainly contributed.

The Spanish influence is also visible in two literary works that are likely to be connected with Leidrad's reform. The first is the canon law collection *Dacheriana*. We have met in Chapter 3.1 its Supplement of 36 *capitula* and discussed how the latter should be seen as an anti-Adoptionist product from Lyon which even echoes Leidrad's own theological thoughts. In fact, as scholars usually believe, the original three-book *Dacheriana* itself was composed in early Carolingian Lyon as well. *Dacheriana* is structurally modeled on the Spanish collection *Collectio Hispana systematica*. Not out of coincidence, two extant codices of *Collectio Hispana systematica* were probably produced in Leidrad's scriptorium of Lyon (Lyon, BM, 336 + Paris, BnF, Baluze

---

1 According to Bernhard Bischoff, *Katalog*, 157.
2 According to Bernhard Bischoff, *Katalog*, 1363.
3 According to CLA, IV.417.
4 Louis Holtz, "Leidrat, évêque de Lyon," p. 316.
5 According to Bernhard Bischoff, *Katalog*, 1220.
6 According to Bernhard Bischoff, *Katalog*, 913.
7 Bernhard Bischoff, "Manuscripts in the Age of Charlemagne," p. 34. Also cf. Sigmund Tafel, "Lyons Scriptorium," 4 (1925): p. 64.

270, fols. 74-75; Paris, BnF, Lat. 11709, cf. Table 3.3). Praised as being "au centre de toutes les collections de la Réforme carolingienne,"[1] *Dacheriana* was one of the most successful canonical collections before Gratian.[2] What distinguished it from other early medieval canonical collections (including its model *Collectio Hispana*) — also one of the major reasons for its great popularity — is the fact that it was purposefully designed to be a convenient judicial compendium for the use of bishops. As Abigail Firey put it, "the *Dacheriana* seems be an episcopal book. The quantity of canons pertaining to episcopal judiciary, governmental, and administrative functions precludes an intended audience of local priests."[3] Apart from a preface compiled from various sources including Augustine's *Enchiridion*, the three books are respectively themed with penance, jurisdiction, and clerical discipline. The composition of *Dacheriana* is usually dated to Charlemagne's reign, which made it very likely a product of Leidrad's Lyon.[4] After all, it would not be surprising to find a connection between the making of a canonical collection that highlighted the episcopal duty and authority and an epoch when the bishop once again became the dominant power in Lyon.

The other literary work is an anonymous martyrology, conserved in a single manuscript (Paris, BnF, Lat. 3879).[5] A martyrology was primarily a calendar comprised of the names and memorial dates of Christian martyrs when this genre emerged in the fifth century as the Pseudo-Hieronymian martyrology. Bede was the first author who created an "historical" martyrology, that is a martyrological calendar attached with the

---

1 Paul Fournier, Gabriel Le Bras, *Histoire des collections canoniques en Occident depuis les Fausses décrétales jusqu'au Décret de Gratien* (Paris: Recueil Sirey, 1931–1932).

2 Its popularity is witnessed by its 52 extant manuscripts, surpassed in number only by *Collectio Dionysio-Hadriana* and *Pseudo-Isidorian Decretals*. Cf. Lotte Kéry, *Canonical Collections*, pp. 87-92; Hubert Mordek, *Kirchenrecht und Reform im Frankenreich: Die Collectio Vetus Gallica, die älteste systematische Kirchenrechtssammlung des Fränkischen Gallien* (Berlin: Walter de Gruyter, 1975); Abigail Firey, *Toward a History of Carolingian Legal Culture Canon Law Collections of Early Medieval Southern Gaul* (Ph.D. dissertation: University of Toronto, 1995). The problem of the edition in Luc d'Achery, Louis-François-Joseph de La Barre, eds., *Spicilegium sive collectio veterum aliquot scriptorum qui in Galliae Bibliothecis delituerant* (Paris: 1723), vol. 1, pp. 509-564, see Abigail Firey, "Ghostly Recensions in Early Medieval Canon Law: The Problem of the *Collectio Dacheriana* and its Shades," *Tijdschrift voor rechtsgeschiedenis* 68 (2000): pp. 63-82.

3 Abigail Firey, "Toward a History of Carolingian Legal Culture," p. 178; also see pp. 177-187 for the best analysis of the orientation and the function of *Dacheriana*.

4 The traditional dating of *Dacheriana* is based on its use of *Collectio Dionysio-Hadriana* which Charlemagne promoted for realm-wide use in *Admonitio generalis* of 789 and the earliest extant manuscript (Cologne, Dombibliothek, 122) which was supposed to be copied ca. 805. Cf. Hubert Mordek, *Kirchenrecht und Reform im Frankenreich*, p. 259. But Abigail Firey proposed to see the composition of *Dacheriana* as an accumulative process during a long time, cf. her "Toward a History of Carolingian Legal Culture," pp. 138-159.

5 For a fundamental study, see Henri Quentin, *Les martyrologes historiques du Moyen Âge: étude sur la formation du martyrologe romain* (Paris: J. Galbada, 1908), pp. 131-221. Also cf. Jacques Dubois, Genevieve Renaud, eds., *Edition pratique des martyrologes de Bede, de l'anonyme lyonnais et de Florus* (Paris: Editions du Centre national de la recherche scientifique, 1976), which reorganized in a calendrical way the martyrological entries listed alphabetically in Quentin's edition.

narrative of each martyr's life and passion. This new format was probably designed for the sake of communal daily readings in monastic communities.[1] The anonymous martyrology under present discussion here was the first known effort to expand the Bedan martyrology. Prefaced by a passage drawn from *Enchiridion* (an Augustinian work which, remarkably, also serves as a major source for the preface to *Dacheriana*, cf. above), the anonymous martyrology contains the narratives of 387 individuals or groups of martyrs and saints (in comparison with 258 in its Bedan model).[2] No fewer than 15 among the newly added individuals or groups of saints are Spanish and their entries are relatively long. According to Henri Quentin's source criticism, the composer of the anonymous martyrology very likely had access to and used a Spanish passionary as his source.[3] More remarkable is the fact that 23 newly added individuals or groups of saints are related to Lyon or its vicinity, and certain entries reveal the details of local cults in Lyon. It is thus almost certain that our anonymous martyrology originated in Lyon.[4] The fact that Florus used it as the model for his own martyrology in the 840s reinforces this provenance.[5]

The Spanish source of this anonymous martyrology likely arrived at Lyon during the frequent connections with the Pyrenean area that characterized Leidrad's episcopate. The *terminus ante quem* of its composition is the translation of a bunch of North African relics, those of Cyprian, Speratus, and Pantaleon, to Lyon Cathedral. This translation, which took place in 807,[6] is absent in the anonymous martyrology of Lyon but present in that of Florus.[7] Leidrad could have ordered such a martyrology to be composed either in order to regularize the celebration of the cult of saints in liturgy, or to provide standard material for communal readings for canonical clerics and monks.

---

1 For the general survey of the genre, see Jacques Dubois, *Les martyrologes du Moyen Âge latin* (Turnhout: Brepols, 1978). For the pseudo-Hieronymian martyrology and its development in the ninth century, see Felice Lifshitz, *The Name of the Saint: The Martyrology of Jerome and Access to the Sacred in Francia, 627–827* (Notre Dame: University of Notre Dame Press, 2006). For Bede's martyrology, see eadem, ed., trans., "Bede, *Martyrology*," *Medieval Hagiography: An Anthology*, ed. Thomas Head (London: Garland, 2000), pp. 167-197.
2 Henri Quentin, *Les martyrologes historiques du Moyen Âge*, pp. 137-138.
3 Ibid., pp. 139-148.
4 Ibid., pp. 219-221.
5 For Florus' martyrology, see ibid., pp. 222-408.
6 The relics were taken by Charlemagne's envoys to Harun al-Rashid, the Abbasid caliph of Baghdad, from North Africa on their way back, and then brought to Gaul in 807. Ado of Vienne in his *Chronicon* copied the narrative of this diplomatic mission from the revised version of *Annales regni Francorum* and then added: "Tunc tempore delata sunt ossa beati Cypriani a Carthagine cum reliquiis beatorum Scillitariorum martyrum, Sperati sociorumque eius, et posita sunt in ecclesia beati Ioannis baptistae in ciuitate Lugdunensi." PL 123, cols. 131-132. Dating the translation to 801 (cf. Michael McCormick, *Origins of the European economy: Communications and Commerce, A.D. 300–900* (Cambridge: Cambridge University Press, 2001, p. 891); Jonathan Conant, "Europe and the African Cult of Saints, circa 350–900: An Essay in Mediterranean Communications," *Speculum* 85 (2010): pp. 1-46) is not correct.
7 Jacques Dubois, Genevieve Renaud, eds., *Edition pratique des martyrologes*, p. 129.

The translation of the relics of these three North African saints was commemorated in a poem of Florus, composed one or two decades after the event. The poem vividly narrates how Charlemagne's envoys to Baghdad saw the relics in a desolated church in Carthage, brought them back to Gaul, and stored them first in Arles.[1] It was at this point, according to Florus, Leidrad "the best presbyter who held the peaceful seat of Lyon, inflamed by the heat of ardent zeal and attentive to sacred objects everywhere (*intentusque sacris rebus ubique*)," begged Charlemagne to allow these relics to be located in Lyon, and the "prosperous and illustrious Cyprian" was finally able to "sleep at the placid altar of John [the Baptist]."[2] In Florus' poem, the triple martyrs, enjoying devotional prayer and festal veneration — Florus mentioned Agobard's sermon on the feast day of Cyprian — and guaranteeing Orthodoxy and Grace from God, have become a crucial part of the collective identity of the church of Lyon.[3]

Leidrad's promotion of the worship of ancient and foreign relics could have reflected the tightened control of the cult of saints that Charlemagne intended.[4] As other poems of Florus whose youth and early clerical formation overlapped the episcopate of Leidrad

---

1   Florus, *Qualiter sanctorum martyrum Cypriani Sperati Pantaleonis reliquiae Lugdunum aduectae sunt*, *Poetae Latini aevi Carolini (II)*, MGH Poetae Latini medii aevi 2, ed. Ernst Dümmler (Berlin: Weidmann, 1884), no. xiii, pp. 544-545. Cf. Louis Holtz, "Les hendécasyllabes de Florus, chantre des saints martyrs Cyprien, Spératus et Pantaléon," *La rigueur et la passion: Mélanges en l'honneur de Pascale Bourgain*, eds. Cédric Giraud, Dominique Poirel (Turnhout: Brepols, 2006), pp. 89-100. Another narrative of this incident can be found in the marytrology of Ado of Vienne, see Jacques Dubois, Genevieve Renaud, eds., *Le martyrologe d'Adon: ses deux familles, ses trois recensions: texte et commentaire* (Paris: Editions du Centre national de la recherche scientifique, 1984), p. 311-315. For the relative unreliability of Ado's account, cf. Henri Quentin, *Les martyrologes historiques du Moyen Âge*, pp. 508-514.

2   "Quod mox comperit optimus sacerdos/Lugduni placidam tenens cathedram/Sollertis studii calore flagrans/Intentusque sacris rebus ubique/Leidradus prece supplici serenum/Regem postulat impetratque raptim/Vt rite sacra martyrum piorum/Nostris moenibus ossa conderentur/Et nunc ad placidam Iohannis aram/Qui Christum uitrea respersit unda/Dignis cultibus et honore claro/Florens, inclyte Cypriane, dormis." Florus, *Qualiter sanctorum martyrum Cypriani Sperati Pantaleonis reliquiae Lugdunum aduectae sunt*, *Poetae Latini aevi Carolini (II)*, no. xiii, pp. 544-545.

3   "Sed, quaeso, uigiles uigilque nostris/Intendas precibus fiasque nobis/Clemens et ualidus dei patronus/Soluas crimina conferasque uota/Sit, quaeso, memor illa lingua nostri/Quae confessa dei perenne uerbum/Ceruicem gladio dedit secandam/Sed Christum recinens silere nescit/Hanc Christus iugiter benignus audit/Vel sacro populos stilo excitantem/Vel prauas hereses deosque falsos/Verbi fulmine funditus cremantem/Hanc et pro populo et patrono nostro/Semper, quaesumus, audiat rogantem/Pastorem foueat, gregem propaget/Det munus fidei, decus salutis/O doctor sacer, o beate martyr/Serua pontificem pius Agobardum/Qui nomen, meritum, tuumque festum/Dictis extulit et honore compsit/O triplex honor, o triforme culmen/O tres magnifici piique testes/Sit nobis triplici fauens precatu/Pollens unica trinitas per aeuum." Ibid., pp. 544-545.

4   Marie-Céline Isaïa, "L'hagiographie contre la réforme dans l'église de Lyon au IXe siècle," *Médiévales* 62 (2012): pp. 83-104; Paul Fouracre, "The Origins of the Carolingian Attempt to Regulate the Cult of Saints," *The Cult of Saints in Late Antiquity and the Middle Ages: Essays on the Contribution of Peter Brown*, eds. James Howard-Johnston, Paul Antony Hayward (Oxford: Oxford University Press, 1999), pp. 143-165. Charlemagne's personal contact with saints and relics, see Julia M. H. Smith, "Rulers and Relics c.750–c.950: Treasure on Earth, Treasure in Heaven," *Past and Present Supplement* 5 (2010): pp. 73-96.

witnessed, the Apostles,[1] Stephen the Protomartyr[2] and the martyr Cyprian[3] occupied the center of devotional imagination in this city in the following generation.

3.3   The Lyon Annotations in the Context of Church Reform and Clerical Instruction

The story of Leidrad the reformer is a legendary one. Born in Bavaria and initiating his ecclesiastical career in his home country — he kept the habit of signing the Germanized *Leidrat* in his *ex-dono* until the end of his life[4] — Leidrad left for Austrasia to serve the king of the Franks, carried out mission in Septimania, worked as the head of an ancient episcopal city of Burgundy for a little less than two decades, and finally retired to one of the most prestigious abbeys in Neustria. His life odyssey was an epitome of his energetic epoch. Equally remarkable were his reform achievements in Lyon. Before his episcopate, even if we take the rhetorical element of our sources into consideration, the church of Lyon, which had had a glorious past, was in a decadent state. It turned out to be Leidrad, a foreigner, who guided the revival of its ecclesiastical and intellectual tradition, and made it a vigorous *plebs ecclesiastica* once again. The "spiritual ethnogenesis" fostered by Leidrad in Lyon,[5] however, was far from isolated, but closely followed the pace of realm-wide Frankish church reform initiated by his master Charlemagne. The making of Carolingian Lyon during Leidrad's episcopate, as this chapter has demonstrated, is a perfect local case of the so-called "Carolingian Renaissance."

Certainly, the historical picture of Leidrad's reform shown in this chapter is restricted by the availability of sources. For example, we know little about how Leidrad performed his metropolitan office over his suffragan bishops of Langres, Autun, Chalon-sur-Saône, and Mâcon. There is no indication of Leidrad's summoning of any provincial synod or

---

1   *Poetae Latini aevi Carolini (II)*, no. xi, pp. 541-542.
2   Ibid., no. xii, pp. 542-544.
3   Ibid., no. xiv, p. 546.
4   As Louis Holtz acutely observed in his "Leidrat, évêque de Lyon (798–814)," p. 315, n.1.
5   The term is borrowed from Martin Claussen, *Reform of the Frankish Church*, pp. 46-47.

his intervention in the episcopal election of suffragan dioceses.[1] Similar is the reform in the rural world. Leidrad mentioned at the very end of his report to Charlemagne that he had rehabilitated St-Willibadus, a country church in the Bugey area around 40 miles east of the city, an indication that his reforming antenna extended somewhat beyond the city wall.[2] One may also wonder whether Leidrad made his baptismal exposition, as presented to Charlemagne, available for the instruction of rural priests. But since there appears to be no episcopal statute,[3] no manuscript for local priests,[4] no examination for local priests,[5] and no clerical inventory[6] extant from Leidrad's Lyon, we can say little

---

1   He was called archbishop, for example, by his former disciple Claudius: "Quod ego in Lucduno ciuitate apud uenerabilem patrem Leidrad, gratiae Dei iamdictae aecclesiae archiepiscopo, incoaui, quo faciente et Deo donante aliquantulum in scripturarum scientiam profecimus." Claudius, Letter 1, *Epistolae Karolini aevi (II)*, p. 592; and by Louis the Pious: "Nos interea missum nostrum uenerabilem scilicet [uirum] Leidrardum archiepiscopum ad hanc rem inuestigandam et diligenter inquirendam misimus..." *Die Urkunden Ludwigs des Frommen*, no. 80, p. 197. In this royal charter, Leidrad worked as Louis the Pious' *missus* to investigate a case of church property in Mâcon. Leidrad certainly spoke as a metropolitan in his reply to Charlemagne's baptism inquiry ("Praecipere nobis dignati estis, ut aut per nostra scripta aut per nos ipsos cognoscatis, qualiter nos et suffraganei nostri doceamus et instruamus sacerdotes Dei..." Cf. Susan Keefe, *Water and the Word*, p. 353). Lyon's metropolitan status was highlighted by Charlemagne's testament in 811, which Leidrad himself witnessed, cf. Einhard, *The Life of Charles the Emperor*, c. 33, p. 50. Agobard exercised the metropolitan authority much more extensively than his predecessor, cf. Alfred Coville, *Recherches sur l'Histoire de Lyon*, pp. 391-393; Michel Rubellin, "Lyon aux temps carolingiens," pp. 162-164. The promotion of metropolitan hierarchy in the Carolingian era and its actual effect, cf. Steffen Patzold, "Eine Hierarchie im Wandel: Die Ausbildung einer Metropolitanordnung im Frankenreich des 8. und 9. Jahrhunderts," *Hiérarchie et Stratification Sociale dans l'Occident Médiéval (400–1100)*, eds. François Bougard, Dominique Iogna-Prat, Régine Le Jan (Turnhout: Brepols, 2008), pp. 161-184; Daniel Pangerl, *Die Metropolitanverfassung des karolingischen Frankenreiches* (Hannover: Hahnsche, 2011).

2   "Aliam quoque ecclesiam in eadem parochia, que est in honorem sancti Vuldaldi, restauraui." Leidrad, *Report to Charlemagne*, p. 287. The identification of the church of St-Willibadus, cf. Alfred Coville, *Recherches sur l'Histoire de Lyon*, p. 269, n. 2.

3   Cf. Carine van Rhijn, *Shepherds of the Lord*.

4   Eadem, "Manuscripts for Local Priests."

5   Eadem, "'Et hoc considerat episcopus, ut ipsi presbyteri non sint idiothae': Carolingian Local *correctio* and an Unknown Priests' Exam from the Early Ninth Century," *Religious Franks: Religion and Power in the Frankish Kingdoms: Studies in Honour of Mayke de Jong*, eds. Rob Meens, Dorine van Espelo, Bram van den Hoven van Genderen, Janneke Raaijmakers, Irene van Renswoude, Carine van Rhijn (Manchester: Manchester University Press, 2016), pp. 162-180.

6   Carl Hammer, "Country Churches, Clerical Inventories and the Carolingian Renaissance in Bavaria," *Church History* 49 (1980): pp. 5-17.

substantial about the effect of his reform of the rural church.[1] However, the general picture is still clear: It was the order, orthodoxy, and spiritual — as well as material — prosperity of clergy, monks, and nuns under the episcopal governance, and the patronage of the Apostles, martyrs, and saints that lay at the center of Leidrad's reform of Lyon. This historical background is of crucial importance to the subject of this book, because it helps explain the social imagination of the Lyon Annotations, as we will discuss in detail in Chapter 7.

Equally helpful is to take into consideration how the intellectual products of Leidrad's reform commonly functioned to instruct clerics and to shape their good faith and way of life, and there are detectable echoes in the Lyon Annotations. We can make a few observations here.

The content of about half of the manuscripts produced or possibly produced by the scriptorium of Lyon during Leidrad's episcopate is exegetical, which confirms our observation on the revival of biblical education in Chapter 2.4.3. Like Paris, BnF, NAL 1740, these exegetical manuscripts were probably library books available to clerics for personal study (cf. Chapter 2.3). From the perspective of church governance, the instruction of biblical knowledge among clerics helped maintain the orthodoxy of the church. For example, Agobard, who received his training in biblical exegesis in Leidrad's schools (as we will see in detail in Chapter 8), turned out to be able to quote biblical quotations extensively, to refute rural superstition and to condemn ordeal.[2] In the Lyon Annotations, we can find references to the Holy Bible as the caliber to identify heresy, for example, the exposition for Deut. 17:6 ("By the mouth of two or three witnesses shall he die that is to be slain. Let no man be put to death, when only one beareth witness against him"):

> The two witnesses refer to the Law and the Gospel; but the three refer to the Law, the Prophet, and the New Testament. Those whom the two or three witnesses do not

---

1   If we allow ourselves the risk of anachronism and too literal reading of rhetorical discourse, Agobard's lament over the rural superstitions and the class oppression of lay landlords on rural priests could be seen as a sign that his predecessor had less success reforming the countryside than he did the city. For superstition, see Agobard, *Liber contra insulsam uulgi opinionem de grandine et tonitruis*, CCCM 52, ed. Lieven Van Acker (Turnhout: Brepols, 1981), pp. 3-15; cf. Paul Dutton, "Thunder and Hail over the Carolingian Countryside," *Charlemagne's Mustache and Other Cultural Clusters of a Dark Age*, idem (New York: Palgrave Macmillan, 2004), pp. 169-188; Rob Meens, "Thunder over Lyons: Agobard, the *Tempestarii*, and Christianity," *Paganism in the Middle Ages: Threat and Fascination*, eds. Carlos Steel, John Marenbon, Werner Verbeke (Leuven: Leuven University Press, 2012), pp. 157-166. For lay landlords and local priests, see Agobard, *De priuilegio et iure sacerdotii*, CCCM 52, ed. Lieven Van Acker (Turnhout: Brepols, 1981), pp. 54-69; cf. Janet Nelson, "Making Ends Meet: Wealth and Poverty in the Carolingian Church," *Studies in Church History* 24 (1987): pp. 25-35; Michael E. Moore, *A Sacred Kingdom: Bishops and the Rise of Frankish Kingship, 300–850* (Washington, D.C.: Catholic University of America Press, 2011).

2   Cf. Agobard, *Liber contra insulsam uulgi opinionem de grandine et tonitruis*; idem, *Liber de diuinis sententiis*, CCCM 52, ed. Lieven Van Acker (Turnhout: Brepols, 1981), pp. 31-49.

condemn, the priests of the Church should not condemn as well.[1]

But secular learning was not totally out of the picture. As we have seen, MS Rome, Archivio della Casa Generalizia dei Padri Maristi, AII, Leidrad's personal book, contains a series of treatises on dialectics, including the works of the non-Christian Apuleius and the anti-Christian Porphyry. Whether the same kind of manual was used for the instruction of clerics at that time is not clear, but we find in the Lyon Annotations one original entry which demonstrates a similarly sympathetic attitude toward pagan authors and secular learning. It is for Deut. 20:19-20 ("When thou hast besieged a city a long time and hath compassed it with bulwarks to take it, thou shalt not cut down the trees that may be eaten of…But if there be any trees that are not fruitful but wild and fit for other uses, cut them down…"):

> The city which was besieged for a long time by holy preachers, that is spiritual fighters, tropologically signifies the philosophers of this world who resorted to human reasons and were willing to convert later than other people. But because those same philosophers wrote certain things morally well in their books, that is, they spoke what is true, just like fruitful trees, the ecclesiastical men shall not refuse these things. But what they understood badly about God or His creatures, or in the praise of their own gods, just like trees not fruitful, shall be cut off by the roots with the sword of severity. Nobody inexperienced was able to carry out this job, but spiritual men who were gifted with both the divine and human learning, could manage to fulfill it.[2]

The veneration of the Apostles and martyrs regularized by the anonymous martyrology and promoted in the translation of relics also reflects in the expositions that recall the glorious martyrdom, for example, the one on Deut. 20:5 ("And the captains shall proclaim through every band in the hearing of the army…"):

> Captains of the people through every band were the Apostles and apostolic men who in the time of persecution encouraged the faithful people in word and deed, lest

---

1   "Duo testes, lex et Euangelium; tres uero: legem prophetiam atque Nouum Testamentum exprimunt. Quos autem hii duo uel tres testes non condemnant, nec sacerdotes ecclesiae condemnare debent." Paris, BnF, NAL 1740, fol. 48r; "Iam superius in hoc libro premissum est quod nemo debeat condemnari uelut hereticus nisi quem lex et Euangelium condemnauerit." Paris, BnF, NAL 1740, fol. 53r, on Deut. 19:15.

2   "Ciuitas que multo tempore a sanctis predicatoribus, id est spiritalibus uellatoribus obsessa est, tropologice significat philosophos huius mundi qui humanas rationes requirendo, tardius quam ceteri homines credere uoluerunt. Sed quia isdem philosophi nonnulla in libris suis moraliter bene scripserunt, hoc quod uerum loquuti sunt, quasi arbores fructuosas, a uiris ecclesiasticis renuenda non sunt. Ea uero que aut de deo aut de eius creatura siue in laude deorum suorum male senserunt, quasi arbores infructuosas ferro seueritatis radicitus abscindende sunt; quod nemo inperitus facere potuit sed uiri spiritales, diuina atque humana scientia prediti, hoc implere ualuerunt." Paris, BnF, NAL 1740, fol. 55v.

they yield to their persecutors, but in order that they fight for their faith until death.[1]

Similarly, the guiding rules of exercising confessions regulated in the conciliar decrees collected in the first book of *Dacheriana*[2] finds an echo in the original exposition for Deut. 24:10 ("When thou shalt demand of thy neighbour any thing that he oweth thee, thou shalt not go into his house to take away a pledge") in the Lyon Annotations:

> None of the priests should extort confession from any offender against his will. It is proper for the Christian believer to do so in the literal sense. But mystically, it can be understood concerning the reconciliation of penitents, to whom the Sacrament of the Body and the Blood of the Lord should not be denied at their deathbed, if his penance has taken place earlier by any length of time.[3]

Last but maybe most important, instruction in biblical knowledge had its pastoral function. Clerics' correct understanding of the Holy Bible and their capability to teach were common pastoral concerns of high ecclesiastics of that time. According to an instructive letter written ca. 800 by Leidrad's friend Arn archbishop of Salzburg to his suffragan bishops:

> The bishop should take care that the priests are not ignorant (*idiothae*), but are able to read and understand the Holy Scriptures, so that they can instruct according to the tradition of the Roman Church, and they ought to deliver the catholic faith, to teach the people entrusted to them, and to celebrate the Mass according to the custom, just as the Roman tradition is transmitted to us.[4]

Leidrad himself was fully aware of the necessity of preaching the Holy Scripture in pastoral care. He explicitly expressed it in his response to Charlemagne's baptism inquiry of 811/812:

> It is not proper for us to avoid saying that in the city in which we preside, there are certain people affected by the vessel of divine mercy, upon whom God shows the

---

1 "Duces populi per singulas turmas apostoli et apostolici uiri fuerunt, qui tempore persecutionis populum fidelem uerbo atque exemplo exortati sunt ne persecutoribus suis cederent sed usque ad mortem propter fidem suam decertarent." Paris, BnF, NAL 1740, fol. 54r.

2 Rob Meens, *Penance in Medieval Europe*, pp. 119-120.

3 "Nemo ex sacerdotibus a quolibet delinquenti confessionem delictorum inuitus extorquere debet. Hoc et secundum litteram fideli cristiano facere conuenit. Mistice uero de reconciliatione penitentum accipi potest, quibus in exitum sacramentum corporis et sanguinis Domini negandum non·est, si tamen quanticumque tempore eius penitentia precesserit." Paris, BnF, NAL 1740, fol. 64r.

4 "Et hoc consideret episcopus ut ipsi presbyteri non sint idiothae, sed sacras scripturas legant et intelligant, ut secundum traditionem Romane ecclesiae possint instruere, et fidem catholicam debeant ipsi agere et populos sibi commissos docere, missas secundum consuetudinem caelebrare, sicut Romana traditio nobis tradidit." Raymond Étaix, "Un Manuel de Pastorale de l'Époque Carolingienne (Clm. 27152)," *Revue Bénédictine* 91 (1981): pp. 105-130.

riches of His goodness, who is even able to bring forth the splendid pearls prepared to adorn the heavenly city from dung. Scriptures should not be silent to these people... And for that reason, scriptures should be preached, the Gospel should make sound, the terrors of admonitions (*terrores comminationum*) and the delights of consolations (*blandimenta consolationum*) should be announced. For there exist people hard in heart in the ecclesiastical city, to whom the thunders and hail-storms of God's speeches which first strike and then irrigate are useful, and there are also gentle people, to whom only the mild and placid speech of the Divine Word is beneficial.[1]

In the Lyon Annotations, for Deut. 32:46 (Set your hearts on all the words, which I testify to you this day: which you shall command your children to observe and to do, and to fulfill all that is written in this law), the exposition goes:

It instructs the teachers of the Church that they should fulfill all that they understand and believe in the Holy Scripture, and deliver to his children, that is students, to observe.[2]

It is in this general historical context that we should understand one of the most important features of the Lyon Annotations as a biblical commentary: It teaches its audience — the clerics of Lyon — the ideas and ideals of a Christian community, as well as the way to interpret Deuteronomy. This topic will be thoroughly treated in Chapter 7. For now, it is sufficient for us to conclude that the Lyon Annotations is a commentary arising from the milieu of the Carolingian church reform, and a manifestation of the reform.

---

1 "Neque enim nos ambigere oportet esse in plebe cui praelati sumus, aliquos uasa diuinae misericordiae effectos, in quibus ostendat Deus diuitias bonitatis suae; qui solet etiam de sterquilinio proferre praeclaras margaritas ornamento supernae ciuitatis aptandas, pro quibus taceri non debent Scripturae... [E]t propterea debent praedicari Scripturae, debet sonare Euangelium, debent annuntiare et terrores comminationum et blandimenta consolationum, quia in plebe ecclesiastica exsistunt et duricordes quibus utilia sunt tonitrua et grando sermonum Dei quae primum percutiant et postea irrigent, existunt et mites quibus tantummodo lenis et placidus sermo uerbi diuini expediat." Leidrad, *Baptismal Exposition*, Susan Keefe, *Water and the Word*, vol. 2, p. 383.

2 "Doctoribus ecclesiae precipit ut cuncta quae in diuinis Scripturis recte intellegunt et credunt, operibus impleant et filiis suis, id est discipulis, ad custodienda tradant." Paris, BnF, NAL 1740, fol. 89v.

PART II

TRADITION AND INNOVATION

CHAPTER 4

THE EXEGESIS OF DEUTERONOMY BEFORE 800 (I): THE RISE OF CHRISTIAN INTERPRETATION

To reach a reliable and fair evaluation of the historical significance of the Lyon Annotations, a retrospective survey of the Christian exegetical practice for Deuteronomy in the Latin west before 800 is essential. This is the task to be undertaken in the following three chapters.

Unlike other books of the Old Testament such as Genesis, Psalms, and the Song of Songs, a history of the early exegesis of Deuteronomy is a subject yet to be written.[1] Much effort needs to be made to fill this lacuna. On one hand, the Lyon Annotations needs to be seen as a part of the diachronic evolution of the exegesis of Deuteronomy in the Latin west. On the other hand, in a synchronic sense, the exposition of Deuteronomy before 800 constitutes the potential sources and models for the Lyon Annotator. Their multiple approaches to the understanding of this biblical book (or part of it) converged as an exegetical repertoire against which both the traditional and the innovative dimensions of the Lyon Annotations are to be measured. In this sense, the exegetical history of Deuteronomy in the following survey is designed to have a certain teleological color. The expositions that were not likely to be known or accessible to the early medieval Latin west, such as Theodoret of Cyrus's *Questions on Deuteronomy*, Cyril of Alexandria's *Glaphyra*, Procopius of Gaza's catena, and Pseudo-Ephrem's Armenian commentary, while no less important exegetical enterprises *per se*, will either be mentioned in passing or ignored.[2]

---

1 Cf. Thomas Renna, "Christian Exegesis of Deuteronomy: Patristic to Scholastic," *Michigan Academician* 23 (1991): pp. 19-29. Despite its promising title, this paper is unfortunately far from a thorough survey of early and medieval "Christian Exegesis of Deuteronomy" and is sometimes misreading (e.g., at p. 22, making no distinction between Wigbod's commentary in PL 93, cols. 409-416 and the Pseudo-Bedan commentary in PL 91, cols. 379-394). Also cf. Charles Kannengiesser, *Handbook of Patristic Exegesis: The Bible in Ancient Christianity* (Boston: Brill, 2004), vol. 1, pp. 285-286.

2 For the works of Theodoret, Cyril, and Procopius, see the discussions in the following chapters. For the Pseudo-Ephrem, see *The Armenian Commentaries on Exodus-Deuteronomy Attributed to Ephrem the Syrian*, ed. Edward Mathews (Louven: Peeters 2001).

The research method in these three chapters is to combine analysis of compositional context, textual reading, and source criticism. Also, starting with Origen, every time when discussing an exegete, the relationship of his work(s) with the Lyon Annotations will be examined.

The present chapter discusses how Christianity developed its own distinctive way of interpreting Deuteronomy during its formative stage, how Origen proposed the idea that Deuteronomy as the second law prefigures the Gospel, and how Jerome decisively transmitted this typological motif to the Latin west. There exists a long tradition behind the opening of the Lyon Annotations: "Deuteronomium est ueteris iteratio legis; quae iteratio ad Nouum pertinet Testamentum." (1r)

4.1   From the Beginning to the Second Century

The fifth book of the Torah mainly consists of three admonitory speeches of Moses (1:1-4:43, 4:44-29:1; 29:2-30:20) to the people of Israel on the plains of Moab right before they entered Canaan, the Promised Land. The subject of Moses' admonitions concerns various aspects of religious, political, and social life. The book ends with a narrative of Moses' death and Joshua's succession to leadership, and two poems of a prophetic nature, known respectively as the Song of Moses (32:1-43) and the Blessings of Moses (33:2-27).

In Jewish tradition, the book is usually named *Devarim*, drawn from the opening sentence of the book, meaning "words" or "speeches." In the Septuagint, the Greek translation of the Hebrew Bible completed in the second century BC, the book is titled *deuteronomos*, meaning "the second law." This Greek name is drawn from a self-reference inside the book. According to the original Hebrew of Deut. 17:18, Moses commanded that the new king of Israel should have "a copy of this law/teaching" (*mishneh ha-torah*) before him. The Septuagint creates the neologism *deuteronomos* as a translation, which significantly misinterprets the original meaning of "the copy" as "the second." It is not totally a misreading to understand the fifth book of Moses as "the second law," though. Moses' second speech (29:1) ends with God's command for Moses to make a covenant in Moab *in addition to* the covenant previously made in Horeb or Sinai.[1]

It is generally accepted in modern scholarship that the book of Deuteronomy in its final form is the outcome of many stages of redaction that initiated with the religious reform of Josiah, King of Judah (640–609 BC), and lasted for centuries.[2] In the

---

1   Patrick D. Miller, *Deuteronomy* (Louisville: John Knox Press, 1990).
2   Christoph Bultmann, "Deuteronomy," *The Oxford Bible Commentary: The Pentateuch*, eds. John Barton, John Muddiman (Oxford: Oxford University Press, 2010), pp. 188-189.

traditional Jewish view, however, it was Moses who composed Deuteronomy as the last book of the Torah. The early Jews received the book as divine word and divine law *par excellence*. During the Second Temple period, Deuteronomy was pivotal in Jewish educational, liturgical, and intellectual life. It was recited in public readings in the Synagogue. Its excerpts were bound to bodies (*tefillin*) and were affixed to dwellings (*mezuzah*) for religious devotion. The recitation of Deut. 6:4 ("Hear, O Israel, the Lord our God is one Lord"), known as the *Shema*, was required daily. Among the Dead Sea Scrolls discovered in Qumran caves, there were a large number of manuscripts of Deuteronomy and writings relevant to it. Jewish authors of the first century AD such as Flavius Josephus and Philo of Alexandria engaged the book intimately to express their own ethical, theological, historical, and political concerns.[1]

The use and interpretation of Deuteronomy played a significant role as Christianity emerged from Judaism and achieved its independent identity. In the New Testament, it is the most utilized Old Testament book together with Psalms and Isaiah.[2] According to the Gospels, Jesus quoted Deuteronomy in his response to the temptation of the devil (Matthew 4:4-10; Luke 4:4-12), and interpreted Deuteronomy in his teaching to disciples (e.g., in the Sermon on the Mount) and his refutation of Jewish teachers (e.g., on the matter of divorce, in Mark 10:2-12). Paul cited Deuteronomy in his epistles extensively as both an ethical (e.g., 2 Corinthians 13:1) and a theological authority (e.g., 1 Corinthians 8:6). More remarkably, through a radical interpretation and rewriting of precepts from the "law of Moses," the Apostle put forth his revolutionary Christological ideas about the history of Israel (Romans 10:19), the spiritual meaning of the Law (Romans 2:25-29), the fulfillment of the Law in Christ (Galatians 3:10, 3:13, Romans 10:6-8), and the inclusion of gentiles (Romans 15:10).[3]

In the second century, when Christianity in the making experienced what Hans von Campenhausen called "the crisis of the Old Testament canon,"[4] there appeared sharply contrasting attitudes toward Deuteronomy. On the one end of the spectrum is Marcion of Sinope (ca. 85–160) who read the Hebrew Bible in a totally literal way, recognized nothing but its discrepancies with the Gospels and Pauline Epistles, and thus claimed

---

1   Timothy H. Lim, "Deuteronomy in the Judaism of the Second Temple Period," *Deuteronomy in the New Testament*, eds. Maarten J. J. Menken, Steve Moyise (London: T & T Clark, 2007), pp. 6-26; David Lincicum, *Paul and the Early Jewish Encounter with Deuteronomy* (Tübingen: Mohr Siebeck, 2010).

2   *Deuteronomy in the New Testament*, eds. Maarten J. J. Menken, Steve Moyise (London: T & T Clark International, 2007).

3   David Lincicum, *Paul and the Early Jewish Encounter with Deuteronomy*, pp. 117-168.

4   Hans von Campenhausen, *The Formation of the Christian Bible*, trans. J. A. Baker (Philadelphia: Fortress Press, 1972), pp. 62-102. For a helpful general survey, see Oskar Skarsaune, "The Development of Scriptural Interpretation in the Second and Third Centuries (except Clement and Origin)," *Hebrew Bible/Old Testament: The History of Its Interpretation. Volume I. From the beginnings to the Middle Ages (until 1300). Part 1: Antiquity*, ed. Magne Sæbø (Göttingen: Vandenhoeck and Ruprecht, 1996), pp. 373-442.

it irrelevant to the teaching of Jesus Christ.[1] Marcion allegedly exposed "the contrast between the law and the gospel, between Moses and Christ" by juxtaposing Deut. 24:1 and Matthew 19:8.[2] The other end of the spectrum can be found in the *Epistle of Barnabas* which refuted any Jewish understanding and literal observance of their scriptures and proposed instead the allegorical/spiritual reading, exemplified in its figurative interpretation of the Deuteronomic food regulations.[3] Later in the second century, Irenaeus of Lyon (ca. 125–202) held a less radical view of Deuteronomy that fit his theory of the economy of salvation.[4] According to this first great theologian in the history of Christianity, the ceremonial and moral precepts in Deuteronomy, such as the laws about divorce and circumcision, are the yoke that God set to restrain stubborn Jews, after they failed the natural laws (the Decalogue) delivered to them earlier on the two stone tables, as "the laws of bondage" (*seruitutis praecepta*) and the deserved discipline; but they also prophesize future things and will be annulled by "the new covenant of

---

1 Heikki Räisänen, "Marcion," *A Companion to Second-Century Christian "Heretics,"* eds. Antti Marjanen, Petri Luomanen (Leiden: Brill, 2005), pp. 100-124.

2 "Sed Christus diuortium prohibet dicens, Qui dimiserit uxorem suam et aliam duxerit, adulterium committit; qui dimissam a uiro duxerit, aeque adulter est. Ut sic quoque prohibeat diuortium, illicitum facit repudiatae matrimonium. Moyses uero permittit repudium in Deuteronomio: Si sumserit quis uxorem, et habitauerit cum ea, et euenerit non inuenire eam apud eum gratiam, eo quod inuentum sit in illa impudicum negotium, scribet libellum repudii et dabit in manu eius, et dimittet illam de domo sua. Vides diuersitatem legis et euangelii, Moysi et Christi?" Tertullian, *Aduersus Marcionem*, IV.34.1, ed., trans. Ernest Evans (Oxford: Clarendon Press, 1972).

3 "Now when Moses said, 'You shall not eat a pig, or an eagle or a hawk or a crow, or any fish that has no scales,' he received, according to the correct understanding, three precepts. Furthermore, he says to them in Deuteronomy, 'I will set forth as a covenant to this people my righteous requirements.' Therefore it is not God's commandment that they should not eat; rather Moses spoke spiritually. Accordingly he mentioned the pig for this reason: you must not associate, he means, with such people, who are like pigs. That is, when they are well off, they forget the Lord, but when they are in need, they acknowledge the Lord, just as the pig ignores its owner when it is feeding, but when it is hungry it starts to squeal and falls silent only after being fed again." *Epistle of Barnabas*, 10.1-3, in *The Apostolic Fathers: Greek Texts and English Translations of Their Writings*, ed. *Michael W. Holmes*. 3rd ed. (Grand Rapids: Baker Book House, 2007), pp. 410-411. For the *Epistle of Barnabas*, cf. James Carleton Paget, "The Epistle of Barnabas," *The Expository Times* (11) 2006: pp. 441-446.

4 Cf. Denis Minns, *Irenaeus: An Introduction* (New York: T & T Clark, 2010).

liberty" (*nouum libertatis testamentum*).[1]

4.2   Origen and the Foundation of Latin Exegetical Tradition

The intermediate role of the Deuteronomic laws in Irenaeus' theology can be seen as
a precursor to the notion later predominant in the Latin west that Deuteronomy as the
second law prefigures the Gospel. In the third century, the effort to make a systematic
Christian interpretation of the book of Deuteronomy emerged in the exegetical enterprise
of Origen of Alexandria (185–254), the first Christian author who consciously took
biblical exegesis as "a way of life, a way of salvation, culminating in the vision of God."[2]
For Origen, all the scriptures are inspired by God, but their true meaning is often obscure
and concealed behind letters, "the veil of flesh" in his own words.[3] A competent exegete's
task, therefore, is to guide his audience beyond the *sensus literalis* to the divine spiritual
understanding through careful and precise interpretation supported by a combination of
proper philological knowledge and right moral-theological perspectives of the Christian
faith. Biblical hermeneutics in this way achieve "a progression of stages in the Christian's
progress toward perfection."[4]

---

1   "Itaque lex et disciplina erat illis et prophetia futurorum. Nam Deus primo quidem per naturalia
praecepta quae ab initio infixa dedit hominibus admonens eos, hoc est per Decalogum - quae si
quis non fecerit, non habet salutem — et nihil plus ab eis exquisiuit, quemadmodum Moyses in
Deuteronomio ait: Hos sermones [omnes quos] locutus est Dominus ad omnem synagogam filiorum
Israel in monte, et <nihil> adjecit, et scripsit ea in duabus tabulis lapideis, et dedit mihi, propter hoc
ut custodirent praecepta hi qui uelint sequi eum. At ubi conuersi sunt in uituli factionem et reuersi
sunt animis suis in Aegyptum, serui pro liberis concupiscentes esse, aptam concupiscentiae suae
acceperunt reliquam seruitutem, a Deo quidem non abscidentem, in seruitutis autem iugo domantem
eos, quemadmodum et Ezechiel propheta causas talis legis datae reddens ait: Et post concupiscentiam
cordis sui erant oculi eorum, et ego dedi eis praecepta non bona et justificationes in quibus non uiuent
in eis." Irenaeus, *Aduersus haereses seu Detectio et euersio falso cognominatae Gnoseos*, IV.15.1,
SC 100, eds. Adelin Rousseau, Bertrand Hemmerdinger, Louis Doutreleau, Charles Mercier (Paris:
Éditions du Cerf, 1965), pp. 548-551; "Seruitutis autem praecepta separatim per Moysen praecepit
populo, apta illorum eruditioni siue castigationi, quemadmodum ipse Moyses ait: Et mihi praecepit
Dominus in tempore illo docere uobis justificationes et judicia. Haec ergo quae in seruitutem et in
signum data sunt illis circumscripsit nouo libertatis testamento." Ibid., IV.16.5, pp. 570-571.
2   Peter Martens, *Origen and Scripture: The Contours of the Exegetical Life* (Oxford: Oxford University
Press, 2012), p. 243. A helpful survey of Origen's biblical interpretation in the context of the lineage
of the Alexandrian exegetical tradition, see James Carleton Paget, "The Christian Exegesis of the
Old Testament in the Alexandrian Tradition," *Hebrew Bible/Old Testament: The History of Its
Interpretation. Volume I. From the beginnings to the Middle Ages (until 1300). Part 1: Antiquity*, ed.
Magne Sæbø, (Göttingen: Vandenhoeck and Ruprecht, 1996), pp. 478-542.
3   "Nam sicut ibi carnis, ita hic litterae uelamine tegitur, ut littera quidem adspiciatur tamquam caro,
latens uero intrinsecus spiritalis sensus tamquam diuinitas sentiatur." Origen, *Homiliae in Leuiticum
secundum translationem Rufini*, I.1, GCS 29, ed. Wilhelm Baehrens (Leipzig: J. C. Hinrichs, 1920), p.
280.
4   Karen Jo Torjesen, *Hermeneutical Procedure and Theological Method in Origen's Exegesis* (Berlin:
De Gruyter, 1986).

It is not surprising that biblical interpretation constitutes the principal axis of Origen's works. In addition to passages of an exegetical nature omnipresent in his theological and apologetic tracts such as *De principiis* and *Contra Celsum*, the number of Origen's exegetical works as such is immense, including at least 400 homilies and 260 volumes (*tomoi*) of commentaries, as well as enormous exegetical scholia or *excerpta*. However, around three-fourths of them were lost not long after him; of the extant works, the majority were preserved only in the Latin translations of Rufinus, Jerome and, in the case of the commentary on Matthew, an anonymous translator.[1]

The homilies on Deuteronomy are among Origen's lost works. Between 238 and 244, he worked as the official preacher in Caesarea and gave homilies there according to a local liturgical schedule designed to cover the whole Bible in a three-year circle.[2] In Homily 1 on Numbers, Origen told his hearers that he felt inadequate to interpret the mysteries in Numbers, but even more inadequate to interpret Deuteronomy, implying that Deuteronomy would be the next subject of his preaching.[3] The homilies were copied and preserved locally. A brief Greek annotation in the so-called "Codex von der Goltz," probably composed in the library at Caesarea in the fourth century, refers to Homily 7 on Deuteronomy. This is the only direct citation of Origen's homilies on Deuteronomy in

---

1 For the counts, see Gilles Dorival, "Origen," *The New Cambridge History of the Bible, Volume 1: From the Beginning to 600*, eds. James Carleton, Joachim Schape (Cambridge: Cambridge University Press, 2013), pp. 624-626. Jerome praised Origen's productivity by comparing him to Varro, the most prolific Greek author, and, based on the list that Eusebius of Caesarea inserted in his lost hagiographical work the *Life of Pamphilus*, enumerated 786 works of Origen. Cf. Jerome, *Epistula XXXIII*, CSEL 54 *Epistulae 1–70*, ed. Isidorus Hilberg (Vienna: Verlag der Österreichischen Akademie der Wissenschaften, 1910), pp. 252-259. A critical analysis of the list according to the extant works, see Pierre Nautin, *Origène: Sa vie et son oeuvre* (Paris: Beauchesne, 1977), pp. 225-260. Nautin's study should be supplemented with the recently discovered twenty-nine Origenian homilies on Psalms in Munich, Bayerische Staatsbibliothek, Graecus 314, see *Die Neuen Psalmenhomilien: Eine Kritische Edition des Codex Monacensis Graecus 314*, GCS Neue Folge 19, ed. Lorenzo Perrone (Berlin: De Gruyter, 2015).

2 According to the study of Pierre Nautin, Origen gave one homily on an Old Testaments book every morning (except Sunday) in the noneucharistic assembly which allowed the attendance of catechumens, and one homily on a New Testament book every Sunday morning, Wednesday evening, and Friday evening in the eucharistic assembly only for the already baptized. Of the Old Testament books, Origen lectured on the Heptateuch last, after the books of Wisdom and the prophetic books. 16 homilies on Genesis, 13 on Exodus, 16 on Leviticus, 28 on Numbers, 26 on Joshua and 9 on Judges survive in Rufinus' translation. Pierre Nautin, *Origène*, pp. 389-409.

3 "Ego enim uere imparem me iudico ad enarranda mysteria, quae liber hic continet Numerorum; multo autem inferiorem ad illa, quae Deuteronomii uolumen includit." Origen, *Homiliae in Numeros secundum translationem Rufini*, I.2, GCS 30, ed. Wilhelm Baehrens (Leipzig: J. C. Hinrichs, 1921), p. 5.

all the extant sources in any language.[1] But the homilies certainly had wider circulation from the fourth to the sixth century. According to the list of Origen's works attached to Jerome's letter to Paula (ca. 384), Origen composed 13 homilies on Deuteronomy.[2] Pierre Courcelle suggested that this list only consisted of the Origenian works that Jerome had access to.[3] Rufinus mentioned his wish to translate the homilies on Numbers and Deuteronomy in the epilogue of his translation of Origen's commentaries on the Epistle to Romans (ca. 405/406).[4] In the letter to Ursacius, the dedicatee of his translation of Origen's homilies on Numbers (ca. 410), Rufinus once again talked about his expectation to translate "the little orations on Deuteronomy" (*in Deuteronomium oratiunculae*) if his health allowed, so that all Origen's writings about the Mosaic Law would be available in his translation.[5] Rufinus died in 411, and it is uncertain whether he had ever managed to carry out the translation.[6] In the middle of the sixth century, Cassiodorus in *Institutiones* referred to 4 (or 13) homilies of Origen on Deuteronomy "in which there was delicate exposition" available in his library at Vivarium.[7] Elsewhere in the same work, the senator mentioned "Origen's most eloquent homilies on the Octateuch contained in three books

---

1   Codex von der Goltz (Athos, Laura, 184 B 64), named after its major scholar and editor Eduard Freiherr von der Goltz, is a tenth-century manuscript of the Acts of the Apostles and the Epistles with a large number of marginal scholia. Cf. Caroline P. Hammond Bammel, "A New Witness to the Scholia from Origen in the Codex von der Goltz," *Origeniana Quinta*, ed. Robert J. Daly (Leuven: Leuven University Press, 1992), pp. 137-141. For the edition of the marginal annotations, see Eduard Freiherr von der Goltz, *Eine textkritische Arbeit des zehnten bezw. sechsten Jahrhunderts herausgegeben nach einem Kodex des Athosklosters Lawra* (Leipzig: J. C. Hinrich, 1899). Annotation no. 32 (in pp. 51-52) mentions "his seventh homily on Deuteronomy." The composer of these marginal annotations customarily referred to Origen by an unspecified third person singular pronoun.
2   "In Deuteronomio omeliae XIII." Jerome, *Epistula XXXIII*, CSEL 54, p. 257.
3   Pierre Courcelle, *Late Latin Writers and Their Greek Sources*, trans. Harry E. Wedeck (Cambridge: Harvard University Press, 1969).
4   "Quod si me Dominus inplere permiserit, redeam rursus et ad tua desideria, ut uel in Numerorum librum et Deuteronomii aliqua, Deo permittente, dicamus (hoc enim solum nobis de Eptateucho deest), uel de reliquis apostoli Pauli epistulis quae possumus, Domino dirigente, dictemus." Rufinus, *Epilogus in Origenis in Epistulam Pauli ad Romanos explanationum libros*, in *Der Römerbriefkommentar des Origenes: kritische Ausgabe der Übersetzung Rufins, Buch 7–10*, ed. Caroline P. Hammond Bammel (Freiburg: Herder, 1998), p. 862.
5   "Iam enim ex omnibus, quae in legem scripta repperi, solae, ut puto, in Deuteronomium desunt oratiunculae, quas, si Dominus iuuerit et sanitatem dederit oculis, cupimus reliquo corpori sociare..." Rufinus' Prologus to Origen, *Homiliae in Numeros*, GCS 30, p. 2.
6   Cf. C. P. Hammond, "The Last Ten Years of Rufinus's Life and the Date of his Move South from Aquileia," *The Journal of Theological Studies* 28 (1977): pp. 372-429.
7   "Reliqui etiam uobis praestante Domino, si legere uolueritis, omelias praedicti Origenis, id est, in Genesi XVI, in Exodo XII, in Leuitico XVI, in Numerorum XXVIIII, in Deuteronomio sermones IIII in quibus est minuta nimis et suptilis expositio, in Hiesu Naue XXVI, in Iudicum VIIII." *Cassiodori Senatoris Institutiones*, I.1.9, ed. R. A. B. Mynors. 2nd ed. (Oxford: Clarendon press, 1961), p. 15. Nautin cogently argued that the number IIII here could be a slip in copying for XIII, the number of the Origenian homilies on Deuteronomy given by Jerome in his letter to Paula. Pierre Nautin, *Origène*, p. 255. The *Monitum ad Origenis selecta in Deuteronomium* in PG 12, col. 805 cited "octo eius in Deuteronomium homilias" from the same passage of *Institutiones*, which must be a misreading of XIII for VIII from an unidentified manuscript.

(*in codicibus tribus*)," without specifying whether in Greek or in Latin.[1] This was the last trace of the transmission of Origen's homilies on Deuteronomy.

Despite this unfortunate disappearance, which decisively changed Christian exegetical history, there are two groups of sources available for us to glimpse Origen's interpretation of the fifth book of Moses. The first is Origen's fragmentary scholia, that is short explanatory notes, preserved in Greek biblical *catenae*. *Catena*, a genre that originated in Judaea-Palestine at the beginning of the sixth century, is an anthology of exegetical excerpts collected in chain (*catena*) from earlier works.[2] While most of published *catenae* of Origen are no more than philological notes for the purpose of elucidating the literal sense of the expounded biblical verses, a few indeed touch the moral or spiritual significance.[3] For example, in one scholium, the ox and the ass in Deut. 22:10 ("Thou shalt not plough with an ox and an ass together") are interpreted morally as the good and bad parts of human soul, and mystically as Israel and the gentiles.[4] Parallel exegesis can be found in Jerome's commentary on Isaiah, very likely taken from Origen.[5]

Another scholium proposes the comparability between the phrase that repetitively appears in Deuteronomy "Take heed to thyself" (Πρόσεχε σεαυτῷ, Deut. 4:9, 6:12, 8:11, 11:16, 12:13, 19:30, 15:9, 24:8) and the well-known Greek philosophical aphorism

---

1 "Item in Octateucho eloquentissimae nimis omeliae sunt Origenis in codicibus tribus." Cassiodorus, *Institutiones*, I.1.8, p. 14.

2 See Robert Devreesse, "Chaînes exégétiques grecques," *Dictionnaire de la Bible, Supplément I*, eds. Louis Pirot, André Robert, Jacques Briend, Édouard Cothenet (Paris: Letouzey & Ané, 1928), cols. 1084-1233; Gilles Dorival, "Des commentaires de l'Ecriture aux chaînes," *Le Monde Grec Ancien et la Bible, ed. Claude Mondésert* (Paris, Beauchesne: 1984), pp. 361-386; idem, "Biblical Catenae between Philology and History," *Commentaries, Catenae, and the Biblical Tradition: Papers from the Ninth Birmingham Colloquium on the Textual Criticism of the New Testament, in Conjunction with the COMPAUL Project*, ed. Hugh A. G. Houghton (Piscataway: Gorgias Press, 2016), pp. 68-81.

3 The editions of the fragments of Origen's scholiae on Deuteronomy, see PG 12, cols. 805-818; PG 17, cols. 23-36; Robert Devreesse, *Les anciens commentateurs grecs de l'Octateuque et des Rois, Fragments tirés des chaînes* (Vatican: Biblioteca Apostolica Vaticana, 1959), pp. 48-49.

4 PG 12, col. 813.

5 "Simul arat in boue et asino Ebion, dignus pro humilitate sensus. Paupertate nominis sui; qui sic recipit Euangelium, ut Iudaicarum superstitionum, quae in umbra et in imagine praecesserunt, caeremonias non relinquat. Beatus est autem qui seminat in eloquiis scripturarum tam ueteris quam noui instrumenti; et calcat aquas occidentis litterae, ut metat fructum spiritus uiuificantis. Bos iuxta anagogen refertur ad Israel, qui legis portauit iugum et mundum animal est. Asinus peccatorum onere praegrauatus, gentium populus accipitur, cui Dominus loquebatur: *Venite ad me omnes qui laboratis et onerati estis; et ego reficiam uos.*" Jerome, *Commentarii in Isaiam*, I.1.3, CCSL 73, ed. Mark Adriaen (Turnhout: Brepols, 1963), p. 9.

"Know thyself" (Γνῶθι σεαυτὸν).[1] After Origen, the Cappadocian Father Basil the Great (329/330–379) composed a homily on LXX Deut. 15:9 ("Take heed to thyself that there be not a secret thing in thine heart"), appealing for constant introspection and attentive contemplation of the soul, one's truer self than the outer body, and its creator.[2] Basil's homily represents part of the Christianized reception of the Delphic maxim.[3] Since it is very likely that Origen was the first author to explicitly connect "Know thyself" with the book of Deuteronomy, it is not impossible that Basil, who happened to be one of the editors of the Origenian anthology *Philocalia*, could have been directly inspired by him.[4] Rufinus translated Basil's homily into Latin, and his translation can be found in several early medieval manuscripts.[5]

The other group of evidence is the sporadic expositions of Deuteronomic verses that appear in Origen's extant tracts, homilies, and commentaries, which had potential influence on later Latin exegesis via translation. At least twice Origen implied a more com-

1 Robert Devreesse, *Les anciens commentateurs grecs*, p. 49. Origen could have inherited this idea from two Alexandrian predecessors, Philo and Clement: "Evermore be coming to know thyself, as Moses teaches thee in many places, saying 'Give heed to thyself,' for in this way shalt thou perceive those to whom it befits thee to shew obedience and those to whom it befits thee to give commands." Philo of Alexandria, *On the Migration of Abraham*, II, in *Philo Volume IV: On the Confusion of Tongues; On the Migration of Abraham; Who Is the Heir of Divine Things? On Mating with the Preliminary Studies*, Loeb Classical Library 261, trans. F. H. Colson, G. H. Whitaker (Cambridge: Harvard University Press, 1932), pp. 136-137. "Moses, transmitting 'Know yourself' with greater clarity, often says, 'Keep an eye on yourself.'" Clement of Alexandria, *Stromateis*, II.15.3, in *Stromateis: Books 1–3*, The Fathers of the Church 85, trans. John Ferguson (Washington, D.C.: Catholic University of America Press, 1991), p. 206.
2 Heinrich Marti, *Nosce te ipsum... animam tuam... Deum: Predigt 3 des Basilius Caesariensis in der Übersetzung des Rufinus: kritische Ausgabe des lateinischen Textes mit Einleitung, griechischer Fassung und deutscher Übersetzung* (Berlin: De Gruyter, 2012).
3 Cf. Pierre Courcelle, *Connais-toi toi-même: De Socrate à Saint Bernard* (Paris: Études augustiniennes, 1974–1975), vol. 1, pp. 97-111.
4 A case study of Origen's influence on Basil's exegetical thought, see Peter Martens, "Interpreting Attentively: The Ascetic Character of Biblical Exegesis according to Origen and Basil of Caesarea," *Origeniana Octava*, ed. Lorenzo Perrone (Leuven: Leuven University Press, 2003), pp. 1115-1121.
5 Paris, BnF, Lat. 10593 ("Century VI, Origin doubtless Italy," in CLA, V.603); Città del Vaticano, Biblioteca Apostolica, Vaticanus Reginensis lat. 141 ("Nordfrankreich (Saint-Denis?), IX. Jh., 1. Hälfte," in Bischoff, *Katalog*, 6624, III, p. 423); Trier, Stadtbibliothek, Historisches Archiv 1245/597 ("9. Jahrh.," in M. Keuffer, A. Becker, G. Kentenich, *Beschreibendes Verzeichnis der Handschriften der Stadtbibliothek zu Trier* (Trier: F. Lintz, 1888–1931; reprinted by Wiesbaden: Harrassowitz, 1973), vol. 8, pp. 256-257). Mistakenly attributed to Zeno of Verona, the same homily was also preserved in a Rheims manuscript that was copied ca. 800, once owned by Hincmar, but got burned in 1774 (Heinrich Marti, *Nosce te ipsum*, p. XXV).

plete discussion of certain Deuteronomic verses elsewhere, probably in his lost homilies.[1]
The exegesis of Deuteronomy that appears in his extant works may thus have shown up
in his lost homilies on Deuteronomy in a more elaborate form. In Homily 7 on Leviticus,
Origen interpreted the beautiful female war captive (Deut. 21:11) as the secular wisdom
(*rationabilis aliqua disciplina*) that is allowed to be embraced by Christians (taken as
wife) after the infidel and impure element have been removed (her hair and nails being
taken).[2] The same exegesis was adopted by later Latin authors including Jerome, Sido-
nius Apollinaris, Isidore, Bede, Hrabanus Maurus, and Alvarus of Cordoba.[3]

Two more examples from Origen's homilies on Jeremiah: for LXX Deut. 19:15 ("By
the mouth of two witnesses, or by the mouth of three witnesses, shall every word be
established"), Origen understood the two and three witnesses respectively as "New and
Old Testaments" and "Gospel, Prophets, and Epistles";[4] for LXX Deut. 16:21 ("You will

---

1 "But these things [in Deut. 25:5-6] ought to be investigated more completely in their own places."
   Origen, *Commentary on the Epistle to the Romans*, VI.7.14, in *Commentary on the Epistle to
   the Romans: Books 6–10*, The Fathers of the Church 104, trans. Thomas P. Scheck (Washington,
   D.C.: Catholic University of America Press, 2002), p. 26; "The matters related to this [Deut. 2:30],
   however, would more properly be examined in the books on Deuteronomy." Origen, *Commentary on
   the Gospel According to John*, XXXII.222, in *Commentary on the Gospel according to John: Books
   13–32*, The Fathers of the Church 89, trans. Ronald Heine (Washington, D.C.: Catholic University of
   America Press, 1993), p. 382.

2 "Scriptum est in Deuteronomio: 'si' inquit 'exieris ad bellum aduersum inimicos tuos, et uideris ibi
   mulierem decora specie, et concupieris eam, adsumes eam, et rades omnem pilum capitis eius et
   ungulas eius, et indues eam uestimentis lugubribus; et sedebit in domo lugens patrem suum et matrem
   suam et domum paternam suam; et post triginta dies erit tibi uxor.' Sed nunc non est propositum, ut
   haec, quae in testimonium uocata sunt, explanentur; sed propterea diximus, quia et hic de ungulis
   mentio facta est. Verum tamen et ego frequenter 'exiui ad bellum contra inimicos meos et uidi ibi'
   in praedam 'mulierem decora specie.' Quaecumque enim bene et rationabiliter dicta inuenimus apud
   inimicos nostros, si quid apud illos sapienter et scienter dictum legimus, oportet nos mundare id et
   ab scientia, quae apud illos est, auferre et resecare omne quod emortuum et inane est - hoc enim sunt
   omnes capilli capitis et ungulae mulieris ex inimicorum spoliis adsumptae - et ita demum facere
   eam nobis uxorem, cum iam nihil ex illis, quae per infidelitatem mortua dicuntur, habuerit, nihil in
   capite habeat mortuum, nihil in manibus, ut neque sensibus neque actibus immundum aliquid aut
   mortuum gerat. Nihil enim mundum habent mulieres hostium nostrorum, quia nulla est apud illos
   sapientia, cui immunditia aliqua non sit admixta... Nos uero, quibus militia spiritalis est et 'arma non
   carnalia, sed potentia Deo ad destruenda consilia,' 'decora' mulier si repperta fuerit apud hostes et
   rationabilis aliqua disciplina, hoc modo purificabimus eam, quo superius diximus." Origen, *Homiliae
   in Leuiticum*, I.1, GCS 29, pp. 390-391.

3 See the fine survey in Henri de Lubac, *Medieval Exegesis: The Four Senses of Scripture* (Grand
   Rapids: William B. Eerdmans, 1998–2009), vol. 1, trans. Mark Sebanc, pp. 211–224. De Lubac
   misses Bede: "At contra mulier captiua ut uiro israhelitae nubere queat, mundatus a lepra ut
   ecclesiae communicare mereatur, omnes sui corporis pilos praecipiuntur eradere quia uidelicet
   omnis sapientium cogitatio quae bona placens et perfecta est saluatur in perpetuum et apud dominum
   est merces eius stultorum uero prauorum que quasi dei aspectibus indigna radix operum cogitatio
   paenitendo debet excidi." Bede, *In Lucae euangelium expositio*, VI.21, CCSL 120, ed. David Hurst
   (Turnhout: Brepols, 1960), p. 366.

4 "*In ore duorum uel trium testium stabit omne uerbum*, magis conuenit ad interpretantis probationem,
   quam ad quorumcumque hominum numerum: ut firmem uerbum intellectus mei, accipiens duos testes
   de nouo et ueteri Testamento, accipiens tres testes de Euangelio, de Prophetia, de Apostolo." Origen,
   Homiliae in Ieremiam secundum translationem Hieronymi, I, PL 25, col. 589.

not plant every tree near the altar of the Lord your God, and you will not make a wood"),
Origen interpreted the fruitless trees only for delight as the useless words and thoughts of
heresies.[1] Through Jerome's translation, both expositions circulated in the early medieval
west (for the detail, see below).

Judging from his extant works, an important theme in Origen's exegetical interest
in Deuteronomy is the Christian-Jewish relationship. Two verses in the Song of Moses
(Deut. 32:1-43) emerge repetitively as his interpretive objects. One of them is Deut.
32:8-9. Origen took it as a revelation that God divided the nations among the children of
Adam and assigned them by lot to "the angels of God"[2] according to merit and strength,
and distinguished Israel from the nations by keeping them as his own portion and
inheritance.[3] But Origen offered a particular interpretation for Israel. According to him,
"the Israel according to the flesh" used to be God's portion but have "been dispersed
through all the nations" for their sins. Meanwhile, Christians, "gentiles in the flesh but
Israel in spirit" became Israel by "seeing God in mind" *(mente Deum uidendo)* and were

---

1   "Sunt autem alii qui ascendunt super colles, et fiunt subtus omne lignum non fructiferum, sed
    nemorosum: siquidem alterius naturae est lignum, quod ubertate fertile est, alterius quod tantum
    abundat fronde foliorum. In nemoribus et lucis nemo plantat ficum, nemo uineam, nemo arbores
    fertiles, sed oblectationi uisus tantum ligna frondentia. Tales sunt haeretici, qui orationem suam
    uerborum decore componunt, non ut conuertant audientes a uitiis, sed ut delectent. Igitur qui
    istiusmodi seductione persuasus est, abiit subtus omne lignum. Simulque attende quare non dixerit,
    omne lignum, et tacuerit, neque rursum addiderit omne lignum fructiferum, sed significanter
    adiecerit: subtus omne lignum frondosum. Quamobrem si intelligas cur praecipiatur in Lege: *Non
    plantabis omne lignum iuxta altare Domini Dei tui, nec facies nemus.*" Origen, *Homiliae in Ieremiam*,
    XIV, PL 25, col. 690.
2   "The angels of God" (ἀγγέλων θεοῦ) is the reading in the majority of Septuagint manuscripts, also
    attested by a Qumran fragment of Hebrew Deuteronomy (4QDeut) which reads "sons of God." But
    the Masoretic text, the Samaritan Pentateuch, and the Septuagint texts of Symmachus, Aquila, and
    Theodotion support the reading "sons of Israel," which the Latin Vulgate also adopts (*iuxta numerum
    filiorum Israel*). For a general survey of this issue, see David E. Stevens, "Does Deuteronomy 32:8
    Refer to 'Sons of God' or 'Sons of Israel'?" *Bibliotheca Sacra* 154 (1997): pp. 131-141.
3   "Non ergo fortuito arbitrandum est per sortem uenisse illi quidem angelo illam gentem suscipere,
    uerbi causa, Aegyptiorum, alii autem Idumaeorum et alii Moabitarum et alii Indiam uel
    unamquamque nationem earum, quae sunt super terram; sed et ibi, etiamsi 'secundum numerum
    angelorum Dei' dicantur sorte 'gentes' esse diuisae, tamen illa sors, sicut in hominibus diximus quia
    Dei iudicium, quod in occulto est, sors pandit in publico, talis etiam ibi fuisse credenda est, qua pro
    merito et uirtute sua unusquisque angelus illam uel illam gentem in diuisione susceperit." Origen,
    Homiliae in Iesu Nave, XXIII.3, GCS 30, p. 433. Also cf. Origen's homily 13 on Ezekiel, where he
    suggested that both the king of Tyre (in Ezekiel 28) and the king of the Assyrians (in Isaiah 10) were
    angels to whom God allotted nations. See Origen, *Homiliae in Ezechielem secundum translationem
    Hieronymi*, XIII.1, GCS 33, ed. Wilhelm Baehrens (Leipzig: J. C. Hinrichs, 1925).

circumcised in heart.[1] The spiritual journey inborn in the Christian faith is a return from the portion of angels back to that of God.[2]

The other verse is LXX Deut. 32:21 ("They have provoked me to jealousy with that which is not God, they have exasperated me with their idols; and I will provoke them to jealousy with them that are no nation, I will anger them with a nation void of understanding"). Origen understood it as a prophetic revelation about "the election of the unmindful nation" (i.e. the conversion of Christians to God) on the account of the sins of the earlier people (i.e. idolatry committed by the Hebrews).[3] The church is God's retribution to the Synagogue for its worship of idols.[4]

Origen was also among the earliest authors to explicitly interpret LXX Deut. 28:44 ("he shall be the head, and thou shalt be the tail") as a prophecy about the rise of Christians and the fall of Jews.[5] For Deut. 23:3-8, he read the Ammonites and the Moabites who are

---

1 "Verum, ne aestimes haec tantum ad illum dici 'Istrahel', qui 'secundum carnem' est, multo magis haec ad te dicuntur, qui Istrahel effectus es mente Deum uidendo et circumcisus es corde, non carne. Nam et si in carne gentes sumus, in spiritu Istrahel sumus, propter eum, qui dixit: 'pete a me, et dabo tibi gentes haereditatem tuam et possessionem tuam terminos terrae' et propter eum, qui iterum dixit: 'Pater, omnia mea tua sunt et tua mea, et glorificatus sum in his'; si tamen ita agas, ut dignus sis 'pars' esse Dei et in 'funiculo haereditatis eius' metiri. Alioquin si indigne agas, exemplo tibi sint illi, qui ad hoc uocati fuerant, ut essent 'pars' Dei, et peccatis suis hoc meruerunt, ut 'dispergerentur per omnes gentes.'" Origen, *Homiliae in Exodum secundum translationem Rufini*, VIII.2, GCS 29, ed. Wilhelm Baehrens (Leipzig: J. C. Hinrichs, 1920).

2 Cf. Origen, *Homily on Jeremiah*, V.3, in *Homilies on Jeremiah, Homily on 1 Kings 28*, The Fathers of the Church 97, trans. Smith John Clark (Washington: Catholic University of America Press, 1998), pp. 42-43. This homily, available in Greek, is not among Jerome's translation of Origen's homilies on Jeremiah. But very similar expression can be found in Jerome's commentary on Ephesians, probably under the influence of Origen: "Verbum haereditatis et sortis, per quas in Christi partem uenimus, ostendit nos de alia potestate ad aliam transmigrasse: et secundum illud quod in Deuteronomio scriptum est: Quando diuidebat Altissimus gentes, cum disseminaret filios Adam, de angelorum ditione ad partem Domini esse translatos. Et illi quidem aliena, et sibi uel commissa uel usurpata tenuerunt. Iste uero recepit sua: et ascendens in altum captiuam duxit captiuitatem, id est, eos qui ante capti fuerant in perditionem, ipse cepit ad uitam, ut reduceret in excelsum: et quodammodo est capta captiuitas, dum per secundam captiuitatem qui prius capti fuerant, liberantur." Jerome, *Commentaria in Epistolam ad Ephesios*, I.1, PL 26, cols. 454-455.

3 "Sed et in Deuteronomii cantico per prophetiam designatur pro peccatis prioris populi futura esse insensatae gentis electio, non alia utique quam haec, quae per Christum facta est. Sic enim ait: 'Exacerbauerunt me in simulacris suis, et ego in zelo concitabo eos, in gente insipiente inritabo eos.' Est ergo satis euidenter agnoscere, quemammodum Hebraei, qui deum 'exacerbasse' dicuntur in his, qui non sunt dii, et inritasse eum 'in simulacris suis,' inritati sunt et ipsi in zelotypia per 'gentem insipientem,' quam deus 'elegit' per aduentum Christi Iesu et discipulos eius." Origen, *De principiis secundum translationem Rufini*, IV.1.4, GCS 22, ed. Paul Koetschau (Leipzig: J. C. Hinrichs, 1913).

4 "Quid est quod synagoga accipit de ecclesia? Puto illud intelligi posse, quod idem Moyses scribit, dicens: 'Ego in non gentem in aemulationem uos inducam, in gentem insipientem in iram uos concitabo.' Et synagoga ergo de ecclesia istud mercedis accipit, ut ultra idola non colat. Videns enim eos, qui ex gentibus sunt, ita ad Deum conuersos esse, ut ultra idola nesciant, Deum praeter unum neminem uenerentur, ipsa erubescit idola ultra iam colere." Origen, *Homiliae in Exodum*, II.4, GCS 29, p. 160.

5 "Et facti sumus propter fidem Christi nos 'sursum,' ille autem populus, qui permansit incredulus, 'deorsum,' secundum Deuteronomii prophetiam. Si qui ergo habet in se Christum, qui est 'omnium caput,' hic efficitur 'in caput;' illi enim negauerunt Christum Iesum et effecti sunt in caudam et qui erant 'primi,' facti sunt 'nouissimi.'" Origen, *Homiliae in Iesu Naue*, VII.5, GCS 30, p. 332.

forbidden to enter the church of God forever as "the generation of the carnal law" (*carnalis generatio legis*),[1] namely Jews; the Egyptians and Idumaeans who are allowed to enter after the third generation as the gentiles after conversion.[2]

Contra Iudaeos is a consistent theme in Origen's biblical interpretation.[3] But the sporadic comments on Deuteronomic verses listed above may more specifically reflect a consciousness of exegetical competition for the fifth book of the Hebrew Bible between Jewish and Christian intellectual groups. Around the time when Origen delivered his homilies in Caesarea, the Sifre to Deuteronomy, which, as a scholar put it, "misses no opportunity to praise the people (of Israel) and to stress God's positive relationship to them, emphasizing the unbroken nature of this relationship,"[4] had just reached or was about to reach its final redaction in the mid-third century after a century-long accumulation of Rabbinic oral tradition. In his *Contra Celsum* (composed in 249), when Origen refuted Celsus *on behalf of* Judaism, he did not forget to emphasize that Christians could defend the Mosaic Law better than the Jews.[5]

However, compared with all the interpretations of Deuteronomic verses that we have surveyed above, it was the exegetical principle for Deuteronomy proposed by Origen in his *On First Principles* (composed ca. 229–230) that would shed a more decisive shadow over the later Christian exegetical history:

It is not irrelevant that Moses heard from God what was written in the law of

---

1   "Neque enim iste sensus aut haec voluntas fuerat legis, ut carnaliter generaret, sed sopitur lex, ut talis posteritas generetur, quae 'non intret in ecclesiam Domini.' 'Ammanitae enim' inquit 'et Moabitae non introibunt in ecclesiam Domini usque in tertiam et quartam progeniem et usque in saeculum;' designans quod carnalis generatio legis non intret in ecclesiam Christi nec tertia generatione pro trinitate nec quarta pro evangeliis nec in saeculum, nisi forte post praesens saeculum, cum 'plenitudo gentium introierit, et sic omnis Istrahel salvus fuerit factus.'" Origen, *Homiliae in Genesim secundum translationem Rufini*, V.5, ed. W.A. Baehrens, GCS 29 (Leipzig: J. C. Hinrichs, 1920), p. 64.

2   "Denique hi, qui in hoc saeculo, ut Israelitae essent, a deo formati sunt et indignam uitam generis sui nobilitate gesserunt atque ab omni familiae suae generositate deciderunt, isti quodammodo ex uasis honoris pro incredulitate sua in saeculo uenturo in uasa contumeliae conuertentur; et rursum multi, qui in hac uita inter Aegyptia uel Idumaea deputati sunt uasa, Israelitarum fide ac conuersatione suscepta, cum opera Israelitarum fecerint, 'ecclesiam domini ingressi' 'in reuelatione filiorum dei' uasa honoris existent." Origen, *De principiis*, III.1.23, GCS 22, p. 241.

3   See A. J. Philippou, "Origen and the Early Jewish-Christian Debate," *Greek Orthodox Theological Review* (15) 1970: pp.140-152. Peter Martens, *Origen and Scripture*, pp. 133-160. Origen's encounter with Rabbinic culture in Palestine, see the classic study of N. R. M. de Lange, *Origen and the Jews: Studies in Jewish-Christian Relations in Third-century Palestine* (Cambridge: Cambridge University Press, 1976).

4   Reuven Hammer, *Sifre: A Tannaitic Commentary on the Book of Deuteronomy* (New Haven: Yale University Press, 1986).

5   "If the Jew were to defend them and support the scripture, we would give our defence, either by a similar argument or an even better one, of what he regards as abuse and threats uttered by Jesus. Moreover, where the Mosaic law is concerned we are better able to give a defence than the Jew, in that we have been taught by Jesus to understand the law more intelligently." Origen, *Contra Celsum*, II.76, trans. Henry Chadwick (Cambridge: Cambridge University Press, 1953), p. 124.

Leviticus, but in Deuteronomy the people became Moses' audience and learnt from him what they could not hear from God. That is why the book is called Deuteronomy, namely the second law. Some people will see it signify the fact that when the first law given through Moses ceases, a second legislation appears to be constituted which was delivered by Moses specially to his successor Joshua, whom people certainly believed to be the figure of our Savior and by whose second law, that is the evangelical precepts, all are brought to perfection.

But it should be considered whether there is more significance in the fact that the legislation is declared more clearly and manifestly in Deuteronomy than in those books written first, so that the more gleaming and glorious second coming "in the glory of his Father" will be indicated by the Savior's [first] coming which he fulfilled in humility when he "took upon the form of a servant." The figure of Deuteronomy will be fulfilled in the second coming, when all the saints live by the laws of that "eternal gospel" in the Kingdom of Heaven. Just as His [first] coming has now fulfilled the law that "has a shadow of the good things to come," through the glorious [second] coming, the shadow of this [first] coming will be fulfilled and brought to perfection.[1]

Focusing on its "secondness" nature, Origen in the passage above offered two approaches to interpreting Deuteronomy. The first is to see the book as the end of the first law and the foreshadowing of Gospel, and its recipient Joshua as the foreshadowing of Christ; the second is to claim that Deuteronomy foreshadows the second coming of Christ in the Last Judgment, just as the law in the first four mosaic books prefigures his first coming in the Incarnation. Either hermeneutical framework transforms Deuteronomy from a book of divine legislation for Israel to that of hidden evangelical messages for Christians.

---

1 "Ubi ne illud quidem otiosum uidebitur, quod Moyses quidem audit a deo ea, quae in Leuitici lege descripta sunt, populus uero in Deuteronomio auditor Moyseos efficitur et ab illo discit ea, quae a deo audire non potuit. Propterea enim uelut secunda lex Deuteronomium dicitur, quod nonnullis significare uidebitur hoc ipsum, quod, cessante 'lege' prima, quae 'per Moysen data est,' uideatur secunda legislatio deformari, quae specialiter a Moyseo traditur Iesu, successori eius; qui utique formam seruare creditur saluatoris nostri, cuius secunda lege, id est praeceptis euangelicis, ad perfectum omnia perducuntur. Sed uidendum est ne forte magis illud indicare uideatur, quod sicut in Deuteronomio euidentior et manifestior legislatio declaratur quam in his, quae primo scripta sunt, ita et ab eo aduentu saluatoris, quem in humilitate conpleuit, cum 'formam serui suscepit,' clarior ille et gloriosior secundus 'in gloria patris eius' indicetur aduentus, et in illo forma Deuteronomii conpleatur, cum in regno caelorum sancti omnes 'aeterni' illius 'euangelii' legibus uiuent; et sicut nunc adueniens 'legem' repleuit eam, quae 'umbram habet futurorum bonorum,' ita et per illum gloriosum aduentum inplebitur et ad perfectum perducetur huius aduentus umbra." Origen, *De principiis*, IV.3.12–13, GCS 22, p. 343. For a theological analysis of this passage, see Shawn W. J. Keough, "The Eternal Gospel: Origen's Eschatological Exegesis," *Interpretation of the Bible in Late Antiquity: Proceedings of the Montreal Colloquium in Honour of Charles Kannengiesser, 11–13 October 2006*, eds. Lorenzo DiTommaso, Lucian Turcescu (Leiden: Brill, 2008), pp. 101-120.

This general interpretation of Deuteronomy creatively offered by Origen found little echo in Greek patristic exegesis after him. Theodoret of Cyrus, the last great exegete of the Antiochian school, at the very beginning of his *Questions on Deuteronomy* (composed ca. 419) explicitly refuted the idea that Deuteronomy is the second law, and instead understood it as "a summary of the legislation and the events of Exodus, Leviticus, and Numbers."[1] What is implicit is Theodoret's discreet, if not negative, attitude toward the allegorical reading of the Hebrew Bible.[2] If the refutation from the opposite exegetical school is predictable, the same Origenian interpretation of Deuteronomy is also absent in the works of the Alexandrian Father Cyril (ca. 376–444).[3] Procopius of Gaza (ca. 475–538) also did not include it in the *catena* on the Octateuch that he composed, although Origen is among his sources.[4]

The accusation of heresy against the theological doctrines presented in *On First Principles* in the fourth century must play a major role in the poor reception of the exegesis of Deuteronomy in it among Greek Fathers.[5] However, it had a much better fortune in the Latin west, through the transmission of Jerome.

***

But before turning to Jerome, we need to deal with a thorny question: Did the Lyon Annotator use Origen's works as a direct source?

While fundamental, the influence of Origenian exegesis of Deuteronomy on later Latin authors was only indirect in some cases. For example, the Christian interpretation of Deut. 15:9 ("Take heed to thyself..."), which may have originated with Origen, as we have demonstrated above, was known in the Latin west, but mainly through Basil's homily, as we can find in the quotation from the latter by Ambrose of Milan and Paschasius

---

1   Theodoret of Cyprus, *The Questions on the Octateuch*, "On Deuteronomy," I.1, Greek text revised by John. F. Petruccione, trans. Robert C. Hill (Washington, D.C.: Catholic University of America Press, 2007), vol. 2, pp. 170-173.

2   "I have, in fact, encountered various such commentaries: some I found taking refuge in allegory with considerable relish, while others make the inspired composition resemble historical narratives of a certain type with the result that the commentary represents a case rather for Jews than the household of the faith. In my opinion, it is for a wise man to shun the extreme tendencies of both the former and the latter: the things that are relevant to stories of the past should be applied to them even today, whereas the prophecies about Christ the Lord, about the Church from the nations, the evangelical lifestyle, and the apostolic preaching should not be applied to anything else, as Jews with their proclivity to malice love to do and contrive a defense for their disbelief." Idem, *Commentary on the Psalms*, "Preface," in *Commentary on the Psalms: 1–72*, trans. Robert C. Hill (Washington, D.C.: Catholic University of America Press, 2000), pp. 40-41. Cf. Agnethe Siquans, "Theodoret von Kyros als Ausleger des Deuteronomiums," *Das Deuteronomium*, ed. Georg Braulik (Bern: Peter Lang, 2003), pp. 343-360.

3   Cyril of Alexandria, *De adoratione et cultu in spiritu et veritate*, PG 68, cols, 133-1126; *Glaphyrorum in Deuteronomium liber*, PG 69, cols. 643-78.

4   Procopius of Gaza, *Commentarii in Deuteronomium*, PG 87.1, cols. 893-991.

5   Cf. Elizabeth A. Clark, *The Origenist Controversy: The Cultural Construction of an Early Christian Debate* (Princeton: Princeton University Press, 1992), pp. 85-158.

Radbertus.[1]

Similarly, the exposition of the ox and the ass in Deut. 22:10 as Israel and the gentiles was received in the west first via Jerome's adoption in his commentary on Isaiah (see above), and then via Isidore's quotation from Jerome as part of Deuteronomy Entry 6 of his *Expositio in uetus testamentum*.[2] The exposition of the same verse in the Lyon Annotations is a loose abbreviation of Isidore's Deuteronomy Entry 6.[3]

Furthermore, Isidore's commentary on Deuteronomy in *Expositio* also contains three pieces (all discussed above) drawn directly from Origen's homilies (via Jerome's and Rufinus' translation). In the Lyon Annotations, we find parallel exegesis in two of them (Table 4.1) .

---

1   "Vnde etiam in Lege scriptum est: *Adtende tibi, ne fiat uerbum absconditum in corde tuo.* Tibi, inquit, adtende; non utique dicit pecuniae tuae, non possessionibus tuis, non uiribus corporis, sed animo tuo ac menti tuae, unde omnia consilia, facta cogitationes que manant. Tibi ergo adtende ibi, ubi potiorem esse te nosti. Nosce te ipsum, quod Apollini Pythio adsignant gentiles uiri, quasi ipse auctor fuerit huius sententiae, cum de nostro usurpatum ad sua transferant et longe anterior Moyses fuerit, qui scripsit librum Deuteronomii, quam philosophi qui ista finxerunt." Ambrose, *Expositio psalmi cxviii*, II.13, CSEL 62, ed. Michael Petschenig (Vienna: Verlag der Österreichischen Akademie der Wissenschaften, 1913). "Unde Moyses in lege: Attende tibi inquit ne fiat uerbum absconditum in corde. Tibi inquit attende et non utique pecuniae tuae non possessionibus non uiribus tuis sed animo tuo ac menti tuae unde omnia consilia et facta cogitationes que manant. Ibi enim te attende ubi potiorem te nosti. Quod Apollini Phitio gentiles assignant quasi ipse auctor fuerit huius sententiae qua dicitur: Nosce te ipsum cum de nostro ut credimus usurpatu ad sua translata sit. Quoniam longe anterior Moyses quam hi philosophi qui ista finxerunt." Paschasius Radbertus, *Expositio in lamentationes Hieremiae,* III, CCCM 85, ed. Beda Paulus (Turnhout: Brepols, 1988).

2   "In boue quippe simul et asino arat, qui sic recipit Euangelium, ut Iudaicarum superstitionum, quae in umbra et imagine praecesserant, caeremonias non relinquat. In bouis nomine populus ex circumcisione positus sub iugo legis, accipitur; in asino autem populus gentium, pertinens ad Euangelium. Item nonnunquam in boue bene operantium uita, in asino stultorum uecordia figuratur. Quid est ergo: Non arabis simul in boue et asino? Ac si diceret: Fatuum sapienti in praedicatione non socies, ne per eum qui rem implere non ualet, et illi qui praeualet obsistas. Bouem quippe et asinum, si necesse sit, unusquisque sine detrimento operis jungit. Sapientem uero et stultum, non ut unus praecipiat, et alter obtemperet, sed ut pariter aequali potestate annuntient uerbum Dei, non sine scandalo quisque comites facit." Isidore, *Expositio in uetus testamentum*, V.6, PL 83, col. 361.

3   "Id est stultum quemlibet sapienti in predicatione ne socies. Aliter: Ita religionem cristianam fide et opere retine, ut cum subprestitionibus Iudoerum nullam societatem abere uelis, ne utroque pede claudus efficiaris." Paris, BnF, NAL 1740, fol. 59r.

Table 4.1   Textual comparison among Origen, Isidore, and the Lyon Annotations

Deut.	Origen	Isidore (*Expositio in uetus testamentum*, V)	The Lyon Annotations (Paris, BnF, NAL 1740)
16:21	Sunt autem alii qui ascendunt super colles, et fiunt subtus omne lignum non fructiferum... In nemoribus et lucis nemo plantat ficum, nemo uineam, nemo arbores fertiles, sed oblectationi uisus tantum ligna frondentia. **Tales sunt haeretici**, qui orationem suam uerborum decore componunt, non ut conuertant audientes a uitiis, sed ut delectent. (*Homiliae in Ieremiam*, XIV, PL 25, col. 690)	Nemus frondentes arbores et infructuosae sunt, sola delectatione uisus plantatae. **Tales sunt et gentiles**, qui rationem suam uerborum decore componunt, ut non conuertantur a uitiis, sed delectentur, atque istiusmodi subiectione persuadeant. (Entry 3, PL 83, col. 360)	*Lucus* est arbor infructuosa que foliis redundat, fructum nullum profert: significat sapientiam huius mundi superuacua uerbositate adornata, sed fructum fidei et bone operationis non habentem; illi enim lucum uel quamlibet arborem infructuosa *iuxta altare domini plantare* conantur qui in sinceritatem fidei, rationes at superuacuas questiones opponere satagunt; **ex qua occasione diuerse hereses in ecclesia emerserunt.** (fol. 47r)
19:15	*In ore duorum uel trium testium stabit omne uerbum*, magis conuenit ad interpretantis probationem, quam ad quorumcumque hominum numerum: ut firmem uerbum intellectus mei, accipiens duos testes de nouo et ueteri Testamento, accipiens tres testes de Euangelio, de Propheta, de Apostolo. (*Homiliae in Ieremiam*, I, PL 25, col. 589)	Vnde magis conuenit ad probationem, ut affirmem uerbum intellectus mei: Adhibeo etiam duos testes, Nouum et Vetus Testamentum; adhibeo etiam et tres, Euangelium, Prophetam, et Apostolum, sicque stabit omne uerbum. (Entry 13, PL 83, col. 364)	Iam superius in hoc libro premissum est quod nemo debeat condemnari uelut hereticus nisi quem lex et Euangelium condemnauerit. (fol. 33r)
21:10	... Nihil enim mundum habent mulieres hostium nostrorum, quia nulla est apud illos sapientia, cui immunditia aliqua non sit admixta... Nos uero, quibus militia spiritalis est et 'arma non carnalia, sed potentia Deo ad destruenda consilia,' 'decora' mulier si repperta fuerit apud hostes et rationabilis aliqua disciplina, hoc modo purificabimus eam, quo superius diximus. (*Homiliae in Leuiticum*, VII.6, GCS 29, pp. 390-391)	Alii putauerunt hanc mulierem decoram specie, rationabilem aliquam disciplinam significare, quae sapienter dicta inuenitur apud gentiles. Hanc igitur a nobis repertam, oportet de ea primum auferre et resecare omnem superstitionis ejus immunditiam, et sic eam in studio ueritatis assumere. Nihil enim mundum habent disciplinae gentilium, quia nulla apud infideles sapientia est cui immunditia aliqua uel superstitio, non sit admixta. (Entry 14, PL 83, col. 368)	No parallel

As we will see in Chapter 6, *Expositio* constitutes a major source for the Lyon Annotations. But as highlighted in bold in Table 4.1, the exposition of Deut. 16:21 in the Lyon Annotations is closer to Origen's original text (fruitless plant as heretics) than Isidore's version (as pagans). Does this suggest that the Lyon Annotator used Origen's *Homiliae in Ieremiam* as a direct source?

Origen's homilies on certain Old Testament books were available at Lyon when the Annotations were composed and copied. Lyon, BM, 402 (CLA, VI.770; Bischoff, *Katalog*, 2547b), one of Leidrad's personal manuscripts (cf. Chapter 3.1), contains Origen's homilies on Joshua, Judges, and Kings in Rufinus' translation. Besides, Leidrad made a number of folios (Lyon, BM, 443, fols. 7-11, 77 and 227-331) produced by the Lyon scriptorium in order to emend an old codex (Lyon, BM, 443 + Paris, BnF, NAL 1591; Bischoff, *Katalog*, 2549a) which contains Origen's homilies on Genesis, Exodus, and Leviticus.[1] It is possible that Origen's *Homiliae in Numeros* was not available to the composer of the Lyon Annotations, since while Deut. 1-3 extensively repeats the account in Numbers, the allegorical exegesis in Origen's *Homiliae in Numeros* is totally absent in the Annotations.[2]

Proximity seems to exist between Origen's *Homiliae in Exodum* and the Lyon Annotations in two places, although it is difficult to determine whether they are really directly related (Table 4.2) .

Table 4.2 Textual comparison between Origen's *Homiliae in Exodum* and the Lyon Annotations

Deut.	Origen, *Homiliae in Exodum* (GCS 29)	The Lyon Annotations (Paris, BnF, NAL 1740)
But the Lord's portion is his people, Jacob the lot of his inheritance. (32:9)	Verum, ne aestimes haec tantum ad illum dici 'Istrahel', qui 'secundum carnem' est, multo magis haec ad te dicuntur, qui Istrahel effectus es mente Deum uidendo et circumcisus es corde, non carne... si tamen ita agas, ut dignus sis 'pars' esse Dei et in 'funiculo haereditatis eius' metiri. Alioquin si indigne agas, exemplo tibi sint illi, qui ad hoc uocati fuerant, ut essent 'pars' Dei, et peccatis suis hoc meruerunt, ut 'dispergerentur per omnes gentes.' (VIII.2, pp. 220-221)	Pars autem Domini: non tantum carnalis Israel uel Iacob sed potius spiritalis Iacob uitiorum subplantator et per fidem uidens Deum accipiendum est. (86r)
They have provoked me with that which was no god, and have angered me with their vanities, and I will provoke them with that which is no people, and will vex them with a foolish nation. (32:21)	Quid est quod synagoga accipit de ecclesia? Puto illud intelligi posse, quod idem Moyses scribit, dicens: 'Ego in non gentem in aemulationem uos inducam, in gentem insipientem in iram uos concitabo.' Et synagoga ergo de ecclesia istud mercedis accipit, ut ultra idola non colat. Videns enim eos, qui ex gentibus sunt, ita ad Deum conuersos esse, ut ultra idola nesciant, Deum praeter unum neminem uenerentur, ipsa erubescit idola ultra iam colere. (II.4, p. 160)	Hoc est in idolis, et ego prouocabo eos in gentibus quae non sunt gens Dei, in quibus dispersi eos. (87r)

---

1 Cf. Louis Holtz, "Leidrat, évêque de Lyon," p. 316, 320.

2 Hrabanus quoted Origen's *Homiliae in Numeros* in his commentary on Deuteronomy for at least five times, cf. Silvia Cantelli, *Hrabani Mauri opera exegetica*, vol. 2, pp. 553-576. According to Vercelli, Archivio Capitolare, 153 (Bischoff, *Katalog*, 7008), each of these five quotations was source-marked as either "AD" or "ADA."

So, back to the question whether the Lyon Annotator used Origen's works as a direct source: Judging from extant evidence, the most reasonable answer is a cautious "possibly." However, the Origenian brand is clearly perceivable throughout the Lyon Annotations, because the latter was within the exegetical tradition initiated by the Alexandrian Father.

4.3   Jerome and the Establishment of the "Deuteronomy-Gospel" Motif

Jerome (347–319/320) left one of the most incomparable legacies of biblical study and exegesis to the Latin west: a Latin translation of the Bible (the Vulgate), commentaries on 23 biblical books (5 on the New Testament and 18 on the Old Testament, including an unfinished one on Jeremiah), and at least 28 exegetical letters.[1] While the Bethlehem monk never expounded the book of Deuteronomy, it is far from true that Jerome left nothing on the exegetical history of this biblical book. First, as we have already seen, a fair amount of Origen's exegesis of Deuteronomy was transmitted through Jerome's translation and his own works. Second, as we will see in Chapter 5, not long after Jerome's death, Eucherius of Lyon resorted to his authority to solve the questions that his son Salonius had met when reading Deuteronomy.

Third, early medieval exegetes of Deuteronomy tended to consult Jerome's Hebrew etymologies mainly preserved in two of his early works as the springboard for their own allegorical reading: *Liber interpretationis Hebraicorum nominum* (a glossary of the Latin translation of Hebrew person and place names, composed ca. 390, based on a lost work of Philo) and *Hebraicae quaestiones in libro Geneseos* (a work composed in 393, aimed to solve problems in Genesis by the authority of the Hebrew text). What the Hieromyian etymologies found in the Lyon Annotations include in Table 4.3 .

---

1   Cf. Aline Canellis, "Jerome's Hermeneutics: How to Exegete the Bible?" *Patristic Theories of Biblical Interpretation: The Latin Fathers*, ed. Tarmo Toom (Cambridge: Cambridge University Press), pp. 49-76, with helpful tables at 58-59 and 67 showing Jerome's exegetical letters and biblical commentaries. For a general survey, see Denis Brown, *Vir Trilinguis: A Study in the Biblical Exegesis of Saint Jerome* (Kampen: Kok Pharos, 1992).

Table 4.3 Hieromyian etymologies in the Lyon Annotations

The Lyon Annotations (Paris, BnF, NAL 1740)	Jerome[1]
Horeb iniquitatem siue foramen (Deut. 1:2, fol. 1r)	Oreb interpretatur foramen, in quo coluber ingreditur. (*Tractatus lix in psalmos*, p. 94)
Seir hispidus... (Deut. 1:2, fol. 1r)	Seir pilosus uel hispidus. (*Liber interpretationis hebraicorum nominum*, p. 72) Seir pilosus uel hircus. (Ibid., p. 84)
Iair qui interpretatur inluminatus. (Deut. 3:14, fol. 10v)	Iairus inluminans uel inluminatus. (Ibid., p. 140)
Bosor interpretatur carneus. (Deut. 4:43, fol. 16r)	Bosor in tribulatione aut carneus siue pelliceus. (Ibid., p. 150)
Ramoth excelsa mors. (Deut. 4:43, fol. 16v)	Ramoth excelsum signum siue uidit mortem uel excelsa. (Ibid., 87)
Gaulon interpretatur uolutabrum. (Deut. 4:43, fol. 16v)	Golan transmigratio eorum uel uolutabrum eorum. (Ibid., 87)
Amalech qui interpretatur populus lingens uel lambens. (Deut. 25:17, fol. 66v)	Amalec populus lambens uel lingens. (Ibid., p. 61)
Syrus qui interpretatur sublimis. (Deut. 26:5, fol. 67r)	Syria sublimis siue humecta. (Ibid., p. 72) Syria sublimitas. (Ibid., p. 101) Syria sublimis iuxta hebraeam etymologiam.(Ibid., p. 149) Syria sublimis. (Ibid., p. 155)
Hebal uorago uetus. (Deut. 27:4)	Ebal uorago uetus. (Ibid., p. 87)
Garisim diuisio seu aduena. (Deut. 27:11, fol. 69v)	Garizin diuisio siue aduena. (Ibid., p. 87)
[Moab] ex patre... (Deut. 32:49, fol. 90r)	Moab de patre. (Ibid., p. 69, 76) Moab interpretatur ex patre. (*Hebraicae quaestiones in libro Geneseos*, p. 24)
Abarim qui interpretatur transitus. (Deut. 32:49, fol. 90r)	Abarim in transitu. (*Liber interpretationis hebraicorum nominum*, p. 79)
Leui qui interpretatur adsumptus. (Deut. 33:8, fol. 91r)	Leui additus siue adsumptus. (Ibid., p. 68)
Per Ioseph qui interpretatur auctus siue ampliatus. (Deut. 33:13, fol. 91v)	Filius auctus Ioseph, filius auctus. (Ibid., 55)
Ephraim frugifer, significat populum gentium. (Deut. 33:17, fol. 92r)	Efraim frugifer siue crescens. (Ibid., 65) Efraim crescens siue frugifer. (Ibid., 81)
Manases obliuiscens siue oblitus, figura est populi Iudeorum. (Deut. 33:17, fol. 92r)	Manasse oblitus uel necessitas. (Ibid., 69) Manasses obliuiosus uel quid oblitus est. (Ibid., 82)
Zabulon interpretatur tabernaculum fortitudinis. (Deut. 33: 18, fol. 92r)	Zabulon habitaculum fortitudinis. (Ibid., 77)
Isachar uero mercis. (Deut. 33: 18, fol. 92r)	Issachar est merces. (Ibid., 67)
Gad qui interpretatur accintus, in hoc loco figurant Dominum ac Redemptorem nostrum uirtute diuinitatis suae accinctum. (Deut. 33:20, fol. 92r)	Gad tentatio siue adcinctus uel latrunculus. (Ibid., 75)

---

1 Jerome, *Liber interpretationis hebraicorum nominum*, CCSL 72, ed. Paul de Lagarde (Turnhout: Brepols, 1959), pp. 57-161; *Hebraicae quaestiones in libro Geneseos*, CCSL 72, ed. Paul de Lagarde (Turnhout: Brepols, 1959), pp. 1-56; *Tractatus lix in psalmos*, CCSL 78, ed. Germain Morin (Turnhout: Brepols, 1958), pp. 3-352.

Continued

The Lyon Annotations (Paris, BnF, NAL 1740)	Jerome
Dan interpratatus iudicium, significat Christum Dominum, cui Pater omne iudicium dedit. (Deut. 33:22, fol. 92v)	Dan iudicium aut iudicans. (Ibid., 64)
Neptalim dilationem sonat, quae interpretatio refertur ad sanctis predicatoribus. (Deut. 33:23, fol. 92v)	Neptalim conuersauit me uel dilatauit me uel certe inplicuit me. (Ibid., 70)
Aser qui interpretatur beatus siue felix, persona pretendit Domini ac Redemptoris nostri qui uere felix ac beatus est in filiis, id est electis suis. (Deut. 33:24, fol. 92v)	Aser beatitudo uel beatus. (Ibid., 61)

Due to the want of a specific study of the early medieval reception of the Hebrew etymologies, it is hard for us to determine whether the Lyon Annotator got to know them via access to Jerome's original works or through miscellanies.[1] But their importance is clear enough to see.

Maybe even more important is Jerome's introduction to the Latin west of Origen's idea that Deuteronomy as the second law prefigures the Gospel. In his letter to Paulinus of Nola (composed in 394), Jerome urged Paulinus to study the Holy Scripture wholeheartedly. He offered a professional "guide to show a way" by attaching a brief description of the themes of certain biblical books, including the Pentateuch, so that Paulinus could have the right exegetical direction.[2] For Genesis, it is "the creation of the world, the origin of human beings, the division of the land, the confusion of languages, and the Hebrew people's entry into Egypt"; for Exodus, "the ten plagues, the Decalogue, and the divine mysteries and precepts"; for Leviticus, "all the sacrifices, the words, the vestments of Aaron, and the whole order of Levites that express the heavenly sacraments"; for Numbers, "the mysteries of arithmetic, the prophecy of Balaam, the 42 camps in the wilderness." For Deuteronomy, he says:

Also, does not Deuteronomy, that is the second law or the prefiguration of the

---

1 For a study of the development in the later Middle Ages, see Gilbert Dahan, "Lexiques hébreu/ latin? Les recueils d'interprétations des noms hébraïques," *Les manuscrits des lexiques et glossaires de l'Antiquité tardive à la fin du Moyen Âge: Actes du Colloque international (Erice, 23–30 septembre 1994)*, ed. Jacqueline Hamesse (Turnhout: Brepols, 1996), pp. 481-526; Eyal Poleg, "The Interpretations of Hebrew Names in Theory and Practice," *Form and Function in the Late Medieval Bible*, eds. Eyal Poleg, Laura Light (Leiden: Brill 2013), pp. 217-236. There are at least 13 extant copies of the intact *On Hebrew Names* by the ninth century, nineteen on *Hebrew Questions on Genesis*, see Bernard Lambert, *Bibliotheca Hieronymiana manuscripta: La tradition manuscrite des oeuvres de Saint Jérôme* (Turnhout: Brepols, 1969), vol. 2, nos. 200, 201, pp. 1-21.

2 "Haec a me perstricta sunt breuiter-neque enim epistularis angustia euagari longius patiebatur - ut intellegeres te in scripturis sanctis sine praeuio et monstrante semitam non posse ingredi... sola scripturarum ars est, quam sibi omnes passim uindicent: scribimus indocti docti que poemata passim." Jerome, *Epistula LIII*, 6-7, CSEL 54, pp. 452-453. Cf. J. N. D. Kelly, *Jerome: His Life, Writings and Controversies* (London: Duckworth, 1975), p. 192.

evangelical law, contain earlier things, but only in order that new things be put forward from the old?[1]

The interpretation of Deuteronomy as the *euangelicae legis praefiguratio* almost certainly originated with Origen, whose biblical scholarship Jerome admired, modeled, and "plagiarized," even after his dispute with Rufinus against the Alexandrian Father's orthodoxy.[2] A similar expression can be found in another letter of Jerome (no. 78, addressing Eustochius in 383 or 384), where he called Deuteronomy "the prelude of the Gospel" (*meditatorium euangelii*).[3]

Jerome's promotion of Origen's "Deuteronomy-Gospel" typological motif was a decisive moment in Latin exegetical history. It pioneered the dominant mystical/figural interpretation of Deuteronomy for the next several hundred years. Some three decades after Jerome composed that letter to Paulinus, Eucherius of Lyon copied the same wording in his own exegetical handbook *Instructiones*.[4] More than a century and a half after Eucherius, Isidore finally made the motif a standard characterization of the fifth biblical book in the Latin west. We will treat Eucherius and Isidore respectively in Chapters 5.2 and 6.1.

4.4 Ambrose: Deuteronomy as *Legis Praecepta*

Before we end this chapter and turn to the first Latin commentary on Deuteronomy composed by Augustine, we need to make an excursus to discuss another Latin Father, Ambrose, whose expositional approach to Deuteronomy shows certain distinctive features that cannot be totally absorbed in the figural/allegorical main stream of early

---

1 "Videlicet manifestissima est Genesis, in qua de creatura mundi, de exordio generis humani, de diuisione terrae, de confusione linguarum et de gente <pergente> usque ad Aegyptum scribitur hebraeorum. Patet Exodus cum decem plagis, cum decalogo, cum mysticis diuinis que praeceptis. In promptu est Leuiticus liber, in quo singula sacrificia, immo singulae paene syllabae et uestes aaron et totus ordo leuiticus spirant caelestia sacramenta. Numeri uero nonne totius arithmeticae et prophetiae balaam et quadraginta duarum per heremum mansionum mysteria continent? Deuteronomium quoque, secunda lex et euangelicae legis praefiguratio, nonne sic ea habet, quae priora sunt, ut tamen noua sint omnia de ueteribus?" Jerome, *Epistula LIII*, 7, p. 454.

2 Pierre Courcelle, *Late Latin Writers and their Greek Sources*, pp. 100-112. "He [Jerome] must have read also the homilies on Exodus, Leviticus, Numbers, Deuteronomy, Joshua, Judges, which Rufinus possessed and Jerome used on several occasions." Also cf. Mark Vessey, "Jerome's Origen: The Making of a Christian Literary Persona," *Studia patristica* 28 (1993): pp. 135-145.

3 "Succedit deuteronomium, secunda lex, meditatorium euangelii." Jerome, *Epistula LXXVIII*, 43, CSEL 55 *Epistulae 71-120*, ed. Isidorus Hilberg (Vienna: Verlag der Österreichischen Akademie der Wissenschaften, 1910), p. 85. Cf. J.N.O. Kelly, *Jerome*, p. 211; Andrew Cain, *The Letters of Jerome: Asceticism, Biblical Exegesis, and the Construction of Christian Authority in Late Antiquity* (Oxford: Oxford University Press, 2009), pp. 175-178.

4 "Deuteronomium secunda lex in quo est euangelicae legis praefiguratio." Eucherius, *Instructionum ad Salonium*, II.15, CCSL 66, ed. Carmela Mandolfo (Turnhout: Brepols, 2004), p. 215.

medieval exegesis determined by Isidore.

Ambrose (337–397) composed 20 exegetical treatises (commentaries or sermons), none of which seemingly has Deuteronomy as its subject.[1] It may seem surprising to say that the fifth book of the Hebrew Bible had particular significance for the bishop of Milan. But this is no exaggeration. On some occasions, we see Ambrose follow the Alexandrian (especially the Origenian) tradition to expound the allegorical sense of Deuteronomic verses.[2] For example, in his commentary on Psalm 43, Ambrose proposed two figural interpretations (*figura erat...*) for the levirate law on the obligation to marry the dead brother's childless widow (Deut. 25:5-6): While it "bound the Jews in the literal sense," it signifies for Christians both that "Christ will come to the lands to resurrect the semen of the deceased nation" and that "the Gospel will restore the terminated Law among the later generation."[3]

But what distinguishes Ambrose from both his Greek predecessors and contemporary Latin Fathers is his interest in the moral precepts recorded in Deuteronomy. Ambrose opened his commentary on Psalm 36 (composed in the last decade of his life) with the following words:

> Every Holy Scripture is either natural, mystical or moral. Genesis is natural, in which is expressed how the heaven, the sea, the earth were made and in which way this world was constituted; Leviticus is mystical, in which the priestly mystery is understood; Deuteronomy is moral, in which the human life is modeled according to the precept of the Law (*secundum legis praeceptum uita humana*).[4]

In Letter 33 (composed in 390), when describing his experience of biblical meditation, Ambrose singled out Genesis, Deuteronomy, and the Gospel:

---

1   See Boniface Ramsey, *Ambrose* (New York: Routledge, 1997), pp. 56-60. Compared with Augustine, Jerome, and Gregory, the biblical exegesis of Ambrose is more or less underappreciated. See Francesco Braschi, "A Comprehensive Reading of Ambrose's *Explanatio psalmorum XII*," *Studia Patristica* 46 (2010): pp. 137-142. For A general survey, see Fotios Ioannidis, "The Interpretation of Scriptures by Ambrose of Milan," *Synthesis* 3 (2016): pp. 68-75.

2   For Origen and Ambrose, see Christoph Markschies, "Ambrosius und Origenes. Bemerkungen zur Exegetischen Hermeneutik zweier Kirchenväter," *Origeniana Septima: Origines in den Auseinanderetzungen des 4. Jahrhunderts*, eds. Wolfgang Bienert, Uwe Kühneweg (Leuven: Peeters, 1999), pp. 545-569.

3   "Sed hoc ex litterae interpretatione Iudaeum ligabat; ceterum figura erat, quod Christus uenturus esset in terras, qui semen defuncti populi resuscitaret merito fratris, quia dictum est: narrabo nomen tuum fratribus meis, et: quorum patres, et ex quibus Christus secundum carnem, uel quia euangelium defunctae legis reparationem operaretur in posteris, ut semen, quod lex non reliquerat, euangelii tenor resuscitaret." Ambrose, *Explanatio psalmorum xii*, Psalm XLIII.64.3, CSEL 64, ed. Michael Petschenig (Vienna: Verlag der Österreichischen Akademie der Wissenschaften, 1919), p. 307.

4   "Omnis scriptura diuina uel naturalis uel mystica uel moralis est: naturalis in Genesi, in qua exprimitur, quomodo facta sunt caelum maria terrae et quemadmodum mundus iste sit constitutus; mystica in Leuitico, in quo comprehenditur sacerdotale mysterium; moralis in Deuteronomio, in quo secundum legis praeceptum uita humana formatur." Ibid., Psalm XXXVI.1.1, CSEL 64, p. 70.

When I read sacred scriptures, God walks in the Paradise. The book of Genesis is a paradise in which the virtues of patriarchs spring forth; Deuteronomy is a paradise in which the precepts of the Law (*legis praecepta*) flourish; the Gospel is a paradise, in which the Tree of Life makes good fruits and spreads the teachings of eternal hope throughout all the nations.[1]

Genesis and the Gospel are the biblical books most important to Ambrose, who composed no fewer than seven treatises on the patriarchs of Genesis[2] and one ten-book commentary on Luke (his sole New Testament commentary). The bishop of Milan juxtaposed Deuteronomy with them, because it contains *legis praecepta* that shape a Christian's moral life. In the prologue of his commentary on Luke, Ambrose adopted the image of the Well of Abundance in Genesis 26:33 as the figure of biblical moral wisdom:

The Well of Abundance refers to ethical wisdom, because Isaac discovered the water of the living soul only after the foreigners who signify the vices of the body had left. From good morals (*boni mores*) flow forth pure water, and the humanly goodness (*bonitas ipsa popularis*) that functions rather as restraint to oneself is an abundant source to others.[3]

One example how Ambrose expounded moral teachings from Deuteronomy appears in his letter (no. 15) to Irenaeus, a Milan citizen. Irenaeus wanted to know how to understand the taboo of cross-dressing presented in Deut. 22:5 ("A woman shall not be clothed with man's apparel, neither shall a man use woman's apparel, for he that doth

---

1 "Et nunc deambulat in paradiso deus, quando diuinas scripturas lego. Paradisus est Genesis liber, in quo uirtutes pullulant patriarcharum, paradisus Deuteronomium, in quo germinant legis praecepta, paradisus Euangelium, in quo arbor uitae bonos fructus facit et aeternae spei mandata diffundit per uniuersos populos." Ambrose, *Epistulae*, VI.33.3, CSEL 82/1, ed. Otto Faller (Vienna: Verlag der Österreichischen Akademie der Wissenschaften, 1968).

2 *De Cain et Abet, De Noe, De Abraham, De Isaac et anima, De Iacob et vita beata, De Joseph* and *De patriarchis*, all available in CSEL 32/1 or CSEL 32/2, ed. Karl Schenkl (Vienna: Verlag der Österreichischen Akademie der Wissenschaften, 1896–1897).

3 "Nam licet Scriptura diuina mundanae euacuet sapientiae disciplinam, quod maiore fucata uerborum ambitu quam rerum ratione subnixa sit, tamen si quis in scripturis diuinis illa etiam illa quae miranda illi putant quaerit, inueniet tria sunt enim quae philosophi mundi istius praecellentissima putauerunt, triplicem scilicet esse sapientiam, quod aut naturalis sit aut moralis aut rationalis. Haec tria iam et in Veteri Testamento potuimus aduertere. Quid enim aliud significant tres illi putei, quorum unus est uisionis, alius abundantiae, tertius iuramenti, nisi triplicem istam in Patriarchis fuisse uirtutem? Rationalis puteus uisionis eo quod ratio uisum mentis acuat et animi purget optutum. Ethicus puteus abundantiae eo quod cedentibus allophylis, quorum specie uitia corporis figurantur, uiuae Isaac liquorem mentis inuenit, purum enim profluunt boni mores et bonitas ipsa popularis abundat aliis sibi restrictior. Tertius puteus iuramenti, hoc est sapientiae naturalis, quae ea quae supra naturam uel naturae sunt conprehendat; quod enim adfirmat et quasi Deo teste iuratur etiam diuina conplectitur, cum dominus naturae fidei testis adhibetur." Ambrose, *Expositio euangelii secundum Lucam*, *prologus*, CCSL 14, ed. Mark Adriaen (Turnhout: Brepols, 1957).

these things is abominable before God").[1] Ambrose interpreted it as a teaching about the natural distinction between the two genders: "Nature clothes each sex in its proper raiment. Moreover, in men and women there are different customs, different complexion, different gestures, gait, and strength, and different qualities of voice."[2] Based on the natural difference are the social norms, which maintain women's inferior social role (*inferioris sexus*). Two quotations from the epistles of Paul are offered as testimony to this interpretation:

> I think it refers not so much to clothing as to manners and to our habits and actions, since one act is proper to a man, another to a woman. Therefore, the Apostle, as the interpreter of the Law (*quasi interpraes legis*), says: "Let your women keep silence in the churches, for it is not permitted them to speak, but to be submissive, as the Law says. But if they wish to learn anything, let them ask their husbands at home." (1 Corinthians 14:34-35) To Timothy he says: "Let a woman learn in silence with all submission. For I do not allow a woman to teach, or to exercise authority over men." (1 Timothy 2:11-12)[3]

Besides gender order, Ambrose also worries about the threat to the virtue of *castimonia*, since cross-dressing is usually a sign of *luxuria*.[4] For the pastor of Milan, to expound this old Deuteronomic precept is to express his present moral concerns.

An even more remarkable case can be found in *De Tobia*, an early treatise of Ambrose in sermonic form against usury and avarice. The treatise (divided into 93 sections by its modern editor) starts and ends with the story of Tobias, the son of Tobit, who gave his money to the poor and asked for no return. Ambrose used this biblical figure as an exemplum in contrast with evil and illegal usurers. The first half of *De Tobia* (ss. 1-45) was built on Basil the Great's *Second Homily on Psalm 14* whose theme is usury. In the second half (ss. 46-93), Basil's influence diminished, and Ambrose made more biblical

---

1   Cf. the analysis in Maria E. Doerfler, "Coming Apart at the Seams: Crossdressing, Masculinity, and the Social Body in Late Antiquity," *Dressing Judeans and Christians in Antiquity*, eds. Kristi Upson-Saia, Carly Daniel-Hughes, Kristi Upson-Saia (Burlington: Ashgate, 2014), pp. 37-51.

2   "Suis unumquemque sexum induit natura indumentis. Denique diuersus usus, diuersus color, motus, incessus, diuersae uires, diuersa uox est in uiro et femina." Ambrose, *Epistulae*, IV.15.2, CSEL 82/1, p. 112. The translation is based on Ambrose, *Letters 1–91*, The Fathers of the Church 26, trans. Mary Melchior Beyenka (Washington, D.C.: Catholic University of America Press, 1954), p. 435-437.

3   "Arbitror autem quod non tam de ueste quam de moribus dixerit uel de usibus nostris adque actibus, quod alius uirum, alius feminam deceat actus. Vnde et Apostolus ait quasi interpraes legis: *Mulieres uestrae in ecclesia taceant; non enim permittitur eis loqui, sed subditas esse, sicut lex dicit. Si quid autem uolunt discere, domi uiros suos interrogent.* et ad Timotheum: *Mulier in silentio discat cum omni subiectione. Docere autem mulieri non permitto neque dominari in uirum.*" Ambrose, *Epistulae*, IV.15.5, CSEL 82/1, p. 113.

4   "Quid de aliis dicimus, qui hoc ad luxuriam diriuandum putant, ut calamistratos et torquatos habeant in ministerio, ipsi promissa barba, illos remissa coma? Merito illic non seruatur castimonia, ubi non tenetur sexus distinctio." Ambrose, *Epistulae*, IV.15.7, CSEL 82/1, p. 114.

quotations and allegorical interpretations of his own. Lois Miles Zucker suggested that the two halves of *De Tobia*, so different in style and source, could have originally been two independent sermons delivered to the public, later combined and revised for publication.[1]

According to my own study, it is quite possible that Ambrose's sermon ultimately presented as the second half of *De Tobia* is in fact an exposition of the Deuteronomic precepts on lending (Table 4.4) .

Table 4.4   Exegesis of Deuteronomy in Ambrose's *De Tobia*

Ambrose, De Tobia	Deut.	Exposition (allegorical exposition in bold)
ss. 48-50	Thou shalt not lend to thy brother money to usury, nor corn, nor any other thing. (23:19)	Loaning to merchants is the fraud and circumvention of this precept.
ss. 51-54	Thou shalt not lend to thy brother... Thou shalt lend [usury] to the stranger. (23:19-20)	Everyone, primarily according to faith, secondarily according to Roman law, is your brother. Be merciful to enemies as well, and do not harm them through the weapon of usury.
ss. 57-58	If he be poor, the pledge shall not lodge with thee that night. (24:10-13) Thou shalt not take the nether, nor the upper millstone to pledge, for he hath pledged his life to thee. (24:6) Neither shalt thou take away the widow's raiment for a pledge. (24:17)	No pledge, not just millstone, should be exacted from no one, not just from the poor or the widow.
ss. 59-62	Thou shalt lend to many nations, and shalt not borrow of any one. (28:12)	**It is not money but *cognitio Dei*, *praedicatio uerbi*, and *gratia Domini* that are to lend.**[1]
ss. 63-66	The stranger that liveth with thee in the land, shall rise up over thee, and shall be higher, and thou shalt go down, and be lower. He shall lend to thee, and thou shalt not lend to him. He shall be as the head, and thou shalt be the tail. (28:43-44)	**When the people of Jews began to fail the observance of the Law, the people of the nations began to teach the interpretation of the Scripture to the old people (*uetusto populo*).**[2]

---

1   Lois Miles Zucker, *S. Ambrosii De Tobia: A Commentary, with an Introduction and Translation* (Ph.D. dissertation: Catholic University of America, 1933). Zucker's Latin text is based on *De Tobia*, CSEL 32/2, ed. Karl Schenkel (Vienna: Verlag der Österreichischen Akademie der Wissenschaften, 1896), pp. 519-573.

2   "Vbi coepit populus Iudaeorum non custodire legem, coeperunt aduenae, hoc est ex populo nationum, qui in Iesum dominum crediderunt, interpretationem scripturarum illi uetusto populo faenerare." Ambrose, *De Tobia*, XVIII.62, p. 78.

3   "Non pecunia utique benedictum facit, sed cognitio Dei, praedicatio uerbi, si gratiam Domini faeneremus, si indigentibus eloquia domini conferamus, si obseruemus mandata caelestia." Ibid., XIX.63, p. 78.

Continued

Ambrose, De Tobia	Deut.	Exposition (allegorical exposition in bold)
ss. 67-77	When thou shalt demand of thy neighbour any thing that he oweth thee, thou shalt not go into his house to take away a pledge. But then shalt stand without, and he shall bring out to thee what he hath. But if he be poor, the pledge shall not lodge with thee that night, But thou shalt restore it to him presently before the going down of the sun, that he may sleep in his own raiment and bless thee, and thou mayst have justice before the Lord thy God. (24:10-13)	**1. The faith is our spiritual trust kept by the Holy Spirit and should not be taken away by force.** **2. The pledge is the holy word heard by the ordinary believers and it should not be snatched away.** **3. "A good cover and garment is the Word of God."**[1]
ss. 83-84	Thou shalt not take the nether, nor the upper millstone to pledge, for he hath pledged his life to thee. (24:6)	"Each is grave and according to the letter, that you should take away from the needy his occupation and means of livelihood, or that you should take the widow's pledge; **but it is more grave if you should retain the word of the soul, which is the widow of the Word, so that you should pronounce the sterility of widowhood upon it."**[2]

The chart above aims to demonstrate that, if we leave aside the epilogue (ss. 88-93), an excursus on Samson's riddle in Judges 14:14 (ss. 53-56) and another on the innocence of Susanna (ss. 78-82), the sermon in the second half of *De Tobia* is in fact Ambrose's systematic exposition of Deuteronomic precepts on lending and pledge (Deut. 23:19-20; 24:6, 10-13, 17; Deut. 28:1, 4, 12-13, 15-16, 18; 28:43-44). His exegetical method is a mixture of both the literal and allegorical understandings. All the Deuteronomic precepts that forbid usury or restrict lending with the expectation of return are to be observed in an even generalized way; precepts such as the command to lend to strangers need to be read allegorically as the order to spread the Word of God. To sum up, we should not be bad usurers who lend money, but be good usurers (*boni faeneratores*) who preach the Christian faith.

Expositions of Deuteronomy for the purpose of moral teachings can also be found in Ambrose's Letter 44, in which he plainly interpreted Moses' curse in Deut. 28:23 ("Be the heaven that is over thee, of brass and the ground thou treadest on of iron") as the

---

1   "Bonus ergo amictus atque uestitus uerbum Dei." Ambrose, *De Tobia*, XX.75, p. 88.
2   "Graue et secundum litteram utrumque, ut usum instrumentum que uiuendi egeno auferas aut uiduae pignus detrahas, sed grauius, si animae, quae uerbi uidua est, uerbum teneas, ut ei sterilitatem uiduitatis indicas." Ibid., XXI.84, p. 96.

threat of miserable famine (*miserandam famem*) to the impious.[1]

In a more allegorical way, Ambrose also occasionally read precepts in Deuteronomy as instruction for the human soul in an exegetical approach that would be named "tropological," a term that Ambrose never used himself, though. The theme of Letter 14 is the meaning of the inheritance law recorded in Deut. 21:15-17. "The two wives, one beloved and the other hated," are interpreted as "diverse qualities of a single soul" (*diuersas qualitates unius animae*), the first carnal and seemingly sweet (*dulcis et suavis ad tempus uidetur*), and the second pious though sadder (*tristior*). It is the right choice for the soul to give preference to the latter's son in inheritance.[2] Similarly, in Letter 13, the beautiful female captive in Deut. 21:10-13 is interpreted as the soul who unites with Christ after her superfluities were removed.[3] Isidore adopted this exposition in Deuteronomy Entry 18 of his *Expositio in uetus testamentum* (For the detail, see Chapter 6.1).

Ambrose's effort to interpret Deuteronomic precepts as still valid moral instructions for Christians, however, found very limited echo during the next four centuries after his death. The main reason seems to be that this exegetical approach was largely outside the Origen-Jerome typological motif that the Deuteronomic law signifies the Gospel, which would become more and more dominant from the sixth century on. Nevertheless, such once marginalized exegetical approach revived in the Lyon Annotations, in which we find multiple exhortations to observe certain Deuteronomic precepts literally (*iuxta historiam a fidelibus obseruandus*). We will treat this issue in detail in Chapter 7.2. It is sufficient here to look at the expositions of the verses related to money lending in the Lyon Anno-

---

1 "His igitur miserandam famem minatur impiis, ut qui pietatem filiorum communi <omni>um domino et patri exhibere nesciunt, careant nutrimento paternae indulgentiae, sit illis caelum aereum concreto aere et solidato in metalli rigorem, sit illis terra ferrea partus suos nesciens et, quod plerumque in<o>pia habeat, discordias serens." Ambrose, *Epistulae*, VII.44, CSEL 82/2, ed. Michaela Zelzer (Vienna: Verlag der Österreichischen Akademie der Wissenschaften, 1990).

2 "Vnde sequenti capitulo legis non duas animas, sed diuersas qualitates unius animae conpraehensas arbitror. Est enim amabilis animae species, quae concupiscit uoluptaria, quae laborem fugit, conpunctiones declinat, iudicium dei neglegit, ideo amabilis, quia dulcis et suauis ad tempus uidetur, quae mentem non adficiat sed oblectet. At illa altera tristior, quae zelo dei conficiatur, sicut uxor seuera scortari conparem suum nolit non patiatur non sinat, nihil indulgeat corpori, nihil uoluptati et delectationi relaxet, abdicet occulta dedecoris, dura laborum sequatur, grauia periculorum. Si igitur pepererint ei ambae, non poterit, inquit, primituum filium amabilis in hereditatis institutione praeponere primituo filio odibilis, cum sciat odibilis filium primituum esse." Ambrose, *Epistulae*, IV.14.2-3, CSEL 82/1, pp. 108-109.

3 "Haec est anima illa, quam lex demonstrat tibi in specie mulieris bonae, quam uideris in praeda et concupieris accipere in uxorem tibi: Induces, inquit, eam in domum tuam, ut tota ei conmittas interiora domus, omnium tuorum uiscerum possessionem, auferas eius superflua, tondeas lapsus et nouacula non satis acuta, ne faciat dolum, tuarum exuuias passionum adque inanes sensus recidas. Ideo ait: Rades eius caput, quo nulla obstacula patiantur oculi sapientis qui sunt in capite eius. Et sedebit, inquit, XXX diebus in domo tua peccata propriae deplorans natiuitatis et conmenta nequissimi *patris diaboli*, qui uult congregare quae non generauit, ut huius mystici numeri purificatione mundata coniugii claues adipiscatur." Ambrose, *Epistulae*, IV.13.11, CSEL 82/1, pp. 106.

tations:

> *Thou shalt lend to many nations.* (Deut. 15:6)
>
> It talks about the Apostles elected from Jews who lent, that is gave out, usury, that is the money of the Word of God, but they did not accept the wisdom of this world from the nations.[1]

> *He shall lend to thee, and thou shalt not lend to him.* (Deut. 28:44)
>
> Just like nations have converted through the preaching of the Apostles not long after the advent of the Lord, so will the nation of Jews believe in Christ the Lord through the preaching of saints from the elected gentiles by the end of the world. It means: He shall lend the money of the Word of God to you, and you shall not lend to him.[2]

> *Thou shalt not lend to thy brother money at usury.* (Deut. 23:19)
>
> Just as is said in a psalm: "He that hath not put out his money to usury," (14:5) and via the prophet Ezechiel: "Thou hast taken usury and increase." (22:12)[3]

It is difficult to determine whether textual parallels of such mean that the Lyon Annotator used *De Tobia* as his source. However, they at least remind us of the broad exegetical spectrum in the Lyon Annotations and its indebtedness to a diverse patristic tradition.

***

In this chapter, we have examined the initial development of Christian interpretation of Deuteronomy in the Latin west. Origen, Jerome, or Ambrose did not leave us any intact commentary on this biblical book. Their exegetical legacy, however, was extremely fundamental. Apart from his multiple expositions of Deuteronomic verses that were to be taken up by later authors, Origen was the first to propose that Deuteronomy foreshadows the Gospel. Jerome elaborated it and shaped a typological motif that would become the commonly accepted hermeneutical principle for Deuteronomy in the Latin exegetical tradition. The same author's Hebrew etymologies would turn out to be an important source of allegorical interpretation for early medieval exegetes. Ambrose's moral expositions of certain Deuteronomic precepts offered an alternative to the Origen-Jerome motif and found an ambiguous echo in the Lyon Annotations. In this sense, the road that would

---

1 "De apostolis dicit ex Iudeis electis qui cunctis gentibus fenus id est pecuniam uerbi Dei fenerauerunt id est comodauerunt, ipsi uero a gentilibus sapientiam huius mundi non acceperunt." Paris, BnF, NAL 1740, fol. 43r.

2 "Sicut enim in primo aduentu Domini per apostolorum predicationem gentes crediderunt, ita secus finem mundi per predicationem sanctorum ex gentibus electis Iudeorum populus in Christo Domino crediturus est, et hoc significat quod ait: Ipse fenerabit tibi pecuniam uidelicet uerbi Dei, et tu non fenerabis ei." Paris, BnF, NAL 1740, fol. 74v.

3 "Sicut est illud in Psalmo: Qui pecuniam suam non dedit ad usuram, et per Ezechihelum prophetam: Ad usuram non commodauerit et amplius non acceperit." Paris, BnF, NAL 1740, fol. 62r.

lead to early medieval exegesis of Deuteronomy had already been well paved before the appearance of the first Latin commentaries on Deuteronomy, which are the subject of our next chapter.

CHAPTER 5

THE EXEGESIS OF DEUTERONOMY BEFORE 800 (II): THE LATIN PATRISTIC COMMENTARIES FROM AUGUSTINE TO GREGORY THE GREAT

In this and the next chapter, the Latin exegesis of Deuteronomy between 400 and 800 will be examined. It's difficult to deal with the use of Deuteronomy in various genres of Christian literature and art as part of the contemporary intellectual "totalizing discourse."[1] Specific aspects of the interrelationship between this biblical book and early medieval social life will be touched in Part III. The present two chapters concentrate on each of early medieval Latin commentaries on Deuteronomy. "Commentaries" mean all the literary enterprises designed to offer explications of the Deuteronomic text.[2] What matters is not only how they interpret this biblical book (the content), but also how they organize the interpretation (the form). The evaluation of the Lyon Annotations cannot be undertaken without the background of this exegetical tradition.

Starting with Augustine, who offered the first Latin commentary on Deuteronomy, and ending with Gregory, whose sporadic expositions of Deuteronomic verses were collected by his secretary Paterius, the survey in this chapter covers five pre-Isidorian Latin commentaries, none of which have undergone close scholarly analysis. These works vary in method, format, length, and originality. While diversity may be the right word to describe the Deuteronomy exegetical practice during this period, we can also perceive the beginning of the triumph of the "spiritual understanding" by 600 in the Latin west which

---

1 Such a wide horizon can be found in Frances Young, *Biblical Exegesis and the Formation of Christian Culture* (Cambridge: Cambridge University Press, 1997), which consciously echoes the thesis of the rise of the Christian "totalizing discourse" initially proposed by Averil Cameron in her *Christianity and the Rhetoric of Empire: The Development of Christian Discourse* (Berkeley: University of California Press, 1991).

2 Biblical commentary in the general sense can include different exegetical genres such as homily, scholia, questions and answers, commentary in the strict sense, and catena. The distinction among them is not always clearly cut. Cf. Mark Elliott, "Exegetical genres in the patristic era," *The New Cambridge History of the Bible, Volume 1: From the Beginning to 600*, eds. James Carleton, Joachim Schape (Cambridge: Cambridge University Press, 2013), pp. 775-797.

would finally lead to the "Isidorian moment" to be treated in the next chapter.

5.1 Augustine of Hippo, *Quaestiones in Heptateuchum*

Augustine composed 57 exegetical entries for Deuteronomy as the fifth book of his *Quaestiones in Heptateuchum*, a collection of his reading notes on the first seven books of the Old Testament. The prologue claims:

> When I read through the sacred scriptures that are called canonical, and compared the translation of the Septuagint with other biblical versions, it pleased me to record by pen these questions that came to my mind, lest they flee from my memory, either by simply proposing them briefly or lengthily, or by offering a solution in a hasty way as much as I could. My purpose was not to interpret them sufficiently, but to be able to check when necessary, either to remind myself of what still needs inquiring, or to prepare myself in thinking and responding on the basis of what it seemed that I had already discovered. If any person does not disdain to read these questions due to its uncouth style caused by my haste, and finds that certain questions proposed are not answered, may he not think that there is nothing beneficial for him there, because knowing what to seek is a certain part of discovering. If the answers to certain questions are satisfying, may he not despise the poor manner of speaking, but rather rejoice over his participation in teaching, for discussion is not sought by way of truth but truth by way of discussion.[1]

It is generally agreed that Augustine wrote out his *Quaestiones* in 419.[2] In his *Retractationes*, Augustine recalled that he had chosen *quaestiones* as the title of the work because he "proposed questions more than answered them, although much more of them

---

1 "Cum scripturas sanctas quae appellantur canonicae legendo et cum aliis codicibus secundum Septuaginta interpretationem conferendo percurreremus, placuit eas quaestiones, quae in mentem uenirent, siue breuiter commemorando uel etiam pertractando tantummodo proponerentur siue etiam qualitercumque tamquam a festinantibus soluerentur, stilo alligare, ne de memoria fugerent: non ut eas satis explicaremus, sed ut, cum opus esset, possemus inspicere, siue ut admoneremur quid adhuc esset requirendum, siue ut ex eo quod iam uidebatur inuentum, ut poteramus, essemus et ad cogitandum instructi et ad respondendum parati. Si quis igitur haec legere propter incultum in nostra festinatione sermonem non fastidierit, quas quaestiones propositas inuenerit nec solutas, non ideo sibi nihil conlatum putet; nonnulla enim pars inuentionis est nosse quid quaeras. Quarum autem solutio placuerit, non ibi uile contemnat eloquium, sed de aliqua participatione doctrinae potius gratuletur; non enim disputatio ueritate sed ueritas disputatione requiritur." Augustine, *Quaestionum in Heptateuchum libri VII, prologus*, CCSL 33, ed. Jean Fraipont (Turnhout: Brepols, 1958).

2 Wilhelm Rüting, *Untersuchungen über Augustins Quaestiones und Locutiones in Heptateuchum* (Paderborn: Schöningh, 1916); Allan Fitzgerald, "*Quaestiones in Heptateuchum*," *Augustine through the Ages: An Encyclopedia*, eds. Allan Fitzgerald, John Cavadini (Grand Rapids: William B. Eerdmans, 1999).

seem to me not without reason to have been so treated that they can be considered solved and expounded."[1] Augustine composed *Quaestiones* together with another work, *Locutiones in Heptateuchum*, in which he collected unidiomatic linguistic phenomena found during his reading.[2]

In three ways, we can contextualize *Quaestiones* within the intellectual career of the bishop of Hippo. First, *Quaestiones* reflects Augustine's continuous research on the Old Testament after the completion of his *De Genesi ad litteram* (ca. 415).[3] The fact that *Quaestiones* passes over Genesis 1–3 for the reason that "I have already discussed them elsewhere as much as I could"[4] implies the intrinsic relationship between these two works, and Augustine applied the same literal exegetical approach to both of them. After completing *Quaestiones*, Augustine turned to the next group of the Old Testament books: *regnorum libri*, that is the books of Samuel, Kings, and Ruth. But he failed to make much progress due to the shortage of time.[5] Second, Augustine composed *Quaestiones* at the same time when he prepared Books 15 and 16 of *City of God*, whose theme is the history from the Fall to the kings of Israel. Some of the unsolved questions in *Quaestiones* are answered there.[6] Lastly, *Quaestiones* is related to Augustine's theoretical reflection on biblical interpretation in his *De doctrina christiana*.[7] The systematic use of

---

1 "Eodem tempore scripsi etiam libros quaestionum de libris eisdem diuinis septem, quos ideo appellare sic uolui, quia ea quae ibi disputantur magis quaerenda proposui quam quaesita dissolui, quamuis multo plura in eis mihi uideantur ita pertractata, ut possint etiam soluta et exposita non inmerito iudicari." Augustine, *Retractationes*, II.55, CCSL 57, ed. Almut Mutzenbecher (Turnhout: Brepols, 1984), p. 132.

2 "Septem libros de septem libris diuinarum scripturarum, id est moysi quinque et uno iesu naue et altero iudicum, feci notatis locutionibus singulorum quae minus usitatae sunt linguae nostrae, quas parum aduertendo sensum quaerunt qui legunt diuinorum eloquiorum, cum sit locutionis genus, et nonnumquam exculpunt aliquid quod a ueritate quidem non abhorreat, non tamen hoc sensisse auctor a quo id scriptum est inuenitur, sed genere locutionis hoc dixisse credibilius apparet." Augustine, *Retractationes*, II.54, CCSL 57, pp. 131-132.

3 Roland Teske, "*Genesi ad litteram liber, De,*" *Augustine through the Ages: An Encyclopedia*, eds. Allan Fitzgerald, John Cavadini (Grand Rapids: William B. Eerdmans, 1999), pp. 376-377.

4 "Exceptis ergo his quae a principio, ubi deus caelum et terram fecisse narratur, usque ad dimissionem duorum primorum hominum de paradiso tractari multipliciter possunt, de quibus alias, quantum potuimus, disseruimus..." Augustine, *Quaestionum in Heptateuchum libri VII, prologus*, p. 1. Notice that Augustine's description of *On the Literal Meaning of Genesis* in his *Retractationes* shows similarity with that of *Quaestiones*: "In quo opere plura quaesita quam inuenta sunt, et eorum quae inuenta sunt pauciora firmata, cetera uero ita posita, uelut adhuc requirenda sint." Augustine, *Retractationes*, II.24, CCSL 57, p. 109.

5 "Regnorum quoque libros eodem modo iam considerare coeperamus; sed non multum progressi in alia, quae magis urgebant, animum intendimus."Augustine, *Retractationes*, II.55, CCSL 57, p. 132.

6 Gerard J. P. O'Daly, *Augustine's City of God: A Reader's Guide* (Oxford: Clarendon Press, 1999), p. 35. Cf. *Quaestionum in Heptateuchum, in Genesim*, IV, VII, XXXIII, XXXV and LXXIV with *De ciuitate Dei*, XV.27, XVI.28-29, XVI.37, CCSL 48, eds. Bernhard Dombart, Alfons Kalb (Turnhout: Brepols, 1955).

7 R. P. H. Green, "Introduction," *Augustine: De Doctrina Christiana*, ed. idem (Oxford: Clarendon Press, 1995), pp. ix-xiv; Cf. Tarmo Toom, "Augustine's Hermeneutics: The Science of the Divinely Given Signs," *Patristic Theories of Biblical Interpretation: The Latin Fathers*, ed. Tarmo Toom (Cambridge: Cambridge University Press), pp. 77-108.

the conceptual pair *locutio* (un-Latin expression in the Latin Bible) and *sensus* (intelligible meaning) can only be found in three Augustinian works: *Quaestiones in Heptateuchum*, *Locutiones in Heptateuchum*, and *De doctrina christiana*.[1] Moreover, certain exegetical methods proposed in *De doctrina christiana*, such as comparing various biblical translations (*interpretum collatio*) and using the rule of faith (*regula fidei*) as caliber, were put into practice in *Quaestiones*.[2]

Question-and-answer is a loosely defined literary format commonly used in early Christian literature. Eusebius of Caesarea was the first known Christian author to adopt it in biblical exegesis, and Ambrosiaster the first Latin author to organize a large-scale biblical commentary in this form.[3] Augustine wrote about a dozen theological and exegetical works as the response to questions raised by his correspondents or his brothers at Hippo.[4] In *Quaestiones*, arguably "the most important work of Augustine belonging to this genre,"[5] the bishop of Hippo raised and answered questions of his own. The 57 entries in the fifth book of *Quaestiones* are presented in the order of the expounded Deuteronomic verses or passages, the first

---

1   Joseph Lienhard, "*Locutio* and *Sensus* in Augustine's Writings on the Heptateuch," *Studia Patristica* 70 (2013): pp. 79-83.

2   "Rarissime igitur et difficillime inueniri potest ambiguitas in propriis uerbis, quantum ad libros diuinarum scripturarum spectat, quam non aut circumstantia ipsa sermonis, qua cognoscitur scriptorum intentio, aut interpretum collatio aut praecedentis linguae soluat inspectio." Augustine, *De doctrina christiana*, III.19, ed. Green, p.140; "Sed cum uerba propria faciunt ambiguam scripturam, primo uidendum est ne male distinxerimus aut pronuntiauerimus. Cum ergo adhibita intentio incertum esse peruiderit quomodo distinguendum aut quomodo pronuntiandum sit, consulat regulam fidei, quam de scripturarum planioribus locis et ecclesiae auctoritate percepit, de qua satis egimus cum de rebus in libro primo loqueremur." Ibid., III.3, p.134. "Vnde quod habent plerique codices 'derelictus est a Raphain,' planius utique dicitur." Augustine, *Quaestionum in Heptateuchum libri VII*, in *Deuteronomium*, IV, CCSL 33, p. 276; "Quoniam portentorum inspectores prohibet esse in populo dei, quaerendum est quomodo ista portenta, quae inspici prohibentur, discernantur ab eis, quae diuinitus ita dantur, ut quid significent dici debeant. Sicut omnia miracula, quae in scripturis reperiuntur, significantia quod pertineat ad regulam fidei; sicut dicimus quid significauerit uellus in area conpluta siccum uel in sicca area conplutum aut uirga Aaron quae floruit et nuces adtulit et cetera huius modi." Ibid., XXVIIII, p. 292.

3   For the question-and-answer as a literary format or genre in the Late Antiquity, see Annelie Volgers and Claudio Zamagni, eds., *Erotapokriseis: Early Christian Question-and-Answer Literature in Context. Proceedings of the Utrecht Colloquium, 13–14 October 2003* (Leuven: Peeters, 2004); Marie-Pierre Bussières, ed., *La littérature des questions et réponses dans l'Antiquité profane et chrétienne* (Turnhout: Brepols, 2013). For a classic study of the patristic exegesis in question-and-answer format, see Gustave Bardy, "La Littérature patristique des quaestiones et responsiones sur l'écriture sainte," *Revue Biblique* 41 (1932): pp. 210-236, 341-369, 515-537; 42 (1933): pp. 14-30, 211-229, 328-352. For a more critical approach, see Claudio Zamagni, "Is the Question-and-Answer Literary Genre in Early Christian Literature a Homogeneous Group?" *La littérature des questions et réponses dans l'Antiquité profane et chrétienne*, ed. Marie-Pierre Bussières (Turnhout: Brepols, 2013), pp. 241-268.

4   Roland Teske, "Augustine of Hippo and the *Quaestiones et Responsiones* Literature," *Erotapokriseis: Early Christian Question-and-Answer Literature in Context. Proceedings of the Utrecht Colloquium, 13–14 October 2003*, eds. Annelie Volgers, Claudio Zamagni (Leuven: Peeters, 2004), pp. 127-144.

5   Claudio Zamagni, "Question-and-Answer Literary Genre," p. 254.

on Deut. 1:29-30, and the last on Deut. 33:17. They vary from concise philological notes to lengthy theological explications. Some focus on certain Greek vocabularies in the Septuagint, for example, "firstborn" (πρωτότοκα) in Question 23 and "evil man" (τὸν πονηρὸν) in Question 39.[1] Augustine also used Jerome's Vulgate – *interpretatio quae est ex hebraeo*, as he called it — as a reference when he considered the Septuagint and its Latin translations ambiguous.[2]

Augustine's major interest lies in "the proper sense" (*secundum proprietatem*) of the Deuteronomic narratives and precepts. For example, Moses' command for the Israelites to write the words of God upon their own thresholds and gates (Deut. 11:20) puzzles Augustine in Question 17: how was one able to copy so many words in so tiny space? Two tentative solutions are offered: either the words were divided and written in different parts of the house, or Moses spoke here in a hyperbolical way.[3] Similarly, apparent discrepancy within biblical text is the subject of many questions. In the long Question 15, Augustine took pains to harmonize the conflicting narratives in Exodus 34:27-28, Deut. 10:1-2, and Deut. 10:3-4, in order to determine whether Moses or God wrote the commandments on the newly made tablets after the first ones had been broken.[4] The inquiry sometimes could be very trivial. In Question 38 on Deut. 23:18 ("Do not offer the salary of prostitutes, nor the price of a dog in the house of the Lord your God for any vow"), Augustine asked why the dog is singled out rather than other unclean animals. "How about pig?" He wondered.[5]

The generally literal approach in *Quaestiones* is not to be confused with modern historical criticism, though. Augustine's exegesis presumes the omnipresence of the double love for God and neighbor in the Holy Scripture.[6] The moral and theological teaching emerges now and then from the literal clarification of biblical text. For example,

---

1   "Quaerendum utrum quae graece dicuntur πρωτότοκα nec latine dici nisi primogenita potuerunt, in his tantum intellegenda sunt, quae nascuntur ex matribus; ipsa enim proprie pariuntur potius quam gignuntur." Augustine, *Quaestionum in Heptateuchum libri VII, in Deuteronomium*, XXIII, CCSL 33, p. 289. "Nam Graecus habet τὸν πονηρόν, quod etiam hic scriptum est; hoc autem potius malignum solet interpretari quam malum. Nec ait: τὸ πονηρόν, id est hoc malignum; sed τὸν πονηρόν, quod est hunc malignum." Ibid., XXXVIIII, CCSL 33, p. 296.

2   E.g., in Question 20, on the command to bring a tithe of fruit to the Levities, strangers, widows and orphans (Deut. 14:28): "Sed in ea interpretatione quae est ex hebraeo apertius hoc distinctum reperimus." Ibid., XX, CCSL 33, p. 288.

3   "Quid est quod praecepit moyses commendans uerba domini et ait: *Scribetis ea super limina domorum uestrarum et ianuarum uestrarum*, cum hoc secundum proprietatem nemo fecisse israhelitarum commemoretur uel legatur, quia nec quisquam potest, nisi forte diuidat ea per multas partes domus suae? An hyperbolica commendatio est, sicut multa dicuntur?" Ibid., XVII, CCSL 33, p. 287.

4   Ibid., XV, CCSL 33, pp. 283-286.

5   Ibid., XXXVIII, CCSL 33, pp. 296.

6   "Manifestum est, non tantum totam legem et prophetas in illis duobus pendere praeceptis dilectionis dei et proximi, quae adhuc sola scriptura sancta erat, cum hoc dominus diceret, sed etiam quaecumque posterius salubriter consecrata sunt memoriae que mandata diuinarum uolumina litterarum." Augustine, *De catechizandis rudibus*, IV.8, CCSL 46, ed. Johannes B. Bauer (Turnhout: Brepols, 1969), p. 128.

Augustine explored the benevolence behind the precept on pledge taking (Deut. 24:10-13) in Question 41 and the precept on the care for widows (Deut. 24:17) in Question 43.[1] A complex theological discussion on the distinction between *similitudo* and *imago* is unfolded in Question 4 (on Deut. 4:16).[2] The relationship between human action and divine intervention stands out as a theme of multiple questions,[3] which echoes Augustine's controversy with Pelagius over Grace and free will.[4]

When Augustine made figural/allegorical interpretations, he did it discreetly. He recognized certain common "signs" in Deuteronomy and related them to what "pertains to the New Testament."[5] Question 30 on Joshua mentions "Deuteronomy that is translated as the second law" in passing, and regards it as one of the signs for the New Testament along with the renewal of the tablets (Exodus 34:1-4) and Joshua's repetition of the covenant (Joshua 24:25).[6] However, Augustine did not elaborate the "Deuteronomy-Gospel" typological motif in any of his Deuteronomy questions. In Question 49 on Deut. 29:1 ("These are the words of the testament which the Lord commanded Moses to establish with the sons of Israel in the land of Moab, beside that testament given to them in Horeb"), Augustine provided a purely literal exposition of "Deuteronomy as the second law":

> It shows why the book of Deuteronomy is called a kind of second law, where there is the repetition of the former law rather than anything else. For there are few things in the second law that are not in the law given earlier.[7]

The conscious restraint from allegorical exegesis in *Quaestiones* can be more clearly revealed in a specific case in comparison with another work of Augustine: *De octo*

---

1 Augustine, *Quaestionum in Heptateuchum libri VII, in Deuteronomium*, XLI, CCSL 33, pp. 297-298.

2 Ibid., IV, pp. 276-277.

3 For example, ibid., XV.4, pp. 285-286; XXX, p. 292.

4 Cf. Gerald Bonner, "Augustine and Pelagianism," *Augustinian Studies* 24 (1993): pp. 27-47; idem, "Augustine, the Bible and the Pelagians," *Augustine and the Bible*, ed. Pamela Bright (Notre Dame: University of Notre Dame Press, 1999), pp. 227-242.

5 The Levites as Christian priesthood: "Nisi per hanc tribum significaretur uniuersum regale sacerdotium, quod ad nouum pertinet testamentum." Augustine, *Quaestionum in Heptateuchum libri VII, in Deuteronomium*, XVI, CCSL 33, pp. 286-287; sheep for Christ: "Boues, cum immolationem paschae de oue tantummodo commendauerit, quam iussit accipi ex ouibus et haedis uel ex capris? Quod mystice accipitur propter Christum, cuius ex iustis et peccatoribus est origo carnalis." Ibid., XXIV, p. 290; horns of bull for the arms of the Cross: "Quod non ita legendum est, tamquam dixerit: primogenitus tauri, sed, cum sit primogenitus, pulchritudo eius tauri est; propter crucis cornua de domino intellegitur figuratum." Ibid., LVII, p. 311.

6 "Repetitio quippe testamenti novum testamentum significat; quod significat et deuteronomium, quod interpretatur secunda lex; quod significant et prioribus confractis tabulae renovatae. Multis enim modis significandum quod uno modo inplendum fuit." Ibid., *in Iosue*, XXX, p. 333.

7 "Ostendit unde appellatus sit liber Deuteronomion quasi secunda lex. Ubi magis illius repetitio est quam aliquid aliud; pauca enim sunt, quae ibi non sint, quod primum datum est." Ibid., *in Deuteronomium*, XLVIIII, p. 304.

quaestionibus ex ueteri testamento. It contains an exposition of the so-called levirate law that an Israelite man is obliged to marry his brother's childless widow and the children born from them are to be reckoned by the name of the dead (Deut. 25:5-6). Augustine's interpretation there is an allegorical one:

> The wife of the dead man is the church, which Christ left among the first believers, and he ascended to the Father through his death and resurrection. In order to beget children, she was joined to the Apostles and the leaders of all the churches. Christ in the Gospel calls the Apostles "brothers." They labored in the church and provided seed, not for themselves but for their dead brother. Also, by His name were called Christians who were to be born from the apostolic fathers via the Gospel.[1]

The theological notes in *De octo quaestionibus* are thought to derive from an unknown Greek author.[2] Augustine adopted the same exposition of the levirate law in his 33-book *Contra Faustum Manichaeum*, a polemical work composed in the early 400s.[3] However, when treating the identical Deuteronomic passage in *Quaestiones*, Augustine totally evaded the allegorical interpretation, and exclusively focused on clarifying how Israel practiced the law, especially in the light of the marriage between Ruth and Boaz.[4]

In a passage in *De Genesi ad litteram*, to which, as we have discussed above, *Quaestiones* can be seen as a sequel, Augustine proclaimed an exegetical principle for the first group of books of the Old Testament:

> As far as the genre of expression (*genere locutionis*) is concerned, the account in these biblical books (*in his libris*) is not of figural things (*figuratarum rerum*) as in the Song of Songs, but entirely of past deeds (*gestarum*) as in the books of the Kingdoms (*regnorum libris*) and others of the same kind. Because the things narrated there pertain to the most common practices of human life, it is not hard that they are most immediately grasped in the literal sense, so that what of future things those deeds

---

1   "Coniux defuncti est ecclesia, quam in illis primis fidelibus Christus reliquit et per mortem ac resurrectionem ascendit ad patrem. Haec ut filios generaret, coniuncta est apostolis et rectoribus quarumque ecclesiarum. Ipse namque in euangelio fratres appellat apostolos, qui operantes in ea suscitarent semen, non sibi, sed defuncto fratri suo, ex cuius etiam nomine uocarentur Christiani, qui patribus apostolis per euangelium nascerentur." Augustine, *De octo quaestionibus ex ueteri testamento*, VII, CCSL 33, ed. Donatien De Bruyne (Turnhout: Brepols, 1958), p. 471.
2   Rainer Jakobi, "Eine Augustinische Echtheitsfrage: De Octo Quaestionibus ex Veteri Testamento," *Augustinianum* 48 (2008): pp. 205-210.
3   Augustine, *Contra Faustum*, XXXII.10, CSEL 25, ed. Josef Zycha (Vienna: Verlag der Österreichischen Akademie der Wissenschaften, 1891), pp. 768-769.
4   Augustine, *Quaestionum in Heptateuchum libri VII, in Deuteronomium*, XLVI, CCSL 33.

themselves may signify may also be dug out from it later.[1]

Book 2 of *De doctrina christiana* divides the Old Testament canons into two classes: *historia* and *prophetia*. *Historia* consists of the Heptateuch, four books of Samuel and Kings (with Ruth), as well as two books of Chronicles, Job, Tobias, Esther, Judith, two books of Esdras (Ezra and Nehemiah), and two books of Maccabees. The catalogue *prophetia* contains Psalms, three books of Solomon (Proverbs, Song of Songs, and Ecclesiastes), two books of Jesus the son of Sirach (Wisdom and Ecclesiasticus), and four major and twelve minor prophets.[2] The exegetical implication behind this special canonical classification could explains why, as mentioned above, Augustine preferred to investigate the literal sense of the Heptateuch in *De Genesi ad litteram* and *Quaestiones*.

The search for *prophetia* is not completely absent in the Deuteronomy questions, though. In Deut. 33:1-5, the prologue to the Blessings of Moses, Moses stated that God came from Sinai, rose up from Seir, hastened from Paran to Cades with many thousands, and spared his people. In Question 56, Augustine read this Deuteronomic passage as a *prophetia* spoken out not from the person of Moses but from Christ.[3] Based on Jerome's Hebrew etymology, He interpreted Sinai ("trial") as Christ's passion; Seir ("hairy") as gentile sinners; Paran ("fruitful mountain") as the church; Cades ("changed" or "sanctity")

---

1 "Narratio quippe in his libris non genere locutionis figuratarum rerum est sicut in Cantico Canticorum, sed omnino gestarum est sicut in regnorum libris et huiuscemodi ceteris. Sed quia illic ea dicuntur, quae uitae humanae usus notissimus habet, non difficile, immo promtissime primitus accipiuntur ad litteram, ut deinde ex illis quid etiam futurorum res ipsae gestae significauerint exculpatur." Augustine, *De Genesi ad litteram libri duodecim*, VIII.1, CSEL 28/1, ed. Josef Zycha (Vienna: Verlag der Österreichischen Akademie der Wissenschaften, 1894), pp. 229-230.

2 "Totus autem canon scripturarum, in quo istam considerationem versandam dicimus, his libris continetur: quinque Moyseos, id est Genesi, Exodo, Levitico, Numeris, Deuteronomio, et uno libro Iesu Nave, uno Iudicum, uno libello qui appellatur Ruth, qui magis ad Regnorum principium videtur pertinere; deinde quattuor Regnorum et duobus Paralipomenon, non consequentibus sed quasi a latere adiunctis simulque pergentibus. Haec est historia, quae sibimet adnexa tempora continet atque ordinem rerum. Sunt aliae tamquam ex diverso ordine, quae neque huic ordini neque inter se conectuntur, sicut est Iob et Tobias et Esther et Iudith et Machabaeorum libri duo et Esdrae duo, qui magis subsequi videntur ordinatam illam historiam usque ad Regnorum vel Paralipomenon terminatam. Deinde prophetae, in quibus David unus liber Psalmorum, et Salomonis tres, Proverbiorum, Cantici Canticorum et Ecclesiastes; nam illi duo libri, unus qui Sapientia et alius qui Ecclesiasticus inscribitur, de quadam similitudine Salomonis esse dicuntur; nam Iesus Sirach eos conscripsisse constantissime perhibetur. Qui tamen quoniam in auctoritatem recipi meruerunt inter propheticos numerandi sunt. Reliqui sunt eorum libri qui proprie prophetae appellantur, duodecim prophetarum libri singuli, qui conexi sibimet, quoniam numquam seiuncti sunt, pro uno habentur; quorum prophetarum nomina sunt haec: Osee, Ioel, Amos, Abdias, Ionas, Micha, Naum, Abacuc, Sophonias, Aggeus, Zacharias, Malachi. Deinde quattuor prophetae sunt maiorum voluminum: Esaias, Hieremias, Daniel, Hiezechiel." Augustine, *De doctrina christiana*, II.26-28, ed. Green, P. 68. Cf. Anne-Marie La Bonnardière, "The Canon of Sacred Scripture," *Augustine and the Bible*, ed. Pamela Bright (Notre Dame: University of Notre Dame Press, 1999), pp. 26-41.

3 "Non neglegenter praetereunda est ista prophetia. Adparet quippe ista benedictio ad nouum populum pertinere, quem dominus christus sanctificauit, ex cuius persona ista dicuntur a Moyse, non ex persona ipsius Moysi, quod in consequentibus euidenter adparet." Augustine, *Quaestionum in Heptateuchum libri VII, in Deuteronomium*, LVI, CCSL 33, p. 309.

as the conversion of the gentiles. The gentiles will become the new people (*populum nouum*) sanctified by God under the name of sons of Israel, and will participate in the ultimate salvation of the nation of Israel.[1]

Quaestiones enjoyed a fairly good manuscript circulation and a high reputation in the early medieval west.[2] However, paradoxically, the *de facto* influence of this Augustinian work was limited at best. Eugippius abbot of Lucullanum composed the first substantial anthology of Augustine's writings, known as *Excerpta ex operibus sancti Augustini* (ca. 500).[3] Organized in thematic order under 384 chapter headings, Eugippius' *Excerpta* was highly recognized as an entrance to Augustine's biblical exegesis in the early Middle Ages, witnessed by the *Notatio de illustribus uiris*, a ninth-century instruction of study composed by the Carolingian monk Notker the Stammerer (840–912) for his former pupil Solomon:

> I think it is useful to you above all to acquire Eugippius, who collected a greatly helpful and very essential volume about the whole authority of the Holy Scripture from all the books of the same most profound and insightful Augustine, in which you will discover many mysteries uncovered about Genesis, Exodus, Leviticus, Numbers,

---

1   "Nimirum ergo prophetia est, ut diximus, populum nouum christi gratia sanctificatum praenuntians ideo sub nomine filiorum israhel, quia semen est Abraham, hoc est filii sunt promissionis, et interpretatio eius est 'uidens deum.' Dominus ergo, qui ex sina uenit, christus intellegendus est, quoniam sina interpretatur 'tentatio.' Venit ergo ex tentatione passionis, crucis, mortis. Et alluxit ex seir. Seir interpretatur 'pilosus,' quod significat peccatorem; sic enim natus est esau odio habitus. Sed quoniam qui sedebant in tenebris et in umbra mortis, lux orta est eis, ideo alluxit ex seir. Simul etiam non absurde intellegitur esse praedictum ex gentibus quae significantur per nomen Seir, quia mons est pertinens ad Esau, uenturam gratiam christi populo Israhel. Unde dicit apostolus: ita et hi nunc non crediderunt in uestra misericordia, ut et ipsi misericordiam consequantur. Ipsi ergo dicunt: alluxit ex seir nobis. Et festinauit ex monte Pharan — id est ex monte fructifero; id enim interpretatur Pharan, quo significatur ecclesia — cum multis milibus cades. Et 'mutata' interpretatur Cades et 'sanctitudo.' Mutata sunt ergo multa milia et sanctificata per gratiam, cum quibus uenit Christus ad Israhelitas postea colligendos." Augustine, *Quaestionum in Heptateuchum libri VII, in Deuteronomium*, LVI, CCSL 33, p. 310.
2   For the early medieval transmission of *Quaestiones*, see CCSL 33, pp. vii-xvi. Cassiodorus in *Institutiones* described *Quaestiones* as "exceedingly essential and syllogistic demonstration" for questions hidden in the Holy Scripture: "Quaestiones etiam quae in uoluminibus sacris ardua difficultate poterant operiri, libris septem necessaria nimis et syllogistica probatione declarauit, enisus magister optimus et uir acer ingenio ut quod ad salutem animarum constat esse concessum nequaquam indiscussum mortifera neglegentia linqueretur." *Institutiones*, I.1.4, ed. Mynors, p. 12. The Carolingian scholar Notker the Stammerer referred to *Quaestiones* as an essential reference book for the interpretation of the Septateuch: "In totum eptatheucum septem libros quaestionum Augustini et alios VI locutionum de diuersitate interpretum..." Notker, *Notatio de illustribus uiris*, in Erwin Rauner, "Notkers des Stammlers 'Notatio de illustribus uiris.' Teil I: Kritische Edition," *Mittellateinisches Jahrbuch* 21 (1986): pp. 34-69.
3   For Eugippius and *Excerpta ex operibus sancti Augustini*, see Abigail Kathleen Gometz, *Eugippius of Lucullanum: A Biography* (Ph.D. dissertation: University of Leeds, 2008), pp. 76-164; Michael Gorman, "The Manuscript Tradition of Eugippius' *Excerpta ex operibus sancti Augustini*," *Revue Bénédictine* 92 (1982): pp. 7-32, 229-265; Joseph Lienhard, "The Earliest 'Florilegia' of Augustine," *Augustinian Studies* 8 (1977): pp. 21-32.

the book of Deuteronomy, Joshua, Judges, books of Samuel, of Kings, and of prophets.[1]

However, Eugippius selected no more than a single entry from the fifth book of *Quaestiones*: Question 42 on Deut. 24:16 ("Fathers shall not die for their sons, and sons shall not die for their fathers. Each one shall die in his own sin") is quoted as one of a cluster of chapters concerning the problem of sin.[2] Eugippius apparently did not find the same kind of theological significance in other Deuteronomy questions of Augustine. The case of Eugippius' *Excerpta* is symptomatic. We cannot find any use of or reference to *Quaestiones* among extant Latin commentaries on Deuteronomy prior to 800.[3] There is also no trace of the influence of this Augustinian work in the Lyon Annotations.

Augustine's technical approach to exploring the subtle literal meaning did not meet the favor of "spiritual" — theological or moral — understanding of the Bible dominant in early medieval exegetical culture. As we will see in the sixth-century compilation by John the Deacon and the seventh-century commentary by Isidore, Augustine's contribution to the exegesis of Deuteronomy that was well received in the early Middle Ages came not from the fifth book of *Quaestiones*, but his *Contra Faustum Manichaeum*.

5.2 Eucherius of Lyon, *Instructiones and Formulae*

Around 430, the year in which Augustine died in North Africa, Eucherius in southern Gaul composed a two-book manual of biblical interpretation, known as *Instructiones*, for his son Salonius. By then, Eucherius had not yet become bishop of Lyon, and lived as an ascetic in the well-known monastic community at Lérins together with his wife and chil-

---

1 "Et quod pre omnibus utile tibi puto, acquire Eugyppium, qui ex omnibus libris profundissimi et penetralissimi eiusdem Augustini in omnem auctoritatem diuinae scripturae utilissimum et ualde necessarium uolumen collegit, in quo multa mysteria de genesi, de exodo, de leuitico, de numero, de libro deuteronomii, Iosue et iudicum, Samuhele et Malachim et prophetis reserata reperies." Notker, *Notatio de illustribus uiris*, ed. Rauner, p. 59.

2 Eugippius, *Excerpta ex operibus sancti Augustini*, c. 376, CSEL 9/2, ed. Pius Knöll (Vienna: Verlag der Österreichischen Akademie der Wissenschaften, 1875).

3 In the early ninth century, Hrabanus copied almost verbatim all the fifty-seven Deuteronomy questions of *Quaestiones* in his encyclopedic commentary on Deuteronomy. Cf. Silvia Cantelli, *Hrabani Mauri opera exegetica*, vol. 2, pp. 553-576.

dren.[1]

Eucherius composed *Instructiones* as a supplement to the prosperous intellectual and educational life at Lérins under the leadership of *magistri* including Hilary, Salvian, Honoratus, and Vincentius.[2] He pointed out its theme in the prologue:

> You often ask me for the solution of many issues that require an interpreter of sacred scriptures. Let me recall those that you, my Salonius, brought forward sedulously and copiously with the zeal of knowing, as they have come back to memory, and let me answer them, not based on my own ingenuity but on the opinion of the famous teachers, not from my own rashness but from the authority of others, following not so much the ostentation of prideful eloquence but the way of necessary brevity. For to be able to satisfy your innumerable quests, I feel free to insert in addition something that I regard helpful to your knowledge. It is about what *alleluia*, *diapsalma*, and *amen* signify, what are *cidaris*, *siclus*, and others that need interpreting, which frequently appear in the Holy Scripture or are used in quantity in the liturgy of the church. Since these terms appear in a great amount to those who read through the whole corpus of scriptures, I consider it reasonable to show them altogether to you in this work, along

---

1   For the life and works of Eucherius, see the critical study of John M. Pepino, *St. Eucherius of Lyons: Rhetorical Adaptation of Message to Intended Audience in Fifth Century Provence* (Ph. D. dissertation: University of Leeds, 2008), pp. 76-164. The study of the exegesis of Eucherius usually focuses on his *Formulae spiritalis intellegentiae* rather than *Instructiones*, e.g.: Joseph F. Kelly, "Eucherius of Lyons: Harbinger of the Middle Ages," *Studia Patristica* 23 (1989): pp. 138-42; Martine Dulaey, "Eucher de Lyon exégète: l'interprétation de la Bible en Gaule du Sud dans la première moitié du Ve siècle," *Mauritius und die Thebäische Legion/Saint Maurice et la légion thébaine: Actes du colloque international Fribourg, Saint-Maurice, Martigny, 17–20 Septembre 2003*, eds. Otto Wermelinger, Philippe Bruggisser, Beat Näf, Jean-Michel Roessli (Fribourg: Academic Press, 2005), pp. 67-95; Charlotte Kempf, "Eucherius von Lyon: *Formulae spiritalis intellegentiae* und *Instructiones*," *Handbuch der Bibelhermeneutiken von Origenes bis zu Gegenwart*, ed. Oda Wischmeyer (Berlin: De Gruyter, 2016), pp. 63-71. For the only study of the structure of *Instructiones*, see Bardy, "La Littérature patristique," 42 (1933): pp. 14-22.
2   According to Eucherius' description: "Dignum namque est quacumque cura mea ingenium tuum remunerari qui uix dum decem natus annos heremum ingressus inter illas sanctorum manus non solum inbutus uerum etiam enutritus es sub Honorato patre, illo, inquam, primo insularum postea etiam ecclesiarum magistro; cum te illic beatissimi Hilarii tunc insulani tironis sed iam nunc summi pontificis doctrina formaret per omnes spiritalium rerum disciplinas, ad hoc etiam te postea consummantibus sanctis uiris Saluiano atque Vincentio eloquentia pariter scientia que praeeminentibus. His igitur tot ac talibus usus magistris ex me quoque minimo omnium audies quae sciscitatus es. In quibus iam nunc et interrogantem te et me respondentem recognosce. Vale in Christo." Eucherius, *Instructionum ad Salonium libri II*, CCSL 66, pp. 77-78. The intellectual background of Lérins at the time of Eucherius, see Clemens M. Kasper, *Theologie und Askese: Die Spiritualität des Inselmönchtums von Lérins im 5. Jahrhundert* (Münster: Aschendorff, 1991). The background of ecclesiastical politics, see Ralph W. Mathisen, *Ecclesiastical Factionalism and Religious Controversy in Fifth-Century Gaul* (Washington, D.C.: Catholic University of America Press, 1989), pp. 69-140.

with their meanings.[1]

Book 1 of *Instructiones* is "on the more difficult questions of the Old and New Testament," organized in question-and-answer format by the order of biblical canons. Book 2 of *Instructiones* is a lexicon of biblical proper nouns, especially those transliterated from Hebrew, Greek, and Aramaic. Most of the items are short *ad litteram* definitions. Eucherius' other exegetical manual, *Formulae spiritalis intellegentiae*, composed between 432 and 434 for his other son Veranus, adopts a similar lexical format. It is a dictionary of the "spiritual meanings" of scriptural symbols supplied with exemplary scriptural citations.[2] Eucherius published *Instructiones* and *Formulae* altogether to a wider audience after he became the bishop of Lyon.[3]

Eucherius in *Formulae* cited Deuteronomy for seven times as examples of biblical symbols. Five of them are from Deut. 32, the Song of Moses, one of the canticles, with which the immediate audience of *Formulae*, that is Veranus and other monks of Lérins, would be greatly familiar from the Divine Office.[4] Besides, Deut. 6:4 is cited to demonstrate *unitas Deitatis*,[5] and Deut. 7:1 cited to demonstrate that nations can be the symbol of sins.[6]

---

1 "Saepe a me requiris multarum rerum absolutionem quae in diuinis uoluminibus interpretem postulant; colligam, prout redierint in memoriam quae a te, mi Saloni, studio cognoscendi sedule copiose que prolata sunt, atque eis non ex meo ingenio sed ex illustrium doctorum iudicio, neque ex propria temeritate sed ex aliorum auctoritate respondeam consectans non tam eloquii exultantis ambitum quam necessariae breuitatis modum. Sic enim et innumeris satisfieri inquisitionibus tuis poterit et mihi insuper liberum erit aliqua extrinsecus quae cognitioni tuae utilia arbitror inserere, ut est illud, quid significet alleluia, diapsalma, amen, quid sit cidaris, ephod, siclus et cetera, quae uel in sacris libris frequentata uel maxime in ecclesiae usu posita interpretationem requirunt. Haec cum se legentibus per totum Scripturarum corpus crebro offerant, non ab re existimaui ea tibi cum significationibus suis in opere hoc quasi coaceruata ostendere." Eucherius, *Instructionum ad Salonium libri II*, CCSL 66, p. 77.

2 The content of the ten books of *Formulae*: "Oremus itaque Dominum, ut reuelet condensa Scripturarum suarum et proferamus, quomodo secretiore intellectu sentiendum sit: I. De his quae appellantur membra Domini uel quae de eo significantur. II. De supernis creaturis. III. De terrenis. IIII. De animantibus. V. De uariis nominum appellationibus. VI. De interiore homine. VII. De his quae in usu atque in medio habentur. VIII. De uariis uerborum uel nominum significationibus. VIIII. De Hierusale uel aduersis eius. X. De numeris." Eucherius, *Formulae spiritalis intellegentiae*, "Epistula ad Veranum," CCSL 66, ed. Carmela Mandolfo (Turnhout: Brepols, 2004) p. 5.

3 Cf. *Epistula Rustici ad Eucherium*, CSEL 31, ed. Karl Wotke (Vienna: Verlag der Österreichischen Akademie der Wissenschaften, 1894), pp. 197-199.

4 "Vinea ecclesia uel populus Israhel... item in malam partem: *Ex uinea enim Sodomorum uitis eorum*." Eucherius, *Formulae spiritalis intellegentiae*, III, CCSL 66, p. 17; "Vitis Christus... item in aliam partem ut supra in cantico Deuteronomii: *Ex uinea Sodomorum uitis eorum*." Ibid.; "Palmites apostoli uel sancti... et in malam partem in cantico Deuteronomii: *Et palmes eorum ex Gomorra*." Ibid.; "Vuae fructus iustitiae... item in malam partem in Deuteronomino: *Vua eorum uua fellis*." Ibid.; "Promptuaria cordis receptacula; in cantico Deuteronomii: *Et in promptuariis timor*." Ibid., VII, p. 49.

5 "Hic numerus ad unitatem Deitatis refertur; in Pentateucho: *Audi Israhel, Dominus Deus tuus Dominus unus est*." Ibid., X.1, p. 72.

6 "Gentes uitia; in Pentateucho: *Cum introduxerit te Dominus Deus tuus in terram quam possessurus ingredieris et deleuerit gentes multas coram te*." Ibid., IX, p. 70.

Book 1 of *Instructiones* contains two questions on Deuteronomy (Pentateuch Questions 41 and 42). The first is on a discrepancy over the number of people going to Egypt with Jacob found between Deut. 10:22 (70) and Acts 7:14 (75). Eucherius' response is:

It is certain that when Jacob went to Egypt, there were as many as seventy souls, including Joseph and his sons Ephraim and Manasse. But when the number of souls is mentioned there as seventy-five, he [the author of the Acts of Apostles] reckoned sons and grandsons of Ephraim and Manasse to be counted by anticipation, who according to the narrative of the Holy Scripture were born in Egypt afterwards.[1]

This interpretation is based on the entry for Genesis 46:26-27 of *Hebraicae quaestiones in Genesim*, a work, as we have mentioned in Chapter 4.3, composed by Jerome to introduce to Christians the original Hebrew text of the Holy Scripture (*hebraica ueritas*) and the Hebrew expositional teachings (*hebraicae traditiones*).[2] As one of Eucherius' major exegetical sources, Jerome serves as, according to Carmela Mandolfo, "un punto di riferimento constante" for *Instructiones*.[3]

Jerome's original exposition for Genesis 46:26-27 focuses on the variance between the Greek and Hebrew readings; that is, 75 souls went to Egypt with Jacob according to the Septuagint, but seventy according to the Hebrew text. Jerome preferred the *hebraica ueritas*. According to him, the 70 include Jacob, Joseph, Manasse, Ephraim, and the 66 descendants of Jacob mentioned in Genesis 46:26. The same number is confirmed by Deut. 10:22 in both the Greek and Hebrew texts. Jerome further noted that, compared with the Hebrew text, the LXX Genesis 46:20 contains an extra clause which lists Machir (Manasse's son), Galaad (Manasse's grandson), Sutallam and Taam (Ephraim's sons), and Edom (Ephraim's grandsons) as Joseph's offspring. He thus drew the deduction that the LXX Genesis 46:27 must have counted these five persons born after Jacob's entrance into Egypt by anticipation (*per anticipationem*), and that is how the number 75 arose. As for the number 75 in Acts 7:14, Jerome's explanation is that its author Luke, who might

---

1   "Constat quidem eo tempore quo Iacob ingressus est Aegyptum cum Ioseph filiisque eius Ephraim et Manasse septuaginta animas tantum fuisse; ibi uero ubi septuaginta quinque animarum numerus refertur, quasi per anticipationem etiam filios nepotesque Ephraim et Manasse numerandos putauit, quos postea in Aegypto natos diuinae relatio lectionis ostendit." Eucherius, *Instructionum ad Salonium libri II*, CCSL 66, p. 100.

2   Robert Hayward, *Saint Jerome's Hebrew Questions on Genesis* (Oxford: Clarendon Press, 1995), pp. 1-27.

3   Carmela Mandolfo, "L'influsso delle 'Hebraicae quaestiones in libro Geneseos' di Girolamo sulle 'Instructiones' di Eucherio di Lione," *Scritti classici e cristiani offerti a Francesco Corsaro*, eds., Carmelo Curti, Carmelo Crimi (Catania: Università degli studi di Catania, Facoltà di lettere e filosofia, 1994), vol. 2, pp. 435-453. Cf. Ilona Opelt, "Quellenstudien zu Eucherius," *Hermes* 91 (1963): pp. 476-483. The use of Jerome in *Formulae*, see Martine Dulaey, "Jérôme maître d'exégèse au monastère de Lérins: le témoignage des *Formulae* d'Eucher de Lyon," *Augustinianum* (44) 2004: pp. 371-400.

have been ignorant of Hebrew, should have adopted the Septuagint, which enjoyed wider circulation and greater authority at that time.[1]

In Pentateuch Question 41 of *Instructiones*, Eucherius summarized Jerome's conclusion in a very concise way, passing over all the complicated philological argumentations in his source.

Pentateuch Question 42 is on the verse "Cursed is everyone who is hung on a tree" (Deut. 21:23):

> How should we respond to the Jews who defame the testimony: Cursed is everyone who is hung on a tree? A guilty person who is hung on a tree is cursed, but not an innocent person. For the curse of innocence cannot be the punishment of sin. And if Mordecai had indeed fulfilled the king's crude sentence and got hung on the tree, would they judge that he deserved this curse? Or, would they consider Maccabees and others who, according to the testimony of the Holy Scripture, suffered similar death in most humiliating way as cursed persons? Similarly, our Savior who would redeem people did not flee the cross and so he died. Therefore, as we glorify the Passion of the Lord in greater deeds, let them not make accusation falsely in smaller deeds. It is not surprising if Christ, who we claim that descended to Hell, is said to have suffered

---

1   "*Omnes ergo animae, quae ingressae sunt cum Iacob Aegyptum et quae exierunt de femoribus eius, absque mulieribus filiorum Iacob, animae sexaginta sex: filii autem Ioseph, qui nati sunt ei in Aegypto, animae nouem. Omnes ergo animae, quae ingressae sunt cum Iacob Aegyptum, septuaginta et quinque.* Quod excepto Ioseph et filiis eius sexaginta sex animae, quae egressae sunt de femoribus Iacob, introierint Aegyptum, nulla dubitatio est. Ita enim et paulatim per singulos supputatus numerus approbat, et in hebraeis uoluminibus inuenitur. Hoc autem, quod in LXX legimus *filii autem ioseph, qui nati sunt ei in Aegypto, animae nouem,* sciamus in hebraeo pro nouem esse duas. Ephraim quippe et Manasse, antequam Iacob intraret Aegyptum et famis tempus ingrueret, nati sunt de Aseneth filia Phutiphare in Aegypto. Sed et illud, quod supra legimus facti sunt autem filii Manasse, quos genuit ei concubina Syra Machir: et Machir genuit Galaad: filii autem Ephraim fratris Manasse Sutalaam et Taam: filii uero Sutalaam Edem additum est, si quidem id, quod postea legimus, quasi per anticipationem factum esse describitur. Neque enim tempore illo, quo ingressus est Iacob Aegyptum, eius aetatis erant Ephraim et Manasse, ut filios generare potuerint. Ex quo manifestum est, omnes animas, quae ingressae sunt Aegyptum de femoribus Iacob, fuisse LXX, dum LXVI postea ingressae sunt et reppererunt in Aegypto tres animas, Ioseph scilicet cum duobus filiis eius, septuagesimus autem ipse fuerit Iacob. Hanc rem, ne uideamur aduersum scripturae auctoritatem loqui, etiam LXX interpretes transtulerunt in Deuteronomio quod in *LXX animabus ingressus est Israhel in Aegyptum.* Si quis igitur nostrae sententiae refragatur, scripturam inter se contrariam faciet. Ipsi enim LXX interpretes, qui hic LXXV animas per πρόλημψιν cum Ioseph et posteris suis Aegyptum ingressas esse dixerunt, in Deuteronomio LXX tantum introisse memorant. Quod si e contrario nobis illud opponitur, quo modo in actibus apostolorum in contione Stephani dicatur ad populum LXXV animas ingressas esse Aegyptum, facilis excusatio est. Non enim debuit sanctus Lucas, qui ipsius historiae scriptor est, in gentes actuum apostolorum uolumen emittens contrarium aliquid scribere aduersus eam scripturam, quae iam fuerat gentilibus diuulgata. Et utique maior opinionis illo dumtaxat tempore LXX interpretum habebatur auctoritas quam Lucas, qui ignotus et uilis et non magnae fidei in nationibus ducebatur. Hoc autem generaliter obseruandum quod ubicumque sancti apostoli aut apostolici uiri locuntur ad populos, his plerumque testimoniis abutuntur, quae iam fuerant in gentibus diuulgata, licet plerique tradant Lucam euangelistam ut proselytum hebraeas literas ignorasse." Jerome, *Hebraicae quaestiones in libro Geneseos*, CCSL 72, pp. 49-50.

the gallows, for he accepted death that originated with the curse of sin, although he had no sin of his own. Therefore, he was hung on the tree, so that by being hung on the tree, he can release us from the transgression, which is the trespass of death on the tree.[1]

Eucherius' response is based on another work of Jerome's, *Commentary on Galatians* composed in 386. On Galatians 3:13-14 in which Paul cites Deut. 21:23, Jerome commented that "it is a notorious question and we are accustomed to hear from the Jews the infamous charge that our Savior and Lord was under the curse of God."[2] He refuted that not everyone who hung on a tree was cursed, but only those who sinned and committed great crime. The Jewish heroes, including Maccabees and Mordecai, were sentenced to crucifixion but not cursed. Then, by comparing different versions (six Greek and one Hebrew) of this Deuteronomic verse, Jerome came to the conclusion that Jews must have interpolated "by God" after "Everyone who hangs on a tree is cursed" in Septuagint manuscripts, in order to slander Christ and Christians, because the word "curse" is never juxtaposed with the word "God" throughout the whole Hebrew Bible. Rather, Christ who had no sin undertook the curse for our salvation: He "descended to Hell, so that we could ascend to Heaven," and "hung on a tree, in order that he could remove the sin that we had committed through the tree of the knowledge of good and evil by being hung."[3]

Again, it is clear that, in Pentateuch Question 42, Eucherius took Jerome's elaborate argument — even Jerome's question[4] — cut off philological analysis, and condensed its theological thesis.

---

1   "XLII. Quid respondendum Iudaeis obicientibus testimonium illud: Maledictus omnis qui pendet in ligno? Maledictum esse hominem qui in ligno pendeat, sed noxium non innocentem. Neque enim innocentiae potest esse maledictum poena peccati. Et enim si Mardochaeus praeparato ligno appensus sententiam regiae crudelitatis explesset, numquid eum hi nunc dignum hac maledictione iudicarent? Aut Macchabaei atque alii quos Scriptura morte simili indignissime testatur adflictos numquid apud eos pro maledictis habentur? Quapropter Saluator noster a morte redempturus hominem ita crucem non refugit ut mortem. Igitur in minoribus non calumnientur, cum pro patientia Domini nos etiam in maioribus gloriemur. Nec mirum, si dicatur patibulum subisse, quem nos etiam ad inferna descendisse fateamur, qui cum proprium ipse peccatum non habuerit, suscepit tamen mortem de peccati maledictione uenientem. Atque idcirco pependit in ligno, ut nos delicto quod in ligno fuerat perditionis admissum ligno appensus absolueret." Eucherius, *Instructionum ad Salonium libri II*, CCSL 66, pp. 100-101.
2   "Haec idcirco congessimus quia famosissima quaestio est et nobis solet a Iudaeis pro infamia obici quod Saluator noster et Dominus sub Dei fuerit maledicto." Jerome, *Commentarium in epistula Paulina ad Galatas*, II.3, CCSL 77A, ed. Giacomo Raspanti (Turnhout: Brepols, 2006), p. 90.
3   "Ille descendit ad inferos ut nos ascenderemus ad caelum, ille factus est stultitia ut nos sapientia fieremus... Ille pependit in ligno ut peccatum quod commiseramus in ligno scientiae boni ac mali ligno deleret appensus." Ibid., p. 93.
4   Eucherius: "Quid respondendum Iudaeis obicientibus testimonium illud: Maledictus omnis qui pendet in ligno?" Jerome: "Haec idcirco congessimus quia famosissima quaestio est et nobis solet a Iudaeis pro infamia obici quod Saluator noster et Dominus sub Dei fuerit maledicto."

The simplification of Jerome in these two Deuteronomy entries of *Instructiones* well exemplifies Eucherius' own claim in the preface to answer questions "not based on my own ingenuity but on the opinion of the famous teachers," and "to follow not so much the ostentation of prideful eloquence but the way of necessary brevity." The combination of the tradition of *doctores* and the style of *breuitas* would have a long future in the medieval exegetical compiling practice.[1]

In Book 2 of *Instructiones*, Eucherius defined the Greek name *Deuteronomium* as "the second law in which there is the prefiguration of the evangelical law."[2] This certainly comes from Jerome's Letter 53 (cf. Chapter 4.3), the addressee of which, Paulinus of Nola, happened to be Eucherius' correspondent as well.[3] This entry makes Eucherius the first Latin author to quote Jerome's "Deuteronomy-Gospel" typological motif.

Therefore, significantly, all the Deuteronomy-related expositions in *Instructiones* are based on the works of Jerome. Martine Dulaey's recent meticulous source criticism of Eucherius' works contends that Eucherius used Augustine most often as his exegetical source.[4] But Eucherius resorted to the authority of Augustine, especially his *Enarrationes in Psalmos*, mainly for the sake of expounding Psalms.[5] In the case of Deuteronomy, as we have demonstrated, Eucherius' primary source was undeniably Jerome. In fact, Augustine did offer his own solutions to both Pentateuch Question 41 and 42 of *Instructiones*: the first in Genesis Question 152 of *Quaestiones in Heptateuchum*; the second in Book 14 of *Contra Faustum Manichaeum*.[6] Given that both the Augustinian works must

---

1 As Joseph F. Kelly commented in his "Eucherius of Lyons," p. 142: "What might we say then about Eucherius' exegesis? It is unimaginative but not uninformed; it is conservative but not reactionary; it takes the biblical text seriously but does little that is serious with the text... Eucherius wrote for a Church which was already living in that future. He apparently did not expect his episcopal sons to do great theology — and in this he was right as Salonius' surviving work demonstrates — and so he provided them with material for pastoral care: brief explanation of biblical passages, choices of interpretations to allow for varied audiences, catchwords to enliven a sermon in days when theology would be transmitted more and more by oral rather than by written means." Also cf. Katharina Greschat, "Spätantike Bildungstraditionen im Umkreis des Klosters von Lerinum: Die Kompendienwerke des Eucherius von Lyon," *Zeitschrift für Antikes Christentum* 10 (2007): pp. 320-335.

2 "Deuteronomium secunda lex in quo est euangelicae legis praefiguratio." Eucherius, *Instructionum ad Salonium*, II.15, CCSL 66, p. 215.

3 Cf. Paulinus of Nola, *Epistulae*, LI, CSEL 29, ed. Wilhelm Hartel (Vienna: Verlag der Österreichischen Akademie der Wissenschaften, 1894), pp. 423-425.

4 Martine Dulaey, "Augustin en Provence dans les premières décennies du Ve s: Le témoignage des Formulae d'Eucher," *Studia Ephemeridis Augustinianum* 90 (2004): pp. 121-146.

5 The exposition of Psalms, the biblical book most familiar to monks, understandably occupies a dominant proportion in both *Instructiones* and *Formulae*. There are 65 questions on Psalms in *Instructiones*, almost half of all the questions on the Old Testament (132 in total). In *Formulae*, 36% of all the cited biblical examples are from Psalms. This count is taken from Martine Dulaey, "Eucher de Lyon exégète," p. 78.

6 Augustine, *Quaestionum in Heptateuchum libri VII*, in *Genesim*, CLII, CCSL 33, pp. 58-59; idem, *Contra Faustum*, XIV.3, CSEL 25, p. 404.

have been available to Eucherius,[1] Eucherius seemed simply to prefer to Jerome's solutions.

After receiving the revised *Instructiones* and *Formulae* from Eucherius ca. 435, Rusticus of Narbonne praised that "as the preacher teaches posterity, you will be glorified in the mouth and love of all the Christians in the future."[2] Eucherius' *Nachleben* in the early medieval west was indeed very considerable.[3] Cassiodorus in his *Institutiones* listed Eucherius as one of the *introductores Scripturae diuinae* together with Tyconius (*Liber regularum*), Augustine (*De doctrina christiana*), Adrian (*Introduction to the Holy Scriptures*), and Junillus Africanus (*Instituta regularia diuinae legis*).[4] In the Carolingian era, according to Notker, Eucherius was known as the one who "proposed and solved many most useful expositions, both tropological and anagogical, of sacred scriptures."[5]

Since Eucherius was once the bishop of Lyon, it is natural to wonder about his influence on the Lyon Annotations. Eucherius' *Instructiones* and *Formulae* were certainly available in Lyon during the episcopate of Leidrad. Two manuscripts show the evidence. The first is Paris, BnF, Lat. 9550 (CLA, V.589), one of the earliest manuscripts of Eucherius' *opera*. According to Louis Holtz, this manuscript was produced in Lyon in the second half of the sixth century at the request of the abbot of the monastery of Condat. Leidrad brought the manuscript back to the episcopal library of Lyon ca. 800, likely for the sake of the biblical education that he initiated, which we have examined closely in Chapter 2.4.3. Florus studied the manuscript and left many corrections and annotations.[6]

The other relevant manuscript is Paris, BnF, Lat. 12236 (Bischoff, *Katalog*, 4783), copied in Lyon after a Spanish model. This manuscript also contains both *Instructiones*

---

1 Martine Dulaey, "Augustin en Provence," pp. 135, 138.

2 "Nam dum erunt superius conprehensa, omnium Christianorum ore et amore celebrabere praedicandus in posterum, dum doces posteros." *Epistula Rustici ad Eucherium*, CSEL 31, p. 199. Cf. Mark Vessey, "The Epistula Rustici ad Eucherium: from the Library of Imperial Classes to the Library of the Fathers," *Society and Culture in Late Antique Gaul: Revisiting the Sources*, eds. Ralph W. Mathisen and Danuta Shanzer (Burlington: Ashgate, 2001), pp. 278-297.

3 Cf. Thomas O'Loughlin's comment on *Formulae*: "I doubt if there is a single work of exegesis between AD 600 and 1,000 without traces of his [Eucherius'] work and method." See his "The Symbol Gives Life: Eucherius of Lyons' *Formula* for Exegesis," *Scriptural Interpretation in the Fathers: Letter and Spirit*, eds. Thomas Finan and Vincent Twomey (Dublin: Four Courts Press, 1995), pp. 221-252; for a survey of the medieval reception of *Formulae*, see pp. 245-249. Also cf. John M. Pepino, *St. Eucherius of Lyons*, pp. 267-300. The manuscript transmission, cf. CCSL 66, pp. x-xvii.

4 "Primum est post huius operis instituta ut ad introductores Scripturae diuinae, quos postea repperimus, sollicita mente redeamus, id est Ticonium Donatistam, sanctum Augustinum *De doctrina christiana*, Adrianum, Eucherium et Iunilium." Cassiodorus, *Institutiones*, I.10.1, ed. Mynors, p. 34.

5 "Habes Eucherium... qui multas et utilissimas interpretationes, tropologias et anagoges sanctarum scripturarum proposuit et dissoluit." Notker, *Notatio de illustribus uiris*, ed. Rauner, p. 64.

6 Louis Holtz, "La tradition lyonnaise," pp. 169-173.

and *Formulae*.[1] It is noteworthy that the text of *Instructiones* in this manuscript contains a third Deuteronomy question which may not be Eucherius' own but would be considered as Eucherius' in Carolingian Lyon:

> QUESTION: How is it said in Deuteronomy (5:9) that God was jealous, when He should suffer no disturbance? RESPONSE: As you say, God cannot be disturbed, but he is jealous in peaceful goodness, lest a soul that owes chastity to the only God be polluted in corruption and shame by many faults.[2]

The Lyon Annotator took up neither this interpolation nor the two authentic Deuteronomy questions in *Instructiones*. However, concerning biblical symbols, the potential influence of Eucherius, especially his *Formulae*, on the Lyon Annotations is identifiable (Table 5.1).

Table 5.1   Textual comparison between Eucherius and the Lyon Annotations

The Lyon Annotations (Paris, BnF, NAL 1740)	Eucherius (CCSL 66)
Robusta manus Dei, Filius eius est per quem omnia facta sunt: ipse et brachium eius a quo uniuersa continentur. (Deut. 4:34, fol. 15v)	Bracchium Domini Filius, per quem omnia operatus est. (*Formulae*, I, p. 6)
In manibus uero id est in bonis operibus semper ostendere. (Deut. 11:18, fol. 33r)	Manus opus. (*Formulae*, VI, p. 43)
Quid per silua nisi condensitatem sanctarum Scripturarum significat. De qua Scriptura in psalmo inscriptum est: Et reuelauit Dominus condensa. (Deut. 19:5, fol. 52r)	Condensa opaca uel contecta scripturae diuinae; in psalmo: *Et reuelabit condensa*. (*Formulae*, III, p. 19)
Quid per uineam nisi plebem significat fidelem et quid per semen nisi uerbum innuit predicationis. (Deut. 22:9, fol. 59r)	Vinea ecclesia uel populus Israhel. (*Formulae*, III, p. 17) Semen diuina praedicatio. (*Formulae*, III, p. 15)
... quem catholicum probauerint illi palmam uictoriae dare oportet. (Deut. 25:1, fol. 65r)	Palma perfectio uel uictoria. (*Formulae*, III, p. 21)
In agro, id est in mundo... (Deut. 28:16, fol. 72r)	Ager hic mundus. (*Formulae*, III, p. 15)

---

1 Philippe Lauer suggested that this manuscript was probably Leidrad's personal book, in his "Observations sur le Scriptorium de Lyon," *Bibliothèque de l'École des chartes* 86 (1925): pp. 380-87. Louis Holtz has reservation for this attribution, cf. Louis Holtz, "Leidrat, évêque de Lyon," p. 321.

2 "Int. Quomodo in Deut. (V, 9) Deus zelatus fuisse dicitur, cum in Deum nulla perturbatio cadat? Resp. Deus perturbari, ut ipse ais, non potest, sed tranquilla bonitate zelat: ne uni Deo debens anima castitatem per multos falsos corrupta et prostituta turpetur." PL 50, col. 782, cf. Paris, BnF, Lat. 12236, fol. 31v. The source of this interpolated entry is Augustine's Exodus Question 158: "Cum praeciperet deus loquens ad Moysen, ut data terra in potestate omnis idolatria euerteretur nec adorarentur dii alieni, ait: Dominus enim deus zelans nomen, Deus zelator est, id est: nomen ipsum, quod dominus deus dicitur, zelans est, quia deus zelator est. Quod non humanae perturbationis uitio facit Deus semper atque omni modo incommutabilis atque tranquillus; sed hoc uerbo indicat non inpune plebem suam per alienos deos fornicaturam. Ductum est enim uerbum tropo metaphora a zelo maritali, quo castitatem custodit uxoris, quod nobis prodest, non Deo." Augustine, *Quaestionum in Heptateuchum libri VII, in Exodum*, CLVIII, CCSL 33, p. 145.

Continued

The Lyon Annotations (Paris, BnF, NAL 1740)	Eucherius (CCSL 66)
Per arietes uero, duces ecclesiae. (Deut. 32:14, fol. 86v)	Arietes apostoli uel ecclesiarum principes. (*Formulae*, IV, p. 33)
Per uineas quoque Sodome et Gomorre, ut dictum est, peccata significat gentilium ignorantium deum. (Deut. 32:32, fol. 88r)	Vinea... in malam partem: Ex uinea enim Sodomorum uitis eorum. (*Formulae*, III, p. 17)
Per uuas uero, amaritudinis quasi nequissimos fructus, opera eorum mala ac peruersa demonstrare uoluit. (Deut. 32:32, fol. 88r)	Vuae... in malam partem in Deuteronomio: Vua eorum uua fellis. (*Formulae*, III, p. 17)
Iuxta anagogen, id est superiorem sensum. (Deut. 32:39, fol. 89r)	Anagoge superior sensus. (*Instructiones*, II, p. 216)
Gladius Domini siue sagitte, ultio illius in impiis et peccatoribus. (Deut. 32,42, fol. 89r)	Gladius uindicta uel sermo Domini. (*Formulae*, I, p. 7)
Ipse figuraliter rinocerota propter inuicta fortitudine. (Deut. 33.17, fol. 91v)	Rinoceron fortis quisque uel in bonam uel in malam partem. (*Formulae*, IV, p. 30)
Scutum, id est protectio. (Deut. 33:29, fol. 92v)	Scutum protectio Dei. (*Formulae*, I, p. 7)

The symbolic expositions that the Lyon annotator could have borrowed from Jerome, Gregory, or Isidore are not included in the chart above. But still, considering the flexible transmission of biblical typology in the early Middle Ages, the influential relationship suggested in the chart above needs to be taken as tentative.

The Lyon Annotations is also related to Eucherius via a mysterious theological piece *De diuinis nominibus*. Supposedly transcribed from an old manuscript, it appeared in Joannes Brassicanus' edition of *Formulae* of 1531 as its first chapter, and eventually got reprinted in Migne's PL (vol. 50, cols. 729-737). Scholars have tended to take *De diuinis nominibus* as an interpolation, not only because not a single extant copy of *Formulae* contains it, but also because parts of its content repeat what can be found in the authentic text of *Formulae*.[1] There is no scholarship at present, as far as we know, to date or to identify the origin of *De diuinis nominibus*. However, four entries in the Lyon Annotations show great resemblance to the text of *De diuinis nominibus* (Table 5.2).

---

1   Both Karl Wotke's CSEL edition and Carmela Mandolfo's CCSL edition of *Formulae* exclude *De diuinis nominibus*. *De diuinis nominibus* is close in content to the first chapter of a no less mysterious text named *De essentia diuinitatis* (PL 42, cols. 1199-1206) ascribed to many medieval authors, including Augustine, Ambrose, Jerome, Anselm, and Bonaventure. Cf. CCSL 66, pp. iv-v.

Table 5.2 Textual comparison between *De diuinis nominibus* and the Lyon Annotations

The Lyon Annotations (Paris, BnF, NAL 1740)	Pseudo-Eucherius, *De diuinis nominibus* (PL 50)
Id est spiritu Dei. (Deut. 9:10, fol. 27bis)	Digitus Dei singulariter Spiritus sanctus accipitur... (col. 732)
... ipse et brachium eius a quo uniuersa continentur. (Deut. 4:34, fol. 15v) Robusta manus Filius Dei est per quem omnia facta sunt; ipse est brachium extentum a quo omnia continetur. (Deut. 11:2, fol. 31v)	Brachia Dei Patris Filius eius et Spiritus sanctus intelliguntur... Idcirco autem Filius Dei Patris brachium dicitur, quia creatura electa ab ipso continetur. (col. 731)
Vsque in hodiernum diem abscondit Dominus faciem suam a Iudeis, subtrahendo illis cognitionem suam ita ut similes forent gentilibus qui non nouerunt Deum. (Deut. 32:20, fol. 87)	Abscondere Deus faciem legitur, cum quibusdam eorum ex gentibus culpis, cognitionem suam abscondit, sicut in populo Iudaeorum nunc impletum esse uidemus, quia negantes Filium Dei, scientiam ueri Dei ita perdiderunt, ut similes forent gentibus, quae Dominum non nouerunt. (col. 734)
Pedes eius apostoli intelleguntur per quos ceteris fidelibus ecclesiae euangelica doctrina tradita est (Deut. 33:3, fol. 90v).	Aliter autem pedes Domini, id est, Iesu Christi significant sanctos praedicatores, de quibus in Deuteronomio scriptum est: Qui appropinquant pedibus ejus, accipient de doctrina eius. (col. 733).

It is an open question whether *De diuinis nominibus* was available in Lyon ca. 800, and used as a source by the Lyon Annotator.

5.3   John the Deacon, *Expositio in Heptateuchum*

Paris, BnF, lat. 12309, a late ninth-century manuscript (Bischoff, *Katalog*, 4829) copied and preserved in the monastery of Corbie, contains a late antique Latin commentary on the first seven books of the Old Testament.[1] The *incipit* (in fol. 1v) gives its author as "John the deacon of the Roman church."[2] Scholars have speculated on the identity of this John. The proposed candidates include the legate of Pope Agatho (r. 678–681) who attended the third council of Constantinople (680/681), and the three namesake popes of the sixth century. Michael Gorman in a paper of 1996 supported the authorship of Johannes Hymonides who worked with Anastasius Bibliothecarius during the pontificate of Pope John VIII (r. 872–882); he was also the author of the ninth-century

---

1   For a thorough study of the manuscript and commentary on the Heptateuch in it, see Anne-Marie Genevois, "Autour de Jean Diacre et de son *Expositio in Heptateuchum*," *Du copiste au collectionneur: Mélanges d'histoire des textes et des bibliothèques en l'honneur d'André Vernet*, eds. Donatella Nebbiai-Dalla Guarda, Jean-François Genest, André Vernet (Turnhout: Brepols, 1999), pp. 35-48. For the manuscript, also see David Ganz, *Corbie in the Carolingian Renaissance*, p. 149, who catalogued the manuscript under "Mid-ninth century volumes in perfected caroline — Datable MSS." For the online facsimile, see http://gallica.bnf.fr/ark:/12148/btv1b90679163, last accessed September 14, 2021.

2   "EXPOSITUM IOHANNIS ROMANAE ECCLESIAE DIACONI." Paris, BnF, lat. 12309, fol. 1v.

hagiography of Gregory the Great.[1] This attribution cannot be right. As Gorman himself was aware, *Expositio in Heptateuchum* was known and used by Lupus of Ferrières (ca. 805–862), a younger contemporary of Johannes Hymonides living in *Francia*.[2] A textual transmission so quick across the Alps is almost impossible to imagine. Moreover, the latest identifiable source in *Expositio* is Victor of Capua (d. 554). If Hymonides were the author, it is hard to believe the man who composed a *uita* of Gregory the Great would not use any Gregorian expositions to compile a commentary on the Heptateuch. Anne-Marie Genevois who is working on an edition of *Expositio* suggests that Pope John III (561–574) was the author of this exegetical compilation.[3] I follow Genevois' authorial attribution.

The *Expositio in Heptateuchum* was one of the first biblical *catenae* in Latin, an exegetical genre that we have encountered in Chapter 4.2. It consists of excerpts selected from the works of various Christian authors. According to Jean Baptiste Pitra, more than 600 excerpts in the *Expositio* were drawn from 24 authors. Augustine and Jerome are quoted most; John Chrysostom, Origen, and Rufinus of Aquileia utilized frequently.[4] In the Corbie manuscript, the sources of excerpts are indicated in red ink by an author's name and a work's title, or by abbreviations such as "c.s." (*cuius supra*) and ub.s. (*uerbis supra*).

According to Genevois' survey of the sections on Genesis (fols. 2r-70r) and Exodus (fols. 70r-104v), John the Deacon's *Expositio* shows exclusive interest in elaborating theological teachings through the Holy Words. Baptismal catechesis or clerical instruction was probably its primary usage.[5] The author's own observation on the Deuteronomy section (fols. 129v-131v) accords with Genevois' evaluation. Deut. 3:23-24 ("And I besought the Lord at that time, saying: Lord God, you have begun to show unto thy servant thy greatness") is quoted at the very beginning, not expounded, but rather as a straightforward claim of Christian doctrine. Following it are seven entries. Except one, all the expositions were excerpted from Augustine's *Contra Faustum*. The only alternative source is Eucherius' *Instructiones*: Pentateuch Question 42 on Deut. 21:23 (cf. Chapter 5.2) is cited to supplement the exposition of the same biblical verse in *Contra Faustum* XIV.3.

It is possible, as scholars have suggested, that the text preserved in Paris, BnF, lat. 12309 is an abridged edition of John's original collection redacted during the copying

---

1   Michael Gorman, "The Commentary on the Pentateuch Attributed to Bede in PL. 91.189-394," *Revue Bénédictine* 106 (1996): pp. 61-108, 255-307, n. 15.

2   "Item Ioannes Ecclesiae Romanae diaconus praedestinatos malos sermonibus beati Augustini expressit, uolens ostendere quid significet illud Genesis." Lupus of Ferrières, *Collectaneum de tribus quaestionibus*, PL 119, col. 657; "Ut scribit Ioannes Romanae Ecclesiae diaconus, in libro ad Petrum de Regula uerae fidei, de praedestinatis, hoc modo disseruit." Ibid., col. 656.

3   Anne-Marie Genevois, "Autour de Jean Diacre," pp. 44-48.

4   Jean Baptiste Pitra, *Spicilegium Solesmense complectens sanctorum scriptorum ecclesiasticorum* (Paris: F. Didot, 1852-58), vol. 1, pp. lv-lxiv.

5   Anne-Marie Genevois, "Autour de Jean Diacre," pp. 35-48.

process in Carolingian Corbie.[1] Nevertheless, John the Deacon's strong theological and doctrinal concern was still clearly perceptible in the present version, and he certainly found that the exegesis of Deuteronomy in Augustine's *Contra Faustum* met his needs.

The *Contra Faustum* is Augustine's response to a doctrinally polemical work known as *capitula* composed by Faustus the Manichean bishop of Milevis (in North Africa) for the purpose of rejecting the Old Testament. Faustus' *capitula* presents the standard Manichean opinions on the Old Law that it is not merely irrelevant but opposed to the New Testament, and therefore useless and even poisonous to Christians. *Contra Faustum* as Augustine's response thus has primarily an exegetical nature, designed to display the defense of Catholic use of the Old Testament.[2] The general attitude toward the Old Testament precepts in *Contra Faustum* is:

> If people of that time and of that race [Jews] scorned those observances at the time when those observances were necessary to foretell the realities that have now been revealed, they would have been guilty, just as we [Christians] would be foolish if we thought that those prophetic observances (*praenuntiatiuas obseruationes*) did us any good, now that the New Testament has been revealed. But, in the same way, we would be sacrilegious and wicked if we thought that we should throw away those same books. For they were written for our sake (*propter nos scripti*) so that we might know and faithfully and firmly hold that those realities, which have now been revealed to us and proclaimed in full clarity, were foretold by those symbols so long before. After all, the Lord now does not command us to observe the things that were written there in a bodily manner, but to understand and to practice them in a spiritual manner... Hence, that scripture once served as a commandment (*praeceptum*) is now a testimony (*testimonium*).[3]

Neither to forsake (*abiciere*) nor to observe in a bodily manner (*obseruare corporaliter*), but to understand and to practice in a spiritual manner (*intellegere et facere spiritaliter*): This is Augustine's exegetical self-positioning for the Old Law in *Contra*

---

1 Anne-Marie Genevois, "Autour de Jean Diacre," p. 37.

2 David F. Wright, "Augustine: His Exegesis and Hermeneutics," *Hebrew Bible/Old Testament: The History of Its Interpretation. Volume I. From the beginnings to the Middle Ages (until 1300). Part 1: Antiquity*, ed. Magne Sæbø (Göttingen: Vandenhoeck and Ruprecht, 1996), pp. 701-730.

3 "Tam rei essent illius temporis et illius populi homines, si obseruare contemnerent, quando illa sic fieri, ista quae nunc reuelata sunt, tunc sic praenuntiari oportebat, quam nos desipientes essemus, si nunc iam manifesto nouo testamento illas praenuntiatiuas obseruationes aliquid nobis prodesse putaremus. Sicut sacrilegi et inpii, si eosdem libros, qui propter nos scripti sunt, ut ea, quae iam nobis reuelata et in manifestatione adnuntiata sunt, tanto ante illis figuris praenuntiata cognoscentes fideliter et firmiter teneremus, ideo putaremus abiciendos. Quia ea, quae ibi scripta sunt, non iam obseruare corporaliter, sed intellegere et facere spiritaliter nos dominus iubet... Unde scriptura ipsa tunc erat praeceptum, nunc testimonium." Augustine, *Contra Faustum*, VI.9, CSEL 25, pp. 299-301. The translation is based on *Answer to Faustus, a Manichean*, ed. Roland Teske, The Works of Saint Augustine: A Translation for the 21st Century 1/20 (Hyde Park: New City Press, 2006), p. 103.

Faustum.

All the excerpts in the Deuteronomy section of John the Deacon's *Expositio* and summarize the theme of each are listed in Table 5.3 .

Table 5.3   Exegesis of Deuteronomy in John the Deacon's *Expositio*

Contra Faustum	Capitula (Paris, BnF, lat. 12309, fols. 129v-131v)	Theme
XVI.19	Prophetam de gente tua et de fratribus tuis sicut me suscitabit tibi Dominus Deus tuus. (Deut. 18:15)	The promised prophet is Jesus Christ of whom Moses' successor Joshua is the figure. Not the Law given through Moses but the grace and truth made through Jesus Christ can lead to the Kingdom of Heaven.
XIV.3 (+Pentateuch Question 42 of Eucherius' *Instructiones*)	Quando peccaverit homo quod morte plectendum est, et adiudicatus morti adpensus fuerit in patibulo. (Deut. 21:23)	Christ embraced death for us who sin.
VI.9	Non arabis in boue simul et asino. (Deut. 22:10)	One should not join a wise and a fool together when proclaiming the Word of God.
XIX.26	Si acceperit homo uxorem et habuerit eam et non inuenerit gratiam ante oculos eius propter aliquam foeditatem. (Deut. 24:1)	Charitable consideration exists behind the law of divorce.
XXXII.10	Quando habitauerint fratres simul et unus ex eis absque liberis mortuus fuerit uxor defuncti non nubet alteri; sed accipiet eam frater eius. (Deut. 25:5-10)	The levirate law signifies how the Apostles "married" the Church after Christ's resurrection and ascension, and raised Christians as Christ's children.
XVI.22	Quod si nolueris audire vocem Domini Dei tui ut custodias et facias omnia mandata eius et caeremonias quae ego praecipio tibi hodie venient super te omnes maledictiones istae. (Deut. 28:15)	Moses' curses are uttered as prophecies.
XVI.22	Et erit vita tua pendens ante te. (Deut. 28:66)	"Your life hanging" prefigures Christ.

By taking *Contra Faustum* as his dominant source, John the Deacon embraced an Augustinian exegetical tradition for Deuteronomy alternative to what we have seen in *Quaestiones in Heptateuchum*. Due to its extremely limited transmission and influence, it is unlikely that John the Deacon's compilation directly influenced the Lyon Annotations. However, as we will see more closely in Chapter 6, via the intermediation of Isidore, the Lyon Annotator did absorb the Augustinian exegesis in *Contra Faustum* for the interpretation of Deut. 25:5-10 and that of Deut. 22:10.

5.4 Verecundus of Junca, *Commentarii super cantica ecclesiastica*

Between 533 and 545, the African Christian priest Verecundus, the future bishop of Junca in the African province of Byzacena, composed an elaborate commentary on Deut. 32:1-43 in his exposition of the Old Testament canticles. In the Christian context, biblical canticles, or odes, are poetic or hymnic passages selected from the Holy Scripture for liturgical use, especially in the singing of the Divine Office. Usually attached to Psalters, the canticles can be conveniently understood as "the psalms outside Psalter."[1]

Verecundus provided the first known Latin attempt to expound these canticles. He related in the preface that "Ezra the scribe of the Law collected certain canticles (*cantica*) from different books of the Holy Scripture that are similar to the Psalms of David, and added them to the book of Psalms, so that they can be sung in the same way as the psalms."[2] In early Christianity, the selection of canticles was not yet unified but greatly diverse.[3] In the lone manuscript that preserves the intact copy (Leiden, Universiteitsbibliotheek, Voss. lat. F 58, produced in Corbie in the first half of the ninth century, cf. Bischoff, *Katalog*, 2192), Verecundus' exposition contains commentaries on nine canticles: Moses' "Song of Sea" after Israel passed the Red Sea (Exodus 15:1-19), the "Song of Moses" at the end of his life (Deut. 32:1-43), the canticle of Jeremiah deploring the Babylonian captivity (Lamentations 5:1-22), the canticle of Azarias (Daniel 3:26-45), the canticle of Ezechias (Isaiah 38:10-20), the canticle of Habacuc (Habacuc 3), the prayer of Manasseh (taken as apocryphal in the western tradition), the canticle of Jonah in the belly of the fish (Jonah 2:3-10), and the canticle of Deborah (Judges 5:1-32). In 1905, Germain Morin discovered a twelfth-century manuscript (Metz, Bibliothèques-Médiathèques, 1212) that contains nine fragmentary pieces under the title *Verecundus presbiter in canticis prophetarum*, one of which is on the canticle of Isaiah (Isaiah 26).[4] Verecundus could thus have commented on more than nine Old Testament canticles.[5]

---

1 For canticles in early and medieval Christianity, see James Mearns, *The Canticles of the Christian Church, Eastern and Western, in Early and Mediaeval Times* (Cambridge: Cambridge University Press, 1914); Heinrich Schneider, "Die biblischen Oden im christlichen Altertum," *Biblica* 30 (1949): pp.28-65; Heinrich Schneider, "Die biblischen Oden seit dem sechsten Jahrhundert," *Biblica* 30 (1949): pp. 239-272; Heinrich Schneider, "Die biblischen Oden im Jerusalem und Konstantinopel," *Biblica* 30 (1949): pp. 433-452; Heinrich Schneider, "Die biblischen Oden im Mittelalter," *Biblica* 30 (1949): pp. 479-500.

2 "Cantica quaedam, quae in diuersis libris dispersa ad similitudinem Dauidicorum psalmorum Esdras scriba legis collegit, libroque psalmorum adiunxit, ut eodem sono cantuque psallantur, quo solent ipsi quoque psalmi cantari." Verecundus, *Commentarii super cantica ecclesiastica*, *In Exodi cantico*, 1, CCSL 93, ed. Roland Demeulenaere (Turnhout: Brepols, 1976), p. 3.

3 See the study of James Mearns and Heinrich Schneider cited above.

4 Germain Morin, "Un écrivain inconnu du XIe siècle: Walter, moine de Honnecourt, puis de Vézelay," *Revue Bénédictine* 22 (1905), pp. 165-180. Cf. CCSL 93, p. xviii.

5 Verecundus held a rather flexible attitude toward the selection of canticles: "Ceterum, quot sint numero cantica, non demonstrantur, quia frequenter ab aliis alia uidimus decantari." Verecundus, *Commentarii super cantica ecclesiastica*, *In Exodi cantico*, 1, CCSL 93, p. 3.

Deut. 32:1-43, known as the Song of Moses, played an important role in Jewish worship during the Second Temple Period. It was sung in the temple, recited in the synagogue, and recognized by Jewish authors such as Philo and Josephus as "the great ode of Moses."[1] It was one of the few Old Testament canticles universally recognized by various Christian churches in the Late Antiquity.[2] Early Christian exegetes generally understood the Song of Moses as a testimony against Israel's perfidy and a prophecy about the coming of Christ, the conversion of gentile nations, and the confession of the true faith, as we have seen exemplarily in Origen's works (cf. Chapter 4.2). Among Latin authors, Niceta of Remesiana (ca. 335–414) in his *De psalmodiae bono* summarized the Song of Moses as:

> When he [Moses] was about to die physically, he recited an awe-inspiring canticle in Deuteronomy. He left the canticle to the people as a testimony, so that the tribes of Israel would know what kind of ruin (*funera*) they would face if they left the Lord. Too pitiable [were] those who still did not want to and were not able to give up unlawful superstitions after hearing such clear denunciation.[3]

Verecundus' commentary on the Song of Moses is in line with the same exegetical tradition. It starts with:

> Deuteronomy that is called the second law — for the Greeks, *deuteros* means "second" and *nomos* "law" — contains a canticle in which Moses, at the end of his life, after instructing the people to celebrate ceremonies, invoked the heaven and the earth for testimony.[4]

Although he occasionally picked up bits from earlier authors such as Jerome, Augustine, and especially Eucherius (only *Formulae*),[5] Verecundus' exposition overall shows an independent exegetical mind. Understanding the Song of Moses as a prophetic testimony of faith, Verecundus took pains to exhaust the theological and doctrinal teachings hidden behind every sentence of the canticle. Christological interpretation is

---

1   Cf. Heinrich Schneider, "Die biblischen Oden im christlichen Altertum," pp. 31-32.
2   See the comparative table of the different early Christian lists of canticles in CCSL 93, pp. xxvi-xxvii.
3   "Ipse tamen Moyses corpore recessurus terrificum carmen in Deuteronomio iterauit, quod scriptum testamenti uice populo dereliquit, unde scirent tribus Israhel quae et qualia funera eos manerent cum a Domino recessissent: nimis miseri atque miserandi, qui tali tamque euidenti denuntiatione praemissa noluerunt aut nequiuerunt ab inlicitis superstitionibus praecauere." Cuthbert H. Turner, ed., "Niceta of Remesiana II: Introduction and Text of *De Psalmodiae Bono*," *The Journal of Theological Studies* 95 (1923): pp. 225-252.
4   "Deuteronomium, quod secunda lex appellator (*deuteros* quippe secunda, *nomos* lex dicitur apud Graecos) canticum habet, quo Moyses, ultimo sui temporis fine, postquam populum seruare ceremonias erudiuit, caelum ac terram in testimonium inuocauit." Verecundus, *Commentarii super cantica ecclesiastica*, *In cantico Deuteronomii*, 1, CCSL 93, p. 16.
5   Cf. the source apparatus in CCSL 93.

unsurprisingly omnipresent. For example, the father in Deut. 32:7 (*Interroga patrem tuum...*) is *spiritaliter* understood as Christ "whom we should call upon with inquiries, because he is the hidden hoard of wisdom and knowledge, from whom we would be able to learn virtue."[1] Another exegetical term frequently used by Verecundus is *mystice*. For example, for the wheat in Deut. 32:15 (*Cum adipe renum tritici et sanguinem uuae...*):

> But it makes sense well mystically (*mystice*). By wheat are signified sacred scriptures whose spiritual flour feeds the mind. Its exterior shell, that is historical reading (*historica lectio*), is to be left behind. The diversity of holocausts and sacrifices does not delight me; nor does the story that Jacob had four spouses, yielded to the hatred of the brother, collected many flocks for Laban, and shepherded both the flocks of one color and those of diverse colors. There are other things as well that can be understood full of mysteries if contemplated spiritually. Thus, all these shells of wheat should be peeled, and what are hidden interiorly seem similar to the marrow.[2]

For Verecundus, the exploration of inner meaning is an essential part of biblical reading. After an extensive exposition — as long as 110 lines in the CCSL edition — over a single verse (Deut. 32:42 "*Inebriabo sagittas meas sanguine, et gladius meus manducabit carnes*"), Verecundus appealed to his readers:

> Wise reader, turn yourself to the meals that have been served! Approach prudently, aware that you have to prepare these: That is, when you eat the tasty food by reading (*legendo*), obtain the understanding (*intellegentiam*) of sacred scriptures, so that you would be considered as the one who understands (*intellector*) just like the food preparer (*praeparator*).[3]

Verecundus himself was certainly such an able *intellector*. The omnipresent biblical citation testifies to his great familiarity with the Holy Bible.[4] Verecundus also had the

---

1 "Spiritaliter Christum patrem intellege, quem debemus interrogationibus prouocare, quoniam ipse est thesaurus sapientiae et scientiae absconditus, a quo uirtutem discere ualeamus." Verecundus, *Commentarii super cantica ecclesiastica, In cantico Deuteronomii*, 8, CCSL 93, p. 25.

2 "Mystice uero recte concurrit. Tritico Scripturae significantur diuinae, quarum spiritali similagine pascitur mens, cuius tamen exterius corium, id est historica lectio, relinquetur. Nec enim me iuuat holocaustorum sacrificiorumque diuersitas. Neque me iuuat Iacob connubia quattuor habuisse, fraternoque odio cedentem, plurima apud Laban pecora conquisisse: nunc uaria, nunc unicoloria pro pastorali labore tulisse. Et cetera, quae si spiritaliter cogitentur, plena mysteria cognoscentur. Haec ergo uniuersa tritici sunt coria conpellenda: quae autem ibi interius latent, medullae esse atque simila uidebuntur." Verecundus, *Commentarii super cantica ecclesiastica, In cantico Deuteronomii*, 15, CCSL 93, p. 32.

3 "Sapiens lector, adpositis adhibe te cibis! Prudenter adtinge, sciens te debere talia praeparare: hoc est Scripturarum sanctarum, dum legendo comedis delicias, intellegentiam para, ut talis intellector habearis, qualis fueris praeparator." Ibid., 43, p. 64.

4 For example, in the commentary on the Song of Moses alone, Verecundus cited the Psalms for fifty-six times. Cf. CCSL 93, pp. 223-226.

patience and learning to enumerate and distinguish multiple senses of a same biblical figure.[1] To give an example: for "A fire is kindled in my anger" (Deut. 32:22), he listed three kinds of fires inflamed by God as recorded in the Bible, cited relevant biblical passages as proof, and decided which fits the context of the Song of Moses best.[2] Verecundus was also not reluctant to juxtapose multiple meanings of the same biblical verse according to different senses, under exegetical catalogues including *historice, secundum litterae textum, secundum litteram, tropologice, moraliter, figuraliter, spiritaliter, mystice, allegorice, secundum spiritalem intellegentiam,* and *spiritali intellectu.*[3]

Verecundus was probably the only late antique Christian author to make a distinction between the tropological and moral senses, while other contemporary exegetes usually equated these two.[4] For instance, Verecundus interpreted Deut. 32:13 ("He fed them from the products of fields in the strength of the earth") respectively in historical, tropological, and moral senses:

> By the strength of the earth, he demonstrates fertility and abundance. By

---

1   E.g.: "Vini genera plura sunt, quae in Scripturis sanctis intellegibiliter demonstrantur..." Verecundus *Commentarii super cantica ecclesiastica, In cantico Deuteronomii,* 16, CCSL 93, pp. 32-33; "Longum est diuersarum genera uinearum praesenti loco subnectere. Sed curioso lectori quaedam intellegentiae semina conculcamus, ut cognoscat quae sit ista differentia uinearum..." Ibid., 33, pp. 52-53.
2   "Non enim unus est ignis qui sumammatur a Domino, sed triplex... Quaeritur ergo nunc cuius ignis speciem demonstrauit: utrum illius qui tantum peccatum consumit, homines autem non laedit, quem Dominus in terra ueniabiliter misit, an illius purgatorii, uel certe quem nuper diximus damnandorum. Vnde aestimo purgatorium dici, qui ad purgationem nostrorum census est delictorum, et usque ad inferos penetrabit, utpote ubi non tantum corpora, sed etiam animae post resurrectionem transibunt." Verecundus, *Commentarii super cantica ecclesiastica, In cantico Deuteronomii,* 23, CCSL 93, pp. 40-42.
3   One may wonder whether Augustine's promotion of this exegetical method could have influenced his later African compatriot: "Quando autem ex eisdem scripturae uerbis non unum aliquid sed duo uel plura sentiuntur, etiam si latet quid senserit ille qui scripsit, nihil periculi est si quodlibet eorum congruere ueritati ex aliis locis sanctarum scripturarum doceri potest, id tamen eo conante qui diuina scrutatur eloquia, ut ad uoluntatem perueniatur auctoris per quem scripturam illam sanctus operatus est spiritus, siue hoc assequatur siue aliam sententiam de illis uerbis quae fidei rectae non refragatur exsculpat, testimonium habens a quocumque alio loco diuinorum eloquiorum." Augustine, *De doctrina christiana,* III.84, ed. Green, p.168.
4   "In tropologia de littera ad maiora consurgimus et, quicquid in priori populo carnaliter factum est, iuxta moralem interpretamur locum et ad animae nostrae emolumenta conuertimus." Jerome, *Epistula CXX,* CSEL 55, p. 514. "Tropologia moralis intellegentia." Eucherius, *Instructionum ad Salonium libri II,* II, CCSL 66, p. 216. "Tropologia est moralis explanatio ad emundationem uitae et instructionem pertinens actualem." John Cassian, *Collationes,* XIV.8, CSEL 13, p. 405. "Historice namque iuxta litteram, tropologice iuxta moralem scientiam, mystice iuxta spiritalem intellegentiam." Isidore, *Sententiae,* I.18.12, CCSL 111, ed. Pierre Cazier (Turnhout: Brepols, 1998), p. 64. "Item mensa tabernaculi quattuor habet pedes quia uerba caelestis oraculi uel historico intellectu uel allegorico uel tropologico, id est morali, uel certe anagogico solent accipi." Bede, *De tabernaculo,* CCSL 119A, ed. David Hurst (Turnhout: Brepols, 1969), p. 145. For the development of the troplogical sense in the early and medieval Christianity, see Henri de Lubac, *Medieval exegesis,* vol. 2, trans. E. M. Macierowski, pp. 127-134.

the products of fields, he reveals the fruits nourished by abundance of fertility. Tropologically, the strength of the earth means the faith of the church. The products of fields is the knowledge of scriptures, by which the people of God is fed and fostered. Morally, the strength of the earth reflects the condition of the human soul that begins to obtain virtue in itself by daily progress. Humility alone should be called the strength of the earth, to which the Lord exhorts us: "Learn because I am meek, and humble of heart." (Matthew 11:29) The products of fields is our feelings and thoughts through which we take spiritual food.[1]

In this case and others in Verecundus' commentary on the Song of Moses, the "tropological" sense usually concerns the economy of salvation, while the "moral" sense pertains to the spiritual conversion of individual souls. The fallacy and danger of heresy frequently appear in Verecundus' tropological expositions.[2] His zeal for the "Catholic" doctrine would be more substantially reflected in his deep involvement in the controversy of Three Chapters in opposition to Emperor Justinian during his episcopate of Junca.[3] Verecundus' disobedience against the emperor whom he believed to have supported the false doctrine was foreshadowed in the declaration on the submission of imperial power to Christian faith presented in his exposition of the Deut. 32:20 ("I will turn my face

1   "Per uirtutem terrae ubertatem, abundantiam monstrat. Nascentia agrorum, fructus ubertatis copia nutritos ostendit. Tropologice uirtus terrae, id est Ecclesiae fides. Agrorum autem nascentia Scripturarum sunt intellectus, quibus Dei populus pascitur et fouetur. Moraliter animae concurrit humanae, quae diurnis profectibus uirtutem in se coeperit obtinere, quae sola est humilitas appellanda, ad quam nos Dominus exhortatur: *Discite quia mitis sum et humilis corde.* Agrorum autem nascentia sensus sunt et cogitationes nostrae quibus spiritales capimus cibos." Verecundus, *Commentarii super cantica ecclesiastica, In cantico Deuteronomii*, 14, CCSL 93, p. 30.

2   On Deut. 32:7: "Tropologice *annos nationis nationum* Ecclesiae haeresumque nobis figuraliter tempora monstrat, quod illa in aeternum, hae temporaliter uiuant." Ibid., 8, p. 24; on Deut. 32:8: "Tropologice, diuisas gentes scismatum distributiones ostendit, quas filiorum Adae uocabulo demonstrauit, quibus non dubitatur malos angelos praesidere, quorum sunt arte diuisae." Ibid., 9, p. 25; on Deut. 32:17: "Sed tropologice deos recentes haeresum doctrinas ostendit quas recentius fingunt, et ut uisum fuerit, deos sibi nouos conponunt. Quis enim nesciat Donatistas alteram sibi Christum induxisse? Similiter Venustianus et ceteri qui ea colunt quae apostoli, patres eoram, non docuerunt. Non quod illorum nunc sint patres, sed quod fuerint aliquando, cum apud nos permansissent in fide." Ibid., 18, p. 34; on Deut. 32:21: "Rectius tropologice conuenit scismaticis dici, ex persona Filii, quem aut minorem dicunt, aut initium non nisi a Virgine praesumpsisse, aut fantasiam esse, et cetera quae sibi confingunt." Ibid., 22, p. 39; on Deut. 32:23: "Nam aliter tropologice currit. Nam quod ait *gladium ad occisionem*, diabolum intellege, animarum uidelicet peremptorem. *Canes ad lacerandum*, haereticos scismaticosque demonstrat, membra Christi sine dubio lacerantes: *Videte*, inquit, *canes*; *uidete malos operarios. Volatilia caeli,* humanorum sunt ignominia uitiorum." Ibid., 24, p. 43.

3   According to the *Chronicon* of Victor of Tunnuna: "POST CONSULATUM BASILI V. C. ANNO XI, Reparatus archiepiscopus Cartaginis ecclesie, Firmus Numidarum episcoporum primatus, et Primasius ac Verecundus concilii Biza[n]ceni episcopi pro fidei causa ad urbem regiam eiusdem precepto principis euocantur... POST CONSULATUM BASILII V. C. ANNO XII... Verecundus uero ecclesie Iuncensis episcopus, in defensione memoratorum perdurans capitulorum, Calcidona, ubi refugium fecerat, in diuersorio gloriose martyris Euphimie de hac uita migrauit ad Deum." CCSL 173A, ed. Carmen Cardelle de Hartmann (Turnhout: Brepols, 2003), pp. 47-48.

away from them"), in which Verecundus originally interpreted the story in 1 Samuel 18:1-4 in a figural way: after seeing David (as the figure of Christ), Jonathan the son of Saul (as the figure of secular rulers who "guard and defend the Christian city") offered his girdle (as the figure of vigilant severity) and bowed (as the figure of defending) to the latter "through the laws issued on the behalf of the churches."[1]

The cases enumerated above exemplify how Verecundus deftly mingled his rich theological and exegetical learning with a strong sense of reality. It is also reflected in his exegetical imagination of Christians' position in this world. When expounding Deut. 32:21 (*Et ego zelabo eos in non gente*), Verecundus focused on why Christians are not called a nation:

> It is said that Christians are not a nation, unlike other peoples of nations that gathered and lived in one place, such as the nation of Jews (six hundred thousand were united there), or whichever nations such as the Gothic, the Parthian, or the Herul. In contrast, dispersed throughout the whole breadth of the world, we are few and distributed in various places, dwelling in the midst of schismatics, heretics, Jews, and unbelievers, and are rightly not called a "nation."[2]

The tumultuous experience of the Catholic church of North Africa in the first half of the sixth century — first the Arian persecution under the rule of the Vandals, then the imperial interventions in the provincial ecclesiastical matters after the Vandalic War —

---

1   "Ionathan figuram saecularium continet regum, qui uidentes nostrum fortissimum Dauid, id est credentes in Domino meo Iesu, balteum circumspectae districtionis suae arcumque defensionis, per leges pro ecclesiis datas, indumentumque suae potestatis eidem religiosius obtulerunt, dum plebem christianam muniunt ac defendunt." Verecundus, *Commentarii super cantica ecclesiastica, In cantico Deuteronomii*, 21, CCSL 93, p. 36. The description of Jonathan's garment as *indumentumque suae potestatis eidem religiosius* echoes the so-called "ministerial theory of the imperial power" that had developed in the late fourth century, aptly defined by Peter Brown: "In this ministerial theory, the imperial power was demystified. The emperor was no longer bathed in a quasi-divine aura in such a way that the image of the emperor wavered between that of a god and an ordinary mortal. The emperor was an ordinary human being. He was expected to behave as a pious Christian. But he was no less powerful for that. The brute weight of the imperial system was enthusiastically accepted provided that it was used for a higher aim – the defense and extension of the Christian faith. In this ministerial view, the emperor was thought of as acting as the servant of God, to whom he owed directly the gift of empire." *Through the Eye of a Needle: Wealth, the Fall of Rome, and the Making of Christianity in the West, 350–550 AD* (Princeton: Princeton University Press, 2012), p. 238.

2   "Non gentem posuit christianos, qui non sicut ceterae gentium nationes uno in loco habitant congregati, sicut gens uidelicet Iudaeorum (ibi sexcenta milia fuerunt adunata) uel sicut quaelibet, Gothica uel Parthica seu Herula. Sed nos dispersi per totum diffusae latitudinis orbem, pauci sumus in diuersis locis distributi, in medio scismatum, haeresum, Iudaeorum, infidelium commorantes, et merito non gens appellamur." Verecundus, *Commentarii super cantica ecclesiastica, In cantico Deuteronomii*, 22, CCSL 93, p. 40. Cf. Gerda Heydemann, "People(s) of God? Biblical Exegesis and the Language of Community in Late Antique and Early Medieval Europe," *Meanings of Community across Medieval Eurasia*, eds. Erik Hovden, Christina Lutter, Walter Pohl (Leiden: Brill, 2016), pp. 48-50.

must have contributed to Verecundus' vision of the true Church amongst enemies.[1] In his exposition of Deut. 32:36 (*eos fatigalos, et defectos in abductione et desolatos*), Verecundus listed four enemies of the true faith: pagans "who go through various arguments of their own inventions and cannot understand the truth"; heretics "who cannot remain in the truth of Christ steadfastly"; pseudo-Christians "who join us in churches physically but are far away in mind"; and Jews "from whose midst Christ withdrew his dwelling."[2] The denunciation of the *pseudochristiani* reflects Verecundus' concern over the way of life worthy of true Christians.[3] For Deut. 32: 41 (*Et retribuam iudicium inimicis, et his qui oderunt me reddam*), Verecundus interpreted the haters of God as the pseudo-Christians "who seem to hold Christ by declaration (*professione*), but are His enemies in life and morals":

> Christ is mercy, sanctity, holiness, goodness, and whatever other names that he can be named. Therefore, if someone is Christian but merciless, he kills mercy in himself, and by killing mercy in himself, he kills Christ. So, it is not the case that Christ was killed by Jews once, but — it cannot be said without sorrow — He is crucified by Christians every day many times. In a similar way, the one who abandons sanctity kills chastity in himself, and he kills nobody else but Christ.[4]

The only medieval echo of Verecundus' elaborately composed exposition on canticles can be found in Paschasius Radbertus (785–865), the Carolingian scholar and abbot of Corbie who extensively adopted Verecundus' canticle of Jeremiah (Lamentations 5:1-22)

---

1 For a general survey of the Christianity in Africa during this period, see François Decret, *Early Christianity in North Africa*, trans. Edward Smither (Eugene: Wipf and Stock Publishers, 2009), pp. 189-201. More specifically, cf. Andy Merrills and Richard Miles, *The Vandals* (Chichester: Wiley-Blackwell, 2010), pp. 177-203; Stanisław Adamiak, *Carthage, Constantinople and Rome: Imperial and Papal Interventions in the Life of the Church in Byzantine Africa (533–698)* (Roma: Gregorian and Biblical Press 2016), pp. 53-114.

2 "Fatigantur pagani qui per diuersa inuentionum suarum argumenta currentes, conprehendere nequeunt ueritatem... Deficiunt haeretici qui perseueranter in Christi manere nequeunt ueritate. Abducuntur pseudochristiani, qui nobiscum in ecclesiis corpore sociantur, mente tamen longius semouentur. Desolantur autem Iudaei, de quorum medio Christus habitator abscessit." Verecundus, *Commentarii super cantica ecclesiastica, In cantico Deuteronomii*, 37, CCSL 93, p. 56.

3 "Pseudo quoque christianos inpulsat, qui propriae redemptionis immemores, fidem, ueniam delictorum, beatitudinem futurorum scientiamque ueritatis secuti, uitia pro uirtutibus offerunt Deo, et bono contumeliam faciunt largitori." Ibid., 7, p. 21, on Deut. 32:5.

4 "Inimici autem tam daemones quam haeretici cognoscuntur, nec non etiam pseudochristiani, qui licet uideantur professione Christum tenere, uita autem et moribus inimici sunt eius... Christus misericordia est, religio, sanctificatio, bonitas et quibuscumque aliis nominibus poterit nuncupari. Si quis ergo christianus est, sed inmisericors, misericordiam in se perimit, misericordiam in se perimendo Christum occidit. Sic ergo fit ut non semel Christus fuerit a Iudaeis occisus, uerum etiam multotiens, quod sine dolore dici non potest, a christianis cottidie crucifigitur. Similiter et qui sanctificationem derelinquit, id est castitatem in se occidit, nihil aliud nisi Christum occidit." Ibid., 42, pp. 60-61.

in his *Expositione in Lamentationes Hieremiae.*[1] The copy that he used must be no other than the Corbie manuscript Leiden, Universiteitsbibliotheek, Voss. lat. F 58. There was no trace of early medieval circulation of *Commentarii super cantica ecclesiastica* beyond this monastery.

In the Lyon Annotations, the expositions of the Song of Moses are introduced by the annotation for Deut. 31:19 ("Now therefore write you this canticle, and teach the children of Israel..."):

> Notice how this canticle pertains not only to the earlier people of Jews but also to the following people, that is Christians. In this canticle, good things are promised to the good ones, and evil things are threatened for the evil ones.[2]

In the early 840s, Hrabanus Maurus composed a commentary "in allegorical sense" (*allegorico sensu*) on ten canticles sung in Lauds for King Louis the German. The section on the Song of Moses was basically drawn from his commentary on Deuteronomy composed in the 820s.[3] Hrabanus in his preface differentiated the significance of the Song for Christians from that for Jews who "received these favors ungratefully and abused them":

> Therefore, similarly, we are instructed in the same song, so that we will not be ungrateful to the favors of God, but rather persist in praising him through the whole time of our life, until the Sabbath comes in which we may possess the eternal peace with Christ perpetually.[4]

Neither the exposition of the Song of Moses in Lyon Annotations nor that by Hrabanus uses Verecundus' work.

---

1   Roland Demeulenaere marked Paschasius' quotations from Verecundus in the source apparatus in CCSL 93, pp. 67-82.

2   "Nota quomodo canticum hoc non tantum ad priorem populum Iudeorum pertineant sed et ad sequentem, hoc est cristianum. In quo cantico bonis bona pollicentur et malis mala minantur." Paris, BnF, NAL 1740, fol. 84r.

3   Hrabanus, *Commentaria in Cantica*, PL 112, cols. 1132-1151= *Enarratio super Deuteronomium*, PL 108, cols. 968-984.

4   "Sabbato quoque bene et congrue canticum Deuteronomii canendum constitutum est, in quo beneficia Dei erga priorem populum demonstrantur, et quam ingrate idem populus ea susceperit, hisque abusus sit, certissime exprimitur; quia ea die antiquitus constitutum est Deuteronomium legis in synagoga recitari, ne obliuio praeceptorum Dei in populo fieret, sed magis incitarentur ad obseruationem praeceptorum illius. Unde in Actibus apostolorum Iacobo dicente ita scriptum legimus: *Moyses enim a temporibus antiquis habet in singulis ciuitatibus, qui eum praedicent in synagogis, ubi per omne sabbatum legitur*; nos ergo similiter eodem carmine spiritualiter instruimur, ut non simus ingrati beneficiorum Dei, sed magis per omne tempus uitae nostrae laudibus eius insistamus, donec ueniat illud sabbatum, in quo perpetualiter cum Christo requiem possideamus aeternam." Hrabanus, *Commentaria in Cantica*, PL 112, cols. 1090-1091.

5.5 Gregory-Paterius, *Liber testimoniorum*

Around 600 in Rome, Paterius, a notary of the apostolic church, edited an expositional compilation for biblical canons. It was titled the *Liber testimoniorum, Book of Testimonies*. Paterius drew all the materials from the works of his bishop, one of the greatest patristic exegetes, Pope Gregory the Great (r. 590–604). *Liber testimoniorum* is the first mono-authorial exegetical florilegium, and also a major pathway by which Gregory's biblical exegesis entered into the Middle Ages. The enormous manuscript survival (123 in total) sufficiently testifies to its great popularity.[1]

Paterius appears in Gregory's *Registrum epistolarum* twice as *notarius* (both in 595) and twice as *secundicerius*, the second rank among notaries (in 599 and 600). To him the pope dictated letters of appointments, manumissions, and wills.[2] Bede called Paterius *beati papae Gregorii discipulus*.[3] Paterius' close relationship with his master was also attested by Gregory's ninth-century biographer Johannes Hymonides who remembered Paterius as one of the pope's "most prudent clerical counselors and intimates" after the latter excluded lay attendants from the Lateran palace: "Paterius, also a notary, who, made by Gregory the *secundicerius*, plucked something most useful from his books."[4] By the early twelfth century, in Sigebert of Gembloux's *De uiris illustribus* (composed in 1111/1112), Paterius' Gregorian florilegium had come to be called the *Liber testimoniorum*.[5] "Testimonies" refer to the verses that Gregory drew from other books of the Scripture as proofs in his exposition of certain biblical texts. The term was used

---

1 Fabrizio Martello, "Paterius," in *La trasmissione dei testi latini del Medioevo*, eds. Paolo Chiesa, Lucia Castaldi (Florence: SISMEL, Edizioni del Galluzzo, 2004–2013), vol. 4, pp. 435-441.

2 "Hanc autem epistulam paterio notario ecclesiae nostrae scribendam dictauimus." Gregory, *Epistolae*, V.26 (February 595), CCSL 140, p. 293; "Hanc autem manumissionis paginam paterio notario scribendam dictauimus et propria manu una cum tribus presbyteris prioribus et tribus diaconibus pro plenissima firmitate subscripsimus uobis que tradidimus." Ibid., VI.12 (September 595), p. 381; "Hanc autem paterio secundicerio nostro scribendam dictauimus, cui que subscripsimus." Ibid., IX.98 (January 599), p. 651; "[P]aterius secundicerius dixit: 'probus abbas monasterii sanctorum andreae et luciae uestris, si praecipitis, desiderat aspectibus praesentari.'" Ibid., XI.15 (October 600), p. 881.

3 "Audiui autem quia Paterius eiusdem beati papae Gregorii discipulus de tota sancta scriptura quaeque ille per partes in suis operibus explanauit collecta ex ordine in unum uolumen coegerit, quod opus si haberem ad manus facilius multo ac perfectius studium meae uoluntatis implerem; uerum quia necdum illud uidere merui ipse per me hoc prout potui imitari domino adiuuante curaui." Bede, *In Cantica canticorum libri VI*, CCSL 119B, ed. David Hurst (Turnhout: Brepols, 1983), p. 359.

4 "Caeterum prudentissimus rector Gregorius, remotis a suo cubiculo saecularibus, clericorum sibi prudentissimos consiliarios familiaresque delegit... Paterium aeque notarium, qui ab eo secundicerius factus, ex libris ipsius aliqua utillima deflorauit." Johannes Hymonides, *Vita Gregorii*, II.11, PL 75, col. 92.

5 "Paterius, Romane ecclesie notarius et secundicerius, colligens omnia diuine scripture testimonia, per que Gregorius obscura sue expositionis dilucidauit, tres libellos edidit, duos de testimoniis ueteris instrumenti et unum de testimoniis noui testamenti, ipsum que codicem appellauit librum testimoniorum." Sigebert of Gembloux, *De viris illustribus*, 43, in *Catalogus Sigeberti Gemblacensis monachi de viris illustribus*, ed. Robert Witte (Bern: Herbert Lang, 1974), p. 65.

by Gregory himself. In his letter to Leander of Seville which served as the preface to his *Moralia in Iob*, Gregory stated that his monastic brothers asked him to expound the book of Job in a way that he should not only fortify his expositions with "testimonies" but also interpret the obscure "testimonies" themselves.[1] In the preface to *Liber testimoniorum*, addressed to an unknown former disciple of Gregory (called *beatitudo uestra*, probably a bishop), Paterius recalled how he had been attracted by the testimonies and his master's expositions of them in the *Moralia* and thus undertaken to collect them:

> The more frequently I read through the words dictated by most blessed and apostolic pontiff Gregory, our as well as your educator, the more ardently his clearest exposition urged me to desire them, and I found something in them extremely incomparable. When he took pains to examine the story of one single holy man, that is the blessed Job, covered with hidden darkness of mysteries, through the triple exposition — that is typological, moral and historical — and to make it clearer than light to all openly through bright revelation by pushing away the cloud of ignorance, he was forced to expound almost the whole Old and New Testaments for the sake of explanation... He was committed to discuss the testimony through the explanation of additional exposition. In some places, he judged the mere exposition of a certain testimony insufficient, if he had not offered a broader teaching by bringing one more testimony to clear interpretation. It has come to pass that, as I have said above, almost all the mysteries of the Old Testament have become clear, which, revealed in the inspiration of the divine will, would satisfy the hunger of our famine with the abundance of celestial food. Driven by extremely ardent desire for this knowledge, I had begun to gather some from these testimonies in a brief way, but to neglect others. My conscience as my witness, although I did not wish anyone should know about my effort and took pains to keep it secret, certain people brought it to the attention of our apostolic pontiff. In his persuasive and uplifting words that the blessed you must know about, he soon began to encourage me to complete zealously what I had begun

---

1   "Qui hoc quoque mihi in onere suae petitionis addiderunt, ut non solum uerba historiae per allegoriarum sensus excuterem, sed allegoriarum sensus protinus in exercitium moralitatis inclinarem, adhuc aliquid grauius adiungentes, ut intellecta quaeque testimoniis cingerem et prolata testimonia, si implicita fortasse uiderentur interpositione superadditae expositionis enodarem." Gregory, *Moralia in Iob*, *Epistola ad Leandrum*, CCSL 143, p. 2.

carelessly.[1]

After Gregory's intervention, Paterius decided to work on his editorial project in a more systematic way. First, following his master's suggestion, in the title of each excerpt, he indicated its subject, and the title of the cited Gregorian work as well as the book number.[2] Second, he broadened the scope of his search to cover Gregorian works other than the *Moralia*.[3] Third, he arranged the testimonies in scriptural order, so that "the earnest reader who desires to find an explanation of a certain obscure question will not be delayed."[4] Fourth, he gathered the expositions of the same verse scattered in different

---

1 "Dum beatissimi atque apostolici Gregorii pontificis nostri uestri quoque addam nutritoris dicta saepius lectione percurrerem, auidiusque mihi eis assiduum esse ipsa luculentissima uerborum eius satisfactio suaderet, quiddam in eis repperi sine comparatione potissimum. Dum igitur unius sancti uiri, hoc est beati Iob historiam abstrusis mysteriorum opacitatibus tectam sub triptici, id est typica, morali, atque historica, studuit expositione discutere, ac repulso ignorantiae nubilo, in aperto cunctis luce clarius serena patefactione monstrare, paene totam ueteris ac noui Testamenti seriem rerum explanandarum necessitate est coactus exponere. Ubi enim occultae nimis rei dilucidandae necessitas imminebat, ne aut obscurum quid apud audientium animos remaneret, aut ipse non liquidissima satisfactione obscuritatis interna ad lucem uideretur eicere; non solum disertissimis uerborum assertionibus quod clausum erat aperuit, sed ita esse prolati quoque testimonii non intellecta si inesset forsitan obscuritas rei explanandae augeret potius caliginem quam auferret, idque testimonium studuit addita expositionis explanatione disserere. In quibusdam namque locis in expositione etiam testimonii non solum uerborum satisfactionem sibi posse sufficere iudicauit, nisi alterius iterum deducti ad medium testimonii euidenti interpretatione latius edoceret. Actumque est ut hac occasione, sicut praefatus sum ueteris Testamenti tota paene series occulta patesceret, quae diuini nutus aspiratione reserata, famis nostrae esuriem superni pabuli copia satiaret. Huius ergo rei ardenti nimis desiderio prouocatus quaedam de eisdem testimoniis coeperam sub quadam breuitate decerpere, aliqua uero negligendo transire, quod dum fieret, sicut conscientia mea mihi testis est, me nolente atque hoc cautius prouidente ne a quoquam aliquo modo nosceretur, per quosdam ad eiusdem apostolici pontificis nostri notitiam usque peruenit. Qui me uerbis mox, quibus beatitudo uestra nouit suasoriis, atque ad superna trahentibus hortando coepit accendere, quatenus hoc quod neglecte coeperam explere studiosius debuissem..." The critical edition of the prologue of Paterius' *Liber testimoniorum*, better than the edition in PL, see Fabrizio Martello, *All'ombra di Gregorio Magno: Il notaio Paterio e il Liber testimoniorum* (Roma: Città nuova, 2012), pp. 192-207.

2 "... Ita ut et opus et librum in quo testimonium positum legeretur, uel ex qua re ortum esset, in tituli eius praenotatione signarem." Ibid., p. 194.

3 "... et iam non solum de beati Iob expositione, sed nec de aliis eius opusculis quicquam curaui, sicut prius facere coeperam, neglectum relinquere." Ibid., p. 194.

4 "Quae dum disperse sicut quippe reperta fuerant in schedis suis relata transcurrerem uisum mihi est licet esset laboris immodici, ut uniuscuiusque rei testimonia iuxta quod in suis ex ordine sunt sita codicibus, per libros suos ordinando componerem, quatenus studiosi lectoris desiderium ad elucidandam sibi quam uelit obscuritatem, inuento libri quem requireret titulo, nihil morae uel ad parum aliquo modo praepediret." Ibid., pp. 194-195.

places among Gregory's works and converged them in a single entry.[1] Finally, since the amount of testimonies was too great, Paterius divided them into three books, two on the Old Testament and one on the New.[2]

According to the fundamental study of André Wilmart in 1927, the authentic survival of Paterius' compilation only covers the expositional excerpts of 14 Old Testament books — Genesis, Exodus, Leviticus, Numbers, Deuteronomy, Joshua, Judges, four books of Kings, Psalms, Proverbs, and the Song of Songs — possibly equivalent to Book 1 of Paterius' original project. It is possible that Paterius never managed to accomplish the other two.[3] The commonly used edition of *Liber testimoniorum* in PL (vol. 79, cols. 683-1136), copied from the Maurist edition of 1705, contains three parts, the latter two of which (cols. 917-1136) have been identified as a twelfth-century continuation.[4] Raymond Étaix in 1958 shed doubt on the authenticity of the sections for Proverbs and the Song of Songs, since they were not only absent in some manuscripts but also edited in a much less careful way than Paterius' usual style.[5] Fabrizio Martello recently offered the hypothesis that the sections for Proverbs and the Song of Songs are Paterius' authentic but unfinished notes, collected by him for the sake of ultimate compilation, which, for uncertain reason, he failed to complete.[6]

Étaix's study also demonstrated that the PL edition of *Liber testimoniorum* contains interpolated entries.[7] According to Paul Meyvaert, the unquestionably authentic part of the whole *Liber testimoniorum* contains 377 *testimonia* from *Moralia*, 62 from *Homilies on Ezechiel*, 46 from *On Pastoral Rule*, 38 from the *Homilies on the Gospel*, and two

---

1   "Hoc autem lectorem huius operis prae omnibus nosse commoneo: ut quia quaedam testimonia diuersis locis sita repperi, et in quibusdam sicut res expetiit typice in quibusdam moraliter, in quibusdam etiam historice in expositione perducta, quae praedictis modis exposita comperi, ita et seorsum sequentia siquidem inuicem translata composui. In quibusdam uero locis quia ita satisfactionis norma poscebat, hoc idem de eodem testimonio retexuit, quod dudum explanasse relegitur. Alicubi autem quaedam quae de eo minus pridem dixerat, inter repetita addens uerba suppleuit. Quod ego de iam dictis excerpens, eidem testimonio, ubi poposcit locus inserendum aptaui, quia res non erat, quae separatim poni utiliter potuisset, dum ex praecedentibus quae dicta iam fuerant subsequentibusque penderent. Si enim propter nouitatem paruae rei rursum dicta ponerentur, facerent procul dubio repetita fastidium. Ne ergo expositionis unde haec excerpta sunt recurrens ordinem, plus in quibusdam huius operis locis aliquid quam in textu libri est positum minusue reperias, causae fecit ratio quam praemisi." Fabrizio Martello, *All'ombra di Gregorio Magno*, p. 196.

2   "Perpendens autem quod utriusque Testamenti in unum uellem testimonia redacta colligere, et uoluminis normam excederet et legentis desiderium impediret; in tribus hoc uoluminibus Domino est cooperante dispositum, ut duo ueteris, tertium noui dicta contineat." Ibid., pp. 197-198.

3   André Wilmart, "Le Recueil Grégorien de Paterius et les Fragments Wisigothiques de Paris," *Revue Bénédictine* 39 (1927): pp. 81-104.

4   For the twelfth-century pseudo-Paterius, see René Wasselynck, "Les compilations des 'Moralia in Job' du VIIe au XIIe siècle," *Recherches de théologie ancienne et médiévale* 29 (1962): pp. 5-32.

5   Raymond Étaix, "Le Liber testimoniorum de Paterius," *Revue des sciences religieuses* 32 (1958): pp. 66-78.

6   Lucia Castaldi and Fabrizio Martello, "Tempera quasi aurum: origine, redazione e diffusione del 'Liber testimoniorum' di Paterio," *Filologia Mediolatina* 18 (2011): pp. 23-107.

7   Raymond Étaix, "Le Liber testimoniorum de Paterius," pp. 73-74.

from the *Dialogues*.[1]

The PL edition also fails to present Paterius' original *mise en page*, which is detectable in early manuscripts, such as Amiens, BM, 220 (CLA, VI.711).[2] For example, the original presentation of Deuteronomy Entry 3 of *Liber testimoniorum* must be:

> In Book 28 of the exposition on the Blessed Job, when the topic of removing superficial thoughts from the mind is examined, the verse "Circumcise therefore the foreskin of your heart" (Deut. 10:16) is attached. What is signified by the circumcision of the foreskin, but that "cut off superficial thoughts from the mind after you extinguish lust in the flesh"?[3]

This entry is based on *Moralia*, XXVIII.3.[4] As this concise example shows, the original format of Paterius' entry usually consists of four elements: (1) the source of the citation; (2) Paterius' summary of its theme; (3) the biblical *testimonium*; (4) Gregory's exposition.

Concerning the Deuteronomy section of *Liber testimoniorum*, the PL edition contains 28 entries. Four of them (nos. XVII, XIX, XX, XXIII) are not in Paterius' original compilation. Furthermore, Nos. IV and V are in fact one single entry in which Paterius merged two Gregorian expositions of Deut. 15:19. So are Nos. 11 and 12 for Deut. 22:11. Three authentic excerpts (nos. IX, XII and XV) cannot be traced back either to the reference offered by Paterius or any known Gregorian work. It is likely that Paterius quoted them from an earlier edition of *Moralia* and the pre-revised draft of *Homilies on Ezechiel*.[5] The following table demonstrates the 22 entries for Deuteronomy in *Liber testimoniorum* (Table 5.4).

---

1 Paul Meyvaert, "The Enigma of Gregory the Great's Dialogues: A Response to Francis Clark," *Journal of Ecclesiastical History* 40 (1988): pp. 335-381.

2 For the online facsimile, see http://gallica.bnf.fr/ark:/12148/btv1b8452176j, last accessed September 14, 2021.

3 "In expositione beati Iob, lib. xxviii, dum de resecandis superfluis a mente cogitationibus tractaretur, adiunctum est: Circumcidite praeputia cordis uestri. Quid per hanc praeputii circumcisionem signatur, nisi postquam luxuriam a carne exstinguitis, etiam superflua a cogitatione resecate?" Amiens, BM, 220, fol. 65v.

4 "Vnde bene per Moysen dicitur: Circumcidite praeputia cordis uestri, id est, postquam luxuriam a carne exstinguitis, etiam superflua a cogitatione resecate." Gregory, *Moralia in Iob*, XXXVIII.3, CCSL 143B, p. 1403.

5 Raymond Étaix, "Le Liber testimoniorum de Paterius," pp. 76-77.

Table 5.4   Deuteronomy section in Paterius' *Liber testimoniorum*

Revised entry	Entry in PL	Deut. verse	Source[1]	Thematical summary offered by Paterius
1	I	6:5	*Moralia*, VII.24	De modo dilectionis Dei, ac proximi, eiusque exercitio
2	II	11:14	*Moralia*, XX.2	De praedicatione Veteris ac Noui Testamenti
3	III	10:16	*Moralia*, XVIII.3	De resecandis superfluis cogitationibus
4	IV+V	15:19	*Moralia*, VIII.47 + *Homiliae in Hiezechihelem*, I.2	De cauenda ostentatione in bonae operationis primordiis
5	VI	16:16	*Moralia*, VII.29	Per cessationem rerum transeuntium, de mansuro bonae operationis exercitio
6	VII	16:20	*Moralia*, IX.25	De seruanda in exhibitione operis mentis rectitudine
7	VIII	19:5-6	*Moralia*, X.7	De seruanda increpationis mensura in proximi correctione
8	IX	22:6	?[2]	De discretione seruandae allegoriae et historiae
9	X	22:10	*Moralia*, I.16	De imperitorum doctorum cauenda societate
10	XI+ XII	22:11	*Moralia*, VIII.51 + ?[3]	De uitando duplicitatis uitio
11	XIII	23:10	*Moralia*, IX.55	De purgatione illicitae cogitationis
12	XIV	23:12	*Moralia*, XXXI.27	De diluendis per compunctionis gratiam occultae tentationis maculis
13	XV	24:1	?[4]	De postponenda cura rei transitoriae ob utilitatem spiritualium
14	XVI	24:6	*Moralia*, XXXIII.12	De seruanda praedicationis mensura doctoribus, circa delinquentium confessionem proximorum
15	XVIII	25:5	*Regula pastoralis*, I.5	De dono regiminis minime subtrahendo
16	XXI	32:13	*Homiliae in euangelia*, XXVI.3-4	De mysteriorum per Christi aduentum reseratione, eiusque fidelium meritis
17	XXII	32:22	*Moralia*, XVIII.22 and XXI.12	De incorrecte delinquentium ultione perpetua
18	XXIV	32:39	*Moralia*, VI.25	De electorum purgatione, et diuinae respectu gratiae
19	XXV	32:42	*Moralia*, XVIII.11	De percussione ultima carnaliter uiuentium
20	XXVI	33:2	*Homiliae in euangelia*, XXX.5	De dilectionis gratia erga diuina praecepta electorum impressa cordibus

---

1   Gregory, *Homiliae in Hiezechihelem*, CCSL 142, ed. Marci Adriaen (Turnhout: Brepols, 1971); *Regula Pastoralis*, SC 381-382, ed. Floribert Rommel (Paris: Éditions du Cerf, 1992); *Homiliae in euangelia*, CCSL 141, ed. Raymond Étaix (Turnhout: Brepols, 1999).

2   "In expositione Ezechielis viiii" according to Amiens, BM, 220, fol. 67r, but cannot be located in the present edition of *Homilies on Ezechiel*.

3   "In commentario Ezechielis, homilia vi" according to Amiens, BM, 220, fol. 68r, but cannot be located in the present edition of *Homilies on Ezechiel*.

4   "In expositione beati Iob, lib. v" according to Amiens, BM, 220, fol. 69r, in a different handwriting, but cannot be located in the present edition of *Moralia*.

Continued

Revised Entry	Entry in PL	Deut. Verse	Source	Thematical summary offered by Paterius
21	XXVII	33:9	*Moralia*, VII.30	De diuino amore proximis praeferendo, eisdemque discretae compassionis studio diligendis
22	XXVIII	33:25	*Moralia*, XXXIV.9	De praedicatione sanctae Ecclesiae

Among them, the expositions in Entries 9 and 15 are ultimately based on Augustinian's *Contra Faustum*.[1] The rest seem to be Gregory's original exegesis. Gregory emphasized the need to go beyond the *historia* and to capture the *allegoriarum sensus* in divine reading.[2] Moreover, the pope's special preference to the tropological sense, that is expounding biblical text as instruction for the good Christian life, is clearly reflected in the Deuteronomy expositions collected in *Liber testimoniorum*. See Deuteronomy Entry 5 as an example:

"You must not appear before the Lord empty-handed." (Deut. 16:16). A man appears before the Lord empty-handed, who takes no fruit of his labor with him. One person is eager to increase fortunes, while another earnestly wants to deserve praise. Yet because everyone will die and lose access to all these things, he appears before the Lord empty-handed, for he takes nothing with himself before the Judge. We are therefore admonished for our benefit by the law that "You must not appear before the Lord empty-handed." Those who do not provide for themselves the reward of meriting eternal life by good actions (*bene agendo*) appear before the Lord empty-handed. That is how the psalmist can say about just people: "When they return they will come

---

1 Entry 9: "In boue simul et asino homo arare prohibetur, ac si aperte diceretur: Fatuos sapientibus in praedicatione non socies, ne per eum qui implere non ualet illi qui praeualet obsistas." Paterius, *Liber testimoniorum*, PL 79, col. 778= Gregory, *Moralia in Iob*, I.16, CCSL 143, p. 36. Cf. "Bouem quippe et asinum, si necesse sit, unusquisque sine detrimento operis iungit; sapientem uero et stultum, non ut unus praecipiat et alter obtemperet, sed pariter ex aequali potestate, ut adnuntient uerbum dei, non sine scandalo quisque comites facit." Augustine, *Contra Faustum*, VI.9, CSEL 25, p. 302.
Entry 15: "Frater defunctus ille est, qui post resurrectionis apparens gloriam dixit: *Ite, nuntiate fratribus meis*. Qui quasi sine filiis obiit, quia adhuc electorum suorum numerum non impleuit. Huius scilicet uxorem superstes frater sortiri praecipitur, quia dignum profecto est ut cura sanctae Ecclesiae ei qui hanc bene regere praeualet, imponatur. Cui nolenti in faciem mulier exspuit, quia quisquis ex muneribus quae perceperit, prodesse aliis non curat, bonis quoque eius sancta Ecclesia exprobrans, ei quasi in faciem saliuam iactat. Cui ex uno pede calceamentum tollitur, ut discalciati domus uocetur. Scriptum quippe est: Calciati pedes in praeparatione Euangelii pacis. Si ergo ut nostram, sic curam proximi gerimus, utrumque pedem per calceamentum munimus. Qui uero suam cogitans utilitatem, proximorum negligit, quasi unius pedis calceamentum cum dedecore amittit." Paterius, *Liber testimoniorum*, PL 79, cols. 779-780= Gregory the Great, *Regula Pastoralis*, I.5, SC 381, p. 146, 148. Cf. Augustine, *Contra Faustum*, XXXII.10, CSEL 25, pp. 768-769.
2 E.g., Paterius' Deuteronomy Entry 8 on the precept in Deut. 22:6-7 to keep the the young in the nest and to release the bird: "Matrem igitur dimittentes pullos edimus, cum historiae exempla dimittimus, sed ex ea allegoriarum sensus in mente retinemus." Paterius, *Liber testimoniorum*, PL 79, col. 777.

with joy, carrying their sheaves." Those who have good works to show for themselves, works by which they merit eternal life, are the ones who come to the Judge's tribunal bearing sheaves.[1]

The moralistic themes can also be found in the first half of Entries 4 and 6 (on doing good works with pious intention); 3, 10, 11, and 13 (on eliminating superfluous and evil thoughts and forsaking *terrena cura*); 1 and 21 (loving God in loving neighbor).

The strong concern over Christians' proper way of life and the spiritual improvement is a major feature of Gregory's biblical exegesis. The best example is no other than Paterius' dominant source, the thirty-five-book *Moralia*. The earliest *Vita Gregorii* composed by an unknown monk or nun of Whitby in England ca. 713 called *Moralia* "the medicine for ailing morals against the vices of human souls."[2] Gregory claimed in the preface to *Moralia* that his fellow-monks had requested him "not only to investigate the words of history (*uerba historiae*) through the allegorical sense (*allegoriarum sensus*), but also to bend the allegorical sense directly toward moral exercise (*exercitium moralitatis*)."[3] Both Origen and Eucherius proposed the literal-moral-spiritual tripartite division in analogy with the classical body-soul-spirit anthropology.[4] Gregory's innovative appropriation of this exegetical model prioritizes *moralitas* — how the spiritual teaching from the Bible is applicable to the life of every faithful — as the ultimate goal of biblical interpretation:

First we lay the foundation of history (*fundamenta historiae*), then we erect the fabric of the mind as the fortress of faith through its allegorical "type" (*per*

---

1   "Non apparebis in conspectu Domini uacuus. In conspectu Domini uacuus apparet, qui nihil secum de fructu sui laboris portat. Alius multiplicandis facultatibus aestuat, alius promerendis laudibus anhelat. Sed quia cuncta haec quisque moriens deserit, ante Dominum uacuus apparet, quia secum ante iudicem nihil tulit. Hinc ergo per legem salubriter admonemur, dicentem: Non apparebis in conspectu Domini uacuus. Qui enim promerendae uitae mercedem bene agendo non prouidet, in conspectu Domini uacuus apparet. Hinc de iustis per Psalmistam dicitur: Venientes autem uenient cum exsultatione, portantes manipulos suos. Ad examen quippe iudicii portantes manipulos ueniunt, qui in semetipsis recta opera, quibus uitam mereantur ostendunt." Paterius, *Liber testimoniorum*, PL 79, col. 776= Gregory, *Moralia in Iob*, VII.29, CCSL 143, p. 363. The translation is based on *Moral Reflections on the Book of Job*, trans. Brian Kerns (Minnesota: Liturgical Press, 2014–2017), vol. 2, p. 126. The anthor changed the translation when the text quoted by Paterius is not exactly the same with the standard edition of Moralia.
2   "Quis et hoc in eo sane mentis non agnoscat, cum illa xxxii consideret uolumina, quae beatum Iob exponendo, dictis Moralibus, in languentium direxit mirabile morum, contra uitia humanorum medicamina animarum." *The Earliest Life of Gregory the Great by an Anonymous Monk of Whitby*, 27, ed. Bertram Colgrave (Lawrence: University of Kansas Press, 1968), pp. 122-123.
3   "Qui hoc quoque mihi in onere suae petitionis addiderunt, ut non solum uerba historiae per allegoriarum sensus excuterem, sed allegoriarum sensus protinus in exercitium moralitatis inclinarem, adhuc aliquid grauius adiungentes, ut intellecta quaeque testimoniis cingerem et prolata testimonia, si implicita fortasse uiderentur interpositione superadditae expositionis enodarem." Gregory, *Moralia in Iob, Epistola ad Leandrum*, CCSL 143, p. 2.
4   Cf. Henri de Lubac, *Medieval exegesis*, vol. 1, trans. Mark Sebanc, pp. 132-159.

significationem typicam), and finally we clothe the building with exterior color through the moral grace (*per moralitatis gratiam*).[1]

Bede in his *Ecclesiastical History* succinctly described Gregory's tripartite exposition of the Bible — historical, typological/allegorical and moral — respectively as *quomodo iuxta litteram intellegendus, qualiter ad Christi et ecclesiae sacramenta referendus*, and *quo sensu unicuique fidelium sit aptandus*.[2] Modern scholars have appreciated Gregory's biblical interpretation as "an exegetical program whose major theological thrust was pastoral, moral, and spiritual, oriented towards illuminating experience, reforming behavior and enflaming desire for God,"[3] and seen the fusion of biblical typology and moral tropology into a coherent spiritual interpretation as its distinct character.[4]

The proper practice of pastoral care constitutes a major theme in Gregory's Deuteronomy exposition. In Paterius' collection, Deuteronomy Entry 7, drawn from *Moralia*, X.7, is one of the most influential for later Christian exegetes. The exposition is on Deut. 19:5-6 ("As when a man goes into the wood with his neighbor merely to hew wood, and the wood of the axe flies from his hand, and the head slips from the helve, and strikes his neighbor that he dies, he shall flee to one of these cities and live: lest perchance the kinsman of him whose blood has been shed pursue the slayer while his heart is hot, overtake him and slay him"). Paterius summarized its theme as "About the measure to use to rebuke when correcting a neighbor." Gregory interpreted the precept in the context of a priest correcting a lay person's vice in preaching or in confession. Going to the wood in interpreted as "scrutinizing our sins," and hewing wood as "cutting away the sins of offenders." The neighbor is accidentally killed by the flying axe when too harsh a rebuke from the preacher or the confessor hurts the spirit of love. Therefore, the unintentional killer must take refuge in three cities, that is, "turn himself to the

---

1 "Nam primum quidem fundamenta historiae ponimus; deinde per significationem typicam in arcem fidei fabricam mentis erigimus; ad extremum quoque per moralitatis gratiam, quasi superducto aedificium colore uestimus." Gregory, *Moralia in Iob, Epistola ad Leandrum*, CCSL 143, p. 4.

2 "Nam hortati sunt eum ut librum beati Iob magnis inuolutum obscuritatibus mystica interpretatione discuteret; neque negare potuit opus quod sibi fraternus amor multis utile futurum imponebat, sed eundem librum, quomodo iuxta litteram intellegendus, qualiter ad Christi et ecclesiae sacramenta referendus, quo sensu unicuique fidelium sit aptandus, per XXX et V libros expositionis miranda ratione perdocuit." Bede, *Historia ecclesiastica gentis Anglorum*, II.1.4, SC 489, ed. Michael Lapidge (Paris: Éditions du Cerf, 2005), p. 274.

3 Scott DeGregorio, "Gregory's Exegesis: Old and New Ways of Approaching the Scriptural Text," *A Companion to Gregory the Great*, eds. Bronwen Neil, Matthew Dal Santo (Leiden: Brill, 2013), pp. 269-290.

4 Stephen Kessler, "Gregory the Great: A Figure of Tradition and Transition in Church Exegesis," *Hebrew Bible/Old Testament: The History of Its Interpretation. Volume I. From the beginnings to the Middle Ages (until 1300). Part 2: The Middle Ages*, ed. Magne Sæbø, (Göttingen: Vandenhoeck and Ruprecht, 1996), pp. 135-147. Also see Brendan Lupton, "Gregory's Hermeneutics: Scripture as a Path to God," in *Patristic Theories of Biblical Interpretation: The Latin Fathers*, ed. Tarmo Toom (Cambridge: Cambridge University Press, 2016), pp. 183-205.

lamentations of repentance and be hidden in the unity of the sacrament of hope, faith, and charity," so that his mistake will be pardoned by the kinsman of the slain, namely God the Judge.[1]

Similar concern over pastoral care can be found in Entries 4 (the second half), 9, 14, 15, and 22. It is possible, as Fabrizio Martello hypothesized, that Paterius compiled *Liber testimoniorum* as "uno strumento in vista della predicazione."[2]

There is no doubt that *Liber testimoniorum* formed a major path to the early medieval reception of the Gregorian exegesis of Deuteronomy. For example, as we will see in the next chapter, the composer(s) of the eighth-century Irish *Bibelwerk* used the Deuteronomy section of Paterius' collection extensively. In the ninth century, Notker listed *Liber testimoniorum* as a standard reference for the exposition of the Pentateuch.[3]

When compiling his own commentary on Deuteronomy, Hrabanus Maurus extensively copied the entries in *Liber testimoniorum* (mostly from the Deuteronomy section, but also occasionally from the sections on other Pentateuch books), and he source-marked all

---

1   "Ad siluam quippe cum amico imus quotiens cum quolibet proximo ad intuenda delicta nostra conuertimur, et simpliciter ligna succidimus cum delinquentium uitia pia intentione resecamus. Sed securis manu fugit cum sese increpatio plus quam necesse est in asperitate pertrahit. Ferrum que de manubrio prosilit cum de correptione sermo durior excedit; et amicum percutiens occidit quia auditorem suum prolata contumelia ab spiritu dilectionis interficit. Correpti namque mens repente ad odium proruit, si hanc immoderata increpatio plus quam debuit addicit. Sed is qui incaute ligna percutit et proximum exstinguit, ad tres necesse est urbes fugiat, ut in una earum defensus uiuat, quia si, ad paenitentiae lamenta conuersus, in unitate sacramenti sub spe, fide et caritate absconditur, reus perpetrati homicidii non tenetur. Eum que exstincti proximus et cum inuenerit non occidit quia cum districtus iudex uenerit, qui sese nobis per naturae nostrae consortium iunxit, ab eo procul dubio uindictam de culpae reatu non expetit quem sub eius uenia spes, fides et caritas abscondit. Citius ergo culpa dimittitur quae nequaquam malitiae studio perpetratur." Paterius, *Liber testimoniorum*, PL 79, cols. 776-777= Gregory, *Moralia in Iob*, 10.7, CCSL 143, p. 545.
2   Fabrizio Martello, *All'ombra di Gregorio Magno*, p. 247.
3   "Quod si excerptum Paterii, quod de libris beati Gregorii per ordinem singulorum librorum deflorando confecit, unquam reperire potueris, illud tibi ad omnimodam sufficiet sapientiam." Notker, *Notatio de illustribus uiris*, ed. Rauner, p. 59.

of them as "GG."[1] No evidence shows that Hrabanus had access to the *Moralia* directly.[2]

The case of Isidore's commentary on Deuteronomy in his *Expositio in uetus testamentum* is just the reverse. As we will discuss in the next chapter, source criticism will demonstrate that Isidore drew Gregorian exegesis directly from his *Moralia* and *Regula pastoralis* — which is not surprising because both the Gregorian works were originally dedicated to Leander, Isidore's brother and predecessor as archbishop of Seville — and it is likely that the Spanish archbishop did not use Paterius' collection to compile his *Expositio*, or maybe he did not have access it at all.

The Gregorian exegesis certainly serves as a major source for the Lyon Annotations, although always in the way of abridged paraphrase rather than of verbatim copy. There is no doubt that the Lyon Annotations absorbs certain Gregorian expositions via Isidore's *Expositio in uetus testamentum*. For example, the exposition on Deut. 22:10 ("Thou shalt not plough with an ox and an ass together") in the Lyon Annotations is an abridgement of Isidore's Deuteronomy Entry 6, and the latter itself is an abbreviated compilation of three sources: Gregory's *Moralia* I.16, Augustine's *Contra Faustum*, VI.9, and Jerome's

---

1 Cf. Silvia Cantelli, *Hrabani Mauri opera exegetica*, vol. 2, pp. 553-576. For Hrabanus' source mark, the author consult Vercelli, Archivio Capitolare, 153, a ninth-century manuscript (Bischoff, *Katalog*, 7008) whose sole content is Hrabanus' commentary on Deuteronomy. It was once owned by Hincmar and dedicated by him to St-Maria Rheims Cathedral. Both directly and indirectly (i.e., via Isidore), Hrabanus integrated the whole Deuteronomy section of *Liber testimoniorum*. Besides, Hrabanus also used other sections of *Liber testimoniorum*: Hrabanus, *Enarratio super Deuteronomium*, PL 108, col. 897 = Paterius, *Liber testimoniorum*, II.xix, PL 79, cols. 730 = Gregory, *Homiliae in euangelia*, II.2.8, CCSL 141, pp. 189-190. Hrabanus, *Enarratio super Deuteronomium*, PL 108, cols. 891-893 = Paterius, *Liber testimoniorum*, II.xxxi, PL 79, cols. 735-737 = Gregory, *Homiliae in Hiezechihelem*, I.3, CCSL 142, pp. 38-41. Hrabanus, *Enarratio super Deuteronomium*, PL 108, col. 885 = Paterius, *Liber testimoniorum*, III.ix-x, PL 79, cols. 757-758 = Gregory, *Homiliae in Hiezechihelem*, II.31.8, CCSL 142, p. 275 + *Moralia in Iob*, V.11, CCSL 143, p. 231. Hrabanus, *Enarratio super Deuteronomium*, PL 108, cols. 854-855 = Paterius, *Liber testimoniorum*, IV.xxiii, PL 79, cols. 773-774 = *Moralia in Iob*, XXVII.13, CCSL 143B, pp. 1348-1350. Hrabanus, *Enarratio super Deuteronomium*, PL 108, col. 973 = Paterius, *Liber testimoniorum*, XI.xxxiv, PL 79, col. 828 = *Moralia in Iob*, XXXIII.10, CCSL 143B, pp. 1688-1689.

2 Meanwhile, Hrabanus in his commentary on Deuteronomy quoted passages from Gregory's *Homilies on Gospel* and *Dialogues* that do *not* appear in Paterius' collection: Hrabanus, *Enarratio super Deuteronomium*, PL 108, col. 973 = Gregory, *Homiliae in euangelia*, II.34.11, CCSL 141, p. 309; Hrabanus, *Enarratio super Deuteronomium*, PL 108, col. 869 = Gregory, *Dialogorum libri iv*, III.14, SC 260, ed. Adalbert de Vogüé (Paris: Éditions du Cerf, 1978), pp. 312, 314.

Commentaria in Isaiam I.1.[1] Isidore's mediating role between Gregory and the Lyon Annotations can also be found in the expositions for Deut. 19:5-6, 22:11, 23:10, 23:12-13, 24:6, and 25:2-3. We will discuss this in detail in the next chapter.

But evidence also suggests the need to regard *Liber testimoniorum* as one of the direct sources of the Lyon Annotations. For example, *Moralia*, VIII.47 interprets Deut. 15:19 ("Thou shalt not work with the firstling of a bullock, and thou shalt not shear the first-lings of thy sheep") as the moral precept that one should not display the primary stage of a good life publicly. Isidore copied this exposition verbatim as his Deuteronomy Entry 5 in *Expositio*.[2] The exposition of the same verse in the Lyon Annotations is:

A man who desires to be master before being a disciple wants to plow with a bull-ock's firstling, who, before learning, is busy with teaching what he has not learned. Similarly, a man wants to shear the firstlings of a sheep prematurely, who, as soon as he does a bit of good work in his primary conversion, is hasty to display it publicly to win human praise.[3]

---

1 Gregory, *Moralia in Iob*, I.16, CCSL 143, p. 36: "Fatuos sapientibus in praedicatione non socies, ne per eum qui implere non ualet illi qui praeualet obsistas." The Lyon Annotations: "Id est stultum quemlibet sapienti in predicatione ne socies. Aliter: Ita religionem cristianam fide et opere retine, ut cum subprestitionibus Iudoerum nullam societatem abere uelis, ne utroque pede claudus efficiaris." Paris, BnF, NAL 1740, fol. 59r; Isidore, *Expositio in uetus testamentum*, V.6, PL 83, col. 361: "Non arabis simul in boue et asino. In bouis nomine populus ex circumcisione positus sub jugo legis, accipitur; in asino autem populus gentium, pertinens ad Euangelium, in boue quippe simul et asino arat, qui sic recipit Euangelium, ut Iudaicarum superstitionum, quae in umbra et imagine praecesserant, caeremonias relinquat. Item nonnunquam in boue bene operantium uita, in asino stultorum uecordia figuratur. Quid est ergo: Non arabis simul in boue et asino? Ac si diceret: Fatuum sapienti in praedicatione non socies, ne per eum qui rem implere non ualet, et illi qui praeualet obsistas. Bouem quippe et asinum, si necesse sit, unusquisque sine detrimento operis jungit. Sapientem uero et stultum, non ut unus praecipiat, et alter obtemperet, sed ut pariter aequali potestate annuntient uerbum Dei, non sine scandalo quisque comites facit."

2 "In primogenito quippe bouis operari est bonae conuersationis primordia in exercitio publicae actionis ostendere. Ouium quoque primogenita tondere est ab occultationis suae tegmine humanis oculis incohantia bona nostra denudare. In primogenito ergo bouis operari prohibemur atque a primogenitis ouium detondendis compescimur, quia et si quid robustum incipimus, exercere hoc in aperto citius non debemus. Et cum uita nostra simplex quid atque innocuum incohat, dignum est ut secreti sui uelamina non relinquat, ne nudum hoc humanis oculis quasi subducto uellere ostendat. Ad sola ergo diuina sacrificia boum primogenita ouium que proficiant, ut quicquid forte innocuum que incipimus, hoc ad honorem intimi iudicis in ara cordis immolemus. Quod ab illo procul dubio tanto libentius accipitur, quanto et ab hominibus occultatum nulla laudis appetitione maculatur. Saepe autem nouae conuersationis primordia adhuc ex carnali sunt uita commixta; et idcirco innotescere citius non debent ne cum laudantur bona quae placent, deceptus laude sua animus deprehendere in eis nequeat mala quae latent." Gregory, *Moralia in Iob*, VIII.47, CCSL 143, pp. 443-444 = Isidore, *Expositio in uetus testamentum*, V.5, PL 83, col. 361.

3 "Ille in primogenito bouis arare uult qui prius magister esse cupit quam discipulus, qui antequam discat, docere satagit quod non didicit. Similiter etiam ille primogenita ouis ante tempus tonde(re) uult qui si aliquid boni operis in prima sua conuersione egerit, ad humana(s) sostentationes laudes publicare contendit." Paris, BnF, NAL 1740, fol. 44v.

This exposition actually has two Gregorian sources: *Moralia*, VIII.47 (on the danger of displaying good deeds publicly), and *Homiliae in Hiezechihelem*, I.2 (about the danger of preaching at a young age).[1] While Isidore quoted only the former, Deuteronomy Entry 4 of *Liber testimoniorum* contains both. It is a logical deduction that Paterius works here as the direct source for the Lyon Annotator.

The entries of the Lyon Annotations which can be traced back to the Gregorian expositions found *not* in Isidore's *Expositio* but in Paterius' *Liber testimoniorum* are listed in Table 5.5 .

Table 5.5   Textual comparison between Paterius' *Liber testimoniorum* and the Lyon Annotations

Deut.	Gregorian exegesis (Paterius's Deut. Entry; ultimate source)	The Lyon Annotations (Paris, BnF, NAL 1740)
11:14	... Temporaneam quippe pluuiam dedit, quia electis suis priori tempore legis intellectum contulit; serotinam quoque pluuiam tribuit, quia praedicari diebus ultimis incarnationis suae mysterium fecit. (2; *Moralia*, XX.2)	Pluuia temporina Vetus significat Testamentum, serotina uero Nouum Testamentum demonstrat... (32v)
15:19	Primogenitum enim bouis accipimus in infirma aetate primi nostri temporis bonam operationem. In qua tamen arandum non est, quia cum prima sunt adolescentiae uel iuuentutis nostrae tempora, nobis adhuc a praedicatione cessandum est... (4, the 2nd part; *Homiliae in Hiezechihelem*, I.2)	... Similiter etiam ille primogenita ouis ante tempus tonde(re) uult qui si aliquid boni operis in prima sua conuersione egerit, ad humana(s) sostentationes laudes publicare contendit. (44v)
16:16	... Qui enim promerendae uitae mercedem bene agendo non prouidet, in conspectu Domini uacuus apparet... (5; *Moralia*, VII.29)	... Sed ille uacuus coram Domino apparet qui se confitetur nosse Deum, factis autem negat. (47r)
16:20	Iniuste quod iustum est exsequitur, qui ad defensionem iustitia non uirtutis aemulatione, sed amore praemii temporalis excitatur... (6; *Moralia*, IX.25)	Iuste quod iustum est persequitur qui non propter obstentatione uane laudis neque pro qualibet alia mala intentione recte iudicature uidetur sed propter amorem iustitiae iuste cuncta decernit. (47r)

---

1 "Primogenitum enim bouis accipimus in infirma aetate primi nostri temporis bonam operationem. In qua tamen arandum non est, quia cum prima sunt adolescentiae uel iuuentutis nostrae tempora, nobis adhuc a praedicatione cessandum est, ut uomer linguae nostrae proscindere non audeat terram cordis alieni. Quoadusque etenim infirmi sumus, continere nos intra nosmetipsos debemus, ne dum tenera bona citius ostendimus, amittamus, quia et arbusta plantata si prius in terra radicata non fuerint, manu tacta citius arescunt; at si semel radicem fixerint, manus tangit et tamen nil officit, uenti impellunt, nec tamen impellentes laedunt. Et constructi parietes si impellantur, eruuntur, nisi a suo prius fuerint humore siccati. Mens itaque quousque ab humore prauitatis suae perfecte non fuerit exsiccata, alienae linguae manu tangi non debet, ne priusquam plene percipiat, perdat soliditatem suam, ne impulsa ruat, ne uelut arbustum sine radicibus, dum plus quam tolerare ualet concutitur flatibus, arescat. Ad exemplum ergo non sunt ostendenda nisi quae firma sunt. Prius etenim conualescere debet mens, atque ad utilitatem proximorum postmodum demonstrari, dum iam nec per laudem eleuata corruat, nec per uituperationem percussa contabescat. Nam etsi Timotheo dicitur: *Praecipe haec, et doce; nemo adolescentiam tuam contemnat*, sciendum est quod in sacro eloquio nonnumquam adolescentia iuuentus uocatur. Vnde scriptum est: *Laetare, iuuenis, in adolescentia tua*." Gregory, *Homiliae in Hiezechihelem*, I.2, CCSL 142, pp. 18-19 = Paterius, *Liber testimoniorum*, PL 79, col. 776.

Continued

Deut.	Gregorian exegesis (Paterius's Deut. Entry; ultimate source)	The Lyon Annotations (Paris, BnF, NAL 1740)
22:6	... Matrem igitur dimittentes pullos edimus, cum historiae exempla dimittimus, sed ex ea allegoriarum sensus in mente retinemus... (8; ?)	... Tertio uero modo, ut quidam uolunt, de historia legis et sensus spiritales accipiendum est in doctoribus et auditoribus. (58v)
32:13	... Sed quia, iuxta Pauli uocem, *Petra erat Christus*, mel de petra suxerunt, qui eiusdem Redemptoris nostri facta et miracula uidere... (16; *Homiliae in euangelia*, XXVI.3-4)	... Velud saxum petra, Apostolo teste, significat Christum secundum carnem a quo sancti apostoli ante eius passionem dulcedinem uerborum quasi durissimum factus... (86v)
32:22	... Quantum ad praesentem etenim percussionem spectat, recte dicitur: *Ignis exarsit ab ira mea*. Quantum uero ad aeternam damnationem, apte mox subditur: *Et ardebit usque ad inferos deorsum*... (17; *Moralia*, XVIII.22 and XXI.12)	Ignis Domini, ultio eius in impiis et peccatoribus, ardens non in brebi tempore sed usque in aeternum sine fine. (87v)
32:42	Dei gladius carnes comedit, quia in extremo iudicio eius sententia eos, qui carnaliter sapiunt, occidit. (19; *Moralia*, XVIII.22)	Gladius Domini siue sagitte, ultio illius in impiis et peccatoribus. Cruor occisorum, mors secunda, id est pena impiorum et peccatorum. (89r)
33:25	... Quia ergo per ferrum uirtus, per aes autem perseuerantia exprimitur, ferrum et aes calceamentum eius dicitur, dum praedicatio illius acumine simul et constantia munitur. Per ferrum enim mala aduersantia penetrat, per aes autem bona quae proposuit longanimiter seruat. (22; *Moralia*, XXXIV.9)	... Cuius calciamentum, euangelica uidelicat predicatio, ferro conparatur propter acumine subtilitatis et here propter tolerantia sanctorum et sonum predictationis. (92v)

There is also a hint that the Lyon Annotator could have consulted Gregory's own works directly. For three times in the Lyon Annotations, we can find the interpretation of orphan as "the chosen people" and widow as "the Holy Church." Their ultimate source is *Moralia* XVI.45 which was absent in either Isidore's *Expositio* or Paterius' *Liber testimoniorum*.[1]

---

1   "Ipse est qui personam non accipit nec munera, qui facit iudicium pupillo, id est populo electo, et uiduae, hoc est sanctae ecclesiae." (Paris, BnF, NAL 1740, fol. 31r, on Deut. 10:17-18); "Aduenae, sancti intelleguntur, ipsi et pupilli quibus dictum est a Domino: Et patrem nolite uocare uobis super terram: unus est enim Pater uester celestis. Uidua, sancta ecclesia accipitur, quam heretici a uestimento fidei spoliare conantur." (Paris, BnF, NAL 1740, fol. 64v, on Deut. 24:17); "Maledicti heretici qui peruertunt iudicium pupilli uel populi electi et uiduae sanctae uidelicet ecclesiae." (Paris, BnF, NAL 1740, fol. 70r, Deut. 27:19) Cf. "Quos hoc loco pupillos accipimus nisi electos dei, in mentis teneritudine positos, qui magna fidei gratia nutriuntur, et patris sui iam pro se mortui faciem necdum uident?... Quae autem uidua nisi sancta ecclesia debet intellegi, quae occisi uiri sui interim uisione priuata est?" Gregory, *Moralia in Iob*, XVI.45, CCSL 143A, pp. 832-833.
   Also, the interpretation of camel as Jews in the Lyon Annotations ("Quid per camelum animal altum, inorme, ni scribas et phariseos significari uult; ruminantes quidem, id est in lege meditantes sed inter litteram et spiritum nequaquam diuidentes." (Paris, BnF, NAL 1740, fol. 41r, on Deut. 14:7) can be found in *Moralia*, II.32 (CCSL 143, p. 91), "Quamuis et eos cameli ruminantes sed tamen ungulam non findentes, indicant qui in iudaea iuxta litteram historiam audierant, sed uirtutem eius discernere spiritaliter nesciebant." But the ultimate source is likely to be Jerome's commentary on Zacharias: "Rectius autem camelus dici potest populus Iudaeorum, qui et ipse legem dei meditatur, et eam ruminat et uoluit in pectore, sed non diuidit ungulam, ut credat in patrem et in filium; et in eo immundus est, quod nequaquam separat litteram a spiritu, umbram a ueritate, et portat legis onera et audit per prophetam: uae gens peccatrix, populus plenus delictis." Jerome, *In Zachariam*, III.14, CCSL 76A, ed. Marci Adriaen (Turnhout: Brepols, 1970), pp. 892-893.

Similar to the case of other sources, the way of using Gregorian exegesis in the Lyon Annotations is flexible. A good example is Deut. 19:5-6 on the manslaughter in the wood, the Gregorian interpretation of which we have already analyzed above.[1] The Lyon Annotator added something innovative within the paraphrase of his source:

By the wood, nothing but the density of sacred scriptures is signified. It is said about the Scripture in a psalm: 'The Lord will discover the thick woods.' (Psalms 28:9) We just go to the wood to hew wood with a neighbor when we distinguish between letter and spirit through mutual conversation. The iron slips from the handle, when the proposed opinion offends a neighbor in faith due to the excess of speech; the iron is certainly the figure of word, but the handle the figure of tongue; this vice certainly arises among the ecclesiastical men (*ecclesiasticos uiros*) through controversy, and it will lead to heresy.[2]

This supplement actually converts the context of preaching and confessing between priest and layperson in Gregory's original exposition into that of the mutual biblical reading (*conlatio mutua*) among clerics. We learn from Agobard that, during the later episcopate of Leidrad, Felix of Urgel organized a salon in Lyon which was accused to spread unorthodox interpretation of the Bible to clerics.[3] The revision in this exposition may thus reflect the annotator's realistic concern over the biblical reading groups and the potential danger in the divergence of biblical interpretation of his own time.

---

1 Gregory, *Regula Pastoralis*, II.10, SC 381, p. 250, 252 = *Moralia in Iob*, 10.7, CCSL 143, p. 545 = Isidore, *Expositio in uetus testamentum*, V.19, PL 83, cols. 368-369 = Paterius, *Liber testimoniorum*, PL 79, cols. 776-777.

2 "Percutit proximum suum quilibet doctor ecclesiae qui per ignorantiam aut per escessum loqutionis proximum suum scandalizat in fide, non per inuidia aut odio sed, ut dictum est, per indiscreta loqutione. Huic facilis uenia conceditur si per sactifactionem penitentiae ad superiores refugerit ciuitates, fidem uidelicet spem atque caritatem. Quid per silua nisi condensitatem sanctarum Scripturarum significat. De qua Scriptura in psalmo inscriptum est: Et reuelauit Dominus condensa. Ad ligna cedenda simpliciter cum proximo imus quando per conlatione mutua inter littera et spiritu discernimus. Ferrum de manubrio excutitur cum per excessum locutionis prolata sententia proximum in fide scandalizat: per ferrum quippe sermo, per manubrium uero lingua figuratur; hoc quippe uitium inter ecclesiasticos uiros per contentiones oritur et usque ad hereses peruenit. Ad unam supradictarum urbium homicidam refugere est sub fide, spe et caritate penitentiam agere. Proximus ultor sanguinis eius qui occisus est, Christum Dominum significat qui per dispensationem carnis nobis proximus fieri dignatus est, qui futurus est iudex uiuorum et mortuorum. Longior uia est tarditas conuertendi ad penitentiam." Paris, BnF, NAL 1740, fol. 52r.

3 Cf. Agobard, *Adversum dogma Felicis*, V, CCCM 52, ed. Lieven Van Acker (Turnhout: Brepols, 1981), pp. 76-77.

5.6   Conclusion: Diversity and Triumph

This chapter discusses in chronological order five commentaries on Deuteronomy. The fifth book of *Quaestiones* reflects Augustine's personal thoughts on the questions that arose in his serious study of Deuteronomy. The Deuteronomy questions in Eucherius' *Intructiones* (if we trust Eucherius' own statement) originated from his son's biblical reading, and the answers that Eucherius offered are based on Jerome's biblical exegesis. By collecting Deuteronomy expositions from *Contra Faustum*, John the Deacon presented us the allegorical dimension of Augustine's biblical exegesis, quite different from the one shown in *Quaestiones*. Verecundus commented on every verse of the Song of Moses in order to exhaust the Christological and ecclesiological teachings hidden in it. Paterius' great compiling enterprise *Liber testimoniorum* comprehensively transmitted his master Gregory's painstaking effort to reveal the spiritual senses behind the biblical *historia* that may benefit Christians' moral and religious life.

John the Deacon cited Eucherius' Hieronymian interpretation to supplement Augustinian excerpts for once; two of the 22 expositional entries of Gregory collected by Paterius ultimately derive from Augustine. Except these two cases, these five exegetical enterprises on Deuteronomy between 400 and 600 do not overlap. As we will see, the situation was quite different for the next two centuries, during which all the commentaries on Deuteronomy after Isidore used the 22 entries in his *Expositio in uetus testamentum* as the framework.

Behind such diversity, to whom would the triumph belong? We can invite here two judges. The first is time. Augustine's *Quaestiones in Heptateuchum* survived in 22 medieval copies;[1] for the complete Book 1 of *Instructiones*, the number is also 22;[2] for John the Deacon, the number is one (Paris, BnF, lat. 12309); for Verecundus, the number is one as well (Leiden, Universiteitsbibliotheek, Voss. lat. F 58); for Paterius, the number is remarkably 123.[3] In the long run, Paterius' compilation enjoyed dominant popularity in the medieval west.

The other judge is the game changer Isidore. According to the source criticism to be demonstrated in the next chapter, in the Deuteronomy section of *Expositio*, the archbishop of Seville cited or paraphrased Gregory ten times (seven times from *Moralia*, three times from *Regula pastoralis*), and Augustine six times (three times from *Contra Faustum*, twice from *Enarrationes in Psalmos*, once from *Epistola*, but *none* from *Quaestiones in Heptateuchum*). If we keep our horizon within 600–800, it was the tropological exposition of Gregory and the allegorical exposition of Augustine that had most influence on the exegesis of Deuteronomy. The triumph belonged to "the spiritual understanding" of the Old Law.

---

1   CCSL 33, pp. vii-xvi.
2   CCSL 66, pp. x-xviii.
3   Fabrizio Martello, "Paterius," p. 435.

CHAPTER 6

THE EXEGESIS OF DEUTERONOMY BEFORE 800 (III): THE ISIDORIAN MOMENT AND ITS AFTERMATH

This chapter discusses the exegesis of Deuteronomy of the Iberian Father Isidore of Seville in his *Expositio in uetus testamentum* and the commentaries on Deuteronomy between the mid-seventh century and 800 under his influence. Isidore was about the same age as Paterius. The former's elder brother (Leander) was a friend of the latter's master (Gregory). Both of them worked as exegetical compilers. But how they did it differed hugely. When Paterius took pains to present the exegetical achievement of a single author in an organized, faithful, and comprehensive way, Isidore had the ambition to summarize the whole exegetical tradition in a concise, clear, and definite way. It was Isidore's success that finally brought an end to the comparatively diverse patristic era, and its dominant influence would last over at least a century and a half. That is why choosing to call the appearance of *Expositio in uetus testamentum* "the Isidorian moment" in the Latin Deuteronomy exegetical history.

Between Isidore and the Lyon Annotations (ca. 800), three groups of Latin expositions on Deuteronomy are detected in three sets of exegetical enterprises: (1) the Pseudo-Bedan Pentateuch commentary in three recensions; (2) *Pauca problesmata de enigmatibus ex tomis canonicis*, better known as the Irish *Bibelwerk*; (3) Wigbod's *Quaestiones* on the Octateuch and his *Lectiones* on the Hexateuch, also known as *Recapitulatio de paradiso, fonte ac fluminibus et ligno uitae*. The Isidorian exegesis is the backbone for all of them.

In the Lyon Annotations, Isidore still serves as a major source, but not a monopolistic one any more. The significance of this exegetical development can only be understood in the light of the discussion in this chapter.

6.1 Isidore of Seville, *Expositio in uetus testamentum*

Isidore (ca. 560–636), archbishop of Seville, marked a watershed for the Latin exegesis of the Old Testament.[1] Isidore's commentary on Deuteronomy can be found in his *Expositio in uetus testamentum* which covers the Pentateuch, Joshua, Judges, four books of Kings, Esdras, and Machabees.[2] The archbishop probably composed *Expositio* between 604 and 615.[3] The work is regarded as "the vast work of his full maturity" and "the culmination of Isidore's work."[4] The distinguished Isidorian scholar Jacques Fontaine saw in *Expositio* the creation of "un genre nouveau de manuels élémentaires de pédagogie biblique et exégétique."[5] Ildefonsus of Toledo around the mid-sixth century in his *De uiris illustribus* described the work in this way:

He [Isidore] also collects from various authors what he called "expositions of the secret mysteries" (*secretorum expositiones sacramentorum*) and compiles them into one volume. The work is also called the Book of Questions (*liber... Quaestionum*).[6]

Isidore himself asserted his goal and method in the preface:

The history of the Divine Law was not carried out and written down without a certain forecasting of things to come; nor would such a manifold shadow of past deeds pertain to the mystery of foreshadowing, otherwise the Apostle would not have said:

---

1   For the general studies, see Jacques Fontaine, *Isidore de Séville: Genèse et originalité de la culture hispanique au temps des Wisigoths* (Turnhout: Brepols, 2000), pp. 183-193; Thomas O'Loughlin, "Isidore's Hermeneutics: The Codification of the Tradition," *Patristic Theories of Biblical Interpretation: The Latin Fathers*, ed. Tarmo Toom (Cambridge: Cambridge University Press, 2016), pp. 206-231.

2   The modern editors have provided other titles for the work, including *Enarrationes, Quaestiones in uetus testamentum, Commentaria in uetus testamentum, Secretorum expositiones sacramentorum*, and, most well known to modern scholars, *Mysticorum expositiones sacramentorum*. I follow Michael Gorman's preference to the title *Expositio in uetus testamentum*. Gorman explained in the editorial introduction to his edition of the Genesis section (*Isidorus episcopus Hispalensis: Expositio in Vetus Testamentum. Genesis* [Freiburg: Herder, 2009] , pp. ix-xii) why the *editio princeps* published by Johannes Soter in 1530 is closer to Isidore's original text than the one first published by Juan de Grial in 1599, reprinted by Faustino Arévalo in 1797, and taken by Migne in 1850 (PL 83, cols. 207-424). However, Soter's edition is not paginated and therefore difficult to cite. To solve this dilemma, the author will cite the text by the PL column number but collate the PL edition by Soter's.

3   For a brief discussion about the historiography of its dating, see Jacques Elfassi, "*Quaestiones in Vetus Testamentum,*" *La trasmissione dei testi latini del Medioevo*, eds. Paolo Chiesa and Lucia Castaldi (Florence: SISMEL, Edizioni del Galluzzo, 2004–2013), vol. 1, pp. 196-201.

4   Claudio Leonardi, "Aspects of Old Testament Interpretation in the Church from the Seventh to the Tenth Century," *Hebrew Bible/Old Testament: The History of Its Interpretation. Volume I. From the beginnings to the Middle Ages (until 1300). Part 2: The Middle Ages*, ed. Magne Sæbø, (Göttingen: Vandenhoeck and Ruprecht, 1996), pp. 180-195; Donald Jacob Uitvlugt, "The Sources of Isidore's Commentaries on the Pentateuch," *Revue Bénédictine* 112 (2002): pp. 72-100, no. 44.

5   Jacques Fontaine, "Isidore de Séville pédagogue et théoricien de l'exégèse," *Stimuli: Exegese und ihre Hermeneutik in Antike und Christentum. Festschrift für Ernst Dassmann*, eds. Georg Schöllgen and Clemens Scholten (Münster: Aschendorff, 1996), pp. 423-434.

6   "Collegit etiam de diuersis auctoribus, quod ipse cognominat secretorum expositiones sacramentorum, quibus in unum congestis, idem liber dicitur Quaestionum." Ildefonsus, *De uiris illustribus*, VIII, CCSL 114A, ed. Codoñer Merino (Turnhout: Brepols, 2007), p. 611.

"For the Law having a figure of the good things to come, not the very image of the things." (Hebrews 10:1) Hence, those that were said or done in figure (*figuratim*) in the Law and that are full of mystical mysteries (*mysticis sacramentis*), with the help of the highest grace, I compiled in this little work by searching and gathering the opinions of previous churchmen, as if I collected flowers from various meadows, pressing together a few briefly from many. I added a lot and changed some partially. I offered not only to zealous but also to fastidious readers who hate an overlong reading. For they are not resentful about brief exposition shortened from prolixity. Prolonged and hidden speech makes people tired, but brief and clear speech makes them delighted. And since now indeed the whole *sermo* was woven together according to the literal sense (*iuxta literam*), it is necessary that with the foundations of *historia* going first, the allegorical understanding *(allegoricus sensus)* should follow. For they can be understood in figure (*figuraliter*) as preceding prophetic signs that prophesize the things to come.[1]

Scholars are not certain which work is the *iuxta literam a nobis sermo totus contextus* that Isidore claimed.[2] There are three minor Isidorian exegetical works, usually copied together in the manuscript transmission:[3] (1) *De ortu et obitu Patrum* about "the births, deeds, and genealogies of certain holy and most noble persons" recorded in the Old and New Testament;[4] (2) *Allegoriae quaedam Sacrae Scripturae* about "certain most

---

1 "Historia sacrae legis non sine aliqua praenuntiatione futurorum gesta atque conscripta est, nec pertineret ad praefigurationis mysterium tam multiplex rerum umbra gestarum, nisi docens Apostolus diceret: *Lex figuram habet futurorum bonorum, non ipsam imaginem rerum.* Proinde quaedam quae in ea figuratim dicta uel facta sunt, et sunt plena mysticis sacramentis, adiuuante superna gratia, in hoc opusculo exsequentes intexuimus, ueterumque ecclesiasticorum sententias congregantes, ueluti ex diuersis pratis flores collectos ad manum fecimus, et pauca de multis breuiter perstringentes, pleraque etiam adiicientes uel ex aliqua parte mutantes, offerimus non solum studiosis, sed etiam fastidiosis lectoribus, quibus nimia longitudo sermonis abhorret. Breui enim expositione succincta non faciunt de prolixitate fastidium. Prolixa enim et occulta taedet oratio; breuis et aperta delectat. Et quia iam pridem iuxta literam a nobis sermo totus contextus est, necesse est, ut praecedente historiae fundamento, allegoricus sensus sequatur. Nam figuraliter quaedam ex his intelliguntur, uere tanquam prophetica indicia praecedentia futurorum." Isidore, *Expositio in uetus testamentum, prologus*, PL 83, cols. 207-208.
2 "Isidore fait-il là une allusion à un ouvrage pour nous disparu? Ou, plutôt, à cet opuscule *Sur la naissance et la décès des Pères* dont on a dit avec justesse qu'il peut être assimilé à un commentaire biblique de caractère littéral?" Jacques Fontaine, *Isidore de Séville*, p. 187. "In the *praefatio* Isidore also refers to a literal commentary, of which we know nothing, that he had evidently composed before (*iam pridem*) his allegorical commentaries." Michael Gorman, ed., *Genesis*, p. ix.
3 Cf. Jacques Elfassi, "*Allegoriae* sive *Liber de interpretatione quorundam nominum Veteris Nouique Testamenti*," *La trasmissione dei testi latini del Medioevo*, eds. Paolo Chiesa and Lucia Castaldi (Florence: SISMEL, Edizioni del Galluzzo, 2004–2013), vol. 1, pp. 196-201; Paolo Chiesa, "*In libros Veteris et Noui Testamenti Prooemia*," ibid., vol. 2, pp. 338-345; idem, "*De ortu et obitu Patrum*," ibid., pp. 345-353.
4 "Quorumdam sanctorum patrum nobilissimorumque uirorum ortus uel gesta cum genealogiis suis in hoc libello indita sunt; dignitas quoque et mors eorum atque sepultura sententiali breuitate notata." Isidore, *De ortu et obitu Patrum*, ed. César Chaparro Gómez (Paris: Belles Lettres, 1985), p. 103.

well-known names of the Law and the Gospels which are covered under the allegory of imaginary";[1] (3) *Prooemia in libros ueteris ac noui testamenti*, "the little introductions of the stories" of the seventy-two canonical books of the Bible.[2] It is likely that Isidore composed the first two as a pair, interpreting the Bible through major characters, respectively in a literal and allegorical way. It is can be suggested that *iuxta literam a nobis sermo totus contextus* is *Prooemia*. Its literal approach to the Bible in canonical order paved the *historiae fundamentum* for the allegorical exposition in *Expositio*.

In the preface to *Expositio*, Isidore also noted that only parts of the Old Testament contain mysteries and they are connected in narrative by other parts which do not foreshadow anything in themselves.[3] He claimed to speak in the words of Church Fathers (*uox mea, ipsorum est lingua*) and to compile them into one brief compendium (*in unam formam compendio breuitatis*). Eight Fathers are listed: Origen, Victorinus of Pettau (ca. 250–303/304), Ambrose, Jerome, John Cassian, Augustine, Fulgentius of Ruspe (462/467–527/533), and Gregory the Great "who is eloquent eminently in our own times."[4] This enumeration does not count all the Church Fathers quoted in *Expositio*, though. According to the study of Martine Dulaey (on the Genesis section) and Donald Uitvlugt (on the Exodus, Leviticus, Numbers, and Deuteronomy sections), we can at least add seven more: Paulinus of Nola (letters), Caesarius of Arles (sermons), Novatian (*De cibis iudaicis*, once attributed to Tertullian in the early Middle Ages), Cyprian (*De ecclesiae catholicae unitate*), Rufinus of Aquileia (*De benedictionibus Patriarcharum*), and Gregory of Elvira (*Tractatus Origenis*, once attributed to Origen), Pelagius (*Expositiones XIII epistularum Sancti Pauli*, once attributed to Jerome). The most frequently quoted works include Origen's homilies, Augustine's *Contra Faustum* and

---

1   "Quaedam notissima nomina legis euangeliorumque, quae sub allegoria imaginarie obteguntur, et interpretatione aliqua egent, breuiter deflorata contraxi celeriter, ut plana atque aperta lectoribus redderem." Isidore, *Allegoriae Sacrae Scripturae*, PL 83, cols. 97-98.

2   "Disposito igitur Veteris ac Noui Testamenti ordine librorum et numero, nunc cursim breuiterque in eos parua prooemia narrationum subiiciamus." Isidore, *Prooemia in libros ueteris ac noui testamenti*, PL 83, col. 160.

3   "Sane non omnia quae in lege et prophetis scripta sunt, aenigmatibus mysteriorum obteguntur; sed pro his quae aliquid significant, etiam quae nihil significant connectuntur. Sicut enim in citharis et huiusmodi organis musicis, non quidem omnia quae tanguntur, canorum aliquid resonant sed cordae, caetera tamen in toto citharae corpore ideo facta sunt, ut esset ubi connecterentur et quo tenderentur illa quae ad cantilenae suauitatem modulaturus est artifex: Ita in his propheticis narrationibus, quae obteguntur aut aliquid sonant in significatione futurorum, aut si nihil sonant ad hoc interponuntur, ut sit unde illa significantia tanquam sonantia connectantur." Isidore, *Expositio in uetus testamentum*, PL 83, col. 208.

4   "Has autem rerum gestarum figuras de mysticis thesauris sapientium, ut praediximus, depromentes, in unam formam compendio breuitatis contraximus. In quibus lector non nostra leget, sed ueterum. Quod enim ego loquor, illi dicunt, et uox mea, ipsorum est lingua. Sumpta itaque sunt ab autoribus Origene, Victorino, Ambrosio, Hieronymo, Cassiano, Augustino, Fulgentio, ac nostri temporis insigniter eloquenti Gregorio." Ibid.

Enarrationes in Psalmos, and Gregory's *Moralia* and *Regula pastoralis*.[1] Nevertheless, except Genesis, the source criticism of *Expositio* is far from thorough and definite, as my examination of Deuteronomy below will modify Uitvlugt's study.

The introduction to Deuteronomy in *Prooemia* is:

> In Deuteronomy, which is the second law, is narrated what Moses spoke to the people between Paran, Tophel, Laban, and Hazeroth, up to Kadesh-barnea, namely the things commanded and promised, the curses of sins and the promises of blessings. There, Moses sang a song, and gave blessing to the sons of Israel. Also, after having a look at the Promised Land there, he died and was buried. Some Jews count the four books, that is, Genesis, Exodus, Leviticus, and Numbers, as books of Law, and they say that Deuteronomy is the repetition of these same books, as if a meditation on the Law (*legis meditatorium*), with good reason, because those four books contain their own subjects of the past events, and this one [Deuteronomy] contains all.[2]

It seems that the wording *legis meditatorium* originated from Jerome's Letter to Eustochius (no.78) where he called Deuteronomy *meditatorium euangelii*, the prelude of the Gospel (cf. Chapter 4.3). The rare word *meditatorium* in classical Latin means "preparation" and "prelude." In the Middle Ages, it developed the new meaning "the place to meditate." It is also not impossible that Isidore has two self-referential verses in Deuteronomy in mind: Deut. 6:7 ("And thou shalt tell them to thy children, and thou shalt meditate (*meditaberis*) upon them sitting in thy house, and walking on thy journey, sleeping and rising") and Deut. 11:19 ("Teach your children that they meditate on them...").

More influential is the allegorical definition of this biblical book in the opening passage of the Deuteronomy section in *Expositio* (It will be called *Commentary on Deuteronomy* for convenience):

> The book of Deuteronomy is the reiteration of the previous four books of Law. For while these four books contain their own subjects, Deuteronomy repeats all. But this book has innumerable mysteries (*sacramenta*) of its own, a few of which I examined

---

1   Donald Uitvlugt, "The sources of Isidore's commentaries on the Pentateuch"; Martine Dulaey, "Les sources du commentaire d'Isidore sur la Genèse," *Genesis*, ed. Michael Gorman (Freiburg: Herder, 2009), pp. xxv-xliii.

2   "In Deuteronomio autem, quae est secunda lex, narrantur ea quae inter Pharan, et Tophel, et Laban, et [H]aseroth, usque ad Cades Barne fuerunt populo dicta a Moyse: mandata, uidelicet, atque promissa, maledictiones peccatorum, et promissiones beatitudinis. Ibi canit canticum Moyses. Ibi canit canticum Moyses. Ibi dat benedictionem filiis Israel; ibique, terra repromissionis conspecta, moritur atque sepelitur. Nonnulli autem Hebraeorum quatuor tantum libros computant legis, id est, Genesim, Exodum, Leuiticum, Numeros. Deuteronomium autem repetitionem eorumdem librorum, et quasi quoddam legis meditatorium dicunt. Ea duntaxat ratione, pro eo quod illi quatuor proprias rerum gestarum continent causas, iste uero omnium." Isidore, *Prooemia in libros ueteris ac noui testamenti*, V, PL 83, cols. 160-161.

for the exercise of the reader. For Deuteronomy is called the second legislation, signifying the Gospel (*significat euangelium*).[1]

The wording *Deuteronomium... secunda legislatio... quod significat Euangelium*
undoubtedly came from Jerome's Letter 53 to Paulinus, which Isidore quoted lengthily in
his *Etymologiae* prior to the composition of *Expositio*.[2] As we have discussed in Chapter
5.2, Eucherius seems to have been the first to cite Jerome's "Deuteronomy-Gospel"
typological motif, but he did not apply it evidently as a hermeneutic principle.[3] Other
exegetes treated in the previous chapter (Augustine, Verecundus, and Gregory) largely
ignored the motif. Isidore argurably was the first author ever in exegetical history to start
a commentary on Deuteronomy with it. After him, it became standard to do so. We can
see its variances in four ninth-century Deuteronomy commentaries, including the Lyon
Annotations (Table 6.1) .

Table 6.1   "Deuteronomy-Gospel" motif in Carolingian exegetical works

The Lyon Annotations (Paris, BnF, NAL 1740), the opening entry (1r)	Deuteronomium est ueteris iteratio legis; quae iteratio ad Nouum pertinet Testamentum... figura est secundae legis, id est Noui Testamenti, uniuersa precepta Domini atque iudicia que ad creationem pertinentia, magis ad nouum populum, hoc est cristianum sed in nouitate tamen spiritalis Israel...
Hrabanus Maurus, *Enarratio super Deuteronomium*, the preface, a letter to Freculf of Lisieux (PL 108, col. 837)	Haec autem quae nouiter a legislatore inserta reperi, diuina gratia largiente, pro modulo nostri ingenioli, quantulumcunque explanare curaui. Deuteronomium quoque, ut beatus Hieronymus in quadam epistola sua ad amicum ait, secunda est lex, et euangelicae legis praefiguratio; sicque ea habet quae priora sunt, ut tamen noua sint omnia. Quapropter haec res operosa indiget solutione: scilicet quod ita historialiter ordinentur uetera, ut spiritaliter omnia demonstrentur noua, et legis per figuram patefecit littera quae sacer Euangelii textus in se continet sacramenta.

---

1   "Liber Deuteronomii repetitio est praecedentium quatuor librorum legis. Nam dum illi in se proprias
contineant causas, iste tamen replicat omnium. Habet autem et ipse proprie innumerabilia sacramenta,
e quibus pauca pro exercitio lectoris studui memoranda. Deuteronomium autem secunda legislatio
dicitur, quod significat euangelium." Isidore, *Expositio in uetus testamentum*, V, PL 83, col. 359.

2   "Deuteronomium Graeco sermone appellatur, quod Latine interpretatur secunda lex, id est, repetitio,
et euangelicae legis praefiguratio, quae sic ea habet quae priora sunt, ut tamen noua sint omnia quae
in eo replicantur." Isidore, *Etymologiarum siue Originum libri XX*, VI.II.7, ed. Lindsay.

3   Isidore knew Eucherius' *Instructiones*, cf. Jacques Elfassi, "Isidore de Séville connaissait-il les
Formulae d'Eucher de Lyon?" *Felici Curiositate: Studies in Latin Literature and Textual Criticism
from Antiquity to the Twentieth Century: In Honour of Rita Beyers*, eds. Guy Guldentops, Christian
Laes, Gert Partoens (Turnhout: Brepols, 2017), pp. 377-382. But there is no reason to assume that
Isidore cited Jerome indirectly via Eucherius.

Continued

Walahfrid Strabo, *Glosa in Deuteronomium*, the first entry (Sankt Gallen, Stiftsbibliothek, 283, p. 621)[1]	[D]EUTERONOMIUM DICITUR SECUNda lex, uel innouatio legis, quia deuteros graece secunda dicitur, nomos uero lex. Huius libri scribendi causa fuit, ut uel eos commonefaceret de actis praeteritis et praeceptis uel breuiter totam legem in unum collectam ad memoriae utilitatem perduceret. Facilius enim pauca retinentur quam latius dispersa. Prefert autem typum euangelii quod apostolus uerbum ad breuiatum nominat, et quod de cunctis scripturis testimonium habet.
Paschasius Radbertus, *De benedictionibus Patriarcharum Iacob et Moysi*, prologue (CCCM 96, ed. Bede Paulus, (Brepols: Turnhout, 1993, p. 8)	Et ideo eo in libro istae recapitulantur sicut et omnis ille liber Deuteronomium quae secunda et noua lex uocatur.

Isidore's *Commentary on Deuteronomy* contains 22 entries, of which Entry 4 as an anomaly expounds not any Deuteronomic verse but Leviticus 19:23 ("you shall take away the firstfruits of them [trees]").[2] Donald Uitvlugt's study offers us a starting point to detect Isidore's use of sources,[3] as showed in the following table with the revisions of the author in footnotes (Table 6.2).

---

1 Burton Van Name Edwards is preparing an edition of this commentary for CCCM, and he kindly offered me the permission to read his draft. The Latin text given here is based on my own transcription of the ninth-century manuscript Sankt Gallen, Stiftsbibliothek, 283 (Bischoff, *Katalog*, 5724). For the online facsimile, see http://www.e-codices.unifr.ch/en/csg/0283/, last accessed September 14, 2018.

2 No satisfying explanation for this anomalous entry has been offered. It is possible that Isidore simply mistakenly regarded Leviticus 19:23 as a Deuteronomic verse. But it is also not impossible to read Entry 4 an extension of Entry 3 (on Deut. 16:21 "Non plantabis omne lignum iuxta altare Dei"), since both are concerned with the allegorical sense of plants. Likewise, it is also possible to treat Entry 4 and Entry 5 (on Deut. 22:10 "Non arabis in boue simul et asino") as a single piece, since they share not only the same theme (the initial stage of good practice) but also the same source (Gregory's *Moralia*, VIII.47).

3 Donald Uitvlugt, "The sources of Isidore's commentaries on the Pentateuch," pp. 99-100.

Table 6.2   Isidore's *commentary on Deuteronomy*

Entry	Deut.	Chapter heading[1]	Source[2]
1		"Liber Deuteronomii repetitio est praecedentium quatuor librorum legis... secunda legislatio dicitur, quod significat Euangelium."	Jerome, *Epistola* LIII.7
	1:2	Quid significet quod undecim diebus Deuteronomium a Moyse scribitur	
2	1:3	De quadraginta annis laboriose peractis a filiis Israel, et uestimentis eorum non attritis	Augustine, *Enarrationes in Psalmos*, XCIV.14; *Epistola* CCV.1
3	16:21	De non plantando ligno iuxta altare Dei	Origen-Jerome, *Homiliae in Ieremiam*, XIV
4	Lev. 19:23	De auferendiis praeputiis ligni pomiferi	Gregory, *Moralia*, VIII.47
5	15:19	De non operando in primogenito bouis, et non tondendis primogenitis ouium	Gregory, *Moralia*, VIII.47
6	22:10	De non arando in boue et asino	Gregory, *Moralia*, I.16; Augustine, *Contra Faustum*, VI.9; Jerome, *Commentaria in Isaiam*, I.1.3[3]
7	25:4	De non alligando os bouis triturantis	Augustine, *Enarrationes in Psalmos*, LXXX.4; Pelagius/Pseudo-Jerome, *Expositiones XIII epistularum Sancti Pauli*[4]
8	14:21	De non coquendo haedo in lacte matris suae	
9	22:11	De non induenda ueste ex lana linoque contexta	Gregory, *Moralia* VIII.51; Augustine, *Contra Faustum*, VI.9
10	24:6	De non accipienda loco pignoris superiore et inferiore mola	Gregory, *Moralia*, XXXIII.12
11	23:7	De non abominando Aegyptio	Cassian, *Collationes*, V.19

1   The old manuscripts of *Expositio* usually contain a list of chapter headings preceding each commentary of *Expositio*. They may reflect Isidore's own design.

2   Origen, *Homiliae in Leuiticum*, GCS 29, ed. Wilhelm Baehrens (Leipzig: J. C. Hinrichs, 1920), pp. 280-507; idem, *Homiliae in Ieremiam*, PL 25, cols. 583-692; Jerome, *Epistula LIII*, CSEL 54, pp. 442-464; idem, *Commentaria in Isaiam*, CCSL 73, 73A, ed. Mark Adriaen (Turnhout: Brepols, 1963); Augustine, *Enarrationes in Psalmos*, CCSL 38-40, eds. Eligius Dekkers, Johannes Fraipont (Turnhout: Brepols, 1956); idem, *Epistula CCV*, CSEL 57, ed. Alois Goldbacher (Vienna: Verlag der Österreichischen Akademie der Wissenschaften, 1911), pp. 323-340; idem, *Contra Faustum*, CSEL 25, pp. 251-797; Pelagius, *Expositions of Thirteen Epistles of St Paul*, ed. Alexander Souter (Cambridge: Cambridge University Press, 1922–1931); Cassian, *Collationes*, CSEL 13; idem, *De institutis coenobiorum*, CSEL 17; Gregory, *Moralia in Iob*, CCSL 143, 143A, 143B; idem, *Regula Pastoralis*, SC 381-382.

3   Uitvlugt's suggestion that this entry uses Augustine's *De ciuitate Dei* and a sermon by Caesarius is not persuasive.

4   Uitvlugt noticed the correspondence between Isidore's text and a fifth-century worked-over form of Pelagius' *Expositiones XIII epistularum Sancti Pauli* (PL 30, col. 884): "Vult illi praestare carnalia, a quibus alii spiritualia consequuntur: quia occupati in doctrina, necessaria sibi prouidere non possunt." But he failed to realize that the same text can be found in Pelagius' original commentary, Pelagius, *Expositions of Thirteen Epistles of St Paul*, vol. 2, p. 497. Also, Uitvlugt's suggestion that this entry uses *Moralia* is not persuasive.

Continued

Entry	Deut.	Chapter heading	Source
12	25:13	De non habendis in sacculo diuersis ponderibus	Cassian, *Collationes*, XXI.22
13	19:15	De trium testimonio uel duorum ualituro	Origen-Jerome, *Homiliae in Ieremiam*, I
14	25:5-10	De uxore fratris accipienda, eiusque semine suscitando	Augustine, *Contra Faustum*, XXXII.10; Gregory, *Regula pastoralis*, I.5
15	20:8	De formidoloso et pauido, quod non egrediatur ad bellum	Cassian, *De institutis coenobiorum*, VII.15
16	7:1	De interpretatione septem gentium, quas dominus tradidit Israeli	Cassian, *Collationes*, V.16, 23[1]
17	7:1	Quod Dominus cum Abraham de futuris loqueretur, non septem sed decem gentes dinumerasse	Cassian, *Collationes*, V.22
18	21:10	De muliere decora capta in bello, et eradendis capillis eius	Origen-Rufinus, *Homiliae in Leuiticum*, VII.6[2]; Ambrose, *Epistulae*, IV.13.11[3]
19	19:5	Quid significet securis ligna caedens, manubriumque effugiens	Gregory, *Regula pastoralis*, II.10
20	23:10	De pollutione somnii nocturni	Gregory, *Moralia*, IX.55
21	23:12-13	De paxillo in baltheo egredientis ad requisita naturae	Gregory, *Moralia*, XXXI.27
22	25:2-3	De quadraginta flagellis delinquentibus adhibendis	Gregory, *Moralia*, VI.22

Isidore depended on five Fathers to compose his *Commentary on Deuteronomy*: Origen, Jerome (including Pelagius' commentary on Pauline epistles which Isidore would probably regard as a Hieronymian work), Augustine, Cassian, and Gregory. The use of Jerome is relatively light. The most frequently quoted father is Gregory, whom Isidore once praised in these terms: "Not only in the present is there no equal teacher, but there has never been at any time."[4] Uitvlugt shed doubt on Thomas O'Loughlin's argument

---

1 Uitvlugt failed to notice the use of *Collationes*, V.23 in this entry.

2 Uitvlugt failed to notice the use of Origen's Leviticus Homily 7 in this entry. He was thus also wrong to claim that Isidore in *Expositio* quoted Origen's *Homiliae in Leuiticum* only in the Leviticus section ("The sources of Isidore's commentaries on the Pentateuch," p. 79).

3 Uitvlugt failed to notice the use of Ambrose in this entry (cf. Chapter 4.4).

4 "Gregorius Papa Romanae sedis apostolicae praesul, compunctione timoris Dei plenus et humilitate summus, tantoque per gratiam Spiritus Sancti scientiae lumine praeditus, ut non modo illi praesentium temporum quisquam doctorum, sed nec in praeteritis quidem par fuerit unquam." Isidore, *De uiris illustribus,* 27, ed. Codoñer Merino (Salamanca: Consejo superior de investigaciones científicas, 1964), pp. 148-149. In the so-called *Versus Isidorii* that is supposed to decorate Isidore's library, the status of Gregory is juxtaposed with Augustine: "XIII GREGORIVS/Quantum Augustino clares tu Hippone magistro/Tantum Roma suo praesule Gregorio." Isidore, *Versus*, CCSL 113A, ed. Sanchez Martin (Turnhout: Brepols, 2000), p. 225.

For the reception of Gregory in Visigoth Spain and especially by Isidore, see Jamie Wood, "A Family Affair: Leander, Isidore and the Legacy of Gregory the Great in Spain," *Isidore of Seville and his Reception in the early Middle Ages: Transmitting and Transforming Knowledge*, eds. Andrew Fear, Jamie Wood (Amsterdam: Amsterdam University Press), pp. 31-56.

that Isidore in the Genesis section of *Expositio* used Paterius' *Liber testimoniorum* rather than Gregory's own works.[1] The source criticism of the Deuteronomy section supports Uitvlugt's view that Isidore quoted or paraphrased Gregory independent of Paterius. As we have seen in Chapter 5.5, Paterius selected expositions of Deuteronomy from four Gregorian works: *Moralia*, *Regula pastoralis*, *Homiliae in Hiezechihelem*, and *Homiliae in euangelia*. In comparison, Isidore in his *Commentary on Deuteronomy* used only *Moralia* and *Regula pastoralis*.[2] Also, the last entry of Isidore's *Commentary on Deuteronomy* is based on *Moralia* VI.22, which is not collected in *Liber testimoniorum*. On most of the occasions when Isidore used Gregory (in Entries 4, 5, 9, 10, 19, 20, 21, and 22), he tended to quote intact passages faithfully, although, in one case (Entry 6), he did make significant change (see below).

Augustine's *Enarrationes in Psalmos* and *Contra Faustum* serve as sources for Isidore's Deuteronomy Entries 2, 7, and 14. As Uitvlugt shrewdly commented, both of these two Augustinian works "are concerned with the unity of the Old and New Testament, demonstrating how the Old Testament finds its spiritual fulfillment in Christ. This sort of spiritual interpretation is exactly what Isidore promises his reader in the Preface to the Commentaries."[3] In Entry 9 (on Deut 22:11), Isidore juxtaposed an excerpt from *Moralia* and one from *Contra Faustum*, calling the former "according to the moral sense," the latter "according to another allegorical understanding."[4]

In comparison with Augustine and Gregory, Isidore's use of Origen (through the translation of Rufinus and Jerome) is more flexible.[5] Entry 3 resorts to Origen to interpret the unfruitful trees forbidden to be planted near the altar of the Lord as the beautiful words void of virtue and faith, but Origen's original reference to heretics is replaced with gentiles. In Entry 13, Isidore took the initiative to contextualize Origen's allegorical exposition of Deut. 19:15 ("two or three witnesses" as New and Old Testament, or Gospel, Prophets, and Epistles) by adding *cum contra quoslibet impios uel haereticos agimus*. In Entry 18 on Deut. 21:10, after interpreting the beautiful female war captive as the soul converting from sins to Christ — an exposition, as we have seen in Chapter 4.4,

---

1   Donald Uitvlugt, "The sources of Isidore's commentaries on the Pentateuch," p. 77; cf. Thomas O'Loughlin, "Isidore's Use of Gregory the Great in the Exegesis of Genesis," *Revue Bénédictine* 107 (1997): pp. 263-269.

2   For instance, Deuteronomy Entry 4 of *Liber testimoniorum* on Deut. 15:19 ("Non operaberis in primogenito bouis, et non tondebis primogenita ovium") contains passages from *Moralia*, VIII.47 and *Homiliae in Hiezechihelem*, I.2. For the same verse, in Entry 4 of *Commentary on Deuteronomy*, Isidore used the former but not the latter.

3   Donald Uitvlugt, "The sources of Isidore's commentaries on the Pentateuch," p. 80.

4   "Hoc secundum moralem sensum. Caeterum iuxta alteram allegoriam..." Isidore, *Expositio in uetus testamentum*, V.9, PL 83, col. 362.

5   For a general study, see Jean Chatillon, "Isidore et Origène: Recherches sur les sources et l'influence des *Quaestiones in Vetus Testamentum* d'Isidore de Séville," *Mélanges bibliques rédigés en l'honneur de André Robert* (Paris: Bloud & Gay, 1956), pp. 537-547. Chatillon's survey is based on the Exodus, Joshua, and Judges sections.

originated with Ambrose — Isidore introduced Origen's exposition in his seventh homily on Leviticus as an exegetical alternative: "*Others thought* that this captive woman, beautiful to the eye, means some discipline of reason, which, wisely said, is among the Gentiles."[1]

Another source that Isidore used very freely is John Cassian. Entry 15 adopts the expositional framework in the latter's *De coenobiorum institutis*, VII.15 to interpret the ban that the fearful and faint-heart people not go to fight (Deut. 20:8) as a warning that a Christian with no determined mind should not enter religious life. But Isidore rewrote Cassian's exposition so greatly that the exegetical focus actually switches from worldly wealth to carnal desire.[2]

Deuteronomy Entries 16 and 17 provide a good example to examine in detail how Isidore manipulated his Cassianic source. The expounded verse is Deut. 7:1 about the command to destroy the seven Canaanite nations. Isidore excerpted from Book 5 of *Conlationes* to demonstrate that "the seven nations are the seven capital sins which by

---

1 All the relevant references were listed in footnotes of Table 4.1.
2 "Homo formidolosus et corde pauido non egrediatur ad bellum. Vadat et reuertatur ad domum suam, ne pauere faciat corda fratrum suorum, sicut et ipse timore perterritus est. Quibus uerbis edocetur non posse quenque professionem contemplationis, uel spiritualis militiae arripere exercitium, qui adhuc nudari terrenis operibus pertimescit. Ne rursus ad infirmitatem mentis reuertantur, suoque exemplo alios ab euangelica perfectione reuocet, et infideli terrore infirmet; jubent itaque tales, ut, discedentes ex pugna, reuertantur in domum, quia non possunt duplici corde bella Domini praeliari. Vir enim duplex animo, inconstans est in omnibus uiis suis. Tales quippe oportet ut ne initium quidem renuntiationis arripiant. Quibus melius est, ut in actiua uita consistant, quam tepide contemplationem exsequentes, majori discrimini semetipsos inuoluant. Melius est enim non uouere, quam uouere et non reddere. Similiter et ille a tali militia prohibetur, qui uxorem duxerit, qui plantauerit uineam, uelut propaginem filiorum, non enim potest seruire diuinae militiae seruus uxoris. Nec potestasse qui studium contemplationis, qui adhuc in delectatione defigitur carnis. Nemo, inquit Apostolus, militans Deo, implicat se negotiis secularibus, ut ei placeat cui se probauit." Isidore, *Expositio in uetus testamentum*, V.15, PL 83, cols. 365-366. Cf. Cassian, *De institutis coenobiorum*, VII.15, CSEL 17, pp. 138-139: "De his igitur, qui dicentes renuntiasse se huic mundo rursus incredulitate fracti nudari terrenis opibus timent, in Deuteronomio mystice praecipitur: si quis est homo formidolosus, et corde pauido, non egrediatur ad bellum: uadat, et reuertatur in domum suam, ne pauere faciat corda fratrum suorum, sicut et ipse timore perterritus est. Hoc testimonio quid euidentius quaeso? Nonne manifeste mauult eos scriptura professionis huius nec initium sibimet usurpare nec nomen, quam exhortatione exemplo que corrupto etiam alios ab euangelica perfectione reuocare et infideli infirmare terrore? Iubetur itaque eis ut discedentes e pugna reuertantur in domum suam, quia non potest quisquam duplici corde bella Domini proeliari (uir enim duplex animo inconstans in omnibus uiis suis), et cogitantes secundum illam euangelii parabolam eum, qui cum decem milibus progreditur, contra regem cum uiginti milibus uenientem non posse confligere, adhuc eo longe posito postulent pacem, id est ut ne initium quidem renuntiationis arripiant potius quam tepide eam post exsequentes maiori discrimine semet inuoluant. Melius est enim non uouere, quam uouere et non reddere. Pulchre autem hic cum decem milibus et ille cum uiginti uenire describitur. Amplior enim inpugnantium nos uitiorum numerus est quam uirtutum pro nobis dimicantium. Nemo autem potest deo seruire et mamonae, nec ponens quisquam manum suam super aratrum et respiciens retro aptus est regno Dei."

God's grace every spiritual soldier is admonished to uproot by overcoming."[1] In Cassian's original scheme, of the ten nations which God promised to Abraham that his progeny would conquer (Genesis 15:18-21), three refer to gentiles' idolatry, Jews' blasphemy, and gluttony. Christians conquer all these three when they leave "the intellectual Egypt" via knowledge of God and baptism. The seven nations mentioned in (Deut. 7:1) refer to the other seven cardinal sins (fornication, avarice, anger, melancholy, sloth, vainglory, and pride), with which Christians need to keep fighting in "the spiritual desert."[2]

The problem that Isidore had with this exposition of Cassian is that the archbishop of Seville preferred the Gregorian pattern of capital sins to the Cassianic. One of major distinctions between the two patterns is how to understand the root of sins, as we have discussed closely in Chapter 2.4.2. Cassian sees gluttony as the root of other seven sins; for Gregory, all the seven cardinal originate from pride, "the queen of sins" and "the root of all evils." To make Cassian's exposition fit the Gregorian model, Isidore edited his source in very extraordinary way (Table 6.3).

Table 6.3   Source using in Isidore's Deuteronomy Entries 16 and 17

Cassian, *Conlationes*	Isidore, *Expositio*
Numerosior enim est quam Israhel carnalium passionum populus, qui de hoc septenario fomite uitiorum ac radice procedit. Exinde enim pullulant homicidia, contentiones, haereses... **alia que conplura his similia. Quae cum sint multo maioris numeri quam uirtutes, deuictis tamen illis octo principalibus uitiis, ex quorum natura eas certum est emanare, omnes protinus conquiescunt ac perpetua pariter cum his internicione delentur**. De gastrimargia namque nascuntur... De fornicatione... De filargyria... De ira... De tristitia... De acedia... De cenodoxia... De superbia contemptus, inuidia, inoboedientia, blasphemia, murmuratio, detractatio. (V.16, pp. 141-142)	Numerosior est enim quam Israel carnalium passionum populus, qui de hoc septenario fomite ac radice procedit uitiorum. De gastrimargia namque nascuntur... De fornicatione... De philargyria... De ira... De tristitia... De accidia... De cenodoxia... De superbia contemptus, inuidia, inobedientia, blasphemia, murmuratio, detractio, **aliaquequam plurima similia, quae cum sint multo majoris numeri quam uirtutes, deuictis tamen illis septem principalibus uitiis, ex quorum natura ista procedunt, omnes protinus conquiescunt, ac perpetua pariter cum his internicione delentur**. (V.16, PL 83, cols. 366-367)

---

1 "Septem istae gentes septem sunt principalia uitia quae per gratiam Dei unusquisque spiritualis miles exsuperans exterminare penitus admonetur." Isidore, *Expositio in uetus testamentum*, V.16, PL 83, col. 366.

2 "Cum ad Abraham de futuris dominus loqueretur, quod uos minime requisistis, non septem gentes legitur dinumerasse, sed decem, quarum terra semini eius danda promittitur. Qui numerus adiecta idololatria atque blasphemia euidenter inpletur, quibus ante notitiam dei et gratiam baptismi uel inpia gentilium uel blasphema Iudaeorum multitudo subiecta est, donec in intellectuali Aegypto conmoratur. Si autem abrenuntians quis et egressus exinde per dei gratiam deuicta pariter gastrimargia ad heremum peruenerit spiritalem, de inpugnatione trium gentium liberatus contra septem tantum, quae per Moysen dinumerantur, bella suscipiet." John Cassian, *Collationes*, V.22, CSEL 13, p. 147.

Continued

Cassian, *Conlationes*	Isidore, *Expositio*
Qui numerus adiecta idololatria atque blasphemia euidenter inpletur, quibus ante notitiam dei et gratiam baptismi **uel inpia gentilium uel blasphema Iudae-orum** multitudo subiecta est, donec in intellectuali Aegypto conmoratur. Si autem abrenuntians quis et egressus exinde per dei gratiam deuicta pariter **gastri-margia** ad heremum peruenerit spiritalem, de inpugnatione trium gentium liberatus contra septem tantum, quae per Moysen dinumerantur, bella suscipiet. (V.22, p. 147)	"Qui numerus, adiecta idololatria gentium, blasphemia Iudaeorum, errore haereticorum, euidentissime adimpletur. Quibus ante notitiam Dei et gratiam baptismi, uel **impia impietate gentium gentilium, uel blasphema Iudae-orum, uel errore haereticorum**, multitudo subjecta est, donec in intellectuali Aegypto commorantur." (V.17, PL 83, col. 367)

In Deuteronomy Entry 16, Isidore played a word game on the sentence which in Cassian's original text bridges the discussion of the numerous "carnal passions" and the enumeration of the eight capital sins: "There are many more such [passions] which are far more numerous than the virtues, but if those eight capital sins from whose nature these passions emanate are overcome, all of them will turn inactive immediately and are deleted thoroughly together with capital sins in perpetual destruction." What Isidore did is to move the whole sentence forwards, after the enumeration of the sins that derive from pride. Meanwhile, he changed "eight capital sins" to "seven capital sins" in the sentence. Therefore, the reader of Isidore's Deuteronomy Entry 16 would have the impression that seven cardinal sins, together with multiple carnal passions, all derive from pride. After Isidore's alteration, the Gregorian sin model emerges from Cassian's words. Furthermore, in Entry 17, Isidore changed the exposition of three nations conquered in Egypt, from gentiles' idolatry, Jews' blasphemy, and gluttony (in Cassian's original text) to gentiles' idolatry, Jews' blasphemy, and the error of heretics. By all these pieces of subtle textual modification, Isidore managed to transform his source into a sin theory of his own: The orthodox faith conquers paganism, Judaism, and heresy, and Christians need to keep fighting in their moral life with the seven capital sins that are rooted in pride.

This case above clearly shows Isidore's exegetical initiative as a *compilator*, defined by himself as a "plunderer" of the preceding *auctores*, the one "who mixes others' words with his own *(aliena dicta suis praemiscet)*, just like pigment-makers are accustomed to crush together diverse and mixed things in a mortar."[1] The seemingly modest claim *"uox mea, ipsorum est lingua"* rather reveals an ambitious effort to synthesize various previous exegetical traditions into one single voice of his own.

Entry 6 (on Deut. 22:10 "Thou shalt not plough with an ox and an ass together") is a

---

1 "Conpilator, qui aliena dicta suis praemiscet, sicut solent pigmentarii in pila diuersa mixta contundere." Isidore, *Etymologiarum siue Originum libri XX*, X.44, ed. Lindsay. Isidore as a *compilator*, cf. Martin Irvine, *The Making of Textual Culture: "Grammatica" and Literary Theory 350–1100* (Cambridge: Cambridge University Press, 1994), pp. 241-243; Jacques Fontaine, *Isidore de Séville*, pp. 329-344.

good example how Isidore mixed diverse patristic sources (Table 6.4).

Table 6.4   Source using in Isidore's Deuteronomy Entry 6

Isidore, Expositio, V.6, cols. 361-362	Sources
In bouis nomine populus ex circumcisione positus sub jugo legis accipitur; in asino autem populus gentium pertinens ad Euangelium: *in boue quippe et simul asino arat qui sic recipit Euangelium, ut Iudaicarum superstitionum, quae in umbra et imagine praecesserant, caeremonias non relinquat.* Item nonnunquam *in boue bene operantium uita,* **in asino stultorum uecordia figuratur.** Quid est ergo: Non arabis simul in boue et asino? Ac si diceret: *Fatuum sapienti in praedicatione non socies, ne per eum qui rem implere non ualet et illi qui praeualet obsistas. Bouem quippe et asinum, si necesse sit, unusquisque sine detrimento operis jungit. Sapientem uero et stultum, non ut unus praecipiat, et alter obtemperet, sed ut pariter aequali potestate annuntient uerbum Dei, non sine scandalo quisque comites facit.*	**JEROME** *Simul arat in boue et asino* Ebion, dignus pro humilitate sensus. Paupertate nominis sui; *qui sic recipit euangelium, ut iudaicarum superstitionum, quae in umbra et in imagine praecesserunt, caeremonias non relinquat.*[1] **GREGORY** In Scriptura autem sacra *boum* nomine aliquando hebetudo fatuorum, aliquando *bene operantium uita signatur.* **Quia enim bouis nomine stultorum uecordia figuratur**, recte per Salomonem dicitur... Asinorum quoque nomine aliquando stultorum pigritia, aliquando immoderata petulantium luxuria, aliquando gentilium simplicitas designatur. Stultorum pigritia asinorum appellatione figuratur sicut per Moysen dicitur: Non arabis in boue simul et asino. Ac si diceret: *Fatuos sapientibus in praedicatione non socies ne per eum qui implere rem non ualet, illi qui praeualet obsistas.*[2] **AUGUSTINE:** Bouem et asinum ad operandum iungere tunc non licebat; nunc licet... *Bouem quippe et asinum, si necesse sit, unusquisque sine detrimento operis iungit: sapientem uero et stultum, non ut unus praecipiat, et alter obtemperet, sed pariter ex aequali potestate, ut annuntient uerbum Dei, non sine scandalo quisquam comites facit.*[3]

This table shows not only how Isidore compressed his three patristic sources (cf. the words in italic in the table), but also how he deliberately altered one of the sources (cf. the words in bold), by changing the ass in Gregory's original to the ox, for the sake of the coherency of his own exegesis.

Among "others' words," Isidore was not timid to insert his own. For four times, we can see Isidore offer expositions of Deuteronomy himself. Aside from the anti-Jewish exegesis in Entry 1 (to be treated in Chapter 8), there is a clear pastoral tone in Isidore's independent exegesis (Table 6.5).[4]

---

1   Jerome, *Commentaria in Isaiam*, I.1.3, CCSL 73, p. 9.
2   Gregory, *Moralia in Iob*, I.16, CCSL 143, p. 36.
3   Augustine, *Contra Faustum*, VI.9, CSEL 25, p. 302.
4   Jacques Fontaine, "Isidore de Séville et la Bible," *Recherches Augustiniennes et Patristiques* 33 (2003): pp. 65-69: "Ils tiennent une place essentielle dans ce qu'on pourrait appeler la pastorale d'ensemble du royaume wisigoth."

Table 6.5 Original exegesis in Isidore's *Commentary on Deuteronomy*

Deut.	Isidore, *Expositio* (PL 83)	Summary
1:2	In cuius principio... per transgressionem Decalogi mandatorum. (V.1, col. 359)	The eleven days during which Moses wrote Deuteronomy signify the fall of the Jews through the transgression of the Decalogue.
16:21	Nos autem secundum praeceptum... sed in doctrina spiritus et uirtute. (V.3, col. 360)	Planting wood near the altar of God signifies speaking unfruitful words in preaching.
14:21	Non coques haedum in lacte matris suae... fortiori disciplina se redimat. (V.8, col. 362)	The ban against boiling a kid in the milk of his dam signifies correcting the one who has committed grave sin by not mild but severe discipline.
24:6	Tollit enim superiorem... et formido fuerit cum spe. (V.10, col. 363)	Taking the nether nor the upper millstone to pledge signifies neither scaring nor flattering sinners.

To appreciate Isidore's *Commentary on Deuteronomy* in the context of Latin exegetical history, it is convenient to borrow Fontaine's appreciation of general exegetical achievement of the archbishop of Seville:

> Origen's exegesis had been diffracted through the preaching and commentaries of the great Latin exegetes of the preceding three centuries. Isidore attempted to carry out an inverse operation: to gather, to extract, and to concentrate the quintessence of the dispersed exegesis; and he managed it with a rare talent of integrating. Meanwhile, his work remained transparent and intelligible to readers who no longer possessed the intellectual capacities of their predecessors. He thus "kept the deposit" and transmitted it. What's better, he made it more easily transmissible to all. Isidore of Seville was one of the favorite *auctores* to subsequent exegetes for many centuries.[1]

Isidore's influence on later Latin exegetes of Deuteronomy is decisive in three ways. First, as we have seen, thanks to Isidore, the idea of Deuteronomy as *secunda lex et euangelicae legis praefiguratio* became the dominant exegetical principle. Second, as we will see in the rest of the chapter, Isidore's *Expositio* serves as the absolute backbone for

---

1 "L'exégèse origénienne s'était diffractée à travers la prédication et les commentaires des grands exégètes latins des trois siècles précédents. Isidore a tenté de réaliser une opération inverse: rassembler, extraire et concentrer la quintessence de cette exégèse dispersée; et il y a réussi avec un rare talent combinatoire, tout en demeurant transparent et intelligible à des lecteurs qui ne possédaient plus les capacités intellectuelles de leurs prédécesseurs. Il a ainsi 'gardé le dépôt' et l'a transmis: mieux encore, il l'a rendu plus aisément transmissible à tous. C'est sans doute pour avoir tenu cette gageure qu'Isidore de Séville allait demeurer pour de longs siècles l'un des *auctores* préférés des exégètes ultérieurs." Jacques Fontaine, "Isidore de Séville et la Bible," p. 69.

the exegetical practice in the Latin West between 650 and 800.[1] Finally, even more lasting is the influence of Isidore's exegetical method of *compilatio*: "to mix others' words with one's own," which pioneered Carolingian exegesis. It might not be exaggerating, at least in the case of Deuteronomy, to claim that "the Isidorian moment" divided the early Christian exegetical world and the medieval one.

6.2 Wigbod, *Quaestiones in Octateuchum and Recapitulatio de paradiso, fonte ac fluminibus et ligno uitae* (*Lectiones* on the Hexateuch)

The reception of Isidore's works in the Latin west is generally considered a crucial intellectual incident characteristic of the early Middle Ages.[2] Jocelyn N. Hillgarth argued for the greatly influential thesis that Ireland played an exclusive role in their earliest dissemination as part of the commercial as well as cultural exchange between northern Iberia and Ireland.[3] Recent scholars have circumscribed Hillgarth's thesis both by cautioning against the arrival of Isidorian works in Ireland before the mid-seventh century,[4] and by proposing the direct transmission from Spain to other parts of the Continent and

---

1   An exception to this "Isidorian domination" is the Spanish Church Father Julian of Toledo (ca. 642–690). His *Liber anticimen*, or *Antikeimonon*, is a collection of over two hundred pairs of question and answer to solve the apparent contradiction between different biblical verses. As Thomas O'Loughlin argued, *Liber anticimen* should be seen as a precursor of the *disputatio* literature that bloomed in the twelfth century: "Julian of Toledo's *Antikeimonon* and the Development of Latin Exegesis," *Proceedings of the Irish Biblical Association* 16 (1993): pp. 80-98. Cc. 35-38 of *Liber anticimen* involve Deuteronomy, sources including Augustine's *Contra Faustum*, *Enarrationes in Psalmos*, and *Tractatus in euangelium Iohannis*, Ambrose's *De Spiritu Sancto*, and Origen's homilies on Genesis. Cf. CCSL 115B, ed. Jose. C. Martín-Iglesias (Turnhout: Brepols, 2014), pp. 136-145. The lack of Isidore's influence in *Liber anticimen* may be explained by the competition over the ecclesiastical and intellectual leadership in Spain between Seville and Toledo in the second half of the seventh century. Cf. Michael Kelly, "The Politics of History-Writing: Problematizing the Historiographical Origins of Isidore of Seville in Early Medieval Hispania," *Isidore of Seville and his Reception in the Early Middle Ages: Transmitting and Transforming Knowledge*, eds. Andrew Fear, Jamie Wood (Amsterdam: Amsterdam University Press), pp. 91-110.

2   Bernhard Bischoff, "Die europäische Verbreitung der Werke Isidors von Sevilla," *Isidoriana: Colección de estudios sobre Isidoro de Sevilla*, ed. Manuel C. Diaz y Diaz (León: Centro de Estudios 'San Isidoro,' 1961), pp. 317-344; Robert McNally, "Isidorian Pseudepigrapha in the Early Middle Ages," ibid., pp. 305-316; Jamie Wood, Andrew Fear, eds., *Isidore of Seville and his Reception in the Early Middle Ages: Transmitting and Transforming Knowledge* (Amsterdam: Amsterdam University Press, 2016).

3   Jocelyn N. Hillgarth, "The East, Visigothic Spain and the Irish," *Studia Patristica* 4 (1961): pp. 422-456; idem, "Visigothic Spain and Early Christian Ireland," *Proceedings of the Royal Irish Academy* 62 (1961–1963): pp. 167-194; idem, "Ireland and Spain in the Seventh Century," *Peritia* 3 (1984): pp. 1-16.

4   Marina Smyth, "Isidorian Texts in Seventh-Century Ireland," *Isidore of Seville and his Reception in the Early Middle Ages: Transmitting and Transforming Knowledge*, eds. Jamie Wood, Andrew Fear (Amsterdam: Amsterdam University Press, 2016), pp. 111-130.

Anglo-Saxon England.[1]

The eleven extant pre-Carolingian copies (three are fragments) witness the early transmission of *Expositio in uetus testamentum*. The provenances disperse widely: Burgundy, Spain, Tours, St-Gall, Freising, Regensburg, North Italy/Bobbio, and England.[2] But all of them were produced after 700. As for the post-Isidorian commentaries on Deuteronomy, while the evidence is too meager to recover the exact transmission route and timetable, it may be more helpful if we take the period between 650 and 800 as a whole, and focus on the correlation between exegetical style and geographical distribution. We will first examine an exegete working in *Francia* and his conservative reception of the Isidorian exposition of Deuteronomy.

***

In 1719, in a manuscript in the library of the Abbey of St-Maximin in Trier (now lost), Edmond Martène discovered a series of commentaries on the Pentateuch, Joshua, Judges, and Ruth, partially in question-and-answer format, composed for Charlemagne by a certain Wigbod. Martène published its first part (on Genesis 1–3), later presented in Migne's PL 96, cols. 1101-1168.[3] The whole *Quaestiones in Octateuchum* is available in PL 93, cols. 233-430, copied from Johannes Hervagius' *editio princeps* of Bede's *opera omnia*. Hervagius regarded it as one of Bede's *dubia et spuria*. Therefore, *Quaestiones in Octateuchum* has often been cited as Pseudo-Bede.[4]

The lost Trier manuscript contains a remarkable colophon which Martène also transcribed: "*Carolus rex Francorum et Longobardorum ac patricius Romanorum hunc codicem ad opus suum scribere iussit.*"[5] "The king of Franks and Lombards and the patrician of Romans" was Charlemagne's standard title before his imperial coronation of 800. This

---

1 Edward James, "Ireland and Western Gaul in the Merovingian period," *Ireland in Early Mediaeval Europe: Studies in Memory of Kathleen Hughes*, eds. Dorothy Whitelock, Rosamond McKitterick, and David Dumville (Cambridge: Cambridge University Press, 1982), pp. 362-386. Henry Mayr-Harting, *The Coming of Christianity to Anglo-Saxon England* (University Park: The Pennsylvania State University Press, 1991), pp. 127-128, radically claiming "Now if we speak of Isidore, the truth is that he quickly became known *everywhere* in the seventh century."

2 Michael Gorman, ed., *Genesis*, pp. xv-xvi.

3 Edmond Martène's handwritten transcription of this lost manuscript, conserved in Paris, BnF, Lat. 17188, now available online: http://gallica.bnf.fr/ark:/12148/btv1b9066627j, fols. 287-360, last accessed September 14, 2021. Martène's original publication of the section on Genesis 1-3, see *Veterum Scriptorum et Monumentorum Historicorum, Dogmaticorum, Moralium Amplissima Collectio* (Paris, 1724–1733), vol. 9, cols. 293-366.

4 For the history of scholarship, see Michael Gorman, "The Encyclopedic Commentary on Genesis," pp. 173-177.

5 PL 96, cols. 1103-1104. The colophon is comparable to the incipit of a commentary on Daniel and grammatical works compiled by Peter of Pisa for Charlemagne in Brussels, Belgium Bibliothèque Royale, II 2572: *INCIPIT LIBER DE DIVERSIS QVAESTIVNCVLIS CVM RESPONSIONIBUS SVIS QVEM IVSSIT DOMNVS REX CAROLVS TRANSCRIBERE EX AVTENTICO PETRI ARCHIDIACONI*. Cf. Michael Gorman, "Peter of Pisa and the *Quaestiunculae* Copied for Charlemagne in Brussels II 2572 with a Note on the Codex Diezianus from Verona," *Revue Bénédictine* 110 (2000): pp. 238-260.

Trier manuscript, therefore, could be the archetype of the codex that Wigbod prepared for Charlemagne's personal use. Before the commentary, there is also a dedicatory poem preceding the commentary which largely recycles the verses of Avitus of Vienne and Eugenius of Toledo. The poem leaks more information on both the compiler and recipient of the commentary:

> Here you have, king, the book you once ordered.
> Take it up, happy man, and use it for many years.
> How great it is to sing of your praise,
> King Charles, happy and known in all lands.
> Your command reaches the ends of the earth.
> Who under the arch of the sky can eloquently recount, great man,
> Your praises in polished language?
> Who can sing your triumphs and your remarkable piety
> And reveal in a long poem your riches?
> Who can even count the quantity of books
> Which you have ordered to be collected from many lands
> To renew the writings of the Holy Fathers who have gone before?
> ...
> Why it should be disdained that, ordered by the great prince
> The small songs of the selected Mosaic book
> I, the humble Wigbod, supplement with a great amount of trifles.
> These to you, the highest king, compelled by the order of the master,
> I, your little servant, dedicated with devoted mind.[1]

Scholars agree that the compiler *Vigbodus humilis* should be identified with "the abbot and priest *Vuigbodus*, a man of upright faith" who, in company with papal legates, at-

---

1   "En habes in promtu, o rex, quod iusseras olim;/suscipe et, o felix, multos utaris per annos/O quam magna tuae clarent praeconia laudis,/rex Carole, felix et notus in omnibus aruis!/Finibus extremis tua, maxime, iussio pollet./Quis ualet urbane laudes sermone polito/fari, magne, tuas caeli sub culmine claras?/Quis tua mixta canat mira pietate trophaea,/diuitiasque tuas longo quis carmine pandat?/Quis saltem poterit seriem enumerare librorum/quos tua de multis copulat sententia terris,/sanctorum renouans patrum conscripta priorum?/... cur dedignetur, quod iussus principe magno/paruula excerpi Mosaici carmina bibli/Vigbodus humilis nugarum mole piaui?/Haec tibi, rex summe, iussu compulsus herili/seruulus, ut potui, deuota mente dicaui." The dedicatory poem is available both in PL 96, cols. 1103-1104 and in *Poetae Latini aevi Carolini (I)*, pp. 96-97. The citation is from the new edition of Luigi Munzi, "Compilazione e riuso in età carolingia: il prologo poetico di Wigbodo," *Romanobarbarica* 12 (1992): pp. 189-210. The translation is based on Gorman, "Wigbod and Biblical Studies under Charlemagne," p. 49, no. 21, with certain modification. "The small songs of the selected Mosaic book" refer to a poem of Eugenius of Toledo attached to the commentary, whose theme is the six days of the Creation.

tended the legatine synods in England of 786 as Charlemagne's observer.[1] It is not likely that Wigbod was from Anglo-Saxon England like Alcuin whom he met in Northumbria during the same journey, for Wigbod never used Bede as a source in his exegetical compilations. The abbacy that Wigbod possessed was possibly either Lorsch or St-Maximin.[2] To Wigbod scholars have also attributed an unpublished commentary on the Gospels (*Quaestiunculae super Euangelica*).[3]

Quaestiones in Octateuchum is certainly not an original work. Wigbod provided his own exegesis only in three short passages, all on Genesis.[4] He even showed no interest in altering his sources. It is not a balanced work, either. Wigbod apparently tried to organize the commentary in questions and answers between a *magister* (M) and a *discipulus* (D), but failed to keep it all through. More than half of the work is not in this format. Speaking of content, Wigbod's exegetical practice gradually slides from integrating various sources to copying Isidore's *Expositio in uetus testamentum* verbatim. Michael Gorman identified thirteen different sources used in the Genesis 1–3 section. The major ones are the three seventh-century works deriving from Augustine's *De Genesi ad litteram*. Only 16% of the material is from Isidore's *Expositio*. On the rest of the book of Genesis (cc. 4–50), Gorman identified eleven sources, of which the major two are Isidore's *Expositio* (48%) and Jerome's *Hebraicae quaestiones in libro Geneseos* (38%). When it comes to Exodus, Isidore's *Expositio* becomes the dominant source, supplemented by one passage from Isidore's *Prooemia* and seven from Paterius' *Liber testimoniorum*. For Leviticus, Numbers, Deuteronomy, Joshua, Judges, and Ruth, Isidore's *Expositio* became the sole source.[5]

As for the Deuteronomy section in *Quaestiones in Octateuchum*, Gorman pointed out that Wigbod combined the introduction to Deuteronomy in Isidore's *Prooemia* with

---

1   According to the report of one of the legates, George of Ostia, to Pope Hadrian I about his journey: "Ego autem adsumpto mecum adiutore, quem filius uester excellentissimus, rex Carolus, ob reuerentiam apostolatus uestri nobiscum misit, uirum probatae fidei, Uuigbodum abbatem atque presbiterum, perrexi in regionem Nordanhymbrorum ad Aelfualdum regem et archiepiscopum sanctae aecclesiae Eboracae ciuitatis Eanbaldum." Alcuin, Letter 3, *Epistolae Karolini aevi (II)*, p. 20. Cf. Wilhelm Levison, *England and the Continent in the Eighth Century* (Oxford: Clarendon Press 1946), pp. 16, 128-129.

2   For a close analysis, see Michael Gorman, "Wigbod and Biblical Studies under Charlemagne," pp. 60-62.

3   Bernhard Bischoff proposed it first in his "Turning-points in the History of Latin Exegesis in the Early Middle Ages", trans. Colm O'Grady, *Biblical Studies: The Medieval Irish Contribution*, ed. Martin McNamara (Dublin: Dominican Publications, 1976), pp. 74-160; then confirmed by Michael Gorman in his "Charlemagne's Commentator."

4   Cf. Michael Gorman, "The Encyclopedic Commentary on Genesis," pp. 181, 187-188; idem, "Charlemagne's Commentator," p. 18. It is noteworthy that all these three original passages are concerned with the relationship between the Old and the New Testament.

5   Cf. Michael Gorman, "The Encyclopedic Commentary on Genesis," pp. 177-192. Gorman noted that two passages respectively from the Exodus and Leviticus sections of *Expositio* are absent in Wigbod's compilation, see ibid., p. 176, n. 21.

the Deuteronomy section in *Expositio*. This observation is based on Hervagius' edition (= PL 93, cols. 409-416). However, if we consult Martène's unpublished transcription of the Trier manuscript which is closer to Wigbod's original compilation for Charlemagne, we will *not* find the part of Isidore's *Prooemia*, which thus must be a later interpolation.[1] According to Martène's transcription, the Deuteronomy section in Wigbod's *Quaestiones* is an unchanged copy of all 22 entries of Isidore's *Commentary on Deuteronomy*. Except the omission of chapter headings, there is even no change in format.

Realizing that Wigbod was indeed capable of compiling various sources into an "encyclopedic commentary on Genesis" of his own, and that he must have had access to Paterius' *Liber testimoniorum* (used as a source for the Exodus section), we have to deduce that, as far as the fifth biblical book is concerned, this courtly exegete of Charlemagne had no exegetical interest in going beyond Isidore.

***

Wigbod's encounter with Deuteronomy is witnessed by another work of his. In an article of 1894, Germain Morin drew attention to a set of commentaries on the first six books of the Old Testament found in two manuscripts. In one of them (Paris, BnF, Lat. 2342), these commentaries have the title *Lectiones uenerabilis Bedae presbiteri super Pentateuchon Moysi*. In medieval transmission, this work was more often known as "*Recapitulatio de paradiso, fonte ac fluminibus et ligno uitae*," drawn from the heading of its first chapter. Of the eleven extant manuscripts (all after 1100), six attribute it to Ambrose.[2]

Morin proposed that *Recapitulatio* might be Bede's *capitula lectionum in Pentateucum Mosi, Iosue, Iudicum*.[3] This attribution cannot be right, since Paul Meyvaert proved later that the *capitula lectionum* in Bede's bibliographic list does not refer to any exegetical works, but rather refers to "summaries of chapters."[4] M. L. W. Laistner listed *Recapitulatio* among "Lost and Doubtful Works" of Bede and correctly noted that they are abbreviations of Isidore's *Expositio*.[5] Michael Gorman is the first scholar who closely studied this commentary, although his interest is limited to the Genesis section. According to his source criticism of the section on Genesis 1–3, *Recapitulatio* is primarily a summary and epitome of Isidore's *Expositio*, occasionally supplemented by other sources including Gregory and Jerome, but remarkably, *not* Augustine.[6]

---

1   Paris, Bnf, Lat. 17188, fol. 353r.

2   Michael Gorman, "Wigbod and the *Lectiones*." Gorman followed Burton Van Name Edwards to add three more manuscripts of *Recapitulatio* in the postscript of his "The Commentary on the Pentateuch Attributed to Bede," p. 108.

3   Germain Morin, "Notes sur plusieurs écrits attribués a Bède le vénérable," *Revue Bénédictine* 11 (1894): pp. 289-295. Cf. Bede, *Historia ecclesiastica gentis Anglorum*, V.24, SC 491, p. 190.

4   Paul Meyvaert, "Bede's *Capitula Lectionum* for the Old and New Testament,' *Revue Bénédictine* 105 (1995): pp. 348-80.

5   M. L. W. Laistner, *A Hand-List of Bede Manuscripts* (Ithaca: Cornell University Press, 1943), 154.

6   Michael Gorman, "Wigbod and the *Lectiones*."

Wigbod cited *Recapitulatio* three times in his *Quaestiones in Octateuchum.*[1] In one of them, the title is presented as *"recapitulatio de paradiso, fonte ac fluminibus et ligno vitae";*[2] in another, it is shortened as *recapitulatio.*[3] Gorman in 1995 proposed that *Recapitulatio* was written sometime between 650 and 750 by "a young exegete at work, extracting and paraphrasing Isidore's commentaries on the Old Testament, while occasionally adding a few passages,"[4] and, "originating as an informal notebook kept by a teacher, it might have been designed for instruction; each *lectio* or *capitulum* could serve as the basis for a discussion on an aspect of the text of the Old Testament."[5] Gorman adjusted his opinion in a paper of 2004, and turned to regard *Recapitulatio* as "a work of his [Wigbod's] own construction" produced during the preparation of *Quaestiones in Octateuchum*, without giving his reason explicitly.[6] Gottfried Kreuz undertook a more critical examination of the authorship and nature of *Recapitulatio*. Based on a meticulous comparative analysis of the Genesis section of *Quaestiones in Octateuchum*, that of *Recapitulatio*, and their sources, Kreuz drew the conclusion that *Recapitulatio* and *Quaestiones in Octateuchum* came out of a single working process of a single author, and that Wigbod very likely composed *Recapitulatio* first as "ein handlicheres Exzerpt" for teaching purpose, and later used it together with more materials to compose *Quaestiones.*[7]

The anthor's examination of the Deuteronomy section of *Recapitulatio* is based on Paris, BnF, Lat. 2342, a manuscript copied at Bec in the twelfth century which, according to Gorman, "seems to preserve the original form of the text."[8] Generally speaking, the Deuteronomy section of *Recapitulatio* is an abbreviated rewriting of Isidore's *Commentary on Deuteronomy*. The Deuteronomy section in Paris, BnF, Lat. 2342 (25v-27r) begins with chapter headings which were defectively copied.[9] The list of numbered headings in the archetype of the manuscript, presumably designed by Wigbod himself, apparently echoes Isidore's original *mise en page*, as we have seen in the previous subchapter. Each of the 22 *lectiones* in the main text (the first eight are numbered) is an abridgement of one Deuteronomy entry of *Expositio*. Isidore's *Commentary on Deuteronomy* contains ca. 3500 words; the Deuteronomy section of *Recapitulatio* has only ca. 1300 words.

---

1 Michael Gorman, "Charlemagne's Commentator," p. 7.
2 PL 96, col. 1148 = PL 93, col. 269.
3 PL 93, col. 290.
4 Michael Gorman, "Wigbod and the *Lectiones*," p. 338.
5 Ibid., p. 341.
6 Michael Gorman, "Charlemagne's Commentator," p. 7.
7 Gottfried Eugen Kreuz, *"Inquiri mihi necesse est...*: Überlegungen zu drei vermuteten kleineren Genesiskommentaren Wigbods," *Wiener Studien* 122 (2009): pp. 223-247.
8 Michael Gorman, "Wigbod and the *Lectiones*," p. 322; for the manuscript description of Paris, BnF, Lat. 2342, see pp. 318-319. The manuscript facsimile is available online: http://gallica.bnf.fr/ark:/12148/btv1b105437825, last accessed September 14, 2021. *Recapitulatio* is in fols. 2v-28v.
9 Apparently, the copyist missed the headings of VII, VIII and XX first, and later made up the headings of VII and of VIII in the blank space nearby. Cf. Paris, BnF, Lat. 2342, fol. 25v.

In some cases, Wigbod simply cut off in his judgment less relevant content for the sake of brevity. For example, for the longest Deuteronomy entry (no. 16 on Deut. 7:1), Wigbod removed the whole elaborate discussion on the capital sins, abbreviating 351 words into 60.[1] In others, he kept Isidore's keywords and compressed the language, as in Entry 3 (on Deut. 16:21), demonstrated in the Table 6.6 (keywords in bold).

Table 6.6   Textual comparison between Isidore and *Recapitulatio*

Isidore, *Expositio* (PL 83, cols. 359-360)	Wigbod, *Recapitulatio* (Paris, BnF, Lat. 2342, fols. 25v-26r)
Non plantabis omne lignum iuxta altare Dei, nec facies nemus. Inter-dicitur quippe ne nemus complantetur in templo. Nemus frondentes arbores et **infructuosae** sunt, sola delectatione uisus plantatae. Tales sunt et **gentiles**, qui rationem suam uerborum decore componunt, ut non conuertantur a uitiis, sed delectentur, atque istiusmodi subiectione persuadeant. Nos autem secundum praeceptum Dei iuxta altare nemus non plantamus, si **circa dominicam fidem** nihil in uerbis infructuosum, nihil audientias secularis illecebrosum componimus, sed sola puritate **ueritatis**, scientiam **praedicationis** tenemus. Hoc nemus in praedicatione sapientiae plantare deuitabat Apostolus, cum dicebat: Et loquimur non in doctis humanae **sapientiae** Verbis, sed in doctrina spiritus et uirtute.	Iuxta altare dei prohibet plantari nemus, quod tantum sit infecundis arboribus. Quia sicut **gentiles infructuosam** et ponposam mundane **sapientiae** non debemus habere orationem, si **circa dominicam fidem** teneamus cum caritate ueram **praedicationem**.

In the last Deuteronomy *lectiones*, Wigbod showed more initiative in reorganizing Isidore's words for the purpose of clarity. For instance, Isidore in Deuteronomy Entry 19 (on Deut. 19:5-6 about the manslaughter in the wood) expounded the kinsmen of the dead who might pursue the perpetrator as *districtus iudex... qui se nobis per naturae consortium iunxit*. In *Recapitulatio*, Wigbod elaborated "severe judge" in a more explicit way: "The friend of the dead person is Christ sharing our flesh, who will judge the bad deeds that we commit to neighbors, unless we resort to penance through hope, faith, and love."[2]

Only in one case did Wigbod explicitly provide his original exegesis. *Lectio* 11 (on Deut. 23:7 "Thou shalt not abhor the Egyptian") is:

We should not abhor the Egyptian, that is the secular thing, as long as it is essential to us. But according to the Apostle, let us be content with daily food and clothing. In

---

1   "XVI. VII sunt principalia uitia quae per gratiam Dei unusquique spiritualis miles exuperans exterminare penitus amonitur. Et maiores numero sunt quia uitia plura sunt quam uirtutes. Fortiores etiam sunt quia fortius militat in membris nostris oblatio carnalium passionum quam studia uirtutum. Sed spiritualibus populis, id est, uirtutibus, pugnantes locum in cordibus nostris uitiis auferamus et Israel, id est, uidentes dominum simus." Paris, BnF, Lat. 2342, fol. 26v. Cf. Isidore, *Expositio in uetus testamentum*, V.3, PL 83, cols. 366-367.

2   "Amicus mortui Christus est per carnis nostrae consortium qui in iudicio iudicabit mala quae proximis facimus, nisi paenitendo per spem, fidem et caritatem debeamus." Paris, BnF, Lat. 2342, fol. 27r. Cf. Isidore, *Expositio in uetus testamentum*, in V.19, PL 83, cols. 368-369.

another sense (*Aliter*): We should not abhor the Egyptian, that is, sinners. See what follows and you will know why to interpret so: "Because thou wast a stranger in the land of Egyptian." (Deut. 23:7), that is what the Apostle said.[1]

While the first half summarizes Isidore's Deuteronomy Entry 11, the second half (*Aliter...*) which interprets the Egyptian as sinners is not to be found in Isidore or any other early medieval work. Except for this glimpse of originality, Wigbod's exposition of Deuteronomy in *Recapitulatio* did not extend beyond Isidore's *Expositio*.

As we have seen in both *Quaestiones in Octateuchum* and *Recapitulatio*, Wigbod's conservative reception of the Isidorian exegetical tradition might be representative in *Francia*. To corroborate this hypothesis, we can raise Paris, BnF, Lat. 15679, an exegetical miscellany designed by Theodulf at the end of the eighth century. It contains patristic expositions, either in the original or epitomized format, on every biblical canons. The section on the Pentateuch (pp. 1-63), including Deuteronomy, copies from Isidore's *Expositio* in entirety.[2] The conservative reception of the Isidorian allegorical exegesis of Deuteronomy in northern Gaul is in sharp contrast with the flexible use of the same Spanish author by his southern Gallic contemporary, the Lyon Annotator.

6.3   The α and γ Recensions of the Pseudo-Bedan Pentateuch Commentary (Milan, Biblioteca Ambrosiana, G.82 inf.)

Migne's PL 91 presents a commentary on the first five books of the Old Testament (cols. 189-394). Its first publisher, Gulielmus Montanus, attributed it to Bede, and this authorship was generally held until the mid-twentieth century, when scholars like F. J. E. Raby and M. L. W. Laistner seriously shed doubt on it. More recently, scholars of Hiberno-Latin literature like Robert McNally, Dáibhí Ó Cróinín, and Joseph Kelly have noted "the Irish symptoms" of this Pentateuch commentary as published in PL 91 and claimed its author an "Irish Ps. Bede."[3]

Alessandro Azzimonti in a paper of 1994 analyzed "un anonimo commentario al pentateuco di età protocarolingia" discovered in a twelfth-century manuscript Milan, Biblioteca Ambrosiana, G.82 inf. 70% of this anonymous commentary overlaps with

---

1   "Non debemus abhominari egyptium, hoc est saeculum in quantum est nobis necessarium. Simus autem secundum Apostolum, contenti uictu cotidiano atque uestitu. Aliter: Non debemus abhomnari egyptium, hoc est peccatores. Quare? Vide quid sequatur: Quia et uos aduenae fuistis in terra Egypti, hoc est quod Apostolus ait." Paris, BnF, Lat. 2342, fol. 26r.

2   Cf. Michael Gorman, "Theodulf of Orléans and the Exegetical Miscellany in Paris lat. 15679," *Revue Bénédictine* 109 (1999): pp. 278-323.

3   For the scholarship, see Michael Gorman, "The Commentary on the Pentateuch Attributed to Bede in PL. 91. 189–394," pp. 61-72.

80% of the Pseudo-Bede commentary in PL 91.[1] In 1996, Michael Gorman published the outcome of his decade-long study of the Pseudo-Bedan Pentateuch commentary, arguing that the commentary in PL 91 and that in Milan, Biblioteca Ambrosiana, G.82 inf. are in fact two recensions (β and γ, as Gorman named) of the same Pentateuch commentary.[2]

According to Gorman, the primordial recension α (reconstructed as the overlap of γ and β) was "probably" produced in Spain in the second half of the seventh century. Augustine's *De Genesi ad litteram* is the major source for the Genesis 1–3 section, and Isidore's *Expositio* for the rest. The γ recension "might" be carried out by the same author as α, perhaps for the purpose of updating and completing the latter, because both recensions share almost the identical source pool. Of its four extant copies of γ, two provide mistaken authorial attribution to Isidore.[3] Gorman also deduced that the β recension was likely produced in the mid-eighth century, and "might be written by students or relatively uneducated clerics or even laymen who were, for the most part, unfamiliar with the patristic tradition." Not γ but β contains many "Irish symptoms" recognized by Hiberno-Latin scholars, although Gorman even refused to see these "symptoms" as really "Irish."[4]

Gorman's opinions as summarized above are predominantly based on his study of the Genesis 1–3 section. In the following examination of the Deuteronomy section of all the three recensions of the Pseudo-Bedan Pentateuch commentary, the author consults Milan, Biblioteca Ambrosiana, G.82 inf., fols. 95v-100 for γ, PL 91, cols. 379-394 for β, and treat their overlap as the primordial α.[5] Since α and γ are probably two stages of the same working process and β shows a departure from it, α and γ in this subchapter will be discussed, and β in the next.

The Deuteronomy section in α can be seen as an enlarged version of Isidore's commentary in *Expositio*. All Isidorian Deuteronomy entries (except the abnormal Entry 9 on

---

1   Alessandro Azzimonti, "'Sicut dictum vidimus': Un anonimo commentario al Pentateuco d'età protocarolingia (Ambr. G 82 inf.)," *Aevum* 68 (1994): pp. 283-302. Azzimonti's paper is based on his *tesi di laurea*, whose advisor, Mirella Ferrari, was the discoverer of this commentary from the manuscript.

2   Michael Gorman, "The Commentary on the Pentateuch Attributed to Bede."

3   Milan, Biblioteca Ambrosiana, G.82 inf., fol. 1v reads "Incipit tractatus Isidori Hispaliensis episcopi super Pentatheucum." Milan, Biblioteca Ambrosiana, D.523 inf., fol. 220r reads "Isodorus super Pentateucon..."

4   For the manuscript description and the stemma codicum, see Michael Gorman, "The Commentary on the Pentateuch Attributed to Bede," pp. 75-84.

5   The twelfth-century Milan, Biblioteca Ambrosiana, G.82 inf. is the best manuscript to study the γ recension. Of the other three extant manuscripts, (1) Monte Cassino, Archivio della Badia, 30 does not contain the Deuteronomy section at all; (2) Oxford, Bodleian Library, Lat.th.d.3 contains the Deuteronomy section but only incomplete; (3) Milan, Biblioteca Ambrosiana, D.523 inf. was copied from Milan, Biblioteca Ambrosiana G.82 inf. I consulted Milan, Biblioteca Ambrosiana, G.82 inf. via the microfilm of Biblioteca Ambrosiana Collection in the Medieval Institute of University of Notre Dame, U.S.

Leviticus 19:23) were either copied or abbreviated, and reorganized in scriptural order.[1]

When this anonymous exegete abbreviated Isidore, he did it in an effective way. For example, Isidore's Deuteronomy Entries 16 and 17 (both on Deut. 7:1, 435 words in total) are combined and rewritten in 87 words.[2] Besides compressing, he also supplemented. Isidore interpreted the duration of forty years before Israel entered the Promised Land (Deut. 1:3) as the figure of the forty days that Jesus spent in the desert (Deuteronomy Entry 1). The author of α added that the number also signifies the multiplication of the Law (ten) and the Gospel (four).[3] To the exposition of the oxen that tread out corns on the floor (Deut. 25:4) as the *doctores* who need material support (Deuteronomy Entry 7 of *Expositio*), the author of α added that "For they are oxen who tread and separate husks and corns on the floor, that is in the church."[4]

More intriguing is the case of Israel's eleven days' journey (Deut. 1:2). According to Isidore, the number signifies "the fall of the Jewish city in the Gospel through the transgression of the mandates of the Decalogue." The author of α expanded it and further connected it with the Apostles:

> First of all, it should be noted that it indicates that Deuteronomy was written by Moses in twelve days. By this statement, it is shown that, just like Deuteronomy, the second law, signifies the Gospel, his testimony in twelve days signifies the number of the Apostles, through whom the Gospel was spread throughout the whole sphere of the earth. Moreover, since it is recorded as eleven days in the Septuagint, the number can signify the eleven Apostles with the betrayer Judas excluded. Alternatively, it certainly signifies the fall of the Jewish city in the Gospel through the transgression of

---

1 The order is: 1, 2, 17, 16, 8, 5, 3, 19, 13, 15, 18, 6, 9, 11, 20, 21, 10, 22, 7, 14, 12. Azzimonti failed to recognize Isidore's Deuteronomy Entry 9 and 11, cf. Azzimonti, "'Un anonimo commentario al Pentateuco," p. 298, n. 55.

2 "Cum uero ad Habraham de futuro Dominus loqueretur, non septem gentes, sed decem legitur denumerasse, quarum terra semini eius danda promittitur, qui numerus adiecta idololatria gentium, blasphemia Iudaeorum, errore haereticorum, euidentissime adimpletur, quibus donec intellectuali Aegypto commoratur, multitudo subiacetur. Si autem egressus quis ad heremum perueniat spiritualem, de impugnatione trium gentium liberabitur. Septem quae per Moysen denunciantur bella suscipiet. Septem autem gentes septem uitia principalia designant, quae per Dei gratiam unusquisque miles exuperat. Quod uero numeri maioris esse dicuntur, haec ratio est, quia plura uitia quam uirtutes." Milan, Biblioteca Ambrosiana, G.82 inf., fol. 96r.

3 "Quadraginta autem anni quibus laboriose Moyse peracti ad terram repromissionis filii Israel peruenerunt significat totum tempus quo ecclesia in laboribus uiuit, quae propter denarium numerum legis obseruat, et quaternum propter Euangelium. Decies autem quatuor, quadraginta sunt." Milan, Biblioteca Ambrosiana, G.82 inf., fol. 96r.

4 "Sequitur, non ligabis os bouis triturantis in area fruges tuas. Quod significat illud quod apostolus dicit: Si nos uobis spiritualia seminauimus, magnum est si uestra carnalia metamus? Quia in bouis nomine uniuscuiusque doctoris uita exprimitur. Vult ergo Scriptura doctoribus praeparari carnalia, a quibus spiritualia consequantur auditores. Ipsi sunt enim boues terentes et separantes in area, id est in ecclesia, paleas fruges." Milan, Biblioteca Ambrosiana, G.82 inf., fol. 98r.

the mandates of the Decalogue.[1]

The reading "twelve days" cannot be identified in any known biblical version. Nevertheless, in the eighth-century Irish *Bibelwerk* (to be discussed below), we find the same reading: *Deuteronomium interpretatur secunda lex, quia replicat Moyses in his duodecim diebus scribens Deuteronomium.*[2]

Another clue to link α to Irish exegesis is its opening of the Deuteronomy section:

It should be known well that in Deuteronomy there is the repetition of the preceding four books, but it contains many things of its own. That Deuteronomy is the second law, or repetition of the Law (*iteratio legis*), signifies that the New Testament succeeded the Old.[3]

While this sentence is certainly based on Isidore's *Expositio*, the expression *iteratio legis* is nowhere to be found in either Isidore's or any other patristic work. Before 800, only two other sources share the same wording, and they are both from seventh-century Ireland: *De mirabilibus sacrae scripturae* of Augustinus Hibernicus and *Expositio quattuor euangeliorum* of Pseudo-Jerome.[4] Does this mean that the primordial α of the Pseudo-Bedan Pentateuch commentary is Irish (despite Gorman's strong objection), or, could such coincidence be explained by the energetic cultural communication between Spain

---

1 "In cuius principio notandum est, quid indicit quod Deuteronomium duodecim diebus a Moyse scribitur. Per quod ostenditur, quia sicut Deuteronomium pro eo quod secunda lex est, Euangelium significant, sic et contestitio eius duodecim diebus apostolorum numerum designat, per quos Euangelium per totum orbem terrae diffusum est. Porro, si iuxta Septuaginta undecim diebus legitur potest sinificare undecim apostolos abiecto Iuda proditore." Milan, Biblioteca Ambrosiana, G.82 inf., fol. 95v. Cf. "In cuius principio notandum est, quid indicet quod undecim diebus idem Deuteronomium a Moyse scribitur; nisi ad significandum Iudaicae plebis lapsum in Euangelio, per transgressionem Decalogi mandatorum." Isidore, *Expositio in uetus testamentum*, V.1, PL 83, col. 208.

2 *Pauca problesmata de enigmatibus ex tomis canonicis*, De Deuteronomio, 445, CCCM 173, ed. Gerard MacGinty (Turnhout: Brepols, 2004), p. 205.

3 "[S]ciendum est sane quod in Deuteronomio repetitio est praecedentium quatuor librorum, et tamen in se multa propria continet. Quod autem Deuteronomium secunda lex, uel iteratio legis dicitur: significat, quod nouum Testamentum ueteri succederet." Milan, Biblioteca Ambrosiana, G.82 inf., fol. 95v.

4 *De mirabilibus sacrae Scripturae* (PL 35, cols. 2149-2200): "Quadragesimo anno egressionis filiorum Israel de Aegypto, quadragesima secunda mansione in campestribus Moab super Iordanem populus sedit, ubi Moyses Deuteronomium, hoc est, iterationem legis praedicauit." PL 35, col. 2174. Cf. Gerard MacGinty, "The Irish Augustine: *De mirabilibus sacrae Scripturae*," *Irland und die Christenheit: Bibelstudien und Mission*, eds. Próinséas Ní Chatháin, Michael Richter (Stuttgart: Klett-Cotta, 1987), pp. 70-83. *Expositio quattuor euangeliorum* (PL 30, cols. 531-589): "Dominum tuum adorabis, et reliqua: per tria exempla Deuteronomii quo significatur Euangelium, id est, iteratio legis..." PL 30, col. 534. Cf. Joseph F. Kelly, "A Catalogue of Early Medieval Hiberno-Latin Biblical Commentaries (II)," *Traditio* 45 (1989): pp. 393-434.

and Ireland in the seventh century?[1]

About 25% of α expounds the Deuteronomic verses uncovered in Isidore's *Expositio* (Table 6.7).

Table 6.7   Original exegesis in α recension of Pseudo-Bede

Deut.	Original exposition in α (PL 91)
... Where there is very much gold. (1:1)	Gold = Gospel (379B)
Thou wilt not be able to destroy them altogether: lest perhaps the beasts of the earth should increase upon thee. (7:22)	Nations = sins; beasts = pride or vainglory (385A-B)
The Lord thy God will raise up to thee a prophet of thy nation and of thy brethren like unto me. (18:15)	Prophet = Christ (387C-D)
A woman shall not be clothed with man's apparel, neither shall a man use woman's apparel. (22:5)	No woman shall teach in the Church; a man in woman's apparel = something "feminine or soft" in the teaching of churchmen (390A-B)
An eunuch, whose testicles are broken or cut away, or yard cut off, shall not enter into the church of the Lord. (23:1)	Eunuch = the one who lives in a soft way (391A)
A mamzer, that is to say, one born of a prostitute, shall not enter into the church of the Lord, until the tenth generation. (23:2)	Those born of a prostitute = those living in a carnal way, or gentiles (391A-B)
The Ammonite and the Moabite, even after the tenth generation shall not enter into the church of the Lord for ever. (23:3)	The Ammonite and the Moabite = heretics (391B)
They that are born of them, in the third generation shall enter into the church of the Lord. (23:8)	Those born of the Edomite and the Egyptian = secular persons who can be associated with holy men through the Trinity, or through Hope, Faith, and Love (391C)
Thou shalt set up great stones, and shalt plaster them over with plaster. (27:2)	Stones = the Law; plaster = the learning of the priest (304B)
These shall stand upon mount Gerizim to bless the people... And over against them shall stand on mount Ebal to curse. (27:12-13)	Gerizim and Ebal = the New and Old Testament (304B-C)
Cursed be he that abideth not in the words of this law, and fulfilleth them not in work. (27:26)	The accursed = the Jews (304C)

These expositions in α show two noteworthy characteristics. First, they are original, that is not copied from Isidore or earlier Church Fathers.[2] Second, the exegetical method of these non-Isidorian expositions is rather Isidorian, i.e., allegorical, especially

---

1   Jocelyn N. Hillgarth, "Visigothic Spain and Early Christian Ireland." Robert McNally pointed out that the Isidorian pseudepigrapha was a distinctive phenomenon in Ireland in the late seventh and eighth century, see Robert McNally, "Isidorian Pseudepigrapha," pp. 305-316.

2   To interpret Deut. 18:15 as a prophetic sign of the coming of Christ is common in early Christian polemical literature, cf. Tertullian, *Aduersus Marcionem*, IV.22.10, pp. 380, 382; Cyprian, *Ad Quirinum testimonia aduersus Iudaeos*, CCSL 3, I.18, eds. Robert Weber and Maurice Bévenot (Turnhout: Brepols, 1972), p. 18. But such exegesis is really not a patristic invention, but can be found in Acts 3:22 and 7:37.

typological. The common mode is that A in the Deuteronomic lemma signifies B in Christian doctrine or church life. The one on Deut. 7:22 is a good example:

But what he says about not to destroy the nations altogether lest perhaps the beasts should increase upon them, shows that we should be aware that when sins have been expulsed out of our flesh and suddenly overcome, the spiritual beasts might approach against us, that is, arrogance, pride or certainly vainglory which would take more labor to root out than carnal sins as long as they creep in. For Lot, who had restrained himself when living in Sodom so that he had not sinned, was polluted by abominable intercourse when abiding in the mountain. And through this it is signified that whenever we expulse any sin, let virtue be planted immediately in its place, lest the expulsed [evil] spirit by any chance discover our empty home and return.[1]

This exposition follows the allegorical interpretation of Canaanite nations as sins in Isidore's Deuteronomy Entries 16 and 17, and extended similar moral teaching to an alternative Deuteronomic verse.[2] In this and other original expositions in the α recension of the Pseudo-Bedan Pentateuch commentary, we see an exegete at work in imitation of Isidore.

***

The α recension ceased at Deut. 27. As its updated version, besides certain supplement to the exposition of Deut. 25:5-10 on the levirate law drawn from Gregory's *Regula*

---

1 "Quod uero dicit, de gentibus non delendis pariter ne forte bestia multiplicarentur contra eos, ostendit nobis cauendum esse, expulsis peccatis a carne nostra, et repente superatis, accedant contra nos bestiae spirituales, hoc est iactantia, aut superbia, uel certe uana gloria, quae si subrepserint maiori labore exstirpabuntur quam carnalia uitia. Loth enim cum esset in monte positus concubito nefario pollutus est, qui in Sodomis habitans se continuit, ut non peccaret. Hac per hoc quodcunque uitium expulerimus, statim in loco illius plantetur uirtus, ne forte expulsus spiritus, iterum reuertens inueniat domum nostram uacantem." Milan, Biblioteca Ambrosiana, G.82 inf., fol. 96r.

2 Hrabanus copied this exposition in his commentary on Deuteronomy. Cf. PL 108, col. 868. According to Vercelli, Archivio Capitolare, 153 (Bischoff, *Katalog*, 7008), Hrabanus marked the source as "BD", namely Bede, implying that he consulted a copy of the β recension of the Pentateuch commentary.

pastoralis,[1] the γ recension contains an extra original exposition on the Song of Moses (Deut. 32:1-43), starting with "After these, Moses sings the song in which the Jewish city is reproached and the calling of gentiles is signified in a mystical way."[2] Arguably the first Latin interpretation of the Song of Moses after Verecundus of Junca (cf. Chapter 5.4), it consists of succinct allegorical notes on selected verses of Deut. 32. Its author seems to be a skilled exegete who comfortably raised scriptural evidence from various biblical canons and took patristic exegesis to support himself.[3] The exposition concentrates on the evangelical messages hidden in Deuteronomic verses and reveals them exclusively through an allegorical method (x refers to y). See the interpretation of Deut. 32:13–14 as an example:

> Other verses that follow apply to Jews according to the historical sense, and Christians spiritually. "Honey out of the rock" refers to divine words out of Christ; "oil out of the hardest stone" refers to the ardor of good works out of the gentile nation who is called stones due to the hardness of heart. "Honey, butter or milk" refers to different precepts; "herd," "sheep," "lamb," "ram," or "goat" refers to different behaviors of men. But "Basan" is translated as confusion: "the breed of Basan" are the sons of gentiles, who enter faith from confusion of gentile belief. "Blood of the

---

1   "Sequitur, quando fratres habitauerint simul, et ex eis absque liberis mortuus fuerit, et reliqua. Quid aliud in figura hoc demonstrat, nisi quia unusquisque Euangelii praedicator ita debet in Ecclesia laborare, ut defuncto fratri, id est Christo, suscitet semen, qui post resurrectionis apparens gloriam, dixit: Ite, nuntiate fratribus meis. Qui quasi sine filiis obiit, quia adhuc electorum suorum numerum non impleuit. Huius scilicet superstes uxorem frater sortiri praecipitur, quia dignum profecto est, ut cura sanctae Ecclesiae ei qui hanc bene regere preualet imponatur. Et semen quod suscitatum fuerit, eius nomen accipiat. Denique hoc intellegens Apostolus, ait: Numquid Paulus pro uobis crucifixus est, aut in nomine Pauli baptizati estis? Tanquam diceret: Defuncto fratre uos genui: Christiani uocamini, non Paulini. At uero qui electus ab Ecclesia ministerium Euangelii renuit, ab ipsa Ecclesia merito contempnitur. Ut dixerat cui nolenti in faciem mulier expuit, quia quisquis ex muneribus quae praecipit prodesse aliis non curat, bonis eius sancta Ecclesia exprobrans, et quae quasi in faciem saliuam iactat. [Non] sane sine signo huius obprobrii calceamentum enim pedis unius exuit, ne sit in eorum numero illorum, de quibus Apostolus dicit: Caltiati pedes in praedicatione Euangelii pacis. Qui enim sic euangelicam fidem tenet, ut et sibi possit Ecclesiae prodesse, et non renuit, bene intelligitur utroque pede caltiatus. Qui autem sibi putat quia credidit satis esse consultum, curam uero aliorum refugit, quasi unius pedis caltiamentum cum decore amittit." Milan, Biblioteca Ambrosiana, G.82 inf., fols. 98r-98v. Cf. Gregory, *Regula Pastoralis*, I.5, SC 381, pp. 146, 148.

2   "Post hec cantat Moyses canticum, in quo Iudaica plebs reprobatur et gentium uocatio mistice designatur." Alessandro Azzimonti transcribed the exposition of the Song of Moses in Alessandro Azzimonti, "Un anonimo commentario al Pentateuco," pp. 301-302.

3   The explicit biblical quotations include: Isaiah 1:2; 1 Corinthians 2:6, 1 Peter 2:10; Colossians 3:9; Luke 12:49. The book of Daniel is also mentioned: "Hoc et in uisione Danihelis ostenditur..." One of Gregory's homilies on the Gospel is briefly cited to bring an alternative reading as well as an exposition of Deut. 32:9, see Alessandro Azzimonti, "Un anonimo commentario al Pentateuco," p. 301, n. 62. Besides, the interpretation of "the breed of Basan" (Deut. 32:14) leans on the Hebrew etymology of Jerome: "Basan autem confusio interpretatur: filii Basan filii sunt gentilium, qui ueniunt in fidem de confusione gentilitatis." Cf. Jerome, *Liber interpretationis hebraicorum nominum*, CCSL 72, p. 114.

grape" is the faith of the Cross of Christ.[1]

After the exposition of the Song of Moses, γ ends with three more passages. The first one, drawn from Jerome's Letter 53 to Paulinus, summarizes the theme of each book of the Pentateuch;[2] the second, drawn from Jerome's prologue to his translation of Samuel and Kings (so-called *galeatum principium*), provides the Hebrew name of each book of the Pentateuch;[3] the third, probably originally composed, counts the number of verses of each book of the Pentateuch.[4]

***

To sum up, from the Deuteronomy section in the α to that in the γ recension of the Pseudo-Bedan Pentateuch commentary, we see a continuous effort not only to preserve Isidore's exegetical framework, but also to apply his allegorical method to more biblical text. If Gorman is right that both the recensions were created in Spain in the second half of the seventh century, they witness the continuing vitality of the exegetical culture in Iberia after the archbishop of Seville.

---

1   "Cetera que secuntur et secundum hystoriam Iudeis conueniunt et spiritaliter Christianis. Mel autem de petra eloquia diuina [de] Christo; oleum de saxo durissimo flagrantia bonorum operum de populo gentili, qui propter duritiam cordis lapides uocantur. Mel autem uel butirum aut lac diuersitas est preceptorum; armenta autem et oues uel agni et arietes aut hyrci diuersitas morum hominum. Basan autem confusio interpretatur: filii Basan filii sunt gentilium, qui ueniunt in fidem de confusione gentilitatis. Sanguis uue fides crucis Christi est." Alessandro Azzimonti, "Un anonimo commentario al Pentateuco," p. 301.

2   "Huc usque de Pentatheuco Moysi in qua de creatura mundi, de exordio generis humani, de diuisione terrae, de confusione linguarum et de gente usque ad Aegyptum scribitur Hebraeorum. De exodo cum decem plagis, cum decalogo, cum mysticis diuinis que praeceptis. De Leuitico in quo singula sacrificia, imo singulae paene syllabae et uestes Aaron et totus ordo leuiticus spirant caelestia sacramenta. De Numeris in quibus totius arithmeticae et prophetiae Balaam et quadraginta duarum per heremum mansionum mysteria continentur. Deuteronomio ubi recapitulantur priora et euangelicae legis est praefiguratio, et de ueteribus noui efficuntur." Milan, Biblioteca Ambrosiana, G.82 inf., fol. 99v. Cf. Jerome, *Epistula LIII*, 7, CSEL 54, p. 454.

3   "Apud Hebreos autem horum primus Bresith uocatur quem nos Genesim dicimus; secundus Celesmoth [*sic*] qui Exodus appellatur; tercius Vagegra [*sic*], id est Leuiticus; quartus Vagadaber [*sic*] quem Numeros uocamus. Quintus Addabarim, qui Deuteronomium praenotatur. Hii sunt quinque libri Moysi quos proprie Thorath, id est Legem appellant." Milan, Biblioteca Ambrosiana, G.82 inf., fol. 99v. Cf. Jerome, *Prologus in libro Regum, Biblia sacra: iuxta Vulgatam versionem*, eds. Bonifatius Fischer, Robert Weber (Stuttgart: Deutsche Bibelgesellschaft, 1994), p. 364.

4   "Genesis uersus habet numero quatuor milia septingentos. [E]xodus tria milia quingentos triginta. Leuiticus habet duo milia quadringentos. Numerus autem liber tria milia trecentos. Deuteronomium tria milia. Et illorum qui secuntur, quorum primus Hiesu Naue habet duo milia et qui sequitur Iudicum duo milia habet." Milan, Biblioteca Ambrosiana, G.82 inf., fols. 99v-100r.

6.4 The β Recension of the Pseudo-Bedan Pentateuch Commentary (PL 91, cols. 189-394)

The β recension of the Pentateuch commentary, as mentioned above, was attributed to Bede in the two extant copies (both ca. 800) and the lost one used by Gulielmus Montanus to make the edition now presented in PL 91, cols. 189-394. The Deuteronomy section in β contains much more interpolation to the primordial α — almost doubling its length — than γ. We will focus on these supplemental parts to explore this recension.[1]

The first thorny issue is whether the β recension is Irish. In 1954, Bernhard Bischoff published a greatly influential article, which proposes that the biblical exegesis composed by Irish authors or under Irish influence from the mid-seventh to ninth century, lying between patristic exegesis (last masters being Gregory and Isidore) and its revival by Bede and Carolingian authors, as a "turning point" (Wendepunkt) in Latin exegetical history. Most of the Hiberno-Latin commentaries or glosses as Bischoff identified are anonymous. They share some "Irish symptoms" in family resemblance. Bischoff identified thirty-nine such works in his article.[2] In the late 1980s, Joseph Kelly published a catalogue which expands the number of early medieval Hiberno-Latin Commentaries from 39 to 114.[3] Kelly aptly summarized Bischoff's *irische Symptomen* in the following words:

> These elements were rarely unique to the Irish and were often borrowed from the Latin Fathers, but the Irish used them so frequently that they could be considered Irish *characteristica*. These included *inter alia* a fondness for rudimentary questions, the citation of the *tres linguae sacrae* (Hebrew, Greek, Latin), the use of the phrase *non difficile* to characterize a question, the adoption of procedures from ancient grammarians, open references to heterodox writers (such as Pelagius) and non-canonical gospels (such as that to the Hebrews), an interest in genealogies, and the determination of a book's *tempus, locus,* et *persona*.[4]

---

1 Despite Michael Gorman appeal for a critical edition of the β recension of the Pseudo-Bedan Pentateuch commentary, the only available edition is still the defected one presented in PL 91.

2 Bernhard Bischoff, "Wendepunkte in der Geschichte der lateinischen Exegese im Frühmittelalter," *Sacris Erudiri* 6 (1954): pp. 189-281; the revised version, see idem, *Mittelalterliche Studien: Ausgewählte Aufsätze zur Schriftkunde und Literaturgeschichte* (Stuttgart: Hiersemann, 1966-1981), vol. 1, pp. 205-273. For The English translation by Colm O'Grady, see "Turning-points."

3 Joseph F. Kelly, "A Catalogue of Early Medieval Hiberno-Latin Biblical Commentaries (I)," *Traditio* 44 (1988): pp. 537-571; idem "Catalogue (II)."

4 Idem, "Catalogue (I)," p. 537. Bischoff also suggested certain other "Irish symptoms": the repeated use of phrases including *pauca de, non difficile, non dubium,* and *more...*; the predilection to the allegorical interpretation of numbers; the use of certain conceptual pairs including *historia/sensus* and *uita/theoretica*. Cf. Bernhard Bischoff, "Turning-points," pp. 83-94.

The "Bischoff thesis" on Irish exegesis has critics, including Gorman.[1] The β recension of Pseudo-Bedan Pentateuch commentary is not in Bischoff's list, but Hiberno-Latin scholars after him agree on its Irish symptoms.[2] Gorman, while deeply suspicious of the notion of "Irish exegesis" itself, also admitted that the interpolations in β have certain special characters.[3]

It is noteworthy that all those scholars base their judgment solely on the Genesis section, and no one has ever studied carefully the remaining β recension.[4] In the author's examination of the interpolations in the Deuteronomy section, three points which remind us of the Bischoff Thesis are noted.

First, different from the section title found in Milan, Biblioteca Ambrosiana, G.82 inf. (*Incipit Deuteronomium qui dicitur Addabarim*), the incipit in β is *EXPLANATIO IN QUINTUM LIBRUM MOSIS, Qui Hebraice ELLEHADDEBARIM, Graece DEUTERONOMIUM, Latine ALTERA LEX dicitur*,[5] a typical example of *tres linguae sacrae*.[6]

Second, the Deuteronomy section of β opens with a grammarian-style exposition, including the distinction between its *natura* and *littera*, and the *tres personae* of its author and audience (God the Father, Moses, and the Israel city).[7]

Third, the interpolations in β show a special interest in numerological symbolism. Scholars have revealed the special keenness in Hiberno-Latin writings and early Irish art

---

1   Critics include Clare Stancliffe, "Early Irish biblical exegesis," *Studia Patristica XII: Papers presented to the Sixth International Conference on Patristic Studies held in Oxford, 1971*, ed. Elizabeth A. Livingstone (Berlin: Akademie Verlag, 1975), vol.1, pp. 361-370; Michael Gorman, "A Critique of Bischoff's Theory of Irish Exegesis: The Commentary on Genesis in Munich Clm 6302 (Wendepunkte 2)," *The Journal of Medieval Latin* 7 (1997): pp.178-233; idem, "The Myth of Hiberno-Latin Biblical Exegesis," *Revue Bénédictine* 110 (2000): pp. 42-85; Mark Stansbury, "Irish Biblical Exegesis," *The Irish in Early Medieval Europe: Identity, Culture and Religion*, eds. Roy Flechner, Sven Meeder (London: Palgrave 2016), pp. 116-130.

2   See Michael Gorman's thorough summary in Michael Gorman, "The Commentary on the Pentateuch Attributed to Bede." The scholars mentioned by Gorman include Robert McNally, Joseph Kelly, David Dumville, Clare Stancliffe, James Cross, Charles D. Wright, Dáibhí Ó Cróinín, and John Carey.

3   Ibid., pp. 86-107. "If the reader is inclined to accept the validity of Bischoff's theories about 'Irish symptoms,' the text printed in Appendix 1 [the interpolations in β] will be regarded to be in some sense 'Irish,' 'of Irish origin', or 'Irish-influenced,' but I suspect the interpolations were compiled sometime in the late seventh or eighth century, in a relatively educated circle which wished to take on the daunting task of emending the original version of the Pentateuch commentary, and I see no reason why this work must have been done in Ireland or in an Irish milieu on the continent."

4   For instance, in Kelly's catalogue, we can only find "Pseudo-Beda, Commentarius in Genesim" (no. 22).

5   PL 91, col. 379.

6   Cf. Robert McNally, "The 'Tres Linguae Sacrae' in Early Irish Bible Exegesis," *Theological Studies* 19 (1958): pp. 395-403.

7   "Sed tamen sciendum, quibus modis hic liber Euangelium figuret: quod ita dicitur, quia hic liber fuerat in natura, antequam fuisset in littera... Tres quoque personae in hoc libro cooperatae erant, id est, Patris, et Moysi, plebisque cui annuntiatur... Hoc quoque Deuteronomium in duobus modis fuit obscurum, id est, in natura et littera." PL 91, col. 379.

to elaborate the allegorical significance of numbers that appear in biblical text.[1] Most of the numerological expositions in the Deuteronomy section of β can be traced back to an Isidorian treatise called *Liber numerorum* (PL 83, cols. 179-200), but some among them still demonstrate an Irish connection. For example, to interpret Number Four as human elements (*humido, arido, frigido,* and *calido*) can only be found in two pre-Carolingian works: β and an Irish Pseudo-Jerome *Expositio quattuor euangeliorum* (Bischoff's no. 11A and Kelly's no. 56A).[2] The use of *decem sensus* (five senses of body plus five senses of soul), identified by Bischoff as a typical "Irish symptom," appears in β as well.[3]

Even if we take one step backwards from the whole debate on the "Irish exegesis," we are still able to claim that the supplemental expositions of Deuteronomy in the β recension was produced in an intellectual context different from either α or γ.

The Deuteronomy section of β contains many lexical explanations of biblical vocabularies similar to glosses. Some of them are purely literal,[4] others allegorical.[5] The literature of biblical glossary arose in the Latin west from the second half of the seventh century on.[6] This exegetical genre originated from Anglo-Saxon England, to be precise, Canterbury. Theodore archbishop of Canterbury (r. 668–690) and Hadrian abbot of Sts-Peter-and-Paul (r. 670–709) established there a school of biblical studies

---

1 Represented by the Pseudo-Isidorian *Liber de numeris*, an Irish work produced in Bavaria in the late-eighth century, cf. Robert McNally, *Der irische Liber de numeris: eine Quellenanalyse des Pseudo-Isidorischen Liber de numeris* (Ph.D. dissertation: Universität München, 1957). Also cf. Hilary Richardson, "Number and Symbol in Early Christian Irish Art," *The Journal of the Royal Society of Antiquaries of Ireland* 114 (1984): pp. 28-47; Marina Smyth, "The Irish Liber de numeris," *The Scriptures and Early Medieval Ireland: Proceedings of the 1993 Conference of the Society for Hiberno-Latin Studies on Early Irish Exegesis and Homilectics*, ed. Thomas O'Loughlin (Turnhout: Brepols, 1999), pp. 291-297.

2 "Hi etiam mentes quadriformem hominem significare possunt, quatuor creaturis consistentem, humido scilicet, et arido, frigido et calido, cui Euangelium praedicatur." PL 91, col. 380. Cf. Pseudo-Jerome, *Expositio Euangelii secundum Marcum*, XVI, CCSL 82, ed. Michael Cahill (Turnhout: Brepols, 1997), p. 82: "Omni creaturae, id est, omni generi humano, quod in se commune habet ab omni creatura, iubentur; id est, angelis, pecoribus, lignis, lapidibus, igni et aquae, calido et frigido, humido, arido, quia mundus minor homo dicitur." But cf. Isidore, *Liber numerorum*, V.23, PL 83, col. 183: "Ipsa denique hominis natura ex quatuor est elementis concreta, ex calido et frigido, humido atque sicco" in which *siccus* is given instead of *aridus*.

3 "Per *decimam partem* quam Dominus a populo postulat significantur decem sensus, quos unusquisque nostrum reddere debet Domino." PL 91, col. 386. Bernhard Bischoff, "Turning-points," p. 86. But cf. Isidore, *Liber numerorum*, XI.57: "Decem sunt praeterea urbes, quas si bene rexeris, cordis et corporis sensus duplicato numero accipies in futurum." PL 83, col. 190.

4 E.g.: "*Argob* mons est. *Aroer* ciuitas, *Galaad* regio. *Moab* ab Occidente... *Gessum* fons est, et *Magati* locus. *Iair* et *Machir* unus uir est." PL 91, col. 382; "*Mare Rubrum*, propter limum rubicundum dicitur." PL 91, col. 385.

5 E.g.: "*Dispe*, id est genus uiperarum, quod haereticorum tenet figuram, qui Trinitatem blasphemans, quod sub iuramento pollicitus est." PL 91, col. 385; "*Crabrones*, id est mali mores illorum." PL 91, col. 385.

6 John Contreni, "Glossing the Bible in the Early Middle Ages: Theodore and Hadrian of Canterbury and John Scottus (Eriugena)," *The Study of the Bible in the Carolingian Era*, eds. Celia Chazelle, Burton Van Name Edwards (Turnhout: Brepols, 2003), pp. 19-38.

of the Antiochene style, witnessed by a set of several biblical glossaries both in Latin and in vernacular.[1] Their multiple derivative formats produced during the early Middle Ages attest to the wide dissemination and influence of these Canterbury glossaries.[2] It is tempting to wonder whether the author of β had knowledge of those glossaries and used them as reference. For example, "the grievous infirmities of Egypt" (*infirmitates Aegypti pessimas*) in Deut. 7:15 are interpreted as *decem plagas Aegypti* in β, close to the entry on the same biblical lemma in the Canterbury glossary so-called "Pentateuch I": *ipsas plagas dicit quas habuerunt.*[3]

A relevant feature is the conscious adoption of Jerome's Hebrew etymologies for allegorical exegesis.[4] The interest in the Hieronymian etymologies is considered a character of early Irish exegesis.[5] It is difficult to know whether the author of β took these etymological notes directly from Jerome (especially his *Liber interpretationis hebraicorum nominum*), or via glossaries.

Whoever composed the supplemental expositions in the Deuteronomy section of β was capable of creating allegorical exegesis of Isidorian style. One such example is the following exposition of Moses' appointment of "tribunes, and centurions, and officers over fifties, and over tens" for Israel (Deut. 1:15):

> The tribune who gives order to a third part of the people, as other ranks, signifies the *doctores* who teach the faith of the Trinity in three laws. The centurion who is the leader of a hundred persons signifies the *doctores* who preach the heavenly rewards in the future and a hundredfold in the present life. In a similar way, an officer over fifties signifies the *doctores* who preach penance. But everyone can find satisfaction from Apostles in all their five senses, for they taught all those these mentioned above. An

---

1 Bernhard Bischoff, Michael Lapidge, *Biblical Commentaries from the Canterbury School of Theodore and Hadrian* (Cambridge: Cambridge University Press, 1995).

2 Including the so-called "Leiden Glossary" and "Reichenau Bible Glosses," see J. D. Pheifer, "Early Anglo-Saxon Glossaries and the School of Canterbury," *Archbishop Theodore: Commemorative Studies on his Life and Influence*, ed. Michael Lapidge (Cambridge: Cambridge University Press, 1995), pp. 281-333. The new editions of those biblical glossaries, see *Glossae Biblicae*, CCCM 189A, 189B, ed. Paolo Vaciago (Turnhout: Brepols, 2004).

3 PL 91, col. 385; Bernhard Bischoff, Michael Lapidge, *Biblical Commentaries from the Canterbury School of Theodore and Hadrian* (Cambridge: Cambridge University Press, 1995).

4 E.g.: "Inter *Pharan*, et *Tophel*, et *Laban*, et *Aseroth*, quorum interpretatio est, auctus, insulsa, dealbatio, et atria, qui quatuor mentes, ut supra diximus, quatuor Euangelia significant, a quibus Ecclesia augetur in fide. Insulsa, contra uitia et diabolum. Dealbata, in baptismo et poenitentia, et resurrectione. Atria, id est, Ecclesia uel Euangelium." PL 91, col. 380, on Deut. 1:1; "*Seir* autem pilosus interpretatur, quo indicatur mortalitas. Sicut enim lex litterae de immolandis uictimis, et de occisione illorum qui proximos occiderent, praeceperat: sic Euangelium de occisione peccatorum et uitiorum est." PL 91, col. 380, on Deut. 1:2; "*Seon* et rex Amorrhaeorum, daemonem regem gentium figurat, uel sensum malum, regem uitiorum." PL 91, col. 381, on Deut. 1:4; "*Hebraeus* transiens interpretatur. Hebraea, id est anima uniuscuiusque perfecti de gentilitate, ad baptismum transiens." PL 91, col. 386, on Deut. 15:12.

5 Joseph F. Kelly, "Hiberno-Latin Exegesis and Exegetes," *Annuale Mediaevale* 21 (1981): pp. 46-60.

officer over tens signifies the one who proclaims the ten commandments of the Law. But this order of multiplying in tribunes and centurions is also the order of believing. But the four orders of those leaders are the numeral figure of the four Gospels which taught the four cardinal virtues, that is, justice, prudence, temperance, and fortitude. But Moses is the figure of Christ in his election of rulers: those elected rulers signify the twelve Apostles who were elected together with the four Evangelists by Christ to ruler over the Church.[1]

This exegete was also familiar with Church Fathers. In the exposition of "Thou shalt love the Lord thy God with thy whole heart" (Deut. 6:5), he adopted the motif of the good builder in Ambrose's *Hexaemeron*, with same words but in totally different context.[2] It is too conservative for Gorman to assume that β was composed "by students or relatively uneducated clerics or even laymen who were, for the most part, unfamiliar with the patristic tradition."[3] Rather, it is better to see the Deuteronomy section of β as a daring and mature effort to enrich the Isidorian tradition with Irish? cultural resource.

6.5 The Irish Reference Bible (*Pauca problemata de enigmatibus ex tomis canonicis*)

Besides the β recension of the Pseudo-Bedan Pentateuch commentary, there is another early medieval commentary on Deuteronomy identified as Irish in the well-known "Bibelwerk." Named by Bischoff, *das Bibelwerk* (Bischoff's no. 1A and Kelly's no. 15A), or the *Reference Bible*, consists of a series of commentaries on all the biblical

---

1 "*Tribunus* dicitur, qui tribui imperat, ut alii; significat doctores, in tribus legibus fidem Trinitatis docentes. *Centurio* uero qui super centum sit, significat doctores qui praedicant praemia coelestia in futuro, uel centuplum in praesenti. *Quinquagenarium* super quinquaginta similiter doctores significat, poenitentiam praedicantes. Unusquisque autem ex quinque sensibus in apostolis impletur. Ipsi enim praedicauerunt uniuersa supradicta. *Decanus* autem imperat super decem, signat decem uerba legis narrantem. Ordo autem crescendi est in tribunis et centurionibus, et est quoque ordo credendi. Quatuor autem ordines quorum principium quatuor Euangelia in numero figurant, quae quatuor uirtutes principales docuerunt, id est, Iustitiam, Prudentiam, Temperantiam, Fortitudinem. Moyses uero Christum signat in electione *principum*: principes quoque qui eliguntur, duodecim apostoli figurantur, cum quatuor Euangeliis a Christo electos, ad principatum super Ecclesiam." PL 91, cols. 381-382.
2 "More quoque artificis dilectio primum ponitur, quia sit omnium mandatorum fundamentum. Ita enim artifex fundamentum primo ponit, et deinde aedificat domum. Sic et nos decet dilectionem fundamentum primum ponere, ac deinde bona opera instituere." PL 91, col. 384. Cf. "Bonus artifex prius fundamentum ponit, postea fundamento posito aedificationis membra distinguit et adiungit ornatum. Posito igitur fundamento terrae et confirmata caeli substantia-duo enim ista sunt quasi uelut cardines rerum-subtexuit: terra autem erat inuisibilis et incomposita." Ambrose, *Hexaemeron*, I.7.25, CSEL 32/1, ed. Karl Schenkl (Vienna: Verlag der Österreichischen Akademie der Wissenschaften, 1896), p. 23.
3 Michael Gorman, "The Commentary on the Pentateuch Attributed to Bede," p. 94.

canons except Lamentations and Baruch. There is a later and abbreviated version extant as well (Bischoff's no. 1B and Kelly's no. 15B). In manuscripts, the *Reference Bible* is titled *Pauca problemata de enigmatibus ex tomis canonicis*. Hiberno-Latin scholars agree on its Irish origin, and tend to date this anonymous work to the mid-eighth century.[1] According to Martin McNamara:

> It is a kind of biblical encyclopedia. Its late eighth-century compiler, an Irishman who had lived some time on the Continent, had behind him a century and a half of Irish exegetical activity. He depends on earlier writings and also, probably, on the oral tradition of the Irish schools. His composition has numerous Irish characteristics.[2]

The *Reference Bible* begins with an introduction to the authorship and subject of each canon, the division of the Bible, and the multiple concepts of the law, mainly based on the works of Isidore and Junilius Africanus. After it, each biblical book is treated in canonical order.[3] Like most of other biblical commentaries between 600 and 800, the *Reference Bible* is a patchwork made of excerpts from various patristic sources. How its compiler or compilers used sources is a complicated issue.[4] Gerard MacGinty, the editor of the Pentateuch section of the *Reference Bible*, hypothesized that the work is a product of multiple layers of excerpting practice:

> I have come to believe we are to understand the summary manner of most of its patristic references, indeed understand the very nature of the text, as rather unevenly developed lecture notes. I suggest they were not those taken by any student, but rather some lecturer's own notes, gathered from various series of excerpts and with excerpts of his own; many possibly could be shorthand references to texts to be cited more

---

1 Bernhard Bischoff, "Turning-points," pp. 97-102; Martin McNamara, "Psalter text and Psalter study in the early Irish Church (A.D. 600–1200)," *The Psalms in the early Irish Church*, idem (Sheffield: Sheffield Academic Press, 2000), pp. 19-142; Gerard MacGinty, "The Pentateuch of the Reference Bible: the Problem Concerning its Sources," *The Scriptures and Early Medieval Ireland: Proceedings of the 1993 Conference of the Society for Hiberno-Latin Studies on Early Irish Exegesis and Homiletics*, ed. Thomas O'Loughlin (Turnhout: Brepols, 1999), pp. 163-177. McNamara would like to date the *Reference Bible* to the late eighth century, and MacGinty to the early half of the eighth century. Michael Gorman, expectably, does not believe it was composed in Ireland or in an Irish mileu, cf. his "The Myth of Hiberno-Latin Biblical Exegesis," pp. 61-62.

2 Martin McNamara, "Psalter Text and Psalter Study," p. 52.

3 For a clear survey of the structure and the content of the *Reference Bible*, see Martin McNamara, "Plan and Source Analysis of *Das Bibelwerk*, Old Testament," *Irland und die Christenheit: Bibelstudien und Mission*, eds. Próinséas Ní Chatháin and Michael Richter (Stuttgart: Klett-Cotta, 1987), pp. 84-112. For the New Testament section, see Joseph Kelly, "*Das Bibelwerk*: Organization and *Quellenanalyse* of the New Testament Section," ibid., pp. 113-123.

4 "I am careful to qualify compiler with (s), although the final editor was probably a single individual." Gerard MacGinty, "The Pentateuch of the Reference Bible," p. 165, n. 9.

fully.[1]

MacGinty believed that the direct sources of the *Reference Bible* are the compilations or epitomes — Paterius' *Liber testimoniorum* for Gregory, Eugippius' *Excerpta* and an Irish epitome of *De Genesi ad litteram* for Augustine, Isidore's *Expositio* for various Fathers, and much more unidentified or lost ones — via which the exegesis of Jerome, Augustine, Ambrose, Ambrosiaster, Eucherius, Junilius, and perhaps Origen are gathered together.[2]

As far as the Deuteronomy section of the *Reference Bible* (33 entries numbered consecutively in Roman numerals in extant manuscripts) is concerned, its compiling practice can be properly described as a well-done enlargement of the exegesis of Deuteronomy on the basis of Isidore's *Expositio*. After the first entry (it will be discussed soon below), the Irish compiler apparently regarded it as his primary task to adopt nearly all the Deuteronomy expositions of Isidore in abridged form, even including the abnormal one on Leviticus 19:23 (cf. Chapter 6.1).[3] To enrich this Isidorian tradition, this compiler resorted to alternative sources, the major one of which is Paterius' *Liber testimoniorum*. Eleven Gregorian expositions drawn from Paterius' collection, also in

---

1 Gerard MacGinty, "The Pentateuch of the Reference Bible," p. 165. MacGinty's critical edition of the commentaries on the Pentateuch in the *Reference Bible*, see CCCM 173. The critical edition of the Apocalypse section in the *Reference Bible* is available in *Commentaria minora in Apocalypsin Iohannis*, CCSL 107, ed. Roger Gryson (Turnhout: Brepols, 2003), pp. 243-295.
2 Gerard MacGinty, "The Pentateuch of the Reference Bible," p. 171.
3 The entries abridged from Isidore without obvious alteration or supplement include:
Pauca problesmata, Deut. II = *Expositio in uetus testamentum*, V.3;
Pauca problesmata, Deut. III = *Expositio in uetus testamentum*, V.4;
Pauca problesmata, Deut. IV = *Expositio in uetus testamentum*, V.5;
Pauca problesmata, Deut. V = *Expositio in uetus testamentum*, V.6;
Pauca problesmata, Deut. VI = *Expositio in uetus testamentum*, V.7;
Pauca problesmata, Deut. VII = *Expositio in uetus testamentum*, V.8;
Pauca problesmata, Deut. VIII = *Expositio in uetus testamentum*, V.9;
Pauca problesmata, Deut. IX = *Expositio in uetus testamentum*, V.10;
Pauca problesmata, Deut. X = *Expositio in uetus testamentum*, V.11;
Pauca problesmata, Deut. XI = *Expositio in uetus testamentum*, V.13;
Pauca problesmata, Deut. XIII = *Expositio in uetus testamentum*, V.15;
Pauca problesmata, Deut. XVII = *Expositio in uetus testamentum*, V.18;
Pauca problesmata, Deut. XVIII = *Expositio in uetus testamentum*, V.19;
Pauca problesmata, Deut. XIX = *Expositio in uetus testamentum*, V.20;
Pauca problesmata, Deut. XX = *Expositio in uetus testamentum*, V.21.

abbreviated style, appear right after the last entry (XXI) abridged from Isidore.[1] The evidence to use Paterius to control Isidore's exposition is also visible in Entry XII.[2]

There are other supplemental sources. In the last entry (XXXIII) about the question "who wrote the ending of Deuteronomy after the death of Moses," the complier adopted Jerome's doctrinal treatise *On the Perpetual Virginity of the Blessed Mary against Helvidius*, with the authorial mark "Hieronimus dicit."[3] Entries XIV–XVI on the seven Canaanite nations, he remarkably resorted to Isidore's own source, Book 5 of Cassian's *Collationes* (with an explicit source mark *Iohannes Cassianus*), to enlarge the relevant exposition in Isidore's *Expositio*.[4]

The only two obvious deviations from the Isidorian tradition are both related to Pseudo-Bedan commentary discussed in the previous two subchapters. In the opening

---

1   *Pauca problesmata*, Deut. XXII = *Liber testimoniorum*, V.2;
   Pauca problesmata, Deut. XXIII = *Liber testimoniorum*, V.3;
   Pauca problesmata, Deut. XXIV = *Liber testimoniorum*, V.5;
   Pauca problesmata, Deut. XXV = *Liber testimoniorum*, V.6;
   Pauca problesmata, Deut. XXVI = *Liber testimoniorum*, V.8;
   Pauca problesmata, Deut. XXVII = *Liber testimoniorum*, V.13;
   Pauca problesmata, Deut. XXVIII = *Liber testimoniorum*, V.16;
   Pauca problesmata, Deut. XXIX = *Liber testimoniorum*, V.18;
   Pauca problesmata, Deut. XXX = *Liber testimoniorum*, V.19;
   Pauca problesmata, Deut. XXXI = *Liber testimoniorum*, V.20;
   Pauca problesmata, Deut. XXXII = *Liber testimoniorum*, V.21.
2   *Pauca problesmata*, CCCM 173, no. 456, p. 208: "XII Uxorem fratris mortui frater uiuus iussus est accipere, ut non sibi sobolis sed fratri mortuo reputetur: id est, ut doctor ecclesiae defuncto fratri, id est Christo, suscitet semen qui pro nobis est mortuus; sicut Paulus dicit, Si multos pedagogos habetis, tamen non multos patres, genui enim uos, reliqua. Item dicit, Numquid Paulus pro uobis crucifixus est, uel in nomine Pauli baptizati estis? Hic apparet Paulus genuit filios, sed non sunt sui filii sed fratris eius, qui dixit, Ite, nuntiate fratribus meis, ut eant in Galileam. Ille cuius debet uxor esse et non uult semen <fratris suscitare>: expuat in faciem eius, et uno pede discalciatur. Id est, qui doctor debet esse ecclesiae et non uult, expuat ecclesia in faciem eius: id est, obprobrium faciet ei ecclesia ut non sit doctor neque pastor; et pes eius discalciatur quia dilectionem proximi habere non uoluit. Duos enim pedes calciatos habet qui se ipsum et proximum diligit; unum habet, qui proximum non diligit." The Irish compiler supplemented one biblical citation (Matthew 28:10), which is present in Gregory's exposition in *Regula pastoralis*, I.5 (SC 381, p. 146) and Paterius' Deuteronomy Entry 15 (PL 79, col. 781).
3   "XXXIII Quis scripsit quod legitur in fine Deuteronomii post mortem Moysi? Cum Moyses suos scripsit quinque libros, nulli dubium est, ut Hieronimus dicit, quod ipse Moyses scripsit per spiritum prophetie, uel Esdras addidit illas historias post mortem Moysi et Iosuae." *Pauca problesmata*, CCCM 173, no. 477, p. 211. Cf. Jerome, *Aduersus Heluidium de Mariae uirginitate perpetua*: "Item in fine Deuteronomii: Et defunctus est Moyses seruus Domini in terra Moab per uerbum Domini, et sepelierunt eum in Geth, prope domum Phegor, et nemo scit sepulcrum eius usque in diem istum. Certe hodiernus dies illius temporis aestimandus est, quo historia ipsa contexta est, siue Moysen dicere uolueris auctorem Pentateuchi, siue Ezram eiusdem instauratorem operis, non recuso." PL 23, col. 199.
4   Entries XIV supplies the Latin names of *gastrimargia*, *philargyria*, and *cenodoxia* (based on *Collationes* V.2); Entry XV groups the eight capital sins in pair (based on Cassian's *Collationes* V.3); Entry XVI resorts to Collationes V.18-19 (not Isidore's source *Collationes* V.22) to explain the discrepancy between the number of nations and that of capital sins. *Pauca problesmata*, CCCM 173, no. 458-460, pp. 209-210.

entry of Deuteronomy section of the *Reference Bible*, the compiler chose not to follow Isidore's allegorical exposition, but to provide a downright literal introduction of the *auctor*, *tempus*, and *res* of the book of Deuteronomy. The same entry also states that Moses composed Deuteronomy in "12 days," reflecting a rather strange reading of Deut. 1:2, different from either the Vulgate or Isidore's *Expositio* (both reading "eleven days").[1] It must have puzzled early medieval readers, since in the shorter and later recension of the *Reference Bible*, "12" is removed.[2] As we have seen in Chapter 6.3, the reading "12 days" also appears in the Pseudo-Bedan commentary. What's more, in Entry XXI on the command not to exceed forty stripes in punishment (Deut. 25:2-3), the interpretation of Number Forty as the multiplication of "ten commandments of the Law and four Gospels" accords with an original exposition in the Pseudo-Bedan commentary, rather than the one offered in Isidore's *Expositio* ("the Decalogue of the Law diffused throughout the four parts of the world").[3] The relationship between the Deuteronomy section of the *Reference Bible* and that of Pseudo-Bedan commentary is yet to be explored deeper.

In sum, the commentary on Deuteronomy in the *Reference Bible* largely takes the whole Isidorian exegetical tradition, and enriches it both by supplementing alternative materials and by resorting to Isidore's own sources.

6.6 The Isidorian Tradition and the Lyon Annotations

Wigbod, the Pseudo-Bedan Pentateuch commentary, and the Irish *Bibelwerk* represent three types of reception of the Isidorian exegesis of Deuteronomy. The degree of dependence varies: Wigbod's commentary on Deuteronomy in both of his *Quaestiones* and *Lectiones* rarely deviates from his Isidorian source; the three recensions of Pseudo-Bede not only absorb the Isidorian exposition as their backbone (more than 50% in the α and γ recensions, around 30% in the β recension) but also adopt his allegorical method (in the format "x signifies y") to make original exegesis; the anonymous Irish compiler(s)

---

1 "I Deuteronomium: interpretatur secunda lex, quia replicat Moyses in his duodecim diebus scribens Deuteronomium, quicquid continent praedicti iiii libri legis scripti per xl annos." *Pauca problesmata*, CCCM 173, no. 475, p. 205.

2 "Deuteronomium: interpretatur secunda lex, quia replicat Moyses in his diebus quicquid continent quattuor libri <scripti> per annos xl." *Pauca problesmata (textus breuior)*, CCCM 173, no. 146, p. 288.

3 "XXI xl flagellatur omnis peccator in lege: id est, ut nos peccatum per x uerba legis et iiii euangelia peccata emendamus." *Pauca problesmata*, CCCM 173, no. 465, p. 212. Cf. "... quod per quadragenarium numerum figura significetur huius temporis, in quo Ecclesia per quatuor mundi partes diffusa, sub Decalogo legis uiuit." Isidore, *Expositio in uetus testamentum*, V.22, PL 83, col. 370. "Quadraginta autem anni quibus laboriose Moyse peracti ad terram repromissionis filii Israel peruenerunt significat totum tempus quo Ecclesia in laboribus uiuit, quae propter denarium numerum legis obseruat, et quaternum propter Euangelium. Decies autem quatuor, quadraginta sunt." Milan, Biblioteca Ambrosiana, G.82 inf., fol. 96r = PL 91, col. 380.

largely depended on Isidore to compile the Deuteronomy section of *Bibelwerk* (ca. 75%), but consciously used alternative sources (Paterius, Jerome, and Cassian) for the sake of enrichment. They altogether attest to the dominant Isidorian tradition for the exposition of the "second law" in the early medieval west between ca. 650 and ca. 800.

Geographically speaking, it seems that the relatively active intellectual life in the Atlantic circle (Spain, Ireland, and Anglo-Saxon England) during this period corresponds to the comparatively creative reception (in the case of the Pseudo-Bedan Pentateuch commentary and the Irish *Bibelwerk*, especially the β recension of the former), while the comparatively weak exegetical tradition in *Francia* before 800 partially explains the conservative use of Isidore by Wigbod.[1]

It is against this background that we should understand the relationship between Isidore and the Lyon Annotations. Isidore's shadow is certainly present in this southern Gallic commentary. On one hand, the Annotator internalized the "Deuteronomy-Gospel" typological motif popularized by Isidore (cf. Chapter 6.1) in a way even more thorough than those earlier post-Isidorian commentaries. The motif itself appears explicitly for four times (one of them being the downright *quasi deuteronomium Euangelium*),[2] and, as we will see more clearly in Chapter 7, the consistent theme of the Lyon Annotations is to expound the evangelical messages embedded in the *secunda lex* for Christians, the "spiritual Israel," once called *secundus... populus* in an annotation.[3]

On the other hand, in the Lyon Annotations, we can detect the clear influence of no fewer than sixteen Deuteronomy entries, *plus* one Exodus entry and one Numbers entry

---

1   Despite the importance of the Holy Bible in the Merovingian social, political and religious life (cf. Yitzhak Hen, "The Uses of the Bible and the Perception of Kingship in Merovingian Gaul," *Early Medieval Europe* 1 [1998]: pp. 277-289; Ian Wood, "Incest, Law and the Bible in Sixth-century Gaul," ibid., pp. 291-304; Pierre Riché, "L'enseignement et la culture des laïcs dans l'Occident précarolingien," *La scuola nell'occidente latino dell'alto Medioevo* [Spoleto: Centro italiano di studi sull'alto medioevo, 1972], vol. 1, pp. 231-253), there are only three extant biblical commentaries from Merovingian Gaul: the fragments of Gregory of Tours' commentary on the Psalms; an anonymous commentary on Hebrews; Pseudo-Theophilus' commentary on the four Gospels, cf. Yitzhak Hen, "A Merovingian Commentary on the Four Gospels," *Revnedes Étndes Augustinienne* 49(2003), pp. 167-187.

2   "[Si enim liber hoc Deuteronomium] figura est secundae legis, id est Noui Testamenti, uniuersa precepta Domini atque iudicia que ad creationem pertinentia, magis ad nouum populum, hoc est cristianum sed in nouitate tamen spiritalis Israel [...] potiusquam ad carnalem populum Iudeorum [qui non] desiit esse caecus." Paris, BnF, NAL 1740, fol. 1r; "Deuteronomium id est iteratio legis, figura est Euangelii quam omnes qui presunt ecclesiae die ac nocte meditare debent..." Paris, BnF, NAL 1740, fol. 49r, on Deut. 17:18; "... in quorum corda Dominus Euangelium, qui est secunda lex, non atramento sed Spiritu sancto scripsit et ad notitiam omnium credentium manifeste proposuit." Paris, BnF, NAL 1740, fol. 69r, on Deut. 27:2; "... per octenarium uero quasi deuteronomium Euangelium accipitur. Annus uero remissionis praesens tempus est, quod post aduentum Saluatoris usque in finem sequitur." Paris, BnF, NAL 1740, fol. 83r, on Deut. 31:10-11.

3   E.g., "Prior ille populus Israheliticus ex Egypto liberatus est potiusquam redemptus; secundus uero populus id est cristianus, heres Noui Testamenti, de spiritali Egypto, tenebras uidelicet huius mundi et potestate diaboli sanguine Domini Ihesu Christi redemptus est." Paris, BnF, NAL 1740, fol. 23r, on Deut. 7:8.

of Isidore's *Expositio* (Table 6.8).

Table 6.8 Use of Isidore's *expositio* in the Lyon Annotations

The Lyon Annotations (Paris, BnF, NAL 1740)	Isidore, Expositio
Undenarius quippe numerus transgressionem significat legis... figura est secundae legis, id est Noui Testamenti... (Deut. 1:2, fol. 1r)	Deut. Entry 1
Vestimenta Israhelitarum que per quadraginta annis \<non\> *consumpta sunt*, significaberunt corpora sanctorum que post resurrectionem incorruptibilia permane\<nt\>. (Deut. 29:5, fol. 78r)	Deut. Entry 2
Lucus est arbor infructuosa que foliis redundat, fructum nullum profert: significat sapientiam huius mundi superuacua uerbositate adornata... (Deut. 16:21, fol. 47r)	Deut. Entry 3
Id est stultum quemlibet sapienti in predicatione ne socies. Aliter: Ita religionem cristianam fide et opere retine, ut cum subprestitionibus Iudoerum nullam societatem abere uelis... (Deut. 22:10, fol. 59r)	Deut. Entry 6
Duplicate mentis in uiro relegio\<so\> uel femina inesse prohibet. In *lana* quippe simulata simplicitas; in *lino* uero, occulta malitia demonstratur. (Deut. 22:11, fol. 59r)	Deut. Entry 9
Prohibet lex sacerdotibus ecclesiae penitentibus *inferiorem* uel *superiorem* molam accipere, id est spem atque formidinem subtraere... (Deut. 24:6, fol. 63v)	Deut. Entry 10
Spiritaliter autem *diuersa pondera* et duplices mensuras illi *in domibus suis*, id est in conscientiis suis, habent qui aliter facta sua pensant ali\<ter\> proximorum suorum qui culpas suas licet graues leuitant et proximorum suorum \<mi\>nima sicut grauiora iudicant. (Deut. 25:13, fol. 66i)	Deut. Entry 12
Duo *testes*, lex et Euangelium; tres uero: legem prophetiam atque Nouum Testamentum exprimunt. (Deut. 17:6, fol. 48r)	Deut. Entry 13
Fratres in unum habitauerunt eo tempore quo Dominus ac Redemptor noster... ideo relictis eius, id est sanctam ecclesiam, fratres illius iuniores hoc est sancti apostoli, ad regendum acceperunt et quoscumque ex Iudeis uel gentibus per sua predicatione adquesierunt... (Deut. 25:5-10, fol. 65r)	Deut. Entry 14
Quicumque enim magis filios ac filias atque uxorem quam uitam aeternam diligit, ad spiritale(m) militiam idoneus esse non potest: sufficit enim illis simplex conuersatio, id est actiua uita, ad salutem anime. (Deut. 20:6-7, fol. 54v)	Deut. Entry 15
Tropologice uero septem principalia uitia insinuant id est... (Deut. 7:1, fol. 22)	Deut. Entry 16
In quorum *numero captiuorum mulier pulcra* significat animam ad imaginem Dei creatam, ex Christi coniugio per fidem aptam... (Deut. 21:10-13, fol. 57)	Deut. Entry 18
Percutit proximum suum quilibet doctor ecclesiae qui per ignorantiam aut per escessum loqutionis proximum suum scandalizat in fide... (Deut. 19:4-5, fol. 52)	Deut. Entry 19
Inter quos si fuerit quispiam ex eis qui *nocturno* id est occulta cogitatione sit *pollutus*, necesse est ut egressus e *castra* alienum se iudicet a societate electorum, donec per satisfactionem penitentiam et lacrimis lauet *uestimenta sua*... (Deut. 23: 9-14, fol. 61v)	Deut. Entries 20 and 21
Hoc quippe significat *quadragenarius numerus* omnis enim culpa quae in ac uita per sactisfactione penitentiae uel quolibet flagello corporali expiata non fuerit, in futuro seculo uelut transacto qudragenario numero expiari omnino non poterit... (Deut. 25:1-3, fol. 65r)	Deut. Entry 22

Continued

The Lyon Annotations (Paris, BnF, NAL 1740)	Isidore, Expositio
Hec sunt decem mandata legis que in libro Exodi continentur, ex quibus decem mandata primum pertinet ad Patrem, secundum preceptum ad Filium, tertium uero ad Spiritum sanctum; septem autem que secuntur ad dilectionem proximi conueniunt; in qua decem mandata, id est decalogum legis, omnia diuina precepta continentur. (Deut. 5:7, fol. 17v)	Exodus Entry 29[1]
Hoc rex Basan qui interpretatur conclusio, rex confusionis atque ignominie, figuram gestauit diaboli. (Deut. 3:11, fol. 10r)	Numbers Entry 39[2]

Generally speaking, the way of using Isidorian exegesis in the Lyon annotations is more flexible than in the three groups of the pre-800 commentaries that we have examined in this chapter. A usual *modus operandi* is to put Isidore's allegorical exegesis in a more specific context of ecclesiastical life. For example, Isidore in his Deuteronomy Entry 12 followed Cassian to interpret the command that "Thou shalt not have divers weights in thy bag, a greater and a less" (Deut. 25:13) as a warning against the habit to treat oneself and one's neighbor with double standards. In the Lyon Annotations, we see the exposition paraphrased, but with a supplemental statement: "Many bishops or priests in the church do such thing, who, as it is said, judge others about the least sins but do not correct their own bad deeds."[3]

A question worth asking is whether the Lyon Annotator absorbed Isidorian exegesis directly through Isidore's *Expositio*, or via a certain post-Isidorian commentary? The manuscript survival does not help much. The only relevant copy that we can connect to Carolingian Lyon is Lyon BM, 447 + 448, which contains the Genesis-Deuteronomy section of Isidore's *Expositio* (448, fols. 150r-178r + 447, fol. 1r-I05v) and the shortened recension of the *Bibelwerk* (447, fols. 106r-152r). But this manuscript was produced in the late ninth century.[4] Considering the wide dissemination of *Expositio* in eighth-century Gaul — plus a complete copy of late eighth century written in Freising, Leidrad's home — there is no reason to deny the possibility that the author of the Lyon Annotations had access to Isidore's original text.[5] But the anthor's source criticism suggests an alternative,

---

1 "Dat igitur inde Dominus Moysi legem innocentiae nostrae, et cognitionis suae. Eamdemque in decem uerba constituit, et saxeis tabulis digito suo scripsit. Et haec quidem praecepta ita sunt distributa, ut tria pertineant ad dilectionem diuinae Trinitatis, septem uero ad amorem fraternam, quibus societas humana non laeditur. Primum Decalogi mandatum ad Deum Patrem pertinet... Secundum praeceptum ad Filium pertinet... Tertio praecepto legis insinuatur de obseruatione Sabbati, quod ad Spiritum sanctum pertinet..." Isidore, *Expositio in uetus testamentum*, II.29, PL 83, cols. 301-303.

2 "Og uero rex interpretatur conclusio, Basan autem confusio; id enim agit diabolus semper, ut concludat uiam ad Dominum, opponendo idola sua, ne credatur in Christum. Conclusio enim praecedit, ut rex; sequitur confusio, ut plebs: quia quos modo concludit, ne credant in Christum, quando apparuerit Christus, omnes confundentur." Ibid., IV.39, PL 83, cols. 355-356.

3 "Hoc quippe faciunt plerique episcopi siue presbiteri in ecclesiam qui alios, ut dictum est, de minimis peccatis iudicant et semetipsos de perpetrata mala non corrigunt." Paris, BnF, NAL 1740, fol. 66r.

4 Bischoff, *Katalog*, 2550, 2552.

5 Michael Gorman, ed. *Genesis*, pp. xv-xvi.

maybe more possible, proposal: the Lyon Annotator could have used the β recension of Pseudo-Bedan Pentateuch commentary or a similar text as his source.

This proposal is based on two facts. First, all the Isidorian expositions detectable in the Lyon Annotations as listed above, including the Exodus Entry and the Numbers Entry,[1] can also be found in the β recension of Pseudo-Bede in abbreviated format. Second, there exists a remarkable parallel between the Lyon Annotations and the *original* parts of β. See Table 6.9.

Table 6.9   Textual comparison between β recension of Pseudo-Bede and the Lyon Annotations

Deut.	The Lyon Annotations (Paris, BnF, NAL 1740)	β recension of Pseudo-Bede (PL 91)
21:15-17	Homo iste, habens duas uxores, figuram pretendit Domini ac Redemptoris nostri qui habet duas plebes, primam scilicet ex circumcisionem, alteram uero ex pretio. Sed quia prima illa, id est synagoga Iudeorum, propter perfidiam suam odiosa effecta est, ecclesia uero, in dilectionem Redemptoris sui perseuerans dilecta appellatur… (fol. 57v)	In hoc Christus cum duabus Ecclesiis potest intelligi, qui non profert filium dilectae, id est populum Ecclesiae gentium, populum Synagogae in diuisionem substantiae, hoc est, in mandatis legis, a populo enim Synagogae, hoc est, a primitiua Ecclesia principium est. (col. 389)
23:1	Eunuchus iste qui non intra ecclesiam Domini, a parte totum significat quosdam intra ecclesiam effeminatos atque uitiis suis resolutos; qui cum sint natura uiri, carnali uitio eneruati, uelut femine efficiuntur quasi abciso ueretro. (fol. 61r)	… ostendit quod omnes qui molliter uiuunt, nec exercent opus uirile, non possunt permanere in numero sanctorum, siue congregationc. (col. 391)
23:3	Sicut enim per manzer Iudei, ita per Amanitas et Moabitidas, heretici atque scismatici accipiuntur qui neque per legem neque per Euangelium quem se recipere gloriantur, in ecclesia sanctorum, propter errorem suum, introibunt. (fol. 61r)	Significat ab Ecclesia haereticos semper esse repellendos. Haereticum autem, inquit, hominem post unam et alteram correptionem deuita. (col. 391)
24:1-4	Tropologice autem mulier haec significat sinagoga Iudeorum quam sibi Dominus retro olim per cognitionem legis sociauit… (fol. 62v)	Hic homo Christum significat, uxor Synagogam Iudaeorum, quae Christum non inuenit persequendo, et ad crucem trahendo… (col. 392)
25:11-12	Viri iurgientes inter se, doctores significant ecclesiam de dispensationem dominice incarnationis diuersa sentientes, e quibus ille qui aduersus alterum preualet, de catholicum demonstrat qui per auctoritatem ueritatis, hereticum conuicit et refutat… (fol. 66r)	Per hos duos uiros doctor perfectus et imperfectus potest intelligi, et per uxorem, haereticorum ecclesia, quae uult haereticum liberare de manu doctoris perfecti, mittens opus haereseos ad opus perfectum boni doctoris: cujus ecclesiae opus abscindendum est. (col. 394)

---

1   Cf. "Basan, confusio. Hoc enim agit diabolus ut semper concludat uiam quae ducit ad uitam. Conclusio enim praecedit ut rex, confusio subsequitur tanquam plebs; quia quos concludit ne credant in Christum, quomodo apparuerit confundatur." PL 91, col. 370; "Dominus denique legem in decem uerba constituit. Nullus numerus crescit amplius, nisi usque ad decem: si enim uiginti numeraueris, decem habes; si triginta, decem triplicabis; et sic inuenies quantumcunque progressus fueris, ac per hoc in plenitudine numeri plenitudinem mandatorum constituit, quae scilicet mandata sic quidam distinguunt, ut tria pertineant ad dilectionem Trinitatis, septem uero ad amorem fraternum, quibus societas humana non laeditur…" PL 91, col. 318.

Continued

Deut.	The Lyon Annotations (Paris, BnF, NAL 1740)	β recension of Pseudo-Bede (PL 91)
27:12-13	Duo hii montes utrumque Testamentum signifi-casse non dubium est; a quibus mons Garizim, in quo ad benedicendum sex tribus steterunt, Nouum significat Testamentum in quo populus electus non in timore seruili sed amore caritatis, Dei precepta implere satagit... (fol. 69v)	In duobus autem montibus Gezirim et Ebal, in quibus benedictiones et male-dictiones inferuntur, utrumque Testa-mentum significare potest... (col. 394)

Leave aside the question how the Lyon Annotator got access to Isidorian exegesis, it is still clear that the Lyon Annotations' dependence on the Isidorian tradition is much looser than those post-Isidorian Deuteronomy commentaries that we have examined in Chapter 6.2–6.5. The Isidorian exegesis in *Expositio* is not the dominant backbone any more, its proportion in the whole commentary is much lower (less than 10%). The Lyon Annotations broke through the Isidorian dominance in exegesis of Deuteronomy.

6.7   Conclusion of Part II: The Patristic Tradition and Innovation of the Lyon Annotations

Margaret Gibson in her fundamental study of Carolingian glossed Psalters described these glosses as "technically innovative but exegetically conservative," because despite the innovation in *mise en page*, their glosses themselves are predominantly based on Cassiodorus' *Expositio Psalmorum* or Bede's revised version of it known as *Titulatio*.[1] Similarly, Michele Ferrari in his study of Zürich, Staatsarchiv, W3.19.XII, the earliest *édition commentée* as he identified it, called the author of the Ezekiel commentary that the manuscript contains "a devout Gregorian," because he excerpted from Gregory's homilies on the Gospels to compose his commentary.[2] In comparison, the marginal annotations on Deuteronomy in Paris, BnF, NAL 1740, a Bible book updated to édition commentée (cf. Chapter 2.3), is anything but "exegetically conservative." Instead, the way it was composed helps enrich our traditional picture of early medieval and Carolingian biblical exegesis.

As we have seen through multiple examples in last three chapters, there is rarely a single entry in the Lyon Annotations that is copied verbatim. This feature makes it difficult to carry out the source criticism of this commentary. The ideal way of presenting it would be a critical edition with source apparatus, which, however, is beyond the goal of this book. Instead, The author chooses to list all the possible direct sources and count the word number of the expositions in the Lyon Annotations that derive from these sources.

---

1   Cf. Margaret Gibson, "Carolingian Glossed Psalters," pp. 78, 96-98.
2   Michele Camillo Ferrari, "Before the 'Glossa ordinaria,'" p. 294.

In Chapters 4–6, most of them have been examined in close detail. For the rest (Isidore's *Sententiae* and Bede's four-book commentary on Song of Songs), the author shows the reason to see them as sources in following footnotes. The whole Lyon Annotations has 14,223 words. The proportions of these expositions within the whole commentary have been accordingly calculated (Table 6.10).

Table 6.10 Statistics of source using of the Lyon Annotations

Identifiable direct sources (possible)	Word count	Percentage
Origen-Jerome, *Homiliae in Ieremiam*	101	0.7
Origen-Rufinus, *Homiliae in Exodum*	41	0.3
Origen-Rufinus, *Homiliae in Iesu Naue*[1]	31	0.2
Jerome's Hebrew etymologies	131	0.9
Ambrose , *De Tobia*	97	0.7
Eucherius, *Formulae*	137	1.0
Pseudo-Eucherius, *De diuinis nominibus*	66	0.5
Gregory-Paterius, *Liber testimoniorum*[2]	206	1.4
Gregory, *Moralia*	97	0.7
Isidore, *Sententiae*[3]	26	0.2
Pseudo-Bede, *the Pentateuch commentary (β)* [Isidore, *Expositio in uetus testamentum*]	1516 [1006]	10.6 [7.1]
Bede, *Cantica canticorum libri VI* [4]	116	0.8
Total	**2565**	**18%**

1 "Et facti sumus propter fidem Christi nos 'sursum,' ille autem populus, qui permansit incredulus, 'deorsum,' secundum Deuteronomii prophetiam. Si qui ergo habet in se Christum, qui est 'omnium caput,' hic efficitur 'in caput;' illi enim negauerunt Christum Iesum et effecti sunt in caudam et qui erant 'primi,' facti sunt 'nouissimi.'" Origen, *Homiliae in Iesu Nave*, VII.5, GCS 30, p. 332. Cf. "Aduena populum significat gentium qu(i) ante aduentum Saluatoris quasi in *cauda* reprobus erat, post eius uero aduentum per gratiam ipsius factu est priori; Iudei uero qui primi erant, facti sunt nouissimi." Paris, BnF, NAL 1740, fol. 74v, on Deut. 28:43-44.

2 As far as Gregory's exposition is concerned, Isidore's *Expositio* is taken as the primary potential source, Paterius's *Liber testimoniorum* as the secondary, and Gregory's original works as the third.

3 "Primum preceptum in hoc loco de destructione idolorum est: idolarie quippe cultus omni peccato deterior sit; nemo enim in culpa maior quam ille qui Deum nescit." Paris, BnF, NAL 1740, fol. 34v, on Deut. 12:1-2. Cf. Isidore, *Sententiae*, II.1.6, CCSL 111, p. 92. "Nullus autem in culpa maior est quam ille qui Deum nescit."

4 "Terra lacte et melle manantem tipice incarnationem Domini significat siue sancta ecclesia que simplici cibo nutrit paruulos suos donec ad perfectam etatem perueniant; melle autem id est spiritali cibo perfectos alit; potest et per terram lacte et melle manantem, supernam significare patriam." Paris, BnF, NAL 1740, fol. 20r, on Deut. 6:3; "Terram lacte et melle manantem tropologice ecclesiam dicit que lacte, id est simplici cibo, paruulos suos nutrit; melle uero hoc est spiritali intellectu perfectos alit; potest et per terram fluentem lacte et melle celestem significare patriam." Paris, BnF, NAL 1740, fol. 32v, on Deut. 11:8-9; "*Terram lacte et melle manantem* ecclesiam dicit que simplici doctrina tamquam lac paruulos nutrit, spiritali uero cibo uelut mel spiritalis aliter qui cum propheta dicere possunt: Quam dulcia faucibus meis eloquia tua, super mel et fauum ori meo." Paris, BnF, NAL 1740, fol. 67v, on Deut. 26:9. Cf. Bede, *Cantica canticorum libri VI*, II.1.6, CCSL 119B, p. 261. "In lacte eruditio paruulorum in melle ea quae perfectioribus competit doctrina signatur."

This source criticism is naturally tentative. Regarding early medieval intellectual transmission, to scholars today, there is always much more hidden than revealed. For example, we never know for sure the literary repertoire accessible to an author living in southern Gaul ca. 800. There could have been a certain lost or to be identified early medieval commentary on Deuteronomy, known to the Lyon Annotator but not to us. However, if we concentrate on the reception of known Church Fathers, it is clear that, on one hand, the Lyon Annotator had an extensive knowledge of patristic exegesis. The comparatively wide spectrum of patristic exegetical tradition that the Lyon Annotator utilized — in comparison with the post-Isidorian commentaries that we have examined in Chapter 6 — was a witness to the initial stage of the increasing availability of the works of Church Fathers that characterized the Carolingian Renaissance.[1]

On the other hand, the overall patristic proportion in the whole Lyon Annotations is not high. W can take two slightly later Carolingian biblical commentaries as comparisons. The first is Claudius of Turin's commentary on Joshua, composed in early 827.[2] As said above, Claudius had been a cleric in Leidrad's Cathedral until he left for the royal court of Louis the Pious, and he could have known the Lyon Annotations either literarily or orally (cf. Chapter 2.4.3). Claudius composed his commentary on the sixth book of the Old Testament by collecting "the words of our precursors who were ahead of us both in learning and in era."[3] According to Pascal Boulhol's study, Claudius' commentary on Joshua consists of approximately 4% original exposition, around 4% biblical citation, and 91% excerpts from the works of Church Fathers, including: Origen-Rufinus' *Homiliae in Iesu Naue*; Augustine's *Quaestiones in Heptateuchum* and *Locutiones in Heptateuchum*; Isidore's *Expositio in uetus testamentum*; Paterius' *Liber testimoniorum*, Jerome's Hebrew etymological works; Bede's *Quaestiones in Regum librum XXX*.[4] If Claudius had managed to carry out his abortive plan to comment on Deuteronomy, it would likely have been a similar scissors-and-paste work, dependent on the *dicta maiorum* on this biblical book, and on Exodus, Leviticus, and Numbers.[5]

About a decade after Claudius' project on the Pentateuch, Hrabanus Maurus, then the abbot of Fulda, undertook to compose a series of commentaries on the same biblical books at the request of Freculf who had just become the bishop of Lisieux to assist

---

1   Bernice Kaczynski, "The Authority of the Fathers."
2   On the dating of the commentary, cf. Pascal Boulhol, *Claude de Turin*, pp. 15-32.
3   "Et ob hoc omitto Deuteronomii librum, qui pene in superioribus libris, id est Exodo, Leuitico atque Numerorum magna ex parte iuxta litteram et spiritum a nobis iam expositus est, et ad librum Iesu Nauae agiographum ex dictis maiorum nostrorum, qui nos et scientia et tempore praecesserunt, transire desidero..." Claudius, Letter 11, *Epistolae Karoli aevi (II)*, p. 609.
4   Cf. Pascal Boulhol, *Claude de Turin*, pp. 281-282.
5   "Et ob hoc omitto Deuteronomii librum, qui pene in superioribus libris, id est Exodo, Leuitico atque Numerorum magna ex parte iuxta litteram et spiritum a nobis iam expositus est..." Claudius, Letter 11, *Epistolae Karolini aevi (II)*, p. 609.

the latter with pastoral care.[1] The last one on Deuteronomy was accomplished in the later 820s, an encyclopedic commentary of great length, four times as long as the Lyon Annotations.[2] Hrabanus lamented to Freculf that he was not able to find sufficient patristic exegetical sources (*dicta maiorum*) to compile his commentary, so he resorted to the relevant expositions that he had compiled for the first four biblical books, and, "for what I found newly inserted by the Legislator [Moses], by the gift of Divine Grace, I took care to bring something trivial according to my little talent."[3] In this arguably most original commentary ever composed by Hrabanus, however, more than 50% consists of passages excerpted verbatim from as many as 26 patristic sources, the backbone of which are the Deuteronomy sections of Augustine's *Quaestiones in Heptateuchum*, of Isidore's *Expositio in uetus testamentum* and Paterius' *Liber testimoniorum*.[4]

Instead of copying related patristic excerpts verbatim or almost verbatim, and pasting them together with a certain amount of original exposition to shape a running commentary as Claudius and Hrabanus did, the Lyon Annotator engaged himself with the patristic tradition in a more active way. In the previous three chapters, we have seen multiple examples of how the Lyon Annotator confidently paraphrased, abridged, and re-contextualized the patristic excerpts. Here are two more examples specifically showing how the Isidorian exposition was adopted in the convenient format "x signifies y" and applied to expounding alternative Deuteronomic verses.

---

1 "Nouit, mi dilectissime, tuae charitatis beneuolentia in occiduo littore Oceani, quamuis nullis suffragantibus meritis, pastoralem me suscepisse curam: ubi populum famem passum uerbi salutaris reperi, sed minime suam sentientem inediam. Non enim spirituales esuriendo desiderabat dapes, quarum suauitatis gustum necdum expertus erat; quem primum lacte alendum, non solido censui cibo. Igitur, annuente Domino, escam iam ambiunt contingere, et quamuis adhuc paruuli, panem sibi dari deposcunt: sed ut eis frangatur, et in uiscera eorum salubriter traiiciatur absque discrimine strangulationis, uestro indigemus solatio, maxime autem in Pentateucho." Freculf's letter to Hrabanus Maurus, PL 107, col. 439.

2 PL 108, cols 837-998 + Paul-Irénée Fransen, "La fin inédite du commentaire de Raban Maur sur le Deutéronome."

3 "Sed quia in hunc librum cuiuspiam explanationem proprie non inueni, necesse habui ut perfectis anteriorum librorum expositionibus, inde ad huius libri enodandas quaestiones assumerem facultatem. Haec autem quae nouiter a legislatore inserta reperi, diuina gratia largiente, pro modulo nostri ingenioli, quantulumcunque explanare curaui." Hrabanus, *Enarratio super Deuteronomium*, PL 108, cols. 838-839.

4 The author's statistics are based upon Silvia Cantelli, *Hrabani Mauri opera exegetica*, vol.2, pp. 553-76. The identified sources include: Josephus, *Antiquitates*; Origen-Rufinus, *Homiliae in Numeros*; Ambrose, *In epistulam ad Romanos*; Ambrose, *Epistula XIV* and *XV*; Jerome, *Epistula XXXIX* and *LXXVIII*; Jerome, *Liber de situ et nominibus locorum hebraicorum*; Jerome, *Liber interpretationis hebraicorum nominum*; Jerome, *Commentarii in Ezechielem*; Jerome, *Commentariorum in Matthaeum libri VIII*; Jerome, *Commentarii in Esaiam*; Augustine, *Quaestiones in Heptateuchum*; Augustine, *Enchiridion*; Augustine-Eugippius, *Excerpta ex operibus sancti Augustini*; Caesarius of Arles, *Sermones*; Hesychius, *Commentarius in Leuiticum*; Cassiodorus, *Expositio Psalmorum*; Gregory-Paterius, *Liber testimoniorum*; Gregory, *Dialogorum libri IV*; Gregory, *Homiliae in Euangelia*; Isidore, *Etymologiae*; Isidore, *Expositio in uetus testamentum*; Bede, *De templo Salomonis*; Bede, *In Lucae Euangelium expositio*; Bede, *Explanatio Apocalypsis*; Pseudo-Bede, *the Pentateuch commentary (β)*; Alcuin, *Expositio in Iohannis Euangelium*.

For Deut. 5:14 ("The seventh is the day of the sabbath, that is, the rest of the Lord thy God. Thou shalt not do any work therein, thou nor thy son nor thy daughter, nor thy manservant nor thy maidservant, nor thy ox, nor thy ass..."), the ox and the ass are interpreted as "docti et indocti" in the Lyon Annotations. Its exegetical origin is the first part of the exposition in Isidore's *Expositio* for Deut. 22:10 ("Thou shalt not plough with an ox and an ass together"): "Fatuum sapienti in praedicatione non socies..."[1] Similarly, for Deut. 6:7 ("And thou shalt tell them to thy children, and thou shalt meditate upon them sitting in thy house..."), the house is interpreted as "our consciences" in the Lyon Annotations. It originates from the exposition in Isidore's *Expositio* for Deut. 25:13–14 ("Thou shalt not have divers weights in thy bag, a greater and a less; neither shall there be in thy house a greater bushel and a less") which instructs: "We shall not have double measures in the house of our conscience."[2]

Meanwhile, the Lyon Annotator was also not timid to resort to the Bible directly to support and elaborate his exposition. The quotations from biblical books other than Deuteronomy constitute around 5% of the whole of the Lyon Annotations. They are overwhelmingly but not exclusively from Psalms, Pauline Epistles, and Gospels (Table 6.11).

Table 6.11   Bible citations in the Lyon Annotations

Biblical books	Frequency		Biblical books	Frequency	
Psalms	22		Romans	10	
Wisdom	2		1 Corinthians	4	
Isaias	1		2 Corinthians	4	
Ezechiel	2		Galatians	1	
Matthew	9		Ephesians	2	
Mark	2	22	Philippians	1	32
Luke	4		1 Thessalonians	1	
John	7		1 Timothy	4	
Acts	2		Titus	1	
James	1		Hebrews	4	
Peter	1				

Almost all these biblical quotations are likely to be supplied by the Annotator himself, rather than copied second-handedly from patristic works.

To sum up, the large proportion of original exposition, the organic utilization of patristic source, and the confident direct appeal to biblical *testimontia* make the Lyon An-

---

1 "Cum dicitur tui, doctoribus ecclesie loquitur; per filis ac filias, utriusque sexus religiosas appellat; per seruum et ancillas, seculares demonstrat; per bouem et asinum doctos et indoctos insinuat..." Paris, BnF, NAL 1740, fol. 18r. Cf. Isidore, *Expositio in uetus testamentum*, V.6, PL 83, col. 361.

2 "In domo sedemus quando intra conscientias nostras a terrenis actibus quiescimus." Paris, BnF, NAL 1740, fol. 20v. Cf. Isidore, *Expositio in uetus testamentum*, V.12, PL 83, col. 364.

notations a challenge to the present understanding of the exegetical practice in the era of Charlemagne. Based on his study of Wigbod's commentary on Genesis, Michael Gorman regarded the age of Charlemagne a modest starting phase of the Carolingian biblical exegesis: "Perhaps the achievement of the second generation of exegetes who worked for Louis the Pious, men such as Claudius of Turin, can be distinguished from those of the first generation who had worked for Charlemagne (Wigbod, Alcuin, Theodulf) in this way: The first generation found and excerpted texts and compiled compendia and sets of *quaestiones*, usually preferring to avoid the patristic works themselves."[1] John Contreni held a similarly conservative opinion when he said that the exegetes in the age of Charlemagne, such as Wigbod, Alcuin, and Josephus Scottus, were "unprepared to confront the patristic tradition directly."[2] Claudio Leonardi also saw Wigbod as "the model for Carolingian exegesis... that would be applied particularly by the first and second generations of scholars and school teachers of the Carolingian era... who reduc[ed] to a minimum or to nil his own personal written contribution... [t]he choice of sources and their integration within the body of the text thus became the absolute criterion of exegesis."[3]

The Lyon Annotations simply does not fit in this traditional narrative. It is not a *catena* like the works of Wigbod or Peter of Pisa's *Quaestiones in Danielem*,[4] nor a compilation like Paul the Deacon's homiliary or Smaragdus' *Liber comitis*,[5] nor an abridgment of patristic commentary like Alcuin's on the Gospel of John and Josephus' on Isaiah,[6] or a florilegium like Theodulf's.[7] This commentary, produced in Lyon ca. 800, is an innovative and coherent exposition that confidently embraces the patristic tradition and integrates it for the purpose of teaching biblical knowledge to clerics and making the Deuteronomic precepts relevant to the present religious, moral, and social life of a Christian community. Its fortunate survival as marginal annotations enriches our imagination of the vitality of the exegetical practice in the age of Charlemagne.

---

1   Michael Gorman, "Wigbod and Biblical Studies under Charlemagne," p. 75.
2   John Contreni, "Carolingian Biblical Culture," p. 8.
3   Claudio Leonardi, "Aspects of Old Testament Interpretation," pp. 188-189.
4   Wigbod, see Chapter 6.2. Peter of Pisa's *Quaestiones in Danielem*, see PL 96, cols. 1347-1362.
5   For Paul the Deacon's homiliary, see PL 95, cols. 1059-1566. Cf. Cyril Smetana, "Paul the Deacon's Patristic Anthology," *The Old English Homily and its Backgrounds*, eds. Paul Szarmach, Bernard Huppe (Albany: State University of New York Press, 1978), pp. 75-97. For Smaragdus' *Liber comitis*, composed ca. 812, see PL 102, cols. 13-552, cf. Matthew Ponesse, "Standing Distant from the Fathers: Smaragdus of Saint-Mihiel and the Reception of Early Medieval Learning," *Traditio* 67 (2012): pp. 71-99.
6   For Alcuin's commentary on Gospel of John, dedicated to Charlemagne's daughters Gisela and Rodtruda, see PL 100, cols. 737-1008. Cf. Michael Gorman, "Rewriting Augustine." For Josephus Scottus' commentary, cf. Joseph Kelly, "The Originality of Josephus Scottus' Commentary on Isaiah," *Manuscripta* 24 (1980), pp. 176-180.
7   Cf. Michael Gorman, "Theodulf of Orléans and the Exegetical Miscellany."

PART III
OLD AND NEW

CHAPTER 7
DEUTERONOMY INTERPRETED AS CHRISTIAN COMMUNITY

Part III turns to analyze the ecclesiastical imaginary in the Lyon Annotations, namely, how the Christian church, its history and its opponents (pagans, heretics, and Jews) are presented via exegetical language. As a genre of medieval historical source, biblical commentary is often comparatively conservative and formulaic. It conveys exegetical stereotypes accumulated through tradition more often than expressing new ideas. However, a handful of recent studies have well demonstrated that this literary genre was not at all detached from contemporary concern, but is potentially revealing for scholars to explore the evolution of social and political thinking.[1]

The Lyon Annotations, as we have seen in Part II, is less dependent on patristic exegetical tradition than our common view of early medieval biblical commentary would suggest. What stands behind such exegetical innovation is not merely an exegete's confidence in his own hermeneutic skill, but also a scheme self-consciously applied to interpreting Deuteronomy as a book that teaches about the ecclesiastical order for a Christian community. To demonstrate how such a scheme is presented necessitates a careful reading of the exegetical lexicons and discourses used in the Lyon Annotations, especially those originally composed. This is the general method for the two chapters of Part III. The present chapter examines the major ways in which an imaginary Christian community is presented through the exposition of Deuteronomy: how Israel is interpreted as the Church, and how Deuteronomic precepts are transformed into Christian teachings applicable to various aspects of the church life.

---

1   For example, Philippe Buc, *L'Ambiguïté du Livre: Prince, pouvoir et peuple dans les commentaires de la Bible au Moyen Âge* (Paris: Beauchesne, 1994), also see his "*Principes gentium dominantur eorum*: Princely Power Between Legitimacy and Illegitimacy in Twelfth-Century Exegesis," *Cultures of Power: Lordship, Status, and Process in Twelfth-Century Europe*, ed. Thomas Bisson (Philadelphia: University of Pennsylvania Press, 1995), pp. 310-328; Sumi Shimahara, *Haymon d'Auxerre*; John Contreni, "By Lions, Bishops are Meant."

7.1 *Spiritalis Israel*: The Chosen People as a Christian *Ecclesia*

In the terminology repertoire in the Lyon Annotations, one phrase that stands out is *spiritalis Israel*. The whole commentary starts with the programmatic entry:

> Deuteronomy is the repetition of the Old Law. This repetition pertains to the New Testament... [For if this book of Deuteronomy] is the figure of the second law, that is of the New Testament; [it contains] all the precepts of the Lord and His judgments regarding creation; [then] more to the new people, that is the Christian people, but in its newness nonetheless the spiritual Israel (*in nouitate tamen spiritalis Israel*)... rather than to the carnal people of Jews [who does not] cease to be blind.[1]

The very last entry of the Annotations is:

> *Blessed are thou, Israel. Who is like to thee, O people, that art saved by the Lord.* (Deut. 33:29)
> "Blessed be Israel," that is the chosen people; the head and the body are evidently Christ and the Church; no one outside Christ have been able to be like the Church, the people saved by the Lord, who is the Lord for this chosen people...[2]

In several other entries of the Lyon Annotations we see the notion that the Christian people (*populus christianus*) or the Church is the "spiritual Israel" and the "heir of the New Testament," the true receiver of the Law delivered by Moses, for example:

> *And Moses called all Israel, and said to them: Hear, O Israel, the ceremonies and judgments, which I speak in your ears this day. Learn them, and fulfill them in work.* (Deut. 5:1)
> Moses signifies that the Law that has been given through him, and the Law gives the precepts of living (*precepta... uiuendi*) not to the carnal Israel, that is Jews, but to the spiritual Israel, that is the Christian people, the heir of the New Testament.[3]

---

1 "Deuteronomium est ueteris iteratio legis; quae iteratio ad Nouum pertinet Testamentum... [Si enim liber hoc Deuteronomium] figura est secundae legis, id est Noui Testamenti, uniuersa precepta Domini atque iudicia que ad creationem pertinentia, magis ad nouum populum, hoc est cristianum sed in nouitate tamen spiritalis Israel [...] potiusquam ad carnalem populum Iudeorum [qui non] desiit esse caecus." Paris, BnF, NAL 1740, fol. 1r.

2 "Beatus Israel, id est populus electus, caput uidelicet et corpus, hoc est Christus et ecclesia, cui nullus similis extra eum esse poterat, populus saluatus a Domino, cui ipse Dominus est..." Paris, BnF, NAL 1740, fol. 92v.

3 "Per Moysen lex que per illum data est; que lex non tantum Israeli carnali id est Iudeis precepta dat uiuendi, sed maxime Israeli spiritali, id est populo christiani heredem Noui Testamenti." Paris, BnF, NAL 1740, fol. 17r.

The Lord, our God, made a covenant with us in Horeb. He made not the covenant with our fathers, but with us who are now present and living. (Deut. 5:2-3)

Take heed with an open mind (*aperta sententia*) how the Law that was delivered to the earlier people of Jews in Mount Sinai through Moses was not delivered for them, but was transmitted via them for us 'upon whom the ends of the world are come.' They were the carriers of the Law, not the doers (*factores*); but the heirs of the New Testament, that is the true Christians, prove to be not only carriers but also doers.[1]

Two Pauline passages are deftly insinuated in the latter annotation. The first is 1 Corinthians 10:11, whose context is the significance of Israelite history for Christians: "Now all these things happened to them in figure, and they are written for our correction, upon whom the ends of the world are come." It leads the discussion to the distinction between Christians and "Israel according to the flesh."[2] The second is Romans 2:13, about law and justification: "For not the hearers of the law are just before God, but the doers of the law shall be justified." It culminates in the well-known Pauline statement about the "inward Jew" and the "spiritual circumcision."[3]

In the Lyon Annotations, there is a clear eschatological implication in the notion of *spiritalis Israel*:

Hear, O Israel: Thou shalt go over the Jordan this day. (Deut. 9:1)

Hear this, you Israel! You deserve to be not the carnal Israel but rather the spiritual Israel, who through the grace of faith [are] the true Israel, and enter the Promised Land, that is the Church, through the grace of baptism as if through River Jordan. In the Church, if you live 'soberly, and justly, and godly in this world' (cf. Titus 2:12), you will be able to go over through it to the heavenly homeland after death, in which you might live forever.[4]

---

1   "Nota aperta sententia quomodo lex que priori populo Iudeorum in montem Sinai per Moysen data est, non ad illos tantum data est, sed per illos ad nos in quos fine(s) seculorum deuenerunt, transmissa est; illi enim portitores legis fuerunt, non factores; heredes uero Noui Testamenti id est ueri cristiani, non solum portitores sed et factores conprobantur." Paris, BnF, NAL 1740, fol. 17r.

2   "Haec autem omnia in figura contingebant illis: scripta sunt autem ad correptionem nostram, in quos fines saeculorum deuenerunt." (1 Corinthians 10:11) "Quoniam unus panis, unum corpus multi sumus, omnes qui de uno pane participamus. Videte Israel secundum carnem: nonne qui edunt hostias, participes sunt altaris?" (10:17-18)

3   "Non enim auditores legis iusti sunt apud Deum, sed factores legis iustificabuntur." (Romans 10:11) "Non enim qui in manifesto, Iudaeus est; neque quae in manifesto, in carne, est circumcisio. Sed qui in abscondito, Iudaeus est; et circumcisio cordis in spiritu, non littera, cuius laus non ex hominibus, sed ex Deo est." (2:28-29)

4   "Audi Israel! Non tantum carnalis Israel sed potius spiritalis qui per gratiam fidei uerus Israel esse meruisti, qui per baptissimi gratiam uelu<t> per fluenta Iordanis terram repromissionis id est ecclesiam, introisti. In qua ecclesia, *si sobriae, iuste et pie uixeris*, per illam ad celestem patriam post mortem transire poteris, in qua in aeternum uiuas." Paris, BnF, NAL 1740, fol. 27r.

Similar are the annotations for Deut. 6:3 and 10:12-13:

> *Hear, O Israel, and observe to do the things which the Lord hath commanded thee...* (Deut. 6:3)
>
> Hear this, you spiritual Israel who deserve to be the true Israel by faith, and do not mean to be unfaithful and to be the despiser of God's precepts like that carnal Israel, that is the Jewish people, who became rebellious against God.[1]

> *And now, Israel, what doth the Lord, thy God, require of thee but that thou fear the Lord, thy God, and walk in his ways, and love him and serve the Lord thy God, with all thy heart and with all thy soul and keep the commandments of the Lord and his ceremonies, which I command thee this day, that it may be well with thee?* (Deut. 10:12-13)
>
> And now, you Israel who are the true and spiritual Israel, pay attention and hear with the whole heart those things that are dictated to you through the Law, and keep in mind, because God requires nothing else from you but that you love Him with all your heart, with all your soul, and all your strength, and guard His precepts that it may be well with you forever.[2]

The message behind the constant use of the phrase "spiritual Israel" is that the Christian church fulfills the Deuteronomic precepts in their truest or spiritual sense. As we have seen in Part II, the spiritual sense had become the primary pursuit of the exposition of Deuteronomy by early Middle Ages. The Lyon Annotator took one step further to emphasize the true recipients of the spiritual sense of the "second legislation" themselves as spiritual. This is the coherent exegetical scheme of the whole commentary.

The "spiritual" understanding of "Israel" played a vital role in the formation of early and patristic Christianity.[3] The exact phrase "spiritual Israel" never appears in the New

---

1 "Audi, spiritalis Israel, qui per fidem meruisti esse uerus Israel and noli esse incredulus et contem<p>tor preceptorum D<dei> sicut carnalis ille Israel id est populus Iudeorum qui rebellis extitit aduersus Deum." Paris, BnF, NAL 1740, fol. 20r.

2 "Et nunc Israel, qui uerus et spiritalis Israel es, intende et ex toto corde audi ea que tibi per legem dicuntur, et scito quia nihil a te aliud Deus requiret nisi ut diliges eum ex toto corde tuo et in tota anima tua et ex totis uiribus tuis et custodias precepta eius ut bene sit tibi in aeternum." Paris, BnF, NAL 1740, fol. 30v.

3 Graham Harvey, *The True Israel: Uses of the Names Jew, Hebrew, and Israel in Ancient Jewish and Early Christian Literature* (Leiden: Brill, 1996), pp. 225-256; Robert Hayward, *Interpretations of the Name Israel in Ancient Judaism and Some Early Christian Writings from Victorious Athlete to Heavenly Champion* (Oxford: Oxford University Press, 2005), pp. 330-351; more generally, see Marcel Simon, *Verus Israel: Study of the Relations Between Christians and Jews in the Roman Empire, AD 135–425*, trans. Henry McKeating (Liverpool: Liverpool University Press, 1996); for the Judaic background, cf. Michael Mach, "Verus Israel: Towards a Clarification of a Jewish Factor in Early Christian Self-Definition," *Concepts of the Other in Near Eastern Religions*, ed. Ilai Alon (Leiden: Brill, 1994), pp. 143-171.

Testament books, but the idea is implicit in the language of Pauline epistles, including the two passages (1 Corinthians 10:18 and Romans 2:28-29) analyzed above.[1] Justin Martyr seems to have been the first Christian author to collocate "Israel" and "spiritual."[2] In the Latin tradition, Jerome in his translation of Origen adopted the phrase *spiritalis Israhel*, and used it in his own writings.[3] Augustine used similar terms extensively in his works.[4] "Spiritalis Israel" or the like, curiously, does not show up often, if ever at all, in the writings of Gregory and Isidore. At the time of Charlemagne, we find the expression *spiritalis Israhel, id est populi Christiani* in Alcuin's commentary on the Gospel of John. The relevant passage, however, is not Alcuin's original, but is drawn from a Gospel homily of Bede.[5] More significant is the following passage found in the *Opus Caroli* composed by Theodulf:

---

1   E.g.: "Israel secundum carnem" (1 Corinthians 10:18), "circumcisio cordis in spiritu, non littera" (Romans 2:28-29), and "Non enim omnes qui ex Israel sunt, ii sunt Israelitae" (Romans 9:6).

2   "We have been led to God through this crucified Christ, and we are the true spiritual Israel, and the descendants of Juda, Jacob, Isaac, and Abraham, who, though uncircumcised, was approved and blessed by God because of his faith and was called the father of many nations. All this shall be proved as we proceed with our discussion." Justin Martyr, *Dialogue with Trypho*, The Fathers of the Church 6, trans. Thomas B. Falls (Washington, D.C.: Catholic University of America Press, 1948), p. 156.

3   "Quapropter consurgentes laudemus Dominum et fiamus pro carnali Israhel spiritalis Israhel." Origen, *Homiliae in Lucam*, XII, GCS 49, p. 88; Cf. Jerome, *Commentarii in Isaiam*, VI.15.1, CCSL 73, p. 254: "Quomodo circumcisio et carnalis est et spiritalis, et de spiritali ab Apostolo dicitur: *Nos enim sumus circumcisio, qui spiritu deo seruimus et gloriamur in domino, et non in carne confidimus. Et rursum ad distinctionem spiritalis israelis, dicitur de carnali: Videte israel secundum carnem*; et: *Vos gentes in carne*." Also cf. Origen, *De principiis*, IV.3.6, GCS 22, p. 332: "Per quod significat utique quod sit et alius Israhel, qui non sit 'secundum carnem' sed secundum spiritum."

4   E.g.: "Sic fit Israel spiritalis non unius gentis sed omnium quae promissae sunt patribus in eorum semine, quod est Christus. Hic ergo Israel spiritalis ab illo Israele carnali, qui est unius gentis, nouitate gratiae non nobilitate patriae et mente non gente distinguitur." Augustine, *De doctrina christiana*, III.113-114, ed. Green, p.184; "Ideo quippe addidit, carnaliter uel secundum carnem, quia est israel spiritaliter uel secundum spiritum, qui ueteres umbras iam non sequitur, sed eam consequentem quae illis umbris praecedentibus significata est ueritatem." Idem, *Contra aduersarium legis et prophetarum*, I, CCSL 49, ed. Klaus-D. Daur (Turnhout: Brepols, 1985), pp. 68-69; "Nos enim sumus Israel populus Dei: *Nos in uerbis dicentis agnoscimus, audi, populus meus, et loquar tibi, Israel, et testificabor tibi.*Quid sumus ad ista dicturi? Nouimus quidem Israel spiritualem, de quo dicit Apostolus: *Et quicumque hanc regulam sequuntur, pax super illos et misericordia, et super israel Dei.*" Idem, *Tractatus aduersus Iudaeos*, PL 42, col. 57; "Quid est autem quod poscis ut astruam, Si Pater et Filius et Spiritus sanctus unus est Deus: cum hoc astruat uoce clarissima Scriptura diuina dicens: *Audi, Israel; Dominus Deus tuus, Dominus unus est.* Quod et uos utique audiretis, si Israel esse uelletis, non carnaliter ut iudaei, sed spiritualiter ut Christiani." Idem, *Contra Maximinum episcopum Arianorum*, II.23, PL 42, col. 796.

5   "Potest etiam haec Domini sententia, qua dixit se Nathanael prius quam uocaretur a Philippo, cum esset sub ficu, uidisse, super electione spiritalis Israhel, id est populi Christiani, mystice intellegi, quem Dominus necdum se uidentem, necdum per apostolos eius ad fidei gratiam uocatum, sed sub tegimine adhuc peccati prementis abditum, misericorditer uidere dignatus est..." Bede, *Homeliae Euangelii*, I.17, CCSL 122, ed. David Hurst (Turnhout: Brepols, 1955), pp. 203-204; cf. Alcuin, *In Evangelium Ioannis*, PL 100, col. 764. For the context of Bede and *spiritalis Israel*, see Andrew Scheil, *The Footsteps of Israel: Understanding Jews in Anglo-Saxon England* (Ann Arbor: University of Michigan Press, 2004), pp. 1-97.

He [Moses] also ordered crimson fringes to be made in the four corners of robes, either for the sake of distinguishing the people of Israel, so that [the fringes] be a sign on clothing, just like circumcision was the sign on the body; or in order that we, the spiritual Israel, may have the justice and the holy way of life (*conuersatio*) as clothing; the rim of the clothing is decorated with fringes, as if we learn in our life the testimonies of sacred scriptures. The good use of fringes was abused badly rather than held by the carnal Israel, but granted well by the legislator to us, the spiritual Israel.[1]

This passage itself is an original exposition of a piece of the Old Law (Numbers 15:38 "Thou shalt tell them to make to themselves fringes in the corners of their garments, putting in them ribands of blue" = Deut. 22:12 "Thou shalt make strings in the hem at the four corners of thy cloak, wherewith thou shalt be covered"). Theodulf's idea that the Old Law was granted to *nos qui spiritalis Israel sumus* is remarkably similar to what we find in the Lyon Annotations.[2]

In an oft-cited paper, Mary Garrison critically analyzed the evolution of the discourse of the Franks as the new Israel or the chosen people during the reigns of Pippin the Short and Charlemagne. She reached a rather conservative conclusion: "The Franks as the New Israel" was far from a common identity during the second half of the eighth century; even as late as ca. 800, its use was still conditional and ambiguous.[3] However, if we switch our perspective, it seems that the identification of the new/true/spiritual Israel with the non-ethnic Christian church was readily in place in the reign of Charlemagne.

The *sancta ecclesia*, sometimes juxtaposed with *populus christianus*,[4] is an important political concept that characterized Carolingian Europe. Its two constituent elements are,

---

1 "Iussit quoque fimbrias iacinctinas fieri in quattuor angulis palliorum, siue ad dinoscendum populum Israel, ut essent signum *in ueste*, sicut *circumcisio signum in corpore*, siue ut nos, qui spiritalis Israel sumus, habeamus pro indumento iustitiam et sanctam conuersationem, huius indumenti extremitas fimbriis iacinctinis sit ornata, quatenus uita nostra sanctarum Scripturarum sit testimoniis erudita. Hic enim fimbriarum bonus usus et bene per legislatorem sive illi carnali Israheli sive nobis, spiritali, bene concessus, male ab illis abusus potius quam habitus est." Theodulf, *Opus Caroli*, I.17, pp. 183-184. For an insightful analysis of this passage, cf. Conor O'Brien, "Empire, Ethnic Election and Exegesis in the *Opus Caroli (Libri Carolini)*," *Studies in Church History* 54 (2018): pp. 96-108.

2 For a good summary of the ecclesiological principles of Theodulf's *Opus Caroli*, see Thomas F. X. Noble, *Images, Iconoclasm, and the Carolingians*, pp. 207-243. More generally, see Elisabeth Dahlhaus-Berg, *Nova antiquitas et antiqua novitas: typologische Exegese und isidorianisches Geschichtsbild bei Theodulf von Orléans* (Köln: Böhlau, 1975).

3 Mary Garrison, "The Franks as the New Israel? Education for an Identity from Pippin to Charlemagne," *The Uses of the Past in the Early Middle Ages*, eds. Yitzhak Hen and Matthew Innes (Cambridge: Cambridge University Press, 2000), pp. 114-161. For further discussion, cf. Conor O'Brien, "Chosen Peoples and New Israels in the Early Medieval West," *Speculum* 95 (2020): pp. 987-1009.

4 E.g., *Annales regni Francorum*: "Inde autem itinere permoto partibus Baioariae perrexit, ad Reganesburg peruenit, ibi exercitum suum coniunxit. Ibique consilio peracto Francorum, Saxonum, Frisonum, disposuerunt propter nimiam malitiam et intollerabilem, quam fecerunt Auari contra sanctam ecclesiam uel populum christianum...", anno 791, MGH Fontes iuris Germanici antiqui in usum scholarum separatim editi VI, ed. Friedrich Kurze (Hannover: Hahnsche, 1895), p. 88.

as Mayke de Jong nicely put it, "a clergy that ministered effectively, and a people that found mercy in the eyes of God."[1] The connoted connection — on one hand, between the Christian community and God; on the other hand, between the sacred history and the present — was crystallized in the Israelite identity which embodied both the anxiety to keep the *cultus diuinus* according to the *norma rectitudinis* and the eschatological pursuit of salvation. Not surprisingly, one of the decisive hinges for such identity structure was the Old Law — the Old Testament in general, but the Mosaic precepts in particular — and how Christians should understand and apply it.[2]

An example of this *par excellence* was Charlemagne's well-known capitulary, the *Admonitio generalis* of 789. Calling himself *gratia Dei eiusque misericordia donante rex et rector regni Francorum et deuotus sanctae ecclesiae defensor humilisque adiutor*, Charlemagne claimed to imitate the Israelite king Josiah, "who was zealous to call back the kingdom committed to him by God to the cult of the true God by visitation, correction, and admonition." He thus "decided to promulgate certain *capitula*" for the secular and ecclesiastical elites of his realm to preach to their subjects.[3] The first 59 *capitula* are conciliar decrees drawn from *Collectio Dionysio-Hadriana*.[4] After them are "some other *capitula* which seem to me advantageous to subjoin to the previous admonition."[5] These entries are largely backed up by direct biblical quotations. This section starts with those that derive from the evangelical command of double love to God and neighbors (cc. 60 and 61). A large proportion of the entries that follow are directly related to the Old Law (nos. 62-67, 71, 72, and 79), including but not limited to the Ten

---

1 Mayke de Jong, "The State of the Church: *Ecclesia* and Early Medieval State Formation," *Der frühmittelalterliche Staat: Europäische Perspektiven*, eds. Walter Pohl, Veronika Wieser (Vienna: Verlag der Österreichischen Akademie der Wissenschaften, 2009), pp. 241-254.

2 Cf. Mayke de Jong, "Old Law and New-Found Power: Hrabanus Maurus and the Old Testament," *Centres of Learning: Learning and Location in Pre-Modern Europe and the Near East*, eds. Jan Willem Drijvers, Alasdair MacDonald (Leiden: Brill, 1995), pp. 161-176; Wilfried Hartmann, "Die Karolingische Reform Und Die Bibel"; Gerda Heydemann, "The People of God and the Law: Biblical Models in Carolingian Legislation," *Speculum* 95 (2020): pp. 89-131.

3 "Nam legimus in regnorum libris, quomodo sanctus Iosias regnum sibi a Deo datum circumeundo, corrigendo, ammonendo ad cultum ueri Dei studuit reuocare, non ut me eius sanctitate aequiperabilem faciam, sed quod nobis sunt ubique sanctorum semper exempla sequenda, et quoscumque poterimus, ad studium bonae uitae in laudem et in gloriam Domini nostri Iesu Christi congregare necesse est. Quapropter, ut praediximus, aliqua capitula notare iussimus, ut simul haec eadem uos ammonere studeatis, et quaecumque uobis alia necessaria esse sciatis, ut et ista et illa aequali intentione predicetis. Nec aliquid, quod uestrae sanctitati populi Dei utile uideatur, amittite, ut pio studio non ammoneatis, quatenus ut et uesstra sollertia et subiectorum oboedientia aeterna felicitate ab omnipotente Deo remuneretur." *Admonitio generalis*, pp. 182, 184.

4 For a challenge to this traditional scholarly view, see Abigail Firey, "Mutating Monsters: Approaches to 'Living Texts' of the Carolingian Era," *Digital Proceedings of the Lawrence J. Schoenberg Symposium on Manuscript Studies in the Digital Age* 2 (2010): pp. 1-14. However, Michael Glatthaar in his introduction to the latest MGH edition of the *Admonitio generalis* still held that the first part of the capitulary is "ein konzises Elaborat einzig und allein aus der Collectio Dionysio-Hadriana."

5 "Sunt quoque aliqua capitula, quae nobis utilia huic praecedenti ammonitione subiungere uisa sunt." *Admonitio generalis*, p. 210.

Commandments. The Pentateuch and Wisdom books are quoted extensively.[1]

The only biblical book cited by name in the *Admonitio generalis* is Deuteronomy.[2] There are four explicit or implicit quotations from Deuteronomy in the capitulary, dealing with four crucial politico-religious issues of Charlemagne's realm: worshiping and loving the single God (c. 60, Deut. 6:4-5); making just judgment and rejecting bribes (c. 62, Deut. 1:16-17);[3] forbidding divinations (c. 64, Deut. 18:10-11); keeping vow (c. 72, Deut. 23:21). As Henry Mayr-Harting observed, "the authors [of the *Admonitio generalis*] were much more thinking *through* Deuteronomy *as a whole* [Mayr-Harting's own emphasis], and its moral implication."[4] It may not be purely coincidence. The law code that King Josiah, Charlemagne's model ruler, discovered and used as a blueprint to reform his kingdom, as recorded in 2 Kings 22–23, is thought by modern scholars to be related to Deuteronomy, if not this biblical book *per se*.[5] It is hard to know for sure whether Charlemagne and his counselors had the same notion in mind and consciously applied Deuteronomic precepts as part of the project of becoming the new Josiah leading the new Israel. One piece of indirect evidence came from several decades later in the *Glosa in Deuteronomium* of Walahfrid Strabo, who introduced this biblical book in the following words: *Hic etiam liber sub Iosia legitur in templo repertus ut uidelicet populo praeuaricanti meritam maledictionem proponeret.*[6]

In sum, the typological thinking that the Christian community is the present mirror of the past chosen people of God was not a notion unfamiliar in the reign of Charlemagne. "The Church" as the object of Charlemagne's reform, however, was not primarily a territorial or demographic unit, but a ministering one. The macro-*ecclesia* under the leadership of Charlemagne consisted of a myriad of local micro-*ecclesiae* governed by political and ecclesiastical elites who were explicitly targeted as the primary audience of *Admoni-*

---

1 The quoted biblical books include Exodus, Leviticus, Deuteronomy, Psalms, Proverbs, Ecclesiastes, and Wisdom.

2 "... non in adolatione nec in consideratione personae, sicut in Deuteronomio dictum est: Quod iustum est, iudicate, siue ciues sit ille siue peregrinus, nulla sit distantia personarum, quia Dei iudicum est." Ibid., LXII, p. 212; "Item habemus in lege Domini mandatum: *Non auguramini*. Et in Deuteronomiio: Nemo sit, *qui ariolo sciscitetur* uel *somnia observet* uel *ad auguria* intenda. Item: *Ne sit maleficus nec incantator nec phitones consolator.*" Ibid., LXIV, p. 216.

3 Notice that the same Deuteronomic citation can be found in Alcuin's *Liber de uirtutibus et uitiis*, XX, PL 101, col. 629: "Non est persona in iudicio consideranda, sed causa. Scriptum est enim: *Non accipies personam in iudicio*. Iniqui iudices errant in ueritatis sententia, dum intendunt qualitatem personae: et nocent saepe iustis, dum improbe defendunt impios. Acceptio munerum in iudiciis, praeuaricatio est ueritatis. Qui Deum timentes iuste iudicant, aeterna a Domino accepturi sunt praemia."

4 Henry Mayr-Harting, "Charlemagne's Religion," *Am Vorabend der Kaiserkrönung: Das Epos "Karolus Magnus et Leo papa" und der Papstbesuch in Paderborn 799*, eds. Peter Godman, Jörg Jarnut, Peter Johanek (Berlin: Akademie Verlag 2002), pp. 113-124.

5 Cf. Christoph Bultmann, "Deuteronomy." As did Mayr-Harting, John Contreni also noticed this connection. See his "Carolingian Biblical Culture," pp. 1-3.

6 Sankt Gallen, Stiftsbibliothek, 283, p. 621.

tio generalis: *omnes ecclesiasticae pietatis ordinibus seu saecularis potentiae dignitates*.[1] The realistic counterpart of the *spiritalis Israel* in the Lyon Annotations is not an ethnic group or a political realm but a *plebs ecclesiastica* under the rule of a bishop and priests, not unlike Leidrad's Lyon as we have examined it in Chapter 3.

In order to prove this argumentation, let us take a close look at a particular Deuteronomic passage. Around 775, an obscure Anglo-Saxon named Cathuulf composed a mirror for princes for Charlemagne in epistolary format.[2] He started it with stating how Charlemagne enjoyed the special grace of God who "exalted you in the honor of glory of the reign of Europe." Charlemagne thus should take up the duty to "guard and rule over all the members of Him [God] on behalf of Him, and render account in the judgment of God." Auxiliary to him are the bishops who are "in the secondary place on behalf of Christ." To all of them Cathuulf exhorted: "Consider diligently between you how to establish the law of God over the people of God."[3] He then provided a set of imitable exempla, the very first of which was based on the Deuteronomic passage on king making (Deut.17:14-20):

> There are a great number of exempla for (*uobis*) to elevate the Law. I am writing down a few first, as the canons bring forth and the law of all of Christendom (*totius christianitatis lex*) contains according to the commands of God. After belief in God and love and fear of God, may you often hold (*habeas*) the handbook (*enchyridion*), that is to say the manual book, the written law of your Lord in your hands; may you read (*legas*) it every day of your life so that you may be imbued with divine wisdom and secular learning, as were David, Solomon, and the other kings. Like God said to Moses about kings: "When he is raised to the throne of his kingdom, the book of the Law will never leave his hands. He shall not have many wives; nor be arrogant over his contemporaries, puffed up or jealous and etc.; but judge rightly between the poor

---

1   *Admonitio generalis*, p. 180.

2   Cf. Mary Garrison, "Letters to a King and Biblical Exempla."

3   "Nunc igitur, domine mi rex, pro his modis beatitudinum nocte et die com omnibus exercitibus tuis da gloriam Deo regi regnorum et gratiarum acciones com omni regno tuo: quod ipse te exaltauit in honorem glorie regni Europe. Et adhuc etiam maiora prestat tibi horum, namque praedictorum, si illum exaltas cum suis hoc modo. Memor esto ergo semper, rex mi, Dei regis tui cum timore et amore, quod tu es in uice illius super omnia membra eius custodire et regere, et rationem reddere in die iudicii, etiam per te. Et episcopus est in secundo loco, in uice Christe tantum est. Ergo considerate inter uos diligenter legem Dei constituere super populum Dei..." *Epistolae Karolini aevi (II)*, pp. 502-503.

and the powerful, rescue the poor from the hand of the powerful [and etc.]."[1]

Notice how Cathuulf in this passage switched the object of his admonition between the second-person plural, namely Charlemagne and bishops, and the second-person singular, namely Charlemagne alone. The Deuteronomic exemplum of law-keeping kings was directed to the Frankish king alone. In 831, the exact same biblical passage was taken by Jonas of Orléans to admonish Charlemagne's grandson, Pippin I of Aquitaine in his *De institutione regia*.[2]

Now, we turn to the five annotations on the same Deuteronomic passage in the Lyon Annotations:

> *When thou art come into the land which the Lord, thy God, will give thee and possessest it and dwellest in it and shalt say: I will set a king over me, as all nations have that are round about, thou shalt set him whom the Lord, thy God, shall choose out of the number of thy brethren. Thou mayst not make a man of another nation king that is not thy brother.* (Deut. 17:14-15)
>
> Land which Lord the God promised to give to holy preachers signifies the Holy Church. In the Church, he orders that nobody other than those elected by the Lord via grace of faith and purity of life to lead the people as kings or judges, that is bishops or priests, not anyone heretical nor spotted with whatever mortal vice.[3]

---

1 "Exempla perplurima sunt, ut legem exaltetis. Primum pauca uobis scribo, sicut canones promunt et totius christianitatis lex continet per Dei mandatum. Post fidem Dei et amorem et timorem, ut sepius habeas enchyridion, quod est librum manualem, legem Dei tui scriptum in manibus tuis; ut legas illum omnibus diebus uite tue, ut tu sis in sapientia diuina et secularibus litteris inbutus, sicut Dauid et Salomon et ceteri reges fuerunt. Item dixit Deus ad Moysen de regibus: 'Cum sederit in solio regni sui, numquam recedet liber legis de manibus suis: non uxores plures habeat; non superbum super coetaneos suos, non elatum, non inuidiosum' et reliqua; sed recte iudicare inter pauperem et potentem, et pauperem eripere de manu potentis [et reliqua]." *Epistolae Karolini aevi (II)*, p. 503.

2 "De rege autem, qualis esse uel quid cauere debeat, ita in Deuteronomio legitur: Cum ingressus fueris terram, quam Dominus Deus tuus dabit tibi et possederis eam habitaueris que in illa et dixeris: constituam super me regem, sicut habent omnes per circuitum nationes, eum constitues quem Dominus Deus tuus elegerit de numero fratrum tuorum, et post pauca: Non habebit uxores plurimas, quae inliciant animum eius neque argenti et auri inmensa pondera. Postquam autem sederit in solio regni sui, describat sibi Deuteronomium legis huius in uolumine, accipiens exemplar a sacerdotibus leuiticae tribus et habebit se cum leget que illud omnibus diebus uitae suae, ut discat timere Dominum Deum suum et custodire uerba et caerimonias eius, quae lege praecepta sunt. Nec extolletur cor eius in superbiam super fratres suos neque declinet in partem dextram uel sinistram, ut longo tempore regnet ipse et filii eius super Israhel. Adtende quod timor Dei et custodia praeceptorum eius et humilitas quae non patitur eum extollere super fratres suos et iustitiae rectitudo non solum regem, sed et filios eius longo faciet regnare tempore." Jonas of Orléans, *De institutione regia*, III, SC 407, ed. Alain Dubreucq (Paris: Éditions du Cerf, 1995), p. 186.

3 "Terram quam Dominus Deus sanctis predicatoribus dare pollicitus est, sanctam signifcat ecclesiam: in qua ecclesia reges uel iudices id est episcopos siue prespiteros, non alios nisi quos Dominus per gratiam fidei et uite puritatem elegerit preponere populo iubet, non hereticos neque quolibet mortali uitio maculosos." Paris, BnF, NAL 1740, fol. 48v.

And when he is made king, he shall not multiply horses to himself nor lead back the people into Egypt... He shall not have many wives, that may allure his mind, nor immense sums of silver and gold. (Deut. 17:16-17)

Salomon neglected to observe this precept, who, allured by the love of women, turned out to fall into the cult of idols. But now (*nunc autem*), the haughty priests in the Church, who love wealth, indulge in pleasure, and live luxuriously, by their own perverse example and word provoke the people subject to them not to the heavenly homeland, but to the concupiscence of this world that they have renounced in baptism, as if lead them back to Egypt. For Egypt is the figure of this world, and the life of Egypt is the way of life (*conuersatio*) of gentiles.[1]

But after he is raised to the throne of his kingdom, he shall copy out to himself the Deuteronomy of this law in a volume, taking the copy of the priests of the Levitical tribe, and he shall have it with him and shall read it all the days of his life... (Deut. 17:18-19)

Deuteronomy, namely the repetition of the Law, is the figure of the Gospel, on which all who preside in the Church should meditate day and night, as the blessed Apostle Paul said to his disciple Timothy who was a bishop himself: "Till I come, attend unto reading, to exhortation, and to doctrine (1 Timothy 4:13)," and slightly later, "Take heed to thyself and to doctrine: be earnest in them. For in doing this thou shalt both save thyself and them that hear thee (1 Timothy 4:16)."[2]

And that his heart be not lifted up with pride over his brethren nor decline to the right or to the left... (Deut. 17:20)

This is what the Apostle says about recently elected bishops: "Not a neophyte, lest being puffed up with pride, he fall into the judgment of the devil." (1 Timothy 4:16) Right refers to the prosperity of the present life or the praise, but left refers to the adversity of this world or the blame of people.[3]

---

1 "Hoc preceptum Salamon custodire neclexit qui amore mulierum inlectus, usque ad idolorum cultum declinauit; nunc autem in ecclesia sacerdotes elati, diuitiarum amatores, deliciis abluentes atque luxoriose uiuentes, subiectas sibi non ad celestem patriam prouocant sed exemplo prauitatis suae et uerbo, ad concupiscentias mundi quas in baptismo renuntiauerunt, quasi ad Egiputm reuocant. Egyptus enim figura est mundi, uita Egypti conuersatio gentilium." Paris, BnF, NAL 1740, fol. 49r.

2 "Deuteronomium id est iteratio legis, figura est Euangelii quam omnes qui presunt ecclesiae die ac nocte meditare debent, dicente beato Paulo apostolo ad Timotheum discipulum suum, qui et ipse erat episcopus: Dum uenio, adtende lectioni et exortatione doctrine; et post pauca: Adtende tibi doctrine, insta in illis: hoc enim faciens, et teipsum saluum facies et qui te audierint." Paris, BnF, NAL 1740, fol. 49r.

3 "Hoc est quod Apostolus de nuper conuersis episcopis ait: Non neofitum, ne in superbia elatus, in iudicium incidat diaboli; per dexteram, prosperitas uitae presentis siue laus humana, per sinistram uero aduersitas seculi huius seu uituperatio hominum." Paris, BnF, NAL 1740, fol. 49v.

... that he and his sons may reign a long time over Israel. (Deut. 17:20)

Not in the present age but in the future one.[1]

Clearly, in the Lyon Annotations, the embodiment of the *spiritalis Israel* is an *ecclesia*, an ecclesiastical community led by the bishop and his priestly team. What shaped this identity is the exegetical transformation of Deuteronomic precepts into Christian religious and ethical teachings, the topic we will turn to now.

7.2 *In Figura and inter Litteram et Spiritum Discernere*: Deuteronomy Transformed into Christian Teachings

Fransen claimed that the Lyon Annotations "ne s'agit donc pas d'une interprétation systématique."[2] If we take a close look, however, clues remain to map the exegetical strategy, and one of them is its exegetical language. The following table shows the hermeneutical terminologies and the frequencies of their appearance in the Lyon Annotations (Table 7.1).

Table 7.1   Hermeneutical terminologies in the Lyon Annotations

Hermeneutical terminologies	Times
x significare y	99
x figura est y/figuraliter/x prefigurabit y/figuram exprimere/figuram gestare/figuram pretendere/figurata est/prefigurata est/prefiguratio/in figura/figurate	34
tipice	1
mistice	4
iuxta historiam	12
iuxta litteram	12
iuxta litteram... non spiritaliter	1
iuxta historiam... fieri non posse/secundum historiam... non convenire	3
spiritaliter/spiritalem intellegentiam/spiritalem intellectum/sensus spiritales	22
non carnaliter sed spiritaliter/non secundum litteram sed spiritaliter/non iuxta litteram sed spiritaliter/spiritaliter magis quam carnaliter/spiritaliter potius... quam iuxta litteram	7
tam carnaliter quam spiritaliter	1
tropologice	10
moraliter	1
iuxta anagogen, id est superiorem sensum	1
allegorice/secundum allegoricum... sensum	2

Foremost, it is clear that the major approach is allegorical or typological. The elements

---

1   "Non presenti seculo sed in futuro." Paris, BnF, NAL 1740, fol. 49v.
2   Paul-Irénée Fransen, "Un commentaire marginal lyonnais," p. 32.

in the biblical narrative (types) are interpreted as *figurae* to signify something pertinent to Christian doctrine (antitypes). The typological mentality is a fundamental heritage of the patristic exegesis of the Old Testament.[1] It is based on the assumption that the Old Testament prefigures the New, as Augustine once aptly put it: *In uetere nouum lateat et in nouo uetus pateat.*[2] The same idea is explicitly expressed in the first and programmatic entry of the Lyon Annotations: *Deuteronomium est ueteris iteratio legis; quae iteratio ad Nouum pertinet Testamentum.* The Christians as the "heirs of the New Testament" (*heredes Noui Testamenti*) are obliged to pursue the mysterious teachings hidden in the Second Law from the evangelical horizon. A set of common biblical typologies comes out repeatedly (Table 7.2).

Table 7.2   Typology in the Lyon Annotations

Type	Antitype
Deuteronomy	New Testament
Moses	the Law
Promised Land	Kingdom of Heaven/the Church
carnal Israel (Jews)	spiritual Israel (Christians)
six days	this world
the seventh day	the rest to come (*futura requies*)
the Canaanite nations	capital sins
Egypt	the secular world
Joshua	evangelical preaching

Many types and antitypes seem to be drawn from specific patristic works, especially Eucherius' *Formulae* and Isidore's *Expositio in uetus testamentum*, as we have already discussed in Part II. Meanwhile, the Lyon Annotator was obviously not timid about composing typological expositions of his own. Here we note three series of original expositions as example to demonstrate his exegetical capacity to turn Deuteronomic precepts into Christian teachings effectively. The first set is on the observance of the principle solemnities (the phase, the festival of weeks, and the solemnity of tabernacles):

> *Observe the month of new corn, which is the first of the spring, that thou mayst celebrate the phase to the Lord, thy God, because in this month the Lord, thy God, brought thee out of Egypt by night. And thou shalt sacrifice the phase to the Lord thy*

---

1   Cf. Frans van Liere, *An Introduction to the Medieval Bible* (Cambridge: Cambridge University Press. 2014), pp. 119-120. For the typological exegesis of the Church Fathers, see Jean Daniélou, *From Shadows to Reality: Studies in Biblical Typology of the Fathers*, trans. Wulstan Hibberd (London: Burns & Oates, 1960). For a theoretical reflection, see Frances Young, "Typology," *Crossing the Boundaries: Essays in Biblical Interpretation in Honour of Michael D. Goulder*, eds. Stanley E. Porter, Paul Joyce, David E. Orton (Leiden: Brill, 1994), pp. 29-48.

2   Augustine, *Quaestionum in Heptateuchum libri VII, in Exodum*, LXXIII, CCSL 33, p. 106.

God, of sheep and of oxen, in the place which the Lord, thy God, shall choose, that his name may dwell there. (Deut. 16:1-2)

Moses gives a command about when it is proper to celebrate the solemnity of the Passover. The place chosen by the Lord is the Catholic Church, outside which neither the Passover nor any other solemnities can be accepted by God. Even if heretics celebrate the solemnities at the same timings as the Church, since they celebrate outside the Catholic Church, they are not accepted by God.[1]

Thou shalt number unto thee seven weeks from that day wherein thou didst put the sickle to the corn. (Deut. 16:9)

Just like Moses admonishes the Church to celebrate the Passover in the figure of the phase, so he admonishes to observe the Pentecost, that is the advent of the Holy Spirit, in the figure of the solemnity of weeks, that is 50 days after the Passover. In the day of the Pentecost, the Holy Apostles put the sickle of their preaching upon those Jewish converts (*credentes ex Iudeis*) as if corn, when 3000 were converted and baptized in that day, and five thousand in another day.[2]

Thou shalt celebrate the solemnity also of tabernacles seven days when thou hast gathered in thy fruit of the barnfloor and of the winepress. (Deut. 16:13)

The festival of tabernacles signifies the perfection of saints. Just like the renewal of life (*innouatio uitae*) via baptism is to be understood in the figure of the Passover, and the consecration via the gift of the Holy Spirit in the figure of the day of the Pentecost, so in the figure of the festival of tabernacles is declared the fulfillment of all the virtues. For they celebrate the festival of tabernacles, who, according to evangelical preaching, sell all that they possess, give them to the poor, and follow the Lord free from secular solicitude.[3]

The second set is on the rite to expiate an unsolved murder:

---

1 "De sollemnitate Pasche preceptum dat quo tempore celebrari oportet. Locus electus a domino ecclesia catholica est extra quam neque Pascha neque alias sollemnitates Deo accepta esse non possunt; siquidem et heretici celebrant sollemnitates hisdem temporibus quibus et ecclesia, sed quia extra fidem catholicam celebrant, Deo accepta non sunt." Paris, BnF, NAL 1740, fol. 44v.

2 "Sicut per Fasse precipitur ecclesiae pascha celebrare ita et per sollemnitatem ebdomadarum id est quinquagesimo ide post pascha, Pentecosten, aduentum uidelicet Spiritus sancti uenerabliter custodire. In quo die Pentecosten sancti apostoli falce predicationis sue, credentes ex Iudeis quasi segete messuerunt cum in eodem die tria milia et in alio quinque milia conuersi ac baptizati sunt." Paris, BnF, NAL 1740, fol. 46r.

3 "Festiuitas tabernaculorum perfectionem sinificat sanctorum. Sicut enim per Pascha innouatio uitae per baptismum et per diem Pentecosten consecratio per donum Spiritus sancti accipitur, ita et per festiuitatem tabernaculorum complementum declaratur omnium uirtutum. Illi enim festiuitatem tabernaculorum celebrant qui secundum euangelicam predicationem uendunt omnia quae possident et dant pauperibus et liberi atque expediti a seculi sollicitudine, Dominum secuntur." Paris, BnF, NAL 1740, fol. 46v.

When there shall be found in the land, which the Lord thy God will give thee the corpse of a man slain and it is not known who is guilty of the murder... (Deut. 21:1)

In my opinion, the body of the man slain signifies the body of the Savior who without any fault was killed by the impious people. Moses certainly reveals this when he says the one guilty of the murder is not known, just like what is said in a psalm: "They asked me things that they knew not." (cf. Psalms 34:11) [1]

... thy ancients and judges shall go out and shall measure from the place where the body lieth the distance of every city round about, and the ancients of that city which they shall perceive to be nearer than the rest, shall take a heifer of the herd that hath not drawn in the yoke nor ploughed the ground... (Deut. 21:2-3)

The nearer city was Jerusalem near which the Lord suffered the Passion. It is without doubt that the ancients of that city were Annas, Caiphas, and other rulers of the people of Jews who went out of Jerusalem and brought the Lord to death. The heifer of the herd signifies the flesh of the same Lord, the posterity of the Patriarchs, and the flesh assumed by the Son of God; this flesh has not drawn the yoke of sin, nor has ploughed the ground, because the virgin born of a virgin did not know the works of corruption, when the blood makes the expiation of all the sinners, that is those who have believed in him. [2]

... and they shall bring her into a rough and stony valley, that never was ploughed, nor sown. (Deut. 21:4)

This *valley* is the figure of the world which had not been cultivated by the holy preachers before the advent of the Savior, nor received the seed of the Word of God. [3]

And the priests, the sons of Levi, shall come, whom the Lord, thy God, hath chosen to minister to him, and to bless in his name and that by their word every matter should be decided and whatsoever is clean or unclean should be judged... and shall say, "Our hands did not shed this blood, nor did our eye see it." (Deut. 21:5)

The priests, the sons of Levi, are to be understood as the Apostles who did not consent in the Passion of the Lord, as was said above; the guilt of Jews, namely what

---

1 "Cadauer hominis occisi, ut suspicor, corpus significat Saluatoris quod ab impiis absque culpa occisum est; hoc quippe demonstrat cum dicit: Ignoratur cedis reus; sicut est illud in psalmo: Que ignorabant, interrogabant me." Paris, BnF, NAL 1740, fol. 56r.

2 "Vicinior ciuitas Hierusalem fuit apud quam Dominus passus est. Seniores ciuitatis illius, Anna et Caifas ceterique principes populi Iudeorum fuisse non dubium est qui egredientes extra Jierusalem, Dominum mort<i> tradiderunt. Vitul<am> de armento, eiusdem d<omini> carnem et patriarch<a>rum posteritatem, carnem assumptam a Filio Dei significat; que caro iugum peccati non traxit nec mouere terram scindit, qu<ia> uirgo ex uirgine nata, corruptionis opera non nouit, cum sanguis expiatio fit omnium peccatorum , illorum uidelicet qui crediderunt." Paris, BnF, NAL 1740, fol. 56r.

3 "Haec uallis figura est mundi quae ante uentum Saluatoris a sanctis predicatoribus exculta non fuit nec semen uerbi Dei recepit." Paris, BnF, NAL 1740, fol. 56r.

were perpetrated upon Christ, could be washed out by those who believed in no other way than through the blood of Him whom they brought to death.[1]

And the guilt of blood shall be taken from them, and thou shalt be free from the innocent's blood that was shed when thou shalt have done what Lord hath commanded thee. (Deut. 21:8-9)

The faithful city, you are innocent of the innocent's blood, that is certainly the Passion of Christ the Lord, if you make penance and are baptized in the mystery of His death and Resurrection.[2]

The third set is on the commandments written on stones and the erection of an altar:

And Moses with the ancients of Israel commanded the people, saying: Keep every commandment that I command you this day. (Deut. 27:1)

By Moses, the Law is to be understood; by the ancients, the prophets.[3]

And when you are passed over the Jordan into the land which the Lord, thy God, will give thee, thou shalt set up great stones and shalt plaster them over with plaster... (Deut. 27:2)

The great stones which he ordered to set up after passing over Jordan and to plaster with plaster assumed the figure of Holy Apostles polished by faith and love, in whose hearts the Lord wrote down the Gospel, that is the Second Law, not by ink but by the Holy Spirit, and asked them to make it manifest to all the believers.[4]

... that thou mayst write on them all the words of this law when thou art passed over the Jordan, that thou mayst enter into the land which the Lord, thy God, will give thee, a land flowing with milk and honey, as he swore to thy fathers. (Deut. 27:3)

By Jordan the grace of baptism was prefigured, for just like the earlier people of Jews were not able to enter the Promised Land unless by passing over Jordan, so the Christian people, the heir of the New Testament, are not able to follow the Kingdom

---

1 "Sacerdotecons filii Leui apostoli accipiuntur qui in passione Domini, ut superius dictum est, non consenserunt; nec enim aliter reatus Iudeorum quod in Christo perpetrati sunt, ab eis qui crediderunt absolui potuit nisi per eius sanguinem quae [quem?] morti tradiderunt." Paris, BnF, NAL 1740, fol. 56v.

2 "Tu autem, plebs fidelis, innocens eris ab innocentis cruore, passione uidelicet Christi Domini, si egeris penitentiam et in sacramento mortis hac resurrectionis eius baptizatus fueris." Paris, BnF, NAL 1740, fol. 56v.

3 "Per Moysen lex, per seniores prophetae accipiuntur." Paris, BnF, NAL 1740, fol. 68v.

4 "Ingentes lapides quos transito Iordane erigere precepit calceque leuigare, figuram pretenderunt sanctorum apostolorum fide et caritate leuigatos; in quorum corda Dominus Euangelium, qui est secunda lex, non atramento sed Spiritu sancto scripsit et ad notitiam omnium credentium manifeste proposuit." Paris, BnF, NAL 1740, fol. 69r.

of Heaven unless they are renewed through the grace of baptism.[1]

... and thou shalt build there an altar to the Lord, thy God, of stones which iron hath not touched and of stones not fashioned nor polished... (Deut. 27:5-6)

This altar made of untouched stones which are not touched by iron signifies the unity of the Holy Church built by living stones, that is the holy people in the unity of faith and love. The iron of evil and division, that is the schism of heretics or any sort of wickedness, does not taint them or split them from the unity of the Catholic Church.[2]

And thou shalt write upon the stones all the words of this law plainly and clearly. (Deut. 27:8)

That is the evangelical preaching, or both the Testaments spiritually expounded.[3]

Besides *significare, figuraliter, figura est* etc., the other system of hermeneutical terminologies used in the Lyon Annotations include *iuxta historiam, spiritaliter, tropologice, allegorice*, and *iuxta anagogen*, which indicate the author's knowledge of the theory of multiple senses of Scripture that took shape in the Latin west during the early Middle Ages. John Cassian divided knowledge (*scientia*) into two categories (practical and theoretical), subdivided the latter into two (*historica interpretatio* and *intellegentia spiritale*), and differentiated three types of *intellegentia spiritale*:

Historia embraces the knowledge of past and of visible things... *allegoria* is related to what happened later, for what actually happened is said to have prefigured the form of another mystery... *Anagoge* ascends from spiritual mysteries even to still more sublime and more sacred secrets of Heaven... *Tropologia* is the moral explanation which

---

1 "Per Iordanem gratia baptismi prefigurata est; sicut enim prior ille populus Iudeorum terram repromissionis ingredi non potuit nisi transito Iordane, ita et populus cristianus, heres Noui Testamenti, regnum caelorum consequi non ualet nisi per baptismi gratia renouatus fuerit." Paris, BnF, NAL 1740, fol. 69r.

2 "Altare hoc ex lapidibus integris quos ferrum non tetigit constructum, unitatem significat sanctae ecclesiae ex uiuis lapidibus id est sanctis hominibus in unitatem fidei et caritatis aedificatum, quos ferrum nequitiae hac diuisionis id est hereticorum scisma uel quaelibet malitia non maculat neque ab unitate ecclesiae catholice scindit." Paris, BnF, NAL 1740, fol. 69r.

3 "Id est euangelicam predicationem siue utrumque Testamentum spiritaliter expositum." Paris, BnF, NAL 1740, fol. 69v.

pertains to improvement of life and actual teaching...[1]

Eucherius in the preface to his *Formulae* proposed the same scheme and specifically applied it to biblical interpretation:

Historia teaches the truth of historical events and the trustworthiness of the account, *tropologia* refers to the mystical understanding for the sake of the amendment of life, and *anagoge* leads to the more sacred secrets of heavenly symbols. Some people think that *allegoria* should be put in the fourth place in the class of knowledge, which, according to them, prefigures the future deeds in the narrative of the past deeds... The whole discipline of our religion has emanated from the double fountain of knowledge: they call the first *practicen* and the second *theoreticen*, that is practical and contemplative (*actualem et contemplatiuam*). One accomplishes a practical life in the correction of his habits; one turns to the other life in the contemplation of Heaven and the discussion of the Holy Scripture. So, the practical knowledge spreads from diverse pursuits, and the contemplative knowledge consists of two derivative parts:

---

1 "Sed ad expositionem scientiae de qua sumptum est sermonis exordium reuertamur. Itaque sicut superius diximus πρακτικὴ erga multas professiones ac studia deriuatur, θεωρητικὴ uero in duas diuiditur partes, id est in historicam interpretationem et intellegentiam spiritalem. Unde etiam Salomon cum ecclesiae multiformem gratiam enumerasset, adiecit: *Omnes enim qui apud eam sunt uestiti sunt dupliciter.* Spiritalis autem scientiae genera sunt tria, tropologia, allegoria, anagoge, de quibus in Prouerbiis ita dicitur: *Tu autem describe tibi ea tripliciter super latitudinem cordis tui.* Itaque historia praeteritarum ac uisibilium agnitionem conplectitur rerum, quae ita ab apostolo replicatur: *Scriptum est enim quia Abraham duos filios habuit, unum de ancilla et alterum de libera.* Sed qui de ancilla, secundum carnem natus est: *Qui autem de libera, per repromissionem.* Ad allegoriam autem pertinent quae sequuntur, quia ea quae in ueritate gesta sunt alterius sacramenti formam praefigurasse dicuntur. Haec enim, inquit, sunt duo testamenta, unum quidem de monte Sina, in seruitutem generans, quod est Agar. Sina enim mons est in Arabia, qui conparatur huic quae nunc est Hierusalem et seruit cum filiis suis. Anagoge uero de spiritalibus mysteriis ad sublimiora quaedam et sacratiora caelorum secreta conscendens ab apostolo ita subicitur: quae autem sursum est Hierusalem libera est, quae est mater nostra scriptum est enim: *Laetare sterilis quae non paris, erumpe et clama quae non parturis, quoniam multi filii desertae magis quam eius quae habet uirum.* Tropologia est moralis explanatio ad emundationem uitae et instructionem pertinens actualem, uelut si haec eadem duo testamenta intellegamus πρακτικὴν et theoreticam disciplinam, uel certe si Hierusalem aut Sion animam hominis uelimus accipere secundum illud: lauda Hierusalem dominum: lauda deum tuum Sion. Igitur praedictae quattuor figurae in unum ita, si uolumus, confluunt, ut una atque eadem Hierusalem quadrifarie possit intellegi: Secundum historiam ciuitas Iudaeorum, secundum allegoriam ecclesia Christi, secundum anagogen ciuitas dei illa caelestis, quae est mater omnium nostrum, secundum tropologiam anima hominis, quae frequenter hoc nomine aut increpatur aut laudatur a Domino." Cassian, *Collationes*, XIV.8, CSEL 13, pp. 404-405.

historica disputatio and *spiritalis intellegentiae interpretatio.*[1]

The Lyon Annotator might have been aware of the tripartite concept of spiritual senses, as he did name them a dozen of times. But the Christological, ecclesiological, eschatological, and moral interpretations are usually not clearly distinguished throughout the Lyon Annotations. Much more consistently implemented is the distinction between the spiritual and literal/historical ways of interpretation. This hermeneutical pair had been essential since the origin of Christian interpretation of the Hebrew Bible. Interpreting a biblical lemma *iuxta litteram* or *iuxta historiam* means taking its narration as historically real, its prophecy fulfilled in reality, or its precept as literally effective. In contrast, reading a biblical text *spiritaliter* is to go beyond sacred letters through a "hermeneutical leap" in the pursuit of a deeper understanding.[2] By the ninth century, the Carolingian exegetes used the two categories in a way as fundamental and extensive as their patristic predecessors, and meanwhile enriched their connotations and functions.[3]

To discern whether a Deuteronomic lemma should be understood *iuxta litteram* or *spiritaliter* was a primary concern for the author of the Lyon Annotations. One annotation describes the practice of biblical reading as "discerning between letter and spirit."[4] In a handful of cases, *inter litteram et spiritum discernere* means determining whether the biblical narrative makes sense historically or it is necessary to introduce spiritual

---

1   "Quapropter historia ueritatem nobis factorum ac fidem relationis inculcat, tropologia ad uitae emendationem mysticos intellectus refert, anagoge ad sacratiora caelestium figurarum secreta perducit. Sunt etiam qui allegoriam in hoc scientiae genere quarto in loco adicientam putent, quam gestorum narratione futurorum umbram praetulisse confirment. Haec uero ipsa ut subiectis plenius manifestentur exemplis, caelum est secundum historiam hoc quod intuemur, secundum tropologiam uita caelestis; aquae secundum allegoriam baptismus, secundum anagogen angeli, iuxta illud: Et aquae quae super caelos sunt laudent nomen Domini. Omnis autem disciplina nostrae religionis ex illo duplici scientiae fonte manauit, cuius primam practicen, secundam theoreticen uocauerunt, id est actualem et contemplatiuam; unam, quae actualem uitam morum emendatione consummet, aliam, quae in contemplatione caelestium et diuinarum scripturarum disputatione uersetur. Ergo actualis scientia in diuersa studia diffunditur, contemplatiua autem in duas deriuata partes, id est in historica disputatione et spiritalis intellegentiae interpretatione consistit." Cf. Eucherius, *Formulae spiritalis intellegentiae, Epistula ad Veranum*, CCSL 66, pp. 3-5.
2   For a good survey, see Robert Morgan, "Spirit and Letter: Mapping Modern Biblical Interpretation," *The Spirit and the Letter: A Tradition and a Reversal*, eds. Paul Fiddes, Günter Bader (London: Bloomsbury, 2013), pp. 43-73.
3   For The development of "literal sense" and "spiritual sense" in the Carolingian era, see Elisabeth Mégier, "Spiritual Exegesis and the Church in Haimo of Auxerre's Commentary on Isaiah," *The Multiple Meaning of Scripture: The Role of Exegesis in Early-Christian and Medieval Culture*, ed. Ineke Van't Spijker (Leiden: Brill, 2008), pp. 155-175; eadem, "*Historia* and *Littera* in Carolingian Commentaries on St Matthew: Elements for an Inventory of Exegetical Vocabulary in the Medieval Latin Church," *Producing Christian Culture: Medieval Exegesis and Its Interpretative Genres*, eds. Giles Gasper, Francis Watson, Matthew Crawford (New York: Routledge, 2017), pp. 89-113.
4   "Quid per silua nisi condensitatem sanctarum Scripturarum significat. De qua Scriptura in psalmo inscriptum est: Et reuelauit Dominus condensa. Ad ligna cedenda simpliciter cum proximo imus quando per conlatione mutua inter littera et spiritu discernimus..." Paris, BnF, NAL 1740, fol. 52r, on Deut. 19:5-6.

interpretation. The Annotator made his judgment discreetly. For instance, the command that the body of the man punished with death shall not remain on the tree but be buried on the same day (Deut. 21:22-23) could be understood *secundum litteram*, because it was fulfilled in the Passion of Christ.[1] Moses' curses to the transgressors of the Law in Deut. 28 can be taken *iuxta historiam*, because it reflects how the Jews suffered in history.[2] The blessing that no one would be barren among Israel (Deut. 7:14) should not be read *iuxta historiam*, since "we find that the spouses of the Patriarchs were barren according to the authority of sacred scriptures; rather, it signifies that "among the elected people, no soul would be barren or infertile, that is barren in faith or infertile in good deeds."[3] "The good land of brooks and of waters and of fountains" promised to Israel (Deut. 8:7) is to be interpreted *spiritaliter* as a foreshadowing of the Holy Church, because "there is no river other than Jordan in Canaan, and, as people say, in that region, when the rainfall is lacking, the shortage of water is a greater need than the necessity of food."[4] On some occasions, it is proper to expound according both to the historical and to the spiritual sense, such as God's promise to give rest to Israel and to subdue all the nations round about (Deut. 25:19) which "we read partly realized during the time of King Saul *iuxtam historiam*, but it will be fulfilled completely in the Judgment Day."[5]

More remarkable is how *inter litteram et spiritum discernere* functions to make Moses' moral precepts applicable to the Christian community. Some laws were thought to be promulgated only for the carnal Israel. For example, the punishment against the one who slanders his wife (Deut. 22:13-19) "was mandated to Jews *ad litteram*, due to their incontinence and in order to refrain their libido, so that they would never loosen the bridles of lust (*luxuria*) through various women everywhere."[6] The "carnal observance"

---

1 "Hoc quippe secundum litteram in eiusdem Domini corporis factum legitur, qui in eodem die quo passus est, et sepultus fuit." Paris, BnF, NAL 1740, fol. 58r.

2 E.g., "Iuxta historiam propter peccata umani generis non solum labores Iudeorum haec potestes deuoraberunt sed et a horum frequenter debasta<ti sunt>." Paris, BnF, NAL 1740, fol. 74r, on Deut. 28:38 ("Lucustae omnia deuoraberunt.") Also cf. "Hoc iuxta historiam Iudeis incredulis sub Romanis accidisse non dubium est." Paris, BnF, NAL 1740, fol. 87v, on Deut. 32:25 ("Foris uastabit eos gladius, et intus pauor, iuuenem simul ac uirginem, lactentem cum homine sene.")

3 "Iuxta historiam fieri non potuit ut in priori populo illo mulier nulla sterelis esset cum secundum auctoritatem sanctarum Scripturarum patriarcharum coniuges stereles fuisse recognoscimus; in populo uero electo nulla sterelis nullaque infecunda anima esse potest quae aut in fide sterelis sit aut in bonis operibus infecunda." Paris, BnF, NAL 1740, fol. 23v.

4 "Haec omnia spiritaliter in sancta ecclesia reperiuntur conlata a Domino, non in terra Canaan ubi preter Iordane fluuio alius nullus est; in qua regione, ut fertur, si quando pluuie desunt, maior penuria de aquarum inopia quam de ciborum necessitate fit." Paris, BnF, NAL 1740, fol. 25v.

5 "Hoc enim iuxtam historiam tempore Saulis regis ex parte factum legimus, perfecte autem in diem iudicii impletum erit." Paris, BnF, NAL 1740, fol. 66v.

6 "Hoc preceptum ad litteram Iudeis, propter incontinentiam eorum atque refrenendam libidinem mandatum est ut nequaquam passim eis frena luxurie per diuersas feminas laxarent." Paris, BnF, NAL 1740, fol. 59r.

of the Law ceased after the advent of Christ.[1] For example, concerning the law of divorce (Deut. 24:1-4):

> The Jews were accustomed to do so *ad litteram*. But because the Lord prohibits such things to be done in the Gospel, the rule is to be understood *spiritaliter* rather than *carnaliter*.[2]

For the command of immediate punishment:

> In the Old Testament, that is in the Law, due to the stubbornness of Jewish people, the punishment of retribution against offenders was not delayed, but as soon as one of them sinned, he was punished immediately so that others who [saw him] punished would fear to perpetrate the same sins lest they suffer similar punishments. But in the New Testament, sinners should be punished not by the death of flesh but by the death of sins, so that they are put to death in the flesh sense, but live according to the spirit of God.[3]

For the command that "thou shalt eat the spoils of thy enemies" (Deut. 20:14):

> These precepts are for the carnal people to follow *iuxta litteram*; it is not proper for the spiritual people under the grace of the Gospel to observe them *secundum historiam*.[4]

Christians are compared to the animals that not only chew the cud but divide the hoof in two parts, because they not only meditate on the Law but also make distinction between letter and spirit, while Jews who meditate on the Law but fail to distinguish between letter and spirit are signified by the animals that chew the cud but do not divide the

---

1   "Sicut per Moysen, ut sepe dictum est, figurata est lex quae in aduentu Saluatoris in carnalibus obseruationibus defuncta est, ita per Iosuae, successore Moysi, significatus est Chrsitus Dominus, qui populum suum ad celestem patriam praebuit." Paris, BnF, NAL 1740, fol. 83v, on Deut. 31:14 ("Abierunt ergo Moyses et Iosue et steterunt in tabernaculo testimonii.")

2   "Hoc Iudei ad litteram facere consueti erant. Sed quia Dominus in Euangelio talia fieri prohibet, idcirco spiritaliter magis quam carnaliter accipiendum est." Paris, BnF, NAL 1740, fol. 62v.

3   "In Vetero Testamento id est in lege propter duritiam populi Iudeorum in delinquentibus pena ultionis non differebatur sed mox ut quis ex illis peccasset, confestim puniebatur ut ceteri uidentes timerent talia perpetrare ne similia paterentur. In Nouo autem Testamento peccatores non morte carnis puniendi sunt sed morte uitiorum ut mortificentur quidem secundum carnem, uiuant autem secundum Domini in spiritum." Paris, BnF, NAL 1740, fol. 39r. Also cf. "Lex peccatores puniri iubet; in Euangelio uero non eosdem delinquentes sed facinora illorum funditus de ecclesia extirpare iubet." Paris, BnF, NAL 1740, fol. 47v, on Deut. 17:5 ("Educes uirum ac mulierem qui rem sceleratissimam perpetrarunt ad portas ciuitatis tuae, et lapidibus obruentur.")

4   "Carnali populo iuxta litteram haec facere precepta sunt; quod spiritalibus sub Euangelii gratia secundum historiam custodire non conuenit." Paris, BnF, NAL 1740, fol. 55r.

hoof.[1]

The major yardstick for discernment is the Gospel or the New Testament. For the commandment "life for life, eye for eye, tooth for tooth, hand for hand, foot for foot" (Deut. 19:21):

> This judgment was put forward in a similar way in the books of Exodus and Leviticus. But because the Lord prohibited to do so in the Gospel, it is to be understood *non secundum litteram sed spiritaliter* about heretics, for those who kill the lives of others by the sword of their tongues put their own lives to death. Concerning other members, it is to be understood in a similar way.[2]

For the command to set free the Hebrew servant after the service of six years (Deut. 15:12):

> You will find the precept in the book of Exodus in a similar way. But because no such thing was admonished in the New Testament, it is thus better to be understood *spiritaliter* rather than *iuxta litteram*.[3]

However, in the Lyon Annotations, there are indeed a handful of Deuteronomic precepts that pass the "Gospel test," i.e., are considered acceptable to the "spiritual Israel" according to the literal sense (Table 7.3).

Table 7.3 Precepts according to literal sense in the Lyon Annotations

Deut.	Precepts
6:5	Thou shalt love the Lord thy God with thy whole heart, and with thy whole soul, and with thy whole strength.[4]
7:2	Thou shalt make no league with them [pagans].[5]
10:20	To Him [God] thou shalt adhere, and shalt swear by His name.[6]

---

1 "...inter littera et spiritu uelut ungulam diuidentes atque in lege diuina die noctuaque meditantes, tamquam munda animalia ruminantes." Paris, BnF, NAL 1740, fol. 40v, on Deut. 14:6; "Quid per camelum animal altum, inorme, ni scribas et phariseos significari uult; ruminantes quidem, id est in lege meditantes sed inter litteram et spiritum nequaquam diuidentes." Paris, BnF, NAL 1740, fol. 41r, on Deut. 14:7.

2 "Hoc iudicium in libro Exodi et in Leuitico similiter premissum est. Sed quia Dominus in Euangelio ita facere prohibuit, ideo non secundum litteram sed spiritaliter de hereticis accipiendum est ut qui aliorum animas gladio in lingue suae interficiunt, suas necent. Similiter et de cetera membra spiritaliter intellegendum est." Paris, BnF, NAL 1740, fol. 53v.

3 "Hoc preceptum in libro Exodi similiter repperies. Sed quia in Nouo Testamento nihil tale preceptum est, idcirco spiritaliter potius est accipiendum quam iuxta litteram." Paris, BnF, NAL 1740, fol. 44r.

4 "Hoc habes in Euangelio." Paris, BnF, NAL 1740, fol. 20v.

5 "Hec omnia iuxta historia et priori populo custodire oportuit et sequenti populo cristiano non neglegere." Paris, BnF, NAL 1740, fol. 22v.

6 "Veraciter, non fallaciter." Paris, BnF, NAL 1740, fol. 31r.

Continued

Deut.	Precepts
15:7-8	If one of thy brethren that dwelleth within the gates of thy city in the land which the Lord thy God will give thee, come to poverty, thou shalt not harden thy heart, nor close thy hand, but shalt open it to the poor man, thou shalt lend him, that which thou perceivest he hath need of.[1]
16:19	Thou shalt not accept person nor gifts.[2]
18:10-11	Neither let there be any wizard, nor charmer, nor any one that consulteth pythonic spirits, or fortune tellers, or that seeketh the truth from the dead.[3]
22:1	Thou shalt not pass by if thou seest thy brother's ox, or his sheep go astray, but thou shalt bring them back to thy brother.[4]
22:3	Thou shalt do in like manner with his ass, and with his raiment, and with every thing that is thy brother's, which is lost, if thou find it, neglect it not as pertaining to another.[5]
22:5	A woman shall not be clothed with man's apparel, neither shall a man use woman's apparel.[6]
22:23-24	*On adultery or/and rape* (see below)[7]
23:21	When thou hast made a vow to the Lord thy God, thou shalt not delay to pay it.[8]
24:10	When thou shalt demand of thy neighbour any thing that he oweth thee, thou shalt not go into his house to take away a pledge.[9]
24:14	Thou shalt not refuse the hire of the needy, and the poor.[10]
24:15	But thou shalt pay him the price of his labour the same day, before the going down of the sun, because he is poor, and with it maintaineth his life.[11]
24:19	When thou hast reaped the corn in thy field, and hast forgot and left a sheaf, thou shalt not return to take it away, but thou shalt suffer the stranger, and the fatherless and the widow to take it away.[12]
24:20	If thou have gathered the fruit of thy olive trees, thou shalt not return to gather whatsoever remaineth on the trees, but shalt leave it for the stranger, for the fatherless, and the widow.[13]

---

1 "Sunt plerique intra ecclesia qui timendo futuram paupertatem, nullam misericordiam plectuntur erga proximos suos indigentes; aiunt enim: Si ea que possideo pauperibus erogauero, unde sum sustentaturus meipsum atque domesticos meos?" Paris, BnF, NAL 1740, fol. 43v.

2 "Audiant haec auari iudices et desinant contemplatione auaritie, personarum acceptores fieri." Paris, BnF, NAL 1740, fol. 47r.

3 "Hoc iuxta historiam fidelibus cristianis omnibus modis uitandum est." Paris, BnF, NAL 1740, fol. 50v.

4 "Patet sensus qui iuxta historiam a fidelibus obseruandus est." Paris, BnF, NAL 1740, fol. 58r.

5 "Hoc enim et Dominus in Euangelio precipit cum dicit: Omnia quecumque uultis ut faciant uobis homines, et uos facite illi<s> similiter. Haec est enim lex et prophetae." Paris, BnF, NAL 1740, fol. 58r.

6 "Hoc enim et iusta historiam facere indecens est..." Paris, BnF, NAL 1740, fol. 58v.

7 "Hoc simpliciter iusta litteram accipiendum est, non spiritaliter." Paris, BnF, NAL 1740, fol. 60r.

8 "Patet manifestus sensus iuxta litteram..." Paris, BnF, NAL 1740, fol. 62v.

9 "... Hoc et secundum litteram fideli cristiano facere conuenit..." Paris, BnF, NAL 1740, fol. 64r.

10 "Et hoc iuxta litteram omnis modis facere conuenit." Paris, BnF, NAL 1740, fol. 64r.

11 "Patet sensus iuxta litteram." Paris, BnF, NAL 1740, fol. 64r.

12 "Patet sensus iuxta litteram..." Paris, BnF, NAL 1740, fol. 64v.

13 "... tamen et ad litteram fideli christiano facere conuenit." Paris, BnF, NAL 1740, fol. 64v.

Continued

Deut.	Precepts
25:13-14	Thou shalt not have divers weights in thy bag, a greater and a less, neither shall there be in thy house a greater bushel and a less.[1]
27:21	Cursed be he that lieth with any beast.[2]

Remarkably, the table above contains all the four Deuteronomic quotations in *Admonitio generalis* that we have seen in Chapter 7.1 — worshiping and loving the single God, making just judgment and rejecting bribes, forbidding divinations and keeping vows — implying a certain shared approach to the reception of the Old Law in the age of Charlemagne. Most of those literally accepted precepts are moral, related to charity, justice, and normal social behavior. They make one of the Lyon Annotations's a few examples of the Christian adoption of the Old Testament Law in the early Middle Ages.[3]

A good example is the annotation *Hoc simpliciter iuxta litteram accipiendum est, non spiritaliter* at the margin of the right column of fol. 60r, nearby the passage about the law of adultery and rape (Deut. 22:23-29):

> If a man have espoused a damsel that is a virgin and some one find her in the city and lie with her, thou shalt bring them both out to the gate of that city, and they shall be stoned, the damsel because she cried not out being in the city; the man because he hath humbled his neighbour's wife. And thou shalt take away the evil from the midst of thee. (Deut. 22:23-24) But if a man find a damsel that is betrothed in the field, and taking hold of her, lie with her, he alone shall die. The damsel shall suffer nothing, neither is she guilty of death, for as a robber riseth against his brother and taketh away his life, so also did the damsel suffer. She was alone in the field, she cried, and there was no man to help her. (22:25-27) If a man find a damsel that is a virgin who is not espoused and taking her lie with her and the matter come to judgment, he that lay with her shall give to the father of the maid fifty sicles of silver and shall have her to wife, because he hath humbled her. He may not put her away all the days of his life. (Deut. 22:28-29)

The annotation is significant because it appeals to a literal reception of death penalty

---

1 "Hoc iuxta historiam fidelibus hominibus omnibus modis seruandum est..." Paris, BnF, NAL 1740, fol. 66r.

2 "Manifestus sensus." Paris, BnF, NAL 1740, fol. 70v.

3 On this topic, see Raymund Kottje, *Studien zum Einfluss des Alten Testamentes auf Recht und Liturgie des frühen Mittelalters (6–8. Jahrhundert)* (Bonn: Ludwig Röhrscheid Verlag, 1970); Rob Meens, "The Uses of the Old Testament in Early Medieval Canon Law: the *Collectio Vetus Gallica* and the *Collectio Hibernensis*," *The Uses of the Past in the Early Middle Ages*, eds. Yitzhak Hen, Matthew Innes (Cambridge: Cambridge University Press, 2000), pp. 67-77.

on adultery/rape in the Old Law.

Comparable cases can be found in some other early medieval and Carolingian sources of a prescriptive nature. One major recension of *Collectio Hibernensis*, an Irish canonical collection that emerged between 669 and 748 and circulated on the Frankish continent by the end of the eighth century, contains Deut. 22:23-29 under the heading *De uirginibus obpresis aut seductis.*[1] The so-called *Liber ex lege Moysi*, a legal collection that consists of 297 prescriptions taken from Exodus, Leviticus, Numbers, and Deuteronomy, produced in Ireland as well ca. 700 and transmitted to the continent by the early ninth century, contains Deut. 22:28-29.[2] Around 850, a monk of Mainz who called himself Benedictus Levita, made a compilation as the continuation of the capitulary collection of Ansegis of Fontenelle, having entries of both Deut. 22:23-24 and 25-26, respectively under the headings *De puella uirgine desponsata* and *De desponsata uirgine in agro reperta.*[3] Prudentius bishop of Troyes composed a florilegium of biblical texts entitled *Praecepta* in the mid-ninth century, and it contains Deut. 22:22-24.[4] Hincmar of Rheims in his treatise against abduction cited Deut. 22:23-24 to prove that "the law of God wanted the contract and bond of marriages to be holy and inviolable," and Deut. 22:25-27 to prove that "the law of God compares these raptors, oppressors, and violators to robbers and murderers, and orders them to be killed."[5]

In the field of secular law, Deut. 22:25-27 appears as the single biblical entry under the rubric *IN VETERI TESTAMENTO IN LIBRO DEVTERONOMII* in an Aquitainian

---

1 Roy Flechner, ed., *The Hibernensis, Volume 1: A Study and Edition* (Washington, D.C.: Catholic University of America Press, 2019), p. 363. Cf. Maurice Sheehy, "The Bible and the *Collectio canonum Hibernensis*," *Irland und die Christenheit: Bibelstudien und Mission*, eds. Próinséas Ní Chatháin, Michael Richter (Stuttgart: Klett-Cotta, 1987), pp. 277-283.

2 Sven Meeder, "The *Liber ex lege Moysi*: Notes and Text," *Journal of Medieval Latin* 19 (2009): pp. 173-218.

3 *Benedicti capitularia*, II. 47-48, MGH Leges II. 2, ed. Fridericus Henricus Knust (Hannover: Hahnsche, 1832), p. 76.

4 PL 115, col. 1429. Cf. Jared Wielfaert, *Prudentius of Troyes (d. 861) and the Reception of the Patristic Tradition in the Carolingian Era* (Ph.D. dissertation: University of Toronto, 2015), pp. 48-49.

5 "Sed et tam sanctum atque inuiolabile uoluit esse lex Dei foedus et uinculum nuptiarum, parentali auctoritate et legitima postulatione initiatum, ut puellam desponsatam, etiam ante copulam nuptiarum, uxorem eius cui desponsata est esse confirmet, dicens: *Si puellam uirginem desponderit uir, et inuenerit eam aliquis in ciuitate, et cubuerit cum illa, educes utrumque usque ad portam ciuitatis illius, et lapidibus obruentur, puella quia non clamauit cum esset in ciuitate, uir quia humiliauit uxorem proximi sui...* Hos autem raptores, et oppressores, ac uiolatores, lex Dei latronibus et homicidis comparat, et interfici iubet, ubi de puella, quae in agro uiolenter oppressa fuerit, loquitur, dicens: *Sin autem in agro uir repererit puellam quae desponsata est, et apprehendens concubuerit cum illa, ipse morietur solus, puella nihil patietur, nec est rea mortis. Quoniam sicut latro consurgit contra fratrem suum, ut occidat animam eius, ita et puella perpessa est: sola erat in agro, clamauit, et nullus adfuit qui liberaret eam.*" Hincmar, *De coercendo et exstirpando raptu uiduarum, puellarum ac sanctimonialium*, PL 125, col. 1021. Cf. Rachel Stone, "The Invention of a Theology of Abduction: Hincmar of Rheims on *Raptus*," *Journal of Ecclesiastical History* 60 (2009): pp. 433-448.

legal codex of the late ninth century, Leiden, Bibliotheek der Riksuniversiteit, Voss. Lat. Q. 119 (fol. 12r), among multiple Roman legal epitomes, Barbarian legal codes, and Carolingian capitularies.[1] Noticeably, the death penalty of adulterers can also be found in the barbarian code *Lex Gundobada*, which, according to Agobard, was still in use in Lyon of his time.[2] All these that we have just enumerated above together provide an intellectual context for the literal reception of the Deuteronomic law of adultery/rape in the Lyon Annotations.

***

To sum up, via apt exegetical technique, the Lyon Annotator effectively transformed the old precepts of Deuteronomy into doctrinal and moral teachings pertinent and applicable to a Christian community. The Lyon Annotations functioned to teach "the heirs of the New Testament" not only how to understand the biblical book, but also how to live according to the Law of God recorded in it.

7.3   A *Plebs Fidelis* Imagined

7.3.1   *The Constituents of the Church*

While Israel is interpreted as an *ecclesia*, and old precepts are transformed into doctrinal and moral teachings pertinent to Christians, the Lyon Annotator also presents the internal hierarchy of the church via typological exegesis:

> *The seventh is the day of the sabbath, that is, the rest of the Lord, thy God. Thou shalt not do any work therein, thou nor thy son nor thy daughter nor thy manservant nor thy maidservant nor thy ox nor thy ass nor any of thy beasts...* (Deut. 5:14)
>
> When "your" is said, he talks about teachers of the church; by "sons" and "daughters," he names the religious people of both genders; by "manservant" and "maidservants," he points to secular people; by "ox" and 'ass,' he refers to learned and unlearned people...[3]

---

1   Hubert Mordek, *Bibliotheca Capitularium*, pp. 210-217.
2   "Si adulterantes inuenti fuerint, et uir ille occidetur et femina." *Liber constitutionum sive Lex Gundobada*, MGH Leges nationum Germanicarum II.1, LXVIII.1, ed. Ludwig Rudolf von Salis (Hannover: Hahnsche, 1892), p. 95. Cf. Agobard, *Aduersus legem Gundobadi*, CCCM 52, ed. Lieven Van Acker (Turnhout: Brepols, 1981), pp. 17-28.
3   "Cum dicitur tui, doctoribus ecclesie loquitur; per filis ac filias, utriusque sexus religiosas appellat; per seruum et ancillas, seculares demonstrat; per bouem et asinum doctos et indoctos insinuat..." Paris, BnF, NAL 1740, fol. 18r.

Who shall give them to have such a mind to fear me and to keep all my command-ments at all times that it may be well with them and with their children for ever? (Deut. 5:29)

['They and their children'] refer to teachers and disciples.[1]

Blessed shalt thou be among all people. No one shall be barren among you of ei-ther sex, neither of men nor cattle. (Deut. 7:14)

[Men and cattle] refer to teachers and disciples.[2]

... for the land which thou goest to possess is not like the land of Egypt from whence thou camest out where, when the seed is sown, waters are brought in to water it after the manner of gardens, but it is a land of hills and plains, expecting rain from heaven... (Deut. 11:10-11)

The land of Egyptians is to be understood as the present world; their waters refer to those philosophers' wisdom, which is not from heaven but rather earthly, beastlike and diabolical; but the Holy Church is watered by heavenly rain, that is, the rain of Divine Word; the church is mountainous because of perfect teachers of the church, and flat because of humble disciples.[3]

There shall you feast before the Lord, your God, you and your sons and your daughters, your menservants and maid-servants and the Levite that dwelleth in your cities... (Deut. 12:12)

When he says "you," he talks about teachers; he calls disciples living religiously of both genders their sons and their daughters; he names lay people of both genders 'menservants and maid-servant'; but he calls priests the Levites.[4]

And thou shalt feast before the Lord, thy God, thou and thy son and thy daughter and thy manservant and thy maidservant and the Levite that is within thy gates and the stranger and the fatherless and the widow who abide with you. (Deut. 16:11)

By these orders, he generally calls the whole church, that is teachers and disciples, religious and lay, the learned and the unlearned.[5]

---

1 "Id est doctoribus et auditoribus." Paris, BnF, NAL 1740, fol. 19v.
2 "Tam in doctoribus quam auditoribus." Paris, BnF, NAL 1740, fol. 23v.
3 "Terra Egyptiorum presens mundus intelligitur: aque eorum sapientia filosoforum quae non est de caelo sed terrena, animalis, diabolica; sancta uero ecclesia imbre celesti id est diuinorum eloquiorum inrigatur; que ecclesia montuosa est perfectis doctoribus, campestris autem in humilibus auditoribus." Paris, BnF, NAL 1740, fol. 32v.
4 "Vos cum dicit, doctoribus loquitur; filios hac filias eorum ex utroque sexum discipulos appellat, religiose uiuentes; seruos et ancillas, seculares ex utroque sexum nominat; leuites autem sacerdotes appellat." Paris, BnF, NAL 1740, fol. 36r.
5 "Per hos ordines omnem contaxat ecclesiam id est doctores et auditores, religiosos et seculares, doctos atque indoctos." Paris, BnF, NAL 1740, fol. 46r.

When the Lord, thy God, hath destroyed the nations whose land he will deliver to thee and thou shalt possess it and shalt dwell in the cities and houses thereof... (Deut. 19:1)

The nations which the Lord promised to destroy in front of the sons of Israel signify the powers of the air and their sins, through which they dominate the humankind subject to them; when these sins are rooted out, in their place in which they ruled by impiety, the sons of Israel, that is Christian believers, teachers and disciples, began to dwell.[1]

Blessed shall be the fruit of thy womb and the fruit of thy ground and the fruit of thy cattle, the droves of thy herds and the folds of thy sheep. (Deut. 28:4)

Cattle of the church tropologically signifies the carnal but faithful people; herds of oxen signify the order of clerics; sheep signify monks or other believers who live innocently.[2]

Two fundamental but overlapping dichotomies stand out: teacher (*doctor*) and disciple (*auditor/discipulus*); the church person (*religiosus*) and the laity (*secularis/carnalis*).

7.3.2 *Doctores, Praedicatores, and Sacerdotes*

In early medieval ecclesiastical discourse, a *doctor* is a church leader learned in divine knowledge and holding the responsibility of guiding the Christian community subject to him by instructing how to believe and to live.[3] Leidrad specified at the beginning of his treatise *De abrenunciatione diaboli* that the worst *scandalum* that the devil spreads is the enmity *inter doctores et auditors*, which tells us how fundamental this hierarchy was to the social structure of his time.[4] In Gregory's *Regula pastoralis*, *doctor* is one of the major appellations, synonymous to *rector*, *pastor*, *sacerdos*, *praedicator*, and *praeposi*-

---

1 "Gentes quos Dominus a facie filiorum Israel disperdendas pollicitus est, significant aerias potestates et uitia eorum per que humanum genus subiectum dominabantur; quibus extirpatis, in eorum loco in quibus ipsi per impietatem regnabant, habitare coeperunt filii Israel id est fideles cristiani, doctores atque auditores." Paris, BnF, NAL 1740, fol. 51v.

2 "Iumenta ecclesie tropologice carnalem significat populum sed fidelem, armenta bouum ordinem clericorum, oues monachi uel ceteri fideles innocenter uiuentes." Paris, BnF, NAL 1740, fol. 71r.

3 Hannah Matis, *The Song of Songs in the Early Middle Ages*, pp. 42-57.

4 Even worse than the scandel between "rulers of the church and administrators of the state": "Intelleximus itaque post uestram benignissimam admonitionem, quia de operibus et pompis diaboli multiplicius respondendum erat, quam de caeteris rebus: quoniam per eas cupiditates, et per cupiditates scandala mundi crebrescunt quotidie, et quod peius est, inter Ecclesiae rectores, et reipublicae administratores discordiae oriuntur; et quod adhuc horum est pessimum, inter doctores et auditores odia se interserunt, inimicitiae concitantur, detractiones agitantur." Leidrad, *De abrenuntiatione diaboli*, PL 99, col. 873.

tus, for the undertaker of pastoral care.[1] *Doctores* "brought the Holy Church to the rude minds of the unfaithful by preaching,"[2] "always mediated on the Divine Word in their hearts," and taught them.[3] The same notion can be found in the Lyon Annotations:

> ... *and thou shalt tell them to thy children, and thou shalt meditate upon them sitting in thy house and walking on thy journey, sleeping and rising. And thou shalt bind them as a sign on thy hand, and they shall be and shall move between thy eyes. And thou shalt write them in the entry and on the doors of thy house.* (Deut. 6:7-9)

He instructs the teachers of the Church that they meditate on the law of God day and night, and teach their children, that is disciples. We sit in the house when we rest from earthly acts in our consciences; we walk on the way when we make progress in good deeds; we sleep and rise according to the weakness of human flesh; binding precepts in hands means always retaining the law in good deeds; always having them between eyes means always keeping the precepts in memory with no oblivion; writing the precepts of the Lord in the entry and on the doors means always keeping and retaining it in highest veneration of mind.[4]

> *Set your hearts on all the words which I testify to you this day, which you shall command your children to observe and to do and to fulfill all that is written in this law...* (Deut. 32:46)

He instructs the teachers of the Church that they should fulfill in deeds all that they understand and believe in sacred scriptures, and deliver to their children, that is students, to observe.[5]

It is remarkable that in the former entry, the author identifies himself and his readers as the *doctores* by using the first-person plural: *sedemus, ambulamus, dorminus* and *consorgimus.*

---

1 Gregory, *Regula pastoralis*, SC 381, p. 63. Cf. Robert A. Markus, *Gregory the Great and His World* (Cambridge University Press, 1998).

2 "Vectibus quippe arcam portare, est bonis doctoribus sanctam Ecclesiam ad rudes infidelium mentes praedicando deducere." Gregory, *Regula pastoralis*, II.11, SC 381, p. 254.

3 "Sed circulis uectes inhaercant. ut doctores semper in suis cordibus eloquia sacra menditantes, testamenti arcam sine mora eleuent: si quid necesse est, protinus docent." Ibid., p. 256.

4 "Doctoribus ecclesie precipit ut et ipsi legem Dei meditentur die ac nocte et filios suos id est discipulos doceant. In domo sedemus quando intra conscientias nostras a terrenis actibus quiescimus; in uia ambulamus cum bonis operibus proficimus; dorminus atque consorgimus secundum infirmitatem humane carnis; in manibus precepta ligare est <cum> bonis operibus eam semper retinere; inter oculos ea semper habere est in memoriam absque ulla obliuione semper recolere; in limine siue in hostiis precepta Domini scribere est in ipsa summa ueneratione mentis eam semper recolere atque retinere." Paris, BnF, NAL 1740, fol. 20v.

5 "Doctoribus ecclesiae precipit ut cuncta quae in diuinis Scripturis recte intellegunt et credunt, operibus impleant et filiis suis, id est discipulis, ad custodienda tradant." Paris, BnF, NAL 1740, fol. 89v.

Doctores could be the leaders of different types of ecclesiastical communities, including monasteries:

> *Thou shalt appoint judges and magistrates in all thy gates which the Lord, thy God, shall give thee, in all thy tribes, that they may judge the people with just judgment and not go aside to either part.* (Deut. 16:18-19)
>
> By judges and magistrates, rulers of the Church (*rectores ecclesie*) are called, that is bishops, priests, and abbots appointed in all the churches, just as in all the tribes; they teach the people subject to them how they are able to believe and live.[1]

But in the context of the Lyon Annotations, *doctor* primarily refers to *sacerdos* and *praedicator* who carry the duty of pastoral care for their neighbors:

> *When thou buildest a new house, thou shalt make a battlement to the roof round about lest blood be shed in thy house and thou be guilty if any one slip and fall down headlong.* (Deut. 22:8)
>
> The new house is to be understood as the faithful city (*plebs fidelis*) renewed via the grace of baptism, and holy preachers need to make sure that every one of them encloses the church entrusted to them within the battlements of faith and discipline lest, due to his negligence, whoever fall from the church into heresy or perish headlong in whichever mortal sin, and the magister is guilty of the blood of the one who perishes in his fault.[2]

It is necessary for them to carry out preaching in the right way:

> *Thou shalt not sow thy vineyard with divers seeds lest both the seed which thou hast sown and the fruit of the vineyard be sanctified together.* (Deut. 22:9)
>
> By vineyard, he signifies the faithful city, and by semen, he implies the speech of preaching. A person is preached to in his own city; one sows with diverse seeds, who preaches what he is not able to affirm, not from the authority of sacred scriptures, nor from the tradition of Holy Fathers, but from the apocryphal books of heretics, from the superstitions of philosophers, or from his own understanding.[3]

---

1 "Iudices et magistri rectores ecclesiae appellantur, id est episcopi, presbiteri atque abbates per cunctas ecclesias uelut per singulas tribus constituti, qui doceant populum sibi subditum quomodo credat et qualiter uiuere queat." Paris, BnF, NAL 1740, fol. 47r.

2 "Domum nouam plebs fidelis intellegitur per baptismi gratiam in noua, et a sanctis predicatoribus necesse est ut unusquisque ecclesiam sibi creditam muro fidei atque discipline circumdet ne quis ex illa, per neglegentiam eius, aut in herese ruat aut in quolibet mortali peccato precipitatus intereat et sit ille magister reus sanguinis eius qui per eius culpam perierit." Paris, BnF, NAL 1740, fol. 59r.

3 "Quid per uineam nisi plebem significat fidelem et quid per semen nisi uerbum innuit predicationis. Ille predicatur in plebem sua; altero semine seminat qui non de auctoritatem sanctarum Scripturarum neque ex traditione sanctorum patrum sed de libris apocrifis hereticorum aut ex subperstitione phisolophorum uel ex proprio sensum quod predicat adfirmare non ualet." Paris, BnF, NAL 1740, fol. 59r.

Taking the priestly honor means being the spiritual soldiers of God.[1] A qualified *spiritalis miles* needs to keep himself from carnal love:

> *What man is there that hath planted a vineyard and hath not as yet made it to be common whereof all men may eat? Let him go, and return to his house lest he die in the battle and another man execute his office. What man is there that hath espoused a wife and not taken her? Let him go and return to his house lest he die in the war, and another man take her.* (Deut. 20:6-7)
>
> By vineyard, he signifies sons or other neighbors, and by wife, the carnal love between man and woman. For whoever loves sons, daughters, and wife more than eternal life, cannot be not suitable to attend the spiritual battle. For a simple way of life (*simplex conuersatio*), that is active life, is sufficient to them for salvation of the soul.[2]

Priests should not "love wealth, indulge in pleasure, and live luxuriously,"[3] nor "embrace earthly possessions."[4] Once joining the priesthood, they shall never return to the carnal life which they have abandoned.[5] They shall sow the seed of the Divine Word by preaching skillfully in the hearts of listeners, making them their spiritual sons.[6] They

---

1 "Domum nouam aedificauit et non dedicabit eam quilibet paterfamilias qui domesticos domus sua necdum fecit cristianos et idcirco ab spiritali militia id est a sacerdotali honore prohibendus est. De talibus ait Apostolus: Qui enim domui sue preesse nescit, quomodo ecclesiae Dei diligentiam abebit?" Paris, BnF, NAL 1740, fol. 54r, on Deut. 20:5 ("Quis est homo qui aedificauit domum nouam et non dedicauit eam?")

2 "Per uineam filios significat uel ceteros propinquos, per uxorem carnalem amorem inter uirum et feminam. Quicumque enim magis filios ac filias atque uxorem quam uitam aeternam diligit, ad spiritale(m) militiam idoneus esse non potest: sufficit enim illis simplex conuersatio, id est actiua uita, ad salutem anime." Paris, BnF, NAL 1740, fol. 54v.

3 "Hoc preceptum Salamon custodire neclexit qui amore mulierum inlectus, usque ad idolorum cultum declinauit; nunc autem in ecclesia sacerdotes elati, diuitiarum amatores, deliciis abluentes atque luxoriose uiuentes, subiectos sibi non ad celestem patriam prouocant sed exemplo prauitatis suae et uerbo, ad concupiscentias mundi quas in baptismo renuntiauerunt, quasi ad Egiputm reuocant. Egyptus enim figura est mundi, uita Egypti conuersatio gentilium." Paris, BnF, NAL 1740, fol. 49r, on Deut. 17:17 ("Non habebit uxores plurimas, quae alliciant animum eius, neque argenti et auri immensa pondera.").

4 "Nota aperta<m> sententiam de sanctis sacerdotibus qui cum Apostolo dicere possunt: Habentes alimenta et quibus tegamur, his contenti sumus. Quorum hereditas Dominus est, terrenas possessiones ambire non debent." Paris, BnF, NAL 1740, fol. 49v, on Deut. 18:1-2 ("Non habebunt sacerdotes et Leuitae, et omnes qui de eadem tribu sunt, partem et haereditatem cum reliquo Israel, quia sacrificia Domini, et oblationes ejus comedent, et nihil aliud accipient de possessione fratrum suorum: Dominus enim ipse est haereditas eorum, sicut locutus est illis.")

5 "Patet sensus iuxta litteram, sed mistice sanctis predicatoribus precipitur ut ad ea que reliquerunt nequaquam reuertantur." Paris, BnF, NAL 1740, fol. 64v, on Deut. 24:19 ("Quando messueris segetem in agro tuo, et oblitus manipulum reliqueris, non reuerteris, ut tollas illum.")

6 "... Abet sacerdos stultus qui per linguam suam semen uerbi in corda audientium infundere non ualet, nec spiritales filios generare..." Paris, BnF, NAL 1740, fol. 61r, on Deut. 23:1 ("Non intrauit eunuchus, attritis uel amputatis testiculis et absciso uereto, ecclesiam Domini.")

shall also perform the sacrament of penance properly.[1] When correcting their subjects' misdeeds, they should not be too harsh in language to the extent of scandalizing them.[2] They shall constantly reflect upon their own faults.[3]

They shall be the perfect sacrifice without blemish before God.[4] There are four major virtues for a good priest: "right activity and detachment from vulgar way of life", "understanding and highest contemplation", "speech of preaching", and "abstinence of belly and what are beneath belly." "Whoever has these four principle virtues will gain the perfect priesthood without defect."[5]

7.3.3 The Laity

Clerics and monks constitute the group of *religiosi* who renounce the world and become the soldiers of God in spiritual battle.[6] In distinction from them, lay believers live

---

1 "Nemo ex sacerdotibus a quolibet delinquenti confessionem delictorum inuitus extorquere debet. Hoc et secundum litteram fideli cristiano facere conuenit. Mistice uero de reconciliatione penitentum accipi potest, quibus in exitum sacramentum corporis et sanguinis Domini negandum non est, si tamen quanticumque tempore eius penitentia precesserit." Paris, BnF, NAL 1740, fol. 64r, on Deut. 24:10 ("Cum repetes a proximo tuo rem aliquam quam debet tibi, non ingredieris domum eius ut pignus auferas.")

2 "Percutit proximum suum quilibet doctor ecclesiae qui per ignorantiam aut per escessum loquutionis proximum suum scandalizat in fide, non per inuidia aut odio sed, ut dictum est, per indiscreta loquutione." Paris, BnF, NAL 1740, fol. 52r, on Deut. 19:5-6 ("Sed abiisse cum eo simpliciter in siluam ad ligna caedenda, et in succisione lignorum securis fugerit manu, ferrumque lapsum de manubrio amicum eius percusserit, et occiderit...")

3 "... spiritaliter autem diuersa pondera et duplices mensuras illi in domibus suis, id est in conscientiis suis, habent qui aliter facta sua pensant ali<ter> proximorum suorum qui culpas suas licet graues leuitant et proximorum suorum <mi>nima sicut grauiora iudicant. Qui festucam <in> oculo proximi sui uiden<t> et trabem in oculo suo non considerant. Hoc quippe faciunt plerique episcopi siue presbiteri in ecclesiam qui alios, ut dictum est, de minimis peccatis iudicant et semetipsos de perpetrata mala non corrigunt. Hoc enim uitium quod ex su<per>bia oritur, uniuersos hereticos atque ypocritas a regno Dei alienos efficit." Paris, BnF, NAL 1740, fol. 66r, on Deut. 25:13-14 ("Non habebis in sacculo diuersa pondera, maius et minus, nec erit in domo tua modius maior, et minor.")

4 "Per bouem a parte totum sacerdotes significat uitiosos; per ouem autem monachos uel ceteros religiosos quos absque macula peccati Dominus sibi offerre uult; criminosos uero omnino non reciptit." Paris, BnF, NAL 1740, fol. 50r, on Deut. 17:1 ("Non immolabis Domino Deo tuo bouem et ouem in quo est macula aut quippiam uitii.")

5 "Alibi armum atque pectusculum siue maxillas quod secum legem sacertibus a populo accipere preceptum erat, sub Nouo Testamento boni sacerdotes non carnaliter sed spiritaliter a semetipsis Deo offerre debent. In armo quippe figuratur recta operatio et uulgari conuersatione seiuncta; in pectusculo autem intellectus et superna contemplatio; in maxilla sermo predicationis. In uentriculo uero continentia uentris et ea quae sub uentre sunt. Quicumque autem has quattuor uirtutes principlaes habuerit, perfectum sacerdotium absque culpa retemptabit." Paris, BnF, NAL 1740, fol. 50r.

6 "Loquitur lex cunctis religiosis clericis ac monachis mundum renuntiantibus et ad spiritalia bella contra hostes inuisibiles ide est inmundos spiritus egredientibus ut in initio conuersionis sue custodiant se ab omni re mala, hereticorum uidelicet errorem atque cetera peccata." Paris, BnF, NAL 1740, fol. 61v, on Deut. 23:10-14.

carnally but inside the Catholic Church, and shall not be looked down upon:

> *Thou shalt not abhor the Edomite, because he is thy brother, nor the Egyptian,*
> *because thou wast a stranger in his land. They that are born of them in the third*
> *generation shall enter into the church of the Lord.* (Deut. 23:7-8)

In a similar way, he instructs all the religious people, that is virgins and *continen-*
tes, lest they ever abhor the married lay people like the Egyptians, just as many heretics did with no doubt. For there is also no religious person who does not need the
help of the laity. For those from them [Egyptians], that is from lay believers, are born
according to flesh, but reborn via the grace of baptism, they enter the church of the
Lord every day. The third generation naturally refers to the baptism that proceeds in
the name of the Father, the Son and the Holy Spirit.[1]

The laity shall be friendly with the church people:

> *And do you therefore love strangers...* (Deut. 10:19)

It is instructed to other believers who hitherto live carnally that they should love
the strangers, such as the Apostles, martyrs, and other perfect people (*perfecti*) who
thoroughly renounce the world and are loved by the Lord, and should make them unto
themselves friends of the mammon of iniquity, who may receive themselves into everlasting dwellings (cf. Luke 16:9).[2]

The distinction between the way of life (*conuersatio*) of *religiosus* and that of *laicus*,
however, should not be blurred:

> *When a man hath lately taken a wife, he shall not go out to war, neither shall any*
> *public business be enjoined him, but he shall be free at home without fault that for one*
> *year he may rejoice with his wife.* (Deut. 24:5)

The Law prohibits married believers who are hitherto overcome by carnal love to
attend to the spiritual battle, that is to renounce the world; nor is whoever preacher al-

---

1 "... similiter precepit cunctis religiosis id est uirginibus et conti<nenti>bus ne ullo modo laicos
coniugatos quasi Egyptios abominent, sicut plerique heretici fecisse non dubium est. Non est enim
religiosus quoque qui laicorum adiutorium non indigeat. Qui enim ex eis, id est ex laicis fidelibus,
secundum carnem generantur, per baptismi gratia regenerati, ecclesiam Domini cotidie intrant; tertia
quippe generatio baptismum demonstrat quod in nomine Patris et Filii et Spiritus sancti datur." Paris,
BnF, NAL 1740, fol. 61v.
2 "Ceteris fidelibus sed adhuc carnaliter uiuentibus precipitur ut diligant peregrinos, quales fuerunt
apostoli et martyres atque ceteri perfecti qui funditus mundum renuntiantes quos Dominus diligit sed
de mamona iniquitatis faciant sibi illos amicos qui eos recipiant in aeterna tabernacula." Paris, BnF,
NAL 1740, fol. 31r.

lowed to impose upon them the burden of a continence that they are unable to bear.[1]

7.3.4 Moral Life in This World

Through the sacrament of baptism, people wash away their previous sins and join in the one single Church.[2] The church, however, does not automatically guarantee final salvation.[3] Instead, "in the church, if you live soberly, and justly, and godly in this world, you are able to go over through it into the heavenly homeland after death, in which you live forever."[4] Baptism requires Christians to keep carrying out divine precepts in practice as well as persisting in faith through the present world until the Final Judgment:

> *Thou shalt make strings in the hem at the four corners of thy cloak wherewith thou shalt be covered.* (Deut. 22:12)
>
> By strings, nothing is signified other than precepts. We join these precepts with our actions, just like we bind crimson ribbons to our cloaks, so that our activity is not dissolved from divine mandates.[5]

> *In the sight of the Lord, thy God, shalt thou eat them every year in the place that the Lord shall choose, thou and thy house.* (Deut. 15:20)
>
> But he says "in the sight of the Lord thy God shalt thou eat them," as if he says, if [you] can do something good at the initial stage of your conversion, do it in order to take pains to please God alone, not human beings. Every year, that is through the

---

1 "Prohibet lex coniugatos fideles qui adhuc carnali amore uicti tenentur, ad spiritale(m) militiam id est mundi renuntiationem procedere nec eis a quolibet predicatore pondus continentiae quod portare non possint eum inponere." Paris, BnF, NAL 1740, fol. 63r.

2 "In uitulo illo quem filii Israel absentem Moyse, secus montem Sinai fecerunt et adorauerunt, tropologice pene omne genus humanum prefigurabit quod per idolorum cultura et cetera peccata diabolo aderentes, humanum corpus eius effecti fuerant; quos tamen Dominus, cuius personam gestabat Moyses, de caelo quasi de montem Sinai descendens, a diaboli societate separabit et ab inuicem fideles ab infidelibus dissociabit atque igne Spiritus sancti eorum peccata conbusit et per baptismi gratiam, quasi in torrentem qui de latere Domini descendit, adsparsos in unitate ecclesiae incorporabit." Paris, BnF, NAL 1740, fol. 28v, on Deut. 9:21 ("Vitulum arripiens igne combusi.")

3 "... siquidem et in ecclesia spiritaliter duodecim tribus, decem tribus propter fidem et operationem accipiuntur." Paris, BnF, NAL 1740, fol. 86r, on Deut. 32:8 ("Iuxta numerum filiorum Israhel.")

4 "Audi Israel! Non tantum carnalis Israel sed potius spiritalis qui per gratiam fidei uerus Israel esse meruisti, qui per baptissimi gratiam uelu<t> per fluenta Iordanis terram repromissionis id est ecclesiam, introisti. In qua ecclesia, si sobriae, iuste et pie uixeris, per illam ad celestem patriam post mortem transire poteris, in qua in aeternum uiuas." Paris, BnF, NAL 1740, fol. 27r, on Deut. 9:1 ("Audi, Israel: tu transgredieris hodie Iordanem...")

5 "Quid per funiculos nisi precepta figuratur; quae precepta si cum actiones nostras coniungimus quasi uittas iacintinas palleis nostris conligamus, ut nostra operatio a diuinis mandatis non dissoluatur." Paris, BnF, NAL 1740, fol. 59r.

progress of virtues, until you are able to reach perfection through the augmentation of good work.[1]

Six days shalt thou labour and shalt do all thy works. The seventh is the day of the sabbath, that is, the rest of the Lord thy God. Thou shalt not do any work therein... (Deut. 5:13-14)

The six days are to be understood as the present world, which was created by God in six days. Therefore, we are admonished that as long as we live in this life, we should do whatever is good; but after the seventh day, that is the rest to come, approaches this life, that will be the time not to work but to render account.[2]

... thou shalt immolate the phase in the evening at the going down of the sun, at which time thou camest out of Egypt. (Deut. 16:6)

Indeed, [the Lord] prohibits the dispensation of his own Incarnation which happened in the evening to be delayed to the first morning, that is to the future resurrection; but [we shall] not anticipate what we have not prepared for ourselves in this life by living well after the day of the Resurrection, but shall complete it by believing and working before the Day of Judgment.[3]

As long as a Christian in the Church sins, he is under the curse of the Law.[4] Sins would exclude him from the community of God's chosen people (*societas electorum*):

But if it have a blemish or be lame or blind or in any part disfigured or feeble, it shall not be sacrificed to the Lord, thy God, but thou shalt eat it within the gates of thy city. The clean and the unclean shall eat them alike, as the roe and as the hart. (Deut. 15:21-22)

A blind animal is the stupid person who does not have the light of faith; a lame

---

1   "Quod uero ait: In conspectu Domini Dei tui comedes ea, ac si dicat: Si quid boni agere potest in initio conuersionis tuae, ita operare ut soli Deo placere studeas, non hominibus. Per annos singulos, hoc est per profectu uirtutum, donec per augmentum bone operationis, ad perfectionem peruenire ualeas." Paris, BnF, NAL 1740, fol. 44v.

2   "In diebus sex presens mundus intelligitur qui in sex dies a Deo factus est. Idcirco precipitur nobis ut in hac uita quamdiu subsistimus, operemur quod bonum est; postquam autem septimus dies, id est futura requies, huic uitae accesserit, non operandi tempus sed retende rationis erit occasio." Paris, BnF, NAL 1740, fol. 18r.

3   "Prohibet etiam dispensationem incarnationis suae quod in uespere mundi factum est, in die primo mane, hoc est ad futuram resurrectionem, reseruare; sed ante diem iudicii credendo et operando implere, nec post diem resurrectionis expectare, quod in hac uita bene uiuendo nobis non preparauerimus." Paris, BnF, NAL 1740, fol. 45v.

4   "Per hanc sententia Iudei sub maledicto legis adicti retinentur; a quo maledicto nemo ex illis immunis esse poterit, nisi qui in Christo Domino nostro crediderit ut per eius gratiam liber eficiatur. Siquidem et omnis homo etiam christianus in ecclesiam quamdiu peccat, sub maledicto legis est." Paris, BnF, NAL 1740, fol. 70r, on Deut. 27:26 ("Maledictus qui non permanet in sermonibus legis huius nec eos opere perficit.")

animal is the person who limps in the way of God and is unable to take a step of good deed; a blemished animal is the vicious person disfigured by bad deeds. But it is added that "thou shalt eat it within the gates of thy city," which signifies that, inside the church, such people are more than good people, but only the chosen ones are accepted in the sacrifice of God.[1]

> *... but whatsoever is dead of itself, eat not thereof. Give it to the stranger that is within thy gates to eat, or sell it to him...* (Deut. 14:21)

By the stranger within the gates of the church, that is the one who stays in his faith, nothing is signified other than carnal Christians living perversely who claim that they know God but negate Him in actions. They are thus considered alienated from the community of the chosen people. For they eat what is unclean when they abstain themselves from no sin, but wallow in the mud of libido in the way of life of gentiles like brutal beasts.[2]

The life in this present world is thus a lasting battle against sins. Behind the battle is the confrontation between the demoniacal seduction and the assistance of God and His saints:

> *The Lord shall cause thy enemies that rise up against thee to fall down before thy face: one way shall they come out against thee, and seven ways shall they flee before thee.* (Deut. 28:7)

The hosts of saints come as if through one way, when the unclean spirits beat the hearts of the chosen people through whichever single sin in thought. These unclean spirits have been beaten with the help of God and the chosen people's own vigilance, as if they are conquered and recede through the sevenfold incitement of sins. For the one who has been seduced by them through whichever sin, will be irreproachable from other sins. These all were offered by God to the chosen people spiritually.[3]

---

1 "Cecum animal est homo stultus qui lumen fidei non habet; claudum est qui in uia Dei claudicat et gressum boni operis agere not ualet; maculosum animal est homo uitiosus, malis actibus deformis. Quod uero addidit: Intra portas tuas commedes illud, hoc significat quod intra ecclesiam pluriores sunt tales quam boni, sed soli electi in Dei sacrificio accipiuntur." Paris, BnF, NAL 1740, fol. 44v.

2 "Quid per peregrinum intra portas ecclesiae id est intra fidem eius manentem nisi cristianos carnales praue uiuentes significat qui confitentur se nosse Deum, factis autem negant, qui idcirco perigrini ducuntur qui a societate electorum alieni existunt. Comedunt enim que inmunda sunt dum a nullis se peccatis contineant sed more gentium tamquam bruta animalia in ceno libidinis uolutantur." Paris, BnF, NAL 1740, fol. 41v.

3 "Quasi per unam uiam ostes sanctorum ueniunt cum inmundi spiritus corda electorum per unum quodlibet uitium in cogitatione pulsant. Qui si per Dei adiutorium et eorum uigilantiam repulsi fuerunt, uelut per septiformem fomitem uiciorum uicti recedunt. Qui enim ab uno quolibet uitio ab eis seductus fuerit, a ceteris peccatis inculpatibilis erit. Haec omnia spiritaliter populo electo a Domino conlata sunt." Paris, BnF, NAL 1740, fol. 71r.

In this life, one cannot expect to win the battle once and for all, but shall keep vigilant all the time:

He will consume these nations in thy sight by little and little and by degrees. Thou wilt not be able to destroy them altogether lest perhaps the beasts of the earth should increase upon thee... (Deut. 7:22)

Certainly, no one of the chosen people was able to be so perfect at the initial stage of his conversion to the extent that whichever kind of sin that fights against him does not last. Even if such thing had happened, he would suffer from the worse detriment due to the security and sloth of his own soul.[1]

It is necessary to lean on the ecclesiastical discipline:

Seven days shalt thou eat without leaven the bread of affliction... (Deut. 16:3)

Seven days signify the whole duration of the present life, during which it is proper for the believers of the church to eat the bread of affliction, that is their previous sins, or to make penance for daily transgressions (*pro cotidianis excessibus*) and to mourn for their own bad deeds.[2]

The major sins are seven: gluttony, fornication, avarice, anger, melancholy, envy, and vainglory, and the queen of them is pride.[3] One particular sin that the Lyon Annotator frequently singled out is *luxuria,* which is contagious for all the ecclesiastical orders:

These shall you eat of all that abide in the waters: all that have fins and scales you shall eat. Such as are without fins and scales, you shall not eat, because they are unclean. (Deut. 14:9-10)

By clean or unclean fishes, he spiritually signifies nothing other than the Christians renewed through the water of baptism; but some of them live spiritually whom he says to be clean, while others are carnal *luxuriose.*[4]

And when he is made king, he shall not multiply horses to himself nor lead back

---

1 "Nemo quippe ex electis ita perfectus in primordio conuersionis sue esse potuit ut qualemcumque uitium qui ei semper repugnet non remaneat; quod si fieri potuisset, deteriorem detrimentum ex securitate atque inertia animae suae sustineret." Paris, BnF, NAL 1740, fol. 24v.

2 "Septem dies omnes tempus significant uitae presentis; in quo tempore fidelibus ecclesiae conuenit afflictionis panem comedere id est preteritis peccatis suis siue pro cotidianis excessibus paenitentiam agere et mala sua deflere." Paris, BnF, NAL 1740, fol. 45v.

3 "Septem hec gentes, licet omnes gentes quas apostoli et ceteri predicatores, in posesionem acceperunt significent; tropologice uero septem principalia vitia insinuant id est ingluuies, forncationem, auaritiam, iram, tristiam, inuidiam, cendoxia, id est vana g<loria> atque nouissima har<um> omnium regina, superbia." Paris, BnF, NAL 1740, fol. 22r, on Deut. 7:1.

4 "Quid per pisces mundos uel inmundos spiritaliter significat nisi cristianos ex aqua baptismi regeneratos; sed alios spiritaliter uiuentes quos mundos esse dicit, alios uero carnales luxuriose conuersantes." Paris, BnF, NAL 1740, fol. 41r.

*the people into Egypt... He shall not have many wives, that may allure his mind, nor
immense sums of silver and gold.* (Deut. 17:16-17)

Salomon neglected to observe this precept, who, allured by the love of women,
turned out to fall into the cult of idols. But now, the haughty priests in the Church,
who love wealth, indulge in pleasure, and live luxuriously, by their own perverse example and word provoke the people subject to them not to the heavenly homeland,
but to the concupiscence of this world that they have renounced in baptism, as if lead
them back to Egypt. For Egypt is the figure of this world, and the life of Egypt is the
way of life of gentiles.[1]

A woman shall not be clothed with man's apparel... (Deut. 22:5)

... but it is not proper in spiritual sense that whoever weak and hitherto living carnally takes up the appearance of the perfect through hypocrisy, nor is it proper that
whoever is religious in the church lives dissolutely and *luxuriose* just like a woman.[2]

With no exact translation in modern language, *luxuria* in the context of antique and
medieval moral discourse is generally related to the excess or superfluous pleasure that
brings about moral corruption.[3] The worry about its corruptive threat to the justice and
morality of the Church may explain the Lyon Annotator's constant urge for charity to the
poor, a communal virtue sharply opposed to the self-satisfactory *luxuria*:

*When thou shalt demand of thy neighbour any thing that he oweth thee, thou shalt
not go into his house to take away a pledge...* (Deut. 24:10)

... It is proper for a Christian believer to carry it out according to literal sense...[4]

Thou shalt not refuse the hire of the needy and the poor... (Deut. 24:14)

It is proper to carry it out according to literal sense in every manner.[5]

*... but thou shalt pay him the price of his labour the same day before the going
down of the sun, because he is poor and with it maintaineth his life...* (Deut. 24:15)

---

1 "Hoc preceptum Salamon custodire neclexit qui amore mulierum inlectus, usque ad idolorum cultum
declinauit; nunc autem in ecclesia sacerdotes elati, diuitiarum amatores, deliciis abluentes atque
luxoriose uiuentes, subiectos sibi non ad celestem patriam prouocant sed exemplo prauitatis suae
et uerbo, ad concupiscentias mundi quas in baptismo renuntiauerunt, quasi ad Egiputm reuocant.
Egyptus enim figura est mundi, uita Egypti conuersatio gentilium." Paris, BnF, NAL 1740, fol. 49r.
2 "... spiritaliter uero non oportet, quamlibet infirmum et adhuc carnaliter uiuentem, per hipocrisin
speciem perfectorum adsumere nec quemlibet religiosum in ecclesiam dissolute atque luxuriose
tamquam mulierem uiuere." Paris, BnF, NAL 1740, fol. 58v.
3 Cf. Christopher Berry, *The Idea of Luxury: A Conceptual and Historical Investigation* (Cambridge
University Press, 1994), pp. 45-98; Eoghan Ahern, "Abundance, *Luxuria*, and Sin in Late Antique
Historiography," *Journal of Early Christian Studies* 25 (2017): pp. 605-631.
4 "... Hoc et secundum litteram fideli cristiano facere conuenit..." Paris, BnF, NAL 1740, fol. 64r.
5 "Et hoc iuxta litteram omnis modis facere conuenit." Paris, BnF, NAL 1740, fol. 64r.

The meaning is clear according to the literal sense.[1]

Thou shalt not pass by if thou seest thy brother's ox or his sheep go astray, but thou shalt bring them back to thy brother. (Deut. 22:1)

The meaning is clear which is to be observed by believers according to the literal sense.[2]

When thou hast reaped the corn in thy field and hast forgot and left a sheaf, thou shalt not return to take it away, but thou shalt suffer the stranger and the fatherless and the widow to take it away that the Lord, thy God, may bless thee in all the works of thy hands. (Deut. 24:19)

The meaning is clear according to literal sense...[3]

If thou have gathered the fruit of thy olive trees, thou shalt not return to gather whatsoever remaineth on the trees but shalt leave it for the stranger, for the fatherless and the widow. (Deut. 24:20)

... but it is proper for a Christian believer to carry it out according to the literal sense.[4]

Remember that thou also wast a bondman in Egypt, and therefore I command thee to do this thing. (Deut. 24:22)

As if he says: "Just like I who took you from the servitude of sin and the power of the devil had mercy on you, so it is necessary that you have mercy on your indigent neighbors."[5]

"The pride of certain rich people" is condemned.[6] Selfishness does harm to the harmonious order of a Christian community:

If one of thy brethren that dwelleth within the gates of thy city in the land which the Lord, thy God, will give thee come to poverty, thou shalt not harden thy heart nor close thy hand but shalt open it to the poor man, thou shalt lend him that which thou perceivest he hath need of. (Deut. 15:7-8)

There are many inside the church who show no mercy to their indigent neighbors due to the fear of future poverty, for they say: "If I distribute what I possess to poor

---

1 "Patet sensus iuxta litteram." Paris, BnF, NAL 1740, fol. 64r.
2 "Patet sensus qui iuxta historiam a fidelibus obseruandus est." Paris, BnF, NAL 1740, fol. 58r.
3 "Patet sensus iuxta litteram..." Paris, BnF, NAL 1740, fol. 64v.
4 "... tamen et ad litteram fideli christiano facere conuenit." Paris, BnF, NAL 1740, fol. 64v.
5 "Ac si dicat: Sicut ego tui misertus sum, qui te de seruitute peccati et potestate diaboli erui, ita et tu erga proximos tuos indigentes, misericors esse debet." Paris, BnF, NAL 1740, fol. 65r.
6 "Potest et per camelum elatio filosoforum et superbia quorundam diuitum figuraliter demonstrare." Paris, BnF, NAL 1740, fol. 41r, on Deut. 14:7.

people, how will I sustain myself and my servants?"[1]

7.3.5 Pagans, Philosophers and Heretics

Four groups are mentioned as the threat to the *plebs fidelis*: Jews, pagans, philosophers, and heretics. "Gentiles, that is pagans, who ignore the true God and worship images (*simulacra*),"[2] appear in the Lyon Annotations primarily in the historical context of the apostolic mission and the conversion of nations, for example:

> *When the Lord, thy God, shall have enlarged thy borders, as he hath spoken to thee, and thou wilt eat the flesh that thy soul desireth, and if the place which the Lord, thy God, shall choose that his name should be there be far off, thou shalt kill of thy herds and of thy flocks, as I have commanded thee, and shalt eat in thy towns, as it pleaseth thee.* (Deut. 12:20-21)

> The Lord enlarged the borders of His church, when, spread through the preaching of the Apostles after His ascension into Heaven and the arrival of the Holy Spirit, it was enlarged in the whole world; at that time, the Apostles just mentioned seized the gentiles who came the faith, as if eating flesh, when they made them [join] with the body of Christ, that is the church, via grace of baptism, as if killing various animals.

> The place which the Lord shall choose signified the primitive church whose way of life (*conuersatio*) was far different from the way of life of gentiles for a long while; but when the nations began to believe, it was not necessary for them to congregate in one place or one province, but it was necessary for everyone to seek and to adore the Lord in his own place, just like the Psalmist says: "In every place of his dominion, O my soul, bless thou the Lord."[3]

Besides their belief, the un-Christian practices, *gentilium consuetudines peruersas*,

---

1 "Sunt plerique intra ecclesia qui timendo futuram paupertatem, nullam misericordiam plectuntur erga proximos suos indigentes; aiunt enim: Si ea que possideo pauperibus erogauero, unde sum sustentaturus meipsum atque domesticos meos?" Paris, BnF, NAL 1740, fol. 43v.

2 "Sicut gentiles, id est pagani, qui ignorantes Deum uerum, simulacra coluerunt." Paris, BnF, NAL 1740, fol. 13v, on Deut. 4:16 ("Ne forte decepti faciatis uobis sculptam similitudinem.")

3 "Dilatabit Dominus terminos ecclesiae suae quando post ascensionem suam in caelis et ad aduentum Spiritus sancti per apostolorum predicationem diffusa, in uniuerso mundo dilatata est; tunc iam dicti apostoli quasi carnes uesci caeperunt quando gentiles ad fidem uenientes, per baptismi gratiam uelut diuersa animalia mactantes, secum unum corpus Christi, quod est ecclesia, fecerunt." Paris, BnF, NAL 1740, fol. 37r. "Locus quem elegerit Dominus primitiuam significabat ecclesiam cuius conuersatio in primordio longe distabat a conuersatione gentilium; postquam uero gentes credere coeperunt, non eis fuit necessarium ad unum locum uel prouintiam conuenire, sed unumquemque in loco suo Dominum querere et adorare sicut psalmista ait: In omni loco dominationis eius, benedic anima mea Domino." Paris, BnF, NAL 1740, fol. 37r.

such as lacerating faces, cutting off hairs of the dead, and consulting the dead for prophecy, are singled out and condemned.[1] Agobard recorded certain *tempestarii* who were
believed to be able to control storms by means of incantation in the rural area of Lyon,
implying that the concern over pagan practice in the Lyon Annotations could have been
more than theoretical.[2]

Juxtaposed with pagan customs are the *superstitiones* of "philosophers," namely ancient pagan authors.[3] Their haughtiness (*elatio*) is condemned and their earthly wisdom
considered inferior to the Divine Wisdom.[4] Meanwhile, one annotation encourages the
adoption of philosophers' pagan knowledge by "spiritual men who were gifted with both
divine and human learning":

> *When thou hast besieged a city a long time and hath compassed it with bulwarks*
> *to take it, thou shalt not cut down the trees that may be eaten of...But if there be*
> *any trees that are not fruitful but wild and fit for other uses, cut them down...* (Deut.
> 20:19-20)

The city which was besieged for a long time by holy preachers, that is spiritual
fighters, tropologically signifies the philosophers of this world who resorted to human
reasons and were willing to convert later than other people. But because those same
philosophers wrote certain things morally well in their books, that is they spoke what
is true, just like fruitful trees, the ecclesiastical men shall not refuse these things. But
what they understood badly about God or His creatures, or in the praise of their own
gods, just like trees not fruitful, shall be cut off by the roots with the sword of severity.

---

1 "Masculinum gentilium diuine predicationi resistentem, superstitiones significat filosoforum atque
gentilium consuetudines peruersas; quas sancti predicatores gladio uerbi dei interfecerunt id est
funditus deleuerunt." Paris, BnF, NAL 1740, fol. 55r, on Deut. 20:13 ("Percuties omne quod in
ea generis masculini est in ore gladii."); "Sicut faciebant gentiles eo tempore super mortuos suos,
exterminantes facies suas et capita decaluantes."; Paris, BnF, NAL 1740, fol. 40v, on Deut. 14:1
("Non uos incidetis nec facietis caluitium super mortuo."); "Hoc iuxta historiam fidelibus cristianis
omnibus modis uitandum est." Paris, BnF, NAL 1740, fol. 50v, on Deut. 18:10-11 ("Nec inueniatur in
te qui lustret filium suum, aut filiam, ducens per ignem : aut qui ariolos sciscitetur, et obseruet somnia
atque auguria, nec sit maleficus, nec incantantor, nec qui pythones consulat, nec diuinos, aut quaerat
a mortuis ueritatem."); "Mortuos inmundos spiritus dicit, a quibus homines praediti futura scistentur."
Paris, BnF, NAL 1740, fol. 50v, on Deut. 18:11 (... quaerat a mortuis ueritatem.")
2 Agobard, *Liber contra insulsam uulgi opinionem de grandine et tonitruis*, CCCM 52; cf. Paul Dutton,
"Thunder and Hail"; Rob Meens, "Thunder over Lyons."
3 "Masculinum gentilium diuine predicationi resistentem, superstitiones significat filosoforum atque
gentilium consuetudines peruersas; quas sancti predicatores gladio uerbi dei interfecerunt id est
funditus deleuerunt." Paris, BnF, NAL 1740, fol. 55r, on Deut. 20:13 ("Percuties omne quod in ea
generis masculini est in ore gladii.").
4 "Potest et per camelum elatio filosoforum et superbia quorundam diuitum figuraliter demonstrare."
Paris, BnF, NAL 1740, fol. 41r, on Deut. 14:7; "Terra Egyptiorum presens mundus intelligitur: aque
eorum sapientia filosoforum quae non est de caelo sed terrena, animalis, diabolica; sancta uero
ecclesia imbre celesti id est diuinorum eloquiorum inrigatur; que ecclesia montuosa est perfectis
doctoribus, campestris autem in humilibus auditoribus." Paris, BnF, NAL 1740, fol. 32v, on Deut.
11:10-11.

Nobody inexperienced was able to carry out this job, but spiritual men who were gifted with both the divine and human learning, could manage to fulfill it.[1]

The ambivalent attitude toward pagan learning as we see in the annotation above has a deep intellectual tradition in the Latin west, from Augustine to Alcuin.[2] In comparison, the condemnation of heresy in the Lyon Annotations is much more unequivocal and harsher:

> *Thou shalt not make peace with them...* (Deut. 23:6)
> It is admonished to the catholic people that they do not keep peace or harmony with heretics at all.[3]

> *If any man be found soliciting his brother of the children of Israel and selling him shall take a price, he shall be put to death, and thou shalt take away the evil from the midst of thee.* (Deut. 24:7)
> This man assumes the figure of heretics who sell all those under sin, whom they cheat.[4]

> *Observe diligently that thou incur not the stroke of the leprosy...* (Deut. 24:8)
> Leprosy is the doctrine of heretics.[5]

> *Cursed be he that removeth his neighbour's landmarks, and all the people shall say, Amen. Cursed be he that maketh the blind to wander out of his way. And all the people shall say, Amen.* (Deut. 27:17-18)
> Cursed be every heretic who dares to remove, that is to change, the landmarks of faith in the church, for he makes whoever is blind and ignorant wander off the way,

---

1 "Ciuitas que multo tempore a sanctis predicatoribus, id est spiritalibus uellatoribus obsessa est, tropologice significat philosophos huius mundi qui humanas rationes requirendo, tardius quam ceteri homines credere uoluerunt. Sed quia isdem philosophi nonnulla in libris suis moraliter bene scripserunt, hoc quod uerum loquuti sunt, quasi arbores fructuosas, a uiris ecclesiasticis renuenda non sunt. Ea uero que aut de deo aut de eius creatura siue in laude deorum suorum male senserunt, quasi arbores infructuosas ferro seueritatis radicitus abscindende sunt; quod nemo inperitus facere potuit sed uiri spiritales, diuina atque humana scientia prediti, hoc implere ualuerunt." Paris, BnF, NAL 1740, fol. 55v.

2 Cf. John Marenbon, *Pagans and Philosophers: The Problem of Paganism from Augustine to Leibniz* (Princeton: Princeton University Press, 2015), pp. 19-72.

3 "Catholicis precipitur ut cum hereticis omnino pacem uel concordiam non habeant." Paris, BnF, NAL 1740, fol. 61r.

4 "Homo iste, hereticorum forma pretendit, qui omnes quos decipiunt, sub peccato uenumdant." Paris, BnF, NAL 1740, fol. 63v.

5 "Lepra hereticorum est dogma." Paris, BnF, NAL 1740, fol. 63v.

that is in faith.[1]

Cursed be he that perverteth the judgment of the stranger, of the fatherless and the widow. And all the people shall say, Amen. (Deut. 27:19)

Cursed be heretics who pervert the judgment of the fatherless, or the chosen people, and of the widow, that is the holy church.[2]

One may wonder whether the Annotator had Adoptionism in mind when he emphasized that heresy would arise when the *doctores* of the Church hold different views on the nature of the second person of God and His incarnation.[3] But he also held a historical view to trace the genealogy of heretics back to the origin of the Christian church:

But the prophet who being corrupted with pride shall speak in my name things that I did not command him to say or in the name of strange gods, shall be slain. (Deut. 18:20)

Taking the part for the whole (*a parte totum*), the proud prophet who, not through the spirit of God but depraved in his own understanding, talks not in truth but in falsehood, signifies the persona of all the heretics who emerged inside the church since the advent of our Savior, among whom were Simon Magus, Nicholas, Ebion, Marcion, Cerinthus, and Basilides.[4]

This heresiological list was very likely taken from the so-called *Decretum Gelasianum* or *Libris recipiendis et non recipiendis*, a sixth-century Frankish doctrinal document, which contains a catalogue of apocryphal books and writings of heretics to be rejected.[5]

---

1 "Maledictus omnis hereticus qui audet transfere, id est mutare, in eccleisa terminos fidei, Ipse enim caecum quelibet ignorantem errare facit in uia, hoc est in fide." Paris, BnF, NAL 1740, fol. 70r.

2 "Maledicti heretici qui peruertunt iudicium pupilli uel populi electi et uiduae sanctae uidelicet ecclesiae." Paris, BnF, NAL 1740, fol. 70r.

3 "Viri iurgientes inter se, doctores significant ecclesiam de dispensationem dominice incarnationis diuersa sentientes, e quibus ille qui aduersus alterum preualet, de catholicum demonstrat qui per auctoritatem ueritatis, hereticum conuicit et refutat. Cuius heretici uxor dicitur plebs carnalis uel qulilibet fautor hereticorum, qui de incarnatione Domini male sentiendo blasphemat, cuius presumptio, uelut manus, ab ecclesia abscidatur." Paris, BnF, NAL 1740, fol. 66r, on Deut. 25:11-12 ("Si habuerint inter se iurgium uiri et unus contra alterum rixari coeperint uolensque uxor alterius eruere uirum suum de manu fortioris miserit manum et adpraehenderit uerenda eius, abscideres manu illius.") Cf. "De hereticis dicit qui Filium Dei non creatorem omnium cum Patrem se creaturam adfirmare conantur sicut Arriani et Eunamiani." Paris, BnF, NAL 1740, fol. 18r, on Deut. 5:11 ("Non usurparis nomen Domini Dei tui frustra.")

4 "Propheta arrogans qui non per spiritum Dei sed sensu proprio deprauatus, mendacio non ueritate loquitur, a parte totum personam significat omnium hereticorum qui per aduentum Saluatoris nostri in ecclesia emerserunt, ex quibus fuit Simon Magus, Nicolaus, Euion, Marcion, Cenrintus, Basilides et ceteri eorum similes." Paris, BnF, NAL 1740, fol. 51r.

5 Ernst von Dobschütz, *Das Decretum Gelasianum de libris recipiendis et non recipiendis* (Leipzig: J. C. Hinrichs, 1912), pp. 58-59.

To determine and to condemn someone as a heretic, the priests need to refer to both the Old and New Testaments and "the opinion of Holy Fathers" (*concilium sanctorum patrum*).[1] When someone is condemned as a heretic through the judgment of priests, he could recognize his error and return to the Catholic Church through penance:

> *If there be a controversy between men and they call upon the judges, they shall give the prize of justice to him whom they perceive to be just, and him whom they find to be wicked they shall condemn of wickedness. And if they see that the offender be worthy of stripes, they shall lay him down, and shall cause him to be beaten before them. According to the measure of the sin shall the measure also of the stripes be, yet so that they exceed not the number of forty, lest thy brother depart shamefully torn before thy eyes.* (Deut. 25:1-3)

That is, the conflict between the catholic and the heretic arises, whose case is delivered to the judgment of priests. It is proper to give the palm of victory to the side whom they prove catholic; but they will condemn the one whom they judge impious, that is heretical. But if the same heretic recognizes his error and wants to return to the catholic faith and make amends for past perfidy, may the opportunity of penance (*penitentiae locus*) not be denied to him according to the priestly judgment, but he shall make penance according to the nature of his fault (*iuxta qualitatem culpe suae*) in a humble way, so that his penance, like his stripes, does not exceed the number of forty. For it is better for any heretic or other repentant sinner to receive what he deserves in this life.[2]

The judgment of ecclesiastical councils first, the penance next: the settlement of heresy described is not dissimilar to what Felix of Urgel experienced in *Francia* (cf. Chapter 3.1). Once again, the seemingly purely theoretical exposition in the Lyon Annotations does not lack realistic color.

---

1   "Iam superius in hoc libro premissum est quod nemo debeat condemnari uelut hereticus nisi quem lex et Euangelium condemnauerit." Paris, BnF, NAL 1740, fol. 53r, on Deut. 19:15 ("Non stabit testis unus contra aliquem."); "Testis mendax hereticus est, catholicum quemlibet tamquam hereticum condemnare uolens; quorum causa in concilio sanctorum patrum diligenter examinata, quem hereticum probauerint, condemnabunt; quem catholicum, illi pluma uictoriae dabunt." Paris, BnF, NAL 1740, fol. 66r, on Deut. 19:16-19 ("Si steterit testis mendax contra hominem ... stabunt ambo... in conspectu sacerdotum... cumque diligentissime perscrutantes... reddent ei sicut fratri suo facere cogitauit.")

2   "Id est inter catholicum et hereticum intentio orta fuerit, quorum causa in iudicio sacerdotum perducta, quem catholicum probauerint illi palmam uictoriae dare oportet; quem uero impium, hoc est hereticum, iudicauerint, condemnabunt; quod si idem hereticus, cognito herrore suo, ad catholicam fidem redire uoluerit et preterita perfidia satisfacere, secundum iudicium sacerdotalem ei penitentiae locus non negetur, sed iuxta qualitatem culpe suae humiliatus peniteat, ita tamen ut eius penitentia quasi uerbera quadrigenarium numerum non excedat. Melius enim est cuilibet heretici uel alio peccatori conuerso in hac uita recipere quod meretur." Paris, BnF, NAL 1740, fol. 65r.

***

In a seminal paper on the voluminous commentary on Leviticus composed by the twelfth-century Benedictine monk Ralph of Flaix, John Van Engen discussed how this Old Testament ritual book was interpreted as a moral and religious guide to Christian community via the technique of biblical exegesis. One of the major achievements of this commentary from the perspective of the Christian hermeneutics of Leviticus, as Van Engen manifested, is how Ralph broke through the predominantly Christology-oriented exegetical tradition, which originated with Origen and culminated in Hrabanus Maurus, and interpreted Leviticus as a "Law": "Law" in the sense not of the literal observance of ritual regulations, but of "the defining marks and divinely sanctioned practices of a religious community."[1] By the discussion in this chapter, the same appreciation is also applicable to what the author of the Lyon Annotations did to Deuteronomy. In the Annotations, we read not merely theological doctrines (which certainly are not absent though), but a colorful representation of the way of life of a Christian church (not a monastic community as in the case of Ralph's, but rather one characterized of pastoral structure): its self-identity (*spiritalis Israel*), its rules (transformed either *secundum litteram* or *spiritaliter* from Mosaic precepts), its internal hierarchy, its moral concern, and its enemies. In short, to borrow Van Engen's impressive wording, in the Lyon Annotations we see "Deuteronomy interpreted as Christian community."

What's more, another major point of the same paper of Van Engen is that the innovative exegetical approach in Ralph's commentary was a reaction to the intellectual challenge of the Jewish interpretation of Leviticus which dangerously attracted the contemporary uneducated Christian clerics. The same "Jewish shadow" is no less significant in the Lyon Annotations. This is the topic that we will turn to now.

---

1   John Van Engen, "Ralph of Flaix: The Book of Leviticus Interpreted as Christian Community," *Jews and Christians in Twelfth-Century Europe*, eds. John Van Engen, Michael Signer (Notre Dame: University of Notre Dame Press, 2001), pp. 150-170.

CHAPTER 8
THE JEWISH QUESTION

Around one quarter of all the exegetical entries in the Lyon Annotations mention the Jews. The language is largely (but not exclusively, though, as we will see) hostile, and even vituperative. In a delicately written paper arguing for a general anti-Jewish intellectual atmosphere in Lyon during the first half of the ninth century, Warren Pezé took the Lyon Annotations as one of his major sources and called it "un commentaire à tendance antijuive." In Pezé's opinion, the violent rhetoric against Jews in the Annotations reflects the common intention among the early-ninth-century clerics of Lyon to exclude Jews from Christians' social life, and Agobard's anti-Jewish polemics composed during the 820s should be understood in this intellectual atmosphere.[1]

The scholar whom Pezé is in implicit dialogue with is Johannes Heil. Heil refuted the idea that there was real campaign against the Jewish community in ninth-century Lyon; instead, the authors of Lyon used anti-Jewish rhetoric for other purposes: in Agobard's case, in order to protest the encroachment of secular power on local church property.[2] Moreover, more pertinent to our concern, Heil doubted that the representations of Jews and Judaism commonly found in Carolingian exegesis had anything to do with exegetes' attitude to actual Jews in social life. They are rather, in a term borrowed from Jeremy Cohen,[3] "hermeneutical Jews":

> [I]n their exegeses the Jews played an eminent, now and then dominant role, and they were for the authors more or less "real." This reality did not depend on physical evidence or social encounters, but was instead defined by the Scriptures, the interpretation inherited from the Fathers, and knowledge about the nature of

---

1 Warren Pezé, "Amalaire et la communauté juive de Lyon." The argument of this chapter can be found summarized in Yin Liu, "Agobard, Deuteronomic Curses, and an Anti-Jewish Exegetical Discourse in Carolingian Lyon," *Viator* 51 (2020): pp. 205-239.

2 Johannes Heil, "Agobard, Amolo, Das Kirchengut und die Juden von Lyon," *Francia* 25 (1998): pp. 39-76.

3 Cf. Jeremy Cohen, *Living Letters of the Law: Ideas of the Jew in Medieval Christianity* (Berkeley: University of California Press, 1999), pp. 2-3, in which the "hermeneutical Jew" is defined as "the Jew as constructed in the discourse of Christian theology, and above all in Christian theologians' interpretation of Scripture."

time and history... The Jews in Carolingian exegesis were imagined, "pneumatic" or "hermeneutic" Jews, a type, and contemporary Jews were, if at all, perceived through the lens of this all-important type. Therefore, the image of the Jews in Carolingian exegesis was the product of fundamental theological views and personal concerns of the exegetes, rather than the role of the Jews in the actual world of the Carolingian domains.[1]

Against this scholarly background, this chapter unfolds our own discussion on "the Jewish question" in the Lyon Annotations. The questions to be asked and examined are: how the Lyon Annotator presented the Jews, their relationship with the Old Law, and their position in the history of salvation; and how the exegesis in the Annotations is related to the anti-Jewish rhetoric that characterizes the writings of Agobard.

8.1   Expounding Deuteronomy Contra Iudaeos

In the Lyon Annotations, there are plenty of entries in which, in Pezé's words, "les juifs sont sévèrement admonestés."[2] The *prior populus*, due to their rejection of the true Savior and the true faith, were kept out of not only the present church but also the King-dom of Heaven:

> *Beware lest perhaps your heart be deceived and you depart from the Lord and serve strange gods and adore them and the Lord being angry shut up heaven that the rain come not down nor the earth yield her fruit and you perish quickly from the excellent land which the Lord will give you.* (Deut. 11:16-17)
>
> Because they despised to observe the precepts of God, expelled from the land which the Lord had given to them, the people of Jews were destroyed and made alien-ated not only from the land, but also from the church of God.[3]

> *Go up to the top of Pisgah, and cast thy eyes round about to the west and to the north and to the south and to the east, and behold it, for thou shalt not pass this Jor-dan.* (Deut. 3:27)
>
> Moses who was prohibited by the Lord from entering the Promised Land in this passage, assumed the figure of the Law through which the earlier people of Jews (*prior*

---

1   Johannes Heil, "Labourers in the Lord's Quarry," pp. 92-93. For more comprehensive argumentation, cf. his monograph *Kompilation oder Konstruktion*.
2   Warren Pezé, "Amalaire et la communauté juive de Lyon," p. 20.
3   "Populus Iudeorum pro eo quod precepta Dei custodire contempsit, idcirco de terra quam ei Dominus dederat expulsi perierunt, et non tantum de illa, sed etiam de ecclesia Dei alieni effecti sunt." Paris, BnF, NAL 1740, fol. 33r.

populus Iudeorum) were not able to receive the Kingdom of Heaven. He was able to foresee the Promised Land through the spirit of prophecy but, as it was said, was not able to enter it; for the Law brought nothing to perfection.[1]

A mamzer, that is to say, one born of a prostitute, shall not enter into the church of the Lord until the tenth generation. (Deut. 23:2)

Mamzer is the name of the one born of fornication; he signifies the unbelieving Jews (*Iudeos incredulos*) whom the Lord accuses through Prophet Isaiah by saying: "But draw near hither, you sons of the sorceress, the seed of the adulterer, and of the harlot." (Isaiah 57:3) Therefore, they will not enter the church of the Lord in the tenth generation, that is by the justification of law, as the Apostle witnessed by saying: "Because by the works of the law no flesh shall be justified before him." (Romans 3:20)[2]

Thou shalt see the land before thee which I will give to the children of Israel, but thou shalt not enter into it. (Deut. 32:52)

Moses, that is the teachers of the Law (*legis doctores*), saw the Promised Land, that is clearly the Incarnation of the Savior, through the books of Law and Prophets, but because they did not want to believe, they thus did not have the right to enter the Kingdom of Heaven.[3]

They are called *perfidi Iudei*, obstinate in the useless "carnal" observance of the Law and morally suspicious:

Circumcise therefore the foreskin of your heart, and stiffen your neck no more... (Deut. 10:16)

Let the faithless Jews (*perfidi Iudei*) hear these, who boast about the circumcision of flesh, and let them believe in the Son of God whom they deny now, and may they be able to pursue the spiritual circumcision through the faith and the grace of baptism;

---

1 "Moyses in hoc loco qui prohibitus est a Domino terram repromissionis ingredi, formam tenuit legis per quam prior populus Iudeorum regnum caelorum accipere non ualuit. Quam terram repromissionis per spiritu propheticae preuidere potuit sed in ea, ut dictum est, ingredi nequiuit; nihil enim ad perfectum perduxit lex." Paris, BnF, NAL 1740, fol. 11v.

2 "Mamzer appellatus de fornicatione natus; significat Iudeos incredulos quos Dominus per Esaiam prophetam sed arguens dicit: Vos autem accedite huc, fili auguriatrices, semen adulteri et fornicariae. Hi enim non intrabunt ecclesiam Domini, per decimam generationem, per iustam uidelicet legis, teste Apostolo qui ait: Quia et operibus legis non iustificabitur omnis caro coram illo." Paris, BnF, NAL 1740, fol. 61r.

3 "Vidit Moyses, id est legis doctores terra repromissionis, incarnationem uidelicet Saluatoris, per libros legis et prophetarum, sed quia credere noluerunt, idcirco in regnum caelorum ingredi non meruerunt." Paris, BnF, NAL 1740, fol. 90r.

for the circumcision of flesh benefits nothing without the cleanness of heart.[1]

But of them that chew the cud but divide not the hoof, you shall not eat, such as the camel, the hare and the cherogril. Because they chew the cud but divide not the hoof, they shall be unclean to you. The swine also, because it divideth the hoof but cheweth not the cud, shall be unclean; their flesh you shall not eat, and their carcasses you shall not touch. (Deut. 14:7-8)

By camel, the tall and enormous animal, nothing other than Scribes and Pharisees are intended to be signified, indeed those who chew the cud, that is meditate on the Law but never divide between letter and spirit.[2]

By hare [is signified] the Jewish city, cowardly, soft, savage, and resistant to nobody.[3]

By Cherogril [is signified] the same infidel city of Jews, covered by spines of their sins and sticking to their impiety stubbornly.[4]

There is no doubt that by swine, that is pig, the same Jews, or heretics, and others who wallow in their mud of libido are signified.[5]

By their flesh, he insinuates nothing other than the carnal superstitions, that is their false tradition; by their carcasses, he points to nothing other than the works of death, from all of which the Christian believer should keep away.[6]

... he shall see that their hand is weakened and that they who were shut up have also failed... (Deut. 32:36)

This is [the hand] of the Jews, whose activity is weakened just like the hand, and who failed in their infidelity, as if shut up in prison.[7]

They are deprived of the knowledge of God:

---

1 "Audiant haec perfidi Iudei qui de circumcisione carnis gloriantur et credant in Dei Filio quem nunc negant et per fidem et baptisimi gratiam spiritalem circumcisionem consequi ualeant; nam circumcisio carnis sine munditia cordis nihil prodest." Paris, BnF, NAL 1740, fol. 31r.

2 "Quid per camelum animal altum, inormen, ni scribas et phariseos significari uult; ruminantes quidem, id est in lege meditantes sed inter litteram et spiritum nequaquam diuidentes." Paris, BnF, NAL 1740, fol. 41r.

3 "Per leporem plebem iudaicam, timidam mollem atque inmansuetam nullique resistentem." Paris, BnF, NAL 1740, fol. 41r.

4 "Per chirogillium eandem plebem perfidam Iudeorum, spinis peccatorum suorum coopertam et impietatem suam pertinaciter defendentem." Paris, BnF, NAL 1740, fol. 41r.

5 "Per sus id est porcum eosdem Iudeos siue hereticos atque ceteros in ceno libidinis suo uolutantes figurare non dubium est." Paris, BnF, NAL 1740, fol. 41r.

6 "Quid per eorum carnes nisi carnales subpretitiones id est uanas eorum traditiones insinuat et quid per cadauera eorum nisi opera mortalitatis demonstrat, a quibus omnibus fidelis christianus abstinere debet." Paris, BnF, NAL 1740, fol. 41r.

7 "Hoc est Iudeorum, quorum operatio uelut manus infirmata est, qui in infidelitate sua, tamquam in carcere conclusi, defecerunt." Paris, BnF, NAL 1740, fol. 88v.

And he said, I will hide my face from them... (Deut. 32:20)

The Lord has hidden His face from Jews until today, by taking away the knowledge of Him from them so that they have been alike to the gentiles who did not know God.[1]

You shall not add to the word that I speak to you, neither shall you take away from it. (Deut. 4:2)

He who preaches what the Holy Scripture does not say from his own understanding will add to or take away the Word of God, just like it is clear that Scribes and Pharisees and all the heretics have done, who transgressed the command of God because of their false traditions.[2]

... burning it with brimstone and the heat of salt so that it cannot be sown any more nor any green thing grow therein... (Deut. 29:23)

The city of Jews set on fire and burnt, by the mire of luxury as if brimstone and by the heat of desire and malice as if fire; the seed of the Word of God cannot be sown, nor can it have any green thing, that is the hope of future happiness.[3]

They are Devil's associates and a sinful nation under the divine curse:

They have sinned against him and are not of his children in their filth; they are a wicked and perverse generation. (Deut. 32:5)

That is the Jews in the filth of idols, who used to be sons of God, but now are sons of the Devil, as the Lord said to them: "You are of your father the devil." (John 8:44)[4]

For only Og, king of Basan, remained of the race of the giants. His bed of iron is shewn, which is in Rabbath of the children of Ammon... (Deut. 3:11)

The king of Basan, which means "conclusion," the king of "confusion" and "ignominy," bore the figure of the Devil. His bed of iron is to be understood as the impious people and the sinners in whom the Devil rules through impiety and injustice. That bed, that is the rest of the Devil, had been extended to the four parts of the world among all the nations living without law before the advent of the Savior; but now, removed from the hearts of nations through the advent of the Lord, the Devil holds

---

1 "Vsque in hodiernum diem abscondit Dominus faciem suam a Iudeis, subtrahendo illis cognitionem suam ita ut similes forent gentilibus qui non nouerunt Deum." Paris, BnF, NAL 1740, fol. 87r.

2 "Ille de Verbum Dei addet uel demet qui ex proprio sensu hoc predicat quod diuina Scriptura non dicit sicut scribae et fariseiat atque omnes heretici fecisse manifestum est, qui propter traditiones suas falsas, mandatum Dei transgressi sunt." Paris, BnF, NAL 1740, fol. 12r.

3 "Plebs Iudeorum fetore luxuriae quasi sulfure et ardore cupiditatis adque malitie uelut igne succensa atque conbusta; semen uerbi Dei seri non potest neque uiride quicquam, id est spem future beatitudinis, habere potest." Paris, BnF, NAL 1740, fol. 80r.

4 "Id est Iudei in sordibus idolorum, qui aliquando filii Dei, (n)unc autem filii diaboli, ipso Domino eis dicentem: Vos ex patre diabolo estis." Paris, BnF, NAL 1740, fol. 86r.

supremacy among Jews and heretics, as if in the citadel of the children of Ammon.[1]

... for I am the Lord, thy God, a jealous God, visiting the iniquity of the fathers upon their children unto the third and fourth generation to them that hate me... (Deut. 5:9)

The one who is jealous is a *zelator*, who will visit the sins of the fathers upon the children unto the third and fourth generation, that is clearly unto those who prove to be the imitators of their evil parents, just like we see have happened to the infidel Jews today (*nunc perfidis Iudeis*).[2]

But if thou wilt not hear the voice of the Lord, thy God, to keep and to do all his commandments and ceremonies which I command thee this day, all these curses shall come upon thee, and overtake thee. (Deut. 28:15)

... after them [the blessings] follow the curses by the Lord upon them, that is the Jews, who have not believed in Christ; these curses abide in their offspring all the time.[3]

Among all the late antique and early medieval exegetes of Deuteronomy whom we have closely examined in Chapters 4–6, Origen's exposition shows the strongest anti-Jewish color (cf. Chapter 4.2), and, in two cases, the Lyon Annotator might have taken over certain of his *contra Iudaeos* motifs:

The stranger that liveth with thee in the land shall rise up over thee, and shall be higher, and thou shalt go down, and be lower. He shall lend to thee, and thou shalt not lend to him. He shall be as the head, and thou shalt be the tail. (Deut. 28:43-44)

The stranger signifies the people of the gentiles who were rejected, as if being the tail, before the advent of the Savior. But after His advent, they were prioritized via His

---

1 "Hoc rex Basan qui interpretatur conclusio, rex confusionis atque ignominie, figuram gestauit diaboli. Lectus eius ferreus uiri sunt homines impii atque peccatores in quibus per impietatem atque iniustitiam regnat accipiuntur. Quod lectum, id est requies eius, ante aduentum Saluatoris in cunctis gentibus sine lege uiuentibus per quattuor mundi partes dilatatum erat; nunc autem per aduentum Domini de corda gentilium exclusus, in Iudeis et hereticis, quasi in arcem filiorum Amon principatum tenet." Paris, BnF, NAL 1740, fol. 10r.

2 "Hemulator id est zelator, qui reddet peccata patrum in filios usque in tertiam et quartam generationem, in his uidelicet qui malorum parentum suorum imitatores existunt, sicut nunc perfidis Iudeis eueniesse uidemus." Paris, BnF, NAL 1740, fol. 17v.

3 "... post haec secuntur maledictiones a Domino in eis, id est Iudeis, qui credere Christo noluerunt; quae maledictiones usque manent super eorum posteritatem." Paris, BnF, NAL 1740, fol. 72r.

grace; but Jews who used to be first were made last.[1]

But the Lord's portion is his people, Jacob the lot of his inheritance. (Deut. 32:9)

But the Lord's portion is to be understood not as the carnal Israel or Jacob, but rather as the spiritual Jacob, the supplanter of vices, seeing God through faith.[2]

However, it is noteworthy that the strong and extensive anti-Jewish accent in the multiple above cited entries of the Lyon Annotations is largely absent in the Latin patristic exegesis of Deuteronomy. For example, Jews rarely appear in Augustine's expositions of Deuteronomy in *Expositio in Heptateuchum* and *Contra Faustum*, or Gregory's as collected in *Liber testimoniorum*. While Augustine and Gregory were in fact among the few most influential contributors to the Jewish question in the west ever,[3] it seems that both Fathers did not intend to deal with this issue when expounding the fifth book of the Bible.

Isidore was the author of *De fide catholica contra Iudaeos*, the most extensive anti-Jewish theological treatise after Tertullian's.[4] However, the anti-Jewish element in his commentary on Deuteronomy in *Expositio* is not strong as well. Of all the twenty-two expositional entries, only in three entries is the theme of *contra Iudaeos* briefly touched. Entry 1 expounds the eleven days during which Moses composed Deuteronomy as "the falling of the Judaic city in the Gospel due to the transgression of the precepts of the Decalogue."[5] In Entry 17 (based on Cassian; cf. Chapter 6.1), "*blasphema Iudaeorum*" is

---

1 "Aduena populum significat gentium qu(i) ante aduentum Saluatoris quasi in cauda reprobus erat, post eius uero aduentum per gratiam ipsius factus est priori; Iudei uero qui primi erant, facti sunt nouissimi." Paris, BnF, NAL 1740, fol. 74v. Cf. Origen, *Homiliae in Iesu Nave*, VII.5, GCS 30, p. 332: "Et facti sumus propter fidem Christi nos 'sursum,' ille autem populus, qui permansit incredulus, 'deorsum,' secundum Deuteronomii prophetiam. Si qui ergo habet in se Christum, qui est 'omnium caput,' hic efficitur 'in caput;' illi enim negauerunt Christum Iesum et effecti sunt in caudam et qui erant 'primi,' facti sunt 'nouissimi.'"

2 "Pars autem Domini non tantum carnalis Israel uel Iacob sed potius spiritalis Iacob uitiorum subplantator et per fidem uidens Deum accipiendum est." Paris, BnF, NAL 1740, fol. 86r. Cf. Origen, *Homiliae in Exodum*, VIII.2, GCS 29, pp. 220-221. "Verum, ne aestimes haec tantum ad illum dici 'Istrahel', qui 'secundum carnem' est, multo magis haec ad te dicuntur, qui Istrahel effectus es mente Deum uidendo et circumcisus es corde, non carne. Nam et si in carne gentes sumus, in spiritu Istrahel sumus, propter eum, qui dixit: 'pete a me, et dabo tibi gentes haereditatem tuam et possessionem tuam terminos terrae' et propter eum, qui iterum dixit: 'Pater, omnia mea tua sunt et tua mea, et glorificatus sum in his'; si tamen ita agas, ut dignus sis 'pars' esse Dei et in 'funiculo haereditatis eius' metiri. Alioquin si indigne agas, exemplo tibi sint illi, qui ad hoc uocati fuerant, ut essent 'pars' Dei, et peccatis suis hoc meruerunt, ut 'dispergerentur per omnes gentes.'"

3 The relevant literature is enormous. For a fine synthesis, see Jeremy Cohen, *Living Letters of the Law*, pp. 19-94.

4 PL 83, cols. 449-538. Cf. Wolfram Drews, *The Unknown Neighbour: The Jew in the Thought of Isidore of Seville* (Leiden: Brill, 2006).

5 "Deuteronomium autem secunda legis latio dicitur, quod significat Euangelium. In cuius principio notandum est quid indicet quod undecim diebus idem Deuteronomium a Moyse scribitur; significat uero Iudaicae plebis lapsum in Euangelio per transgressionem Decalogi mandatorum." Isidore, Expositio in uetus testamentum, V.1, PL 83, col. 359.

signified by one of the three nations vanquished by Israel in Egypt.[1] Among the multiple expositions in Entry 6 on Deut. 22:10 ("Thou shalt not plough with an ox and an ass together"), the one based on Jerome (cf. Chapter 6.1) is anti-Jewish:

> In the name of ox, the people of circumcision who are placed under the yoke of the Law are to be understood; in ass, the people of nations who are related to the Gospel are to be understood. He who ploughs with an ox and an ass together receives the Gospel but does not abandon the ceremonies of Jewish superstitions which had preceded in shadow and image.[2]

The Lyon Annotator picked up this exposition, but adapted it to a more aggressive format:

> Another way to interpret: hold the Christian religion (*religionem cristianam*) fast in both faith and deed, so that you want to have no connection with the superstitions of the Jews, lest you become lame in both feet.[3]

Among the original expositions in the Deuteronomy section of the Pseudo-Bedan Pentateuch commentary, a few contain anti-Jewish element. The most significant one is to connect Jews to Moses' curses for the transgressors of the Law, which can be found in all the three recensions.[4] We will discuss it in the next subchapter. The β recension contains two other entries of *contra Iudaeos* reference. The first expounds the lame animal (mentioned in Deut. 15:21) as "the Jewish people who believe in letters rather than true understanding (*sensum*)."[5] The second is an allegorical reading of the law of

---

1 "Qui numerus, adiecta idololatria gentium, blasphemia Iudaeorum, errore haereticorum, euidentissime adimpletur. Quibus ante notitiam Dei et gratiam baptismi, uel impia impietate gentium gentilium, uel blasphema Iudaeorum, uel errore haereticorum, multitudo subjecta est, donec in intellectuali Aegypto commorantur." Isidore, *Expositio in uetus testamentum*, V.17, PL 83, col. 367.

2 "In bouis nomine populus ex circumcisione positus sub jugo legis accipitur; in asino autem populus gentium pertinens ad Euangelium. In boue quippe et asino simul arat qui sic recipit Euangelium, ut Iudaicarum superstitionum, quae in umbra et imagine praecesserant, caeremonias non relinquat." Isidore, *Expositio in uetus testamentum*, V.6, PL 83, col. 361.

3 "Id est stultum quemlibet sapienti in predicatione ne socies. Aliter: Ita religionem cristianam fide et opere retine, ut cum subprestitionibus Iudoerum nullam societatem abere uelis, ne utroque pede claudus efficiaris." Paris, BnF, NAL 1740, fol. 59r.

4 "In duobus autem montibus Garizim, Balim, quibus benedictiones et maledictiones inferuntur, utrumque Testamentum significare potest, quia populus sub lege positus, sub maledicto tenebatur. Quia scriptum est: Maledictus qui non permanet in sermonibus huius legis, nec eos opere facit. Denique Iudaei, traditiones phariseicas obseruantes, mandata legis contempserunt. In Nouo autem Testamento gratiae benedictio in populum Christianum redundauit, quo Christus eleuans manum benedixit apostolos. Utrumque Testamentum tamen mons est, quia utrumque spirituale intellectum habet, quem Iudaei non intelligentes, sub occidente eos littera uiuebant." PL 91, col. 394 = Milan, Biblioteca Ambrosiana, G.82 inf., fol. 98v.

5 "Potest quoque claudus populum Iudaicum significare, credentem tantum litteram, et non sensum." PL 91, col. 387.

divorce:

> *If a man take a wife and have her and she find not favour in his eyes for some*
> *uncleanness, he shall write a bill of divorce and shall give it in her hand, and send her*
> *out of his house. And when she is departed and marrieth another husband and he also*
> *hateth her and hath given her a bill of divorce, and hath sent her out of his house or*
> *is dead, the former husband cannot take her again to wife, because she is defiled, and*
> *is become abominable before the Lord, lest thou cause thy land to sin, which the Lord,*
> *thy God, shall give thee to possess.* (Deut. 24:1-4)

This man signifies Christ, and the wife the synagogue of Jews which did not discover Christ but pursued him and dragged him to the cross. The bill of divorce is the
Gospel; her hand is the works of infidelity; the house is the church or the Kingdom of
Heaven; another husband is the Apostle whose house signifies the church. Or if he is
dead, [he died] when helping sinners. The former husband, that is Christ, [cannot take
her again to wife], that is the synagogue, because she is impenitent. The land which
you shall not cause to sin is the body or the church.[1]

In the Lyon Annotations, we can find a piece of exposition similar to the one shown
above on the same lemma:

> But in the tropological sense, this wife signifies the synagogue of Jews which the
> Lord formerly used to unite with Himself through the knowledge of the Law; but be-
> cause she displeased [Him] in His eyes due to her own unbelief, like her uncleanness,
> in the advent of the Son of God, He gave her the bill of divorce, that is the books of
> Law and of Prophets in which this divorce was written, and sent her out of his house,
> that is, separated her from the Holy Church. But the synagogue which the Lord repu-
> diated preferred to stay under the Law rather than under Grace, as if she was united
> with another man. The Law itself repudiates her for her transgression. For if they had
> believed in Moses, they would have certainly received the Son of God. Thus, the said
> city of Jews [was] repudiated by both Christ and the Law, as if by two men. As long

---

1 "Hic homo Christum significat, uxor synagogam Iudaeorum, quae Christum non inuenit persequendo,
et ad crucem trahendo. Liber autem repudii, id est Euangelium; Manus autem illius, id est opera
infidelitatis; domus ecclesia est, siue regnum coelorum; alter maritus, apostolum, cujusque domus
ecclesiam significat. Vel si mortuus fuerit, in adiutorio peccatoribus. Non poterit prior maritus, id est
Christus, synagogam, quia impoenitens est. Nec peccare facies terram, id est, corpus uel ecclesiam."
PL 91, cols. 392.

as she is like such, she is unclean and filthy, and cannot go back to the former man.[1]

The β recension of Pseudo-Bede might have been one of the sources for the Lyon Annotations, as we have discussed in Chapter 6.6. If the exposition in the Lyon Annotations above indeed derives from Pseudo-Bede, its adaptation highlights a particular thesis: Jews are the transgressor of the Law. The same theme appears repeatedly.[2] Behind the strong anti-Jewish tone of the Lyon Annotations lies a general exegetical theme: Jews or Christians, who are the true observers of the Law of God? One can argue that such a question must be taken as purely exegetical rhetoric, exclusively serving Christians' theological construction.[3] However, while the Jewish-Christian interconnection in the Latin west was less intensive in the early Middle Ages than later periods, wherever Christianity and Judaism ever coexisted and competed with each other, the Law, its interpretation, and its observance could become a real intellectual battlefield.

A well-known ninth-century case of such is the apostate Bodo. In 838/839, Bodo who had served as a court deacon of Louis the Pious abandoned Christianity, converted to Judaism, and fled from the Christian Frankish Empire to Muslim Spain. He later had himself circumcised, grew his hair and beard, and changed his name to Eleazar. This incident not only shocked the Frankish world, but also led to a religious dispute in Spain with the Mozarab author Alvarus who tried to persuade Bodo/Eleazar to return to the Christian faith, only to arouse the latter's hostile response. Four letters from Alvarus and three from Bodo are extant. They record a theological debate which consists of harsh attacks on each other's religion. In the lone manuscript, the three letters of Bodo were almost completely erased by a later reader (maybe of the thirteenth century) who apparently

---

1   "Tropologice autem mulier haec significat sinagoga Iudeorum quam sibi Dominus retro olim per cognitionem legis sociauit; sed quia in aduentum Filii Dei ob incredulitatem suam quasi feditatem displicuit in oculis eius, ideo dedit ei libellum repudii, ide est libros legis et prophetarum, in quibus scriptum est hoc repudium, et emisit eam de domo sua, id est ab a sancta ecclesia separabit. Quae tamen sinagoga quam Dominus repudiauit, quasi alteri uiro coniuncta est, cum maluit sub lege esse quam sub gratia, quem (quam?) etiam et ipsa lex propter eius preuaricationem repudiat. Si enim credidissent Moysi, recipissent utique Filium Dei. Et idcirco iam dicta plebs Iudeorum a Christo et lege quasi a duobus uiris repudiata. Quamdiu talis fuerit inmunda atque sordida est; et ad priorem uirum reuertere non poterit." Paris, BnF, NAL 1740, fol. 62v.

2   E.g.: "Prima generatio peccati est originale delictum quod ex Adam in omne genus hominum propagatum est. Secunda generatio peccati est preuaricatio naturalis legis de qua in psalmo scriptum est: Preuaricatores reputaui omnes peccatores terrae. Tertia generatio peccati est transgressio legis que per Moysen data est. Quarta generatio peccati est in eis qui Filium Dei negant et eius Euuangelium recipere nolunt; que generatio peccati deterior est omni peccato. <H>ec sunt quattor generationes delic<t>orum que ex malorum parentum in nequissimis filiis eorum a Domino redduntur. De Iudeis quippe <Domi>nus in Euangelio ait: Et uiderunt me et oderunt me et Patrem meum; quod uero addidit: Et faciens misericordiam in multa <m>ilia, id est sine finem, ad electis pertinet." Paris, BnF, NAL 1740, fol. 17v, on Deut. 5:9.

3   Cf. Johnannes Heil, "Goldenes Zeitalter," pp. 106-110.

tried to stop the circulation of those blasphemous words.[1] However, from the remaining fragments and especially Alvarus' verbatim quotations from his rival, we are still able to recover the general argumentation of Bodo, whose central theme is the interpretation of the Hebrew Bible and the observance of the Law.[2]

Bode described his own conversion as "from the idolatry to the cult of the highest God." In Judaic faith, he "devoted [him]self to standing fast sedulously in the law of the Lord (*in lege Domini*)."[3] He acutely pointed out the intrinsic link between the Holy Scripture, its interpretation, and worship:

> Jerome whose translation of scriptures you [Christians] use presented the whole Psalms word by word; for other books of the Holy Scripture, however, he composed false translation. Among Jews alone there is an integral text of scriptures and an integral interpretation of this text. Among you Christians, there are as many understandings as interpreters. We Jews have a single text of scriptures and a single way of worship (*cultum*). But I saw in the palace of the king of the Franks [Louis the Pious] fourteen 'catholic' men whose ways of cult were diverse from each other.[4]

According to Bodo, Judaism is characterized by the consistency between the way of life and the Law as given by God, while the Christians did not observe the Law but interpreted it erroneously:

> Since you always adhere to the witnesses of Law and of Prophets, I ask you: why you do not observe the ceremonies of the Law? In fact, [what good] are all these laws for you who are inspired by the love of money and seized by libido? There is no surprise that the laymen are rarely chaste. Your clerics themselves are proud of having pleasant embraces by sleeping with diverse women.

---

1 For the background, see Allen Cabaniss, "Bodo-Eleazar: A Famous Jewish Convert," *The Jewish Quarterly Review* 43 (1953): pp. 313-28; Bernhard Blumenkranz, "Du nouveau sur Bodo-Eleazar?" *Revue des Études Juives* 112 (1953): pp. 35-42; Frank Riess, "From Aachen to Al-Andalus: The Journey of Deacon Bodo (823–876)," *Early Medieval Europe* 13 (2005): pp. 131-157; idem, *The Journey of Deacon Bodo from the Rhine to the Guadalquivir: Apostasy and Conversion to Judaism in Early Medieval Europe* (London: Routledge, 2019).

2 The anthor consult the reconstruction of Bodo artfully made by Bernhard Blumenkranz in Bernhard Blumenkranz, "Un pamphlet juif médio-latin de polémique antichrétienne," *Revue d'histoire et de philosophie religieuses* 34 (1954): pp. 401-413.

3 "Ex idololatria ad summi Dei cultum reuersus sum. Ob meritum eterne retributionis deuoui me seculum in lege Domini consistere." Blumenkranz, "Pamphlet," p. 404.

4 "Iheronimus cuius interpretatione Scripturarum utimini, in Psalmis cuncta uerbum ex uerbo expressit, in ceteris autem Scripturarum libris falsam translationem confecit. Apud Iudeos solos integer Scripturarum textus et huius textus integra interpretatio inuenitur; apud uos Christianos, quot interpretes, tot sensus. Nos Iudei unum Scripturarum textum et unum cultum habemus. Vidi autem in Francorum regis palatio quatuordecim uiros catholicos inter se ipsos cultu diuersos." Ibid., p. 406, 408.

Because you live loosely (*dissolute*), you say that the Law has been loosened (*solutam*). But the Law which had been written down by the finger of God was never loosened, the Law about which the Lord says in Deuteronomy: "Lay up these my words in your hearts and minds." (Deut. 11:18) It reads in another place in the same book: "Moses commanded us a law, the inheritance of the multitude of Jacob." (Deut. 33:4) Again in the same book: "Take heeds that you do not forget the words that thy eyes have seen, and let them not drop from thy heart all the days of thy life." (Deut. 4:9) Listen, you Christians, what was written: "all the days of thy life." Pay attention and take heed firmly, lest you not see when seeing, or not understand what hearing.

I prove that your authors, or rather compilers (*auctores uel potior compilatores*) from whose books you draw proofs, have made many mistakes. But I strengthen my Law with truthful witnesses.[1]

Bodo's harsh arguments are extremely precious to our knowledge of the early medieval Jewish-Christian relationship, because they provide a rare glimpse of how the Jewish side could reflect upon the different attitudes toward the observance and the understanding of the Law both in their belief and in Christianity. It is also remarkable how Bodo quoted Deuteronomy to attest to the eternal validity of the Law as "the inheritance of the multitude of Jacob."

Different from the al-Andaluz under the Umayyad regime where Bodo/Eleazar and Alvarus carried out their epistolary polemics, the early-ninth-century Lyon was a Christian city. Nevertheless, unless we take the description in Agobard's anti-Jewish writings as purely fictional, the Jewish community in Lyon apparently offered an option of belief and cult alternative to and in competition with the Christian church in the early ninth century.

In Agobard's epistolary treatise *On Cautioning Dining and Associating with Jews* addressed to Nibridius bishop of Narbonne, then the archbishop of Lyon talked about "the

---

1 "Quia semper testimonia legis et prophetarum adhibetis, rogo uos cur cerimonias legis non obseruatis. Reuera autem, quid he omnes leges uobis qui amore pecunie iniecti et libidinibus capti estis. Haud mirum quod laici raro casti! Clerici ipsi uestri per diuersarum feminarum concubitos in ipso templo uestro gloriantur dulces sibi habere complexos.
"Quia dissolute uiuitis, dicitis legem esse solutam. Non autem soluta est lex que digito Dei scripta est, lex de qua Dominus dicit in libro Deuteronomio: 'Ponite hec uerba mea in cordibus et in animis uestris.' Et in eodem libro alibi legitur: 'Legem precepit nobis Moyses hereditatem multitudinis Iacob.' Et iterum in eodem libro: 'Caue ne obliuiscaris uerborum que uiderunt oculi tui, et ne descendant de corde tuo cunctis diebus uite tue.' Audite, Christiani, quod scriptum est: 'Cunctis diebus uite tue'; firmiter adtendite et cauete, ne uidentes non uideatis, et ne audientes non intelligatis.
"Auctores uel potior compilatores uestros, de quorum libris argumenta trahitis, multum errasse probo. Ego autem legem meam uerificis testimoniis firmo." Blumenkranz, "Pamphlet," p. 408.

Jews who seem to be spread in this city of ours and some other neighboring cities"[1] and their close connection with and strong influence on local Christians:

> ... due to great familiarity and regular cohabitation, some ones from the Christian flock eventually observe the Sabbath with the Jews, violate the Lord's day with illegal activity, and break the regular fasts... They [the Jews] boast with proud mouth that they are the offspring of Patriarchs, the race of the just ones, and the descendant of prophets, while the wretched people who hear these are ignorant that their prophets are accustomed to call them the sinful nation, a people laden with iniquity, a wicked seed, and ungracious children (Isaiah 1:4); to call their father an Amorrhite and their mother a Cethite (Ezechiel 16:3); to call the rulers of Sodom and the people of Gomorrha (Isaiah 1:10). They also do not know that John the forerunner of the Lord called them the offspring of vipers (Luke 3:7), and the Lord himself frequently called them the serpents, or an evil, wicked, perverse, and adulterous generation (cf. Matthew 12:39). Thus, some of the common and rural people (*ex uulgaribus ac rusticis*) are seduced into such a sea of error that they suspect with a mind astray and speak out with impious mouths among their peers and those like them that the Jews is the sole people of God (*solum Dei... populum*) and their observance of pious religion is much more reliable (*multo certiorem*) than our faith.[2]

Slightly before composing the passage above, in his letter to Louis the Pious known as *On the insolence of the Jews*, Agobard mentioned that the Jews of Lyon "dared to preach to Christians disrespectfully what to believe and to hold, blaspheming the Lord God and

---

1 "... tamquam ueri cultores christiane fidei, omni obseruantia ab infidelium consortio segregarent, non utique gentilium, qui inter nos minime commorantur, sed Iudeorum, qui in nostra hac et in nonnullis aliis uicinis urbibus uidentur esse diffusi." Agobard, *De cauendo conuictu et societate iudaica*, CCCM 52, ed. Lieven Van Acker (Turnhout: Brepols, 1981), p. 231.

2 "... dum ex familiaritate nimia et assidua cohabitatione aliqui de grege christiano sabbatum quidem cum Iudeis colunt, diem uero dominicam inlicita operatione uiolant, nec et ieiunia statuta dissoluunt... dum se patriarcharum progeniem, iustorum genus, prophetarum sobolem superbo ore proloquuntur, ignorantibus miseris, qui hec audiunt, quod ipsi eorum prophetae gentem peccatricem, populum grauem iniquitate, semen nequam, filios sceleratos, patrem ipsorum Amorreum, matrem Cetheam, Sodomorum principes et Gomorre populum soleant appellare, sed et illud pariter nescientibus, quod precursor Domini Iohannes genimina eos dixerit uiperarum, et ipse Dominus frequenter illos nunc serpentes, nunc generationem malam, prauam, peruersam atque adulteram uocitarit. Vnde et in tantum erroris pelagus nonnulli ex uulgaribus ac rusticis abducuntur, ut hunc solum Dei esse populum, aput hos pie religionis obseruantiam, ac multo certiorem, quam nostra sit, fidem, et seducto suspicentur animo, et ore impio inter pares et consimiles fateantur." Agobard, *De cauendo conuictu et societate iudaica*, pp. 231-232.

our Savior Jesus Christ right in front of them."[1] Certain ignorant Christians (*imperiti christiani*) even claim that the Jews preach better than Christian priests.[2]

Both the treatises of Agobard were composed in the late 820s. One or two decades earlier, when the Lyon Annotations was composed, Judaism in Lyon may not have been so aggressive yet. However, it is still probable that a prosperous Jewish community with stable religious practice and strong self-identity had already existed in Lyon during the episcopate of Agobard's predecessor. Since the Lyon Annotations was a product of local clerical education, we could reasonably deduce that the strong *contra Iudaeos* tone in it reflects the Christian reaction to the intellectual pressure of Judaism, especially Jews' claim of their exclusively right observance of the Law. Just like Bernhard Blumenkranz asserts: "Every anti-Jewish writing presupposes the existence of an active and energetic Jewish group the fight against which is the purpose of the polemical writings."[3]

8.2   The Accursed Jew

A remarkable exegetical innovation of the Lyon Annotations is its systematic exposition of Jews as the object of Moses' curses for the transgressor of the Law. Moses' promise of blessings and curses first appears in Deut.11:26-28: "Behold! I set forth in your sight this day a blessing and a curse: a blessing, if you obey the commandments of the Lord, your God, which I command you this day, a curse, if you obey not the commandments of the Lord, your God, but revolt from the way which now I shew you and walk after strange gods which you know not." He ordered Israel to put the blessing and the curse respectively on Mount Gerizim and Ebal (11:29). Later in Deuteronomy, Moses stipulated how the curse should be pronounced (27:11-26), and made a long litany of curses on the city, the field, and all kinds of properties; the punishments for the accursed include plagues, military defeat, servitude of the nation, and other calamities (28:15-68).

In Carolingian public discourse, the Mosaic curses were not necessarily of anti-Jewish function. A good example is the *acta* of Aachen Council of 836, also known as *De Re-*

---

1   "His causis laetificati sunt Iudaei ultra modum, et contristati christiani, non solum illi qui fugerunt, aut qui absconditi sunt, uel qui districti, sed et caeteri, qui uiderunt uel audierunt, maxime ideo, quia sententia Iudeorum ita confirmata est, ut auderent inreuerenter praedicare christianis, quid potius credendum esset ac tenendum, blasphemantes coram eis Dominum Deum ac Saluatorem nostrum Iesum Christum." Idem, *De insolentia Iudaeorum*, CCCM 52, ed. Lieven Van Acker (Turnhout: Brepols, 1981), p. 192.

2   "... ad hoc peruenitur, ut dicant imperiti christiani melius eis praedicare Iudeos quam presbiteros nostros..." Ibid., p. 194.

3   Bernhard Blumenkranz, "Anti-Jewish Polemics and Legislation in the Middle Ages: Literary Fiction or Reality?" *Journal of Jewish Studies* 15 (1964): pp. 125-140.

bus ecclesiasticis non inuadendis, most likely drawn by Jonas of Orléans.[1] Jonas warned those who encroach church property with the Mosaic curses in Deuteronomy:

> It continues in the book of Deuteronomy, in which, among many other precepts that Moses delivered to the sons of Israel, it is read: "Behold I set forth in your sight this day a blessing and a curse: a blessing, if you obey the commandments of the Lord your God, which I command you this day; a curse, if you obey not the commandments of the Lord your God, but revolt from the way which now I shew you." (Deut. 11:26-28) It should be noted carefully that those who obey the divine precepts deserve a blessing, while those who disobey them merit a curse. It is clearer than light that those who steal ecclesiastical properties inflict insult upon and disobedience to God and thus become transgressors of His precepts. Thus, they should look out carefully lest they undergo curse of the sort that the lawgiver proposed instead of blessing. Whoever wishes to know what that curse is really like should read the earlier and later declarations of the divine law and find out for certain how terrible, horrible, and frightening that curse is.[2]

Also, as Lester Little's study shows, the Mosaic curses functioned as one of the major elements in the formulas of monastic maledictions that took shape in *Francia* not long after the ninth century.[3]

The use of the Mosaic curses in patristic anti-Jewish literature is not extensive.[4] Mere-

---

1 *De rebus ecclesiasticis non inuadendis, Concilia aevi Karolini [742–842]. Teil 2 [819–842]*, MGH Leges, no. 56B, ed. Albert Werminghoff (Hannover and Leipzig: Hahnsche, 1908), pp. 724-767. For the discussion of this document, cf. Steffen Patzold, *Episcopus: Wissen über Bischöfe des späten 8. bis frühen 10. Jahrhunderts* (Ostfildern: Thorbecke, 2008), pp. 218-221.

2 "Sequitur in libro Deuteronomii, in quo inter cetera multa mandata, quae Moyses locutus est ad filios Israhel, ita legitur: *En, inquit, propono in conspectu uestro hodie benedictionem et maledictionem, benedictionem, si oboedieritis mandatis domini Dei uestri, quae ego hodie precipio uobis, maledictionem, si non obaudieritis mandata Dei uestri, sed recesseritis de uia, quam ego nunc ostendo uobis.* Notandum diligenter est, quod oboedientes preceptorum diuinorum benedictionem, inoboedientes uero maledictionem mereantur. Luce enim clarius constat, quod surreptores ecclesiasticarum rerum iniuriam et inoboedientiam Deo inrogent suorumque preceptorum transgressores existant. Unde prouidendum est, ne huiuscemodi maledictionem, quam legifer proponit, pro benedictione subeant. Qui autem nosse uult, quae sit eadem maledictio, scrupulosissime diligenterque precedentia et subsequentia diuinae legis legat eloquia et pro certo inueniet, quantum sibi terribilis et horribilis atque pertimescenda sit eadem maledictio." *Concilia aevi Karolini [742–842]. Teil 2 [819–842]*, no. 56B, p. 725. The translation is based on Lester K. Little, *Benedictine Maledictions: Liturgical Cursing in Romanesque France* (Ithaca: Cornell University Press, 1993), pp. 104-105, with select modifications.

3 Ibid., pp. 59-62.

4 For the *contra Iudaeos* literature, see Arthur Williams, Adversus Judaeos: *A Bird's Eye View of Christian* Apologiae *until the Renaissance* (London: Cambridge University Press, 1935). Also cf. Rosemary Ruether, "The *Adversus Judaeos* Tradition in the Church Fathers: The Exegesis of Christian Anti-Judaism," *Aspects of Jewish Culture in the Middle Ages*, ed. Paul Szarmach (Albany: State University of New York Press, 1979), pp. 27-50.

ly two relevant lemmata are cited repeatedly. The one is "He shall be as the head, and thou shalt be the tail" (Deut. 28:44), interpreted as a prophetic sign of the fall of Jews and rise of the gentiles. Cyprian bishop of Carthage (d. 258) in his anti-Jewish *Testimonia* lists it under the heading "That the gentiles would have faith in Christ instead."[1] His interpretation became so popular that we can find it copied verbatim in later anti-Jewish writings, even together with the African bishop's identical non-vulgate Deuteronomic text.[2] The other frequently quoted verse is "thy life shall be as it were hanging before thee. Thou shalt fear night and day, neither shalt thou trust thy life" (Deut. 28:66), usually interpreted to signify the Passion of Christ ("thy life") on the Cross ("hanging before thee") and Jews' rejection of him ("neither shalt thou trust thy life"). Tertullian (d. 220) in his *Aduersus Iudaeos* quoted it as the prophecy of the Passion and the perfidy of Jews,[3] and Cyprian listed it under the heading "That the Jews would fix him [Jesus Christ] to the Cross."[4] Both Deut. 28:44 and 28:66 appear in Isidore's *De fide catholica contra Iudaeo.*[5] But the archbishop of Seville's anti-Jewish use of the Mosaic curses does not go beyond them.

The exposition of the Mosaic curses in the commentaries on Deuteronomy before 800 is tenuous as well. Augustine in his *Contra Faustum* picked up Deut. 28:66 — in line with the *contra Iudaeos* tradition just mentioned above — as the prophecy of Christ.[6] Isidore, in the Joshua section of his *Expositio*, interpreted the six tribes standing on

---

1 "Quod gentes magis in Christum crediturae essent... In Deuteronomio: eritis gentes in caput, incredulus autem populus in cauda." Cyprian, *Ad Quirinum*, I.21, CCSL 3, p. 22.

2 Cf. *Altercatio legis inter Simonem Iudaeum et Theophilum Christianum*, 5, CCSL 64, ed. Rolando Demeulenaere (Turnhout: Brepols, 1985), p. 274; Zacchaeus Christianus, *Consultationes*, II.10, PL 20, col. 1124.

3 "Huius autem signi sacramentum uariis modis praedicatum est: 'in quo uita hominibus praestruebatur', 'in quo Iudaei non essent credituri', sicut Moyses ante nuntiarat in Exodo dicens: *Eiciemini de terra in quam introibitis ***, et in nationibus illis non eritis in requiem, nec erit stabilitas uestigio pedis tui, et dabit tibi deus cor taedians et tabescentem animam et oculos deficientes, ut non uideant, et erit uita tua pendens in ligno ante oculos tuos, et non credes uitae tuae.*" Tertullian, *Aduersus Iudaeos*, XI.9, CCSL 2, ed. Emil Kroymann (Turnhout: Brepols, 1954), p. 1382.

4 "Quod cruci illum fixuri essent Iudaei... Item in Deuteronomio: et erit pendens uita tua ante oculos tuos, et timebis die et nocte et non credes uitae tuae." Cyprian, *Ad Quirinum*, II.20, CCSL 3, pp. 57-58.

5 "His ergo tot tantisque testimoniis erubescant Iudaei gentium conuersarum aemulatores, tandemque conuicti cognoscant atque audiant in Deuteronomio Dominum proclamantem: *Eritis gentes ad caput, incredulus autem populus ad caudam.*" Isidore, *De fide catholica contra Iudaeo*, II.1.15, PL 83, col. 502; "Iam et quia prius gentes credere poterant in Christum, et postea Iudaei... et in Deuteronomio: *Eritis gentes ad caput, incredulus autem populus ad caudam.*" Ibid., II.4.1, col. 508; "Nam quid est lignum in pane missum, nisi Christi affixio carnis in ligno? Panem enim corpus eius agnoscimus; lignum in pane esse, fides nostra crucem agnoscit in corpore. Quia uita corporis sui panis est. Scriptum est enim: Et erit uita tua pendens ante oculos tuos, et timebis die ac nocte, et non credes uitae tuae." Ibid., I.35.2, PL 83, col. 484. "Sed quia plurimi ex Iudaeorum populo non essent credituri in Christum, Moyses legislator eamdem eorum incredulitatem ante praenuntiauit: Et erit uita tua pendens ante oculos tuos, et timebis die ac nocte, et non credes uitae tuae." Ibid., II.6.1, col. 510.

6 Augustine, *Contra Faustum*, XVI.22, CSEL 25, pp. 464-466.

Mount Gerizim and giving blessings as those who "come to salvation inspired not but the fear of punishment but by the love of heavenly promise," and the other six tribes standing on Mount Ebal and giving curses as those who "fulfill what were written in the Law due not to not the love of blessings or promises but to the fear of future punishments so that they come to salvation."[1] There is no anti-Jewish hint in either case.

This thin patristic precedent only makes the unprecedentedly systematic anti-Jewish expositions of the Mosaic curses in the Lyon Annotations more remarkable, as translated entirely here:

> *Behold! I set forth in your sight this day a blessing and a curse...* (Deut. 11:26)
> The blessing pertains to the chosen people, but the curse to the condemned people, namely the despisers of the Law.[2]

> *And when the Lord, thy God, shall have brought thee into the land whither thou goest to dwell, thou shalt put the blessing upon mount Gerizim, the curse upon mount Ebal...* (Deut. 11:29)
> Some people understand the Gospel and the new people in Mount Gerizim, but in Mount Ebal, the Law and the people of Jews who prefer to be on that mount with curse rather than under the grace of the Gospel with blessing.[3]

> *These shall stand upon mount Gerizim to bless the people when you are passed the Jordan: Simeon, Levi, Judah, Issachar, Joseph and Benjamin. And over against them shall stand on mount Ebal to curse: Ruben, Gad and Aser and Zabulon, Dan and Nephtali.* (Deut. 27:12-13)
> There is no doubt that these two mounts have signified the two Testaments. Of them, Mount Gerizim on which the six tribes stood for blessing signifies the New Testament in which the chosen people occupy themselves with fulfilling the precepts of God not in servile fear but in love of charity. But Mount Ebal on which we read the other six tribes stood to be cursed signified the Law of Moses by which the people of Jews who denied the Son of God preferred to be under curse rather than under the

---

1 "Qui sunt ergo isti qui incedunt iuxta montem Garizim? et qui sunt qui incedunt iuxta montem Hebal? Illi namque qui in hoc loco iuxta montem Garizim incedunt, electi ad benedictionem, eos figuraliter indicant qui non metu poenae, sed coelestis promissionis amore succensi, ueniunt ad salutem, illi uero dimidii, qui iuxta montem Hebal incedunt, in quo maledictiones prolatae sunt, illos indicant qui non amore benedictionum, uel promissionum, sed futurorum suppliciorum timore complent quae in lege scripta sunt, ut perueniant ad salutem." Isidore, Expositio in uetus testamentum, VI.10, PL 83, col. 376.

2 "Benedictio ad electos pertinet; maledictio uer<o> ad reprobos, contemptores legis." Paris, BnF, NAL 1740, fol. 34r.

3 "Plerique in montem Ga<rizim> Euangelium et nouu<m> populum accipiun<t >. In monte uero Eba<l>, legem et populun Iud<e>orum qui malunt su<per> illa cum maledictione esse, quam gratia Euangelii cum benedictione." Paris, BnF, NAL 1740, fol. 34r.

blessing of evangelical teaching. Christ has liberated us from such curse of the Law by being cursed for our sake.[1]

Cursed be he that abideth not in the words of this law and fulfilleth them not in work. (Deut. 27:26)

In this sense, Jews remain struck under the curse of the Law; from this curse no one of them will not be able to be immune, unless he believe in Christ our Lord so as to be made free via His grace.[2]

But if thou wilt not hear the voice of the Lord, thy God, to keep and to do all his commandments and ceremonies which I command thee this day, all these curses shall come upon thee and overtake thee. (Deut. 28:15)

To this point, the blessings of saints were assigned to bring to them by God. After them [the blessings] follow the curses by the Lord upon them, that is Jews who did not want to believe in Christ. These curses always abide on their offspring.[3]

Cursed shalt thou be in the city, cursed in the field. Cursed shall be thy barn and cursed thy stores. Cursed shall be the fruit of thy womb and the fruit of thy ground, the herds of thy oxen, and the flocks of thy sheep. Cursed shalt thou be coming in, and cursed going out. (Deut. 28:16-19)

The infidel people of Jews were certainly cursed in the city of Jerusalem in which they shouted with wicked voices against the Son of God, saying: "Crucify him, crucify him," (Luke 23:21) and "His blood be upon us and our children." (Matthew 27:25) They are cursed in the field, that is in the world, in which they are dispersed and serve nations; their barn is certainly cursed, that is the perverse teaching handed over to them by perfidious teachers; Their stores, namely their posterity, are also cursed; the fruit of their womb is certainly cursed, that is the carnal generation which is conceived and begotten in sin, or surely cursed are their perverse mind and activity; their herds, that is their teachers, are cursed, and the remaining common people [are cursed] just like "sheep for the slaughter" (cf. Psalms 43:22 and Romans 8:36); not only Jews but

---

1   "Duo hii montes utrumque Testamentum significasse non dubium est; a quibus mons Garizim, in quo ad benedicendum sex tribus steterunt, Nouum significat Testamentum in quo populus electus non in timore seruili sed amore caritatis, Dei precepta implere satagit. Mons uero Ebal in quo aliae sex tribus a maledicendum stetisse legitur, prefigurabit lege Moysi qua populus Iudeorum, Dei Filium negantes, sub maledicto esse maluerunt quam sub benedictionem euangelice predicationis; de quo maledicto legis nos Christus liberabit, factus pro nobis maledictus." Paris, BnF, NAL 1740, fol. 69v.

2   "Per hanc sententia Iudei sub maledicto legis adicti retinentur; a quo maledicto nemo ex illis immunis esse poterit, nisi qui in Christo Domino nostro crediderit ut per eius gratiam liber eficiatur. Siquidem et omnis homo etiam christianus in ecclesiam quamdiu peccat, sub maledicto legis est." Paris, BnF, NAL 1740, fol. 70v.

3   "Hucusque benedictiones sanctorum a Domino eis conlate discripte sunt; post haec secuntur maledictiones a Domino in eis, id est Iudeis, qui credere Christo noluerunt; quae maledictiones usque manent super eorum posteritatem." Paris, BnF, NAL 1740, fol. 72r.

also all impious who are begotten in sin are cursed, and they leave this world through bodily death together with the same sin.[1]

The Lord shall send upon thee famine and hunger and a rebuke upon all the works which thou shalt do... (Deut. 28:20)

There is no doubt that all these evils have fallen upon the perfidious people of Jews both carnally and spiritually.[2]

... until he consume and destroy thee quickly for thy most wicked inventions, by which thou hast forsaken me. (Deut. 28:20)

No sin is substance but invention of the Devil and of bad men; for God did not commit a bad deed, that is sin, but sin was invented by the Devil. Those "follow him that are of his side," (Wisdom 2:25) among whom are Jews who have moved away from God due to their own evil inventions by denying His son, and He thus "gave them up to the desires of their heart" (Romans 1:26) "to do those things which are not convenient." (Romans 1:28)[3]

Be the heaven that is over thee, of brass and the ground thou treadest on of iron. (Deut. 28:23)

The heaven of Jews signifies Scribes and Pharisees who shout out lies and do not have faith in the charity of God; the ground signifies the same city of Jews devoid of every fruit justly due to the hardness of their heart.[4]

The Lord give thee dust for rain upon thy land... (Deut. 28:24)

Since it blinds eyes, the dust is the figure of Jews' carnal understanding which does

---

1 "Maledictus utique populus Iudeorum incredulus in ciuitate Iherusalem in qua inprouis uocibus aduersus Filium Dei clamaberunt dicentes: Crucifige, crucifige et Sanguis huius super nos et super filios nostros. Ipsi etiam maledicti in agro, id est in mundo, in quo dispersi gentibus seruiunt; ipsorum denique maledictum orreum, hoc est peruersa doctrina que illis a perfidis magistris tradita est; maledicte quoque reliquie illorum, posteritas uidelicet ipsorum; maledictus denique fructus uentris eorum, id est carnalis generatio que in peccato concipitur et generatur uel certe maledictus intellectus eorum et operatio peruersa; maledicta armenta eorum, doctores uidelicet ipsorum, et reliquum uulgus quasi obes occisionis; maledicti quoque non solum Iudei sed et omnes impii qui in peccato generantur et cum eodem peccato de hoc seculo per mortem carnis egrediuntur." Paris, BnF, NAL 1740, fol. 72r.

2 "Vniuersa mala haec tam carnaliter quam spiritaliter populo Iudeorum perfido accidisse non dubium est." Paris, BnF, NAL 1740, fol. 72v.

3 "Omne peccatum substantia non est sed adinuentio diaboli et malorum hominum; Deus enim malum non fecit, quod est peccatum, sed a diabolo prius inuentum est. Imitantur enim illum qui sunt ex parte eius, ex quibus et Iudei fiunt qui propter adinuentiones suas malas recesserunt a Deo, negantes Filium eius, et ideo tradidit illos in desideria cordis sui ut faciunt quae non conueniunt." Paris, BnF, NAL 1740, fol. 72v.

4 "Caelum Iudeorum significat scribas et fariseos, uaniloquia personantes fidem et in caritatem Dei non habentes; terra uero plebem eandem Iudeorum ab omni fructu iuste uacuam propter duriciam cordis ipsorum." Paris, BnF, NAL 1740, fol. 73r.

not allow them to see the true light, that is Christ.[1]

The Lord make thee to fall down before thy enemies; one way mayst thou go out against them, and flee seven ways... (Deut. 28:25)

Jews, abandoned by God, were handed to their enemies according to just judgment, so that they are not able to resist either demons or humans, either spiritual or carnal. The seven ways in which they flee signify seven principle sins through which they yield to their enemies.[2]

... and be scattered throughout all the kingdoms of the earth... (Deut. 28:25)

In manifest sense, it is about the dispersion of Jews.[3]

The Lord strike thee with the ulcer of Egypt and the part of thy body by which the dung is cast out with the scab and with the itch so that thou canst not be healed. (Deut. 28:27)

As it was written about Jews elsewhere: "And he smote them on the hinder parts: he put them to an everlasting reproach." (Psalms 77:66)[4]

The Lord strike thee with madness and blindness and fury of mind. And mayst thou grope at midday as the blind is wont to grope in the dark and not make straight thy ways. (Deut. 28:28-29)

Madness is the numbness of mind; blindness is ignorance; fury is disturbance of heart. Jews groped in midday when they erred, not seeing in the bright light, that is Christ.[5]

And mayst thou at all times suffer wrong... (Deut. 28:29)

Jews always suffer wrong by their enemies as long as they persist in their perfidy.[6]

... and mayst thou have no one to deliver thee. (Deut. 28:29)

---

1   "Puluis pro eo quod oculos caecat figurat carnalem intellectum Iudeorum qui eos non sinit uerum lumen uidere quod est Christus." Paris, BnF, NAL 1740, fol. 73r.

2   "Iudei a Deo derelicti iusto iudicio traditi sunt hostibus suis, spiritalibus uidelicet adque carnalibus ita ut nec demonibus neque hominibus resistere ualeant. Septem uias per quas fugiunt, septem significant principalia uitia per quod inimicis suis cedunt. Quod et de ceteris reprouis accipiendum est qui dum primo cuilibet uitio resistere non ualent, ceteris peccatis omnis subcumbunt." Paris, BnF, NAL 1740, fol. 73r.

3   "Aperta sententia de dispersione Iudeorum." Paris, BnF, NAL 1740, fol. 73r.

4   "Hoc est quod alibi de Iudeis scriptum est: Et percussit eos in posteriora, obprobrium sempiternum dedit illis." Paris, BnF, NAL 1740, fol. 73r.

5   "Amentia est alienatio mentis, cecitas, ignorantia, furor, perturbatio cordis. In meridie Iudei palpaberunt quando in clara luce quae est Christus non uidentes, offenderunt." Paris, BnF, NAL 1740, fol. 73r.

6   "Omnique tempore Iudei calumniam ab inimicis suis sustinent quamdiu in sua perfidia perseuerant." Paris, BnF, NAL 1740, fol. 73v.

It is clearly in manifest sense about the bad things that Jews suffered from the Romans.[1]

Thou shalt cast much seed into the ground and gather little, because the locusts shall consume all. (Deut. 28:38)

According to the historical sense, due to the sins of humankind, these powers not only consumed the labors of Jews but also frequently devastated the labors of the same people.[2]

The stranger that liveth with thee in the land shall rise up over thee, and shall be higher, and thou shalt go down, and be lower. He shall lend to thee, and thou shalt not lend to him. He shall be as the head, and thou shalt be the tail. (Deut. 28:43–44)

The stranger signifies the people of the gentiles who were rejected, as if being the tail, before the advent of the Savior. But after His advent, they were prioritized via His grace; but Jews who used to be first were made last.[3]

He shall lend to thee, and thou shalt not lend to him. (Deut. 28:44)

Just like nations have converted through the preaching of the Apostles not long after the advent of the Lord, so will the nation of Jews believe in Christ the Lord through the preaching of saints from the elected gentiles by the end of the world. It means: He shall lend the money of the Word of God to you, and you shall not lend to him.[4]

And all these curses shall come upon thee and shall pursue and overtake thee till thou perish because thou heardst not the voice of the Lord, thy God... (Deut. 28:45)

On that account, all these bad things overwhelmed the people of Jews because they did not want to believe in the Son of God nor receive His Gospel.[5]

... and he shall put an iron yoke upon thy neck till he consume thee. (Deut. 28:48)

---

1 "Manifestus sensus patet de malis que Iudeis per Romanis acciderunt." Paris, BnF, NAL 1740, fol. 73v.

2 "Iuxta historiam propter peccata umani generis non solum labores Iudeorum haec potestes deuoraberunt sed et a horum frequenter debasta<ti sunt>." Paris, BnF, NAL 1740, fol. 74r. The handwriting for the second half of this entry in the manuscript is blurry. Fransen's reading seems reasonable.

3 "Aduena populum significat gentium qu(i) ante aduentum Saluatoris quasi in cauda reprobus erat, post eius uero aduentum per gratiam ipsius factus est priori; Iudei uero qui primi erant, facti sunt nouissimi." Paris, BnF, NAL 1740, fol. 74v.

4 "Sicut enim in primo aduentu Domini per apostolorum predicationem gentes crediderunt, ita secus finem mundi per predicationem sanctorum ex gentibus electis Iudeorum populus in Christo Domino crediturus est, et hoc significat quod ait: Ipse fenerabit tibi pecuniam uidelicet uerbi Dei, et tu non fenerabis ei." Paris, BnF, NAL 1740, fol. 74v.

5 "Idcirco omnia mala haec in populo Iudeorum renundaberunt quia noluerunt in Dei Filio credere neque eius Euuangelio recipere." Paris, BnF, NAL 1740, fol. 75r.

The iron yoke signifies the eternal servitude of Jews; it humbles the neck of their pride so that they are not able to raise it high.[1]

The Lord will bring upon thee a nation from afar and from the uttermost ends of the earth... (Deut. 28:49)

[The nation] signifies the Romans who devastated the nation of Jews worse than all [other] nations.[2]

... and [a most insolent nation] will devour the fruit of thy cattle and the fruits of thy land until thou be destroyed... (Deut. 28:51)

There is no doubt that all these bad things occurred to Jews through Romans.[3]

... and thou shalt eat the fruit of thy womb and the flesh of thy sons and of thy daughters... (Deut. 28:53)

We read this bad thing realized in Jerusalem during the time when it was besieged by Romans.[4]

The Lord shall scatter thee among all people from the farthest parts of the earth to the ends thereof.... (Deut. 28:64)

The manifest sense does not lack spiritual understanding. Who doubts that all these bad things have happened to Jews after the resurrection of the Lord?[5]

... and thy life shall be as it were hanging before thee. (Deut. 28:66)

Christ, the life of saints, is the one who hung before the eyes of Jews in the gibbet of the Cross in the time of the Passion; but they did not believe in him, because they discovered what they did not have to fear, saying: 'If we let him alone so, all will believe in him; and the Romans will come, and take away our place and nation.' (John 11:48)[6]

In the morning thou shalt say, "Who will grant me evening?" and at evening, "Who will grant me morning?" for the fearfulness of thy heart wherewith thou shalt

---

1 "Iugum ferreum perpetuam significat seruitutem Iud<e>orum; que ceruic superuie illorum it<a> adeprimet ut sursum eleuar<e> non ualeant." Paris, BnF, NAL 1740, fol. 75r.
2 "Romanos significat qui Iudeorum gentem deterius cun<c>tis gentibus uastati sunt." Paris, BnF, NAL 1740, fol. 75r.
3 "Cuncta haec mala Iudeis per Romanos accedisse non dubium est." Paris, BnF, NAL 1740, fol. 75v.
4 "Hoc malum in Hierusalem eo tempore quo a Romanis obsessa est impletum fuisse legibus." Paris, BnF, NAL 1740, fol. 75v.
5 "Manifestus sensus spiritalem intellegentiam non indiget. Vniuersa enim mala haec Iudeis post Domini resurrectionem accedisse quis dubitat?" Paris, BnF, NAL 1740, fol. 77r.
6 "Vita sanctorum Christus est qui in patibulo crucis tempore pascionis suae ante oculos Iudeorum pependit; sed ideo non crediderunt illi, quia illud inuenerunt quod timere non debuerunt, dicentes: Si dimittimus eum, sic omnes credunt in illum, et uenient Romani et tollent <nos>trum locum et gentem." Paris, BnF, NAL 1740, fol. 77v.

be terrified and for those things which thou shalt see with thy eyes. The Lord shall bring thee again with ships into Egypt by the way whereof he said to thee that thou shouldst see it no more. There shalt thou be set to sale to thy enemies for bondmen and bondwomen, and no man shall buy you. (Deut. 28:67-68)

As some people would like to say, this was fulfilled in the time of Emperor Hadrian.[1]

The repeated message given is that Jews suffer the curses of the Law due to their refusal to believe, and that the curses prophesied by Moses have been fulfilled in their history after the advent of Christ and their status quo. Speaking of the use of sources, the multiple references to the Romans' oppression of the Jews are likely based on Books 6 and 7 of Josephus' *Jewish War* or its epitome, whose circulation was widely extensive in the early Middle Ages.[2] A possible inspiration for the entire set of expositions, however, is one original entry in the primordial recension of the Pseudo-Bedan Pentateuch commentary:

By the two mounts Gerizim and Ebal on which blessings and curses are given are signified both the Testaments, because the people placed under the Law are constrained under curse. For it is said: "Cursed be he that abideth not in the words of this law, and fulfilleth them not in work." (Deut. 27:26) Jews indeed observed Pharisaic traditions and despised precepts of the Law. The blessing of grace was abundant to Christian people in the New Testament, in which Christ blessed the Apostles by raising his hand. The two mounts are the two Testaments, because both

---

1 "Hoc enim, ut quidam uolunt, tempore Adrani imperatoris factum est." Paris, BnF, NAL 1740, fol. 77v.

2 Cf. the editorial apparatus in Paul-Irénée Fransen "Un commentaire marginal lyonnais," pp. 360-362. On Josephus and the epitome of his Jewish War, see Richard Matthew Pollard, "Flavius Josephus: The Most Influential Classical Historian of the Early Middle Ages," *Writing the Early Medieval West, Studies in Honour of Rosamond McKitterick*, eds. Elina Screen, Charles West (Cambridge: Cambridge University Press, 2018), pp. 15-32; idem, "The De Excidio of 'Hegesippus' and the Reception of Josephus in the Early Middle Ages," *Viator* 46 (2015): pp. 65-100. The knowledge of Josephus in Carolingian Lyon was witnessed by Amulo: "Et quia de falsis et caecis Iudaeorum doctoribus nobis sermo est, de quibus dominus testatur dicens: Omnis plantatio, quam non plantauit Pater meus caelestis, eradicabitur. Sinite illos: Caeci sunt duces caecorum. Caecus autem si caeco ducatum praestet, ambo in foueam cadunt, breuiter admonendum putamus, ut etiam libri Iosephi et Philonis, qui homines quidem docti, sed Iudaei impii exstiterunt, quia eos nonnulli nostrorum nimis admirari solent et plus etiam quam diuinas litteras legere delectantur, non multum sequenda existimentur. Qui homines alieni a ueritate, non carent errore et diuinas historias uelut latius replicando et exponendo multa de sua falsa et superflua inserunt et sanos sensus uerborum dei iuxta fallacem opinionem suam aut deprauant aut eneruant. Unde antiqui doctores ecclesiae illa sola ex eis sumunt, quae in eorum libris, de rebus gestis consonanter scripturis nostris referuntur et haec ipsa perpauca et raro et ea maxime, quae ipsi oculis inspecta scripserunt, sicut de excidio Hierosolymorum et templo ac sacerdotio Iudaeorum." Amulo, *Liber de perfidia Iudaeorum*, XXIV, MGH Quellen zur Geistesgeschichte des Mittelalters 29, ed. Cornelia Herbers-Rauhut (Wiesbaden: Harrassowitz, 2017), p. 44.

have spiritual significance which Jews did not understand and lived under the letter [that was] killing them.[1]

We can also find the connection made between specific curses and Jews in an anonymous collection of biblical verses known as *Book of Various Questions Collected from both the Testaments against Jews, Other Infidels, or Many Judaizing Heretics.* Who compiled it and when has been a long-debated issue. For the present purpose, it suffices to know that recent studies tend to attribute its composition to the region of Zaragoza or Toledo in the early eighth century.[2] The compiler claimed that his purpose is to reveal the true meaning of the Bible against those who are "not really Christians, nor totally Jews, but rather more wicked than bad Christians and Jews."[3] It consists of 87 chapters, each of which contains a handful of biblical verses to verify a certain Christian doctrine. Three Deuteronomic lemmata are listed in Chapter 8 titled "That all who want to live under the Law and do not want to believe in Christ are constrained under the curse of law"; "Cursed be he that abideth not in the words of this law, and fulfilleth them not in work. And all the people shall say, Amen" (Deut. 27:16); "Cursed shalt thou be in the city, cursed in the field. Cursed shall be thy barn, and cursed thy stores" (28:16-17); "Cursed shalt thou be coming in, and cursed going out" (28:19). The author cites them to prove that "the Law itself is the witness that the Law makes transgressors without the grace of Christ and

---

1 "In duobus autem montibus Garizim and [E]balim, quibus benedictiones et maledictiones inferuntur, utrumque Testamentum significare potest, quia populus sub lege positus, sub maledicto tenebatur. Quia scriptum est: Maledictus qui non permanet in sermonibus huius legis, nec eos opere facit. Denique Iudaei, traditiones phariseicas obseruantes, mandata legis contempserunt. In Nouo autem Testamento gratiae benedictio in populum Christianum redundauit, quo Christus eleuans manum benedixit apostolos. Utrumque Testamentum tamen mons est, quia utrumque spiritale intellectum habet,quem Iudaei non intelligentes, sub occidente eos littera uiuebant." Milan, Biblioteca Ambrosiana, G.82 inf., fol. 98v = PL 91, col. 394.

2 Angel Vega and August Anspach, eds., *Liber de uariis quaestionibus aduersus Iudaeos seu ceteros infideles uel plerosque haereticos iudaizantes ex utroque Testamento collectus* (El Escorial: Augustinianis Monasterii Escurialensis, 1940). Vega and Anspach argued for its Isidorian authorship. Other scholars (esp. José Madoz) have attributed the work to Felix of Urgel, cf. Robert McNally, "Isidoriana," *Theological Studies* 20 (1959), pp. 432-442. This question of authorship remains unanswered, but Jocelyn N. Hillgarth's suggestion perhaps provides a future solution: "I think it is in the direction of the late Seventh Century and towards Toledo or Saragossa that one should look for an answer to this important question." Cf. Jocelyn N. Hillgarth, "The Position of Isidorian Studies: A Critical Review of the Literature 1936–1975," *Studi Medievali*, 3d ser. 24 (1983): pp. 817-905. For a recent association of the collection with early-eighth-century Zaragoza, see Federico-Mario Beltrán Torreira, "Siervos del Anticristo (la creación del mito histórico del enemigo interno en las fuentes hispanovisigodas,)" *Memoria, mito y realidad en la historia medieval: XIII Semana de Estudios Medievales, Nájera, del 29 de julio al 2 de agosto de 2002*, eds. José Ignacio de la Iglesia Duarte, and José-Luis Martín (Logroño: Instituto de Estudios Riojanos, 2003), pp. 85-127.

3 "... renituntur et omnino non intellegentes, cum eisdem Iudais infidelibus desipiunt, atque hoc modo utroque pede claudicantes, nec uere Christiani, nec in toto Iudaei, sed potius malorum Christianorum atque Iudaeorum deteriores." *Liber de uariis quaestionibus*, eds. Vega and Anspach, p. 1.

constrains them under curse."[1]

About a century later, in the controversy between Alvarus and Bodo/Eleazar (cf. Chapter 8.1), one of Alvarus' epistles contains his response to Bodo's anti-Christian interpretation of Jeremiah 17:5 ("Cursed be the man that trusteth in man"). Apparently, Bodo had argued that because Alvarus believed in Jesus, a pure human, he was under this curse. Against this "most serious problem" (*grabissimum molem*), Alvarus replied that he adored Jesus not as a human but as God; rather, it is Bodo who contradicted himself since he would not be able to clarify if the Messiah whom Jews are expecting is indeed God or a man. "Thus," concluded Alvarus, "it is you who are cursed at home and cursed in the field..."[2] This is clearly a flexible use of Deut. 28:16 ("Cursed shalt thou be in the city, cursed in the field"). Alvarus made a biblical counterattack to Bodo's claim that Christians were under curse, by calling his opponent accursed by the Law.

It is noteworthy that all these three early medieval cases of associating Jews with the Mosaic curses as raised above — the Pseudo-Bedan commentary, *Book of Various Questions*, and Alvarus' epistle — are Spanish. *Book of Various Questions* is also in a certain way related to Felix of Urgel, one of the intellectual figures active in Lyon at the beginning of the ninth century.[3] It is thus possible that the Lyon Annotator developed a Spanish tradition of expounding Jews as the object of the Mosaic curses.

The innovative interpretation of the accursed Jew in the Lyon Annotations has a remarkable echo in *De iudaicis superstitionibus et erroribus*, the most elaborate anti-Jewish work of Agobard, composed ca. 827 for Emperor Louis the Pious. This treatise consists of, in Agobard's own words, "a small portion from the examples and statutes of the Fathers, then from the Acts of Apostles, the Gospels, and the Old Testament, for the

---

1 "De eo quod omnes, qui sub lege uiuere uolunt, et in Christo erdere nolunt, sub maledicto legis constringuntur... Quod autem lex absque Christi gratia praeuaricationes faciat, atque sub maledicto constringat, lex ipsa testis est, scriptum quippe est in Deuteronomio: 'Maledictus qui non permanet in sermonibus legis huius, nec eos opere perficit, et dicit omnis populus, Amen.' Et paulo post aduersus Iudaeos in Christo credere nolentes: 'Maledictus eris in ciuitate, maledictus in agro, maledictum horreum et maledictae reliquiae tuae; maledictus eris ingrediens et maledictus egrediens.'" Ibid., VII.2, pp. 20-21.

2 "Et ideo maledictus tu in domo, maledictus in agro, psalmista pariter concrepante: Deficiant peccatores a terra et iniqui, ita ut non subsistant." Paulus Alvarus, *Liber epistolarum*, XVIII.13, Corpus Scriptorum Mozarabicorum 1, ed. Juan Gil Fernández (Madrid: Consejo Superior de Investigaciones Científicas, Instituto Antonio de Nebrija, 1973), p. 256.

3 José Madoz proposed that Felix was the author of Book of Various Questions, which has been refuted by other scholars including Manuel Díaz y Díaz, see Jocelyn Hillgarth, "The Position of Isidorian Studies," pp. 843-844. It is more likely that Book of Various Questions was known to and utilized by Felix.

purpose of confirming the pious watchfulness of ruling of good pastors."[1] Traditionally divided into 27 chapters, *De iudaicis superstitionibus* is a carefully structured work. Agobard unfolded his arguments by a clearly-designed strategy of source using. Apart from a prologue (c. I) and an epilogue (XXVII), he put forth patristic materials (Cyprian, Jerome, Eusebius, several *vitae* of holy fathers, and the anti-Jewish canons from Gallic councils) first (II–IX); then follows a report of contemporary Jewish beliefs (X);[2] finally, Agobard accumulated biblical quotations as his ultimate testimony (XI–XXVI).

As the last, in a certain sense also conclusive, piece of Agobard's argumentation, cc. XXV–XXVI of *De iudaicis superstitionibus* turn out to be a tiny exegesis of the Mosaic curses. Agobard treated them as realized punishment of God upon Jewish people. the whole passage is translated here:

But since we come to write about the curses that God has imposed upon the infidel Jews, let us recall the curses from above a little more carefully. It is said that Moses spoke to the whole Israelite people beyond Jordan, in the plain wilderness: "I set forth in your sight this day a blessing and a curse: a blessing, if you obey the commandments of the Lord; a curse, if you hear not the commandments of your God. When the Lord, thy God, shall have brought thee into the land whither thou goest to dwell, thou shall put the blessing upon Mount Gerizim, the curse upon Mount Ebal, which are beyond the Jordan." (Deut. 11:26-30) These words, though full of splendid meaning, were not able to be fulfilled before, unless the River Jordan be crossed, that is to say, the baptismal sacrament be consecrated by the water of Jordan which was touched by Christ's body. For Gerizim, which means division, signifies the apostolic city that divides itself from the synagogue of infidels, as Paul spoke about himself: "But when it pleased him, who separated me from my mother's womb, and called me by his grace, I condescended not to flesh and blood." (Galatians 1:15-16) But Ebal, which means old chasm, signifies the carnal and infidel synagogue, which did not consent to cross to the renewal of the spirit that gives life, but preferred to remain in

---

1   "Et quidem si, sicut nunc multa necessitas poscit, ausi essemus aut ualuissemus auribus uestris ingerere dampna animarum, que per uasa diaboli, mentes uidelicet Iudeorum, fidelibus inferuntur, adhiberi omnino iuberet pietas uestra remedium; nunc autem, quia periculosissimum nobis est dicere et innotescere, quod, sicut tempore passionis sue Dominus noster Iesus Christus, pacificaturus omnia per sanguinem crucis sue, uenditus est a falso discipulo et comparatus a ueris persecutoribus ad inludendum et crucifigendum, ita nunc comparetur ab impiis Iudeis quodammodo ad uituperandum licentius et blasphemandum, scribimus tantum pauca de exemplis et statutis patrum, ac deinde de actis apostolicis, siue de Euangeliis et Veteris Testamenti scripturis, ad confirmandam piam gubernationis uigilantiam bonorum pastorum." Agobard, *De iudaicis superstitionibus et erroribus*, I, CCCM 52, ed. Lieven Van Acker (Turnhout: Brepols, 1981), p. 199.

2   On Agobard's knowledge of Hebrew sources, cf. Robert Bonfil, "Cultural and Religious Traditions in Ninth-Century French Jewry," *Jewish Intellectual History in the Middle Ages*, ed. Joseph Dan (Westport: Praeger, 1994), pp. 1-17; Bat-Sheva Albert, "*Adversos Iudaeos* in the Carolingian Empire," pp. 135-138.

the obsolescence of the letter that kills; an immense flood of curses ran over those who had remained there, as it was written: "The princes of Judah are become as they that take up the bound: I will pour out my wrath upon them like water." (Osee 5:10) Just like all the promises and blessings that were shed upon the apostolic city, all the menaces and curses were imposed upon the synagogue of Satan in a series of events as Moses had predicted in the following words: "Cursed shalt thou be in the city," that is Jerusalem; "cursed in the field," <that is to say,> scattered <in the field> of the world. "Cursed shall be thy barn" — here, another translation is "Cursed shall be thy store-room," and <cursed shall> be all your stores. "Cursed shall be the fruit of thy womb, and the fruit of thy ground." (Deut. 28:16-18) "Cursed shalt thou be coming in," when being born to this life, and "cursed going out," when dying from this life (Deut. 28:19). Later in this passage, it goes: "The stranger that liveth with thee in the land," that is the people of the gentiles, "shall rise up over thee, and shall be higher," (Deut. 28:43) that is to say, being made son of Patriarchs, and "made partaker of the root, and of the fatness of the olive tree" (Romans 11:17); "thou shalt go down, and be lower," (Deut. 28:43) severed from the olive tree and fixed in the land of fire and dry. "He shall be as the head, and thou shalt be the tail." (Deut. 28:44) Nowadays, certain people dare to try to lift them up to the head whence they fell, as if they should not be the tail. But they would be there by all means, "until the fulness of the gentiles should come in, and so all Israel should be saved," (Romans 11:25-26) namely all should be saved. For "the Lord shall increase plagues" of those who are now (nunc) infidels, "plagues great and lasting, infirmities grievous and perpetual" — here, another translation is "the truest plagues and true infirmities" (Deut. 28:59). It is also said in this passage: "And he shall bring back on thee all the afflictions of Egypt, which thou wast afraid of, and they shall stick fast to thee. Moreover, the Lord will bring upon thee all the diseases, and plagues, that are not written in the volume of this law till he consume thee." (Deut. 28:60-61) This is exactly what we referred to above in this tract from the Gospel: the last state of that man, to whom the unclean spirit entered together with seven other spirits more wicked than himself, "is made worse than the first." (Matthew 12:45)

We said these things briefly and selected a few from many, wishing to demonstrate in a summary way how many gifts of blessing God prepared for the apostolic city that merited them, and, on the contrary, with how many deserved curses he repelled the infidel synagogue filled with them, so that there might be fulfilled among the elect what had been predicted: "For the lawgiver shall give a blessing" (Psalms 83:8), God blessed them, according to the Apostle, "with spiritual blessings in heavenly places, in Christ." (Ephesians 1:3) For those who believed neither in the letters of Moses nor in the words of Christ and were condemned for this sake by the just judgment of God, that curse overcame them, as had been preannounced by the same Moses: "Cursed is every one, that abideth not in the words of this law to do them." (Deut. 27:26) They did not wish to hear what was written in the law: "But the word is very nigh unto thee, in thy mouth and in thy heart, that thou mayst do it" (Deut. 30:14), as the Apostle interprets: "This is the word of faith, which we preach. For if thou confess with thy mouth the Lord Jesus, and believe in thy heart that God hath raised him up from the dead, thou shalt be saved. For, with the heart, we believe unto justice; but, with the mouth, confession is made unto salvation." (Romans 10:8-10)[1]

---

1 "Sed quia ad maledictiones infidelibus Iudeis a Deo inpositas scribendo peruenimus, paulo diligentius a superioribus eas repetamus. Ait itaque Moyses omni populo Israhelitico trans Iordanen in solitudine campestri: *En propono in conspectu uestro hodie benedictionem et maledictionem: benedictionem, si oboedieritis mandatis Domini, maledictionem, si non audieritis mandata Dei uestri. Cum introduxerit te Dominus Deus tuus in terram, ad quam pergis habitandam, pones benedictionem super montem Garizim, maledictionem super montem Hebal, qui sunt trans Iordanen.* Que uerba, cum permagnificis sensibus plena sint, non ante potuerunt impleri, nisi Iordane transito, id est babtismi sacramento corpore Christi tactis aquis Iordanicis dedicato. Garizim namque, qui interpretatur diuisio, significat apostolicam plebem diuisam ab infidelium synagoga, sicut Paulus de se ipso ait: *Cum autem complacuit ei, qui me segregauit de utero matris meae, ut reuelaret filium suum in me, non adquieui carni et sanguini.* Hebal autem, qui interpretatur uorago uetus, significat carnalem et infidelem synagogam, que non adquieuit transire ad nouitatem spiritus uiuificantis, sed maluit remanere in uetustate littere occidentis; ibi que eis perseuerantibus superuenit inmensus fluuius maledictionum, iuxta quod scriptum est: *Facti sunt principes Iuda quasi adsumentes terminum; super eos effundam quasi aquam iram meam.* Et sicut omnes omnino promissiones et benedictiones requieuerunt super apostolicam plebem, sic omnes comminationes et maledictiones confirmate sunt super synagogam Satane ipso ordine rei, quo Moyses praedixerat uerbis, dicens: *Maledictus eris in ciuitate*, id est Hierusalem, *maledictus in agro*, <id est in agro> mundi dispersus. *Maledictum horreum tuum* (quod alia translatio sic dicit: *Maledicte apothece tue*), *et maledicte omnes reliquie tue. Maledictus fructus uentris tui, et fructus terrae tue. Maledictus eris ingrediens*, nascendo in hanc uitam, et maledictus egrediens, moriendo uidelicet de hac uita. Et post multa *Aduena*, inquid, *qui te cum uersatur in terra*, id est populus gentium, *ascendet super te, erit que sublimior*, effectus uidelicet filius patriarcharum et *socius radicis oliuae et pinguedinis factus; tu autem descendes, et eris inferior*, abscisus ab olea, et siccus in terra iacens igni destinatus. *Ipse erit in caput, et tu eris in caudam*, et nunc ueniunt quidam per se eos conantes leuare in caput, unde ceciderunt, quasi non debeant esse in caudam, quod utique semper erunt, donec plenitudo gentium introeat et sic omnis Israhel saluus fiat, omnis uidelicet saluandus. Nam istorum qui nunc sunt infidelium *augebit Dominus plagas, plagas magnas et perseuerantes, infirmitates pessimas et perpetuas* (quod alia translatio dicit *plagas uerissimas et infirmitates ueras*); item ibi: *Et conuertet in te omnes afflictiones Aegypti, quas timuisti, et adherebunt tibi. Insuper et uniuersos langores et plagas, que non sunt scripte in uolumine legis huius, inducet Dominus super te, donec te conterat.* Hoc profecto est quod supra de Euangelio posuimus: *Erunt nouissima hominis illius*, id est ad quem spiritus inmundus cum aliis septem se ipso nequioribus ingressus fuerit, *peiora prioribus*.

"Et hec quidem breuiter diximus, ac de multis pauca libauimus, strictim scilicet uolentes ostendere, quantis benedictionum muneribus dignam praeparauerit Deus apostolicam plebem, quantis que e contrario maledictionibus suis meritis repletam infidelem reppulerit synagogam, quatinus et in electis impleretur quod predictum fuerat: *Etenim benedictiones dabit qui legem dedit*, benedicens eos, uidelicet iuxta apostolum, *in omni benedictione spiritali in celestibus in Christo*, et illis, qui nec Moysi litteris nec uerbis Christi crediderunt, ac per hoc iusto Dei iudicio reprobati sunt, illa maledictio superueniret, que ab ipso Moyse ita fuerat praenuntiata: *Maledictus omnis qui non permanserit in uerbis legis huius, ut faciat ea*, nolens audire quod in ea scriptum est: *Iuxta te est uerbum ualde in ore tuo et in corde tuo, ut facias illud*, quod apostolus sic exponit: *Hoc est uerbum fidei quod praedicamus. Quoniam si confessus fueris in ore tuo Dominum Iesum, et credideris in corde tuo, quod Deus eum suscitauit a mortuis, saluus eris; corde enim creditur ad iustitiam, ore autem confessio fit ad salutem.*" Agobard, *De iudaicis superstitionibus*, XXV-XXVI, CCCM 52, pp. 219-221.

It is not hard to find that a number of exegetical elements in Agobard's passages remarkably match the expositions of the Mosaic curses (which have been translated earlier in this subchapter) and of other Deuteronomic lemmata (cf. the following footnotes) in the Lyon Annotations (Table 8.1).

Table 8.1 Identical exegesis between the Lyon Annotations and
Agobard's *De iudaicis superstitionibus*

Deut.	Subject	Exposition
11:26-30	Jordan	baptism[1]
	Mount Gerizim	(etymologically) "division"[2]
		Christians
	Mount Ebal	(etymologically) "old chasm"[3]
		Jews
28:16-19	cursed city	Jerusalem
	cursed field	this world
	"Cursed shall be you going out."	Jews dying in sin
28:43-44	stranger	gentiles converted to Christians
	tail	Jews
27:26	"Cursed be he that abideth not in the words of this law, and fulfilleth them not in work."	Jews under the curse of the Law
30:14	"But the word is very nigh unto thee, in thy mouth and in thy heart, that thou mayst do it."	the Christian way of salvation expressed in Romans 10:8-10[4]

In fact, almost all the expositions of Deuteronomy found in Agobard's *De iudaicis superstitionibus* can be found in the Lyon Annotations as well. The single exception is the curse of diseases and plagues (28:60-61). Agobard put it forth to reintroduce the image of the man occupied by evil spirits in Matthew 12:43-45 — which he has already expounded in detail earlier in the same treatise[5] — in order to signify the uncleanness of Jews. Apart from it, there is strong evidence to argue for Agobard's conscious use in *De iudaicis superstitionibus* the exegesis of Deuteronomy as recorded in the Lyon Annotations.

Agobard's early life is not clear. Traditional scholarship tends to believe that he was born in Spain, moved to Narbonne in 782, arrived at Lyon in 792, and was ordained a

---

1 "Per Iordanem gratia baptismi prefigurata est; sicut enim prior ille populus Iudeorum terram repromissionis ingredi non potuit nisi transito Iordane, ita et populus cristianus, heres Noui Testamenti, regnum caelorum consequi non ualet nisi per baptismi gratia renouatus fuerit." Paris, BnF, NAL 1740, fol. 69r, on Deut. 27:3.

2 "Garisim diuisio seu aduena." Paris, BnF, NAL 1740, fol. 69v, on Deut. 27:4.

3 "Hebal uorago uetus." Paris, BnF, NAL 1740, fol. 69r., on Deut. 27:11.

4 "Hoc est quod Apostolus ait: Quoniam si confiteris Dominum Ihesum in ore tuo et in corde tuo credereis quod Deus illum suscitabit a mortuis, saluus eris. Corde enim creditur ad iustitiam, oris autem confessio fit ad salutem." Paris, BnF, NAL 1740, fol. 81bis r, on Deut. 30:14.

5 Agobard, *De iudaicis superstitionibus*, XX, CCCM 52, p. 215.

priest in 804. Anna Langenwalter recently challenged this view, suggesting that Agobard was more likely a native of Lyon and was sent to Lyon Cathedral as an oblate.[1] No matter which side we choose to take, it is certain that when Leidrad came to Lyon and carried out his reform in 798, Agobard was already a young cleric there and won the new archbishop's favor quickly. It is reasonable to assume that he was among the beneficiaries of Leidrad's revival of biblical education (cf. Chapter 2.4.3). His other writings also prove him as a professional biblical reader and an able interpreter.[2] There would thus be no surprise if Agobard would have known the exegesis of Deuteronomy preserved in Lyon Annotations in either a textual or an oral way.

From the perspective of authorial intention, it seems that it was Agobard's deliberate choice to conclude *De iudaicis superstitionibus* with an exposition of the Mosaic curses. On one hand, it offers a dramatic twist to the image of Jews presented in this treatise, from the cursing people who "curse the Lord and his body [i.e., the Christian church] in all their prayers"[3] to the accursed one. On the other hand, labeling Jews with God's lasting curse makes an ultimate endorsement for the necessity to separate them from the Christian church, the sole theme of the discussed treatise and the consistent anti-Jewish pursuit of Agobard.[4] It is no coincidence that Agobard also chose to expound the Mosaic curses in the concluding section of his epistolary treatise *On Cautioning Dining and Associating with Jews* addressed to his fellow bishop Nibridius of Narbonne:

> Venerable father, you know that all who are under the law are under a curse; they are dressed in curse like clothes; the curse has entered into their insides like water and into their bones like oil; they are also cursed in the city and cursed in the fields; cursed when coming in and cursed when going out; cursed are the fruit of the womb, the fruit of the ground, and their flocks; cursed are their storehouses, barns, store-rooms, rooms, foods, and stores of those foods. (cf. Deut. 28:16-19) None of them will be rescued from such frightful and horrible curse, unless through Him, who was accursed for our sakes... May you stick to the observance of the divine law, persist in canons, control those whom you can, frighten those whom you can, and not ask or allow any of the faithful people to join with such great curses and such horrible condemnations

---

1   Anna Langenwalter, *Agobard of Lyon*, pp. 60-65. For the traditional narrative, cf. Allen Cabaniss, *Agobard of Lyons: Churchman and Critic* (Syracuse: Syracuse University Press, 1953), pp. 1-16.

2   Cf. Marie-Celine Isaïa, "'[...] *correctionis gratia iuxta ministerium sibi iniunctum* [...]': Agobard and the Episcopal School of Lyons." Paper presented at the Leeds International Medieval Congress, 5 July 2016. I appreciate Dr. Isaïa's generosity to share this paper with me prior to its publication. For Agobard and the Bible, see Caroline Chevalier-Royet, "La Bible d'Agobard," *Lyon dans l'Europe carolingienne: Autour d'Agobard (816–840)*, eds. François Bougard, Alexis Charansonnet, Marie-Céline Isaïa (Turnhout: Brepols, 2019), pp. 131-143.

3   "[P]ropter hoc maledicere eos Dominum et corpus eius in omnibus orationibus suis, sicut et ante prophetatum est uoce Domini dicentis ad Patrem: *Maledicent illi, et tu benedices*." Agobard, *De iudaicis superstitionibus*, IX, CCCM 52, p. 205.

4   Cf. Jeremy Cohen, *Living Letters of the Law*, pp. 123-145; Anna Langenwalter, *Agobard of Lyon*.

through the profane association with the accursed and the condemned people.[1]

The use of Mosaic curses makes an intriguing case to observe how Agobard applied the biblical knowledge that he had learned in his youth to serve his own elaborate — and radical, as we will see in the next subchapter — anti-Jewish argumentation. What makes it even more significant is how Amulo, the successor to Agobard as the archbishop of Lyon (r. 841–852), also resorted to the Mosaic curses in his own anti-Jewish treatise *Liber de perfidia Iudaeorum*, written for Charles the Bald in the 840s:

> For when the faithful emperors and the holy rulers of the church established these [anti-Jewish laws and canons], they followed the authority of the divine law altogether, and they asked us to follow this divine law as well, which shows that this Jewish people, due to their own infidelity and impiety, has been cursed and detestable in all aspects, by speaking to them via Moses: "But if thou wilt not hear the voice of the Lord thy God, to keep and to do all his commandments, all these curses shall come upon thee, and overtake thee. Cursed shalt thou be in the city, cursed in the field; cursed shall be thy barn, and cursed thy stores; cursed shall be the fruit of thy womb; cursed shalt thou be coming in, and cursed going out; the Lord shall send famine upon thee" etc. (cf. Deut. 15-20) Now we clearly see all these fulfilled upon this unhappy nation. Due to the iniquity by which they denied the Son of God, they appeared cursed in the city of Jerusalem before the Captivity, cursed in the field of the whole world after the Captivity; not only their barn and stores were accursed, but also the fruit of their womb, that is sons, just like their worse fathers cursed themselves and their sons, saying: "His blood be upon us and our children." (Matthew 27:25) "Cursed was this people coming in, <namely,> being born to this life, and cursed going out, <namely,> dying from this life. (Deut. 28:19) The Lord sent upon thee famine." (Deut. 28:20) which was admonished via Prophet Amos: "Behold the days come, and I will send forth a famine into the land: not a famine of bread, nor a thirst of water, but of hearing the word of the Lord. And they shall go about from sea to sea, and from the north to the east: seeking the word of the Lord, they shall not find it." (cf. Amos 8:11-12) For

---

1 "Sciens itaque, pater uenerabilis, omnes, qui sub lege sunt, sub maledicto esse, et indutos maledictione, sicut uestimento, que intrauit sicut aqua in interiora eorum et sicut oleum in ossa eorum, maledictos quoque in ciuitate et maledictos in agro, maledictos in ingressu et maledictos in egressu, maledictum fructum uentris et terrae et peccorum eorum, maledicta eorum cellaria, horrea, apothecas, cybos, et ipsorum cyborum reliquias, nec posse quempiam eorum ab hoc tam inmani tam que horribili maledicto legis eripi, nisi per eum, qui pro nobis factus est maledictum, sciens etiam in eos, qui praedicationem apostolicam nolunt recipere, non solum nullo eorum utendum, sed et puluerem ciuitatis domus eorum de pedibus excutiendum, remissius que in die iudicii Sodome et Gomorre futurum quam illis: permane et tu in diuine legis obseruantia, persiste in canonicis institutis, tene quos potes, terre quos potes, noli dicere nec sinatis quemquam fidelium tantis maledictionibus tam que horrendis damnationibus per maledictorum et condempnatorum prophana consortia communicare." Agobard, *De cauendo conuictu et societate iudaica*, CCCM 52, pp. 233-234.

when they seek and meditate on the Law and the prophets now, dispersed throughout the world, they cannot find the word of the Lord, that is the Son of God, the Lord Jesus Christ. When the knowledge about Him shines in the whole world, as if the midday sun from Heaven, they grope in the dark just like the blind, as it was said in the curses of the Law upon them: "The Lord strike thee with madness and blindness and fury of mind. And mayst thou grope at midday as the blind is wont to grope in the dark, and not make straight thy ways." (Deut. 28:28-29) Through such blindness, they encounter this curse which is the cause of all the curses, and, as it was written in their own Hebrew language, it is stated as such among other curses: "And thy life shall be as it were hanging before thee. Thou shalt fear night and day, neither shalt thou trust thy life." (Deut. 28:66) For what else is this life of the people of God but the one who speaks in the Gospel: "I am the resurrection and the life" (John 11:25)? About Him, Jeremiah speaks in the personality of all the elected people: "the breath of our mouth, Christ the Lord, is taken in our sins, to whom we said: Under thy shadow we shall live among the Gentiles." (Lamentations 4:20) Jews saw this life of theirs hanging before them in the tree of the Cross, hesitating to trust His presence, and feared night and day, that is when His majesty concealed in suffering and when it was revealed in miracles. So, when they hesitated and despised in these, they did not trust their life. This curse certainly remains in them until today... Because like natural branches, they degenerated and were broken from the root of the Patriarchs, and the wild olive was grafted on the good olive, still let them hear these curses: "The stranger that liveth with thee in the land, shall rise up over thee, and shall be higher: and thou shalt go down, and be lower. He shall lend to thee, and thou shalt not lend to him. He shall be as the head, and thou shalt be the tail." (Deut. 28:43-44) As we see clearly, the church of gentiles lends to that people the money of the Word of God, but they do not have the money to lend out. The gentile people, having the Lord Jesus Christ, is the head, but that people is the tail, because they have fallen from the head. They would be there by all means, "until the fulness of the gentiles should come in, and so all Israel should be saved," (Romans 11:25-26) that is to say, all of them should be saved. For now (nunc), for those infidel, according to what was written in these curses: "the Lord shall increase their plagues, plagues great and lasting, infirmities grievous and perpetual" — here, another translation is "the truest plagues and true infirmities." (Deut. 28:59). The Lord speaks to Prophet Haggai: "Ask the priests the law, saying: If one that is unclean by occasion of a soul touch any of all these things, that is bread, or wine, or oil, or pottage, or any meat, shall it be defiled? And the priests answered, and said: It shall be defiled. And the Lord said: So is this people, and so is this nation before my face." (cf. Aggeus 2:12-15) About this, the Apostle confirms, saying: "all things are clean to the clean: but to them that are defiled, and to unbelievers, nothing is clean: but both their mind and their conscience are defiled." (Titus 1:15) It is clear that we know the tables of the unclean people are unclean. For how these tables of them could be not unclean, whose barns and store-rooms were cursed? (cf. Deut. 28:17) [1]

---

1 "Iuxta haec exempla et constituta priorum principum et beatissimi patris atque pontificis monita fideliter et uigilanter auxiliante domino instare debemus, ne fidelium populi impiorum consortiis et contagiis maculentur et deprauentur, quia, ut talia fideles imperatores et sancti rectores ecclesiae constituerent, auctoritatem omnino diuinae legis secuti sunt et nobis sequendam commendauerunt. Quae hunc populum Iudaicum, merito infidelitatis et impietatis suae in omnibus maledictum et detestandum ostendit, dicens illi per Moysen: Si audire nolueris uocem domini dei tui, ut custodias et facias omnia mandata eius, uenient super te omnes maledictiones istae, et apprehendent te. Maledictus eris in ciuitate, maledictus in agro, maledictum horreum tuum et maledictae reliquiae tuae, maledictus fructus uentris tui, maledictus eris ingrediens et maledictus egrediens. Mittet dominus super te famem et cetera. Quae omnia nunc in isto infelici populo manifeste uidemus impleta, cum propter iniquitatem suam qua dei filium denegauit, maledictus extitit in ciuitate Ierusalem ante captiuitatem et maledictus est in agro totius mundi post captiuitatem, et non solum maledictum est horreum eius et reliquiae, sed etiam maledictus fructus uentris eius, id est filii. Sicut ipsi pessimi patres et se et illos maledixerunt dicentes: Sanguis eius super nos et super filios nostros, maledictus est hic populus ingrediens nascendo in hanc uitam, et maledictus egrediens moriendo ex ea. Misit dominus super eum famem, quam per Amos prophetam comminatus est dicens: Ecce dies uenient et mittam famem in terram, non famem panis, nec sitim aquae, sed audiendi uerbum domini. Et circuibunt a mari usque ad mare et ab aquilone usque ad orientem quaerentes uerbum domini et non inuenient. Vere enim nunc quaerentes et meditantes in lege et prophetis et in toto mundo dispersi non inueniunt uerbum domini, id est dei filium dominum Iesum Christum. Et cum eius notitia in uniuerso orbe uelut sol meridianus de caelestibus refulgeat, illi tanquam caeci in tenebris palpant sicut eis in ipsis maledictionibus legis dictum est: Percutiat te dominus amentia et caecitate ac furore mentis: et palpes in meridie sicut palpari solet caecus in tenebris et non dirigas uias tuas. Per hanc enim caecitatem etiam illam maledictionem incurrunt, quae istarum omnium causa est et inter ceteras, ut in Hebraico proprie scriptum est, sic ponitur: Et erit uita tua suspensa ante te. Timebis nocte et die et non credes uitae tuae. Quae est enim haec uita populi dei nisi ille, qui in euangelio loquitur: Ego sum resurrectio et uita, et de quo ex omnium persona electorum Ieremias ait: Spiritus oris nostri christus dominus captus est in peccatis nostris, cui diximus: In umbra tua uiuemus in gentibus. Hanc uitam suam uiderunt Iudaei in ligno crucis suspensam ante se, et in eius praesentia dubitantes credere timuerunt nocte et die, id est et quando eis illius maiestas passionibus occultabatur et quando miraculis declarabatur. Ita dum in istis hesitarent, in illis contemnerent, non crediderunt uitae suae. Quae maledictio utique usque hodie in eis permanet, quia uitam suam, quae illis primum fuerat destinata dicente domino: Non sum missus nisi ad oues, quae perierunt domus Israel, dum nolunt credere a mortuis resuscitatam, ut ex hac fide uiuificentur et possint dicere cum propheta: Viuificabit nos post duos dies, in die tertia suscitabit nos, usque hodie quasi in patibulo suspensam irrident. Unde et in nostra editione recte translatum est: Et erit uita tua quasi suspendens ante te, uidelicet quia ignominia crucis, quae in Christo a mortuis resurgente iam praeteriit, apud istorum impietatem et caecitatem quasi adhuc permaneat, irridetur. Et quia isti tanquam rami naturales degenerauerunt et fracti sunt a radice patriarcharum et oleaster gentium insertus est in bonam oliuam, audiunt adhuc in ipsis maledictionibus: Aduena, qui tecum uersatur in terra, ascendet supra te eritque sublimior. Tu autem descendes et eris inferior. Ipse fenerabit tibi et tu non fenerabis ei. Ipse erit in caput et tu eris in caudam, sicut manifeste uidemus, quia ecclesia ex gentibus fenerat illi populo pecuniam uerbi dei, illi uero unde fenerent, non habent. Et populus gentium est in caput habens dominum Iesum Christum, illi uero in caudam, quia a capite ceciderunt. Quod utique semper erunt, donec plenitudo gentium introeat et sic omnis Israel saluus fiat, omnis uidelicet saluandus. Nam istorum, qui nunc sunt infidelium, iuxta quod in illis maledictionibus scriptum est, augebit dominus plagas, plagas magnas et perseuerantes, infirmitates pessimas et perpetuas; quod alia translatio dicit plagas uerissimas et infirmitates ueras. Loquitur dominus ad Aggaeum prophetam: Interroga sacerdotes legis dicens: Si tetigerit immundus in anima ex omnibus his, id est panem aut uinum aut oleum aut pulmentum aut omnem cibum, numquid contaminabitur? Et responderunt sacerdotes: Contaminabitur. Et ait dominus: Sic gens ista et sic populus iste ante faciem meam. Unde et Apostolus confirmat dicens: Omnia munda mundis, coinquinatis autem et infidelibus nihil est mundum, sed inquinata sunt eorum et mens et conscientia, ut uidelicet immundorum immundas esse nouerimus mensas. Quomodo enim immundae non erunt mensae, quorum maledicta sunt horrea et apothecae?" Amulo, *Liber de perfidia Iudaeorum*, LI, pp. 106-110.

Apparently, also a tiny exegetical work on the Mosaic curses itself, this passage of Amulo is a revised and enlarged version of Agobard's. While some of Amulo's Deuteronomic expositions are copied or paraphrased from cc. XXV–XXVI of *De iudaicis superstitionibus*, some others are not, but rather show striking similarity with the relevant entries of the Lyon Annotations (Table 8.2).

Table 8.2   Identical exegesis between the Lyon Annotations and
Amulo's *Liber de perfidia iudaeorum*

Deut.	Amulo	The Lyon Annotations
Cursed shall be the fruit of thy womb. (28:18)	womb = sons	"... the fruit of their womb is certainly cursed, that is the carnal generation which is conceived and begotten in sin..." (fol. 72r)
And mayst thou grope at midday as the blind is wont to grope in the dark, and not make straight thy ways. (28:29)	blind = unable to see Christ	"Jews groped in midday when they erred, not seeing in the bright light, that is Christ." (fol. 73r)
He shall lend to thee, and thou shalt not lend to him. (28:44)	usury = the money of the Word of God	"Just like nations have converted through the preaching of the Apostles not long after the advent of the Lord, so will the nation of Jews believe in Christ the Lord through the preaching of saints from the elected gentiles by the end of the world. It means: He shall lend the money of the Word of God to you, and you shall not lend to him." (fol. 74v)
And thy life shall be as it were hanging before thee. Thou shalt fear night and day, neither shalt thou trust thy life. (28:66)	your life hanging before thee = Christ on the Cross	"Christ, the life of saints, is the one who hung before the eyes of Jews in the gibbet of the Cross in the time of the Passion; but they did not believe in him, because they discovered what they did not have to fear, saying: 'If we let him alone so, all will believe in him; and the Romans will come, and take away our place and nation." (77v)

We thus come to the conclusion that the expositions of the Mosaic curses in the Lyon Annotations served as a pool of anti-Jewish rhetoric for two of the most important *contra Iudaeos* treatises produced in the ninth-century Lyon. Our survey in this subchapter has also demonstrated a micro-history of how a piece of biblical culture was transmitted and transformed within a Carolingian local intellectual circle across three generations.

8.3   An Anti-Jewish Tradition yet to be Radicalized

The previous subchapter builds a connection between the Lyon Annotations and Agobard's and Amulo's anti-Jewish rhetoric. However, if we take one further step, evidence also allows us to differentiate between the more balanced attitude toward Jews in the

Lyon Annotations and the more radical one in Agobard's writings. To demonstrate it, it is helpful to examine two particular issues: the primitive church and the final salvation of Jews.

Primitiua ecclesia appears now and then in the Lyon Annotations.[1] Originating from the synagogue, the primitive church was constituted by "those who took their beliefs from the Jews." For example:

> *He hath appeared from Mount Paran, and with him thousands of saints...* (Deut. 33:2)
> Thousands of saints signify the primitive church of Jewish converts.[2]

> *Let Ruben live and not die, and be he small in number.* (Deut. 33:6)
> ... But Ruben prefigures the primitive church of Jewish converts to Christ.[3]

The Apostles came out of the primitive church and spread the evangelical message to the gentiles through their missions:

> *Now if thou wilt hear the voice of the Lord, thy God, to do and keep all his commandments which I command thee this day, the Lord, thy God, will make thee higher than all the nations that are on the earth. And all these blessings shall come upon thee and overtake thee, yet so if thou hear his precepts: Blessed shalt thou be in the city, and blessed in the field.* (Deut. 28:1-3)
> This promise was fulfilled in the Holy Apostles and other chosen people who took their beliefs in Christ from Jews, of whom the primitive church consisted. For they sought the blessing from God in the city of Jerusalem; but they [were blessed] in the field, that is in this world, in which God sent them to preach.[4]

Via the primitive church and the Apostles, the key role played by Jews in the origin of the Christian church is stressed:

---

1 Two insightful analyses of the use of the image of the primitive church in the early medieval exegesis of Isaiah can be found in Glenn Olsen, "The ecclesia primitiua in John Cassian, the Ps. Jerome Commentary on Mark, and Bede," *Biblical Studies in the Early Middle Ages*, eds. Claudio Leonardi, Giovanni Orlandi (Firenze: Edizioni del Galluzzo, 2005), pp. 3-25; Elisabeth Mégier, "Jewish Converts in the Early Church and Latin Christian Exegetes of Isaiah, c. 400-1150," *Journal of Ecclesiastical History* 59 (2008): pp. 1-28.

2 "Sanctorum milia significant illam primitiuam ecclesiam quae ex Iudeis credidit." Paris, BnF, NAL 1740, fol. 90v.

3 "Nota de Ruben patriarcha, qui fuit primogenitus Iacob, hoc accipiendum est, qui ante annos plurimos iam obierat. Sed per Ruben prefiguratio est illa primitiua ecclesia ex Iudeis in Christo credidit." Paris, BnF, NAL 1740, fol. 90v.

4 "Haec promissio in sanctis apostolis et ceteris electis qui ex Iudeis in Christo crediderunt, ex quibus primitiua illa ecclesia extitit, inpleta est. Ipsi enim in ciuitate Hierusalem a Domino benedictionem consecuti sunt; ipsi etiam in agro, id est in hunc mundum, in quo ab ipso Domino ad predicandum misi sunt." Paris, BnF, NAL 1740, fol. 71r.

The Lord our God spoke to us in Horeb, saying: You have stayed long enough in this mountain. Turn you, and come to the mountain of the Amorrhites... (Deut. 1:6–7)

This was fulfilled in the Apostles and other preachers who had taken their beliefs in Christ from Jews after the advent of the Savior, who, after leaving Judea just like Mount Sinai, goes over to the mountain of the Amorrhites, that is the people of gentiles, to preach.[1]

Praise his people, ye nations, for he will revenge the blood of his servants. (Deut. 32:43)

May nations, that is those gentile converts, praise the people of the Lord, namely the Apostles and other saints elected from Jews, through whose preaching gentiles turned to believe.[2]

The particular esteem shown to the primitive church in the Lyon Annotations is most clearly revealed in the exposition of Deut. 21:15-17:

If a man have two wives, one beloved and the other hated, and they have had children by him and the son of the hated be the firstborn and he meaneth to divide his substance among his sons, he may not make the son of the beloved the firstborn and prefer him before the son of the hated, but he shall acknowledge the son of the hated for the firstborn and shall give him a double portion of all he hath, for this is the first of his children, and to him are due the first birthrights.

The man with two wives assumes the figure of our Lord and Redeemer, who has two cities — the first certainly from circumcision, but the second from price (*ex pretio*). But since the first wife, the synagogue of Jews, became hateful due to her own perfidy, the church, persevering in the love of its Redeemer, is called beloved. However, the synagogue bore the firstborn son, that is, the chosen people, and the church bore the Later people. Therefore, the son of the church, despite being the son of the beloved wife, is not to be preferred to the son of the hateful wife, that is of the synagogue. For Apostles from it, the primitive church, and whatever is considered

---

1 "Hoc etiam post aduentum Saluatoris in apostolis et ceteris predicatoribus qui ex Iudeis crediderant impletum est, qui post relicta Iudea tamquam montem Sinai, ad montem Amorreorum, populum uidelicet gentium, predicando transierit." Paris, BnF, NAL 1740, fol. 1v.

2 "Laudate gentes, id est credentibus ex gentibus, populum Domini, apostolos uidelicet et ceteros sanctos ex Iudeis electos, per quorum predicationem gentes crediderunt; sanguinem seruorum suorum apostolorum atque martyrum Dominus ab impiis in diem iudicii requisiturus est; in quo die sancti iudicabunt eos iuste, hoc est impios qui illos iniuste indicauerunt." Paris, BnF, NAL 1740, fol. 89r.

more sublime in the Kingdom of Heaven came from this same synagogue.[1]

To put it in other words, the repeated positive image of the primitive church and the Apostles in the Lyon Annotations highlights the Jewish origin of the Christian church. A similar notion has no echo at all in any of the writings of Agobard.

To make this contrast clearer, let's see how the biblical book Acts of the Apostles was used both in the Lyon Annotations and by Agobard. The most manifest reference to the narrative of Acts in the former is the entry for Deut. 16:9 ("Thou shalt number unto thee seven weeks from that day, wherein thou didst put the sickle to the corn") which expounds the Israelite Feast of Weeks as the Pentecost:

> ... In the day of the Pentecost, the Holy Apostles put the sickle of their preaching upon those Jewish converts as if corn, when three thousand were converted and baptized in that day, and five thousands on another day.[2]

The relevant biblical verses are Acts 2:41 and 4:4. Clearly, the Lyon Annotator put particular emphasis upon the Jewish origin of the converts on Pentecost.

Agobard carefully narrated part of the story of Acts in cc. XII–XIV of his *De iudaicis superstitionibus*. His sole concern is to demonstrate how Jews rejected the preaching of Paul (*uas electionsi et magister gentium*, as Agobard called him) and Barnabas, disputed with them, and persecuted them (cf. Acts 13:45-52; 18:5-7; 19:8-9), and how Paul undertook his mission outside Judea and finally arrived in Rome. Here, it is sufficient to take a look at the words by which Agobard began his narrative:

> It begins to be fulfilled by such an order: First, the Lord said to his preachers: "Go ye not into the way of the Gentiles, and into the city of the Samaritans enter ye not." (Matthew 10:5) Then, when He was about to ascend to Heaven, he said: "Go ye into the whole world, and preach the gospel to every creature," (Mark 16:15) so that Judea first rejected Apostles' preaching, then the apostolic preaching came to help us.

---

1 "Homo iste, habens duas uxores, figuram pretendit Domini ac Redemptoris nostri qui habet duas plebes, primam scilicet ex circumcisionem, alteram uero ex pretio. Sed quia prima illa, id est synagoga Iudeorum, propter perfidiam suam odiosa effecta est, ecclesia uero, in dilectionem Redemptoris sui perseuerans, dilecta appellatur. Verumtamen synagoga primogenitum filium id est electum populum genuit, ecclesia autem posteriorem; idcirco non potest filius ecclesiae quamuis dilecte preferri filio odiose, hoc est syangoge; ex ipsa enim apostoli et primitiua ecclesia et quicquid sublimius in regno caelorum dinoscitur, ex eadem syagogam asumptum est. Quod uero ait: Dabit ei de omnibus que possidet duplicia, ad scientiam utriusque Testamenti pertinet." Paris, BnF, NAL 1740, fol. 57v.

2 "Sicut per Fasse precipitur ecclesiae pascha celebrare ita et per sollemnitatem ebdomadarum id est quinquagesimo ide post pascha, Pentecosten, aduentum uidelicet Spiritus sancti uenerabliter custodire. In quo die Pentecosten sancti apostoli falce predicationis sue, credentes ex Iudeis quasi segete messuerunt cum in eodem die tria milia et in alio quinque milia conuersi ac baptizati sunt." Paris, BnF, NAL 1740, fol. 46r.

When the arrogant Judea had rejected the apostolic preaching, which testified to their own damnation, and when this had begun to be fulfilled, the time had already come to fulfill the prophecies about the rise of gentiles and the rejection of Jews, as Paul and Barnabas preached and assembled to hear the Word of the Lord, just like it was written in the Acts of the Apostles...[1]

It is clearly visible how Agobard deftly removed the episode of the conversion of thousands of Jews as recorded in Acts — an episode specifically emphasized in the Lyon Annotation — from his narrative of apostolic mission.

In sharp contrast with Agobard's consistent effort to prove the absolute segregation between Jews and Christians both in history and at present,[2] it seems that the Lyon Annotator was intended to stress the interaction between the two in the history of salvation, reflecting not only on the origin of the church, but also on its final stage:

> *He shall lend to thee, and thou shalt not lend to him.* (Deut. 28:44)
> Just like nations have converted through the preaching of the Apostles not long after the advent of the Lord, so will the nation of Jews believe in Christ the Lord through the preaching of saints from the elected gentiles by the end of the world. It means: He shall lend the money of the Word of God to you, and you shall not lend to him.[3]

In fact, the ultimate salvation of Jews is repeatedly stated in the Lyon Annotations:

> *And when thou shalt seek there the Lord, thy God, thou shalt find him...* (Deut. 4:29)
> This will be the case when Jews believe in Christ in the last days, as Elias prophesized.[4]

> *Now when all these things shall be come upon thee, the blessing or the curse which I have set forth before thee, and thou shalt be touched with repentance of thy heart*

---

1 "Quod tali ordine coepit impleri: Dixit primum Dominus predicatoribus suis: *In uias gentium ne habieritis, et in ciuitates Samaritanorum ne intraueritis*; ascensurus uero ad caelos ait: *Euntes in mundum uniuersum praedicate Euangelium omni creature*, ut scilicet prius a Iudea apostolorum repulsa praedicatio tunc nobis in adiutorium fieret, cum hanc illa ad damnationis sue testimonium superba reppulisset, cumque hoc impleri coepisset, et iam tempus aduenisset, ut implerentur prophetiae de assumptione gentium et repulsione Iudeorum, praedicantibus Paulo et Barnaba, et concurrentibus audire uerbum Domini, sicut scriptum est in Actibus apostolorum..." Agobard, *De iudaicis superstitionibus*, XII, CCCM 52, p. 209.

2 Cf. Jeremy Cohen, *Living Letters of the Law*, pp. 123-145; Anna Langenwalter, *Agobard of Lyon*.

3 "Sicut enim in primo aduentu Domini per apostolorum predicationem gentes crediderunt, ita secus finem mundi per predicationem sanctorum ex gentibus electis Iudeorum populus in Christo Domino crediturus est, et hoc significat quod ait: Ipse fenerabit tibi pecuniam uidelicet uerbi Dei, et tu non fenerabis ei." Paris, BnF, NAL 1740, fol. 74v.

4 "Hoc erit in nouissimis diebus quando predicante Helia Judei in Christo crediderint." Paris, BnF, NAL 1740, fol. 14v.

among all the nations into which the Lord, thy God, shall have scattered thee and shalt return to him and obey his commandments as I command thee this day, thou and thy children, with all thy heart and with all thy soul, the Lord, thy God, will bring back again thy captivity and will have mercy on thee and gather thee again out of all the nations into which he scattered thee before. (Deut. 30:1-3)

Take heed that the promise of God is revealed that Jews will believe in Christ at the end of the world.[1]

... he will make thee more numerous than were thy fathers. (Deut. 30:5)

Reader, take heed how many of the believers from Jews there will be around the end of the world to the extent that they surpass the number of ancient fathers and of the primitive church.[2]

But for the wrath of the enemies I have deferred it, lest perhaps their enemies might be proud... (Deut. 32:27)

In view of the pride of the gentiles to whom Jews were handed to be devoured, the Lord did not want to destroy the same Jews thoroughly, just like what is said in this psalm: "Slay them not." For the nation is spared to do penance for the sake of those who will believe in Christ from that nation at the end of the world.[3]

In these annotations, we see two biblical lemmata of crucial importance to the shaping of Christian attitudes to Jews in the Latin west cited or paraphrased: "[U]ntil the fulness of the Gentiles should come in, and so all Israel should be saved" (Romans 11:25-26) and "Slay them not, lest at any time my people forget" (Psalms 58:12). Based on his expositions of these two lemmata and others, Augustine developed a theory about the Jews, which would have immense influence on western history. To put it simply, in the opinion of the Father of Hippo, Jews possess a unique position in God's economy of salvation: they are not only the historical witness to the Old Testament, but also the reluctant witness to its replacement by the Gospel and Christ's grace to Christian believers. The existence of Jews and their carnal and useless observance of the Law therefore should be tolerated by the Christian society in the *saeculum*, and their final conversion at the end of time will finally complete God's scheme of human salvation.[4]

---

1 "Nota aperta promissione Dei de Iudeis qui secus fine mundi in Christo credituri sunt." Paris, BnF, NAL 1740, fol. 80v.

2 "Nota, lector, quanta multitudo credentium ex Iudeis circa fine mundi erit ut antiquorum patrum et primitiue ecclesiae numero superent." Paris, BnF, NAL 1740, fol. 81r.

3 "Propter superbia gentilium quibus Iudei traditi sunt ad deuorandum: noluit eosdem Iudeos Dominus funditus delere, sicut est illud in psalmo: Ne occideris eos; reseruatur enim ad penitentiam propter illos qui ex ipsa gente secus fine mundi Christo credituri sunt." Paris, BnF, NAL 1740, fol. 88r.

4 Cf. Jeremy Cohen, *Living Letters of the Law*, pp. 23-65; Paula Fredriksen, *Augustine and the Jews: A Christian Defense of Jews and Judaism* (New York: Doubleday, 2008).

It seems that the Lyon Annotator's attitude toward Jews is closer to this Augustinian theory than that of Agobard. In the Lyon Annotations, Jews, their deicidal past, their transgression of the Law, their rejection of the Gospel, and their stubborn "carnal" way of living are extensively criticized and refuted, sometimes rather harshly; but meanwhile, their positive role in the history and the future of the salvation is equally specified.

In contrast, Agobard in his extensive anti-Jewish writing showed sole interest in excluding Jews both from ecclesiastical history and from present Christian society. Admittedly, Agobard did hint (only once though) at the final salvation of Jews by citing Romans 11:25-26 when expounding Deut. 28:44 ("He shall be as the head, and thou shalt be the tail"). But he immediately conditioned it by adding that "for now (*nunc*)," those infidels certainly deserve the Lord's curses of plagues and diseases.[1]

Therefore, the Lyon Annotations represented a balanced and relatively mild anti-Jewish intellectual tradition of Lyon before Agobard radicalized it in the third decade of the ninth century. It may not be irrelevant that, among all the Carolingian commentators on Pauline epistles examined by Johannes Heil, Claudius of Turin, who was educated in Leidrad's Lyon by 811, turned out to be the most lenient when presenting Jews in his exegetical language.[2]

***

In this chapter, we have closely examined the presentation of Jews in the Lyon Annotations, its historical context, and its relationship with Agobard's anti-Jewish rhetoric and stance. To conclude it, we now return to the recent scholarship of anti-Judaism of Carolingian Lyon. It seems that our analysis of the Lyon Annotations suggests the need for revision of both Johannes Heil's thesis and Warren Pezé's.

Heil held a skeptical opinion about the utility of biblical exegesis for understanding the real Jewish-Christian relationship. But as we have seen, the anti-Jewish element in the Lyon Annotations is simply far more extensive and stronger than all the earlier Latin Deuteronomy commentaries. It would be hard to explain it unless we take into consideration the existence of an intellectually active Jewish community in the neighborhood of the Christian church in Lyon, which was indeed testified to other witnesses. We have also suggested that the competition over the identity of the legitimate keeper and interpreter of the Old Law may have contributed to the shaping of anti-Jewish exegesis of Deuteronomy as presented in the Annotations.

Pezé claimed to have detected a common anti-Jewish trend shared in Agobard's

---

1   "*Ipse erit in caput, et tu eris in caudam*, et nunc ueniunt quidam per se eos conantes leuare in caput, unde ceciderunt, quasi non debeant esse in caudam, quod utique semper erunt, donec plenitudo gentium introeat et sic omnis Israhel saluus fiat, omnis uidelicet saluandus. Nam istorum qui nunc sunt infidelium *augebit Dominus plagas, plagas magnas et perseuerantes, infirmitates pessimas et perpetuas...*" Agobard, *De iudaicis superstitionibus*, XXV, CCCM 52, pp. 220.
2   Johannes Heil, "Labourers in the Lord's Quarry," pp. 80-82; idem, *Kompilation oder Konstruktion*, pp. 236-250.

writings, the Lyon Annotations, and some other texts from early-ninth-century Lyon. This view is largely tenable, especially in view of our discussion of how Agobard inherited the anti-Jewish rhetoric recorded in the Lyon Annotations, which he could have learned in Leidrad's biblical school. However, Pezé did not pay enough attention to the evolution of this anti-Jewish tradition of Lyon. As we have seen, the Lyon Annotator and Agobard differed in their overall attitudes toward Jews. While the former seemed inclined to embrace Jews in God's plan of human salvation, the latter simply wanted to segregate them (as a sheer "other") from Christian society. How to explain such an intellectual transformation is beyond the purpose of this book, but it seems safe to say that the Lyon Annotations preserves a sample of the anti-Jewish tradition of Carolingian Lyon prior to the radicalization of Agobard.

CHAPTER 9

CONCLUSION: A LOCAL CAROLINGIAN RE- FORM THROUGH THE LENS OF A BIBLICAL COMMENTARY

Ann Matter in a paper of 2007 laments that "Carolingian biblical interpretation is still the neglected step-child of Medieval Studies."[1] A Carolingianist perhaps could reply that biblical commentary is not always a very "juicy" historical source. The fundamental reason may be that biblical exegesis as a type of Carolingian learning is accumulative in nature. Its aim — if we are allowed to cite T. S. Eliot's famous depiction of a mature poet, surprisingly not so anachronistic here — is to "obtain tradition by great labour" through "a process of depersonalization."[2] This is not to say that Carolingian authors lacked literary creativity. When they undertook biblical exegesis, they seemed — to cite Eliot again — "to escape from personality" intentionally, to a greater or lesser degree. A personal brand so distinct in Alcuin's epistles is largely absent in, let's say, his *Compendium in Canticum Canticorum*.[3] The striking spontaneity shown in Radbertus' *Epitaphium Arsenii* is simply less appreciable in the same author's commentary on Lamentations, although the latter is considered among the most original biblical commentaries of the ninth century.[4] While biblical commentaries *collectively* reveal crucial characteristics of Carolingian culture, it is often a challenge to determine the immediate historical context of an *individual* commentary, let alone to reconstruct a particular historical situation through it.[5]

The nature of early medieval texts also contributes to the challenge presented by Carolingian commentaries to modern historians. The more popular a commentary was in its own times, the more likely it survives in manuscripts today. The paradox here is that a popular exegetical work was usually composed for an audience wider than a local

---

1 Ann Matter, "Haimo's Commentary on the Song of Songs and the Traditions of the Carolingian Schools," Études d'exégèse carolingienne: *Autour d'Haymon d'Auxerre*, ed. Sumi Shimahara (Turnhout: Brepols, 2007), pp. 89-101.
2 T. S. Eliot, "Tradition and the Individual Talent," *The Sacred Wood: Essays on Poetry and Criticism*, idem (New York: Alfred A. Knopf, 1921), pp. 42-53.
3 Hannah Matis, *The Song of Songs in the Early Middle Ages*, pp. 120-124.
4 Ann Matter, "The Lamentations Commentaries of Hrabanus Maurus and Paschasius Radbertus," *Traditio* 38 (1982): pp. 137-163.
5 The preface to a commentary, if there is ever one, could offer useful information, but sometimes it is formalistic itself.

one, and its style was thus usually less circumstantial than universal. This could have made it more successful as an intellectual product, but less useful as a historical source. For example, Hrabanus dedicated his commentaries on the five books of the Pentateuch to Freculf bishop of Lisieux who had ordered them from the abbot of Fulda in order to enrich the book collection of the bishopric newly entrusted to him.[1] But Hrabanus chose to compose them in his usual encyclopedic style, and they turned out to arouse interest and circulated widely through *Francia*.[2] These five commentaries, beautiful samples of Carolingian exegetical practice *per se*, barely helps with our historical picture of Carolingian Neustria beyond the mere fact that the bishop of Lisieux once wanted them.

The methodological reflections above remind us of the great historical value of the Lyon Annotations, the subject of this book. If Paris, BnF, NAL 1740 were not extant, we would have had no chance to get to know this commentary. There is no evidence of its circulation beyond Lyon. Its extreme localness turns out to be its great advantage as a historical source to illuminate Carolingian Lyon. The Lyon Annotations is intrinsically pertinent to the reform of Lyon during the episcopate of Leidrad. In a certain sense, we can see it as a historical fossil of this local reform during the age of Charlemagne.

As argued, several clues, internal and external, strongly suggest that the Lyon Annotations originated from the pedagogical practice in the biblical school established by Leidrad for the episcopal church of Lyon. Its physical presentation as marginalia copied in a scribal style of the episcopal scriptorium in a Bible codex of the episcopal library assures us that the archbishop wanted the present and future cathedral canons to have the opportunity to meditate on this commentary together with the biblical book of Deuteronomy. The intellectual life revived by Leidrad's reform project provided conditions for the making of this unique exegetical treatise. In turn, the Lyon Annotations served Leidrad's goal of creating a well-educated team of elite clergy.

The source criticism of the Lyon Annotations against the Christian exegetical history of the fifth book of the Old Testament in the Latin west has revealed how extensive a legacy of Church Fathers was available to an exegete at Lyon which had one of the best cathedral libraries in *Franica* ca. 800. The diversity within the patristic exegesis which this exegete was able and willing to integrate into his own composition is far beyond any post-Isidorian commentaries on Deuteronomy before 800. Meanwhile, his dependence on the Church Fathers is much less than that of his predecessors. The initiative absorption of exegetical tradition and the confident composition of original expositions make the Lyon Annotations an example for us to reevaluate the vitality of the exegetical practice in the age of Charlemagne, which so far has been underappreciated.

---

1 Cf. Freculf's letter to Hrabanus, PL 107, cols. 439-440.
2 For the manuscript transmission, see Rossana Guglielmetti, "Hrabanus Maurus." Around 838, Humbert bishop of Würzburg attempted to obtain these commentaries from Hrabanus. Cf. Hrabanus' Letters 26 and 27, *Epistolae Karolini aevi (III)*, pp. 439-442.

One charm of the Lyon Annotations is that it has a consistent exegetical scheme, the core of which is the Christian church as the spiritual Israel, namely the true recipient of the spiritual understanding of Moses' precepts in Deuteronomy. This innovative scheme is developed from the traditional Origen-Jerome typological motif to interpret Deuteronomy, "the second law," as the foreshadowing of the Gospel. This scheme makes the exegesis of Deuteronomy also a process of identity building for a Christian community. Cathedral canons of Lyon would have sympathy when reading that such an imagined community is under the leadership of the *doctores*, who guide and instruct the church by their knowledge of the Holy Scripture. Different orders of the community not only share certain common rules but also have distinctive norms of life. Via spiritual or literal interpretation, Moses' ceremonial and ethical precepts are transformed into religious and moral admonitions pertinent to Christians. Like the canon law collection *Dacheriana* and the first Lyon martyrology, both very likely produced in Leidrad's Lyon as well, the Lyon Annotations functioned to instruct the right order of an ideal Christian community.

The Lyon Annotations also presents the "others" of the Christian church, including philosophers, pagans, heretics, and Jews. The last group, the old and carnal Israel, is the object of extensive exegetical treatment. Its conspicuous anti-Jewish tone distinguishes the Lyon Annotations from previous Latin commentaries on Deuteronomy, which is probably a symptom of the church of Lyon's reaction to the active or maybe even aggressive intellectual activity of the Jewish community in the same city. Agobard inherited and radicalized this anti-Jewish local tradition both by adopting the exegetical motif of the accursed Jew as recorded in the Lyon Annotations and by overlooking its other expositions that emphasize the legitimate position of Jews in the history of salvation. The future archbishop's selective use of the Annotations offers the most explicit case of the reception of the Lyon Annotations after the 810s.

Lyon remained an important intellectual and ecclesiastical center throughout the ninth century. It cultivated Claudius, one of first Carolingian exegetes; Agobard, the formidable polemicist, but at the same time the charismatic and learned church leader; and Florus, one of the most learned Carolingian scholars of the Church Fathers. Its local intellectual and ecclesiastical tradition was so cherished in the mid-ninth century that when outsiders like Amalarius and Modoin intervened on behalf of the imperial power in the late 830s, the counterattack from the church of Lyon under the leadership of Florus was fierce and effective.[1] Such a strong local tradition originated with the episcopate of the Bavarian Leidrad, whose episcopate forms the historical context of the present study.

Leidrad's epistolary report to Charlemagne provides the backbone source for us to reconstruct his reform project. However, without the Lyon Annotations, we would not have known what kind of biblical and exegetical knowledge was taught in the newly

---

1   Cf. Klaus Zechiel-Eckes, *Florus von Lyon als Kirchenpolitiker und Publizist.*

established cathedral school; how extensively the patristic works were accessible to the scholars there; how the local elite ecclesiastics imagined themselves and the Christian community under their leadership in biblical discourse; how the anti-Jewish atmosphere existed in the church of Lyon even before its radicalization in the 820s. Better than any other extant sources, the Lyon Annotations mirrors the intellectual and mental world of the *doctores* and *doctores*-to-be of the episcopal church of Lyon at the beginning of the ninth century, whose formation was the greatest achievement of Leidrad's reform.

The Lyon Annotations also provides a rare opportunity to explore the potential of Carolingian exegesis for historical study. This book has tried every method — contextual study, close reading, source criticism, and discourse analysis — to squeeze every drop of "historical juice" out of this commentary. The outcome is rewarding. The Lyon Annotations proves to be a product of church reform, a capsule of an exegetical history, and a carrier of ecclesiastical ideology. Thus, the potential of the historical value of Carolingian biblical commentaries, especially those with a clear local identity, is alluring. A genre considered as the highest knowledge by Carolingians could indeed tell us much about the social and intellectual experience of that exciting era, as long as historians today have patience to ask the right questions.

BIBLIOGRAPHY

Manuscripts Consulted

Amiens, BM, 220 (online facsimile: http://gallica.bnf.fr/ark:/12148/btv1b8452176j, last accessed September 14, 2021)

Milan, Biblioteca Ambrosiana, G.82 inf. (microfilm of Biblioteca Ambrosiana Collection in the Medieval Institute of University of Notre Dame, U.S.)

Paris, BnF, lat. 2342: (online facsimile: http://gallica.bnf.fr/ark:/12148/ btv1b105437825, last accessed September 14, 2021)

Paris, BnF, lat. 12309 (online facsimile: http://gallica.bnf.fr/ark:/12148/ btv1b90679163, last accessed September 14, 2021)

Paris, BnF, lat. 17188: (online facsimile: http://gallica.bnf.fr/ark:/12148/ btv1b9066627j, last accessed September 14, 2021)

Paris, BnF, NAL 1740 (online facsimile: http://gallica.bnf.fr/ark:/12148/ btv1b85856056, last accessed September 14, 2021)

Sankt Gallen, Stiftsbibliothek, 283 (online facsimile: http://www.e-codices.unifr.ch/ en/csg/0283/, last accessed September 14, 2021)

Vercelli, Archivio Capitolare, 153 (photocopy provided by Museo del Tesoro del Duomo e Archivio Capitolare)

Primary Sources

Ado of Vienne. *Chronicon*. PL 123, cols. 23-138. Ed. Georg Heinrich Pertz. MGH Scriptores 2. Hannover: Hahnsche, 1829, pp. 317-323.

---. *Martyrology*. Ed. Jacques Dubois, Genevieve Renaud. *Le martyrologe d'Adon: ses deux familles, ses trois recensions: texte et commentaire*. Paris: Editions du Centre national de la recherche scientifique, 1984.

Alcuin of York. *De Grammatica*. PL 101, cols. 849-902.

---. *In Euangelium Ioannis*. PL 100, cols. 737-1008.

---. *Liber de uirtutibus et uitiis*. PL 101, cols. 613-638.

Alvarus, Paulus. *Liber epistolarum*. Ed. Juan Gil Fernández. Corpus Scriptorum Mozarabicorum 1. Madrid: Consejo Superior de Investigaciones Cientificas, Instituto Antonio de Nebrija, 1973, pp. 144-270.

Agobard of Lyon. *Adversum dogma Felicis*. Ed. Lieven Van Acker. CCCM 52. Turnhout: Brepols, 1981, pp. 73-111.

---. *Aduersus legem Gundobadi*. Ed. Lieven Van Acker. CCCM 52. Turnhout: Brepols, 1981, pp. 17-28.

---. *De cauendo conuictu et societate iudaica*. Ed. Lieven Van Acker. CCCM 52. Turnhout: Brepols, 1981, pp. 231-234.

---. *De insolentia Iudaeorum*. Ed. Lieven Van Acker. CCCM 52. Turnhout: Brepols, 1981, pp. 191-195.

---. *De iudaicis superstitionibus et erroribus*. Ed. Lieven Van Acker. CCCM 52. Turnhout: Brepols, 1981, pp. 199-221.

---. *De priuilegio et iure sacerdotii*. Ed. Lieven Van Acker. CCCM 52. Turnhout: Brepols, 1981, pp. 54-69.

---. *Liber contra insulsam uulgi opinionem de grandine et tonitruis*. Ed. Lieven Van Acker. CCCM 52. Turnhout: Brepols, 1981, pp. 3-15.

---. *Liber de diuinis sententiis*. Ed. Lieven Van Acker. CCCM 52. Turnhout: Brepols, 1981, pp. 31-49.

Ambrose of Milan. *De Tobia*. Trans. Lois Miles Zucker, Ambrosii De Tobia S.: A Commentary, with an Introduction and Translation. Washington: Catholic University of America, 1933.

Ambrose of Milan. *De Tobia*. Ed. Karl Schenkel CSEL 32/2, Vienna: Verlag der Österreichischen Akademie der Wissenschaften, 1896, pp. 519-573.

---. *Epistulae*. Eds. Otto Faller, Michaela Zelzer. CSEL 82/1-4. Vienna: Verlag der Österreichischen Akademie der Wissenschaften, 1968-1996.

---. *Explanatio psalmorum xii*. Ed. Michael Petschenig. CSEL 64. Vienna: Verlag der Österreichischen Akademie der Wissenschaften, 1919.

---. *Expositio euangelii secundum Lucam*. Ed. Mark Adriaen. CCSL 14. Turnhout: Brepols, 1957.

---. *Expositio psalmi cxviii*. Ed. Michael Petschenig. CSEL 62. Vienna: Verlag der Österreichischen Akademie der Wissenschaften, 1913.

---. *Hexaemeron*. Ed. Karl Schenkl. CSEL 32/1. Vienna: Verlag der Österreichischen Akademie der Wissenschaften, 1896, pp. 3-261.

---. *Letters 1-91*. Trans. Mary Melchior Beyenka: The Fathers of the Church 26. Washington, D.C.: Catholic University of America Press, 1954.

Amulo of Lyon. *Liber de perfidia Iudaeorum*. Ed. Cornelia Herbers-Rauhut. MGH Quellen zur Geistesgeschichte des Mittelalters 29. Wiesbaden: Harrassowitz, 2017.

Annales Laureshamenses. Ed. Georg Pertz. MGH Scriptores 1. Hannover: Hahnsche,

1826, pp. 22-39.

Annales Lugduneses. Ed. Georg Pertz. MGH Scriptores 1. Hannover: Hahnsche, 1826, p. 110.

Annales regni Francorum. Ed. Friedrich Kurze. MGH Fontes iuris Germanici antiqui in usum scholarum separatim editi VI. Hannover: Hahnsche, 1895.

Anonymous Martyrology of Lyon. Ed. Henri Quentin. *Les martyrologes historiques du Moyen Âge: étude sur la formation du martyrologe romain.* Paris: J. Galbada, 1908, pp. 131-221.

Anonymous Martyrology of Lyon. Eds. Jacques Dubois, Genevieve Renaud. *Edition pratique des martyrologes de Bede, de l'anonyme lyonnais et de Florus.* Paris: Editions du Centre national de la recherche scientifique, 1976.

Augustine of Hippo. *Contra aduersarium legis et prophetarum.* Ed. Klaus-D. Daur. CCSL 49. Turnhout: Brepols, 1985, pp. 35-131.

---. *Contra Faustum.* Ed. Josef Zycha. CSEL 25. Vienna: Verlag der Österreichischen Akademie der Wissenschaften, 1891, pp. 251-797.

---. *Contra Faustum.* Trans. Roland Teske. Answer to Faustus, a Manichean. The Works of Saint Augustine: A Translation for the 21st Century 1/20. Hyde Park: New City Press, 2006.

---. *Contra Maximinum episcopum Arianorum,* PL 42, cols. 743-814.

---. *De catechizandis rudibus.* Ed. Johannes B. Bauer. CCSL 46. Turnhout: Brepols, 1969, pp. 121-178.

---. *De ciuitate Dei.* Eds. Bernhard Dombart , Alfons Kalb. CCSL 47, 48. Turnhout: Brepols, 1955.

---. *De doctrina christiana.* Ed. R. P. H. Green. Oxford: Clarendon Press, 1995.

---. *De fide et operibus.* Ed. Ioseph Zycha. CSEL 41. Vienna: Verlag der Österreichischen Akademie der Wissenschaften, 1900, pp. 35-97.

---. *De Genesi ad litteram libri duodecim.* Ed. Josef Zycha. CSEL 28. Vienna: Verlag der Österreichischen Akademie der Wissenschaften, 1894, pp. 3-435.

---. *De octo quaestionibus ex ueteri testamento.* Ed. Jean Fraipont. CCSL 33. Turnhout: Brepols, 1958, pp. 469-472.

---. *Epistulae 185-270.* Ed. Alois Goldbacher. CSEL 57. Vienna: Verlag der Österreichischen Akademie der Wissenschaften, 1911.

---. *Enarrationes in Psalmos.* Eds. Eligius Dekkers, Johannes Fraipont. CCSL 38, 39, and 40. Turnhout: Brepols, 1956.

---. *Enarrationes in Psalmos.* Eds. Franco Gori, Hildegund Müller, Clemens Weidmann. CSEL 93/1A, 93/1B, 94/1, 95/1-5. Vienna: Verlag der Österreichischen Akademie der Wissenschaften, 2003-2015.

---. *Quaestionum in Heptateuchum libri VII.* Ed. Jean Fraipont. CCSL 33. Turnhout: Brepols, 1958, pp. 1-377.

---. *Retractationes*. Ed. Almut Mutzenbecher. CCSL 57. Turnhout: Brepols, 1984.

---. *Tractatus aduersus Iudaeos*. PL 42, cols. 51-64.

Bammel, Caroline P. Hammond. Ed. *Der Römerbriefkommentar des Origenes: kritische Ausgabe der Übersetzung Rufins, Buch 7-10*. Freiburg: Herder, 1998.

Basil of Caesarea. *Nosce te ipsum*. Ed. Heinrich Marti. *Nosce te ipsum... animam tuam... Deum: Predigt 3 des Basilius Caesariensis in der Übersetzung des Rufinus: kritische Ausgabe des lateinischen Textes mit Einleitung, griechischer Fassung und deutscher Übersetzung*. Berlin: De Gruyter, 2012.

Bede the Venerable. *De tabernaculo*. Ed. David Hurst. CCSL 119A. Turnhout: Brepols, 1969, pp. 5-139.

---. *In Cantica canticorum libri VI*. Ed. David Hurst. CCSL 119B. Turnhout: Brepols, 1983, pp. 167-375.

---. *In Lucae euangelium expositio*. Ed. David Hurst. CCSL 120. Turnhout: Brepols, 1960.

---. *Historia ecclesiastica gentis Anglorum*. Ed. Michael Lapidge. SC 489, 490, and 491. Paris: Éditions du Cerf, 2005.

---. *Homeliae Euangelii*. Ed. David Hurst. CCSL 122, Turnhout: Brepols, 1955, pp. 1-378.

---. *Martyrology*. Ed. Trans. Felice Lifshitz. *Medieval Hagiography: An Anthology*. London: Garland, 2000, pp. 167-197.

Benedicti capitularia. Ed. Fridericus Henricus Knus MGH Leges II.2 Hannover: Hahnsche, 1832, pp. 17-158.

Biblia sacra iuxta latinam Vulgatam versionem ad codicum fidem, III: Libros Numerorum et Deuteronomii. Rome: Typis Polyglottis Vaticanis, 1936.

Bischoff, Bernhard ,Michael Lapidge. *Biblical Commentaries from the Canterbury School of Theodore and Hadrian*. Cambridge: Cambridge University Press, 1994.

Bitterauf Theodor. *Die Traditionen des Hochstifts Freising, 744-926*. Aalen: Scientia-Verlag, 1967.

Blumenkranz Bernhard. "Un pamphlet juif médio-latin de polémique antichrétienne," *Revue d'histoire et de philosophie religieuses* 34 (1954): pp. 401-413.

Boretius Alfred. *Capitularia regum Francorum I*. MGH Leges. Hannover: Hahnsche, 1883.

Brenton, Lancelot Charles Lee. *The Septuagint version of the Old Testament with an English Translation*. London: Samuel Bagster and Sons, 1879.

Cassian John. *Collationes*. Ed. Michael Petschenig. CSEL 13. Vienna: Verlag der Österreichischen Akademie der Wissenschaften, 1886.

---. *De institutis coenobiorum*. Ed. Michael Petschenig. CSEL 17. Vienna: Verlag der Österreichischen Akademie der Wissenschaften, 1888, pp. 3-231.

Cassiodorus. *Institutiones*. Ed. R. A. B. Mynors. Cassiodori Senatoris Institutiones.

Oxford: Clarendon Press, 1961.

Charlemagne. *De litteris colendis*. Ed. Luitpold Wallach. "Charlemagne's *De litteris colendis* and Alcuin: A Diplomatic-Historical Study," *Speculum* 26 (1951): pp. 288-305.

---. *Admonitio generalis*. Eds. Hubert Mordek, Klaus Zechiel-Eckes, Michael Glatthaar. MGH Fontes iuris Germanici antiqui in usum scholarum separatim editi XVI. Hannover: Hahnsche, 2012.

---. *Capitula de causis cum episcopis et abbatibus tractandis*. Ed. François Louis Ganshof. "Note sur les 'Capitula de causis cum episcopis et abbatibus tractandis' de 811," *Studia Gratiana* 13 (1967): pp. 1-25

Christianus, Zacchaeus. *Consultationes*. PL 20, col. 1071-1166.

Chrodegang of Metz. *Regula canonicorum*. Ed. Wilhelm Schmitz. *S. Chrodegangi Metensis Episcopi (742–766) Regula canonicorum, aus dem Leidener Codex Uossianus Latinus 94 mit Umschrift der Tironischen Noten*. Hannover: Hahnsche, 1889.

Clement of Alexandria. *Stromateis*. Trans. John Ferguson. *Stromateis: Books 1-3*. The Fathers of the Church 85. Washington, D.C.: Catholic University of America Press, 1991.

Colgrave Bertram. *The Earliest Life of Gregory the Great by an Anonymous Monk of Whitby*. Lawrence: University of Kansas Press, 1968.

Collectio Dacheriana. Eds. Luc d'Achery, Louis-François-Joseph de La Barre. *Spicilegium sive collectio veterum aliquot scriptorum qui in Galliae Bibliothecis delituerant*, vol. 1, 509-564. Paris: 1723.

Confraternitates Augienses. Ed. Paul Pieper. MGH Antiquitates, Supplement: Libri confraternitatum Sancti Galli, Augiensis, Fabariensis. Berlin: Weidmann, 1884, pp. 145-352.

Cyprian of Carthage. *Ad Quirinum testimonia aduersus Iudaeos*. Eds. Robert Weber, Maurice Bévenot. CCSL 3. Turnhout: Brepols, 1972, pp. 3-179.

Das Verbrüderungsbuch der Abtei Reichenau. Eds. Johanne Autenrieth, Dieter Geuenich, Karl Schmid. MGH Libri memoriales et Necrologia, Nova series I. Hannover: Hahnsche, 1979.

Die Urkunden Ludwigs des Frommen. Eds. Theo Kölzer, Jens Peter Clausen, Daniel Eichler. MGH Diplomata [Urkunden]. Wiesbaden: Harrassowitz Verlag, 2016.

Douay-Rheims Bible. Baltimore: John Murphy Company, 1914.

Einhard. *The Life of Charles the Emperor*. Trans. Thomas F. X. Noble. *Charlemagne and Louis the Pious: Lives by Einhard, Notker, Ermoldus, Thegan, and the Astronomer* .University Park: Pennsylvania State University Press, 2009, pp. 7-50.

Epistle of Barnabas. Ed. Trans. Michael W. Holmes. *The Apostolic Fathers: Greek Texts and English Translations of Their Writings*. 3rd ed. Grand Rapids: Baker Book House, 2007, pp. 370-440.

Epistolae Karolini aevi (II). Ed. Ernst Dümmler. MGH Epistolae 4. Berlin: Weidmann, 1895.

Epistolae Karolini aevi (III). Ed. Ernst Dümmler. MGH Epistolae 5. Berlin: Weidmann, 1895.

Eucherius of Lyon. *Formulae spiritalis intellegentiae*. Ed. Carmela Mandolfo. CCSL 66. Turnhout: Brepols, 2004, pp. 1-76.

---. *Instructionum ad Salonium*. Ed. Carmela Mandolfo. CCSL 66. Turnhout: Brepols, 2004, pp. 77-216.

Eugippius of Lucullanum. *Excerpta ex operibus sancti Augustini*. Ed. Pius Knöll. CSEL 9/2. Vienna: Verlag der Österreichischen Akademie der Wissenschaften, 1875.

Eutropius of Valencia. *Epistola de octo vitiis ad Petrum Papam*. Ed. Manuel Díaz y Díaz. *Anecdota Wisigotica I*. Salamanca: Universidad de Salamanca, 1958, pp. 27-35.

Evagrius. *Altercatio legis inter Simonem Iudaeum et Theophilum Christianum*. Ed. Rolando Demeulenaere. CCSL 64. Turnhout: Brepols, 1985, pp. 255-302.

Florus of Lyon. *Liber de diuina psalmodia*. Eds. Klaus Zechiel-Eckes, Erwin Frauenknecht. CCCM 260. Turnhout: Brepols, 2014, pp. 33-38.

Fortunatus, Venantius. *Carmina*. Ed. Friedrich Leo. MGH Auctores antiquissimi 4.1. Berlin: Weidmann, 1881.

Frede, Hermann Josef. *Ein neuer Paulustext und Kommentar*. Freiburg: Herder, 1973.

Gregory the Great. *Dialogorum libri iv*. Ed. Adalbert de Vogüé. SC 260. Paris: Éditions du Cerf, 1978.

---. *Epistolae*. Ed. Dag Norberg. CCSL 140 and 140A. Turnhout: Brepols, 1982.

---. *Homiliae in euangelia*. Ed. Raymond Étaix. CCSL 141. Turnhout: Brepols, 1999.

---. *Homiliae in Hiezechihelem*. Ed. Marci Adriaen. CCSL 142. Turnhout: Brepols, 1971.

---. *Moralia in Iob*. Ed. Marci Adriaen. CCSL 143, 143A, and 143B. Turnhout: Brepols, 1979-1985.

---. *Moralia in Iob*. Trans. Brian Kerns. Moral Reflections on the Book of Job. Minnesota: Liturgical Press, 2014-2017.

---. *Regula Pastoralis*. Ed. Floribert Rommel. SC 381 and 382. Paris: Éditions du Cerf, 1992.

Guigue, Marie-Claude. *Obituarium Lugdunensis Ecclesiae: Nécrologe des Personnages Illustres et des Bienfaiteurs de l'Église Métropolitaine de Lyon du IXe au XVe Siècle, Publié pour la Première Fois avec Notes et Documents Inédits*. Lyon: N. Scheuring, 1867.

Halitgar of Cambrai. *Penitential*. PL 105, cols. 652-710.

Hammer, Reuven. *Sifre: A Tannaitic Commentary on the Book of Deuteronomy*. New Haven: Yale University Press, 1986.

Hincmar of Rheims. *De coercendo et exstirpando raptu uiduarum, puellarum ac sanctimonialium*, PL 125, cols. 1017-1036.

Ildefonsus of Toledo. *De uiris illustribus*. Ed. Codoñer Merino. CCSL 114A.

Turnhout: Brepols, 2007, pp. 597-616.

Irenaeus. *Aduersus haereses seu Detectio et euersio falso cognominatae Gnoseos IV*. Eds. Adelin Rousseau, Bertrand Hemmerdinger, Louis Doutreleau, Charles Mercier. SC 100. Paris: Éditions du Cerf, 1965.

Irish Augustine. *De mirabilibus sacrae Scripturae*. PL 35, cols. 2149-2200.

Isidore of Seville. *Allegoriae Sacrae Scripturae*, PL 83, cols. 97-130.

---. *De uiris illustribus*. Ed. Codoñer Merino. Salamanca: Consejo superior de investigaciones científicas, 1964.

---. *Etymologiarum siue Originum libri XX*. Ed. W.M. Lindsay. Oxford: Oxford University Press, 1911.

---. *Expositio in uetus testamentum*. PL 83, cols. 207-424.

---. *Expositio in uetus testamentum*. Ed. Johannes Soter. *Enarrationes doctissimae brevissimae in Genesim, Exodum, Leviticum, Numeros, Deuteronomiū, Iosue, Iudicum, Regū IIII, Esdram, Machabae*. Cologne, 1530.

---. *Expositio in uetus testamentum*. Ed. Michael Gorman. Isidorus episcopus Hispalensis: Expositio in Vetus Testamentum. Genesis. Freiburg: Herder, 2009.

---. *Liber numerorum*. PL 83, cols. 179-200.

---. *Prooemia in libros ueteris ac noui testamenti*, PL 83, cols. 155-180.

---. *Sententiae*. Ed. Pierre Cazier. CCSL 111. Turnhout: Brepols, 1998.

---. *Versus*. Ed. Sanchez Martin. CCSL 113A. Turnhout: Brepols, 2000.

Jerome. *Aduersus Heluidium de Mariae uirginitate perpetua*. PL 23, cols. 183-206.

---. *Commentaria in Epistolam ad Ephesios*, PL 26, cols. 439-554.

---. *Commentarii in Isaiam*. Ed. Mark Adriaen. CCSL 73, 73A. Turnhout: Brepols, 1963.

---. *Commentarium in epistula Paulina ad Galatas*. Ed. Giacomo Raspanti. CCSL 77A. Turnhout: Brepols, 2006, pp. 1-227.

---. *Epistulae 1-70*. Ed. Isidorus Hilberg. CSEL 54. Vienna: Verlag der Österreichischen Akademie der Wissenschaften, 1910.

---. *Epistulae 71-120*. Ed. Isidorus Hilberg. CSEL 55. Vienna: Verlag der Österreichischen Akademie der Wissenschaften, 1910.

---. *Hebraicae quaestiones in libro Geneseos*. Ed. Paul de Lagarde. CCSL 72. Turnhout: Brepols, 1959, pp. 1-56.

---. *Hebraicae quaestiones in libro Geneseos*. Trans. Robert Hayward. *Saint Jerome's Hebrew Questions on Genesis*. Oxford: Clarendon Press, 1995.

---. *In Zachariam*. Ed. Marci Adriaen. CCSL 76A. Turnhout: Brepols, 1970, pp. 747-900.

---. *Liber interpretationis hebraicorum nominum*. Ed. Paul de Lagarde. CCSL 72. Turnhout: Brepols, 1959, pp. 57-161.

---. *Prologus in libro Regum, Biblia sacra: iuxta Vulgatam versionem*. Ed. Bonifatius

Fischer, Robert Weber. Stuttgart: Deutsche Bibelgesellschaft, 1994.

---. *Tractatus lix in psalmos*. Ed. Germain Morin. CCSL 78. Turnhout: Brepols, 1958, pp. 3-352.

Johannes Hymonides. *Vita Gregorii*, II.11, PL 75, cols. 59-242.

Jonas of Orléans. *De institutione laicali*. PL 106, cols. 121-278.

---. *De institutione regia*. Ed. Alain Dubreucq. SC 407. Paris: Éditions du Cerf, 1995.

Justin Martyr. *Dialogue with Trypho*. Trans. Thomas B. Falls. The Fathers of the Church 6. Washington, D.C.: Catholic University of America Press, 1948.

Leidrad of Lyon. *Baptismal Exposition*. Ed. Susan Keefe. *Water and the Word: Baptism and the Education of the Clergy in the Carolingian Empire*. Notre Dame: University of Notre Dame Press , vol. 2, no. 25, 2002, pp. 353-384.

---. *De abrenuntiatione diaboli*. PL 99, cols. 873-884.

---. *Report to Charlemagne*. Ed. Alfred Coville. *Recherches sur l'Histoire de Lyon du Ve siècle au IXe siècle (450-800)*. Paris: Picard, 1928, pp. 283-287.

Liber constitutionum sive Lex Gundobada. Ed. Ludwig Rudolf von Salis. MGH Leges nationum Germanicarum. Hannover: Hahnsche, 1892, pp. 29-116.

Liber de uariis quaestionibus aduersus Iudaeos seu ceteros infideles uel plerosque haereticos iudaizantes ex utroque Testamento collectus. Ed. Vega Angel, August Anspach. El Escorial: Augustinianis Monasterii Escurialensis, 1940.

Liber ex lege Moysi. Ed. Sven Meeder. "The Liber ex lege Moysi: Notes and Text," *Journal of Medieval Latin* 19 (2009): pp. 173-218.

Lupus of Ferrières. *Collectaneum de tribus quaestionibus*, PL 119, cols. 647-666.

Maurus, Hrabanus. *Commentaria in Cantica*, PL 112, cols. 1089-1166.

---. *Commentaria in Exodum*. PL 108, cols. 9-246.

---. *De clericorum institutione*. Ed. Trans. Detlev Zimpel. Turnhout: Brepols, 2006.

---. *De ecclesiastica disciplina*. PL 112, cols. 1191-1262.

---. *De universo*. PL 111, cols. 9-614.

---. *Enarratio super Deuteronomium*. PL 108, cols. 837-998.

---. *Enarratio super Deuteronomium*. Ed. Paul-Irénée Fransen, "La fin inédite du commentaire de Raban Maur sur le Deutéronome," *Revue Bénédictine* 108 (1998): pp. 80-103.

Mordek, Hubert. *Bibliotheca Capitularium Regum Francorum Manuscripta: Überlieferung und Traditionszusammenhang der fränkischen Herrschererlasse*. München: Monumenta Germaniae Historica, 1995.

Niceta of Remesiana. *De Psalmodiae Bono*. Ed. Cuthbert H. Turner. "Niceta of Remesiana II: Introduction and Text of De Psalmodiae Bono," *The Journal of Theological Studies* 95 (1923): pp. 225-252.

Notker the Stammerer. *Notatio de illustribus uiris*. Ed. Erwin Rauner. "Notkers des Stammlers 'Notatio de illustribus uiris.' Teil I: Kritische Edition," *Mittellateinisches*

Jahrbuch 21 (1986): pp. 34-69.

Origen. *Commentary on the Epistle to the Romans*. Trans. Thomas P. Scheck. *Commentary on the Epistle to the Romans: Books 6-10*. The Fathers of the Church 104. Washington, D.C.: Catholic University of America Press, 2002.

---. *Commentary on the Gospel of John*. Trans. Ronald Heine. *Commentary on the Gospel according to John: Books 13-32*. The Fathers of the Church 89. Washington, D.C.: Catholic University of America Press, 1993.

---. *Contra Celsum*. Trans. Henry Chadwick. Cambridge: Cambridge University Press, 1953.

---. *De principiis secundum translationem Rufini*. Ed. Paul Koetschau. GCS 22. Leipzig: J. C. Hinrichs, 1913.

---. *Homiliae in Exodum secundum translationem Rufini*. Ed. Wilhelm Baehrens. GCS 29. Leipzig: J. C. Hinrichs, 1920, pp. 145-279.

---. *Homiliae in Ezechielem secundum translationem Hieronymi*. Ed. Wilhelm Baehrens. GCS 33. Leipzig: J. C. Hinrichs, 1925, pp. 318-454.

---. *Homiliae in Genesim secundum translationem Rufini*. Ed. Wilhelm Baehrens. GCS 29. Leipzig: J. C. Hinrichs, 1920, pp. 1-144.

---. *Homiliae in Ieremiam secundum translationem Hieronymi*. PL 25, cols. 583-692.

---. *Homiliae in Iesu Nave secundum translationem Rufini*. Ed. Wilhelm Baehrens, pp. 287-463. GCS 30. Leipzig: J. C. Hinrichs, 1921.

---. *Homiliae in Leuiticum secundum translationem Rufini*. Ed. Wilhelm Baehrens, pp. 280-507. GCS 29. Leipzig: J. C. Hinrichs, 1920.

---. *Homiliae in Numeros secundum translationem Rufini*. Ed. Wilhelm Baehrens, pp. 3-285. GCS 30. Leipzig: J. C. Hinrichs, 1921.

---. *Homily on Jeremiah*. Trans. Smith John Clark. *Homilies on Jeremiah, Homily on 1 Kings 28*. The Fathers of the Church 97. Washington: Catholic University of America Press, 1998.

---. *Scholiae on Deuteronomy*. PG 12, cols. 805-818.

---. *Scholiae on Deuteronomy*. PG 17, cols. 23-36.

---. *Scholiae on Deuteronomy*. Robert Devreesse, *Les anciens commentateurs grecs de l'Octateuque et des Rois, Fragments tirés des chaînes* (Vatican: Biblioteca Apostolica Vaticana, 1959), pp. 48-49.

Paterius. *Liber testimoniorum*. PL 79, cols. 683-916.

Pauca problesmata de enigmatibus ex tomis canonicis: Praefatio - De Pentateucho Moysi. Ed. Gerard MacGinty. CCCM 173. Turnhout: Brepols, 2002.

Paul the Deacon. *Gesta episcoporum Mettensium*. Ed. Georg Heinrich Pertz. MGH Scriptores 2. Hannover: Hahnsche, 1829, pp. 260-268.

---. *Homiliary*. PL 95, cols. 1059-1566.

Pelagius. *Expositions of Thirteen Epistles of St Paul*. Ed. Alexander Souter.

Cambridge: Cambridge University Press, 1922.

Peter of Pisa. *Quaestiones in Danielem*. PL 96, cols. 1347-1362.

Perrone, Lorenzo. Ed. *Die Neuen Psalmenhomilien: Eine Kritische Edition des Codex Monacensis Graecus 314*. GCS Neue Folge 19. Berlin: De Gruyter, 2015.

Philo of Alexandria. *On the Migration of Abraham*. Trans. F. H. Colson, G. H. Whitaker. *Philo Volume IV: On the Confusion of Tongues; On the Migration of Abraham; Who Is the Heir of Divine Things? On Mating with the Preliminary Studies*. Loeb Classical Library 261. Cambridge: Harvard University Press, 1932, pp. 123-269.

Robert, Ulysse. *Heptateuchi partis posterioris versio latina antiquissima e Codice Lugdunensi*. Paris: A. Rey et cie, 1900.

---. *Pentateuchi versio latina antiquissima e Codice Lugdunensis*. Paris: Librairie de Firmin-Didot, 1881.

Poetae Latini aevi Carolini (I). Ed. Ernst Dümmler. MGH Poetae Latini medii aevi 1. Berlin: Weidmann, 1881.

Poetae Latini aevi Carolini (II). Ed. Ernst Dümmler. MGH Poetae Latini medii aevi 2. Berlin: Weidmann, 1884.

Prudentius of Troyes. *Precepta*. PL 115, cols. 1421-1440.

Pseudo-Alcuin. *Disputatio puerorum*. Ed. Liam Ethan Felsen. *The Disputatio puerorum: A Ninth-Century Monastic Instructional Text Edited from Vienna, Österreichische Nationalbibliothek, 458*. Toronto: Pontifical Institute of Mediaeval Studies: 2017.

Pseudo-Bede. *Commentary on the Pentateuch (β)*. PL 91, cols. 189-394.

Pseudo-Jerome. *Expositio Euangelii secundum Marcum*. Ed. Michael Cahill. CCSL 82. Turnhout: Brepols, 1997.

Pseudo-Jerome. *Expositio quattuor euangeliorum*. PL 30, cols. 531-589.

Quadripartitus. PL 112, cols. 1337-1398.

---. Edmond Martène, *Veterum scriptorum et monumentorum historicorum, dogmaticorum, moralium amplissima collectio* (Paris, 1724-1733), vol. 1, cols. 70-71.

Radbertus, Paschasius. *De benedictionibus patriarcharum Iacob et Moysi*. Ed. Beda Paulus. CCCM 96. Turnhout: Brepols, 1993.

---. *Expositio in lamentationes Hieremiae*. Ed. Beda Paulus. CCCM 85. Turnhout: Brepols, 1988.

Ratio de cursus qui fuerunt eius auctores. Ed. Kassius Hallinger. *Consuetudines saeculi octavi et noni*. Corpus Consuetudinum Monasticarum 1. Siegburg: F. Schmitt 1963, pp. 83-91.

Paulinus of Nola. *Epistulae*. Ed. Wilhelm Hartel. CSEL 29. Vienna: Verlag der Österreichischen Akademie der Wissenschaften, 1894, pp. 423-42.

Rusticus. *Epistula Rustici ad Eucherium*. Ed. Karl Wotke. CSEL 31. Vienna: Verlag der Österreichischen Akademie der Wissenschaften, 1894, pp. 197-199.

Sigebert of Gembloux. *De viris illustribus.* Ed. Robert Witte. *Catalogus Sigeberti Gemblacensis monachi de viris illustribus.* Bern: Herbert Lang, 1974.

Smaragdus, Ardo. *Vita Benedicti abbatis Anianensis et Indensis.* Ed. Georg Waitz. MGH Scriptores 15.1. Hannover: Hahnsche, 1887, pp. 198-220.

Smaragdus of Saint-Mihiel. *Liber comitis.* PL 102, cols. 13-552.

Tertullian. *Aduersus Iudaeos.* Ed. Emil Kroymann. CCSL 2. Turnhout: Brepols, 1954, pp. 1339-1396.

---. *Aduersus Marcionem.* Ed. Trans. Ernest Evans. Oxford: Clarendon Press, 1972.

The Fourth Book of the Chronicle of Fredegar: With its Continuations. Ed. Trans. John M. Wallace-Hadrill. London: Nelson, 1960.

The Lyon Annotations. Ed. Fransen, Paul-Irénée. "Un commentaire marginal lyonnais du Deutéronome du milieu du IXe siècle," *Revue Bénédictine* 117 (2007): pp. 31-63, 339-82.

Theodoret of Cyprus. *Commentary on the Psalms.* Trans. Robert C. Hill. *Commentary on the Psalms: 1-72.* Washington, D.C.: Catholic University of America Press, 2000.

---. *The Questions on the Octateuch.* Rev. John. F. Petruccione. Trans. Robert C. Hill. Washington, D.C.: Catholic University of America Press, 2007.

Theodulf of Orléans. *Praefatio Aureis litteris praefixa Bibliis Theodulfi.* PL 105, cols. 305-306.

---. *Opus Caroli regis contra synodum.* Ed. Ann Freeman. MGH Concilia II Supplementum I. Hannover: Hahn, 1998.

----------. *Zweites Kapitular.* Ed. Peter Brommer. MGH Capitula episcoporum Teil 1. Hannover: Hahnsche, 1984, pp. 142-184.

Vaciago, Paolo, ed. *Glossae Biblicae.* CCCM 189A and 189B. Turnhout: Brepols, 2004.

Verecundus of Junca. *Commentarii super cantica ecclesiastica.* Edited by Roland Demeulenaere. CCSL 93. Turnhout: Brepols, 1976, pp. 3-203.

Victor of Tunnuna. *Chronicon.* Edited Carmen Cardelle de Hartmann, pp. 3-55. CCSL 173A. Turnhout: Brepols, 2003.

von der Goltz, Eduard Freiherr. *Eine textkritische Arbeit des zehnten bezw. sechsten Jahrhunderts herausgegeben nach einem Kodex des Athosklosters Lawra.* Leipzig: J. C. Hinrich, 1899.

von Dobschütz, Ernst. *Das Decretum Gelasianum de libris recipiendis et non recipiendis.* Leipzig: J. C. Hinrichs, 1912.

Werminghoff, Albert, ed. *Concilia aevi Karolini [742-842]. Teil 1 [742-817].* MGH Leges. Hannover and Leipzig: Hahnsche, 1906.

----------. *Concilia aevi Karolini [742-842]. Teil 2 [819-842].* MGH Leges. Hannover and Leipzig: Hahnsche, 1908.

Wigbod. *Quaestiones in Octateuchum.* PL 93, cols. 233-430.

Secondary Sources

Adamiak, Stanisław. *Carthage, Constantinople and Rome: Imperial and Papal Interventions in the Life of the Church in Byzantine Africa (533-698)*. Roma: Gregorian and Biblical Press 2016

Ahern, Eoghan. "Abundance, *Luxuria*, and Sin in Late Antique Historiography," *Journal of Early Christian Studies* 25 (2017): pp. 605-631.

Airlie, Stuart. "The Aristocracy in the Service of the State in the Carolingian Period," *Staat im frühen Mittelalter*. Eds. Stuart Airlie, Walter Pohl, Helmut Reimitz. Wien:Verlag der Österreichischen Akademie der Wissenschaften, 2006, pp. 93-111.

Alberi, Mary. "'The Sword Which You Hold in Your Hand': Alcuin's Exegesis of the Two Swords and the Lay *Miles Christi*," *The Study of the Bible in the Carolingian Era*. Eds. Celia Chazelle, Burton Van Name Edwards. Turnhout: Brepols, 2003, pp. 117-131.

Albert, Bat-Sheva. "*Adversos Iudaeos* in the Carolingian Empire," *Contra Iudaeos: Ancient and Medieval Polemics between Christians and Jews*. Eds. Ora Limor , Guy G. Stroumsa. Tübingen: Mohr, 1996, pp. 119-142.

---. "Anti-Jewish Exegesis in the Carolingian Period: the Commentaries on Lamentations of Hrabanus Maurus and Pascasius Radbertus," *Biblical Studies in the Early Middle Ages*, eds. Claudio Leonardi and Giovanni Orlandi. Firenze: Edizioni del Galluzzo, 2005, pp. 175-192.

Alibert, Dominique. "La transmission des textes patristiques à l'époque carolingienne," *Revue des Sciences philosophiques et théologiques* 91 (2007): pp. 7-21.

Amos, Thomas. *The Origin and Nature of the Carolingian Sermon*. Michigan: Michigan State University, 1983.

Ampère, Jean-Jacques. *Histoire litteraire de la France avant le douzième siècle*. Paris: L. Hachette, 1839.

Anton, Hans Hubert. *Fürstenspiegel und Herrscherethos in der Karlolingerzeit*. Bonn: L. Röhrscheid, 1968.

Azzimonti, Alessandro. "'Sicut dictum vidimus': Un anonimo commentario al Pentateuco d'età protocarolingia (Ambr. G 82 inf.)," *Aevum* 68 (1994): pp. 283-302.

Bachrach, Bernard. *Early Medieval Jewish Policy in Western Europe*. Minneapolis: University of Minnesota Press, 1977.

Bammel, Caroline P. Hammond. "A New Witness to the Scholia from Origen in the Codex von der Goltz," *Origeniana Quinta*. Ed. Robert J. Daly. Leuven: Leuven University Press, 1992, pp. 137-141.

Bardy, Gustave. "La Littérature patristique des quaestiones et responsiones sur l'écriture sainte," *Revue Biblique* 41 (1932): pp. 210-236, 341-369, 515-537.

Bardy, Gustave. "La Littérature patristique des quaestiones et responsiones sur l'écriture sainte," *Revue Biblique* 41 (1933) :pp. 14-30, 211-229, 328-352.

Barrow, Julia. "Grades of Ordination and Clerical Careers, c. 900-c.1200," *Anglo-Norman Studies: Proceedings of the Battle Conference* 30 (2007): pp. 41-61.

---. "Review Article: Chrodegang, his Rule and its Successors," *Early Medieval Europe* 14 (2006): pp. 200-212

Bateson, Mary. "The Supposed Latin Penitential of Egbert and the Missing Work of Halitgar of Cambrai," *The English Historical Review* 34 (1894): pp. 320-326.

Bayard, François, and Pierre Cayez. *Histoire de Lyon, des origines à nos jours. Tome I, Antiquite et Moyen Âge.* Le Coteau: Horvath, 1990.

Beaujard, Brigitte, Paul-Albert Février, et al. *Topographie chrétienne des cités de la Gaule des origines au milieu du VIIIe siècle. 4, Province ecclésiastique de Lyon (Lugdunensis prima).* Paris: De Boccard, 1986.

Berry, Christopher. *The Idea of Luxury: A Conceptual and Historical Investigation.* Cambridge University Press, 1994.

Billett, Jesse D. *The Divine Office in Anglo-Saxon England, 597-c.1000.* Woodbridge and Rochester: Boydell Press, 2014.

Bischoff, Bernhard. "Die europäische Verbreitung der Werke Isidors von Sevilla," *Isidoriana: Colección de estudios sobre Isidoro de Sevilla.* Ed. Manuel C. Diaz y Diaz. León: Centro de Estudios 'San Isidoro,' 1961, pp. 317-344.

---. *Die südostdeutschen Schreibschulen und Bibliotheken in der Karolingerzeit.* Wiesbaden: Harrassowitz, 1960-1980.

---. *Katalog der festländischen Handschriften des neunten Jahrhunderts (mit Ausnahme der wisigotischen).* Wiesbaden: Harrassowitz, 1998-2017.

---. *Manuscripts and Libraries in the Age of Charlemagne.* Ed.Trans. Michael Gorman. Cambridge: Cambridge University Press, 1994.

---. "The Court Library of Charlemagne," *Manuscripts and Libraries in the Age of Charlemagne.* Trans. Ed. Michael Gorman. Cambridge: Cambridge University Press, 1994, pp. 56-75.

---. "Turning-points in the History of Latin Exegesis in the Early Middle Ages", *Biblical Studies: The Medieval Irish Contribution.* Trans. Colm O'Grady. Ed. Martin McNamara. Dublin: Dominican Publications, 1976, pp. 74-160.

---. "Wendepunkte in der Geschichte der lateinischen Exegese im Frühmittelalter," *Sacris Erudiri* 6 (1954): pp. 189-281.

---. "Wendepunkte in der Geschichte der lateinischen Exegese im Frühmittelalter," rev. Bernhard Bischoff, *Mittelalterliche Studien: Ausgewählte Aufsätze zur Schriftkunde und Literaturgeschichte,* vol. 1 .Stuttgart: Hiersemann, 1966-1981, pp. 205-273.

Bischoff, Bernhard ,Virginia Brown. "Addenda to *Codices Latini Antiquiores*," *Mediaeval Studies* 47 (1985): pp. 317-366.

Bischoff, Bernhard, Virginia Brown, et al. "Addenda to *Codices Latini Antiquiores* (II)," *Mediaeval Studies* 54 (1985): pp. 286-307.

Blanchard, Pierre. "Un traité de Benedictionibus Patriarcharum de Paschase Radbert?" *Revue Bénédictine* 28 (1911): pp. 425-432.

Bloomfield, Morton W. *The Seven Deadly Sins: An Introduction to the History of a Religious Concept, with Special Reference to Medieval English Literature*. East Lansing: Michigan State College Press, 1952.

Blumenkranz, Bernhard. "Anti-Jewish Polemics and Legislation in the Middle Ages: Literary Fiction or Reality?" *Journal of Jewish Studies* 15 (1964): pp.125-140.

---. "Du nouveau sur Bodo-Eleazar?" *Revue des Études Juives* 112 (1953): pp. 35-42.

Bonfil, Robert. "Cultural and Religious Traditions in Ninth-Century French Jewry," *Jewish Intellectual History in the Middle Ages*. Ed. Joseph Dan. Westport: Praeger, 1994, pp. 1-17.

Bonner, Gerald. "Augustine and Pelagianism," *Augustinian Studies* 24 (1993): pp. 27-47.

---. "Augustine, the Bible and the Pelagians," *Augustine and the Bible*. Ed. Pamela Bright. Notre Dame: University of Notre Dame Press, 1999, pp. 227-242.

Boucaud, Pierre. "*Corpus Paulinum*: L'exégèse grecque et latine des Épîtres au premier millénaire," *Revue de l'histoire des religions* 230 (2013): pp. 299-332.

---. "Tous libres devant Dieu: Société carolingienne, Église et esclavage d'après l'exégèse de Claude de Turin († ca. 827/828)," *Revue de l'histoire des religions* 228 (2011): pp. 349-387.

Boulhol, Pascal. *Claude de Turin: Un évêque iconoclaste dans l'Occident carolingien: Étude suivie de l'édition du Commentaire sur Josué*. Paris: Institut d'études augustiniennes, 2002.

Braschi, Francesco. "A Comprehensive Reading of Ambrose's *Explanatio psalmorum XII*," *Studia Patristica* 46 (2010): pp. 137-142.

Brown, Denis. *Vir Trilinguis: A Study in the Biblical Exegesis of Saint Jerome*. Kampen: Kok Pharos, 1992.

Brown, Giles. "Introduction: The Carolingian Renaissance," *Carolingian Culture: Emulation and Innovation*. Ed. Rosamond McKitterick. Cambridge: Cambridge University Press, 1994, pp. 1-51.

Brown, Peter. *Through the Eye of a Needle: Wealth, the Fall of Rome, and the Making of Christianity in the West, 350-550 AD*. Princeton: Princeton University Press, 2012.

Buc, Philippe. *L'Ambiguïté du Livre: Prince, pouvoir et peuple dans les commentaires de la Bible au Moyen Âge*. Paris: Beauchesne, 1994.

---. "*Principes gentium dominantur eorum*: Princely Power Between Legitimacy and Illegitimacy in Twelfth-Century Exegesis," *Cultures of Power: Lordship, Status, and Process in Twelfth-Century Europe*. ed. Thomas Bisson, pp. 310-328. Philadelphia: University of Pennsylvania Press, 1995.

Bullough, Donald. *Alcuin: Achievement and Reputation. Being Part of the Ford*

Lectures Delivered in Oxford in Hilary Term 1980. Leiden: Brill, 2004.

---. "Three 'Men of God' in Charlemagne's Service: Alcuin, Hildebald, Arno," *Charlemagne: Empire and Society.* Ed. Joanna Story. Manchester: Manchester University Press, 2005, pp. 136-150.

Bultmann, Christoph. "Deuteronomy," *The Oxford Bible Commentary: The Pentateuch.* Eds. John Barton, John Muddiman. Oxford: Oxford University Press, 2010, pp. 188-189.

Bussières, Marie-Pierre, ed. *La littérature des questions et réponses dans l'Antiquité profane et chrétienne.* Turnhout: Brepols, 2013.

Cabaniss, Allen. *Agobard of Lyons: Churchman and Critic.* Syracuse: Syracuse University Press, 1953.

---. "Bodo-Eleazar: A Famous Jewish Convert," *The Jewish Quarterly Review* 43 (1953): pp. 313-28.

Cain, Andrew. *The Letters of Jerome: Asceticism, Biblical Exegesis, and the Construction of Christian Authority in Late Antiquity.* Oxford: Oxford University Press, 2009.

Cameron, Averil. *Christianity and the Rhetoric of Empire: The Development of Christian Discourse.* Berkeley: University of California Press, 1991.

Canellis, Aline. "Jerome's Hermeneutics: How to Exegete the Bible?" *Patristic Theories of Biblical Interpretation: The Latin Fathers.* Ed. Tarmo Toom. Cambridge: Cambridge University Press, pp. 49-76.

Cantelli, Silvia. *Angelomo e la scuola esegetica di Luxeuil.* Spoleto: Centro Italiano di Studi sull'alto Medioevo, 1990.

---. "L'esegesi della rinascita carolingia," *La Bibbia nel medioevo.* Eds. Giuseppe Cremascoli, Claudio Leonardi. Bologna: Dehoniane, 1996, pp. 167-198.

---. *Hrabani Mauri opera exegetica: repertorium fontium.* Turnhout: Brepols, 2006.

Castaldi, Lucia, and Fabrizio Martello, "Tempera quasi aurum: origine, redazione e diffusione del 'Liber testimoniorum' di Paterio," *Filologia Mediolatina* 18 (2011): pp. 23-107.

Cavadini, John. *The Last Christology of the West: Adoptionism in Spain and Gaul, 785-820.* Philadelphia: University of Pennsylvania Press, 1993.

Chambert-Protat, Pierre. "Liste de Charlier," last accessed September 14, 2021, https://florus.hypotheses.org/liste-de-charlier.

Chambert-Protat, Pierre, Franz Dolveck, et al., eds. *Les douze compilations pauliniennes de Florus de Lyon: Un carrefour des tradition patristiques au IXe siècle.* Rome: École française de Rome, 2017.

Chandler, Cullen. "Heresy and Empire: The Role of the Adoptionist Controversy in Charlemagne's Conquest of the Spanish March," *The International History Review* 24 (2002): pp. 505-527.

Charlier, Célestin. "Les manuscrits personnels de Florus de Lyon et son activité littéraire," *Mélanges Emmanuel Podechard. Études de sciences religieuses offertes pour son éméritat au doyen honoraire de la faculté de théologie de Lyon* (Lyon: Faculté de théologie catholique: 1945): pp. 71-84.

Chatillon, Jean. "Isidore et Origène: Recherches sur les sources et l'influence des Quaestiones in Vetus Testamentum d'Isidore de Seville," *Mélanges bibliques rédigés en l'honneur de André Robert*. Paris: Bloud & Gay, 1956, pp. 537-547.

Chazelle, Celia. *The Crucified God in the Carolingian Era. Theology and the Art of Christ's Passion*. Cambridge: Cambridge University Press, 2001.

Chazelle, Celia, and Burton Van Name Edwards, eds. *The Study of the Bible in the Carolingian Era*. Turnhout: Brepols, 2003.

Chevalier-Royet, Caroline. "Des prédicateurs au service de la réforme de la société carolingienne: l'exemple des homélies de Raban Maur (vers 780-856)," *Gouverner les hommes, gouverner les âmes. XLVIe Congrès de la SHMESP*. Paris: Publications de la Sorbonne, 2016, pp. 49-58.

---. "Entre tradition et innovation: Raban Maur, un érudit carolingien face à ses sources," *Érudition et culture savante de l'Antiquité a l'époque moderne*. Eds. François Brizay, Véronique Sarrazin. Rennes: Presses universitaires de Rennes, 2015, pp. 53-70.

---. *Les Livres de Rois dans l'empire carolingien: Exégèse et actualité*. Paris: Classiques Garnier, 2021.

---. "La Bible d'Agobard," *Lyon dans l'Europe carolingienne: Autour d'Agobard (816–840)*. Eds. François Bougard, Alexis Charansonnet, Marie-Céline Isaïa. Turnhout: Brepols, 2019, pp. 131-143.

---. "Saül et David, premiers rois oints: L'interprétation de ces modèles royaux par deux exégétes carolingiens, Raban Maur et Angélome de Luxeuil," *The Multiple Meaning of Scripture: The Role of Exegesis in Early-Christian and Medieval Culture*. Ed. Ineke Van't Spijker, pp. 61-76. Leiden: Brill, 2008.

Chiesa, Paolo. "*De ortu et obitu Patrum*," *La trasmissione dei testi latini del Medioevo*. Eds. Paolo Chiesa, Lucia Castaldi, vol. 2. Florence: SISMEL, Edizioni del Galluzzo, 2004-2013, pp. 345-353.

---. "*In libros Veteris et Noui Testamenti Prooemia*," *La trasmissione dei testi latini del Medioevo*. Eds. Paolo Chiesa, Lucia Castaldi, vol. 2. Florence: SISMEL, Edizioni del Galluzzo, 2004-2013, pp. 338-345.

Clark, Elizabeth A. *The Origenist Controversy: The Cultural Construction of an Early Christian Debate*. Princeton: Princeton University Press, 1992.

Claussen, Martin. *The Reform of the Frankish Church: Chrodegang of Metz and the Regula canonicorum in the Eighth Century*. Cambridge: Cambridge University Press, 2004.

Close, Florence. *Uniformiser la foi pour unifier l'Empire:. Contribution à l'histoire de la pensée politico-théologique de Charlemagne*. Bruxelles: Académie royale de Belgique, 2011.

Cohen, Jeremy. *Living Letters of the Law: Ideas of the Jew in Medieval Christianity*. Berkeley: University of California Press, 1999.

Cointe, Carolus Le. *Annales Ecclesiastici Francorum*. Paris: Typographia regia, 1665-1683.

Conant, Jonathan. "Europe and the African Cult of Saints, circa 350–900: An Essay in Mediterranean Communications," *Speculum* 85 (2010): pp. 1-46.

Constable, Giles. *Monastic Tithes: From Their Origins to the Twelfth Century*. Cambridge: Cambridge University Press, 1964.

Contreni, John. "'By Lions, Bishops are Meant; by Wolves, Priests': History, Exegesis, and the Carolingian Church in Haimo of Auxerre's Commentary on Ezechiel," *Francia* 29 (2002): pp. 29-56.

---. "Carolingian Biblical Culture," *Iohannes Scottus Eriugena: The Bible and Hermeneutics*. Eds. Gerd van Riel, Carlos Steel, James McEvoy. Leuven: Leuven University Press, 1996, pp. 1-23.

---. "Carolingian Biblical Studies," *Carolingian Essays: Andrew W. Mellon Lectures in Early Christian Studies*. Ed. Uta-Renate Blumenthal. Washington, D.C.: Catholic University of America Press, 1983, pp. 71-97.

---. *Carolingian Learning, Masters and Manuscripts*. Aldershot: Variorum, 1992.

---. "Glossing the Bible in the Early Middle Ages: Theodore and Hadrian of Canterbury and John Scottus (Eriugena)," *The Study of the Bible in the Carolingian Era*. Eds. Celia Chazelle, Burton Van Name Edwards. Turnhout: Brepols, 2003, pp. 19-38.

---. "Inharmonious Harmony: Education in the Carolingian World," *Annals of Scholarship: Metastudies of the Humanities and Social Sciences* 1 (1980): pp. 81-96.

---. *Learning and Culture in Carolingian Europe: Letters, Numbers, Exegesis, and Manuscripts*. Farnham: Variorum, 2011.

----------. "Learning for God: Education in the Carolingian Age," *The Journal of Medieval Latin* 24 (2014): pp. 89-129.

---. "The Carolingian Renaissance," *Renaissances before the Renaissance: Cultural Revivals of Late Antiquity and the Middle Ages*. Ed. Warren Treadgold. Stanford: Stanford University Press, 1984.

---. "The Carolingian Renaissance: Education and Literary Culture," *The New Cambridge Medieval History*, vol. 2. Ed. Rosamond McKitterick. Cambridge: Cambridge University Press, 1995, pp. 709-57.

---. *The Cathedral School of Laon from 850 to 930: Its Manuscripts and Masters*. München: Arbeo-Gesellschaft, 1978.

---. "The Patristic Legacy to c. 1000," *The New Cambridge History of the Bible From 600 to 1450*. Eds. Richard Marsden, Ann Matter. Cambridge: Cambridge University

Press, 2012, pp. 505-535.

---. "The Pursuit of Knowledge in Carolingian Europe," *The Gentle Voices of Teachers: Aspects of Learning in the Carolingian Age*. Ed. Richard Sullivan. Columbus: Ohio State University Press, 1995, pp. 106-141.

Courcelle, Pierre. *Connais-toi toi-même: de Socrate à Saint Bernard*. Paris: Études augustiniennes, 1974-1975.

----. *Late Latin Writers and Their Greek Sources*. Trans. Harry E. Wedeck. Cambridge: Harvard University Press, 1969.

Couser, Jonathan. "A Usable Past: Early Bavarian Hagiography in Context," *Studies in Medieval and Renaissance History* III.4 (2007): pp. 1-56.

Dahan, Gilbert. "Lexiques hébreu/latin? Les recueils d'interprétations des noms hébraïques," *Les manuscrits des lexiques et glossaires de l'Antiquité tardive à la fin du Moyen Âge: Actes du Colloque international (Erice, 23-30 septembre 1994)*. Ed. Jacqueline Hamesse. Turnhout: Brepols, 1996, pp. 481-526.

Dahlhaus-Berg, Elisabeth. *Nova antiquitas et antiqua novitas: typologische Exegese und isidorianisches Geschichtsbild bei Theodulf von Orléans*. Köln: Böhlau, 1975.

Daniélou, Jean. *From Shadows to Reality: Studies in Biblical Typology of the Fathers*. Trans. Wulstan Hibberd. London: Burns & Oates, 1960)

de Jong, Mayke. "Becoming Jeremiah: Paschasius Radbertus on Wala, Himself and Others," *Ego Trouble: Authors and Their Identities in the Early Middle Ages*. Eds. Richard Corradini, Matthew Gillis, Rosamund McKitterick, Irene van Reenswoude. Wien:Verlag der Österreichischen Akademie der Wissenschaften, 2010, pp. 185-196.

---. "Carolingian Political Discourse and the Biblical Past: Hraban, Dhuoda, Radbert," *The Resources of the Past in Early Medieval Europe*. Eds. Clemens Gantner, Rosamond McKitterick, Sven Meeder. Cambridge: Cambridge University Press, 2015, pp. 87-102.

---. "Charlemagne's Balcony: The Solarium in Ninth-Century Narratives," *The Long Morning of Medieval Europe: New Directions in Early Medieval Studies*. Eds. Jennifer R. Davis and Michael McCormick. Burlington: Ashgate, 2008, pp. 277-290.

---. "Charlemagne's Church," *Charlemagne: Empire and Society*. Ed. Joanna Story. Manchester: Manchester University Press, 2005, pp. 103-135.

---."Exegesis for an Empress," *Medieval Transformations: Texts, Power, and Gifts in Context*. Eds. Esther Cohen, Mayke de Jong Leiden: Brill, 2001, pp. 69-100.

---. "Jeremiah, Job, Terence and Paschasius Radbertus: Political Rhetoric and Biblical Authority in the *Epitaphium Arsenii*," *Reading the Bible in the Middle Ages*. Eds. Janet Nelson, Damien Kempf. London: Bloomsbury Academic, 2015, pp. 57-76.

---. "Old Law and New-Found Power: Hrabanus Maurus and the Old Testament," *Centres of Learning: Learning and Location in Pre-Modern Europe and the Near East*. Eds. Jan Willem Drijvers, Alasdair MacDonald. Leiden: Brill, 1995, pp. 161-176.

---. "The Emperor Lothar and His *Bibliotheca Historiarum*," *Media Latinitas: A*

Collection of Essays to Mark the Occasion of the Retirement of L. J. Engels. Eds. R. I. A. Nip, H. van Dijk, E. M. C. van Houts, C. H. J. M. Kneepkens, G. A. A. Kortekaas,Turnhout: Brepols, 1996, pp. 229-235.

---. "The Empire as *Ecclesia*: Hrabanus Maurus and Biblical *Historia* for Rulers," *The Uses of the Past in the Early Middle Ages*. Eds. Yitzhak Hen, Matthew Innes. Cambridge: Cambridge University Press, 2000, pp. 191-226.

---. *The Penitential State: Authority and Atonement in the Age of Louis the Pious, 814-840*. Cambridge: Cambridge University Press, 2009.

---. "The State of the Church: *Ecclesia* and Early Medieval State Formation," *Der frühmittelalterliche Staat: Europäische Perspektiven*. Eds. Walter Pohl, Veronika Wieser. Vienna: Verlag der Österreichischen Akademie der Wissenschaften, 2009, pp. 241-254.

de Lange, N. R. M. *Origen and the Jews: Studies in Jewish-Christian Relations in Third-century Palestine*. Cambridge: Cambridge University Press, 1976.

de Lubac, Henri. *Medieval Exegesis: The Four Senses of Scripture*. Trans. Mark Sebanc , E. M. Macierowski. Grand Rapids: William B. Eerdmans, 1998-2009.

Dekkers, Eligius, and Emil Gaar. *Clavis patrum Latinorum*. Turnhout: Brepols, 1995.

Delisle, Léopold. "Notes sur quelques manuscrits du Baron Dauphin de Verna," *Bibliothèque de l'École des Chartes* 56 (1895): pp. 651-655.

Depreux, Philippe. "Ambitions et limites des réformes culturelles à l'époque carolingienne," *Revue historique* 623 (2002): pp. 721-753.

---. "Les juifs dans le droit carolingien," *Jews in Early Christian Law: Byzantium and the Latin West, 6th-11th Centuries*. Eds. Capucine Nemo-Pekelman, Laurence Foschia, John V. Tolan, Nicholas de Lange. Turnhout: Brepols, 2014, pp. 131-152.

---. *Prosopographie de l'Entourage de Louis le Pieux (781-840)*. Sigmaringen: Thorbecke, 1997.

Depreux, Philippe, Stéphane Lebecq, Michel Perrin, and Olivier Szerwiniack, eds. *Raban Maur et son temps*. Turnhout: Brepols, 2010.

Devreesse, Robert. "Chaînes exégétiques grecques," *Dictionnaire de la Bible, Supplément I*, Ed. Louis Pirot, André Robert, Jacques Briend, and Édouard Cothenet. Paris: Letouzey & Ané, 1928, cols. 1084-1233.

Devroey, Jean-Pierre. "'Mansi absi': indices de crise ou de croissance de l'économie rurale du haut Moyen Âge?" *Le Moyen Âge* 31 (1976): pp. 421-452.

Diesenberger, Maximilian. *Predigt und Politik im frühmittelalterlichen Bayern: Arn von Salzburg, Karl der Große und die Salzburger Sermones-Sammlung*. Berlin: De Gruyter, 2016.

Doerfler, Maria E. "Coming Apart at the Seams: Crossdressing, Masculinity, and the Social Body in Late Antiquity," *Dressing Judeans and Christians in Antiquity*. Eds. Kristi Upson-Saia, Carly Daniel-Hughes, Kristi Upson-Saia. Burlington: Ashgate, 2014, pp. 37-51.

Dorival, Gilles. "Biblical Catenae between Philology and History," *Commentaries, Catenae, and the Biblical Tradition: Papers from the Ninth Birmingham Colloquium on the Textual Criticism of the New Testament, in Conjunction with the COMPAUL Project.* Ed. Hugh A. G. Houghton. Piscataway: Gorgias Press, 2016, pp. 68-81.

---. "Des commentaires de l'Ecriture aux chaînes," *Le Monde Grec Ancien et la Bible.* Ed. Claude Mondésert. Paris, Beauchesne: 1984, pp. 361-386.

---. "Origen," *The New Cambridge History of the Bible, Volume 1: From the Beginning to 600.* Eds. James Carleton, Joachim Schape. Cambridge: Cambridge University Press, 2013, pp. 605-628.

Drews, Wolfram. *The Unknown Neighbour: The Jew in the Thought of Isidore of Seville.* Leiden: Brill, 2006.

du Cange, Fresne, *Glossarium Mediae et Infimae Latinitatis.* Ed. Léopold Favre. Niort: L. Favre, 1883.

Dubois, Jacques. *Les martyrologes du Moyen Âge latin.* Turnhout: Brepols, 1978.

---. "Moines et monastères du Bugey," *Le Bugey* 49 (1962): pp. 1-63. Reprinted in Jacques Dubois, *Histoire monastique en France au XIIe siècle: les institutions monastiques et leur évolution* (London: Variorum, 1982), VII.

Dulaey, Martine. "Augustin en Provence dans les premières décennies du Ves: Le témoignage des Formulae d'Eucher," *Studia Ephemeridis Augustinianum* 90 (2004): pp. 121-146.

---. "Eucher de Lyon exégète: l'interprétation de la Bible en Gaule du Sud dans la première moitié du Ve siècle," *Mauritius und die Thebäische Legion/Saint Maurice et la légion thébaine: Actes du colloque international Fribourg, Saint-Maurice, Martigny, 17-20 Septembre 2003.* Eds. Otto Wermelinger, Philippe Bruggisser, Beat Näf, Jean-Michel Roessli. Fribourg: Academic Press, 2005, pp. 67-95.

---. "Jérôme maître d'exégèse au monastère de Lérins: le témoignage des Formulae d'Eucher de Lyon," *Augustinianum* (44) 2004: pp. 371-400.

---. "Les relations entre Lérins et Marseille: Eucher et Cassien," *Lérins, une île sainte de l'Antiquité au Moyen Âge.* Eds. Yann Codou, Michel Lauwers. Turnhout: Brepols, 2009, pp. 63-82.

---. "Les sources du commentaire d'Isidore sur la Genèse," *Isidorus episcopus Hispalensis: Expositio in Vetus Testamentum. Genesis.* Ed. Michael Gorman. Freiburg: Herder, 2009, pp. xxv-xliii.

Dutton, Paul. "Thunder and Hail over the Carolingian Countryside," *Charlemagne's Mustache and Other Cultural Clusters of a Dark Age.* Ed. Paul Dutton. New York: Palgrave Macmillan, 2004, pp. 169-188.

Earl, Douglas. "The Christian Significance of Deuteronomy 7," *Journal of Theological Interpretation* 3 (2009): pp. 41-62.

Edwards, Burton Van Name. "Deuteronomy in the Ninth Century: The Unpublished

Commentaries of Walahfrid Strabo and Haimo of Auxerre," *The Study of the Bible in the Carolingian Era.* Eds. Celia Chazelle, Burton Van Name Edwards. Turnhout: Brepols, 2003, pp. 97-113.

---. "The Transmission of Carolingian Bible Commentaries in Manuscripts and Printed Editions," last accessed September 14, 2021, https://risd.digication.com/bvnedwards/Bibliography.

Elfassi, Jacques. *"Allegoriae* sive *Liber de interpretatione quorundam nominum Veteris Nouique Testamenti,"* *La trasmissione dei testi latini del Medioevo.* Eds. Paolo Chiesa, Lucia Castaldi. Florence: SISMEL, Edizioni del Galluzzo, 2004-2013, vol. 1, pp. 196-201.

---. "Isidore de Séville connaissait-il les Formulae d'Eucher de Lyon?" *Felici Curiositate: Studies in Latin Literature and Textual Criticism from Antiquity to the Twentieth Century: In Honour of Rita Beyers.* Eds. Guy Guldentops, Christian Laes, Gert Partoens. Turnhout: Brepols, 2017, pp. 377-382.

--- *"Quaestiones in Vetus Testamentum,"La trasmissione dei testi latini del Medioevo,* Eds. Paolo Chiesa, Lucia Castaldi. Florence: SISMEL, Edizioni del Galluzzo, 2004-2013, vol. 1, pp. 196-201.

Eliot, T. S. "Tradition and the Individual Talent," *The Sacred Wood: Essays on Poetry and Criticism.* New York: Alfred A. Knopf, 1921, pp. 42-53.

Elliott, Mark W. "Exegetical genres in the patristic era," *The New Cambridge History of the Bible, Volume 1: From the Beginning to 600.* Eds. James Carleton, Joachim Schape. Cambridge: Cambridge University Press, 2013, pp. 775-797

Elukin, Jonathan. "Judaism: From Heresy to Pharisee in Early Medieval Christian Literature," *Traditio* 57 (2002): pp. 49-66.

Étaix, Raymond. "L'homéliaire composé par Raban Maur pour l'empereur Lothaire," *Recherches Augustiniennes* 19 (1984): pp. 211-240.

---. "Le Liber testimoniorum de Paterius," *Revue des sciences religieuses* 32 (1958): pp. 66-78.

----. "Un Manuel de Pastorale de l'Époque Carolingienne (Clm. 27152)," *Revue Bénédictine* 91 (1981): pp. 105-130.

Ewig, Eugen. "Milo et eiusmodi similes," *Spätantikes und fränkisches Gallien: gesammelte Schriften (1952-1973).* Eds. Hartmut Atsma, Matthias Becher. München: Artemis Verlag, 1976-2009, vol. 2, pp. 189-219.

Ferrari, Michele Camillo. "Before the 'Glossa ordinaria': The Ezekiel Fragment in Irish Minuscule Zürich, Staatsarchiv W3.19.XII, and Other Experiments towards a 'Bible commentée' in the Early Middle Ages," *Biblical Studies in the Early Middle Ages.* Eds. Claudio Leonardi, Giovanni Orlandi. Firenze: Edizioni del Galluzzo, 2005, pp. 283-307.

Favier, H. *Essai historique sur Leidrad Archevêque de Lyon (740?-816-7).* Lyon: Typographie et lithographie J. Gallet, 1898.

Fédon, René. "Les temps obscurs (Ve-Xe siècles)," *Histoire de Lyon et du Lyonnais*. Ed. André Latreille. Toulouse: Université de la France, 1975, pp. 61-75.

Fichtenau, Heinrich. *The Carolingian Empire*. Trans. Peter Munz. Oxford: Blackwell, 1957.

Firey, Abigail. "A Carolingian Lyonnaise Supplement to the *Collectio Dacheriana*," *Proceedings of the Tenth International Congress of Medieval Canon Law: Syracuse, New York, 13-18 August 1996*. Eds. Kenneth Pennington, Stanley Chodorow, Keith Kendall. Città del Vaticano: Biblioteca apostolica Vaticana, 2001, pp. 27-54.

---. *A Contrite Heart: Prosecution and Redemption in the Carolingian Empire*. Leiden: Brill, 2009.

---. "Carolingian Ecclesiology and Heresy: A Southern Gallic Juridical Tract against Adoptionism," *Sacris erudiri* 39 (2000): pp. 253-316.

---. "Ghostly Recensions in Early Medieval Canon Law: The Problem of the Collectio Dacheriana and its Shades," *Tijdschrift voor rechtsgeschiedenis* 68 (2000): pp. 63-82.

---. "Mutating Monsters: Approaches to 'Living Texts' of the Carolingian Era," *Digital Proceedings of the Lawrence J. Schoenberg Symposium on Manuscript Studies in the Digital Age* 2 (2010): pp. 1-14.

---. *Toward a History of Carolingian Legal Culture Canon Law Collections of Early Medieval Southern Gaul*. Toronto :University of Toronto, 1995.

Fischer, Bonifatius. "Bibeltext und Bibelreform unter Karl Dem Grossen," *Karl der Grosse: Lebenswerk und Nachleben*, vol. 2, Das geistige Leben. Ed. Bernhard Bischoff. Düsseldorf: L. Schwann, 1965, pp. 156-216.

Fitzgerald, Allan. "Quaestiones in Heptateuchum," *Augustine through the Ages: An Encyclopedia*. Eds. Allan Fitzgerald, John Cavadini. Grand Rapids: William B. Eerdmans, 1999, pp. 692-693.

Flechner, Roy, ed. *The Hibernensis, Volume 1: A Study and Edition*. Washington, D.C.: Catholic University of America Press, 2019.

Fleckenstein, Josef. *Die Bildungsreform Karls des Grossen als Verwirklichung der Norma Rectitudinis*. Bigge-Ruhr: Josefs-Druckerei, 1953.

Fontaine, Jacques. "Isidore de Séville et la Bible," *Recherches Augustiniennes et Patristiques* 33 (2003): pp. 65-69.

---. *Isidore de Séville: Genèse et originalité de la culture hispanique au temps des Wisigoths*. Turnhout: Brepols, 2000.

---. "Isidore de Séville pédagogue et théoricien de l'exégèse," *Stimuli: Exegese und ihre Hermeneutik in Antike und Christentum. Festschrift für Ernst Dassmann*. Eds. Georg Schöllgen, Clemens Scholten. Münster: Aschendorff, 1996, pp. 423-434.

Fouracre, Paul. *The Age of Charles Martel*. Harlow: Longman, 2000.

---."The Origins of the Carolingian Attempt to Regulate the Cult of Saints," *The Cult of Saints in Late Antiquity and the Middle Ages: Essays on the Contribution of Peter*

Brown. Eds. James Howard-Johnston, Paul Antony Hayward. Oxford: Oxford University Press, 1999, pp. 143-165.

Fournier, Paul, and Gabriel Le Bras, *Histoire des collections canoniques en Occident depuis les Fausses décrétales jusqu'au Décret de Gratien*. Paris: Recueil Sirey, 1931-1932.

Fox, Michael. "Alcuin the Exegete: The Evidence of the *Quaestiones in Genesim*," *The Study of the Bible in the Carolingian Era*. Eds. Celia Chazelle, Burton Van Name Edwards. Turnhout: Brepols, 2003, pp. 39-60.

---. "Alcuin's *Expositio in epistolam ad Hebraeos*," *The Journal of Medieval Latin* 18 (2008): pp. 326-345.

François, Decret. *Early Christianity in North Africa*. Trans. Edward Smither. Eugene: Wipf and Stock Publishers, 2009.

Fransen, Paul-Irénée. "La discipline de l'Église dans un commentaire anonyme au Deutéronome écrit à Lyon au IXe siècle," *Zeitschrift der Savigny-Stiftung für Rechtsgeschichte* 83 (1997): pp. 52-66.

Fredriksen, Paula, *Augustine and the Jews: A Christian Defense of Jews and Judaism*. New York: Doubleday, 2008.

Gadille, Jacques, René Fédou, Henri Hours, and Bernard de Vregille, *Le Diocèse de Lyon*. Paris: Beauchesne, 1983.

Gameson, Richard. *The Early Medieval Bible: Its Production, Decoration and Use*. Cambridge: Cambridge University Press, 1994.

Ganshof, François Louis. "Charlemagne et la revision du texte latin," *Bulletin de l'Institut historique belge de Rome* 44 (1974): pp. 271-281.

Gantner, Clemens, Rosamond McKitterick, and Sven Meeder, eds. *The Resources of the Past in Early Medieval Europe*. Cambridge: Cambridge University Press, 2015.

Ganz, David. "Carolingian Bibles," *The New Cambridge History of the Bible From 600 to 1450*. Eds. Richard Marsden, Ann Matter. Cambridge: Cambridge University Press, 2012.

---."Carolingian Manuscripts: The Verdict of the Master," *Francia* 42 (2015): pp. 252-274.

---. *Corbie in the Carolingian Renaissance*. Beihefte der Francia 20. Sigmaringen: Thorbecke Verlag, 1990.

---. "Mass Production of Early Medieval Manuscripts: The Carolingian Bibles from Tours," *The Early Medieval Bible: Its Production, Decoration and Use*. Ed. Richard Gameson. Cambridge: Cambridge University Press, 1994, pp. 53-62.

Garrison, Mary. "Letters to a King and Biblical Exempla: The Examples of Cathuulf and Clemens Peregrinus," *Early Medieval Europe* 7 (1998): pp. 305-328.

---. "The Bible and Alcuin's Interpretation of Current Events," *Peritia* 16 (2002): pp. 68-84.

---. "The Franks as the New Israel? Education for an Identity from Pippin to Charlemagne," *The Uses of the Past in the Early Middle Ages*. Eds. Yitzhak Hen , Matthew Innes. Cambridge: Cambridge University Press, 2000, pp. 114-161.

Gauthiez, Bernard. "La topographie de Lyon au Moyen Âge," *Archéologie du Midi médiéval* 12 (1994): pp. 3-38.

Genevois, Anne-Marie. "Autour de Jean Diacre et de son Expositio in Heptateuchum," *Du copiste au collectionneur: Mélanges d'histoire des textes et des bibliothèques en l'honneur d'André Vernet*. Eds. Donatella Nebbiai-Dalla Guarda, Jean-François Genest, André Vernet. Turnhout: Brepols, 1999, pp. 35-48.

Gometz, Abigail Kathleen. *Eugippius of Lucullanum: A Biography*. Leeds :University of Leeds, 2008.

Glaser, Hubert. "Bischof Arbeo von Freising," *Christenleben im Wandel der Zeit: Lebensbilder aus der Geschichte des Erzbistums München und Freising*. Ed. Georg Schwaiger. Munich: E. Wewel, 1987, pp. 21-34.

Gorman, Michael. "A Critique of Bischoff's Theory of Irish Exegesis: The Commentary on Genesis in Munich Clm 6302 (Wendepunkte 2)," *Journal of Medieval Latin* 7 (1997): pp.178-233.

---. *Biblical Commentaries from the Early Middle Ages*. Firenze: SISMEL edizioni del Galluzzo, 2002.

---. "Charlemagne's Commentator: The *Quaestiunculae super Euangelium*," *Revue Bénédictine* 117 (2004): pp. 5-74

---. "Peter of Pisa and the *Quaestiunculae* Copied for Charlemagne in Brussels II 2572 with a Note on the Codex Diezianus from Verona," *Revue Bénédictine* 110 (2000): pp. 238-260.

---. "Rewriting Augustine: Alcuin's Commentary on the Gospel of John," *Revue Bénédictine* 119 (2009): pp. 36-85.

---. "The Commentary on Genesis of Angelomus of Luxeuil and Biblical studies under Lothar," *Studi medievali* 40 (1999): pp. 559-632.

---. "The Commentary on Genesis of Claudius of Turin and Biblical Studies under Louis the Pious," *Speculum* 72 (1997): pp. 279-329.

---. "The Commentary on the Gospel of John by Haimo of Auxerre," *Revue Bénédictine* 105 (1995): pp. 61-111.

---. "The Commentary on the Pentateuch Attributed to Bede in PL. 91.189-394," *Revue Bénédictine* 106 (1996): pp. 61-108, 255-307.

---. "The Encylopedic Commentary on Genesis Prepared for Charlemagne by Wigbod," *Recherches Augustiniennes et Patristiques* 17 (1982): pp. 173-201.

---. "The Epitome of Wigbod's Commentaries on Genesis and the Gospels," *Revue Bénédictine* 118 (2008): pp. 5-45.

---. "The Manuscript Tradition of Eugippius' *Excerpta ex operibus sancti Augustini*,"

Revue Bénédictine 92 (1982): pp. 7-32, 229-265.

---. "The Myth of Hiberno-Latin Biblical Exegesis," *Revue Bénédictine* 110 (2000): pp. 42-85.

---. *The Study of the Bible in the Early Middle ages*. Firenze: SISMEL edizioni del Galluzzo, 2007.

---. "Wigbod and Biblical Studies under Charlemagne," *Revue Bénédictine* 107 (1997): pp. 40-76.

---. "Wigbod and the *Lectiones* on the Hexateuch Attributed to Bede in Paris Lat. 2342," *Revue Bénédictine* 105 (1995): pp. 305-347.

Greschat, Katharina. "Spätantike Bildungstraditionen im Umkreis des Klosters von Lerinum: Die Kompendienwerke des Eucherius von Lyon," *Zeitschrift für Antikes Christentum* 10 (2007): pp. 320-335.

Grifoni, Cinzia. "Reading the Catholic Epistles: Glossing Practices in Early Medieval Wissembourg,"*The Annotated Book in the Early Middle Ages: Practices of Reading and Writing*. Eds. Mariken Teeuwen, Irene van Renswoude. Turnhout: Brepols, 2018, pp. 705-742.

Guglielmetti, Rossana. "Hrabanus Maurus," *La trasmissione dei testi latini del Medioevo*. Eds. Paolo Chiesa, Lucia Castaldi. Florence: SISMEL, Edizioni del Galluzzo, 2004-2013, vol.3 pp. 275-332.

---. "Un'esegesi incontentabile," *Il secolo di Carlo Magno: istituzioni, letterature e cultura del tempo carolingio*. Eds. Ileana Pagani, Francesco Santi. Firenze: SISMEL edizioni del Galluzzo, 2016, pp. 177-200.

Hammer, Carl. "Arbeo of Freising's Life and Passion of St Emmeram: The Martyr and his Critics," *Revue d'histoire ecclésiastique* 161 (2006): pp. 5-36.

---. "Country Churches, Clerical Inventories and the Carolingian Renaissance in Bavaria," *Church History* 49 (1980): pp. 5-17.

Hammond, C. P. "The Last Ten Years of Rufinus's Life and the Date of his Move South from Aquileia," *The Journal of Theological Studies* 28 (1977): pp. 372-429

Hartmann, Wilfried. "Die Karolingische Reform und die Bibel," *Annuarium Historiae Conciliorum* 18 (1986): pp. 58-74.

Harvey, Graham. *The True Israel: Uses of the Names Jew, Hebrew, and Israel in Ancient Jewish and Early Christian Literature*. Leiden: Brill, 1996.

Hayward, Robert. *Interpretations of the Name Israel in Ancient Judaism and Some Early Christian Writings from Victorious Athlete to Heavenly Champion*. Oxford: Oxford University Press, 2005.

Heil, Johannes. "Agobard, Amolo, Das Kirchengut und die Juden von Lyon," *Francia* 25 (1998): pp. 39-76.

---. "Goldenes Zeitalter? Juden und Judentum in der Karolingerzeit," *"Wie schön sind Deine Zelte, Jakob, deine Wohnungen, Israel?": Beiträge zur Geschichte europäisch-*

jüdischer Kultur. Ed. Rainer Kampling. Frankfurt am Main: Peter Lang, 2009, pp. 99-114.

---. *Kompilation oder Konstruktion? Die Juden in den Pauluskommentaren des 9. Jahrhunderts*. Hannover: Hahnsche, 1998.

---. "Labourers in the Lord's Quarry: Carolingian Exegetes, Patristic Authority, and Theological Innovation, a Case Study in the Representation of Jews in Commentaries on Paul," *The Study of the Bible in the Carolingian Era*. Eds. Celia Chazelle, Burton Van Name Edwards. Turnhout: Brepols, 2003, pp. 75-95.

---. "Theodulf, Haimo, and Jewish Traditions of Biblical Learning: Exploring Carolingian Culture's Lost Spanish Heritage," *Discovery and Distinction in the Early Middle Ages: Studies in Honor of John J. Contreni*. Eds. Cullen Chandler, Steven Stofferahn. Kalamazoo: Medieval Institute Publications, Western Michigan University, 2013, pp. 88-115.

Hen, Yitzhak. "A Merovingian Commentary on the Four Gospels," *Revue des Études Augustiniennes* 49 (2003): pp. 167-187.

---. "Educating the Clergy: Canon Law and Liturgy in a Carolingian Handbook from the Time of Charles the Bald," De Sion exibit lex et verbum domini de Hierusalem: *Essays on Medieval Law, Liturgy and Literature in Honour of Amnon Linder*. Ed. Yitzhak Hen. Turnhout: Brepols, 2010, pp. 43-58.

---. "Knowledge of Canon Law Among Rural Priests: The Evidence of Two Carolingian Manuscripts from around 800," *The Journal of Theological Studies* 50 (1999): pp. 117-134.

---. "The Romanization of the Frankish Liturgy: Ideal, Reality, and the Rhetoric of Reform," *Rome across Time and Space, c. 500-1400: Cultural Transmission and the Exchange of Ideas*. Eds. Claudia Bolgia, Rosamond McKitterick, John Osborne. Cambridge: Cambridge University Press, 2011, pp. 111-124.

---. "The Uses of the Bible and the Perception of Kingship in Merovingian Gaul," *Early Medieval Europe* 1 (1998): pp. 277-289.

Hen, Yitzhak, and Matthew Innes, eds. *The Uses of the Past in the Early Middle Ages*. Cambridge: Cambridge University Press, 2000.

Heydemann, Gerda. "People(s) of God? Biblical Exegesis and the Language of Community in Late Antique and Early Medieval Europe," *Meanings of Community across Medieval Eurasia*. Eds. Erik Hovden, Christina Lutter, Walter Pohl. Leiden: Brill, 2016, pp. 27-60.

---. "The People of God and the Law: Biblical Models in Carolingian Legislation," *Speculum* 95 (2020): pp. 89-131.

Hillgarth, Jocelyn N. "Ireland and Spain in the Seventh Century," *Peritia* 3 (1984): pp. 1-16.

---. "The East, Visigothic Spain and the Irish," *Studia Patristica* 4 (1961): pp. 422-

456.

---. "The Position of Isidorian Studies: A Critical Review of the Literature 1936-1975," *Studi Medievali*, 3d ser. 24 (1983): pp. 817-905.

---. "Visigothic Spain and Early Christian Ireland," *Proceedings of the Royal Irish Academy* 62 (1961-1963): pp. 167-194.

Holtz, Louis. "La bibliothèque de Florus de Lyon," *Le sense du temps: actes du VIIe Congres du Comite International de Latin Medieval (Lyon, 10-13.09.2014)*. Eds. Pascale Bourgain, Jean-Yves Tilliette. Genève: Librairie Droz, 2017, pp. 897-914.

---. "La tradition lyonnaise d'Eucher de Lyon et le manuscrit Paris, BNF, lat. 9550," *Revue d'Histoire des Textes* 3 (2008): pp. 135-200.

---. "Leidrat, évêque de Lyon (798-814): ses livres, son écriture," *Amicorum societas: mélanges offerts à François Dolbeau pour son 65e anniversaire*. Eds. Jacques Elfassi, Cécile Lanéry, Anne-Marie Turcan-Verkerk, François Dolbeau. Firenze: SISMEL edizioni del Galluzzo, 2013, pp. 315-333.

---. "Les hendécasyllabes de Florus, chantre des saints martyrs Cyprien, Spératus et Pantaléon," *La rigueur et la passion: Mélanges en l'honneur de Pascale Bourgain*. Eds. Cédric Giraud, Dominique Poirel. Turnhout: Brepols, 2006, pp. 89-100.

---. "Les manuscrits latins à gloses et à commentaires de l'Antiquité à l'époque carolingienne," *Il Libro e il Testo: Atti del Convegno Internazionale: Urbino, 20-23 Settembre 1982*. Eds. Cesare Questa, Renato Raffaelli. Urbino: Università degli Studi di Urbino, 1984, pp. 139-167.

Hoyt, Franceen S. *The Carolingian Episcopate: Concepts of Pastoral Care as Set Forth in the Capitularies of Charlemagne and His Bishops (789-822)*. New Haven:Yale University, 1975.

Ioannidis, Fotios. "The Interpretation of Scriptures by Ambrose of Milan," *Synthesis* 3 (2016): pp. 68-75.

Irvine, Martin. *The Making of Textual Culture: "Grammatica" and Literary Theory 350-1100*. Cambridge: Cambridge University Press, 1994.

Isaïa, Marie-Céline. "L'hagiographie contre la réforme dans l'église de Lyon au IXe siècle," *Médiévales* 62 (2012): pp. 83-104.

---. "'[…] *correctionis gratia iuxta ministerium sibi iniunctum* […]': Agobard and the Episcopal School of Lyons." Leeds International Medieval Congress, 5 July 2016.

Jaeger, Stephen. *The Envy of Angels: Cathedral Schools and Social Ideals in Medieval Europe, 950-1200*. Philadelphia: University of Pennsylvania Press, 1994.

Jahn, Joachim. "Bischof Arbeo von Freising und die Politik seiner Zeit," *Ethnogenese und Überlieferung: Angewandte Methoden der Frühmittelalterforschung*. Eds., Karl Brunner, Brigitte Merta. Vienne: Oldenbourg, 1994, pp. 157-162.

Jakobi, Rainer. "Eine Augustinische Echtheitsfrage: De Octo Quaestionibus ex Veteri Testamento," *Augustinianum* 48 (2008): pp. 205-210.

James, Edward. "Ireland and Western Gaul in the Merovingian period," *Ireland in Early Mediaeval Europe: Studies in Memory of Kathleen Hughes*. Eds. Dorothy Whitelock, Rosamond McKitterick, David Dumville. Cambridge: Cambridge University Press, 1982, pp. 362-386.

Jones, Christopher A. "Review of *The Study of the Bible in the Carolingian Era*. The Medieval Review.

Jullien, Marie-Hélène. *Clavis scriptorum Latinorum medii aevi: Auctores Galliae 735-987*. Turnhout: Brepols, 1994-2015.

Kaczynski, Bernice. "Reading the Church Fathers: Notker the Stammerer's 'Notatio de illustribus viris,'" *Journal of Medieval Latin* 17 (2007): pp. 401-412.

----. "The Authority of the Fathers: Patristic Texts in Early Medieval Libraries and Scriptoria," *Journal of Medieval Latin* 16 (2006): pp. 1-27.

Kannengiesser, Charles. *Handbook of Patristic Exegesis: The Bible in Ancient Christianity*. Boston: Brill, 2004.

Kasper, Clemens M. *Theologie und Askese: Die Spiritualität des Inselmönchtums von Lérins im 5. Jahrhundert*. Münster: Aschendorff, 1991.

Kasten, Brigitte. "Alkuins erbrechtliche Expertise für Karl den Großen?" *Annales de Bretagne et des Pays de l'Ouest* 111 (2004): pp. 301-315.

Kramer, Rutger. "Adopt, Adapt and Improve: Dealing with the Adoptionist Controversy at the Court of Charlemagne," *Religious Franks: Religion and Power in the Frankish Kingdoms: Studies in Honour of Mayke de Jong*. Eds. Rob Meens, Dorine van Espelo, Bram van den Hoven van Genderen, et al. Manchester: Manchester University Press, 2016, pp. 32-50.

Keefe, Susan. *A Catalogue of Works Pertaining to the Explanation of the Creed in Carolingian Manuscripts*. Turnhout: Brepols, 2012.

---. *Water and the Word: Baptism and the Education of the Clergy in the Carolingian Empire*. Notre Dame: University of Notre Dame Press 2002.

Kelly, J. N. D. *Jerome: His Life, Writings and Controversies*. London: Duckworth, 1975.

Kelly, Christopher J. "Cassian's Hermeneutics: Purity of Heart and the Vision of God," *Patristic Theories of Biblical Interpretation: The Latin Fathers*. Ed. Tarmo Toom. Cambridge: Cambridge University Press, 2016, pp. 109-132.

Kelly, Joseph F. "A Catalogue of Early Medieval Hiberno-Latin Biblical Commentaries (I)," *Traditio* 44 (1988): pp. 537-571.

---. "A Catalogue of Early Medieval Hiberno-Latin Biblical Commentaries (II)," *Traditio* 45 (1989): pp. 393-434.

---. "*Das Bibelwerk*: Organization and *Quellenanalyse* of the New Testament Section," *Irland und die Christenheit: Bibelstudien und Mission*. Eds. Próinséas Ní Chatháin, Michael Richter. Stuttgart: Klett-Cotta, 1987, pp. 113-123.

---. "Eucherius of Lyons: Harbinger of the Middle Ages," *Studia Patristica* 23 (1989): pp. 138-142.

---. "Hiberno-Latin Exegesis and Exegetes," *Annuale Mediaevale* 21 (1981): pp. 46-60.

---. "The Originality of Josephus Scottus' Commentary on Isaiah," *Manuscripta* 24 (1980), pp. 176-180.

Kelly, Michael. "The Politics of History-Writing: Problematizing the Historiographical Origins of Isidore of Seville in Early Medieval Hispania," *Isidore of Seville and his Reception in the Early Middle Ages: Transmitting and Transforming Knowledge*. Eds. Andrew Fear, Jamie Wood. Amsterdam: Amsterdam University Press, pp. 91-110.

Kempf, Charlotte. "Eucherius von Lyon: *Formulae spiritalis intellegentiae* und *Instructiones*," *Handbuch der Bibelhermeneutiken von Origenes bis zu Gegenwart*. Ed. Oda Wischmeyer. Berlin: De Gruyter, 2016, pp. 63-71.

Keough, Shawn W. J. "The Eternal Gospel: Origen's Eschatological Exegesis," *Interpretation of the Bible in Late Antiquity: Proceedings of the Montreal Colloquium in Honour of Charles Kannengiesser, 11-13 October 2006*. Eds. Lorenzo DiTommaso, Lucian Turcescu. Leiden: Brill, 2008, pp. 101-120.

Kerff, Franz. *Der Quadripartitus: ein Handbuch der karolingischen Kirchenreform:Überlieferung, Quellen und Rezeption*. Sigmaringen: J. Thorbecke, 1982.

Kéry, Lotte. *Canonical Collections of the Early Middle Ages (ca. 400-1140): A Bibliographical Guide to the Manuscripts and Literature*. Washington, D.C.: Catholic University of America Press, 1999.

Kessler, Stephen. "Gregory the Great: A Figure of Tradition and Transition in Church Exegesis," *Hebrew Bible/Old Testament: The History of Its Interpretation. Volume I. From the beginnings to the Middle Ages (until 1300). Part 2: The Middle Ages*. Ed. Magne Sæbø. Göttingen: Vandenhoeck and Ruprecht, 1996, pp. 135-147.

Keuffer M., A. Becker, and G. Kentenich. *Beschreibendes Verzeichnis der Handschriften der Stadtbibliothek zu Trier*. Trier: F. Lintz, 1888-1931.

Kottje, Raymund. *Die Bussbücher Halitgars von Cambrai und des Hrabanus Maurus: Ihre Überlieferung und ihre Quellen*. Berlin: de Gruyter, 1980.

---. *Studien zum Einfluss des Alten Testamentes auf Recht und Liturgie des frühen Mittelalters (6.-8. Jahrhundert)*. Bonn: Ludwig Röhrscheid Verlag, 1970.

---. *Verzeichnis der Handschriften mit den Werken des Hrabanus Maurus*. Hannover: Hahnsche, 2012.

Kreuz, Gottfried Eugen. "*Inquiri mihi necesse est...*: Überlegungen zu drei vermuteten kleineren Genesiskommentaren Wigbods," *Wiener Studien* 122 (2009): pp. 223-247.

La Bonnardière, Anne-Marie. "The Canon of Sacred Scripture," *Augustine and the Bible*. Ed. Pamela Bright. Notre Dame: University of Notre Dame Press, 1999, pp. 26-41.

Laistner, M. L. W. *A Hand-List of Bede Manuscripts*. Ithaca: Cornell University Press.

---. *Thought and Letters in Western Europe: A. D. 500 to 900*. Ithaca: Cornell University Press, 1957.

Lambert, Bernard. *Bibliotheca Hieronymiana manuscripta: La tradition manuscrite des oeuvres de saint Jérôme*. Turnhout: Brepols, 1969.

Langenwalter, Anna. *Agobard of Lyon: An Exploration of Carolingian Jewish-Christian Relations*. Toronto : University of Toronto, 2009.

Lapidge, Michael. "The Study of Latin Texts in Late Anglo-Saxon England: The Evidence of Latin Glosses," *Latin and the Vernacular Languages in Early Medieval Britain*. Ed. Nicholas Brooks. Leicester: Leicester University Press, 1982, pp. 99-140.

Lauer, Philippe. "Observations sur le Scriptorium de Lyon," *Bibliothèque de l'*École des chartes 86 (1925): pp. 380-387

Lehmann, Paul. "Das Problem der Karolingischen Renaissance," *I Problemi Della Civiltà Carolingia*.Spoleto: Centro italiano di studi sull'alto medioevo, 1954 ,pp. 309-58.

Leonardi, Claudio. "Aspects of Old Testament Interpretation in the Church from the Seventh to the Tenth Century," *Hebrew Bible/Old Testament: The History of Its Interpretation. Volume I. From the beginnings to the Middle Ages (until 1300). Part 2: The Middle Ages*. Ed. Magne Sæbø. Göttingen: Vandenhoeck and Ruprecht, 1996, pp. 180-195.

Leonardi, Claudio and Giovanni Orlandi. *Biblical Studies in the Early Middle Ages*. Firenze: Edizioni del Galluzzo, 2005.

Levison, Wilhelm. *England and the Continent in the Eighth Century* . Oxford: Clarendon Press, 1946.

Lexikon des Mittelalters. Stuttgart: Metzler, 1977-1999.

Lienhard, Joseph. "*Locutio* and *Sensus* in Augustine's Writings on the Heptateuch," *Studia Patristica* 70 (2013): pp. 79-83.

---. "The Earliest 'Florilegia' of Augustine," *Augustinian Studies* 8 (1977): pp. 21-32.

Lifshitz, Felice. *The Name of the Saint: The Martyrology of Jerome and Access to the Sacred in Francia, 627-827*. Notre Dame: University of Notre Dame Press, 2006.

Lim, Timothy H. "Deuteronomy in the Judaism of the Second Temple Period," *Deuteronomy in the New Testament*. Eds. Maarten J. J. Menken, Steve Moyise. London: T & T Clark, 2007, pp. 6-26.

Lincicum, David. *Paul and the Early Jewish Encounter with Deuteronomy*. Tübingen: Mohr Siebeck, 2010.

Little, Lester K. *Benedictine Maledictions: Liturgical Cursing in Romanesque France* Ithaca: Cornell University Press, 1993.

Liu, Yin. "Agobard, Deuteronomic Curses, and an Anti-Jewish Exegetical Discourse in Carolingian Lyon," *Viator* 51 (2020): pp. 205-239.

---. "Baptismal Renunciation and the Moral Reform of Charlemagne's Christian Empire," *Traditio* 76 (2021): pp. 117-155.

Lowe, Elias A. *Codices Latini Antiquiores: a Palaeographical Guide to Latin Manuscripts prior to the Ninth Century*. Oxford: Clarendon Press, 1934-1971.

---. *Codices Lugdunenses Antiquissimi. Le scriptorium de Lyon, le plus ancienne école calligraphique de France*. Lyon: Aux dépens des "Amis de la Bibliothèque de Lyon," 1924.

Löwe, Heinz. "Arbeo von Freising: Eine Studie zu Religiosität und Bildung im 8. Jahrhundert," *Von Cassiodor zu Dante: Ausgewählte Aufsätze zur Geschichtsschreibung und politischen Ideenwelt des Mittelalters*. Berlin: De Gruyter, 1973, pp. 75-110.

Lupton, Brendan. "Gregory's Hermeneutics: Scripture as a Path to God," *Patristic Theories of Biblical Interpretation: The Latin Fathers*. Ed. Tarmo Toom. Cambridge: Cambridge University Press, 2016, pp. 183-205.

MacGinty, Gerard. "The Irish Augustine: De mirabilibus sacrae Scripturae," *Irland und die Christenheit: Bibelstudien und Mission*. Eds. Próinséas Ní Chatháin, Michael Richter. Stuttgart: Klett-Cotta, 1987, pp. 70-83.

---. "The Pentateuch of the Reference Bible: the Problem Concerning its Sources," *The Scriptures and Early Medieval Ireland: Proceedings of the 1993 Conference of the Society for Hiberno-Latin Studies on Early Irish Exegesis and Homilectics*. Ed. Thomas O'Loughlin. Turnhout: Brepols, 1999, pp. 163-177.

Mach, Michael. "Verus Israel: Towards a Clarification of a Jewish Factor in Early Christian Self-Definition," *Concepts of the Other in Near Eastern Religions*. Ed. Ilai Alon. Leiden: Brill, 1994, pp. 143-171.

Malkiel, David. "Jewish-Christian Relations in Europe, 840-1096," *Journal of Medieval History* 29 (2003): pp. 55-83.

Mandolfo, Carmela. "L'influsso delle 'Hebraicae quaestiones in libro Geneseos' di Girolamo sulle 'Instructiones' di Eucherio di Lione," *Scritti classici e cristiani offerti a Francesco Corsaro*. Eds., Carmelo Curti, Carmelo Crimi. Catania: Università degli studi di Catania, Facoltà di lettere e filosofia, 1994, vol. 2, pp. 435-453.

Marenbon, John. *From the Circle of Alcuin to the School of Auxerre: Logic, Theology and Philosophy in the Early Middle Ages*. Cambridge: Cambridge University Press, 1981.

---. *Pagans and Philosophers: The Problem of Paganism from Augustine to Leibniz*. Princeton: Princeton University Press, 2015.

Margaret Gibson, "Carolingian Glossed Psalters," *The Early Medieval Bible: Its Production, Decoration and Use*. Ed. Richard Gameson. Cambridge: Cambridge University Press, 1994, pp. 78-100.

"Marginal Scholarship: The Practice of Learning in the Early Middle Ages (c. 800-c. 1000)," NWO-VIDI Research Project, last accessed September 14, 2021, https://www.marginalscholarship.nl/.

Markschies, Christoph. "Ambrosius und Origenes. Bemerkungen zur Exegetischen

Hermeneutik zweier Kirchenväter," *Origeniana Septima: Origines in den Auseinanderetzungen des 4. Jahrhunderts*. Eds. Wolfgang Bienert, Uwe Kühneweg. Leuven: Peeters, 1999, pp. 545-569.

Markus, Robert A. *Gregory the Great and His World*. Cambridge: Cambridge University Press, 1998.

Martello, Fabrizio. *All'ombra di Gregorio Magno: Il notaio Paterio e il Liber testimoniorum*. Roma: Città nuova, 2012.

---. "Paterius," *La trasmissione dei testi latini del Medioevo*. Eds. Paolo Chiesa, Lucia Castaldi. Florence: SISMEL, Edizioni del Galluzzo, 2004-2013, vol. 4, pp. 435-441.

Martens, Peter. "Interpreting Attentively: The Ascetic Character of Biblical Exegesis according to Origen and Basil of Caesarea," *Origeniana Octava*. Ed. Lorenzo Perrone. Leuven: Leuven University Press, 2003, pp. 1115-1121.

---. *Origen and Scripture: The Contours of the Exegetical Life*. Oxford: Oxford University Press, 2012.

Martyn, John R. C. *Gregory and Leander: An Analysis of the Special Friendship between Pope Gregory the Great and Leander, Archbishop of Seville*. Cambridge: Cambridge Scholars Publishing, 2013.

Matis, Hannah. *The Song of Songs in the Early Middle Ages*. Leiden: Brill, 2019.

Mathisen, Ralph W. *Ecclesiastical Factionalism and Religious Controversy in Fifth-Century Gaul*. Washington, D.C.: Catholic University of America Press, 1989.

Matter, Ann. "Exegesis and Christian Education: The Carolingian Model," *Schools of Thought in the Christian Tradition*. Ed. Patrick Henry. Philadelphia: Fortress Press, 1984, pp. 90-105.

---. "Haimo's Commentary on the Song of Songs and the Traditions of the Carolingian Schools," *Études d'exégèse carolingienne: Autour d'Haymon d'Auxerre*. Ed. Sumi Shimahara. Turnhout: Brepols, 2007, pp. 89-101.

---. "The Lamentations Commentaries of Hrabanus Maurus and Paschasius Radbertus," *Traditio* 38 (1982): pp. 137-163.

Mayr-Harting, Henry. "Charlemagne's Religion," *Am Vorabend der Kaiserkrönung: Das Epos "Karolus Magnus et Leo papa" und der Papstbesuch in Paderborn 799*. Eds. Peter Godman, Jörg Jarnut, Peter Johanek. Berlin: Akademie Verlag 2002, pp. 113-124.

---. *The Coming of Christianity to Anglo-Saxon England*. University Park: The Pennsylvania State University Press, 1991.

McCune, James. "The Sermon Collection in the Carolingian Clerical Handbook, Paris, Bibliothèque nationale de France lat. 1012," *Mediaeval Studies* 75 (2013): pp. 35-92.

McCormick, Michael. "A New Ninth-Century Witness to the Carolingian Mass Against the Pagans (Paris, B.N., Lat. 2812)," *Revue Bénédictine* 97 (1987): pp. 68-86.

---. *Origins of the European economy: Communications and Commerce, A.D. 300-*

900. Cambridge: Cambridge University Press, 2001.

McKitterick, Rosamond, ed. *Carolingian Culture: Emulation and Innovation.* Cambridge: Cambridge University Press, 1994.

---. *History and Memory in the Carolingian World.* Cambridge: Cambridge University Press, 2004.

---. "Manuscripts and scriptoria in the reign of Charles the Bald, 840-877," *Giovanni Scoto nel suo tempo. L'organizzazione del sapere in eta Carolingia.* Eds. Claudio Leonardi, Enrico Menestò. Spoleto: Centro italiano di studi sull'alto medioevo, 1989, pp. 200-233.

---. *The Carolingians and the Written Word.* Cambridge: Cambridge University Press, 1989.

---. *The Frankish Church and the Carolingian Reforms, 789-895.* London: Royal Historical Society, 1977.

McNally, Robert. *Der irische Liber de numeris: eine Quellenanalyse des Pseudo-Isidorischen Liber de numeris.* München :Universität München, 1957.

---. "Isidorian Pseudepigrapha in the Early Middle Ages," *Isidoriana: Colección de estudios sobre Isidoro de Sevilla.* Ed. Manuel C. Diaz y Diaz. León: Centro de Estudios 'San Isidoro,' 1961, pp. 305-316.

---. "Isidoriana," *Theological Studies* 20 (1959), pp. 432-442.

---. "The 'Tres Linguae Sacrae' in Early Irish Bible Exegesis," *Theological Studies* 19 (1958): pp. 395-403.

McNamara, Martin. "Plan and Source Analysis of *Das Bibelwerk*, Old Testament," *Irland und die Christenheit: Bibelstudien und Mission.* Eds. Próinséas Ní Chatháin, Michael Richter. Stuttgart: Klett-Cotta, 1987, pp. 84-112.

---. "Psalter text and Psalter study in the early Irish Church (A.D. 600-1200)," *The Psalms in the early Irish Church.* Ed. Martin McNamara. Sheffield: Sheffield Academic Press, 2000, pp. 19-142.

Mearns, James. *The Canticles of the Christian Church, Eastern and Western, in Early and Mediaeval Times.* Cambridge: Cambridge University Press, 1914.

Meeder, Sven. "The Irish Foundations and the Carolingian World," *L'Irlanda e gli Irlandesi nell'alto Medioevo.* Spoleto: Centro italiano di studi sull'alto medioevo, 2010, pp. 467-494.

Meens, Rob. *Penance in Medieval Europe, 600-1200.* Cambridge: Cambridge University Press, 2012.

---. "The Uses of the Old Testament in Early Medieval Canon Law: the Collectio Vetus Gallica and the *Collectio Hibernensis*," *The Uses of the Past in the Early Middle Ages.* Eds. Yitzhak Hen, Matthew Innes. Cambridge: Cambridge University Press, 2000, pp. 67-77.

---. "Thunder over Lyons: Agobard, the *Tempestarii*, and Christianity," *Paganism in the Middle Ages: Threat and Fascination.* Eds. Carlos Steel, John Marenbon, Werner Verbeke. Leuven: Leuven University Press, 2012, pp. 157-166.

Menken, Maarten J. J., and Steve Moyise, ed. *Deuteronomy in the New Testament.* London: T & T Clark International, 2007.

Merrills, Andy and Richard Miles. *The Vandals.* Chichester: Wiley-Blackwell, 2010.

Meyvaert, Paul. "Bede's Capitula Lectionum for the Old and New Testament,' *Revue Bénédictine* 105 (1995): pp. 348-80.

---. "The Enigma of Gregory the Great's Dialogues: A Response to Francis Clark," *Journal of Ecclesiastical History* 40 (1988): pp. 335-381.

Mégier, Elisabeth. "*Historia* and *Littera* in Carolingian Commentaries on St Matthew: Elements for an Inventory of Exegetical Vocabulary in the Medieval Latin Church," *Producing Christian Culture: Medieval Exegesis and Its Interpretative Genres.* Eds. Giles Gasper, Francis Watson, Matthew Crawford. New York: Routledge, 2017, pp. 89-113.

---. "Jewish Converts in the Early Church and Latin Christian Exegetes of Isaiah, c. 400-1150," *Journal of Ecclesiastical History* 59 (2008): pp. 1-28.

---. "Spiritual Exegesis and the Church in Haimo of Auxerre's Commentary on Isaiah," *The Multiple Meaning of Scripture: The Role of Exegesis in Early-Christian and Medieval Culture.* Ed. Ineke Van't Spijker. Leiden: Brill, 2008, pp. 155-175.

Miller, Eric. "The Political Significance of Christ's Kingship in the Biblical Exegesis," *Biblical Studies in the Early Middle Ages.* Eds. Claudio Leonardi, Giovanni Orlandi. Firenze: Edizioni del Galluzzo, 2005, pp. 193-213.

Miller, Patrick D. *Deuteronomy.* Louisville: John Knox Press, 1990.

Minns, Denis. *Irenaeus: An Introduction.* New York: T & T Clark, 2010.

Moore, Michael E. *A Sacred Kingdom: Bishops and the Rise of Frankish Kingship, 300- 850 .*Washington, D.C.: Catholic University of America Press, 2011.

Mordek, Hubert. *Kirchenrecht und Reform im Frankenreich: Die Collectio Vetus Gallica, die älteste systematische Kirchenrechtssammlung des Fränkischen Gallien.* Berlin: Walter de Gruyter, 1975.

Moretus, Henri. "Les Bénédictions des Patriarches dans la littérature du IVe au VIIIe Siècle," *Bulletin de Littérature Ecclésiastique*, ser. 4th, 1 (1909): pp. 398-411.

---. "Les Bénédictions des Patriarches dans la littérature du IVe au VIIIe Siècle," *Bulletin de Littérature Ecclésiastique*, ser. 4th, 2 (1910), pp. 28-40, 83-100.

Morgan, Robert. "Spirit and Letter: Mapping Modern Biblical Interpretation," *The Spirit and the Letter: A Tradition and a Reversal.* Eds. Paul Fiddes, Günter Bader. London: Bloomsbury, 2013, pp. 43-73.

Morin, Germain. "Notes sur plusieurs écrits attribués a Bède le vénérable," *Revue Bénédictine* 11 (1894): pp. 289-295.

---. "Un écrivain inconnu du XIe siècle: Walter, moine de Honnecourt, puis de

Vézelay," *Revue Bénédictine* 22 (1905), pp. 165-180.

Müller, Heribert. "Die Kirche von Lyon im Karolingerreich: Studien zur Bischofsliste des 8. und 9. Jahrhunderts," *Historisches Jahrbuch* (107) 1987, pp. 225-253.

Munzi, Luigi. "Compilazione e riuso in età carolingia: il prologo poetico di Wigbodo," *Romanobarbarica* 12 (1992): pp. 189-210.

Nautin, Pierre. *Origène: Sa Vie et Son Oeuvre*. Paris: Beauchesne, 1977.

Nelson, Janet. "Lay Readers of the Bible in the Carolingian Ninth Century," *Reading the Bible in the Middle Ages*. Eds. Janet Nelson, Damien Kempf. London: Bloomsbury Academic, 2015, pp. 43-56.

---. "Making Ends Meet: Wealth and Poverty in the Carolingian Church," *Studies in Church History* 24 (1987): pp. 25-35.

---. "The Voice of Charlemagne," *Belief and Culture in the Middle Ages: Studies Presented to Henry Mayr-Harting*. Eds. Richard Gameson, Henrietta Leyser. Oxford: Oxford University Press, 2001, pp. 77-88.

Newhauser, Richard. *The Treatise on Vices and Virtues in Latin and the Vernacular*. Typologie des Sources du Moyen Âge Occidental 68. Turnhout: Brepols, 1993.

Niederkorn-Bruck, Meta, and Anton Scharer, eds. *Erzbischof Arn von Salzburg*. Wien: R. Oldenbourg Verlag.

Noble, Thomas F. X. *Images, Iconoclasm, and the Carolingians*.Philadelphia: University of Pennsylvania Press, 2009.

---. "The Varying Roles of Biblical Testimonies in the Carolingian Image Controversies," *Medieval Transformations: Texts, Power, and Gifts in Context*. Eds. Esther Cohen , Mayke de Jong. Leiden: Brill, 2001, pp. 101-119.

---. "Tradition and Learning in Search of Ideology: The *Libri Carolini*," *The Gentle Voices of Teachers: Aspects of Learning in the Carolingian Age*. Ed. Richard Sullivan. Columbus: Ohio State University Press, 1995, pp. 228-260.

O'Brien, Conor. "Chosen Peoples and New Israels in the Early Medieval West," *Speculum* 95 (2020): pp. 987-1009.

---. "Empire, Ethnic Election and Exegesis in the Opus Caroli (*Libri Carolini*)," *Studies in Church History* 54 (2018): pp. 96-108.

O'Daly, Gerard J. P. *Augustine's City of God: A Reader's Guide*. Oxford: Clarendon Press, 1999.

O'Loughlin, Thomas. "Individual Anonymity and Collective Identity: The Enigma of Early Medieval Latin Theologians," *Recherches de théologie et philosophie médiévales* 64 (1997): pp. 291-314.

---. "Isidore's Hermeneutics: The Codification of the Tradition," *Patristic Theories of Biblical Interpretation: The Latin Fathers*. Ed. Tarmo Toom. Cambridge: Cambridge University Press, 2016, pp. 206-231.

---. "Isidore's Use of Gregory the Great in the Exegesis of Genesis," *Revue*

Bénédictine 107 (1997): pp. 263-269.

---. "Julian of Toledo's *Antikeimonon* and the Development of Latin Exegesis," *Proceedings of the Irish Biblical Association* 16 (1993): pp. 80-98

---. "The Symbol Gives Life: Eucherius of Lyons' Formula for Exegesis," *Scriptural Interpretation in the Fathers: Letter and Spirit*. Eds. Thomas Finan, Vincent Twomey. Dublin: Four Courts Press, 1995, pp. 221-252.

---. "Tradition and Exegesis in the Eighth Century: The Use of Patristic Sources in Early Medieval Scriptural Commentaries," *The Scriptures and Early Medieval Ireland: Proceedings of the 1993 Conference of the Society for Hiberno-Latin Studies on Early Irish Exegesis and Homilectics*. Ed. Thomas O'Loughlin. Turnhout: Brepols, 1999, pp. 217-239.

O'Sullivan, Sinéad. "Glossing Vergil and Pagan Learning in the Carolingian Age," *Speculum* 93 (2018): pp. 132-165.

---. "Text, Gloss, and Tradition in the Early Medieval West: Expanding into a World of Learning," *Teaching and Learning in Medieval Europe: Essays in Honour of Gernot R. Wieland*. Eds. Greti Dinkova-Bruun, Tristan Major. Turnhout: Brepols, 2017, pp. 3-24.

Olsen, Glenn. "The *ecclesia primitiua* in John Cassian, the Ps. Jerome Commentary on Mark, and Bede," *Biblical Studies in the Early Middle Ages*. Eds. Claudio Leonardi, Giovanni Orlandi. Firenze: Edizioni del Galluzzo, 2005, pp. 3-25.

Opelt, Ilona. "Quellenstudien zu Eucherius," *Hermes* 91 (1963): pp. 476-483.

Otten, Willemien. "The Texture of Tradition: The Role of the Church Fathers in Carolingian Theology," *The Reception of the Church Fathers in the West: From the Carolingians to the Maurists*. Ed. Irena Backus. Leiden: Brill, 1997, pp. 3-50.

Paget, James Carleton. "The Christian Exegesis of the Old Testament in the Alexandrian Tradition," *Hebrew Bible/Old Testament: The History of Its Interpretation. Volume I. From the beginnings to the Middle Ages (until 1300). Part 1: Antiquity*. Ed. Magne Sæbø. Göttingen: Vandenhoeck and Ruprecht, 1996, pp. 478-542.

---. "The Epistle of Barnabas," *The Expository Times* (11) 2006: pp. 441-446.

Pangerl, Daniel. *Die Metropolitanverfassung des karolingischen Frankenreiches*. Hannover: Hahnsche, 2011.

Patzelt, Erna. *Die karolingische Renaissance: Beiträge zur Geschichte der Kultur des frühen Mittelalters*. Wien: Österreichischer Schulbücherverlag, 1924.

---. "Die Kontinuitätsfrage," *Wirtschaft und Kultur: Festschrift zum 70. Geburtstag von Alfons Dopsch*. Frankfurt: Verlag Sauer & Auvermann, 1966, pp. 18-33.

Patzold, Steffen. "Eine Hierarchie im Wandel: Die Ausbildung einer Metropolitanordnung im Frankenreich des 8. und 9. Jahrhunderts," *Hiérarchie et Stratification Sociale dans l'Occident Médiéval (400-1100)*. Eds. François Bougard, Dominique Iogna-Prat, Régine Le Jan. Turnhout: Brepols, 2008, pp. 161-184.

---. *Episcopus: Wissen über Bischöfe des späten 8. bis frühen 10. Jahrhunderts.*

Ostfildern: Thorbecke, 2008.

Pepino, John M. *St. Eucherius of Lyons: Rhetorical Adaptation of Message to Intended Audience in Fifth Century Provence*. Leeds: University of Leeds, 2008.

Peters, Edward. "*Vox populi, vox Dei*," *Law in Medieval Life and Thought*. Eds. Edward King, Susan Ridyard. Sewanee: The University of the South, 1990, pp. 91-120.

Pezé, Warren. "Amalaire et la communauté juive de Lyon: À propos de l'antijudaïsme lyonnais à l'époque carolingienne," *Francia* 40 (2013): pp. 1-25.

Pheifer, J. D. "Early Anglo-Saxon Glossaries and the School of Canterbury," *Archbishop Theodore: Commemorative Studies on his Life and Influence*. Ed. Michael Lapidge. Cambridge: Cambridge University Press, 1995, pp. 281-333.

Phelan, Owen Michael. "Catechising the Wild: The Continuity and Innovation of Missionary Catechesis under the Carolingians," *The Journal of Ecclesiastical History* (61) 2010: pp. 455-474.

---. "New Insights, Old Texts: Clerical Formation and the Carolingian Renewal in Hrabanus Maurus," *Traditio* (71) 2017: pp. 63-89.

---. "The Carolingian Renewal and Christian Formation in Ninth Century Bavaria," *Texts and Identities in the early Middle Ages*. Ed. Richard Corradini. Vienna: Verlag der Österreichischen Akademie der Wissenschaften, 2006, pp. 389-399.

---. *The Formation of Christian Europe: The Carolingians, Baptism, and the Imperium Christianum*. Oxford: Oxford University Press, 2014.

Philippou, A. J. "Origen and the Early Jewish-Christian Debate," *Greek Orthodox Theological Review* (15) 1970: pp.140-152.

Pitra, Jean Baptiste. *Spicilegium Solesmense complectens sanctorum scriptorum ecclesiasticorum*. Paris: F. Didot, 1852.

Poleg, Eyal. "The Interpretations of Hebrew Names in Theory and Practice," *Form and Function in the Late Medieval Bible*. Eds. Eyal Poleg, Laura Light. Leiden: Brill 2013, pp. 217-236.

Pollard, Richard Matthew. "Flavius Josephus: The Most Influential Classical Historian of the Early Middle Ages," *Writing the Early Medieval West, Studies in Honour of Rosamond McKitterick*. Eds. Elina Screen, Charles West. Cambridge: Cambridge University Press, 2018, pp. 15-32.

---. "The *De Excidio* of 'Hegesippus' and the Reception of Josephus in the Early Middle Ages," *Viator* 46 (2015): pp. 65-100.

Ponesse, Matthew. "Standing Distant from the Fathers: Smaragdus of Saint-Mihiel and the Reception of Early Medieval Learning," *Traditio* 67 (2012): pp. 71-99.

Pourrat, Joseph. *L'antique école de Leidrade: XIe centenaire de sa fondation*. Lyon: E. Vitte, 1899.

Prinz, Friedrich. "Arbeo von Freising und die Agilulfinger," *Zeitschrift für Bayerische Landesgeschichte* 29 (1966): pp. 580-590.

---. "Aristocracy and Christianity in Merovingian Gaul," *Gesellschaft, Kultur, Literatur: Rezeption und Originalität im Wachsen einer europäischen Literatur und Geistigkeit. Beiträge Luitpold Wallach gewidmet.* Ed. Karl Bosl. Stuttgart: Hiersemann, 1975, pp. 153-165.

Raaijmakers, Janneke. "I, Claudius. Self-Styling in Early Medieval Debate," *Early Medieval Europe* 25 (2017): pp. 70-84.

Radl, Clemens. "The Second Benedict: A Review of Recent Scholarship," *Benedict of Aniane, the Emperor's Monk: Ardo's Life.* Allen Cabaniss. Kalamazoo: Cistercian Publications: 2008, pp. 1-26.

Räisänen, Heikki. "Marcion," *A Companion to Second-century Christian "Heretics."* Eds. Antti Marjanen, Petri Luomanen. Leiden: Brill, 2005, pp. 100-124.

Ramsey, Boniface. *Ambrose.* New York: Routledge, 1997.

Renna, Thomas. "Christian Exegesis of Deuteronomy: Patristic to Scholastic," *Michigan Academician* 23 (1991): pp. 19-29.

Reynolds, Roger. "Clerics in the Early Middle Ages: Hierarchies and Functions," *Clerics in the Early Middle Ages: Hierarchy and Image.* Brookfield: Ashgate, 1999, pp. 1-31.

Riess, Frank. "From Aachen to Al-Andalus: The Journey of Deacon Bodo (823-76)," *Early Medieval Europe* 13 (2005): pp. 131-157.

---. *The Journey of Deacon Bodo from the Rhine to the Guadalquivir: Apostasy and Conversion to Judaism in Early Medieval Europe.* London: Routledge, 2019.

Richardson, Hilary. "Number and Symbol in Early Christian Irish Art," *The Journal of the Royal Society of Antiquaries of Ireland* 114 (1984): pp. 28-47.

Riché, Pierre. "Divina pagina, ratio et auctoritas dans la theologie carolingienne," *Nascita dell'Europa ed Europa carolingia, un'equazione da verificare*, vol. 2. Spoleto: Centro italiano di studi sull'alto medioevo, 1980-1981, pp. 719-758.

---. *Education and Culture in the Barbarian West: Sixth through Eighth Centuries.* Trans. John Contreni. Columbia: University of South Carolina Press, 1975.

---. "Instruments de travail et méthodes de l'exégète à l'époque carolingienne," *Le Moyen Âge et la Bible.* Eds. Pierre Riché, Guy Lobrichon. Paris: Beauchesne, 1984, pp. 147-61.

---. "L'enseignement et la culture des laïcs dans l'Occident pré-carolingien," *La scuola nell'occidente latino dell'alto Medioevo.* Spoleto: Centro italiano di studi sull'alto medioevo, 1972, vol. 1, pp. 231-253.

---. "La Bible et la vie politique dans le haut Moyen Âge," *Le Moyen Âge et la Bible.* Eds. Pierre Riché, Guy Lobrichon. Paris: Beauchesne, 1984, pp. 385-400.

---. *Les écoles et l'enseignement dans l'Occident chrétien de la fin du Ve siècle au milieu du XIe siècle.* 3rd ed. Paris: Picard, 1999.

Rieber, Ernst. *Die Bedeutung alttestamentlicher Vorstellungen für das Herrscherbild*

Karls des Grossen und seines Hofkreises. Tübingen : Universität Tübingen, 1949.

Rigg, Arthur and Gernot Wieland, "A Canterbury Classbook of the Mid-eleventh century (the 'Cambridge Songs' Manuscript)," *Anglo-Saxon England* 4 (1975): pp. 113-130.

Roberts, Edward. "Church Building in Bavaria under Bishop Arbeo of Freising,"last accessed September 14, 2021, http://www.charlemagneseurope.ac.uk/blog/church-building-in-bavaria-under-bishop-arbeo-of-freising/.

Rubellin, Michel. "Les monastères du diocèse de Lyon: Le poids de l'héritage carolingien," *Eglise et société chrétienne d'Agobard à Valdès*. Ed. Michel Rubellin. Lyon: Presses Universitaires Lyon, 2003, pp. 243-294.

---. "Lyon aux temps carolingiens," *Eglise et société chrétienne d'Agobard à Valdès*. Ed. Michel Rubellin. Lyon: Presses Universitaires Lyon, 2003, pp. 133-177.

Ruether, Rosemary. "The *Adversus Judaeos* Tradition in the Church Fathers: The Exegesis of Christian Anti-Judaism," *Aspects of Jewish Culture in the Middle Ages*. Ed. Paul Szarmach. Albany: State University of New York Press, 1979, pp. 27-50.

Rüting, Wilhelm. *Untersuchungen über Augustins Quaestiones und Locutiones in Heptateuchum*. Paderborn: Schöningh, 1916.

Saltman, Avrom. "Rabanus Maurus and the Pseudo-Hieronymian *Quaestiones Hebraicae in Libros Regum et Paralipomenon*," *The Harvard Theological Review* 66 (1973): pp. 43-75.

Sheehy, Maurice. "The Bible and the *Collectio canonum Hibernensis*," *Irland und die Christenheit: Bibelstudien und Mission*. Eds. Próinséas Ní Chatháin, Michael Richter. Stuttgart: Klett-Cotta, 1987, pp. 277-283.

Scheil, Andrew. *The Footsteps of Israel: Understanding Jews in Anglo-Saxon England*. Ann Arbor: University of Michigan Press, 2004.

Schneider, Heinrich. "Die biblischen Oden im christlichen Altertum," *Biblica* 30 (1949): pp. 28-65.

---. "Die biblischen Oden im Jerusalem und Konstantinopel," *Biblica* 30 (1949): pp. 433-452.

---. "Die biblischen Oden im Mittelalter," *Biblica* 30 (1949): pp. 479-500.

---. "Die biblischen Oden seit dem sechsten Jahrhundert," *Biblica* 30 (1949): pp. 239-272.

Schramm, Percy Ernst. "Karl Der Große: Denkart und Grundauffassungen. Die von Ihm Bewirkte Correctio ('Renaissance')," *Historische Zeitschrift* 198 (1964): pp. 306-345.

Scott DeGregorio, "Gregory's Exegesis: Old and New Ways of Approaching the Scriptural Text," *A Companion to Gregory the Great*. Eds. Bronwen Neil, Matthew Dal Santo. Leiden: Brill, 2013.

Semmler, Josef. "Karl der Große und das Fränkische Mönchtum," *Karl der Grosse:*

Lebenswerk und Nachleben, vol. 2, Das geistige Leben. Ed. Bernhard Bischoff. Düsseldorf: L. Schwann, 1965, pp. 255-289.

Simon, Marcel. *Verus Israel: Study of the Relations Between Christians and Jews in the Roman Empire, AD 135-425*. Trans. Henry McKeating. Liverpool: Liverpool University Press, 1996.

Siquans, Agnethe. "Theodoret von Kyros als Ausleger des Deuteronomiums," *Das Deuteronomium*. Ed. Georg Braulik. Bern: Peter Lang, 2003, pp. 343-360.

Shimahara, Sumi. "Charlemagne, premier souverain chrétien commanditaire d'exégèse biblique?" *Charlemagne: les temps, les espaces, les hommes. Construction et déconstruction d'un règne*. Eds. Rolf Grosse, Michel Sot. Turnhout: Brepols, 2018, pp. 101-117.

---. "Citations explicites ou recours implicites? Les usages de l'autorite des Pères dans l'exegese carolingienne," *Les réceptions des Pères de l'Église au Moyen Âge: le devenir de la tradition ecclésiale*. Eds. Rainer Berndt, Michel Fédou. Münster: Aschendorff Verlag, 2013, vol. 1, pp. 369-388.

---. "Daniel et les visions politiques à l'époque carolingienne," *Médiévales: Langues, Textes, Histoire* 55 (2008): pp. 19-32.

---, ed. *Études d'exégèse carolingienne: Autour d'Haymon d'Auxerre*. Turnhout: Brepols, 2007.

---. "Gouverner avec la Bible: Les lettres de dédicace adressées aux souverains à l'époque carolingienne," *Épistolaire politique*. Ed. Bruno Dumézil, vol. 1. Paris: Presses de l'Université Paris-Sorbonne, 2014, pp. 107-141.

---. *Haymon d'Auxerre, exegete Carolingien*. Turnhout: Brepols, 2013.

---. "Prophètes scripturaires et hagiographie à l'époque carolingienne," *Hagiographie et prophétie (VIe-XIIIe siècles)*. Eds. Patrick Henriet, Klaus Herbers, Hans-Christian Lehner. Firenze: Edizioni del Galluzzo, 2017, pp. 71-110.

---. "Prophétiser à l'époque carolingienne: l'exégète de la Biblie, nouveau prophète et prédicateur par l'écrit," *Études d'exégèse médiévale offertes à Gilbert Dahan par ses élèves*. Ed. Annie Noblesse-Rocher. Turnhout: Brepols, 2012, pp. 51-80.

---. "Renovatio et réforme dans l'exégèse carolingienne," *Au Moyen Âge, entre tradition antique et innovation: Actes du 131e Congrès des Sociétés Historiques et Scientifiques*. Eds. Michel Balard, Michel Sot. Grénoble: Editions du Comité des Travaux Historiques et Scientifiques, 2009, pp. 57-74.

Skarsaune, Oskar. "The Development of Scriptural Interpretation in the Second and Third Centuries (except Clement and Origin)," *Hebrew Bible/Old Testament: The History of Its Interpretation. Volume I. From the beginnings to the Middle Ages (until 1300). Part 1: Antiquity*. Ed. Magne Sæbø. Göttingen: Vandenhoeck and Ruprecht, 1996, pp. 373-442.

Smalley, Beryl. *The Study of the Bible in the Middle Ages*. Oxford: Basil Blackwell,

1952.

Smetana, Cyril. "Paul the Deacon's Patristic Anthology," *The Old English Homily and its Backgrounds*. Eds. Paul Szarmach, Bernard Huppe. Albany: State University of New York Press, 1978, pp. 75-97.

Smith Julia M. H. "Rulers and Relics c.750-c.950: Treasure on Earth, Treasure in Heaven," *Past and Present Supplement* 5 (2010): pp. 73-96.

Smyth, Marina. "Isidorian Texts in Seventh-Century Ireland," *Isidore of Seville and his Reception in the Early Middle Ages: Transmitting and Transforming Knowledge*. Eds. Jamie Wood, Andrew Fear. Amsterdam: Amsterdam University Press, 2016, pp. 111-130.

----. "The Irish Liber de numeris," *The Scriptures and Early Medieval Ireland: Proceedings of the 1993 Conference of the Society for Hiberno-Latin Studies on Early Irish Exegesis and Homilectics*. Ed. Thomas O'Loughlin. Turnhout: Brepols, 1999, pp. 291-297.

Sot, Michel. "Renovatio, renaissance et réforme à l'époque carolingienne: recherche sur les mots," *Au Moyen Âge, entre tradition antique et innovation: Actes du 131e Congrès des Sociétés Historiques et Scientifiques*. Eds. Michel Balard, Michel Sot. Grénoble: Editions du Comité des Travaux Historiques et Scientifiques, 2009, pp. 117-140.

Stancliffe, Clare. "Early Irish biblical exegesis," *Studia Patristica XII: Papers presented to the Sixth International Conference on Patristic Studies held in Oxford, 1971*. Ed. Elizabeth A. Livingstone. Berlin: Akademie Verlag, 1975, vol. 1, pp. 361-370.

Stansbury, Mark. "Irish biblical exegesis," *The Irish in Early Medieval Europe: Identity, Culture and Religion*. Eds. Roy Flechner, Sven Meeder. London: Palgrave 2016, pp. 116-130.

Stevens, David E. "Does Deuteronomy 32:8 Refer to 'Sons of God' or 'Sons of Israel'?" *Bibliotheca Sacra* 154 (1997): pp. 131-141.

Stone, Rachel. "Beyond David and Solomon: Biblical models for Carolingian laymen," *Gott handhaben: Religiöses Wissen im Konflikt um Mythisierung und Rationalisierung*. Eds. Steffen Patzold, Florian Bock. Berlin: De Gruyter, 2016, pp. 189-202.

---. "The Invention of a Theology of Abduction: Hincmar of Rheims on *Raptus*," *Journal of Ecclesiastical History* 60 (2009): pp. 433-448.

Straw, Carole, "Gregory, Cassian, and the Cardinal Vices," *In the Garden of Evil: The Vices and Culture in the Middle Ages*. Ed. Richard Newhauser. Toronto: Pontifical Institute of Mediaeval Studies, 2005, pp. 35-58.

Sullivan, Richard. "The Context of Cultural Activity in the Carolingian Age," *The Gentle Voices of Teachers: Aspects of Learning in the Carolingian Age*. Ed. Richard Sullivan. Columbus: Ohio State University Press, 1995, pp. 51-105.

---. ed. *The Gentle Voices of Teachers: Aspects of Learning in the Carolingian Age*.

Columbus: Ohio State University Press, 1995.

Szarmach, Paul. "The Latin Tradition of Alcuin's 'Liber de Virtutibus et Vitiis,'" *Mediaevalia* 12 (1986): pp. 13-41.

Tafel, Sigmund. "The Lyons Scriptorium," *Palaeographia Latina* 2 (1923): pp. 66-73.

---. "The Lyons Scriptorium," *Palaeographia Latina* 4 (1925): pp. 40-70.

Teeuwen, Mariken. "Carolingian Scholarship on Classical Authors: Practices of Reading and Writing," *Manuscripts of the Latin Classics 800-1200*. Ed. Erik Kwakkel. Leiden: Leiden University Press, 2015, pp. 23-52.

---. "Marginal Scholarship: Rethinking the Function of Latin Glosses in Early Medieval Manuscripts," *Rethinking and Recontextualizing Glosses: New Perspectives in the Study of Late Anglo-Saxon Glossography*. Eds. Patrizia Lendinara, Loredana Lazzari, Claudia Di Sciacca. Turnhout: Brepols, 2011, pp. 19-37.

---. "Voices from the Edge: Annotating Books in the Carolingian Period," *The Annotated Book in the Early Middle Ages: Practices of Reading and Writing*. Eds. Mariken Teeuwen, Irene van Renswoude. Turnhout: Brepols, 2018, pp. 13-36.

---. "Writing in the Blank Space of Manuscripts: Evidence from the Ninth Century," *Ars Edendi Lecture Series*, Volume IV. Eds. Barbara Crostini, Gunilla Iversen, Brian M. Jensen. Stockholm: Stockholm University Press, pp. 1-25.

Teeuwen, Mariken and Irene van Renswoude, eds. *The Annotated Book in the Early Middle Ages: Practices of Reading and Writing*. Turnhout: Brepols, 2018.

Teske, Roland. "Augustine of Hippo and the *Quaestiones et Responsiones* Literature," *Erotapokriseis: Early Christian Question-and-Answer Literature in Context. Proceedings of the Utrecht Colloquium, 13-14 October 2003*. Eds. Annelie Volgers, Claudio Zamagni. Leuven: Peeters, 2004, pp. 127-144.

---. "Genesi ad litteram liber, De," *Augustine through the Ages: An Encyclopedia*. Eds. Allan Fitzgerald, John Cavadini. Grand Rapids: William B. Eerdmans, 1999, pp. 376-377.

Toom, Tarmo. "Augustine's Hermeneutics: The Science of the Divinely Given Signs," *Patristic Theories of Biblical Interpretation: The Latin Fathers*. Ed. Tarmo Toom. Cambridge: Cambridge University Press, pp. 77-108.

Toom, Tarmo, ed. *Patristic Theories of Biblical Interpretation: The Latin Fathers*. Cambridge: Cambridge University Press.

Torjesen, Karen Jo. *Hermeneutical Procedure and Theological Method in Origen's Exegesis*. Berlin: De Gruyter, 1986.

Torreira, Federico-Mario Beltrán. "Siervos del Anticristo (la creación del mito histórico del enemigo interno en las fuentes hispanovisigodas)," *Memoria, mito y realidad en la historia medieval: XIII Semana de Estudios Medievales, Nájera, del 29 de julio al 2 de agosto de 2002*. Eds. José Ignacio de la Iglesia Duarte, José-Luis Martín. Logroño: Instituto de Estudios Riojanos, 2003, pp. 85-127.

Trompf, G. W. "The Concept of the Carolingian Renaissance." *Journal of the History of Ideas* 34 (1973): pp. 3-26.

Uitvlugt, Donald Jacob. "The Sources of Isidore's Commentaries on the Pentateuch," *Revue Bénédictine* 112 (2002): pp. 72-100.

Ullmann, Walter. "The Bible and Principles of Government in the Middle Ages," *La bibbia nell'alto medioevo*. Spoleto: Centro italiano di studi sull'alto medioevo, 1963, pp. 181-228.

---. *The Carolingian Renaissance and the Idea of Kingship*. London: Methuen, 1969.

Van Engen, John. "Ralph of Flaix: The Book of Leviticus Interpreted as Christian Community," *Jews and Christians in Twelfth-Century Europe*. Eds. John Van Engen, Michael Signer. Notre Dame: University of Notre Dame Press, 2001, pp. 150-170.

van Liere, Frans. *An Introduction to the Medieval Bible*. Cambridge: Cambridge University Press. 2014.

van Renswoude, Irene. "The Art of Disputation: Dialogue, Dialectic and Debate around 800," *Early Medieval Europe* 25 (2017): pp. 38-53.

van Rhijn, Carine. "Charlemagne's *Correctio*: A Local Perspective," *Charlemagne: les temps, les espaces, les hommes. Construction et déconstruction d'un règne*. Eds. Rolf Grosse, Michel Sot. Turnhout: Brepols, 2018, pp. 43-60.

---. "'Et hoc considerat episcopus, ut ipsi presbyteri non sint idiothae': Carolingian Local correctio and an Unknown Priests' Exam from the Early Ninth Century," *Religious Franks: Religion and Power in the Frankish Kingdoms: Studies in Honour of Mayke de Jong*. Eds. Rob Meens, Dorine van Espelo, Bram van den Hoven van Genderen, et al. Manchester: Manchester University Press, 2016, pp. 162-180.

---. "Manuscripts for Local Priests and the Carolingian Reforms," *Men in the Middle: Local Priests in Early Medieval Europe*. Eds. Steffen Patzold, Carine van Rhijn. Berlin: De Gruyter, 2016, pp. 177-198.

---. *Shepherds of the Lord: Priests and Episcopal Statutes in the Carolingian Period*. Turnhout: Brepols, 2014.

Verhulst, Adriaan. *The Carolingian Economy*. Cambridge: Cambridge University Press, 2002.

Versluis, Arie. *The Command to Exterminate the Canaanites: Deuteronomy 7*. Leiden: Brill, 2017.

Vessey, Mark. "Jerome's Origen: The Making of a Christian Literary Persona," *Studia patristica* 28 (1993): pp. 135-145.

---. "The Epistula Rustici ad Eucherium: from the Library of Imperial Classes to the Library of the Fathers," *Society and Culture in Late Antique Gaul: Revisiting the Sources*. Eds. Ralph W. Mathisen, Danuta Shanzer. Burlington: Ashgate, 2001, pp. 278-297.

Vogel, Cyril. "Saint Chrodegang et les Débuts de la Romanisation du Culte en Pays Franc," *Saint Chrodegang: Communications Présentées au Colloque Tenu à Metz à l'Occasion du 12e Centenaire de sa Mort*. Metz: Lorrain, 1967, pp. 91-109.

Volgers, Annelie, and Claudio Zamagni. *Erotapokriseis: Early Christian Question-and-Answer Literature in Context. Proceedings of the Utrecht Colloquium, 13-14 October 2003*. Leuven: Peeters, 2004.

von Campenhausen, Hans. *The Formation of the Christian Bible*. Trans. J. A. Baker. Philadelphia: Fortress Press, 1972.

Waitz, Georg. "Handschriften der Bibliothek zu Lyon," *Archiv der Gesellschaft für Ältere Deutsche Geschichtskunde zur Beförderung einer Gesamtausgabe der Quellenschriften deutscher Geschichten des Mittelalters* 7 (1839): pp. 211-214.

Wallace-Hadrill, John M. "The *via regia* of the Carolingian Age," *Trends in Medieval Political Thought*. Ed. Beryl Smalley. Oxford: Blackwell, 1965, pp. 22-41.

Wallach, Luitpold. "Alcuin on Virtues and Vices: A Manual for a Carolingian Soldier," *Harvard Theological Review* 48 (1955): pp. 175-195

Ward, Anthony. "The Codex Pagesianus: Witness to Church Renewal," *American Benedictine Review* 44 (1993): pp. 308-333.

Wasselynck, René. "Les compilations des 'Moralia in Job' du VIIe au XIIe siècle," *Recherches de théologie ancienne et médiévale* 29 (1962): pp. 5-32.

Wielfaert, Jared. *Prudentius of Troyes (d. 861) and the Reception of the Patristic Tradition in the Carolingian Era*. Toronto: University of Toronto, 2015.

Wickham, Christopher. *Framing the Early Middle Ages: Europe and the Mediterranean, 400-800*. Oxford: Oxford University Press, 2005.

Wieland, Gernot. "The Glossed Manuscript: Classbook or Library book?" *Anglo-Saxon England* 14 (1985): pp. 153-173.

Williams, Arthur. Adversus Judaeos: *A Bird's Eye View of Christian Apologiae until the Renaissance*. London: Cambridge University Press, 1935.

Wilmart, André. "Le commentaire des Bénédictions de Jacob attribué a Paulin de Milan," *Revue Bénédictine* 10 (1920): pp. 57-63.

---. "Le Recueil Grégorien de Paterius et les Fragments Wisigothiques de Paris," *Revue Bénédictine* 39 (1927): pp. 81-104.

---. "Membra Disiecta," *Revue Bénédictine* 36 (1924): pp. 131-136.

Wolfram, Herwig. *The Roman Empire and Its Germanic Peoples*. Trans. Thomas Dunlap. Berkeley: University of California Press, 1997.

Wood, Ian. "Incest, Law and the Bible in Sixth-century Gaul," *Early Medieval Europe* 1 (1998): pp. 291-304.

---. *The Merovingian Kingdoms 450-751*. London: Longman, 1994.

Wood, Jamie. "A Family Affair: Leander, Isidore and the Legacy of Gregory the Great in Spain," *Isidore of Seville and his Reception in the early Middle Ages: Transmitting and Transforming Knowledge*. Eds. Andrew Fear, Jamie Wood. Amsterdam: Amsterdam University Press, pp. 31-56.

Wood, Jamie, and Andrew Fear, eds., *Isidore of Seville and his Reception in the Early Middle Ages: Transmitting and Transforming Knowledge*. Amsterdam: Amsterdam University Press, 2016.

Wright, David F. "Augustine: His Exegesis and Hermeneutics," *Hebrew Bible/Old Testament: The History of Its Interpretation. Volume I. From the beginnings to the Middle Ages (until 1300). Part 1: Antiquity*. Ed. Magne Sæbø. Göttingen: Vandenhoeck and Ruprecht, 1996, pp. 701-730.

Young, Frances. *Biblical Exegesis and the Formation of Christian Culture*. Cambridge: Cambridge University Press, 1997.

---. "Typology," *Crossing the Boundaries: Essays in Biblical Interpretation in Honour of Michael D. Goulder*. Eds. Stanley E. Porter, Paul Joyce, David E. Orton. Leiden: Brill, 1994, pp. 29-48.

Zamagni, Claudio. "Is the Question-and-Answer Literary Genre in Early Christian Literature a Homogeneous Group?" *La littérature des questions et réponses dans l'Antiquité profane et chrétienne*. Ed. Marie-Pierre Bussières. Turnhout: Brepols, 2013, pp. 241-268.

Zechiel-Eckes, Klaus. *Florus von Lyon als Kirchenpolitiker und Publizist: Studien zur Persönlichkeit eines karolingischen "Intellektuellen" am Beispiel der Auseinandersetzung mit Amalarius (835-838) und des Prädestinationsstreits (851-855)*. Stuttgart: Thorbecke, 1999.

图书在版编目（CIP）数据

教授"二次立法"：《申命记》与里昂地区的查理曼改革 = Teaching the Secunda Lex: Deuteronomy and Church Reform at Lyon in the Age of Charlemagne : 英文 / 刘寅著. —— 杭州 : 浙江大学出版社, 2022.3

ISBN 978-7-308-22221-1

Ⅰ.①教… Ⅱ.①刘… Ⅲ.①《圣经》—研究 Ⅳ.①B971

中国版本图书馆CIP数据核字（2022）第005380号

Teaching the *Secunda Lex*: Deuteronomy and Church Reform at Lyon in the Age of Charlemagne

教授"二次立法"：《申命记》与里昂地区的查理曼改革

刘　寅　著

责任编辑	陈佩钰　宁　檬
责任校对	李瑞雪
封面设计	周　灵
出版发行	浙江大学出版社
	（杭州天目山路148号　邮政编码：310007）
	（网址：http://www.zjupress.com）
排　　版	浙江时代出版服务有限公司
印　　刷	杭州钱江彩色印务有限公司
开　　本	710mm × 1000mm　1/16
印　　张	22.75
字　　数	662千
版 印 次	2022年3月第1版　2022年3月第1次印刷
书　　号	ISBN 978-7-308-22221-1
定　　价	88.00元